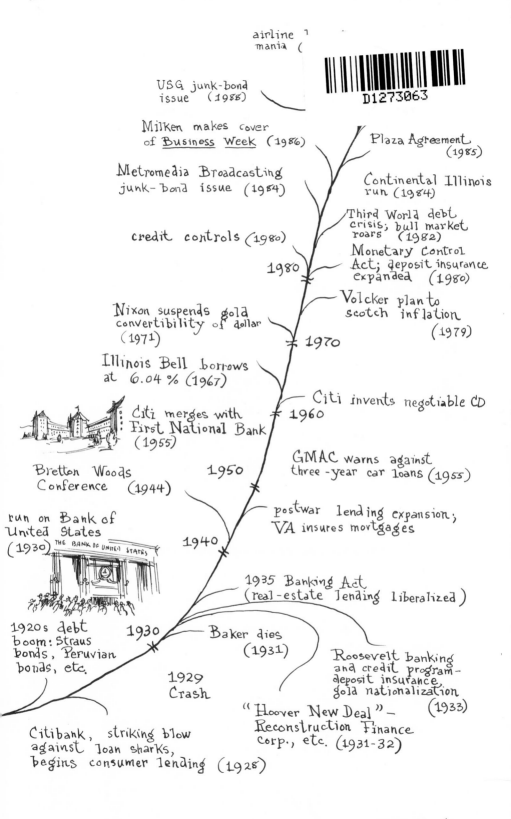

airline mania

USG junk-bond issue (1988)

Milken makes cover of *Business Week* (1986)

Plaza Agreement (1985)

Metromedia Broadcasting junk-bond issue (1984)

Continental Illinois run (1984)

Third World debt crisis; bull market roars (1982)

credit controls (1980)

Monetary Control Act; deposit insurance expanded (1980)

1980

Volcker plan to scotch inflation (1979)

Nixon suspends gold convertibility of dollar (1971)

1970

Illinois Bell borrows at 6.04% (1967)

Citi invents negotiable CD

Citi merges with First National Bank (1955)

1960

GMAC warns against three-year car loans (1955)

Bretton Woods Conference (1944)

1950

postwar lending expansion; VA insures mortgages

run on Bank of United States (1930)

THE BANK OF UNITED STATES

1940

1935 Banking Act (real-estate lending liberalized)

1920s debt boom: Straus bonds, Peruvian bonds, etc.

1930

Baker dies (1931)

Roosevelt banking and credit program— deposit insurance, gold nationalization (1933)

1929 Crash

"Hoover New Deal"— Reconstruction Finance Corp., etc. (1931-32)

Citibank, striking blow against loan sharks, begins consumer lending (1928)

Houk Blanstein 1991

MONEY
OF THE MIND

MONEY
OF THE MIND

*Borrowing and Lending in America
from the Civil War to Michael Milken*

JAMES GRANT

Farrar Straus Giroux

NEW YORK

For Patricia
and also for Emily, Philip, Charles, and Alice,
and Dorothy, too

Acknowledgments

It is only fitting that a story of the evolution of credit should itself be capitalized by debts. Dozens of good Samaritans contributed to making this book. Thanks, first, to John D. Britton, reporter, researcher, and fact gatherer par excellence, whose purview ranged from current financial news to century-old reports of federal bank examiners.

The point of view of this book, as well as its contemporary reporting, comes from the pages of *Grant's Interest Rate Observer*, a twice-monthly journal that chronicled the 1980s (and is in the thick of chronicling the 1990s). Thanks, then, to the staff: Patricia Kavanagh, Jay Diamond, Susan Egan, Catherine Fitzgerald, Ruth Hlavacek, and Caroline McLoughlin. Hank Blaustein, our illustrator, created the endpapers.

In addition to the sources named in the text and notes, I would like to thank a number of people who contributed ideas or suggestions that helped to improve the tone, style, or content of the text. They include, in alphabetical order: David Abrams, Eric Billings, Harry Bingham, Robert F. Boyd, Victoria Brown, Philip Carret, James Chanos, John Exter, John A. Flanders, William Fleckenstein, Michael Harkins, H. Erich Heinemann, John Holman, Fred Kalkstein, Lisa Keefe, Seth Klarman, Tom Knott, Nancy Lazar, John Lee, Sheridan A. Logan, James Lowe, William M. McGarr, Geoffrey H. Moore, George Moore, Leslie Nolan, Charles Peabody, Steven Peck, Russ Ramsey, William F. Rickenbacker, David Shulman, Joan Spriggs, Susan M. Sterne, David Stockman, Craig Zabel, and Manuel Zevron. Walter B. Wriston, the former chairman of Citibank, generously consented to an interview knowing full well how little he would probably like the book. (It should be noted on the subject of Citi that the bank's official biography, *Citibank: 1812–1970*, by Harold van B. Cleveland and Thomas F.

Huertas, is an indispensable work on American financial history. I have used it extensively and with growing admiration for the scholarship of the authors.) Paul J. Isaac and Gert von der Linde both read the manuscript and contributed valuable comments.

Thanks, too, to numerous librarians, archivists, and public relations people. They are: J. Richard Abell, Public Library of Cincinnati; Carol Baerman, Orchard Lake, Mich., Schools; John Calkins, formerly of the First National Bank of Boston; William Creech and William Sherman, National Archives; Dean DeBuck and Ellen Stockdale, Office of the Comptroller of the Currency; The George F. Baker Trust; Ann Gibson and Jean Hrichus, Chase Manhattan archives; Henry Gillett, Bank of England; Nancy Kearse, Allendale, S.C., librarian; Mary Keefe, Cohoes, N.Y., librarian; Barbara L. Kreiger, archives assistant, Dartmouth College; Rosemary A. Lazenby, Federal Reserve Bank of New York; Micki Trager, Brooklyn Heights Business Library; Marsha Trimble, University of Virginia Law Library.

Thanks to Jonathan Galassi, editor-in-chief of Farrar, Straus & Giroux, and to Elisheva Urbas, managing editor, for their judgment and forbearance and to Jack Lynch and Ruth Hlavacek for their copy editing. Thanks to my family for reasons too numerous to mention.

J.G.

Contents

MONEY
OF THE MIND

Introduction

Where did the 1980s come from? Work on this book was begun to answer that question. One thing led to another, however, and the story of the 1980s in American finance became the history of American credit over the past century. The portrait of the Age of Milken became instead the history of George F. Baker, Arthur J. Morris, Daniel Tolman, John M. (One Hundred Percent) Nichols, George Champion, Walter Wriston, and other figures, great and small, in the evolution of banking and credit in the United States. It became a history of financial practices from the National Bank Act of 1864 to the five-year loan on the Yugo automobile, circa 1988. As the institutions of credit and the quality of the currency have both been going downhill, it is necessarily a story of decline. On the other hand, in finance, decay is more colorful than probity, and the prevailing direction of change in the past generation has only enriched the content of the narrative.

"The whole progress of the legislative attitude toward the debtor, from the Roman republic to the present day, has been steadily, though with occasional backward lapses, toward making debt easier to incur, lightening the burden of carrying and softening the consequences of default." Freeman Tilden, who wrote those words in the Great Depression (his wonderful study *A World in Debt* was published in 1935), lived until 1980, long enough to see the liberalizing tendencies of the 1950s, 1960s, and 1970s. Still, he missed their culmination in the 1980s when the world made him a prophet. If, in the early decades of the century, it was impossible for a working man or woman to secure a loan from a legitimate lender, in the 1980s he or she could hardly refuse one. The descendants of the clientele of loan sharks became the valued credit-card "members" of leading banks. In the 1980s, the home-equity loan proliferated, and personal bankruptcy lost its stigma. (Nor did the banks limit their search for potential borrowers to the universe of bona fide adults. "Like a lot of mothers, Zabau Shepard has some charge cards," *The Daily Progress*, Charlottesville, Virginia, reported in 1990, "but she can't use them. It's not that her credit has gone to the dogs; it's that she is a dog.") At the peak of the boom in the 1980s, home-mortgage loans were offered without the usual documentation and junk bonds were sold despite clear warning that the investor was unlikely to see his principal again. Commercial banks seemed to compete to finance the most redundant office buildings, the greatest number of feckless Third World governments, or both.

Animal spirits are an American staple, and the tendencies of the 1980s do not constitute some alien strain in the national character. Real-estate speculation must be as old as the land—in the United States, it is certainly as old as the frontier—and the first bad bank loan was no doubt made around the time of the opening of the first bank. It would be hard to find a more corrupt, reckless, and incompetent lending institution today than the Second Bank of the United States, which closed in 1836.

Still, the boom of the 1980s was unique. Not only did creditors lend more freely than they had in the past, but the government intervened more actively than it had ever done before to absorb the inevitable losses. Two important trends converged in the boom: the democratization of lending and the socialization of risk; more and more people were able to borrow, and more and more debt was federally subsidized. The combination stimulated lending and borrowing and thus the nation's financial markets (and, for that matter, the world's). One of the signal features of the 1980s was the absence of a coast-to-coast bank run. Unafraid for their insured deposits, people did not queue up to demand cash from all the banks that had overlent against the dubious collateral of commercial real estate. The passing of the system-wide bank run has gone unmourned, and understandably so, but it cannot be denied that the resulting public complacency has brought its own costs, most visibly the unpaid invoice for the banking and savings and loan debacles. By standing behind good banks and bad banks alike, the government in effect removed the oldest franchise in banking— that is, safekeeping.

The reinvention of unsecured paper money similarly played an expansive role in the boom of the 1980s. Up until 1971, the dollar had been convertible into gold on demand, at a fixed and certain price (even if the right of convertibility had been steadily narrowed; it was vested at last only with foreign governments or their central banks). As the last remnant of the international gold standard was abolished by President Richard Nixon, the great inflation of the 1970s was accelerated. Interest rates rose for a decade, conditioning a generation of investors to expect the high yields that the junk-bond salesmen of the 1980s subsequently promised them.

Risk-taking is inseparable from lending. Every loan, even if fully secured, is a kind of speculation. The degree of risk varies according to the character and strength of the borrower and the quality of the collateral. "If A lends $1,000 to B, A is speculating upon B's honesty, industry, skill and promptness," Tilden wrote. "That is precisely what debt is, and precisely what credit is; and it is basically nothing else —a speculation."

With the partial socialization of the banking business, a process materially and ironically advanced in the Reagan years, the element of speculation was not removed, but its costs were shifted. The public sector's credit increasingly supplanted the private sector's. Government guarantees—of bank deposits, residential mortgages, farm loans, student loans—became widespread, and thereby expanded the volume of borrowing. As the marginal debtor received the marginal loan, the extra car (or house, boat, or corporation) was sold. All this worked to enlarge the national income. In the 1920s and 1930s, an abundance of lending was succeeded by a drought, and an inflation of prices was duly followed by a deflation. The riddle of the years to come is whether the government has succeeded in breaking this cycle: not the upswing, which in fact it has enthusiastically subsidized, but the downswing. It is whether the sheer bulk of the federal guarantees will forestall the kind of contraction that paralyzed business activity in the Depression and demoralized speculative activity for a generation after that. The fundamental investment question is whether even the government is big enough to underwrite, with good money, the losses born of the lending practices of the 1980s. If the answer to that question is "yes" (and I happen to doubt it), one would want to know why the government does not guarantee everyone. If every debtor had a call on the Treasury, and if the Treasury were none the worse for that commitment, interest rates would be lower and the nation more prosperous. The stock market would never have another bad day.

"Credit" is a financial term with a moral lineage. Its first meaning is "debt." "Trust given or received," Webster's elaborates; "expectation of future payment for property transferred, or of fulfillment of promises given." To "credit" is to believe, and to lend money is necessarily to trust someone. In 1912, Congress conducted an investigation into the existence of a "Money Trust," a financial analogue to the combinations in steel, tobacco, gypsum, leather, and the like. Progressive congressmen listened skeptically as the leading Wall Street bankers explained that the basis of credit is not gold or interlocking directorships but character. To the reformers who had prepared diagrams to document the overarching reach of George F. Baker or J. P. Morgan, such assertions seemed unctuous and self-serving. The Progressive agenda carried the day, and the government became a banker and a guarantor of other bankers. The process accelerated in the 1970s and 1980s, with stimulating results. As the volume of federally subsidized lending increased, so did the prices of things obtainable with borrowed money. Buildings, farmland, and stocks all appreciated, and the stock market climbed. But I think it is far too soon to pronounce this experiment with the taxpayers' credit an unqualified success. The break in farm prices, the real-estate crack-up, and the alarming rise in the incidence of personal bankruptcies in the past several years suggest that the "credence" element of credit may yet prove as significant as the moguls insisted it was.

Credit is not money, exactly,* but the expectation of getting a loan constitutes a real financial medium. Believing that a lender will say "yes," a loan applicant may behave expansively. Expecting to be denied, he or she may behave guardedly. The relaxation of lending standards in the 1980s, I believe, prompted more and more expansive behavior—for example, the purchase of businesses or office buildings for little or no money down. The ripple effects of these purchases created jobs (real-estate-related employment, for example) and helped to create the great bull market. It would be hoping for a great deal if, in the wake of the tightening of lending standards, the ripples did not eventually work in reverse, reducing employment and securities prices.

The money supply can be counted, and so can the supply of debt. However, the potential supply of debt can only be imagined. No one government statistic measures the inclination of bankers to lend or of

---

* The distinction can be elusive, especially in a paper-money regime. The borrower of $10,000 has borrowed "money" and incurred a "debt." The lender, a bank, has acquired an "asset" and also a "liability." The loan, from the bank's point of view, is an asset; the $10,000 deposit (the bank simply credits the loan to the borrower's checking account) is a liability.

Repaying the loan, the borrower extinguishes not one balance-sheet entry, but two. Gone is the $10,000 asset; gone too is the $10,000 liability. The monetary statistics thereby are made lighter in two categories, money and debt.

customers to borrow. Insofar as those inclinations are reduced, by regulatory fiat or through the impairment of bank capital or some other means, so will the vitality of business activity be reduced.

Although my favorite President was Grover Cleveland, I have not meant to write a brief for nostalgia. The gold standard, which President Cleveland championed a century ago, was a system for coordinating the growth of money and credit with the growth of production and population. It was a less imperfect system than its successors, I believe, but it was no panacea, and it was inextricably bound up with the politics and society of the day. Those politics were libertarian, whereas ours are not. My political and financial sympathies are with the free market, but I do not mean to impose them on the champions of George McGovern, for instance. (Some years ago, the former President's son, Francis G. Cleveland, told me that he was a McGovern man. He said that neither he nor his mother ever did understand what the monetary commotion of his father's presidency was all about.)

In general, things seem to get better, not worse. People live longer, run faster, jump higher, eat better, and work more efficiently than they did at the turn of the century. Nevertheless, the art of lending has not improved in the intervening generations. The First National Bank of New York, George F. Baker's bank, earned high profits, lent safely yet imaginatively, conducted an active investment-banking business, an active venture-capital business, and stood by its customers when they needed help. At this writing, Citibank, into which the First National Bank was absorbed in 1955, is making heavy weather of it. The state of banking has been considerably weakened all around, so much so that the General Accounting Office has pronounced the Bank Insurance Fund to be insolvent. To judge by the tripling of the public debt in the decade of the 1980s, the caliber of the government's fiscal management has not shown much evolutionary progress either.

Progress is cumulative in science and engineering but cyclical in finance. Whatever might have been wrong with credit in the 1980s, it was not a lack of financial technology. By the end of the decade, some $800 billion a day in electronic payments was speeding over the Clearinghouse Interbank Payments System, or CHIPS, from bank to bank across continents. Automatic teller machines, "smart" credit cards, and bond-trading software would have left Baker and Morgan thunderstruck. In technology, therefore, banking has almost never looked back. On the other hand, this progress has paid scant dividends in judgment. Surrounded by computer terminals, bankers in the 1980s committed some of the greatest howlers in American financial history.

People in markets are more suggestible than a layman might imagine. Try as they might, they can never know the one thing they really want to know—that is, the future. Not knowing, they compare notes with others. They work in units, not alone. They are brave together at the tops of markets and meek together at the bottoms. I believe that there is an important kernel of truth in the idea that financial errors recur every other generation. Thus, sons and daughters tend to reenact the errors of their grandparents more so than those of their parents. There is not one shred of scientific proof to support this proposition, but I have seen the characteristic financial mistakes of the 1920s repeated with only slight variations in the 1970s and 1980s. In the 1920s, Wall Street sold Latin American bonds to a credulous public. In the 1970s and 1980s, Latin America borrowed money from credulous banks. In the 1920s, Simon Straus issued high-yield bonds secured by commercial real estate; many came to grief in the 1930s. In the 1970s and 1980s, banks lent heavily against the collateral of commercial real estate; many banks failed, or required federal assistance (without the exculpatory fact of a worldwide depression). In both eras, prolonged prosperity wore down the skepticism of creditors. In recent times, that skepticism has been further diminished by the "too big to fail" doctrine, federal deposit insurance, federal mortgage insurance, and other government guarantees. It is the heavy element of subsidy in American credit, I believe, that contributed so enjoyably to the upside and that may ultimately prolong—certainly complicate —the downside.

"Credit," wrote John Locke, "is nothing but the expectation of money, within some limited time." But that is too dry a definition for late-twentieth-century America. The questions are: What kind of money, and how much time? Based on past experience, the answers would be "inflated" and "more," respectively.

1

Gloomy Sewell

On June 23, 1987, a well-heeled Cincinnati investment adviser, Paul David Herrlinger, age forty-six, called the Pittsburgh bureau of the Dow Jones News Service to make an announcement. In a level and businesslike voice, Herrlinger said that he was prepared to buy Dayton-Hudson Corp., the Minneapolis department-store chain, for $6.8 billion. He identified himself as a representative of Stone Inc., a local family firm, and of Capital Management Corp., a local investment-management company.

By chance, Richard Miller, president of Capital Management, was passing Herrlinger's office and overheard the call. Only the day before, Herrlinger had stuck his head into Miller's office and proposed, out of the blue, "Let's make a bid for Dayton-Hudson." Miller had gaily replied, "Oh, sure." The sum total of invested funds at Capital Management was some $6.7 billion short of the purchase price that Herrlinger had in mind.

The Dow Jones organization, however, not knowing what Miller knew, took the news more seriously. On the face of things, there was no reason to doubt it. It was a fact of the bull market that companies were routinely gobbled up by buyers that did not have the full purchase price or anything like it. (In one extreme case, in 1986, the Chicago, Missouri & Western Railway Company borrowed 100 percent of the purchase price of a short-line railroad. The CMW subsequently sued its creditors, Citibank and Heller Financial, for lending it too much.) It was understood that the funds could be borrowed and that, as a matter of fact, if the debtor could not afford to pay the interest on the loan, that problem too could be overcome. A deferred-interest loan could be tailor-made. Having no reason to suspect that Herrlinger would be fired almost as soon as he placed the phone back on its cradle, or that Stone Inc. did not exist, much less have designs on a

New York Stock Exchange-listed department-store chain, Dow Jones proceeded to verify what it could of Herrlinger's story. The bare outline seemed to check, and the Herrlinger bid for Dayton-Hudson became news.

In the open market on the morning before Herrlinger's call, Dayton-Hudson was valued at approximately $4.5 billion, a price representing the collective judgment of all the buyers and sellers except Herrlinger. It was the distillation of everything that every investor but one considered relevant to the retailer's future earning power. The $6.8 billion valuation represented the unique judgment of Herrlinger. As word of the Herrlinger proposition crossed the Dow Jones news ticker at 9:49 a.m., Wall Street unconsciously began to part into the camps of those who would subsequently be able to laugh at the day's events and those who would not. The mirthless contingent was smaller, consisting largely of arbitrageurs who, though not knowing Herrlinger, were nevertheless prepared to invest with him. Thus, news of the putative bid lifted the stock instantly. The reflexive jump was a mark both of the market's insecurity about its own collective judgment and of the accessibility of borrowed money (the subject of how Herrlinger proposed to finance the purchase was not immediately raised for discussion). When, later that day, Herrlinger's lawyer, Anthony Covatta, described his client's telephone call as the work of a troubled mind, Dayton-Hudson gave up everything it had gained, about $10 a share. "This is a medical story, not a financial story," Covatta said that afternoon. "The man is ill; he's not himself."

Herrlinger himself, however, gave a wonderfully lucid interview to the financial press on the lawn of his spacious Cincinnati home. Asked how he proposed to finance the bid, he replied, "That's still undecided." Asked point-blank if the bid was a hoax, he said, "I don't know. It's no more a hoax than anything else . . . an offer is really an intangible thing."

Sane or not—Herrlinger was diagnosed as a manic-depressive, and the Securities and Exchange Commission would make his readmission to the investment business contingent on a clean bill of health—the Cincinnati investor had put his finger on something. In the froth of every bull market, fact becomes blurred with fantasy. By the end of a boom, all things seem possible. Those who believed Herrlinger had been conditioned by the careers of Robert Campeau, Donald Trump, and other titanic debtors to believe almost anything.

Furthermore, as a general proposition in the 1980s, it was easy to come by a loan. There were home-equity loans, liposuction loans,

Third World government loans, art-equity loans, teaser-rate mortgage loans, and five-year loans with which to purchase a Yugo, an automobile with a shorter-than-five-year life expectancy. There were loans to purchase entire companies. There was, of course, nothing revolutionary about buying a company, lock, stock, and barrel. Waves of merger activity have occurred periodically in American financial history. What was unique about the 1980s was the chosen medium of exchange of the deal makers. Rather than issue stock to buy the desired company, an up-to-date buyer would borrow. It was frequently understood that the loan would be repaid with the subsequent sale of parts of the acquired company. An article of faith was that the price paid for the sum of the parts would exceed the market value of the whole—which is to say that the public market was systematically pessimistic in its own valuations. Someone like Herrlinger, having lined up a loan, or the promise of a loan, would call the newspapers to declare that the stock market in effect was misinformed. The price of a certain company, he would say, was too low. Every buyer and seller except himself had failed to see the future clearly. In any case, he proposed to pay a significantly higher price than the one publicly quoted. At that moment, the company was, in banking argot, "in play," and more than one Herrlinger would enter the bidding to compete for the prize.

In corporate finance, the 1980s were a leveling decade. Access to credit, which had been getting progressively easier since the turn of the century, now became wide open. In exchange for the promise to pay high interest rates, a borrower could command vast sums. The lender's oldest fear—default by the borrower, or a panic in which one bankrupt pulled down another—faded. So ubiquitous was credit that, for a few merry hours, there seemed nothing cockeyed in the idea that an unknown Cincinnati investor could have laid his hands on $6.8 billion. The relentless rise in stock prices had taught the market to put the best face on the news. The most profitable state of mind in a bear market is doubt, but in a bull market it is faith, and Wall Street had been watching stock prices go up, or sideways (in any case, not decisively down), since 1975.

Among the still active skeptics, the Herrlinger demonstration was taken as proof that the market had finally slipped its moorings. The gullibility of Wall Street seemed remarkable, even making allowances for normal boom-time credulousness. ("Hey Wall Street, Wanna Buy the Brooklyn Bridge?" was the headline in *Business Week*.) Yet a monied majority harbored no such concern, and in early October, about two weeks before the crash of October 19, a pair of rich Texas oilmen, calling themselves Desert Partners, disclosed the purchase of a sizable stake in U.S. Gypsum Co. It was clear that this was to be no friendly investment undertaken for the long pull. What Cyril Wagner, Jr., and Jack E. Brown sought, evidently, was a profit on their stock. Control of the company, to judge them on past form, was secondary. For the incumbent executives of Gypsum, what was threatened was loss of employment and the upset of the corporate structure to which they had devoted their careers. They had been similarly threatened by First City Financial Corp. of Canada, flagship of the Belzberg interests, in 1986, and they had repulsed the Belzbergs by paying them to go away. Thus, to the Gypsum officer corps, the October 19 collapse seemed heaven-sent. If the break meant anything, it was that debt-financed takeovers had suddenly become obsolete. If the value of common stock was going to fall, not rise, no sane banker would want to lend against the collateral of corporate assets. By mid-January 1988, Wagner and Brown had suffered a paper loss on their Gypsum investment of some $80 million. According to *Forbes* in 1987, the two were among the 400 richest people in the country, but they had apparently run out of willing lenders. On January 14, 1988, the Texans withdrew their takeover bid, citing a lack of financing.

Gypsum management had hardly stopped shaking hands over that good news, however, when Wagner and Brown resurfaced with a new plan and a new commitment for a half-billion-dollar loan from Wells Fargo National Bank. "They're back," the *Chicago Sun-Times* reported, quoting from the horror movies. Great sums would be borrowed to buy out the existing stockholders—no shortage of credit was anticipated after all. To pay interest and principal on the acquisition loan, the company would be streamlined, redirected, and, as necessary, dismembered.

Gypsum chairman Robert J. Day's reaction to the Texans' bid was clinical but not without an undercurrent of annoyance. He said, "The offer is a two-tiered, coercive, front-end-loaded cash tender for approximately 41% of the stock of the company with an expressed indication to propose, subject to significant conditions and uncertainties, a back-end merger for junk bonds and warrants reportedly worth $42 a share." The gist of Day's remark was that the offer lacked both financial substance and sincerity. It was management's conviction that Messrs. Desert Partners had one goal in mind—namely, the levitation of their Gypsum stock to a price at which they could profitably unload it. In truth, nothing the Texans could do, except vanish (as they had done in previous corporate raiding episodes), would mollify the Gypsum executives. If the stockholders accepted Desert Partners' offer, the company would never be the same again. Existing management, understandably, liked things the way they were. They liked the tendency of sales and earnings to increase and of retained earnings to fatten. They liked the career opportunities that a growing company afforded them and their families and friends. They knew as well as anyone that the demand for gypsum wallboard, their staple product, rose and fell with residential-construction activity. They wondered: What was supposed to happen in the next down cycle if there wasn't enough money to pay the interest on the loan that Desert Partners had taken out to buy the company? Even if the lenders didn't drive the company into some ghastly bankruptcy proceeding, what would happen to Gypsum's competitive position? What would happen to them?

One option, at least, was permanently foreclosed by the Desert Partners overture. This was the chance to return to the status quo. Management, though it identified personally with Gypsum, collectively owned less than 1½ percent of its common stock. The majority of the stockholders, who perhaps did *not* identify personally with the company, would be offered a premium of 33 percent of the price of the stock prevailing in late February 1988. Management could remonstrate against the folly of overloading a cyclical manufacturing company with debt. It could throw up legal defenses against an unwanted acquisitor (unwanted, that is, by management). The stockholders, however, would almost certainly tender their shares to the interlopers at the Herrlinger-type premium. Gypsum was in play, and someone would buy it with borrowed money. The only practical course for management, attempting to repulse Wagner and Brown, was to top that hostile offer with one of its own. Management itself would plunge the company into debt, sell off surplus divisions, fire redundant colleagues (including—it was a family-type enterprise—brothers-in-law), and run the risk of future bankruptcy. It was this proposition that management took to the stockholders in the spring of 1988. Approval was promptly forthcoming. Desert Partners, which at last was able to take a profit on the stock it had bought for itself, withdrew. At Gypsum, the summer was occupied with preparations for borrowing money.

The soul-searching that followed the Great Depression produced myriad financial reforms, among them a curious convention of reverse salesmanship. The Securities Act of 1933 bound an issuer of bonds or stock in the public market to furnish a prospectus to would-be buyers.

The prospectus would describe the new offering in detail. It would describe the finances and recent history of the issuing company and set forth every good reason why a prudent man or woman would want to have nothing to do with it. It would divulge the size of the fees that the bankers and investment bankers would receive for their handiwork (in the Gypsum transaction, the number was $38 million). Reformers believed that the cure for shady investments was the sunlight of publicity. In the wake of the Great Depression, it was thought that the public would remain on its guard indefinitely. Before leaping, it would look. It would read the fine print carefully.

On July 7, 1988, Gypsum produced an 80-page prospectus detailing the nuts and bolts and risks associated with $600 million in new debentures. A debenture is a bond, and a bond is a loan. A mortgage bond is a loan secured by property; a debenture is a bond secured by the general credit of the issuing company. A debenture, being unsecured by specific assets, is therefore of lower caste than a mortgage. The new U.S. Gypsum debentures were junk bonds (so called for their low credit rating). They would pay an investor 13¼ percent a year until they matured in the year 2000. On July 1, 2000, if all went according to plan, an investor would get his principal back. In keeping with the pessimistic tone of the genre (and especially appropriate in this case), the Gypsum prospectus was guarded on the prospects for ultimate recovery. The cost of making Desert Partners go away, as it noted, was a drastic overhaul of the company's finances. The money with which to pay the stockholders a high price would have to be borrowed, and the rise in indebtedness would turn the corporate accounts on their head. Before the overhaul, Gypsum's balance sheet showed $636 million of stockholders' equity—funds that the stockholders contributed and that the business had managed to earn, and keep. The balance sheet also showed $781 million in long-term debt. These were conventional numbers. Post-overhaul, the data were highly unconventional. The readings were *minus* $1.6 billion in stockholders' equity and $3.1 billion of long-term debt (of which the $600 million in junk bonds was merely a fraction). The balance sheet of the new Gypsum was indistinguishable from that of a bankrupt.

Before Desert Partners arrived on the scene, Gypsum's bond rating had been investment grade, or conventionally sound. Afterward, its rating became speculative, or junk caliber, meaning that an element of suspense now figured into its bill-paying capacity. The company would need the wind at its back to meet its obligations as they came due, the prospectus said. The risks were described in hypothetical terms—what the company would have looked like if the transaction had been completed in early 1988. "Higher than historical debt levels and interest costs to be incurred by the Company . . . will have a substantial adverse effect on the Company's net earnings," it said on page 10. It was stated that if the overhaul, or "recapitalization," had been in effect in 1988, the company would have reported a $23 million loss for the three months ended March, instead of the actual $40 million net profit. Under the new regime, the company would scarcely cover its interest bill. Under the old regime, there was a comfortable measure of redundancy. Earnings sufficed to cover interest charges by a ratio of almost five to one.

On the same cheerful note, the text continued on page 11: "The Company will need substantial amounts of cash in order to meet its interest expense and principal repayment obligations for the foreseeable future, including approximately $750 million in principal repayments due through the end of 1990. . . . The Company does not expect that it will be able to generate sufficient cash flow from operations to make such payments during such period, and the Company's ability to make such payments will therefore be dependent on the Company's ability to implement the restructuring plan"—that is, to do the kinds of things that Desert Partners had proposed to do. "In addition, the Company's business historically has been cyclical in nature and sensitive to changes in general economic conditions, including conditions in the housing and construction industries."

Naturally, management had formulated plans and projections for survival after the recapitalization. Corporate jets, marginal divisions, expendable channels of distribution, and unpromising products would be eliminated. Fortunately, there would be no recession, the company and its advisers decided. They projected rising sales for five consecutive years. (In 1986, the management of R. H. Macy & Co., in connection with its leveraged buyout, had projected rising sales for ten consecutive years, a vote of confidence such as the Reagan administration could only dream of.) If, however, plans went awry, the prospectus acknowledged, Gypsum "would have to derive funds from alternative sources or seek renegotiation or refinancing of all or a portion of the Company's indebtedness . . . in order to avert default under such indebtedness." Standing ahead of the new bondholders in line for repayment were the bank lenders, numbering 135. Led by Bankers Trust, Chemical Bank, and Citibank, they would lend $2.3 billion, as against the public's $600 million, and they would have first claim on the company's heavily mortgaged assets.

In so many words, then, the prospectus described a roll of the dice. Unless everything went according to plan, the company would be in trouble. As it was, the price of USG's mainstay product, gypsum wallboard, known by its trade name Sheetrock, was falling. House building was on a downswing. If the weakness in prices and construction activity continued, the creditors could count on some form of disaster, in or out of bankruptcy court. In the event, almost nothing went right. Wallboard prices, which had peaked in 1986, at $106 per thousand square feet, were quoted in the neighborhood of $76 in 1990. The company had projected annual rates of construction on the order of 1.5 million houses; the actual number, between 1988 and 1990, averaged 1.35 million units. Late in the day on December 31, 1990, the company publicly admitted that it had borrowed itself into a corner. By the time and date of the release (after the close of trading on New Year's Eve), it was possible to infer that Gypsum's management was sheepish about the news. However, the text was far from contrite. "USG Corp. announced today that it is well along in developing a long-term plan to restructure the corporation's debt and deal with future cash-flow needs," the release led off optimistically. Just the same, the inescapable fact was that the bankers and bondholders would not be paid at all in the short term. For the longer term, they would have to settle for less. The company was going to recapitalize its recapitalization.

In other times and places, few financial observers would have marveled that a hugely indebted wallboard manufacturer had, after all, failed. What would have astonished them was that any reputable lender had financed such a dubious transaction in the first place. By the summer of 1988, however, Wall Street was receptive to heresy. For one thing, National Gypsum, USG's main competitor, had undergone a leveraged recapitalization in 1986. Overburdened with debt, it had nonetheless managed to stump along, just as similarly indebted companies had survived in other industries. Even more important was the fact that, in the investment-banking business, heresy paid better than orthodoxy. With every passing year, the conventional, investment-grade bond business became less profitable, the junk-bond business more so. As for commercial banking, there was money to be made in lending, but not to blue-chip companies (which frequently had better credit ratings than the banks that sought their business). Of necessity, bankers had turned to companies like USG. As for the gypsum maker specifically, prosperity had inspired the notion that house building was no longer a cyclical activity but a perennial one, like eating. Because the mortgage market had been deregulated, capital would flow freely from savers to borrowers, alleviating the droughts that had periodically stymied the construction business in times of regulated interest rates. The USG transaction was ill conceived, but it was also, in some sense, inevitable. By 1988, both the will and the way had become irresistible. There were raiders and there were corporate targets. There were lenders, investment bankers, and junk-bond buyers. (There was also a tax code that favored debt over equity, but that bias had been present in federal law since the enactment of the first income tax.) There were, in growing numbers, fiduciaries who invested not their own money but someone else's. Wagner and Brown were creatures of the times. But no less was their chief lender, Wells Fargo, and their financial adviser, Merrill Lynch & Co.

Goldman Sachs & Co. and Salomon Brothers, investment bankers to USG, conceived a plan of borrowing, drafted the prospectus, lined up investors, and sold the bonds. Bankers Trust, Citibank, and Chemical Bank arranged for a loan of $1.6 billion. Standard & Poor's, the bond-rating agency, softened its warning against the transparent risk of the new structure with a few mitigating sentences about the possibility of future asset sales and/or still more borrowing from the accommodating banks. In the late 1980s, no Wall Street promotion was complete without a Japanese interest, and in July 1988, shortly after the bonds were sold, Settsu Corp., a Japanese paperboard maker, disclosed that it had purchased 9.6 percent of the reconstituted USG "for investment purposes only."

An investment banker involved in the deal recalled that USG borrowed reluctantly and with every intention of discharging its debts. He said that this commitment distinguished it, more than you might imagine, from many junk-bond borrowers with which he had dealt in the decade of the 1980s. Not wanting to encumber a cyclical business, USG's management had nonetheless decided that if anybody was going to do that ill-advised thing, it might as well be them. "These guys embodied the best and the worst of corporate America," the banker went on. "They were insular. Most of them had worked there all their lives. But you could eat off the floor of one of their factories. In 'Sheetrock,' they had the 'Kleenex' or the 'Xerox' brand name of their industry. They were the low-cost producer. It's just that finance never mattered to them." By late 1990, as the company careened toward bankruptcy, almost nothing but finance mattered.

The company had never before been anything except solvent and profitable. It had turned a profit even in the bottom of the Great

Depression (it was, according to *Fortune*, one of the few American manufacturing companies to manage that feat). Gypsum was organized in 1901 as a consolidation of thirty-five little gypsum companies. "The officers of the company are said to be shrewd, practical men who have made money in the business," *The Wall Street Journal* reported after the organization. What the "shrewd" and "practical" man of business favored at the turn of the century was monopoly. Like debt in the 1980s, the trust form of corporate organization was in vogue. It was believed that big companies worked better than small ones and that behemoths worked best. In the same year that Gypsum was strung together, U.S. Steel, the first billion-dollar corporation and the biggest trust of the era, was organized. It was a trust of trusts—a consolidation of smaller merged steel makers—and the apex of the era.

In financial markets, a law of excess applies. Prices tend to go to extremes, on both the upside and the downside, and investment bankers conform to the unwritten rule that every good idea must be driven into the ground like a tomato stake. The merger movement of the turn of the century started in a small way but inevitably gathered steam, adherents, and abandon. It ended with the so-called Rich Man's Panic of 1903, a stock-market break that did particular damage to the securities of the new trusts (and to their newly rich owners). In sizing up the trust boom, the corporate-finance scholar Arthur Stone Dewing wrote not just for his time but for ours too: "At first the consolidations were few in number, but the movement, once begun again, quickly reached beyond anything thought of in the preceding period. Every conceivable line of manufacturing had its trust. Conservative bankers, shrewd businessmen, and doctrinaire economists became infected with the virus of large-scale production. People condemned the trusts one moment and bought their securities the next. It was the harvest-time of promoters."

Gypsum was on the top of the building-products heap from the start (even if, at first, it was malnourished; its sole initial working capital was a $200,000 loan from the old Corn Exchange Bank, later absorbed by Chemical Bank, one of Gypsum's lenders in the 1988 recapitalization). Then, as later, the constituent gypsum companies produced about half the nation's plaster requirement. And almost from the start, the company was identified with a single commanding executive, Sewell Lee Avery, its president from 1905 to 1936, its chairman to 1951, and a member of its board until his death in 1960.

The Avery Era

Avery was born in Saginaw, Michigan, in 1873, the son of Waldo Allard Avery, a prosperous lumberman. He attended public schools in Saginaw and Detroit and the Michigan Military Academy in Orchard Lake. In 1894, a depression year, he was graduated with a bachelor of laws degree from the University of Michigan. The dilemma of what to do for a job was solved by his father, who by then was an investor in a pair of gypsum plants, one in Chicago and the other in Alabaster, Michigan. The one in Chicago had been built to accommodate the construction of the 1893 Chicago World's Fair. Young Avery was taken on at Alabaster. His first decision, according to *Fortune*, was to change the name of the company from the Western Plaster Works to the Alabaster Co. "Sounded better, Sewell thought." The magazine went on: "Avery lived with his young wife (Hortense Lenore Wisner) in a couple of rooms by the lake, had the first bathtub in town, and made a couple of hundred dollars a month. Industrious, persuasive, ambitious, he got along well."

The Alabaster Co. was absorbed by the Gypsum trust—U.S.G., as it was originally called—in 1901, and Avery was named a director of the corporation and its sales manager in Buffalo. By 1905, he was the manager of a larger sales territory and was living in Cleveland. Also in 1905, intracompany politics came to a boil. Avery liked to explain that there had been an explosion: "I came down last, and, lighting on top, I stuck."

In the early years, Gypsum, or Gyp, or Big Gyp, grew slowly and steadily. The Panic of 1907 was dealt with, and market share was wrested from the makers of lime wall plaster. New uses were contrived for alabaster—much was made of its fire-resistant qualities—and gypsum wallboard, a sandwich of plaster between two sheets of paper, emerged as the prefabricated wall of the future. When construction activity leaped in the 1920s, Avery and Gypsum were prepared to furnish the plaster walls. In 1919, the first year of this golden age, net profits totaled $1.1 million, almost twice the earnings of any prior year. The depression year of 1921 actually yielded a small profit. In 1923, Gyp's net earnings totaled $5 million. In 1926, the peak, they topped $10 million.

The next several years illuminate Gypsum and Avery and the intersection of man and organization. So big was the boom of the mid-1920s that new competitors pushed into the gypsum business. Trying to build sales, they cut prices. Gypsum matched those reductions. The price of wallboard fell to $15 per thousand square feet from $27. For two years, Gyp and Certain-teed Products, one of the boom-time entrants, waged a price war. It was Certain-teed that asked for terms from Gypsum, in 1929. It agreed to produce Gyp-type wallboard under license, to halt the sale of its own low-end wallboard, and to accept Gyp's minimum wallboard price. The outcome was satisfactory to Gypsum, although not as satisfactory as life before the price war.

Avery, who had begun his career in the economically depressed 1890s, never joined the new-era chorus of the 1920s, and for his skepticism won the sobriquet "Gloomy Sewell." It was said that as early as 1928 he believed that a financial blow was imminent (although, knowing Avery as we know him now, it is hard to believe that he wasn't bearish long before that). He was flexible enough, however, and Gyp was liquid enough, so that corporate growth proceeded nevertheless. In the late 1920s, Gypsum acquired or built new wallboard plants in New York, Boston, Philadelphia, Detroit, and Chicago. All these locations are accessible by water, and Avery scored a competitive coup by having his gypsum rock supplied by ship. Avery went from strength to strength. In September 1929—exactly the beginning of the Great Depression, the National Bureau of Economic Research determined, and a month before the stock-market break—Gyp quietly laid off 2,000 workers. *Fortune* reported this masterstroke as if it were nothing: "When building failed to show its usual spring increase in 1930, Gyp was neither surprised nor upset. With $35 million in surplus, it could afford to sit and wait a while."

This was the summertime of Sewell L. Avery. U.S. Gypsum turned a profit in 1930, 1931, 1932, and 1933 (and, indeed, in every year thereafter). It did not reduce its Coolidge-era dividend until 1933. In 1931, a year of debt liquidation, currency crisis, and general end-of-the-world upset, its balance sheet resembled Fort Knox. The treasury was brimful with cash, and there was virtually no long-term debt. The numbers, in fact, represented almost the mirror image of the horrific balance sheet produced by the recapitalization of 1988, when there was no depression.

The prescience of Sewell Avery, though little noticed outside Chicago, deeply registered on the partners of J. P. Morgan. The boom had created many business geniuses, but few had retained their gifts in the slump; Avery, evidently, was a man for all seasons. In the summer of 1931, Morgan tapped him for bigger things by inviting him on the board of U.S. Steel. In the fall of 1931, it sounded him out for the chairmanship of Montgomery, Ward & Co., the venerable catalogue and retail house, in which Morgan held an investment that it probably had begun to wish it didn't. Gloomy Sewell was just the man the partners were looking for. Twice in the 1920s, Ward had fallen victim to overoptimism. In the depression of 1920–21, it had been caught with excess inventories. The result was a terrific slump in sales, to $69 million in 1921 from $102 million in 1920, and back-to-back annual losses of $8 million and $10 million, respectively. Later in the decade, emboldened by the new era, Ward had set to work building a national chain of retail outlets. From just 10 stores in 1926, it had accumulated 248 by 1928 and no fewer than 554 by 1930.

Ward in 1931 was on its way to showing an operating loss of almost $9 million. The price of a share of its common stock, which had sold for as much as 156⅞ in 1929, changed hands for as little as 6⅝. Quick to expand, Ward had been slow to contract. It opened 49 new stores in the unprosperous year of 1930. Belatedly noticing the chill in the air, it extended the range of goods it offered for sale on the installment plan. Ten stores were opened in 1931, even though three-quarters of the existing stores were taking losses.

Though a civic-minded Chicagoan, Avery was reluctant to take the helm of this foundering local vessel. He was happy at Gypsum, which was not shipping water. He was fifty-eight years old. "He was asked to reconsider but promptly forgot the matter," wrote the official Ward corporate biographer. "He finally was cornered one Sunday on a golf course and offered the Ward chairmanship at $100,000 a year, plus a stock option. The negotiators told Avery that Eastern directors of the company, meeting in New York, were awaiting his answer. He phoned them and the connection was so poor that his promise to consider the offer was interpreted, perhaps deliberately, as an acceptance and an announcement was released to the press. Avery acknowledged acceptance, although he felt he had been shanghaied." Once Avery quipped, "I banana-peeled into this place, and then couldn't get out."

The 1930s were Avery's miracle-working period. Arriving at Ward, he called in Arthur Andersen and encouraged the public accountant to conduct a thorough and ruthless audit. The result was a "big bath" that arguably made the past look worse than it was and certainly helped management to make the future seem brighter than it otherwise would have been. Avery upgraded the merchandise, redesigned the catalogues, redecorated the offices, brought in new executive talent, and recruited a cadre of experienced chain-store managers to replace the catalogue merchants who had been running the company's retail outlets. He suspended publication of the employee magazine, *Forward*. Years later, a Ward employee remembered this time nostalgically: "I never saw such a mass movement forward in a business. Avery turned the place inside out, even to the fixtures and decorations. All the fellows were bustling and hustling to make the grade in a big way. Everyone wanted to get in there and pitch for the old man."

If anyone had a reason to feel nostalgic for that time, it was Avery. For signing up, he received the option to buy 100,000 shares (out of some 4½ million outstanding) of Ward's common stock at a price of $11 each. Even in the down-and-out year of 1932, the so-called book value of Ward was about $24 a share. This was what the stockholders owned, free and clear. In 1933, the first full fiscal year of the Avery regime, Ward reduced its loss, to $5.6 million from $8.7 million in the preceding year. It showed a sliver of earnings, $2 million, in 1934, and a jump to something resembling commercial normalcy in 1935: more than $9 million in earnings on the back of a 33 percent rise in sales. Also in 1935, the company paid all the dividends it had neglected to pay on its preferred stock during the Depression. In 1936, for the first time since 1931, it paid a dividend on its common. To *Fortune*, in 1936, Avery was "pretty generally held to be the No. 1 Chicago businessman." The magazine invited its readers to imagine the hero in person: "Picture a man of average height, straight with a stomach kept down by plenty of golf, dressed in a dark gray suit, wearing a rather high collar and a dark tie and, when he goes out, a bowler on the top of his head. He has thick brown hair, iron gray at the temples, and the deepest, brightest eyes you have ever seen—eyes that show you how fast the brain behind them works. Such is Mr. Avery. He represents that peculiar combination of qualities that marks the successful Chicagoan—he is shrewd, frank, honest, persuasive, hard-boiled when he needs to be, sentimental when he pleases to be."

In Franklin D. Roosevelt, Avery had an unwelcome partner in the turnaround at Ward. A little like Avery, Roosevelt assumed the leadership of a great institution at a temporary low ebb. In the nation's affairs, as in the company's, things got better and perhaps were bound to get better, the policies of the new chief executive notwithstanding. At all events, Ward was the beneficiary, after 1933, of a rise in consumer purchasing power. In part, the rise in farm income was the result of federal price-support programs, not in any fundamental improvement in the economics of farming. ("Some of our best business is in the most distressed areas," Avery conceded.) The rise in urban incomes owed something to federal employment programs, and the pickup in building activity was partly attributable to the federal insurance of mortgages. Help his companies as they might in the short term, Avery rejected these measures on principle. He was a balanced-budget and a supply-and-demand man, a member of the Liberty League, a Republican, and an absolutely hopeless prospect for conversion to the new gospel of government intervention. When the National Recovery Administration, which was trying to regiment the nation back to prosperity, dunned Ward for $30,000 in 1935, calling the bill a charge for "code administration," Avery refused to pay. For his principle, Ward was denied the right to display the Blue Eagle, the insignia of compliance, or, as Avery might have had it, capitulation.

Fortune, in an admiring piece on Avery in 1935, had remarked on the chairman's resemblance to Henry Ford, and some disaffected Ward employees a few years later drew the same comparison in a less flattering way. Avery, according to a pamphlet that the employees distributed during one of the chronic labor disputes in which the company and they were engaged, "talks a lot, tells long stories and can turn on a considerable voltage of charm when he wants to. . . . Avery is an 1890-model unreconstructed industrialist. Most of his colleagues have more or less accepted the income tax. . . . Not so Avery. He never loses a chance to denounce it as the work of the Satan, and he is one of the chief financial backers of an outfit called the Western Tax Council, whose chief ambition is to repeal the 16th Amendment. If Avery were a Southerner, he would probably be financing a movement to restore slavery." The political left, condemning Avery's views as medieval or Edwardian, inaccurately dated them. In fact, his ideas seemed to derive from Adam Smith, Al Smith, and other libertarian sources. The drift of American politics and fiscal policy in the 1930s troubled him deeply and reinforced his native caution. They led him to take business decisions on the assumption that the chickens of statism would imminently be coming home to roost. The New Deal's attempts at price-fixing, he said, would inevitably blow up, causing a reaction of price-cutting. "And what will happen? Why, we'll get another new dollar," he replied to his own question, alluding to the abrogation of the gold-backed dollar in 1933, an event long since forgotten but then vivid and, to Avery, menacing.

It is notable what Avery didn't do as he, Roosevelt, and the natural course of economic events combined to pry Ward out of its hole. He did not borrow to build new stores or acquire new businesses. Under Avery, the company never borrowed a dollar, sky-high tax rates and rock-bottom interest rates notwithstanding. By the lights of the 1980s, his conservatism was not so much quaint as astounding. To the modern investment banker, to whom debt is a kind of legal tender, it will be hard to imagine the financial climate in which Avery carried his perpetually unfurled umbrella. From 1933 to 1936, business activity did, in fact, rebound, and commodity prices climbed. The stock market rallied. However, millions were still unemployed, and the nation's economy labored under a kind of nagging, low-level virus. Montgomery, Ward & Co., newly prosperous, was capitalized almost entirely with common stock. It could have borrowed, had Avery not been Avery, and the times not been as fragile as they were, but the fear of debt ran deep among lenders and borrowers. Interest rates charged to risky borrowers were high in relation to interest rates charged to investment-grade borrowers, but interest rates in general were strikingly low. In 1938 and 1939, the average yield on a three-month Treasury bill was less than one-tenth of 1 percent. Yields on Treasury bonds declined irregularly, but significantly, to 2.36 percent in 1939 from 3.60 percent in 1929. Corporate borrowing costs fell too. For strong companies, like Montgomery Ward, long-term loans were available at an annual interest cost of 2.45 percent in 1939, down from 4.47 percent in 1929. In 1939, the average business-loan rate offered by the average commercial bank was 2.78 percent, down from 6.02 percent a decade earlier. Europe had confidence enough in America (or fear enough of Hitler) to send large shipments of gold across the Atlantic, but no such bullishness was evident in American business. The devastating bear market and the short, sharp recession of 1937–38 caused stock-taking of what the New Deal had accomplished and what it had obstructed. Avery was convinced that the government had stifled enterprise. Capital was cheap, he must have believed, because prospective returns were low. His political convictions notwithstanding, Avery also saw that the threat of war was a commercial stimulant. Thirty-nine stores were added in 1940, but Avery then called a halt. In the long run, he apparently decided, a mobilized economy would produce inflation, and the false prosperity of inflation, but not profits. Frank M. Folsom, one of a long line of vice presidents whom Avery drove off, was supposed to have asked Gloomy Sewell to stop haranguing his employees about the dismal prospects for the American economy. Under the chairman's influence, the story went, the men were losing their will to carry on.

Ward, though it had some peripheral defense business, was mainly a civilian enterprise, and World War II for Avery was a struggle waged chiefly against his own intrusive government. Sales held up in the war years, but net earnings were whittled down by taxes and the costs of a dizzying rate of labor turnover. "With an average monthly payroll of about 73,000 employees," according to Ward's history, "the departure of 114,000 and the hiring of 121,000 in a year was about par for the course. More than half those who left went into war industries for better pay, or, as in the case of young married men, to avoid being drafted."

Of the many government agencies with which Avery could, on principle, have quarreled, the one that he engaged at the greatest cost and along the widest front was the War Labor Board. Avery for some time had been warring with the United Mail Order, Warehouse, and Retail Employees Union, CIO. The chairman had little enough sympathy for the institution of organized labor and was largely successful in resisting the attempts of John L. Lewis to organize the Gypsum mine workers. But the specific condition of the closed shop inspired him to new feats of obstinacy. When, after a long campaign, the union won an election and was duly certified to represent 7,000 workers in Chicago, Ward refused to sign the contract until President Roosevelt twice commanded it. The sticking point was a so-called maintenance-of-membership clause, under which Ward was bound to discharge any union member who failed to pay his union dues. Avery at first contended that the WLB had no legal authority to compel Ward to do anything; the board was merely an advisory body. When Congress defined the power of the WLB in law, Avery went to court, but the litigation slogged on inconclusively.

So great was the turnover of hourly workers that, when the time came to renew the union's contract, in December 1943, Avery said he doubted that the union still represented a majority of the employees. Over the union's protests, the WLB agreed to propose another election. But it also directed the company to extend the contract until a new vote could be taken. Avery, declining to meet the government halfway, replied that the reimposition of maintenance-of-membership clauses would violate an employee's rights. With that, the union struck.

When, in April 1944, the contest was referred to the President for settlement, the odds on Avery instantly shortened. Roosevelt called on both sides to desist and wired Avery that the strike was delaying the delivery of farm equipment and other essential goods. "Further action" was threatened if the chairman refused to yield. This action turned out to be the seizure of Montgomery, Ward & Co. by the United States government. Avery resisted this too.

"He Seemed Upset"

In defiance, the chairman made photojournalistic history. In the authoritative judgment of *Time* magazine, the picture of Avery being carried out of the Ward headquarters building by a pair of steel-helmeted MPs was the "most startling newspicture since a press agent set a midget on J. P. Morgan's lap in 1933." The legal and ceremonial side of the operation was handled for the government by Attorney General Francis Biddle. It was Biddle who asked Avery to turn over the corporate books to federal accountants, to call a staff meeting to introduce his executive corps to the new, temporary owner, or, finally, to leave voluntarily under his own power.

"Did they actually carry him out?" reporters later asked the Attorney General.

"He was actually picked up and carried out of this chair," Biddle replied.

"How did he react?"

Biddle smiled. "Well, I'll tell you something. He got pretty mad when I said he had to go. Then the blood came to his face and he said to me, 'You New Dealer!' "

"An hour later," according to the *Chicago Daily News*, "Mrs. Avery, reached by telephone at the Avery residence, 209 Lake Shore Dr., said her husband had been home a few minutes previously but had departed.

" 'He seemed upset,' was her only comment."

Avery was more forthcoming to a reporter who asked him what he was going to do next.

"Why, keep right on fighting, of course," the chairman answered. "When you know something is wrong you do not quit because someone takes you out feet first, do you? Somebody has got to awaken the American people to the fact that the government has been and is coercing both employers and employees to accept a brand of unionism which in all too many cases is engineered by people who are not employees of a plant. . . . All of these devices such as the labor board, the conciliation board, etc., only appear to make workers free to choose their bargainers. Most of them are a disguise for slowly leading the nation into a government of dictators."

The legality of the government's action was never settled, either in that occupation or in a subsequent Army takeover, which began in late December 1944 and ended in October 1945, two months after the

*Sewell Avery, president of Montgomery, Ward & Co., and financial archconservative, makes one of the most famous exits in U.S. corporate history: Chicago, April 27, 1944 (*USG CORP.*)*

surrender of Japan. (In November, Avery notified the Federal Bureau of Investigation of the receipt by his office of a poison-pen letter. "One of these days you will find yourself hanged on a lamppost where you belong, you stinking fink," his correspondent wrote. "Chicago's greatest pest to the working class. Filthy slave driver beware.") The second seizure, like the first, was provoked by Avery's rejection of the closed shop and by the government's insistence that he bend to the law. The U.S. District Court held that the government had overreached itself, but it also decided that the Army could remain on the premises while the Attorney General mounted an appeal. When the case came up before the Supreme Court after the war, the Army had already decamped and the justices declined to review the legal merits of the occupation.

Thus, Avery awoke in the morning of postwar America on the wrong side of the bed. In any event, being Avery, he was inclined to expect the worst. He read extensively and was schooled in the cyclical nature of economic phenomena. Then, too, he so completely rejected the liberal economic program that he could hardly allow himself to be optimistic about its consequences. When an economist at Montgomery Ward handed him a diagram of commodity prices reaching back to the beginning of the nineteenth century, the chairman studied it raptly. Prices rose and fell recurrently. They rose in wartime inflations and fell in subsequent postwar deflations. The pattern had repeated itself as recently as 1920–21 (the damage in that episode was compounded by the perverse behavior of interest rates; instead of falling, as they were, and are, expected to do in a business slump, they stayed up). To Avery, a postwar depression was therefore a foregone conclusion. "Who am I to argue with history?" he asked, and kept on asking.

An irony of Avery's postwar term was that he invested heavily in the securities of the federal government, an organization on which he was not otherwise bullish. Faced with the choice of husbanding cash in safe but low-yielding governments, or of investing in the future of the American economy, Avery chose cash. He wanted to let the stockholders know that he wasn't going to take any wooden nickels. "As a result of a consistent record of sales growth, steady earnings, a conservative dividend policy, and no debt, the company is prepared with ample working capital and cash resources to meet postwar conditions as they develop," he assured them.

If any Ward chairman was going to repeat the Panglossian errors of the 1920s, that man would not be Avery. His policy was to wait out the postwar debacle, and he patiently did nothing. Of the next depression, he was certain of two things. First, it would be a doozy; second, it would arrive despite the government's stated policy of guaranteeing full employment. "His policy meant no immediate plans for expansion—no new stores or money for modernization," Ward's corporate biography related. "It meant squirreling away cash. Avery's associates fidgeted as they saw Wards, with inadequate inventory for customer demand, refund over $270 million in 1946 because of unfilled orders. These were lost sales which, if added to actual sales, would have boosted Wards over the top of its first billion dollars. Avery refused to budge. His distrust of the administration in Washington made him all the more certain that conditions were 'rotten' and that 'the axe was about to fall.' "

Avery, at least, proved that his enmity toward Roosevelt was nothing personal or meanly partisan. He was just as bearish under the Truman and Eisenhower administrations as he had been during the New Deal. In 1944, the United Mail Order workers had charged that "Sewell Avery's ideas about things are just what you'd expect in a rich man 70 years old—only more so." The passing years had failed to open his mind. "Unlike the Sears management," Ward's historian wrote, "Avery opposed pension funds, insurance and profit sharing. Questioned about Ward's failure to expand, Avery replied that normal construction costs of $3 per square foot would return (with the recession he still expected), and there was no sense spending money on $14-a-foot buildings."

Looking the Wrong Way

If the government could be taken at its word, business in the postwar world faced not a standard deflation but a newfangled, state-sponsored inflation. The historical pattern of commodity prices would fly off the known charts. It would pay to borrow, because consumer prices would certainly rise. Debtors would be able to repay their loans in the future with depreciating money. Shell Union Oil Co., for one, understood this new world or gave every lucky appearance of understanding it. On April 17, 1946, the company made one of the best bargains in the history of the capital markets, borrowing $125 million (then a huge sum for an American corporation) for twenty-five years at an interest cost of just 2.42 percent. At just about that time, interest rates, which had been irregularly falling since 1920, started rising. Like Avery, the creditors of 1946 feared depression more than inflation, and they insisted that the issuer's lawyers warrant that Shell Union Oil and subsidiaries would not borrow excessively in the future. When the New York State Banking Department gave the issue its imprimatur—the bonds were held to be an appropriate investment for savings banks—investors heaved a collective sigh of relief. What they could not imagine was how little the future would resemble the past or how irrelevant the state's assurances would be in the face of rising interest rates. Shell Union Oil would be able to repay its debt, all right, but not in the kind of dollars it had borrowed from its trusting creditors. It would repay in inflated dollars. (In retrospect, it was almost impossible to miss the inflationary signs. Labor was tight, wages were rising, and bank credit was starting to expand. The lead story in *The Wall Street Journal* of April 3, 1946, dealt with a decline in the nation's savings rate—"Individuals Keep Less for 'Rainy Day' as Cost of Living Mounts.")

The cost of borrowed money would continue to rise, slowly at first, alarmingly at last, until September 30, 1981, when long-dated government bonds would yield almost 15 percent. It is an interesting psychological exercise to wonder if Avery could have brought himself to borrow even if he had been a financial clairvoyant. As it was, he turned Ward into "the bank with a storefront." U.S. Gypsum, of which he remained chairman until 1951, similarly trod the straight and narrow. No debt was taken aboard in the postwar years and holdings of government securities—the bills and notes of the Truman administration, for which Avery undoubtedly did not cast a vote—piled up. Unlike Ward, however, Gypsum continued to invest in plant and equipment in the immediate postwar years. It pulled back at the first inkling of the mild 1949 recession and lay low during the Korean War. Yet its market share—a commanding 50 percent—suffered no erosion, and its profits continued to grow.

Avery's refusal to install air conditioning might have been put down to conservative eccentricity. His all-season caution became a matter for worry, however, as archrival Sears, Roebuck & Co. expanded and modernized at a gallop. In 1946, the Chicago competitors were almost evenly matched in stores (628 for Ward vs. 603 for Sears) and sales ($974 million for Ward vs. $1,045 million for Sears). By 1951, Ward had nothing to brag about but its cash and its unrivaled preparation for the next depression. Sears had pulled ahead in stores and was doing more than double the annual volume of Ward in dollars ($2.6 billion vs. $1.1 billion). All this had been done without a financial stretch. Until 1951, successive postwar balance sheets showed not a dime of debt. In 1952, Sears took out a $200 million bank loan at an interest rate of 2¾ percent. To weigh the cost of borrowing against the return on those funds, the retailer, in the early 1950s, was earning 13 percent and up, after taxes, on its owners' equity. It was earning more than 8 percent after tax on its overall assets. To express the prudence of General Robert E. Wood, Avery's opposite number at Sears, in another way, Sears's net income sufficed to cover its annual interest expense by 39 times in 1952 and by 19 times in 1953 and 1954. Sears evidently felt—and no contemporary financial theorist would disagree—that it could hardly afford not to borrow.

Although lying back on his oars in retail matters, Avery was compulsively active in personnel decisions. He did not needlessly stir up dissension at U.S. Gypsum, which was a model of stability and employee dedication. At Ward, however, he could not, or would not, keep the executives he had carefully recruited. He hated to delegate even minor decisions, liked to gossip, and brooked no dissent, real or imagined. His wife was said to exercise veto power over the buyers' selections of hats. "Don't you know," he once said impishly, "that in the ideal corporation there is no difference of opinion? But, of course, if anybody ventures to differ with me, I throw them out of the window." The result was perpetual motion in the executive suite. Between 1931 and 1948, twenty-seven vice presidents and three presidents resigned (or as *The Wall Street Journal* interpreted it, sarcastically using quotation marks, "resigned"). In 1948, J. P. Morgan's two representatives withdrew from the board; No. 23 Wall Street had despaired of its favorite financial conservative. The mass departure of a new class of right-hand men in 1949, which briefly put Avery in the unusual position of being the company's only incumbent officer, prompted the *Chicago Journal of Commerce* to report, "Ward Runs Out of Vice Presidents."

"The trouble with Wall Street," Avery once said, "is that every time you make a dollar this year, they figure you will make three next." Avery did his best to keep his stockholders' expectations under control. At the 1952 annual meeting, he declared that the national economy might "topple very soon." He repeated his warning in 1953, charging that his critics "didn't know what they were talking about." In 1954, the year in which the Dow Jones Industrial Average finally recovered its losses from the Great Depression, Avery told the stockholders, "From the looks of things, the country is in a distressful condition." When a newsman asked for details, Avery almost bit his head off. "You know damn well what I think," he snapped.

Proxy Battle Royal

On August 26, 1954, Louis E. Wolfson, forty-two years old, a hand-some, well-set-up former right end from the University of Georgia, called a press conference in New York to declare that he was buying stock in Montgomery Ward with an eye to winning control. He said that his associates and he controlled the largest single block of stock in the company, bigger than Avery's 64,000 shares (the chairman had evidently done some selling, for he had once held 100,000 shares, which had made him the largest individual holder). Wolfson attacked Ward's management but not the eighty-year-old chief personally. "We intend to do all we legally and properly can to change the management in order to achieve progressive and essential reforms and to restore Montgomery Ward to its position of the great American institution it deserves to be," he told the press—some fifty representatives of news-papers, television, magazines, and newsreels were on hand at the meeting at the Biltmore Hotel. Wolfson, who reportedly controlled corporate assets worth $200 million, accused the Avery regime of "hoarding money." He noted that, as Sears grew, Ward was actually shrinking—not only in relative terms but also in dollars. Postwar sales had peaked in 1948 and no new stores had been opened since 1941 because Avery kept saying that building costs were inflated and bound to collapse. Ward's management, Wolfson charged, had "blindly and obstinately hitched the company's future to a depression."

Avery, who appreciated a well-turned phrase, refused to acknowl-edge Wolfson's. "Mr. Avery," a Ward spokesman told the press, "is not making any comment and I am quite sure that he will not recognize the Wolfson campaign in any way." Even in those days, entrenched corporate management was sometimes less entrenched than it believed itself to be, but the great offensive weapons of corporate warfare were not yet invented or put into service. No commercial lender was offering credit to would-be takeover artists. There was no junk-bond market (Michael Milken in 1954 was eight years old) and no ideology of financial leverage. Great American universities had not yet produced a body of theory to explain the social benefits of extreme indebtedness. Interest rates were, of course, low and federal tax rates high. In 1954, Ward paid 52 percent of its operating income to the Treasury. So a corporation could borrow at 2½ percent or 3 percent and deduct most of that negligible expense from its federal tax bill. It was cheap capital, but bankers had still not shaken the Depression-era habit of saying "no" to loan applicants. Credit was cheap but not abundant. In the 1980s, credit would become abundant but not cheap. (In 1989, Donald P. Kelly, a corporate executive well known for feats of indebtedness, reflected on earlier financial attitudes. "The trouble is that you had the Sewell Avery type of thinking for so long in this country. I would go to a meeting and the CFO [chief financial officer] would say, 'We are moving toward our goal of having a 25 percent debt-to-equity ratio. Hopefully someday we will have a debt-free company.' I would say, 'That makes no sense at all. If we have a debt-free company, somebody will take it over.' ")

Unable to borrow the money with which to buy the company, Wolfson had a mammoth job of persuasion ahead of him. By the next annual meeting, in April 1955, he would have to line up enough votes to defeat Avery, Mr. Montgomery Ward himself. In the mid-1950s, individual Americans still owned more than half of all the stock in investor-owned American businesses. The now familiar apparatus for collecting and concentrating the ownership of stock during a takeover contest—eager bank lenders and a class of professional accumulators called arbitrageurs—did not exist. Wolfson's difficulties were compounded by the legal obstructions that Ward had thrown up against any unsolicited advance. Only three of Ward's nine directors were up for election in any one year. On the other hand, at the next election one of those directors would be Avery.

The challenger announced that he would tour the nation to solicit the votes of the other 67,731 stockholders in person, over coffee. And in the meantime, Wolfson told the newsmen, "I invite all Montgomery Ward stockholders to express their views on my program by writing me at Wolfson-Montgomery Ward Stockholders Committee." What loomed before Wall Street, then, was an old-fashioned proxy fight. In the prior year, there had been thirty such contests for the control of American corporations, and six had been won by insurgents. Robert H. Young had won control of the New York Central Railroad, and Patrick McGinnis had taken over the New York, New Haven & Hartford Railroad. Affiliated Fund and American Business Shares, institutions which together held 105,000 shares of Ward, that day issued a sympathetically noncommittal statement promising a careful hearing to any proposal that Wolfson might advance. All in all, it was a propitious start for this son of an immigrant junk dealer.

The economic and financial winds were certainly blowing Wolfson's way. On November 23, 1954, Wall Street finally put the Crash behind it by cheering the highest closing level on the Dow Jones Industrial

Average since October 22, 1929. The market's surge that day was unambiguous: 200 issues made new 1954 highs, while only five made new lows. Montgomery, Ward & Co., which closed at 75⅞ on the day Wolfson disclosed his plans, was quoted at 72⅜, down 3½. Altogether, the stock had appreciated by 26 percent from the low price of 1946, the first postwar year in which, contrary to the Avery analysis, the Depression did not resume.

The proxy contest began on a civil note but promptly became rancorous. The first stone was hurled in the Ward annual report for the fiscal year ended January 31, 1955. Avery wrote: "The Kefauver Crime Committee questioned Mr. Wolfson about his part in financing the successful campaign of Fuller Warren for governor of Florida."

Wolfson responded in an open letter, which led off: "Your so-called Annual Report to the stockholders . . . obviously is intended to becloud the issue and to conceal the dismal record of your management in 1954. . . ."

Each man had his point. Ward was almost moribund commercially and Wolfson was questionable personally. In later years, Wolfson would be indicted, convicted, and imprisoned for violations of the securities laws, despite courtroom testimony by character witnesses including such luminaries as Ed Sullivan and Joe DiMaggio. In 1955, however, the Avery forces had no bill of particulars against the handsome industrialist except the self-interested hunch that he didn't add up.

Stockholders of Montgomery, Ward & Co. convened at 10:30 a.m. on April 22 at the Medina Shrine Temple in Chicago. The meeting had been planned for the Conrad Hilton Hotel but was relocated to accommodate an expected crush of investors, reporters, and photographers. Avery, dressed in a blue double-breasted suit, was grinning. He stepped to the dais and, ignoring every woman in the house (these included a nominee for director on the Wolfson slate, Wolfson's wife, and Avery's two daughters) said, "Gentlemen, the meeting will come to order."

Avery, whose age had been given as eighty-one, corrected the record by saying that he was really eighty-two. He looked and sounded all of those years. Photographs the next day showed him at the end of the meeting in a victory gesture, arms raised over his head, white cuffs thrusting out of his sleeves, and white handkerchief peeking nattily out of his jacket pocket. However, for much of the day he had seemed vague and distracted, and the opposition consistently scored points on him. After Avery opened the meeting, he promptly sat down, turning over the chair to a vice president. Wolfson protested: "Without showing or intending any disrespect for Mr. Avery, it seems clear that the chairman is not able to conduct this meeting." When Avery did return to the dais to deliver his remarks on the state of the company and to field stockholders' questions, the results were alarming. "I can't hear anything," he said. "Everything they're saying is a jumble. I am utterly confused by our friend who has a very hungry eye for Montgomery Ward." Periodically, the chairman appeared to forget about the stockholders, turning his back on the audience to address his fellow executives, lined up in seats behind him. At one point, he interrupted himself in the middle of an exposition on the nature of economic cycles. "Oh, that's enough," he said suddenly, not necessarily disappointing the audience but certainly startling it. "He . . . talked for a while about company affairs in a voice so low that I missed a good deal of what he said," John Brooks, *The New Yorker*'s man on the scene, reported, "although I once caught the phrase 'When the economic rain arrives' and knew that he was not letting his public down."

After the meeting, the president of Montgomery Ward, Edmund A. Krider, delivered a parting shot to the corporation's unwanted suitors. It was his personal opinion, said Krider, that if management had had "another month to expose the background and the financial machinations of the Wolfson group, he would not have elected a single director outside of the stock upon which he and his group had claims through various deals and promises."

Harsh words—and in view of Wolfson's subsequent brushes with the law, not implausible ones. But it must also be said of Wolfson, who, in fact, elected three out of nine directors, that his cause was worthy, and his words were graceful and well chosen. Commenting on the restrictive corporate voting practices that he had successfully challenged, he said, "This is not a Wolfson nor an Avery corporation. This is your corporation." Later, putting the best face on things, he said, "As the significance of this victory becomes understood, shareholders will recognize that they are not voiceless and directors and executives will become aware of the power of the investor to hold management to account for their stewardship."

With clairvoyance, Wolfson might have said "the power of the investor, as magnified by the power of the lender." As it was, no banker in 1955 would have considered advancing him the fortune with which to buy Montgomery Ward outright. And it is hard to imagine an issue of Montgomery Ward junk bonds being met by the creditors of the day with any attitude except bewilderment or revulsion. (The early 1950s did see the advent of so-called incentive financing—an insurance company would lend to an unseasoned company at an interest rate of 5 percent or 6 percent in exchange for the future purchase of that company's common stock at an advantageous price. But it was tame stuff by the lights of the 1980s.) The collective attitude of lenders toward risk was not unlike the attitude of Bertha Bauer, a former Republican national committeewoman from Illinois, toward Avery. "I'm on the right side—Avery's," she told the *Chicago Tribune*. "He's a conservative businessman. He retains a large surplus because in this hectic age no one knows what will happen."

Then again, every age is hectic, and markets are always uncertain. Even the chairman's friends had come to see that his time had passed, and shortly after the meeting he announced his resignation. The story went out from Montgomery Ward that the old man had been planning to retire anyway, but had chosen to stay on just long enough to repel Wolfson. "At the outset of the proxy contest," said Avery in a statement, "I announced our intention to resist this raid with every legitimate means at our command. We have done so to the extent that the Wolfson contest was ingloriously repudiated by the stockholders. . . . I now lay down the responsibilities which I have carried at Montgomery Ward since 1931. I leave the chairmanship with the company in a sound financial condition."

There could be no quibbles on that point. Ward had cash and marketable securities on the order of $600 million and was, of course, debt-free. It was well positioned to deal with any economic calamity that the Eisenhower administration might serve up. For his part, Wolfson said he welcomed Avery's resignation as chairman but was glad of his continued presence on the board, "because I sincerely believe that the directors will benefit from his years of experience."

Perhaps the least guarded and most prophetic comment on the day's events was delivered by the stock market. "Immediately before word of the resignation hit the New York Stock Exchange floor," according to *The New York Times*, "Montgomery Ward . . . was selling at 76¾, up 1¾ from its Friday close. Orders to buy flooded in, and at 12:24 p.m. trading had to be suspended, because selling orders were in short supply. By 1:17 p.m. the exchange was able to open the stock at 80 on a block of 16,000 shares, up 2 points from its last sale and 4½ points from the Friday close. Thereafter it increased to 81½, but closed at 80, up 4½ points on the day. Ward's was the most active issue on the exchange yesterday, trading 48,300 shares."

The Great Depression was, at long last, over.

2

Mr. Baker's Bank

In 1933, the critic Lewis Mumford, in high dudgeon about a new colonial-style bank building at Madison Avenue and Sixty-third Street (he said it reminded him of a monument to the Daughters of the American Revolution), pleaded, "Has it ever occurred to any architect that the best protection for money not in the vaults would be a complete glass front, which would make it impossible for anyone to stage a holdup without the whole world knowing it? Columns and heavy masonry fronts look safe but glass would *be* safe." Mumford's vision, in the form of a branch of Manufacturers Trust Company, began to rise two decades later on the southwest corner of Fifth Avenue and Forty-third Street. It bore no resemblance to any other bank branch in New York. As Mumford had proposed, the building was transparent. Sheathing the outside walls were enormous panes of glass, some of which measured ten feet by twenty-two feet, the largest such glass sheets ever cast. They were one-half inch thick (thought to be the ideal gauge for transparency and strength), weighed 1,500 pounds, and cost a dollar a pound, uninstalled. The glass curtain, ingeniously suspended on only eight interior columns, actually hung in place. So close were the tolerances and so precise the sizing and fitting that the builder's superintendent described the job as "more like jewelry than building." Not one of these glass gems was lost in construction: a bullish omen.

The building hardly looked like a bank, inside or out. Up until the mid-1950s, the most popular style of bank design had been the impregnable look. As bankers dressed in dark suits, so banks were built along classical lines. When, in those days, the classical forms were broken, the result was not informality but a new style of grandeur— a double-breasted blue suit, rather than a single-breasted one. Reformers of the Progressive era had demanded that banks disclose their

*Vision of things to come: Manufacturers Trust Co.'s new transparent branch at Fifth Avenue and Forty-third Street, 1954 (*MANUFACTURERS HANOVER TRUST CO.*)*

investments to enable the public to make an informed judgment about the safety of its deposits. Manufacturers and its architect, Skidmore, Owings & Merrill, had adapted this philosophy of sunshine by literally opening the bank walls. At Fifth Avenue and Forty-third Street, the vault was displayed in plain sight at street level. The safe itself was naturally opaque—banks were not (and are not) bound to divulge the details of their securities or loans, except to examiners—but the public could see that there was a safe. It was set in the window like the gowns at Saks. Daylight and floodlight alternately shone on the stainless steel and polished bronze of the vault's door, and the heavy pedestrian traffic assured the bank of an ever-changing, twenty-four-hour watch for its depositors' money.

"The thing about many another bank in this area," said Horace Flanigan, president of the company, "is that you can never tell what goes on inside; it might be a funeral parlor or they might be selling policy slips." For all the modern art and daylight, there was no mistaking the function of the Manufacturers fishbowl. The vault gave it away. "According to the architects," *The New York Times* commented editorially in September 1954, a few weeks before the branch opened, "the idea is to make complete transparency provide for other people's money in the bankers' charge the protection for which steel and concrete vaults have been the traditional reliance." The architect, Gordon Bunshaft, reflected years later that the chief legacy of his design was that it "broke the masonry-fortress psychology of branch banks up to then. . . . From then on, banks all across the country became friendly." Or even seductive. "The bank appeared to be beckoning suggestively to passersby to come in and borrow money and in the passersby came, not awestruck and humble as in times past but eager to be caressed and seduced," ventured the critic Brendan Gill.

Fifteen thousand people, not satisfied with looking into the bank from Fifth Avenue, trooped through it on opening day, and thousands more visited when President Flanigan ordered the new branch to keep its doors open for the next three days until 9 p.m. The *Times*, reporting on the inaugural crowd, remarked that the building seemed more like a hotel lobby than a bank. Not every banker was pleased by the break from tradition, the paper reported, but one, in particular, had reason to be gratified: "To Harold Miner, vice president in charge of the branch who will observe his thirtieth anniversary on the staff in December, it 'still seemed a little unreal' compared to the gloomy quarters from which the bank had moved directly across the street."

Altogether, money was becoming more cheerful. In the autumn of 1954, the stock market was ascendant, business activity was expanding, and the stigma that had attached to Wall Street in the Great Depression was disappearing. If Manufacturers Trust built its bank of glass, it was perhaps because money was regaining its good looks. Debt had not lost its capacity to jar the American sensibility, but people no longer feared for the safety of their deposits as they used to. Capital was becoming braver.

The rise in the new, transparent style of banking was matched by the decline in the old, impregnable approach. The epitome of the monumental institution was, by the early 1950s, in a paradoxically weak position. This was the First National Bank of the City of New York, still known to graybeards as "Baker's Bank" long after the death of its chairman, guiding light, and controlling stockholder, George F. Baker, in 1931. The First National Bank was the first national bank to be chartered in New York City under the National Currency Act of 1863. In New York, it was first in reputation, in conservatism, and in its refusal to bend to new ways. For years it would not accept an account of less than six figures, and it confined its lending to the kind of solid American corporation that didn't really need the money. In return, the same corporations made large, non-interest-bearing deposits which the First could do with as it saw fit. It was in the certainty that the bank would do something wholly safe—for instance, buy Treasury bills—that the depositors turned over their money. Until his death in 1947, Henry Ford left $5 million on deposit for his own account and the Ford Motor Company kept $50 million. U.S. Steel favored the bank with $10 million, and the National Biscuit Co. with as much as $30 million. After World War II, the First found itself with deposits of $715 million but depositors numbering only 1,200. At that, the depositors easily outnumbered the 240 employees.

The First National Bank occupied only one discreet line in the Manhattan telephone directory. It had no branch offices—Baker disapproved of "chain-store banking"—and no separately listed departments. It had no overseas offices. In all its ninety-two-year existence, the bank had occupied quarters at, or near, the corner of Broadway and Wall Street. For most of that time, it was housed in a Victorian brownstone, which, at the time of its completion in 1881, was one of the larger Manhattan office buildings. Although well appointed with window glass and radiating an undeniable antique charm, "Old Fort Sherman" (so named for services the bank rendered a Secretary of the Treasury, John Sherman, in 1879) beckoned no passersby indoors to apply for a small loan.

George Fisher Baker was descended from Richard Baker, who landed in the Massachusetts Bay Colony in 1635 and settled in Dorchester. Five generations of Bakers stayed put. The family of Baker's father moved to Dedham, Massachusetts, in 1816. Moving still further afield, Mr. Baker's father, George Ellis Baker, subsequently opened a shoe store in Troy, New York. Not succeeding in Troy, he moved to the village of Williamsburg, now part of Brooklyn, in the early 1840s. He opened another shoe store, on Maiden Lane in Manhattan, and commuted. This store too failed to catch on. What did succeed was Baker himself, in politics. He was clerk of the board of trustees of the village of Williamsburg and a census taker. In 1850, he was elected on the Whig ticket to the New York State Assembly. In Albany, he fastened himself to the career of William H. Seward, a former governor and incumbent U.S. senator and (it was thought by Baker and others) a future President.

George F. Baker was born in 1840 in Troy. His proud father recorded glimpses of his two-year-old son in letters home to Massachusetts: "He knows every letter whenever he sees it on signs or in the newspaper. Today—Sunday—in the morning he had on his new velvet cap, green dress with sleeves and cape, and his cane, and with his red morocco hymn book under his arm he started off with me to Meeting." George liked kittens and would use his cane to stir up the pigs. "Perhaps I am vain," wrote his father, "but I see a great many folks stop and say, 'See that sweet little boy.' "

Because of his father's long absences on legislative business, George, at the age of ten, was sent to live with his grandmother and an aunt and uncle in Massachusetts. Young Baker spent his summers working on the farm of his father's uncle by marriage and his winters attending school in Dedham. The eleven-year-old George received a letter from his father that said, in part, "Your Mother [Eveline] is glad that you are having your tooth out and that you are not going to dancing school—you can do that some other time."

At the age of fourteen, George entered the S. S. Seward Institute, Florida, New York (owned by the political Sewards), where he studied geography, bookkeeping, history, and algebra. His academic career was brief. "I should like to go to school for a year longer," he wrote to his uncle in May 1855, "but I can't; so I am going to study as hard as I can this term." He added, "I wish I had my fishing pole." Finishing school that fall, George rejoined his family, who had moved to Albany, the state capital. He clerked in a grocery store for $2.00 a week and became a night watchman for a small bank at $5.00 a week. His father, who had become secretary to Governor Myron H. Clark, was able to secure him the post of juniormost clerk in the New York State Banking Department, at $500 a year. "George Fisher has a good salary for one his age," his mother wrote in 1856.

George must have been one of the most industrious clerks in the history of the public sector. "I like my situation very much indeed," he wrote to another uncle in 1856. "Although the hours are short (9 to 5) I am pretty busy while I am there. We are very busy just at present as there is a great call for circulation and I keep busy numbering the bank notes. Yesterday I numbered 300 in 36 minutes so you can see I keep my fingers busy, sometimes for three or four hours steady."

George lived at home with his family. He saved money, went riding, and successfully raced his own scull on the Hudson River. He was able to chin himself with one arm (a feat he would drop into conversations for the rest of his life). He made his first investment: a share of stock in American Express Co. The uncle after whom George took his middle name was Fisher Baker. Fisher was three years older than George. They were playmates as children and fast friends as young men. In 1859, George traveled to Hanover, New Hampshire, to attend the commencement exercises of Fisher's class at Dartmouth College. The train on which George was returning to Albany plunged forty-two feet from a bridge. It killed a number of passengers and crushed George's leg. On September 2, 1859, George wrote to Fisher: "The bones have not yet begun to knit. My leg will be strong but always shorter than the other—we hope by not more than one inch."

At the start of the Civil War, Fisher enlisted with the 18th Regiment of the Massachusetts Volunteers and rose to the rank of first lieutenant and adjutant. He survived the siege of Petersburg and the battles of Fredericksburg, Chancellorsville, Gettysburg, Wilderness, and Cold Harbor. George, who stayed out of the war, began to chafe under the routine of the Banking Department. On March 27, 1861, he came of age: "21 years old," he wrote in his diary. "Father gave me five shares of stock in the Williamsburgh Gas Light Company." George's father had gone to Washington. Lincoln had appointed Seward Secretary of State, and Seward had appointed George E. Baker disbursing clerk and administrator of the Secret Service Fund.

Great events filled the newspapers and the lives of his friends and his father. "I was reading your account of having a Commercial Agent in the Pacific Islands," George wrote to his father, "and supposed it was going to finish by asking me if I would not like to go instead of saying you did not like that place for me. What would be the objection if I could have it and get $2,000 a year and make a good deal more besides?" Shortly after the declaration of war, George was made an assistant to the military secretary in the governor's office in Albany. He joined the Zouave Cadets and drilled daily for an hour and a half. "Have I told you I was a soldier?" he offhandedly asked his father in April 1861.

The thought of returning to the Banking Department—"to make of myself a machine again"—oppressed him. He wanted the job in the South Seas. He attended to his family's finances and kept the minutes of the Military Board and the Board of State Officers. He advised his father that Lincoln "ought to exercise more." He wrote that it was hard to break away from his work to attend the weekly meetings of his reading circle. The title on the circle's agenda for May 3, 1861, was *King Lear*. In the course of his work, George learned military secrets, which raised his self-esteem. "Of course I have to know a great many things which are purely confidential," he let his father know.

Though George was removed from the banking routine, he kept

his father abreast of the financial gossip. He told a story about the failure of the Bank of Albany. The cashier, Kendrick by name, had been earning only $3,000 a year but spending $10,000. "An incident occurred two or three weeks before the Bank of Albany failed," George wrote. "A gentleman who had invested about $7,000 in the Stock, thinking it as secure as real estate, was walking down the street with another gentleman, who remarked to him: 'This is one of the finest turnouts in the City,' speaking of Kendrick's establishment. 'Who owns it?' 'Kendrick does.' The man thought it over and concluded if a Cashier could keep such an establishment and live in style on a $3,000 annual salary, there must be a screw loose in the Bank somewhere."

On May 29, 1861, Baker wrote earnestly to his father: "I shall stick to my exercise at all hazards as imperatively necessary."

A recurrent topic in George's letters was money. He asked his father to send it, acknowledged its receipt, and proposed plans to invest it. On May 31, he suggested the purchase of U.S. Treasury bonds at the then depressed price of 79 cents on the dollar. "It would pay good interest—equal to 7½% and then it will probably rise to par or over within a few years if not in one," he wrote. By "par," George meant 100 cents on the dollar. With his father's financial help, he conducted a business in American flags. When his father once questioned his ethical judgment in a flag-related business matter, George wrote that he was "surprised and pained."

Banking Prodigy

Baker made his mark as the most imaginative, yet prudent, banker in the country, but neither then nor later was he unalterably opposed to debt. On June 8, he thought of another reason why his father should send him funds to use in speculating in government securities. He said that the debt hanging over his head would make him save.

George wrote to his father on August 26, 1861: "For two weeks I have felt a point under the flesh of my leg as if a piece of bone was working up. Last night I was a little nervous about it and took my knife and cut it open just over the place and probed it with a knitting needle. I discovered quite a large piece of bone there."

On October 8, 1861: "Yesterday Dr. Armsley made an unsuccessful attempt to remove a piece of bone from my leg. He used a pair of forceps but was unable to get it out. He broke off several pieces. It didn't feel very good I assure you."

George suffered recurrent splitting headaches. He continued to drill with the militia and rub shoulders with senior New York politicians. "Plenty of champagne," he reported to his father about a dinner party at which one colonel, one lieutenant governor, two generals, the state attorney general, and he (among others) were present, "though I only took one glass." He owned a share in a horse and buggy.

George, at the age of twenty-two, showed signs of mature financial judgment. He had become a student of the government-bond market and advised his father on buying and selling particular issues. He had evolved his own ideas about interest rates, monetary affairs, and stock prices. He recognized, for example, that high interest rates are tantamount to high risk. This timeless wisdom he shared with his father: "I believe it to be a pretty safe rule that whenever you get over 7% interest you must take a corresponding amount of risk. Like the Bank of Albany even paid 12% and thought to be safe as gold, yet went up higher than a kite. . . . What do you gain at 10 or 20% interest if you lose your principal or part of it? Rich men can afford to risk their money but we poor folks must look out for the principals [sic] as well as interest."

At all times and in all markets, there is the choice between selling a good thing and standing pat. In his mature years, Baker hardly ever sold. He believed that, over the long run, things would invariably get better in America. On March 20, 1862, however, he approached the question less rigidly. He ventured that stock prices would continue to rise because the government would continue to issue paper currency to finance the war. The issuance was inflationary, but not (as one may read between the lines) a permanent blessing. "When things go up then is the time to sell," he counseled his father.

"As I grow older," George reflected on the eve of his twenty-second birthday, "I feel more and more the want of a better education and I have been trying since this Winter to improve myself and shall keep on hoping I may in some degree make up for my deficiency. The greatest trouble I have is in my memory—I cannot retain what I read or hear sufficiently well. I think I shall commit some pieces to memory and see if it will not produce a beneficial result."

George F. Baker had come under the appraising eye of John Thompson, a financial publisher and dealer in bank notes. Thompson, who wore oval-shaped, wire-rim spectacles and a lush, white beard, lived in New York. He was a frequent visitor to the State Banking Department in Albany and could see as well as anyone else that George F. Baker was destined for bigger things than the civil service. Thompson was born near Pittsfield, Massachusetts, in 1802. His father had fought in the Revolutionary War. Thompson *fils* taught school, dealt in lottery tickets, and, in 1832, moved to New York to set up as a broker in money, bank notes, and foreign exchange.

Thompson arrived in the same year that President Andrew Jackson vetoed the rechartering of the Second Bank of the United States. The bank was a forerunner to the Federal Reserve System and, like many another financial creation of government, it owed its existence to wartime necessity (in this case, to the debts run up in the War of 1812). It also excited political opposition on the ground that the Constitution did not list the ownership and management of a bank among the federal government's enumerated powers. This was eighty years before the enactment of the Federal Reserve and a century before the creation of the Federal Deposit Insurance Corporation. In Thompson's time, there was no national banking system and no uniform national currency. The essentially local character of the banking system had both advantages and drawbacks. Thousands of state banks competed with each other to issue paper money—that is, bank notes. The notes of solvent, upstanding banks changed hands at par. Those of distant or crooked banks traded at a discount. Shoddy notes were called "shinplasters."

Competition was all to the good, and Hugh Rockoff, a scholar writing in the 1970s, estimated that noteholders' losses from all "free" banks in 1860 were less than 2 percent, substantially less than the great inflation of his time annually cost the holders of uniform United States government money. On the other hand, the plethora of notes was confusing, and by the time of the Civil War, counterfeiters in search of originals to forge had some 7,000 different varieties and denominations to choose from. This confusion John Thompson seized upon as a business opportunity.

Thompson's Bank Note Reporter, first published in 1842, was a weekly devoted to sorting out good banks and their notes from the bad banks and theirs. "Fraudulent and unsafe banks will be pointed out and the public put on their guard where failures may be expected regardless alike of the favor or ill will of the great financiers," an advertisement promised.

Thompson loved to deliver on that claim. He had a lusty, American style, and his journalistic credo was unswerving. "We have no sympathies to influence, no favors to ask, no fears to consult," he wrote to his readers. "In our editorial character, the above is our motto, and as we put it in type, we impress it deeper in our heart. We reproduce this motto at this time because we see that several of the Western bank note reporters are denounced and condemned for quoting and puffing shinplasters. We are too old to be trapped by fog financiers. It is our delight to crush them. It is our sport to agonize them. It is our duty to exterminate them. We see them on their winding way. We discover them tampering with the engravers, puffing their swindles in advertisements, occasionally buying up an editor and often fastening upon green publishers of bank note lists. We have felt the slimy skin of a shinplaster banker grasping us by the hand, but we much prefer a libel suit to any such contact."

Thompson was a businessman first and a journalist second, and he never relinquished his trading business; he simultaneously dealt in bank notes and wrote about them. When the Panic of 1857 struck, he was caught holding a large block of notes of a failed Ohio bank. His bankruptcy he blamed, somewhat gracelessly, on "greedy creditors." A few weeks later, he was found making paraffin candles in a room on Greenwich Street. To all callers, he cheerfully offered a free sample.

Although out of capital, Thompson was far from out of commission. Among his nonmonetary assets were two capable sons, Samuel C. and Frederick F., and a pair of loyal clerks from his former business. Thompson Brothers, organized in May 1858, was a vehicle for further triumphs. *Thompson's Bank Note Reporter* now came under Thompson Brothers ownership (it was the seedling from which eventually grew the daily trade paper *American Banker*). At the outbreak of war, John Thompson, though surely distracted by his own affairs, nonetheless was able to participate in the national debate over how to organize the banking system to serve the Union cause.

The change for which Thompson lobbied was, seemingly, against his personal interest. He advocated "government money," a national currency to circulate in place of gold. It would be a currency free of confusion, free of the risk of bank failure, and free of the risk that Americans would refuse to accept it at face value. In short, it would be a currency free of the very eccentric qualities on which Thompson had built his financial career. In 1863, a variation on Thompson's idea was adopted. The National Currency Act established a uniform currency and a new national banking system. The Currency Act constitutes a milestone in the history of the government's dealing with money and credit. It was, first and foremost, a wartime expedient, a law to promote the sale of government bonds. It created a link between the government's debt, on the one hand, and the government's paper money, on the other hand. In effect, the government undertook to socialize the money supply, or an important part of it. It was a measure that anticipated many of the financial expedients of the twentieth century. If the Civil War was the first modern war, the National Currency Act was the first modern financial legislation.

What distinguished the "greenback" from private-issue bank notes was that the government's money was convertible into nothing. It was "legal tender" by force of law rather than by virtue of intrinsic value. As a check on the solvency of note-issuing banks, Thompson had dispatched his sons in horse and buggy to present them with their own notes. To redeem one's notes was to pay gold coin for them. A bank that was incapable of meeting this demand was, prima facie, insolvent, and Thompson would fry it in his paper and perhaps precipitate its closing. The National Currency Act was a force for financial uniformity. The risk it introduced was that the national finances would become uniformly unsound rather than only irregularly unsound, as in antebellum days.

In the Currency Act (and in an 1864 revision of the law, the National Bank Act), Congress first began to look over the shoulders of the nation's bankers. In exchange for a national charter and the privilege of issuing national bank notes, a bank was obliged to conform to the regulations of the newly created office of the Comptroller of the Currency. Federal regulatory standards were harsher than those imposed by most of the states. For instance, a national bank was obliged to hold a sizable reserve, roughly equivalent to a quarter of its deposits. This "reserve" could not be lent out or invested, but was to be set aside to meet unexpected contingencies. It was to lie fallow. Also, lending against the collateral of real estate was virtually prohibited and the range of permissible investments was narrower than that allowed by the states. All in all, to most of the nation's bankers, a national charter seemed no great bargain. (One apprehension was what might happen to a national bank if the Union should lose the war; a close identification with the U.S. government would have been no valuable business asset.)

So when Thompson's sons applied for a charter shortly after the passage of the 1863 Currency Act, they were the first in line, and their bank was the first to receive a charter in the nation's financial capital. The sons' names were used for discretion's sake. The Panic of 1857 was still fresh in mind, and in the days before the socialization of credit risk, personal character weighed heavily in a banker's reputation. (As late as 1872, a federal bank examiner described the senior Thompson as "for many years somewhat notorious as the publisher of 'Thompson's Bank Note Reporter' and who made a most disastrous failure in 1857.")

It was about 1857 when Baker and Thompson met. Baker was seventeen years old and Thompson was fifty-five. When the elder Thompson invited the young Baker to join him and his sons in their new banking venture, Baker, recalling the ignominy of 1857, was unsure. The sum total of Baker's savings was $3,000, but Thompson offered him as much of the new stock as he wanted; the Thompsons would lend him the money. Baker naturally turned to his father for advice, and his letter came back:

> Washington, April 30, 1863
>
> My dear son:
>
> I guess you had better let the Bank or Thompson Brothers lend you what you want—and take as much stock as you can—depositing everything you have as collateral. It is, I think, the best investment you can have.
>
> It is a great satisfaction that in your business of Banking—selling U.S. Bonds etc.—you are not only making money but helping the Government more than anybody can help, unless it be in the Army.

Baker showed the rare capacity to become less averse to risk as he grew older. For instance, he was unguardedly bullish in 1929, at the age of eighty-nine. But he was conservative—to a fault, he later said—in 1863, at twenty-three. In any case, he refused the Thompsons' offer of a loan. He subscribed for 30 shares, for which he paid cash on the barrelhead. On July 2, 1863, a commanding telegram was handed him at the State Banking Department in Albany: "We want you here by noon tomorrow. Thompson Brothers." The First National Bank of the City of New York opened its doors for business on July 22.

Examiners Pay Tribute

From the start, the First National Bank was a hybrid. Its principal line of business was buying and selling bonds instead of traditional moneylending. It was part bank and part brokerage house. Besides his intelligence and character, George F. Baker brought the asset of political pull to his job with the Thompsons. His father was an intimate of Secretary of State Seward; and Seward, it was expected, would bring the merits of the new bank to the attention of Secretary of the Treasury Salmon P. Chase. In January 1864, the bank was appointed an agent bank for the sale of the Union's 5 percent bonds. "We propose to keep on hand a full supply of Coupon Bonds for immediate delivery," declared an ad for the bank in the hospitable pages of *Thompson's Bank Note Reporter.* "We deal in all classes of Government Securities at favorable rates."

If the bank enjoyed political preferment in Washington, it had no particular standing in New York. Evidently, it rented its modest quarters at 2½ Wall Street. "If you had a proper banking house," Baker's father wrote, "you would become an important institution, I believe." Also, the First was blackballed by the New York Clearing House Association. The Clearing House was the organization through which New York institutions settled their accounts. The state-chartered banks then ruled the roost, and they wanted no truck with a nationally chartered upstart. They were soon forced to reconsider, however, when the growth of the First's business rendered its exclusion impracticable—to them.

As early as the spring of 1864, the First was well launched. The bank's capital was increased to $500,000, and George F. Baker was hitting his stride. In March 1865, he was scolded by his mother for declining an invitation to Lincoln's second inaugural ball: "Don't let money be your idol," she wrote. In May 1865, he was made cashier. At twenty-five, he was more or less the bank's chief operating officer. "Is a young man," an examiner wrote of him in 1866, "but a very faithful and promising officer."

So quickly and profitably did the bank grow, yet so conservatively was it managed, that the examiners soon adopted a tone of outright admiration in describing its operations to their superiors in Washington. Charles A. Meigs, who was assigned to the First in the 1870s, was frequently moved to punctuate his reports with exclamation points and underscoring. For example, he noted in 1872 that the stockholders numbered just 20, and that the directors held "*4,630* shares out of 5,000!" Also, Ebenezer Scofield, besides serving as a director, was also "*assist. cashier!*" All in all, a taut ship. "This Association," Meigs remarked, "presents a case of successful Banking which is, I think, without *precedent* in the history of Banking in the City of New York, considering the time in which the parties have been engaged in it."

A contemporary banker would be struck as much as Meigs was by the breadth and variety of the First National Bank's activities. "It has combined the business of a Broker's Office into that of Banking, and the entire establishment, being as it were in the Thompson family, they have been at a little of everything in which Capital could be profitably employed," the examiner wrote. For instance, the First had cultivated business relationships with new national banks "in all parts of the United States and in fact it may well be called a Manufactory of National Banks!" It purchased Treasury bonds for its customers and performed the classical banker's function of lending against the collateral of trade bills, or invoices—one merchant's promise to pay another. In bankers' jargon, it "discounted" those bills, yet it lent in such a way as to circumscribe its own risk. "Almost all of their Discounted Paper," however, noted Meigs, "they have discounted for their Country Correspondents, with the endorsement of the Bank from whom it was discounted, and, as a consequence, *losses* in this line are of very rare occurrence."

The term "junk bond" had not yet entered the language, but the First National Bank had invested in the First Mortgage Sinking Fund 7 percent Gold Bonds of the Lake Superior & Mississippi Railroad Co. (Translation: a first mortgage is the seniormost loan; a sinking fund is a sum of money earmarked for the repayment of principal; and "gold bonds" were bonds that were bound to be repaid in U.S. dollars defined as a certain weight of gold bullion.) For the time, 7 percent was a fancy rate of interest and suggested the presence of a speculative element in a debtor's finances. U.S. government bonds yielded only 5 percent and higher-grade railroad issues returned a little over 6 percent. However, any inclination toward risk-taking on the part of the officers of the First National Bank was tempered by the fact that it was their bank. As Meigs had remarked, the directors owned most of the stock. Any mistake they made would necessarily be a sincere one. "The character of their accounts is peculiar," remarked Meigs, "but it is specially adapted to the nature of the business in which they are engaged." A favorite investment of the First was the District of Columbia. "In looking over their affairs," wrote Meigs to the home office in March 1873, "I find that over $6,500,000 of the bonds for the grading, paving, services etc. of your City has passed thro the hands of this Institution during the past two years!" And he added, admiringly: "Their Loans and Discounts are remarkably well Secured and they are doing the most remarkably Successful and profitable business of any Bank I have ever heard of."

To be well secured in the plague year of 1873 was what every banker should have been. Two months after the examiner signed his report, panic struck Vienna. In the summer, the City of London suffered a bout of tight money. In the fall, New York was convulsed by the failure of Jay Cooke & Co., the champion bond-selling house of the Union side in the Civil War. After Appomattox, Cooke became the preeminent American investment bank. It had made its reputation with government securities but overreached with Northern Pacific Railroad bonds. Jay Cooke, who had built a huge Philadelphia mansion with his Civil War earnings, certainly knew the difference between public and private finance. A sovereign government, unlike a railroad, could levy taxes. It could print money, unless it was on the gold standard. Thus the odds were against a sovereign government defaulting on securities denominated in its own currency. Railroads can now, and did then, default. Offered the chance to lead the financing of the Union Pacific in 1867, Cooke had at first declined. However, with the completion of that transcontinental line in 1869, he was moved to reconsider. The country was joined. Who could imagine the bullish vistas? To the proposition that he undertake the sale of $100 million of Northern Pacific bonds, Cooke enthusiastically said "yes."

Bigger Than Both Delawares

Baker was on record as distrusting the safety of yields in excess of 7 percent. The Northern Pacific debt, which carried no federal guarantee, yielded 7.30 percent, or three-tenths of 1 percent over the young man's line. Above the desk of one of the partners of Jay Cooke & Co. in New York hung a small, disingenuous sign: "A safe and sure investment. Buy Northern Pacific 7.30% Bonds. As good as governments. Secured by mortgage and land grants." This land Cooke urgently tried to fill with productive settlers, and an anonymous wit wrote a parody of the slightly hyperbolic Cooke advertisements. The land grant, the parodist explained, was larger than the "nine" New England states, plus the northern part of European Russia, all of France, except Alsace and Lorraine, Turkey, a portion of New Jersey and Coney Island, all in all a landmass as large as the "two states of Delaware combined." Earnestly, Cooke endorsed the safety of the bonds and pronounced them safe for widows and orphans. His dilemma was monumental. Not only was the railroad earning no money; it was also spending at a faster rate than Cooke was able to borrow for it.

However fabulous the ultimate prospects—the Northern Pacific was the largest business undertaking in the history of the United States up until that time—the immediate, prosaic truth was that it could not pay its bills. In fact, settlers were not raising oranges and bananas along the Cooke right-of-way, and Duluth did not outshine Paris. Ever greater sums of money were needed to keep the creditors at bay. Some of this money Jay Cooke & Co. itself lent. The firm had expected that the public would buy the Northern Pacific's bonds, even as it had bought the Treasury's, and that the Northern Pacific would repay its debts to Cooke. But the bonds sold slowly. In July 1873, Cooke, in desperation, advertised a kind of close-out sale. Notice was served that the railroad had decided to pay no more than 6 percent on future bond issues but that it would continue to offer 7.30 percent on one last $9 million slice. An unconscionable commission—17 cents on the dollar—was dangled in front of Cooke's best bond-selling agents. Shrewdly, however, the public refused the bait. So the firm itself went unpaid. The devastating announcement came on September 18, 1873: Jay Cooke & Co. had failed.

In inflationary times, interest rates rise and government bonds carry high yields. In the wake of inflations, however, interest rates fall. Those who demand high yields must sacrifice a measure of safety to get them. In the 1870s, yield-minded investors bought the junk bonds of the day—railroad issues—rather than Treasurys. In 1864, the directors of the First National Bank had resolved never to lend except against the collateral of U.S. government bonds. In effect, they would lend to nobody who did not have unimpeachable collateral—in other words, to nobody who really needed the loan. Inasmuch as risk is usually commensurate with reward, the policy was tantamount to a resolution against profitable lending, except that the board promptly ignored it. Meigs had been right about the bank's general fitness in March 1873. What he could not have foreseen were the extraordinary circumstances of the next autumn.

A panic exposes the essence of banking as no lecture, book, or diagram can do. The essential truth about the ordinary bank is that it is no safe-deposit box. Every dollar of the depositors' money is not in storage on the premises all the time. Some of it is, indeed, stacked in the safe, but rare is the bank in that time (and rarer still today) that could meet a demand for cash from all its depositors at once. The art of banking is always to balance the risk of a run with the reward of a profit. The tantalizing factor in the equation is that riskier borrowers pay higher interest rates. Ultimate safety—a strongbox full of currency—would avail the banker nothing. Maximum risk—a portfolio of loans to prospective bankrupts at usurious interest rates—would invite disaster. A good banker safely and profitably treads the middle ground.

The milling crowds at the corner of Broad and Wall streets and the black headlines of the evening newspapers in September 1873 must have caused more worry at the First National Bank than the officers dared to let on. For among the "remarkably well" secured loans and discounts that Meigs had noted was a recent payment to Jay Cooke & Co. for upwards of $200,000. Unluckily enough, the money was sent on September 16, just two days before the Cooke failure. Baker later tried to explain the situation to a suspicious Charles Meigs, and Meigs forwarded Baker's account to his superiors in Washington (". . . the circumstances of the case are very peculiar"). Baker claimed that the First National Bank had commissioned Jay Cooke & Co. to purchase some bills in London. By error, the bank's funds were not properly deposited but were commingled with Cooke's own accounts. In consequence, First National's funds were lost in the bankruptcy— or, as Baker tried to contend, temporarily misplaced. The mortification was worse than that. The money lost was, in fact, the money of the bank's customers. No matter: it was treated by the bank as its own. And although Baker assured Meigs that ultimate payment was certain (the advance was carried on the balance sheet as "due from a . . . Redeeming Agent, Jay Cooke"), the last dollar of the loss was not recovered until 1890, or seventeen years after the event.

The precise condition of the First National Bank in the crisis is beyond knowing. However, one of Thompson's sons recalled it as being parlous. The bank was "loaded with bad debts," wrote Frederick, a vice president of the bank, five years later. In a panic, of course, many formerly good debts suddenly turn bad, and "loaded" is a word that quite possibly was overdrawn (certainly, it was never Meigs's word). Whatever the state of the balance sheet, the panic put the Thompsons on the defensive. John Thompson, who had been through the mill in 1857, would soon be seventy-one. He was by no means ready to retire—still ahead of him was the founding of Chase National Bank, forerunner to Chase Manhattan—but he was not as inclined as Baker to defend the First to the last cent of borrowed money. His other son, Samuel, was president. According to the Baker camp, Sam lost his nerve and urged that the bank wind up in an orderly way before the depositors staged a run and closed it forcibly. Baker, then thirty-three, had invested his life's savings in the bank.

He had a wife, two small children, and an abiding optimism toward the future. To judge by the growth of the bank, not to mention Meigs's detached opinions of it, this confidence was not misplaced. In the heat of the crisis, the officers met to decide what to do.

"Sam, if you are so anxious to get out, I'll buy your stock myself," Baker remembered saying.

"What with?" Sam asked him.

Sam's shares represented a cash investment of $200,000. Not happening to have that kind of money, Baker said nothing.

Then Fred Thompson spoke. "You might just as well know where I stand," he told his brother and father. "George controls this bank. He has 652 shares and I have 2,000. I vote them with George."

Sam asked Baker what he proposed to do.

"I propose to pay every claim presented as long as the money lasts," Baker replied. "When we stop paying it will be because there is not another dollar in the till, and none obtainable."

"Well," said Sam, glancing at the package of unmarketable securities pledged toward payment of the Jay Cooke & Co. loans (not identified but perhaps identical to the involuntary advance mentioned above). "We've been cooked by the Cookes and baked by the Bakers."

For the United States and the rest of the Western financial world, 1873 marked the beginning of a monumental, five-year depression. It was the kind of epidemic that weakens even well-managed banks, but the First National Bank more than survived it. It grew, enriched its stockholders, and astounded and confounded the examiner Meigs. Early in 1874, Baker lined up the financing with which to buy control of the bank. Joining him in this investment were, among others, Harris C. Fahnestock, a former partner of Cooke's. Fahnestock, who was five years older than Baker, had made a brilliant success by running Cooke's New York office. In 1872, a year before the Northern Pacific panic, he had warned Cooke against overreaching and had protested against the fraudulent claims of the bond-selling campaign.

Young President Baker

When George F. Baker was elected president of the First National Bank on September 1, 1877, at the age of thirty-seven, Fahnestock was his vice president, in place of the aged but still spry John Thompson. Less than two weeks after the installation of Baker in the First's presidency, Thompson and his son Samuel founded Chase National.

It was an act of grit and serendipity. "I have just come from the Dry Goods Bank which is closing up its affairs," Thompson, then seventy-four and distinctive in his hand-knitted wool stockings and circa 1850 linen, told a reporter. "I told them this is just the time to start a bank. Everything is at the ebb. Everything has touched bottom and has got as low as it can. If there be any change at all, it must be for the better. A bank which has no real estate, not a debt in the world, no law suits and plenty of cash need fear for nothing. I leave the First National sound as a nut and hope it may be kept so."

Old John Thompson was right all around. By late 1877, the worst of the depression was over, and the First National Bank was most assuredly sound. "[T]he late Panic has left its *mark* upon their Investments," Meigs told Washington in April 1874, "and in my opinion they will suffer to the extent of $100,000 at least as a result. They have reduced their Dividends from 20% to 12% [of capital, which was $500,000] and intend to clear off all the rubbish during this year, even if they have to stop all Dividends, and, as the Stock is all held by the *family*, the public have little interest in the matter, as they could lose *1 Million* and still pay off their debts!"

"So the panic didn't bother you very much, did it?" Baker was asked years later at a congressional hearing. "I guess if you had been there you would have thought so," he replied dryly. Still, the clouds of 1873 were silver-lined. Baker was propelled into the ranks of capitalists, and he set about building a bank that was imaginative and conservative alike.

To Meigs's consternation, it was also complex. In those days, national bank examiners were paid a flat fee, and they were paid by the banks they examined, not by the Treasury Department. The more straightforward a bank's accounts, therefore, the better it was for the examiner. The First's accounts were "very neatly but rather intricately kept," Meigs observed with uncharacteristic understatement, and the standard examiner's form could hardly contain them. On April 6, 1874, the assets of the First National Bank totaled $10.1 million. On February 1, 1875, they were up to $15.3 million. The panic had taken its toll, but the bank was quickly making up its losses. It was a leading member of the syndicate engaged in refunding the Treasury's Civil War debt: exchanging new, low-interest bonds for the old, high-yielding ones. Meigs's head swam. In connection with the bond-selling work, money and gold were borrowed. In connection with the Cooke disaster, new collateral was obtained. A charge was taken to the surplus account, and there was some question as to the value of the District

George F. Baker, age thirty-five, casts a cool, acquisitive glance (GEORGE F. BAKER TRUST)

of Columbia investments. "I and my clerk have been there 6 days, *early and late*, and it is the hardest bank job I ever had in my life," wrote Meigs in February 1875. He was back in December and marveled anew at the scale of the First's bond-underwriting operations. Nine months' profits, the examiner noted, amounted to "$460,000!" Furthermore, questionable debts had been successfully reduced. But what a time he had had. "I really think you should assess them for a larger amount than now used, in payment of my labor in examining them, and I wish you would say to them that it is well worth twice the sum paid!"

Because it was not a conventional bank making ordinary loans, the First was spared most of the commercial distress of the 1870s. It rolled up profits in Wall Street, where it now cut a commanding figure. In exchange for the government's new 4 percent bonds, it stood ready to swap other U.S. bonds. The country was preparing to return to the gold standard, and the First took precautions against unexpected swings in the value of gold pending the restoration of a convertible dollar (that is, convertible into gold at a fixed weight). The size and astuteness of these operations impressed Meigs deeply: "Their great success in placing the 4½% and 4% Bonds is due to the fact that they are always ready to *trade*—on the instant—with Bankers and Capitalists who wish to *sell* the *old* Bonds, and re-invest in the *new ones*, and the promptness and liberality of their terms of doing such business has given them almost a *monopoly* of the U.S. Bond trade, in this City, and the *amounts* so turned over by them—whether by taking in *one* kind of *old* Bonds, and giving *new* Bonds for them . . . is simply enormous, and Vice President Fahnestock informs me that the amount 'turned over' during 1877 is $255,500,000!!" In the prior thirteen months—a disastrous time for American banking—the First had earned no less than $670,000.

As examiner Meigs continued, the First National Bank was also steadfast. In fat times, it accepted the deposits of country banks and paid them a small rate of interest, relending at a higher rate. In lean times, it would anticipate the role of the Federal Reserve System, standing ready to lend to a correspondent in trouble, as it had in 1877. "As a further illustration of the character of the managers for daring, and energy of action," the examiner related,

> I will cite the case of their correspondent—"the Rochester Savings Bank" with $8 Million Deposits—very *sound*—but upon whom a *run* was commenced about 10 days since.
>
> Two of the Trustees at once applied to the 1st National Bank for *help*—having 2 Million of U.S. and other good Bonds, in their hands.
>
> The Bank loaned them $500,000 Currency, on the spot, and hurried it to Rochester, by Express.
>
> Within a day or two $600,000 *more* was loaned them—in Currency—and hurried to Rochester—to the rescue of a solvent Institution! and a virtual agreement made to make the amount up to $2 Million, if needed—Securities to this amount being left in their hands.
>
> This prompt action saved the Savings Bank, and on the 4th Instant, $500,000 of this currency *came back* from Rochester, while I was in the 1st Nat, and they expect the balance to be returned to them in a few days, as the run was "squelched" and Deposits returning.
>
> Now, all this was done *so quietly* that the world knew not from whence the mighty "help" came.
>
> It is a great "feather in their cap" and I commend them for their energy of action at a time of most urgent need, and would *offset* this against some of their "Brokerage" business, as there

is not a single Bank in our City who *would* or *could* have helped a country correspondent to such gigantic figures, and on such short notice!

Can you wonder that this Institution gets such enormous Country Bank Deposits when *this* is the way they will come to the rescue?

In his fortieth year, 1880, George F. Baker bought his family a bigger house and a carriage, their first. In conjunction with a Broadway business neighbor, Bank of the Republic, the First National submitted construction plans for a nine-story office building at the northeast corner of Broadway and Wall Street. The fortresslike specifications included a twenty-two-foot-deep foundation, iron beams, forty-inch-thick upper walls, and a gravel-and-copper roof. Approval was obtained, work begun, and the United Bank Building (eight stories high, in fact) was completed in May 1881.

Like E. H. Harriman, the railroad titan, George F. Baker was the recipient of Wall Street's highest accolade, "moneymaker." As a rule, his stocks rose, his bank grew, his bonds paid interest, and his venture-capital investments bore fruit. (His good fortune extended beyond money. At the exclusive Jekyll Island Club, to which the banker belonged, a run of fair skies and bright sunshine was known as "Baker weather.") In banking, he struck an instinctive, lucrative balance between safety and risk. On the one hand, the First was irreproachably liquid and well capitalized. On the other, it was unusually profitable. As reward is commensurate with risk, Baker, plainly, did not owe his stupendous wealth to prudent investments in 3 percent bonds.

The venturesome side of the banker's personality did not escape detection by the federal examiners. "Of a naturally speculative nature," appraised A. M. Scuba. "[I]s engaged in many undertakings of that character which generally turn out favorably." Baker made his first big venture-capital investment in 1882 when he and a fellow First National director were invited to join a syndicate in the purchase of a controlling interest in the Richmond & Danville Railroad. Baker did not take a shot in the dark. He toured the railroad, one of the better Southern lines, for ten days. Reaching a bullish conclusion, he committed funds. He became a director and actively involved himself in management. "In 1888," writes Sheridan Logan, "the value of the road was generally recognized and another group of men decided to purchase it. The transaction took place at Mr. Baker's desk and the price paid was $240 a share." Baker's cost had been $51 a share.

Baker repeated his success with the Central Railroad of New Jersey. Again, he invested not only with his money but also with his time and executive talent. When, in 1901, he sold out to J. P. Morgan, the price was $160 a share, or four times more than his cost.

A modern banker will look back at these transactions with unalloyed nostalgia. Each antedated the federal income and capital-gains tax. Each occurred in an era of low interest rates. Each preceded the forced separation of commercial banking and investment banking. Lightly taxed (and, in comparison with late-twentieth-century standards, lightly regulated), Baker operated in what now seems a capitalist Garden of Eden. When the Jersey Central chose to consolidate its debts, for instance, the interest rate on its $50 million bond issue was 5 percent. The creditors, evidently an optimistic lot, lent their money for a hundred years. To both of Baker's railroads, Baker's bank furnished accommodation: An 1887 examiner's report lists loans of almost $300,000 and bond investments of more than $500,000 to the Richmond & Danville and the Jersey Central. To put those numbers in perspective, the bank's overall assets—loans, securities, cash, etc.— totaled just $30 million. The examiners found nothing objectionable in these arrangements. It was an exceptionally sound bank, and it was Baker's. Long after Baker's death, however, the First National Bank would decline an invitation for its officers to accept an ownership interest in a company that had applied to it for a loan. Different standards of conduct and different circumstances prevailed in the 1880s. "The small number of Shareholders," wrote examiner Scuba in 1884, "makes it [the First National Bank] practically a private Bank and they are keenly alive to their own interests and sensitive against loss."

Street-level space at the United Bank Building was rented to one of the patron saints of the Union (and thus of the national banking system and therefore of the First itself), General Ulysses S. Grant. Following his second term in the White House, Grant had embarked on a round-the-world tour. He had returned to his old home in Galena, Illinois, supposedly to live out his days in peace, but had soon removed himself to New York, where he fell into partnership with a sharpster named Ferdinand Ward. Grant & Ward, stockbrokers, promptly came to grief. The firm's failure on May 4, 1884, was astonishing for its lopsidedness. As against liabilities of $16 million, the company was able to muster assets of only $7 million. The president of Marine National Bank was a partner in Grant & Ward; the Marine too went bankrupt. The ranks of trusting bank depositors were further thinned by news of the theft of $2 million from the vault of the Second National Bank by the president of that bank himself. Now investors staged a footrace for cash, arriving at the banks on the double and queuing up outside their doors to make withdrawals. To raise cash, bankers called in loans and sold securities. No class of investment, including government bonds, was spared in the ensuing panic. "To state briefly the causes of the disturbance of the market," commented the *Commercial & Financial Chronicle*, "it may be said that they were strictly due to a complete loss of confidence, not so much in the market prices of the securities as in the stability and soundness of various institutions and firms." The federal government did not stand idly by, but it did not send money to the rescue. The Comptroller's contribution to the restoration of pre-panic conditions was to order "expert and reliable examiners to the assistance of the national-bank examiner stationed at New York to protect the public."

As for Baker's bank, no other institution in New York had done a better business in Treasury bonds. Certainly, none was more intimately bound up in the financing of the Civil War. Blinded by affection for the former President, perhaps, Baker failed to detect the fraud at Grant & Ward. "The great experience of the managers enables them to avoid any serious losses in making loans," said an examiner's report in 1885. "When they do occur, the loss is promptly charged off." Even in error, the First National Bank distinguished itself.

3

The Timid Bank

The First National did not have a monopoly on the safety-minded New York depositor. Another bank with the word "National" in its name, the National City Bank, forerunner of Citibank and its holding company, Citicorp, had nearly come a cropper in the Panic of 1837, and new management never seemed to forget that near miss. Under the watchful eye of the merchant Moses Taylor, City Bank ("National" was added to the name in 1865, as it was subsequently added to the names of thousands of other banks, thereby introducing a permanent element of confusion in the nomenclature of American finance) quickly righted itself. Its slogan became "ready money." Taylor saw to it that there was enough cash on the premises, or quickly obtainable outside, to see the bank through any emergency. There weren't many stockholders of City Bank in those days, and Taylor insisted that they come to collect their dividends in person—"makes 'em take an interest in their money," he would say. Three financial panics shattered the peace and prosperity of the administration of Taylor and his son-in-law, Percy R. Pyne. In each episode—1857, 1873, and 1884—City Bank gained deposits at the expense of weaker institutions. "When a bank's safety became the depositors' paramount concern," the official Citibank history records, "depositors rushed to the safest bank around. In New York that was City Bank."

By somewhat debased modern standards, banks in the late nineteenth century seem almost prudishly conservative. The National City Bank's equity capital was equivalent to 16 percent of its assets. A century on, Citicorp's capital would be equivalent to 8 percent of its assets. In 1891, the last year of the Taylor-Pyne regime, "capital" was purely equity capital; it was the owners' investment in the business. A century later, "capital" was also borrowed money. Citicorp's equity capital alone is equivalent to less than 4 percent of its assets. In 1891, "assets" included loans and interest-bearing securities and a large reserve of gold and silver. There were no gold bars on Citicorp's balance sheet a century later. As for the evolution of the art of lending, there were loans on Citicorp's books that would have curled the hair on Taylor's and Pyne's heads. Among the most controversial of these, even by late-twentieth-century lights, were those to Donald Trump, the New York real-estate developer; some of them were secured by little more than the Donald's stated intention to repay. Lending against the collateral of land and buildings was one of the original taboos of the national banking system. The argument against real estate was that it was inherently illiquid. It was a "slow" asset, as distinct, for instance, from a broker's loan secured by stock-exchange collateral. It was not until 1960 that Citibank, by then well launched in the new era (and faced with decline in its traditional corporate-lending business), seriously entered the field of commercial real-estate lending. In the James Stillman years, 1891–1918, a golden age for Citi and for banking in general, the bank's only real-estate asset had been its headquarters building, which it conservatively carried at $200,000, significantly below its estimated market value. (To the mild consternation of at least one federal examiner, the bank did not insure its building. "Supposed to be fire proof," the examiner noted.) Thomas P. Kane, a longtime senior official of the Comptroller's office, reminisced in 1922, "There is no doubt that the elimination from the National Bank Act of the power to make loans upon the security of real estate removed a dangerous principle from the banking laws, and contributed largely to the safety and success of the national banking system."* In recent years, that view has come to seem less quaint.

In 1891, a depression year in which more national banks failed than in any other year since the start of the national banking system in 1864, A. Barton Hepburn, the federal examiner for New York City and a future Comptroller of the Currency, paid a call on the National City Bank. What he found at 52 Wall Street bore a striking resemblance to a safe. For one thing, reserve balances were extraordinarily high. "Reserve has *not* been short for many years," he noted approvingly. On the day he began his investigation, funds set aside in gold and silver and other non-interest-bearing money amounted to 60 percent of deposits; the minimum stipulated by law for a bank of that size was 25 percent. National City was plainly prepared for any contingency imaginable, including war, insurrection, or Bryanism. As the bank

---

* The legal prohibition against real-estate lending was relaxed in 1913, with passage of the Federal Reserve Act, and subsequently in 1916, 1927, 1935, and 1968.

made loans, however, it inevitably suffered losses. Hepburn found that charge-offs—loans written off as doubtful—exceeded $230,000. But the bank was as conservative in accounting policy as it was in its reserve policy. Let a borrower be so much as twenty-four hours delinquent and his loan was charged off; it was consigned to the loss heap. Only as delinquent borrowers became current were overdue funds credited to income. As most delinquent borrowers strove to restore their credit, recoveries increased. The net loss borne on the reported $230,000 in charged-off loans was, in fact, just $7,909 in 1891.

If Hepburn admired the National City Bank, he also felt that impulse of contempt for its excessive caution that a grade-school teacher may feel for an apple-polishing pupil. "The Department need never have any anxiety on account of this Bank, so long as present management continues," he wrote to Washington. "The president is a very timid man. He pays no interest, carries the strongest reserve of any bank in the city and gets a large line of deposits from equally timid people who feel that their money is a little safer in this bank than it would be in government bonds."

It was James Stillman, succeeding Percy Pyne as president in November 1891, who put National City on the way to becoming the world's largest bank. In this great work, Stillman took the world as it was, the bad along with the good. The 1890s were a time of epic consolidation in American business. Railroads failed and were reorganized, and industrial corporations were merged into monopolies. Accordingly, the National City Bank became a leading underwriter of corporate securities and a merchant bank in the image of Baker's. It became Standard Oil's bank and it helped to reorganize the Union Pacific Railroad. The decade was also a time of political and economic upheaval. Depression and the rise of populist politics frightened monied people. The National City Bank became a beacon to them. It is laudable, though not unusual, for a businessman to turn a constructive trend to profit, and Stillman anticipated the rise of big business. It is still more laudable, because uncommon, for a businessman to turn adversity to profit. Absent federal deposit guarantees and the doctrine that some banks are too big to fail, safety constituted an opportunity—an economic franchise—and Stillman adeptly seized it.

The era in which Stillman lived exactly suited his personal gifts. He was unrivaled at saying "no." Refusing a loan was an art more highly developed in Stillman's time than ours because it was more widely practiced then. Bankers and depositors had more to lose in the days before the federal safety net was rigged up across the country.

Stillman himself, for instance, was not only the president of the National City Bank but also its controlling stockholder. If, through some disaster, the bank were to fail, he would be out of more than a job.

Until 1935, the stockholders of a national bank were subject to a risk called "double liability." If their bank failed, they were personally liable for the depositors' losses up to the full, or par, value of their stock. In the case of the Marine National Bank, for instance, the bankruptcy of which uncharacteristically caught out George Baker in 1884, the stockholders' capital was $400,000. Assets totaled $6,700,000. Upon the Marine's insolvency, the Comptroller assessed the stockholders for $400,000—that is, 100 percent of what they had invested. As can be imagined, the last communiqué an investor in a failed bank wished to receive was a dunning notice from the Comptroller of the Currency, and many found reasons not to pay. The Marine's investors scraped up only $273,000 of the $400,000 demanded of them. No doubt, more than a few stockholders of bankrupt banks were themselves broke. Bankers and their stockholders found ways to circumvent the spirit of the double-liability rule. One was to show as little "capital," as legally defined, as possible. In the case of the National City Bank in 1893, for example, paid-in capital was $1 million. It was this sum on which Stillman and the other investors would be assessed if worst came to worst. There was another $2.8 million of "surplus" and "other undivided profits," however, that constituted capital in every sense but the legal one. In case of failure, National City's stockholders would be assessed on $1 million, not on the inclusive, all-in capital of $3.8 million.

One universal lesson of the American banking experience is that no monetary system is foolproof. Notwithstanding the double-liability rule, national banks sometimes failed, and unscrupulous managements connived without the knowledge of presumably vigilant stockholders. Though the rule was no panacea against bad banking, its mere existence implied a relationship between owners and depositors that was lost in the reforms of the 1930s. In Stillman and Baker's time, it was the owners of a bank, not the taxpayers, who owed a financial duty to the depositors. The government was never indifferent to the condition of the banks it had chartered. Nor were the banks indifferent to the public-relations value of the government's oversight. "The right to advertise the institution as being under the supervision of the Government of the United States always has been regarded by national banks as one of their most valuable assets," wrote Kane, "and this fact has been prominently displayed and extensively advertised from the day the banks first opened their doors for business in competition with other banking institutions in their respective communities." Though the federal government regulated, however, it did not at first bear risk. It increasingly tried to forestall panics, but it did not underwrite depositor losses until the New Deal, and it was not forced to honor the promises it had made in any significant amount until the 1980s.

The Stillman Regime

It was a close competition between Stillman and George F. Baker as to who was inclined to say the least in public. Baker gave his first newspaper interview in 1922, at the age of eighty-two. On that historic occasion, he told a newspaperwoman (she had begged for an interview, saying that without it she would lose her job), "Businessmen of America should reduce their talk by at least two-thirds. Everyone should reduce his talk. There is rarely good enough reason for anybody to talk." Stillman, who at home, unless there were guests, presided over a two-hour formal dinner in silence, once accommodated the press with a puckish comment that he jointly signed with another publicity-shy businessman, Henry Clay Frick. After keeping the reporters waiting for an hour, the two sent them this:

The U.S.A. is a great and growing country.
[signed]
Jas. Stillman
H. C. Frick

This is confidential and not for publication unless names are omitted.

Baker was a bull and an "upbuilder," but Stillman had a keener sense of the downside. Of Stillman, Baker once grumbled that he "always looks on the dark side of things." Certainly, the National City Bank president was not a blind optimist. John Winkler, writing from the perspective of the Great Depression (not a flattering vantage point from which to regard any financier), offered this description of the composite unsuccessful loan applicant at Stillman's institution:

A caller would enter Stillman's office, assured, perhaps a little enthusiastic. Without a word the dark, elegant little man at the big, clean desk would motion him to a chair upon which the light fell full. He would look at him, quite impassively, through veiled, impersonal eyes. The man would begin stating his case.

Minutes would pass. The caller would make assertions that seemed to require response. Not a sound from the grave, composed Buddha at the desk, whose eyes seemed to have penetrated through the other to some distant spot in the room. The visitor would fidget, cough, finally finish what he had come to say.

Invariably would follow a long, cruel pause.

Then, as if from far away, the president of the National City Bank would begin to speak. In low, impressive tones he would rip the proposal to shreds.

Indiscriminate prudence was no more the secret of Stillman's success than it was of Baker's, however, and National City eagerly prospected for new business. Under Stillman's management, the bank expanded the stable of corporate customers it had inherited from Taylor and Pyne. Stillman, who was a wealthy man in his own right, joined Jacob H. Schiff of Kuhn, Loeb & Co. in reorganizing the Union Pacific Railroad. Extrication of the Union Pacific from bankruptcy proved long, complex, and profitable, and Stillman ventured his own capital along with the bank's. "In the various reorganization syndicates," according to the Citicorp history, "Stillman had personally risked far more than Harriman and nearly as much as Kuhn, Loeb." Through this alliance, Stillman's bank entered the top tier of Wall Street underwriters. Its success in garnering the investment-banking and lending business of the forerunners to the Fortune 500 is revealed by a partial list of Stillman's directors around the turn of the century: Henry O. Havemeyer (American Sugar Refining), Cyrus H. McCormick (International Harvester), P. A. Valentine (Armour & Co.), and E. H. Harriman (Union Pacific Railroad). Striking an extrafinancial alliance, two of Stillman's daughters would marry two of the sons of William Rockefeller, a National City director who was also the brother of John D.

All this lay in the future. Stillman's first job was to remold the National City Bank in his own image. When he assumed the presidency in 1891, this bank for timid people had only four officers and seventy employees. "Punctuality was rigidly enforced," wrote Winkler of the new regime. "The lunch hour was cut to thirty minutes, the working day lengthened. Even the most minute items of overhead, such as the cost and distribution of pads and pencils, were thoroughly scrutinized. Stenography and the typewriter were making their debut in the business world. The new boss jolted the chief clerk with a dozen 'suggestions' for economy in repairs, cost of ribbons, notebooks, etc. Each hour, each minute (it seemed to the beridden employees), a laconic order for a change in methods bloomed upon the bulletin board, signed in small, straight script: 'Jas. Stillman, president.' "

Stillman's bank expanded in several directions at once. It opened a foreign-exchange department (Baker, a commercial homebody, had no use for international banking and developed a far-flung domestic correspondent network). The unexpected failure of the Third National Bank, which had made a specialty of correspondent banking, brightened Stillman's springtime in 1897. National City quickly agreed to merge with the stricken Third, and none other than A. B. Hepburn, the former national bank examiner for New York, was brought in to supervise the transition. (Hepburn was uniquely qualified for the job. He was, at that moment, Comptroller of the Currency. He had been president of the Third in its better days. And as we have already seen, he had been inside National City to examine it.) One result of the consolidation was a burst of growth for National City. In the decade beginning in 1895, the bank's loans and investments rose at an annual rate of 22 percent, three times greater than that of the average national bank. By 1905, the National City Bank had taken a commanding lead as the largest bank in the country with assets of more than $300 million, some 27 percent larger than the runner-up, the National Bank of Commerce.

Growth at an exceptional rate is a red flag in banking. It is hard enough to manage an ordinary bank; to control a sprouting weed is well-nigh impossible. If loans are expanding too quickly, the lending officers have probably been saying "yes" too frequently. Evidently, the prejudice against pell-mell expansion is deeply rooted, for turn-of-the-century examiners marveled that Stillman's institution had sacrificed nothing in safety and soundness for the sake of growth and size. As in the Taylor-Pyne years, loans continued to be well protected. In general, the value of the collateral securing a loan was 20 percent greater than the sum lent. Losses were rare and in some years non-existent. Of National City, an examiner commented in 1898: "Its assets are clean and contain in cash, demand loans, U.S. bonds and other unquestionably quick items, 91% of the $92,000,000 of liabilities due the public—a sum sufficiently large to eliminate all elements of danger which might be deemed to arise from the magnitude of its resources and operations."

Because interest rates were low, there was no severe penalty for being liquid. A conservative bank could maintain a sizable rainy-day fund, lend to blue-chip borrowers at low rates (National City Bank's loans fetched returns ranging from 1 percent to 6 percent), and nonetheless earn a profit. On the public's deposits, Stillman's bank continued to pay no interest at all. What it offered its depositors was safety, convenience, and accommodation (although not yet boat loans, vacation loans, or first- or second-mortgage loans). "This bank is in its usual strong and prosperous condition," an examiner reported to Washington in 1896. "Its management is able and very conservative and seeks a record for size and solidity rather than for large profits."

Large profits presently began to take care of themselves. As recently as 1895, the bank was making no loans to the companies in which its board was interested (a fact relayed to Washington in these words: "The bank is free from all schemes promoted by the directors"). As the decade wore on, however, Stillman more and more steered the bank in the same direction as his own substantial capital was bound, to Union Pacific, Amalgamated Copper, and Consolidated Gas, for instance. Great sums were lent. When a loan exceeded the maximum allowed under the law (the equivalent of 10 percent of capital to any one borrower), Stillman lent to employees, dummies, and straw men. This subterfuge was winked at by the examiners, acknowledged in reports to Washington, and rationalized by the examiners' judgment that the loans were sound and well secured. In 1901, a bumper year for mergers, one such examiner, Forrest Raynor, advised the Comptroller of the Currency not to worry:

With the growth of the consolidation of large interests has come the necessity for large banking transactions, and as evidenced by the list of large loans herewith, this bank is affording facilities for such requirements.

The board of directors are men of high standing in financial circles, representing large interests, and either themselves or those whom they represent are large owners of the bank's stock. . . . the President of this bank has powers for manipulation with which it would be difficult to cope if used. He is, however, a man of unquestioned integrity, and as the largest owner in many of these institutions, has their interest and his own at stake in their management.

The earnings for the year were about 17% [of capital] and their business is most ably and successfully handled.

Of all the large borrowers with which the National City Bank did business in the 1890s, the United States government was, to Stillman, the most vexing. In recent years, the government has frequently bailed out large banks. In the 1890s, the leading banks, unquestionably solvent, repeatedly rescued the government. It is not easy now to conceive of a Treasury in need of rescue. Since the advent of the progressive income tax in 1913, the entire resources of the United States have been theoretically placed at the government's disposal. When the top income-tax rate was pushed to 67 percent in World War I, the philosophical issue was settled: the government's claim on a taxpayer's income was potentially complete. The power to tax constituted a latent call on as much of the national income as the government happened to need.

When, as in recent years, the Treasury suffered a persistent budget deficit, no financial crisis resulted. The government paid its bills in a currency that, if necessary, it could print itself at negligible cost. And if the global financial markets refused to countenance an outright inflation, it was understood that the government could exercise the prerogatives of the twentieth-century state by raising income taxes.

In Stillman's time the government's field of action was circumscribed. There was no income tax and no unsecured paper currency. There was no tradition of peacetime deficit finance. Money, being gold, was intrinsically valuable. A gold dollar was money in substance and symbol alike. In the greenback period, the Civil War through 1878, monetary value was conferred on a dollar bill by act of Congress (as it is today). It was legal tender in law: except for that federal insignia, a dollar bill was worth only the market price of its paper and printing. On January 1, 1879, the greenback era ended and the gold standard was restored: the dollar was redefined as a weight of gold bullion. The government resumed its compact with the population to redeem unwanted paper currency in gold coin at the legally fixed rate of 25.8 grains to the dollar.

There was, however, a political impetus toward inflation. This was the silver movement, a Populist program for the nation's currency and the politics of debt. If the Federal Reserve had been in existence, the Populists would have petitioned its board of governors for easier money and lower interest rates. In the absence of the Fed, they demanded a larger monetary role for a cheaper metal. They asked that the government buy silver with newly printed paper money. The paper money would be redeemable in either silver or gold. As gold was the more intrinsically valuable metal, any rational holder of dollars would choose gold—if he chose either. Paper money was more portable than coin, and bank deposits (or some of them) paid interest. Monied people were therefore inclined to store their wealth in paper unless and until they came to doubt the size of the government's gold reserve.

By proposing the coinage of silver on liberal terms, the Western mining states and Southern Populists were really proposing the exile of gold. According to Gresham's law, bad money drives good money out of circulation. Under the silver program, prices would rise, or (to say the same thing) the value of paper money would fall. A debt is a promise to pay a sum of money. Cheapen that money, and the burden of debt becomes lighter.

It is not hard to guess which side of the great debate appealed to James Stillman. Like J. P. Morgan and George F. Baker, Stillman was for gold and national solvency (he viewed them as inseparable). To him, as to former Treasury Secretary Charles J. Folger, the Treasury Department was essentially a bank. So many greenbacks were in circulation, and so much gold was available to redeem them. As a sound bank held ample reserves, so did a creditworthy government. For either to suffer a loss of confidence was to invite a run. A run on a government was a run on its gold reserve.

The Sherman Silver Purchase Act of 1890, which directed the government to double its monthly purchase of silver, was the immediate cause of the monetary crisis. On its face, the law seemed innocuous. It required the Treasury to purchase four and a half million ounces of silver a month with a newly created paper money. But its effect was subversive of what Baker and Stillman believed to be the natural monetary order. It did not increase the nation's gold reserves, but it enlarged the number of paper claims against them. The paper was a legal promise of the Treasury to pay gold or silver upon demand, but there was every reason not to demand silver. In 1891, the intrinsic value of a silver dollar, measured in gold, was 76 cents. It fell to 67 cents in 1892 and to 60 cents in 1893. Those who doubted the government's will or capacity to continue to exchange paper for gold trooped to the Treasury offices for gold before the supply ran out. To exchange a Treasury note for a gold coin in 1893 was literally to buy a dollar for 60 cents.

One banker, at least, who could say "no": James Stillman, president of the National City Bank, forerunner to Citibank (BETTMANN ARCHIVE)

As the monetary debate turned on politics as much as it did on financial theory, the arguments were hot. To its friends, the gold standard was the rule of law applied to money. As the Constitution restricted the freedom of action of the Justice Department, so did the gold standard curb the activities of the Treasury. Bound by a legal definition of money, the government could not print its way out of a jam. It could neither bribe the voters—the Treasury could not create money out of thin air any more than a private citizen could—nor run a permanent deficit in international payments. A nation that chronically purchased more from abroad than it sold would suffer an outflow of gold. The drain would set in motion a self-reversing series of events. If the loss of gold precipitated a recession, the former prodigal country's imports would fall. As it spent less abroad, it lost less gold. In time, accounts would painfully swing back toward balance. Gold, in search of the highest return, would flow back to the country that had lost it in the first place.

What Baker, Morgan, and Stillman saw in the gold standard was not what Western miners, Southern farmers, and debtors from every section saw. "You do not want an honest dollar," a Pennsylvania silverite accused the opposition. "You want a scarce dollar." The 1890s were beset by economic and financial ills, and the inflationists blamed them on an alleged shortage of money. It was to make money plentiful, they claimed, that silver must be given parity.

In retrospect, what is most striking about the hard times of the 1890s was how little they yielded in radical politics. In 1893, President Grover Cleveland succeeded in prodding Congress to overturn the Sherman Silver Purchase Act. When the Democrat William Jennings Bryan turned the 1896 presidential race into a monetary referendum, liberating silver vs. the "cross of gold," he was shellacked by the gold-standard Republican, William McKinley. An economic historian, surveying the 1890s with detachment, contended that the silver agitation was never as menacing to established institutions as it seemed. "If the threat to the gold standard had been really dangerous," wrote Rendigs Fels, "the outflow of gold would have assumed proportions great enough to have forced its abandonment."

Gold in Doubt

No doubt. In the thick of the monetary battle, however, the outcome seemed anything but foregone. Investors, as they are sometimes wont to do, focused obsessively on one bellwether statistic. In the period from 1893 to 1896, this fixation was the Treasury's gold reserve. One hundred million dollars was considered the prudent minimum, so that when the balance fell below $70 million in January 1894, an emergency plan was set in motion. ("There was absolutely but one way to avert national calamity and our country's disgrace," was the way Cleveland recalled the moment.) The government would issue bonds with which to secure more gold. This it did, but the drain continued. Another gold bond issue was announced in November 1894. It too proved no more than a stopgap, and the courageous Cleveland fell into a brief brown study. The law required that Treasury notes, once redeemed for gold, be reissued, so that the process of issue and redemption became (in the phrase of the day) an "endless chain." Within two months of the deposit of the proceeds of the second bond sale in the

Treasury's account, the gold reserve had sunk to $41,340,181. Futilely, the sale had yielded $59 million.

The circumstances that cause a government to go hat in hand to its bankers are paradoxically noble ones. They imply, in the first place, the existence of a rule of law. Otherwise, the government could confiscate what it needed. For another thing, they suggest that the money being sought is beyond the capacity of the government to counterfeit. Needing gold in the mid-1890s, the government had to petition its creditors, who naturally included the leading bankers. "[I]t never occurred to any of us to consult, in this emergency, farmers, doctors, lawyers, shoemakers, or even statesmen," Cleveland recalled laconically. "We could not escape the belief that the prospect of obtaining what we needed might be somewhat improved by making application to those whose business and surroundings qualified them to intelligently respond."

Objectively, Stillman and Baker were better financial risks in the early 1890s than the national government. Of the First National, Baker's bank, an examiner summed up neatly in 1892, "This bank has methods peculiar to itself. While they are free and easy, they are conservative and successful." Of National City, we have already noted that a careful clientele preferred it to government bonds. Under Stillman, the City laid in gold coins against the possibility of the Populists winning the day. Records Winkler:

> Just prior to the panic of 1893, when the country's economic structure was weakening and other banks were shipping gold to London for harborage, the National City paid a premium to bring gold across the Atlantic to its vaults. . . . While other banks were drained of cash, there was never a day when Stillman, puffing at a delicate little cigar, could not escort a favored or prospective customer to the cellar and display shining bars of gold. The psychological effect was enormous.

In hard times, conservative bankers rarely command the affection of the man on the street, and the silver wing of the Democratic Party accused the White House of capitulating to "goldbuggery and Shylockism." In defense of the gold standard, Cleveland held up the alternative of barbarism. To succumb to silver inflation, he said, would align the United States "not with the enlightened nations of Christendom, but side by side with China, with the republic of Mexico, with the republics of Central and South America, and with every other semicivilized country on the globe."

On Christmas Eve 1895, J. P. Morgan, joined by National City and other big banks, formed a syndicate to underwrite a new $100 million loan for the beleaguered Cleveland administration. The loan went through, but the gold crisis festered. In the summer of 1896, the Democratic Party repudiated Cleveland and nominated William Jennings Bryan. Months before that alarming event, Stillman was writing to the Secretary of War, Daniel Lamont, about the personal abuse that he had suffered at the hands of the New York press for his role in assisting the Treasury. "To have one's motives misinterpreted and reviled in the manner in which it is being done is very trying," complained Stillman, "and I think that the disposition exists among some of those prominently interested to withdraw from their efforts to cooperate to place a large amount of gold in the Treasury and save the Government from suspension of gold payments and the nation from bankruptcy."

With the help of the bankers (who did not resign out of pique), the nation saved itself. By 1897, the National City Bank had become the government's leading bank. When, in 1899, Lyman Gage, Secretary of the Treasury, advised Stillman that he would have to raise City's capital if he expected to keep the government's sizable deposits, the banker obliged. The pointedness of this federal suggestion was, we may all see now, a straw in the wind.

4

Democratizing Credit

Seen from the present day—a time of general disrepair in banking and of a centibillion-dollar crisis in the so-called thrift industry—the turn of the century has a powerful nostalgic appeal. It was the epiphany of financial arrangements that now seem unattainable. As a rule, the federal budget was balanced. With the defeat of William Jennings Bryan and passage of the Gold Standard Act of 1900, the dollar was anchored in value (as it then seemed) for all time. In the bond market in 1900, blue-chip corporations were able to borrow at less than 3½ percent, well-regarded municipalities at less than 3¼ percent, and the U.S. Treasury at no more than 2 percent.

It was not the golden age of the people's credit, however. For a time in the 1980s, it seemed that anyone could get a loan; that, indeed, almost nobody would be given the opportunity to refuse one. The opposite condition ruled around the turn of the century. The "democratization of credit," as Arthur J. Morris, one of the pioneers of the movement, liked to call it, did not happen all at once or without reversals. But a general trend toward accessibility became unmistakable in the years preceding World War I.

For the working man or woman, the place to raise some sorely needed cash was not the First National Bank. What made that institution impregnable was, in good part, Baker's austere philosophy of credit (and compared with other big-city bankers, he was almost a soft touch). To most loan applicants, he was inclined to say "no," and his bearing was so formidable that a good many potential borrowers evidently didn't bother to ask him.

It was not that Baker or Morgan or other commercial lenders less Olympian were indifferent to the financial needs of Americans as individuals. Rather, they did not view people—consumers, as succeeding generations of bankers learned to call them—as a potential banking market. Lending to the working class was a philanthropic obligation, they believed, and they treated the unmet credit demands of low-income New Yorkers the same way they dealt with the social problems of orphans, newsboys, or unmarried mothers. When an appeal was made on behalf of the working poor in the depression of the early 1890s, the bankers responded in character. A special committee of the Charity Organization Society was formed to investigate the creation of a philanthropic pawnshop. James Speyer, scion of the international banking family, undertook an inspection of the charitable pawnshops in Europe, some of which dated back to the fourteenth century. Speyer reported favorably, Seth Low of the Mayor's Relief Committee got behind the idea, and some of the richest men on Wall Street, Baker included, subscribed a total of $100,000 in seed capital. The Provident Loan Society of New York opened for business in 1894.

Unquestionably, Americans had had extensive experience in borrowing before this event. Robert Morris, the financier of the American Revolution, overextended himself in real estate after the war, was unable to borrow the money to keep his creditors at bay (even at the then prevailing rates of 2 percent or 3 percent a month—that is, 24 percent or 36 percent a year), and spent three and a half years in debtors' prison. The first building and loan association in the United States was established in Frankford, Pennsylvania, in 1831. Boston businessmen petitioned the Massachusetts legislature for repeal of the state usury law in 1834: the legal maximum rate of 6 percent was driving ordinary credit transactions underground. Anticipating the organization of the Provident Loan Society by almost forty years, the Collateral Loan Company of Boston was founded in 1857 to put a more humane and low-cost face on pawnbroking.

In Chicago, according to the recollection of one lenders' lawyer, personal loans were made against the collateral of household furniture as early as 1850. Historians, however, have found no documentary evidence of personal lending for profit until some twenty years later. The earliest known advertisement for a small-loan service in an American newspaper appeared in the *Chicago Tribune* in November 1869. Getting right to the point, the copy said: "Money to Loan in Small Sums on Short Time. Room 14, Major Block." By November 1872, to judge by the *Tribune*'s classified advertising lineage, the personal lending business was prospering. Seven ads offered chattel loans on the collateral of furniture, diamonds, warehouse receipts, houses, and pianos. Outside of Chicago, the *Boston Globe* became the first known American newspaper to advertise the services of a professional lender in the household-goods line. The year was 1873.

Frank J. Mackey opened a chattel-mortgage office in Minneapolis in 1878. So doing, he laid the first brick in what was to become the tower of Household Finance Corporation. Mackey was one of the earliest personal lenders to expand through branch offices. "The chains lending on chattel mortgages expanded slowly, however, compared with the amazing growth of several chains lending on wage assignments," according to Louis N. Robinson and Rolf Nugent, authors of *Regulation of the Small Loan Business*, one of a series of authoritative studies on this arcane topic produced by the Russell Sage Foundation starting in the 1920s. "One of these was developed by John Mulholland, who opened a salary loan office in Kansas City about 1893, established branches in neighboring cities on the profits of his Kansas City office, raised additional capital by the sale of stock, and within fifteen years had more than one hundred offices scattered across the country. It was said that he sold more than a million dollars' worth of stock from his New York office alone."

Back East, Daniel H. Tolman duplicated Mulholland's economic success despite (at the end of his career) some blisteringly bad press. Tolman, who operated a chain in some sixty-three American and Canadian cities, was credited with the innovation of using female employees to defuse the sometimes irate male debtors. In Tolman's obituary, in 1918, *The New York Times* described the breakthrough unsympathetically: ". . . he originated and perfected the well-known plan of conducting his occupation shielded behind the skirts of women."

It might have gratified Tolman, who always maintained that he "only did what every banker does," to learn how the banking establishment has come to share his business vision, albeit at lower profit margins than those he was able to extract. In the credit-card age, the standard rate of interest on unsecured consumer debt is 20 percent a year. A century ago, the going rate on a chattel loan was likely to be 20 percent a month. Ten percent a month was a standard rate on chattel loans of less than $50. Slightly less onerous terms were available on larger chattel loans: in the $100 to $300 range, for example, 5 percent to 7 percent a month. On the fringes of usury, truly astonishing rates were obtained. An Atlanta grand jury in 1903 uncovered interest rates of up to 1,728 percent a year, or 144 percent a month.

Compound interest is a hard and relentless master. Money lent at

6 percent a year—the then maximum bank lending rate—doubles in twelve years. Money lent at 10 percent a month, or 120 percent a year—a typical usurer's rate—doubles within eight months. It is bliss to receive interest payments at extortionate rates. By just that measure is it ruinous to pay them.

Not everyone did pay, of course. A first-person account of the small-loan business describes the risks and rewards of chattel lending: "In 1883–1884, Minneapolis had about 75,000 inhabitants and the office had about $60,000 invested, upon which an excellent return was received. Times were good; in fact, were booming. In 1885–1886 the reaction set in and the bottom dropped out of everything and the losses in the loan business were very large. Because of these losses and the pursuing of a more conservative policy in making loans, the investment went down to around $20,000 and remained at that figure for several years with a reduction of income almost to the vanishing point."

But so high were the rates charged that losses could ordinarily be absorbed as the cost of doing business. In this respect, the nineteenth-century small-loan business was a forebear of the twentieth-century junk-bond business. Unlike the junk-bond salesmen, however, who had recourse to the law in cases of default or bankruptcy, the small-loan men operated on the fringe of society and often outside the law. When, about 1899, a credit-information exchange was organized by the small-loan men of Indianapolis to collect the identities of known deadbeats, the exchange's office door was discreetly unmarked and its telephone number unlisted. Because of the social and legal isolation of the creditors, no legal recourse was ordinarily available to a usurer against a defaulting borrower. Lenders therefore fell back on psychological collection techniques. Through ostentatious dunning or the threat of exposure to neighbors or family, a lender might induce a delinquent borrower to pay. Some employers considered that merely taking out a salary loan was cause for dismissal. In those cases, a lender held information that, if disclosed, could cost the debtor his job.

Forrest Halsey's *The Bawlerout*, a novel published in 1911, explored the usury business from the debtor's point of view. In the opening chapter, an indebted motorman dropped by his lender's office to pay some interest he owed and to beg for time in which to scratch together the principal. The clerk—female, of course—was unmoved.

" 'See here, you,' said the woman, 'we are getting sick of you and your renewals. Mr. Charker is gettin' sick of it.'

" 'Can't help it this time, ma'am—you see, the wife is sick.'

" 'Say, what has that got to do with us? Can we help your wife getting sick? If you didn't intend to pay back that money, what did you come here for . . . ?' "

The clerk had a weapon in reserve—the threat of unloosing the company's paid scold and dispenser of public abuse. "We can't go on this way, Jackson," she told the motorman, "and that's all there is to it. If we don't get that money, we got to go after it. Do you want the bawlerout to come round for the money, or will you come down with it?" With that, the motorman promised to take his daughter out of school and put her to work in a box factory—"It's rather hard on the kid, ma'am, because we was hopin' to keep her a year longer in the school, but she's gotta help." She looked a little young to be working, he allowed, "but me an' the old woman is goin' to swear she is old enough."

More striking than the extraordinary profits of the small-loan business is their persistence. "During the late nineties when the profits that could be made in the small loan business, especially in the salary loan business, began to be noised about," Robinson and Nugent relate, "loan offices in the cities sprang up overnight like mushrooms." Yet ten years later, according to the same authors, the Ohio office of a chain company was able to earn brilliant returns over the course of a full decade. The unnamed office, lending mainly on chattel mortgages (its financial statements were obtained by the Russell Sage Foundation), was able to earn no less than 46 percent a year on its invested capital. The profits of salary lenders were said to be even higher.

Fabulous returns don't last in a market economy, because competition tends to reduce them. In the small-loan business, competition was held in check both by the law and by social convention. Thus, the opportunity to double one's capital every twenty-three months failed to lure much outside capital into the personal lending business. "Occasionally," according to Robinson and Nugent, "a lender induced some wealthy person to put money in his business as a silent partner. Usually, however, a large proportion of the lender's capital had been made in the small loan business itself from a very small original investment."

To established bankers like Speyer, Baker, and Morgan, the usury laws were moot, because the customers to whom they lent so rarely defaulted. The best customers, paying low rates, borrowed because they found it expedient to turn Grade A collateral temporarily into cash. They did not need the money as Tolman's customers needed it. Presenting a bank with New York Stock Exchange-listed securities, they obtained money. This accommodation yielded the bank only a small rate of interest, but the bank (if it was of the caliber of Stillman's) paid nothing at all for its deposits. What the bank offered the depositor in the days before federal deposit insurance was safety.

Regulating Interest Rates

With the laws and attitudes then prevailing, the small-loan men could no more have raised capital on the Stock Exchange than they could have joined the Union Club. The states could not legislate against improvidence, but they could try to regulate the terms on which people borrowed. In 1884, New Jersey prohibited so-called salary loans— loans made against the collateral of wage assignments—at interest rates above 8 percent a year. It was a quixotic rate. Massachusetts became the first state to attempt to regulate all small lending by statute. In 1888, a maximum interest rate was enacted—18 percent a year—but a minimum charge amounting to six months' interest regardless of the term of the loan was also established. By lending for short periods of time at the minimum rate, a usurious yield was obtained in fact. In 1891, Missouri moved to invalidate the pledge of property to secure a loan made at extralegal interest rates.

In the depression winter of 1893–94, the Citizens' Permanent Relief Committee of Philadelphia made an investigation of usurious lending practices. It publicized the pathetic case of an electrician who lost his job through sickness and exhausted his savings. Needing funds, he borrowed $50 from a loan company, signing over a bill of sale on his furniture as collateral. Terms of the loan were severe: repayment in thirteen weeks in equal weekly installments of $5.10, amounting in all to $66.30. The annual rate of interest therefore amounted to no less than 240 percent. "After paying back $35.70, he was unable to continue," the committee reported, "and was threatened with a Sheriff's levy on his household goods." The man's wife appealed to the committee. "Charity they did not ask," the report continued, "but if the constable could be kept off, their household goods saved, and they be enabled to rent a cheaper home, they would be grateful. The two [daughters], fifteen and seventeen years of age, had the promise of positions where they could earn three or four dollars a week, sufficient to keep the family from actual suffering, provided they did not lose their home and household effects."

The committee took up the electrician's cause. It paid a visit to the small-loan office and demanded to pay the outstanding balance on his behalf. What the committee knew full well was that the usurer was bound by law to accept payment at the low legal rate of interest, not the high contracted one. Addressing the usurer's clerk—a man, not one of Tolman's kind—the committeemen announced their mission. "The clerk politely informed us," the report said, "that the balance due on the note amounted to $30.60, but he was as politely told that that must be a mistake; that he was at liberty to accept the balance due on the original loan, plus legal interest, in full settlement. Quite taken aback, he retired to the manager for consultation, returning in a few minutes with the request for us to see that gentleman. On his asking our business, he was in pointed language tendered payment plus legal interest, and after some hesitation accepted."

The legal interest came to exactly 60 cents. The usurious rate was $15.70. It was this $15.10 that the committee saved the electrician and his family—"enough to keep them from absolute want for a number of weeks."

The loan sharks' press did not noticeably improve with the upturn in business activity, and the gait of reform only quickened. In 1895, legislation enabling the incorporation of the Provident Loan Society of New York also directed the chartering of the state's small-loan men and the enactment of maximum interest rates. On loans of $200 or less, the ceiling was 3 percent a month for the first two months and 2 percent a month thereafter. The "loan-shark problem" was the object of reform legislation in other states as well. Six percent was the top legal lending rate set in North Carolina, and 12 percent was the maximum rate established in Utah. Other states, more financially sophisticated, attempted to set rates high enough to allow a small-loan man to make an honest living, but those experiments usually came to naught. So high were the ruling market rates and so lax was the enforcement that lenders often continued to get what the traffic would bear.

"The net result of these sporadic legislative efforts up to 1910 was just about zero," Robinson and Nugent found. "Statutes which invalidated certain forms of security caused lenders merely to switch to other forms. Prohibitive regulations resulted in increased charges to borrowers to compensate the lender for his additional risk. Statutes which recognized the need for a commercial business in this field failed either to provide sufficient gross income to the lender or to force him to comply. In all these states, the loan-shark problem continued apparently without abatement."

In 1904, a man who borrowed $25 wound up losing his furniture to the loan company. "Took Even Baby's Cradle," *The New York Times* reported. In 1908, a debt-ridden father of eight took out a newspaper advertisement to threaten suicide if someone didn't lend him another $500 with which to fend off loan sharks. The crisis was delayed when a pair of Good Samaritans advanced him $250.

To understand the utter contempt in which personal-loan men were held, it is only necessary to compare the obituaries of two contemporaries in finance, each from the *Times*: Speyer, the establishmentarian who helped to organize the Provident Loan Society, and Tolman, the outcast who lent for profit.

The Speyer headline, from 1941: "James Speyer, 80, Banker, Dies Here; Member of the Famous House Long was Leader in Civic and Philanthropic Work; Retired Three Years Ago; A Founder of Provident Loan Society and Trustee of the United Hospital."

And Tolman's, from 1918: "Daniel H. Tolman, 'Loan Shark,' Dies; Usurer Once Offered to Pay Back $500,000 for Pardon from Prison; Failed to Move Gov. Glynn; Operated Loan Offices Throughout the Country in Charge of Women."

The Tolman obituary revealed that the dead man had been sent to jail for six months on a usury charge in 1913, and it unsentimentally quoted the verbal blast that the defendant had received from the sentencing judge: "You are one of the most contemptible usurers in your unspeakable business. The poor people must be protected from such sharks as you, and we trust that your conviction and sentence will be a notice to you and all your kind that the courts have found a way to put a stop to usury. Men of your type are a curse to the community, and the money they gain is blood money."

From time to time, reformers in New York would send loan sharks scurrying across the river to New Jersey, and Tolman had evidently followed this migratory path. But he had been caught in New Jersey too and fined $1,000. Twelve hours later, returning to New York, he was again arrested. The charge was lending $10 for three months at the cost of $5, or at an annual rate of interest of 200 percent. In court, Tolman protested that he had retired from business and was planning a trip around the world. When, instead, he was convicted and sent to prison, his lawyers, family, and friends offered to buy his release by making a bonfire of 25,000 unpaid notes with a face value of $500,000.

The governor took this proposition under advisement, but Tolman himself declared that he would rather serve out his term than "thus forego my manhood."

"Tolman was unpopular with many of the prisoners," the *Times* had reported on the occasion of his release from jail, in 1914. "He was punished for several infractions of prison rules, and was finally set to work with the 'burying gang,' digging graves for those convicts who were about to be buried in Potter's Field." In the spirit of objectivity, the paper also noted that the prisoner's sentence had been shortened a few weeks for good behavior. Even so, a faithful reader of the paper's coverage of the "loan-shark problem" probably wasn't surprised to read: "None of his relatives met him when he stepped from the ferryboat after leaving [Blackwell's Island] yesterday. His hair was white and he seemed sadly altered."

Just as telling of the financial climate was a scolding *Times* editorial in 1913. Headed "Victims of Their Own Folly," the essay bade good riddance to Tolman (he had just been sentenced) but also shook a disapproving finger at the victim of Tolman's crime, a man who had borrowed "not because he really had to have it, but because he wanted to give his father a golden wedding present. Such a gift, for those who can afford it, is highly commendable," the *Times* inveighed, "and many a much worse use of money can be imagined, but the father would have been better honored if the son had shown more sense."

For any New Yorker with sense and some jewelry to pawn, the best place to borrow was the Provident Loan Society. Almost from the day it opened, the Provident was a financial success and an inspiration to the reform movement. In 1895, the first full year of its operation, the institution made 20,804 loans in the sum of $378,000. Twenty years later, it was making 571,059 loans in the sum of almost $20 million. On amounts of less than $100, private pawnshops in New York could legally charge 3 percent a month for the first six months and 2 percent thereafter. The Provident lent at 1 percent a month. Besides jewelry, it accepted pledges on watches, plate, and clothing. Loans were made for a year and were renewable if interest payments were current.

Evidently, no surviving record describes the attitude of pawnbrokers toward the Provident, but the attitude of the Provident toward the pawnbrokers is strongly implied in two official sentences. "At the start," said the society's twenty-fifth anniversary history, "a practical pawnbroker was employed as manager. After ten years the extent of the Society's operations and the character of its problems dictated the engagement, as vice president and executive head, of a man of greater capacity and wider knowledge of social and financial matters." So much for the man of narrow knowledge who had put in the first ten years. His successor was one Frank Tucker, formerly the head of the Association for Improving the Condition of the Poor.

The Provident was, first and foremost, a charitable and uplifting organization, not a profit-making one. It aimed not only to relieve distress through enlightened and liberal lending but also, through competition, to force lower margins on profit-making pawnbrokers. Both of these ends it accomplished. By 1919, in a preview of the almost limitless horizons of modern consumer banking, it was making more loans than the largest domestic savings bank. It had eclipsed the private pawnbroking business in New York and the Crédit Municipal de Paris, the largest of the European municipal loan organizations, which was known affectionately to Parisians as "my aunt." To New Yorkers, the appellation was "uncle," and the Provident was both a rich and an understanding one. Its policy was, first, to make small and costly loans and, only second, to make large and profitable ones. It made loans of as little as one dollar. In financial crises, its policy was to reduce the size of its maximum loan for the sake of making a great number of small (and therefore costly) loans to the needy. In the panic year of 1907, for instance, the maximum was cut to $50 from $1,000.

It is a good bet that the pawnbrokers of New York wished that the big-money philanthropists had applied themselves to reforming Wall Street instead of the pledge-loan business. They were stuck, however. Not only had Provident burst on the scene with the capital and moral authority of the Morgans and Bakers and Vanderbilts; it had also pushed through a strict new regulatory regime. The details may be illustrated by a description of the hypothetical pledge of a cornet for $15. The hapless musician who had hocked his instrument was in good hands at the Provident. If he should happen to fall behind on his payments, he would be reminded of that fact. If he remained in arrears, his horn would be sold at public auction to satisfy his debt. Such sales were undertaken with reluctance by the Provident, and with good reason. There was nothing to be gained by them. If the cornet fetched more than $15 at auction, the net profits (after deducting arrearages on the loan) reverted to the musician. If the price realized was less than $15, the house alone bore the loss. Such was the new, humane face of pawnbroking.

The Provident's offices, in fact, looked like little Greek temples. They were designed to radiate the same qualities of strength, stability, and discretion that Baker's architecture was meant to project. In place

*The pledge-loan aesthetic, then and now: (*left*) the Provident Loan Society of New York, 1915 (*NEW YORK PUBLIC LIBRARY*); (*right*) E-Z Pawn, Austin, Texas, 1991*

of the ancient symbol of the trade, three balls suspended over the door, the Provident had its stately and slightly ambiguous name carved in stone: The Provident Loan Society of New York. Peter Schwed, an ex-employee of the Provident who began work in the Great Depression, relates that the society's name was "almost unknown, particularly in the poorer non-English-speaking districts, but everyone knew where the 'Penny Pein (pawn) Bank' was located." Entering a branch of the Provident, a new customer might have suffered a rush of intimidation. The brasswork and marble shone, and the staff (entirely male, *contra* Tolman) was dressed in uniform black coats and low-voltage neckwear. "Only among borrowers in those offices was the word 'pawn' used," Schwed recalled. "The Provident's nomenclature for a transaction is that an article is 'pledged,' and its staff winces ever so slightly if a customer innocently inquires, 'What can I hock this for?' "

Until the advent of the Provident, Wall Street had spurned consumer finance. Thanks to the imprimatur of established New York bankers, however, this taboo was now broken. The Provident was capitalized with 4½ percent bonds—that is, loans—and something called Certificates of Contribution. The certificates bore a passing resemblance to preferred stock. They paid a 6 percent dividend. However, this dividend was payable solely at the discretion of the trustees out of the society's surplus earnings, if any. Furthermore (and unlike ordinary preferred), the certificates represented no interest in ownership. Nevertheless, the securities did pay 6 percent, year in and year out, and they were admitted to trading on the New York Stock Exchange. The "Provident Perpetual Sixes" became a favorite investment, and their redemption at face value in the 1930s came as a sharp disappointment to the income-minded investors who held them. In the Depression, as Schwed recalled, "the Society's business was so big that earnings more than supplied working capital. The certificates had been as safe as money in the bank—safer in view of the bank closings in 1933—and banks weren't paying anything like six percent interest then."

The Provident drew its clientele from across the New York social spectrum. The truly indigent, almost by definition, were excluded, as they had nothing to pawn. But the poor pledged wedding rings and watches for cash with which to buy medicine. Middle-class businessmen pledged jewelry to raise working capital. "A fish peddler for years borrowed money each week to finance his stock of herring and mackerel and as regularly redeemed his wife's jewelry at the end of the week so that she might wear it to the synagogue," according to Rolf Nugent. As for the formerly rich, the society has lent against the collateral of golf cups and polo trophies.

Banking at the Post Office

Little knowing how much their successors would covet the consumer and his money, the profit-making bankers of Baker and Stillman's generation were content to relinquish the small-deposit franchise to mutual savings banks and building and loan societies. If these institutions were chiefly concerned with the safety of hard-earned family capital, they were still not safe enough for everyone. In unknown numbers, Americans continued to do their banking in stockings, mattresses, and behind loose chimney bricks. It was to serve the market of small and timid savers that the postal savings system was brought into being.

Britain established a postal savings system in 1861. A decade or so later, President Grant's Postmaster General, John A. J. Creswell, proposed that the United States follow suit. A banking crisis made Creswell even more determined, and he devoted a section of his 1873 annual report to arguing his case. "The events of the past few weeks," he wrote of the Panic of 1873, "have awakened a lively interest in a plan heretofore submitted, for securing the savings of the great body of the people by a pledge of the credit and faith of the United States."

The plan went nowhere, but the idea survived. The ball that Creswell helped to start rolling was soon to gather speed. It was the notion that the government's credit is really the people's and that the people, by right, may use it to improve their credit. It would lead, by the 1930s, to the creation of federal deposit insurance and to the enactment of myriad federal credit guarantees for the benefit of farmers, homeowners, small-business owners, students, and classes of borrowers that had not then come into existence. It would facilitate the gross credit expansion of the 1980s, more than a century after Creswell resigned from office in favor of a Republican more closely in step with prevailing ideas about the relationship of government to business. If it was true, as another Postmaster General would remark, that confidence in the government's credit was "universal," why not share the wealth?

The People's Party could see no reason why not, and its 1892 platform demanded the creation of postal savings banks by the government "for the safe deposit of the earnings of the people and to facilitate exchange." In this as in so many other particulars, the Populists lost the election but won the future. By 1910, the postal savings idea was back on the national agenda, and its champion was the Republican President, William Howard Taft.

What Taft proposed was a network of government savings banks under postal administration. The patrons would be Americans who feared banks (a population enlarged by the Panic of 1907) and newly arrived immigrants who had banked with the government in their native countries or had become the targets of "immigrant bank" hoaxes in this one. They would pass up returns of 4 percent at state-chartered mutual savings banks for the certainty of a government-guaranteed rate of 2 percent. They were, in fact, the people who were already buying postal money orders payable to themselves as a makeshift kind of savings account. On these they earned nothing.

The President had another motive, and it will strike a modern investor as quaint. The government borrowed little enough in those years, but it had issued some $700 million in bonds at an interest rate of 2 percent. Rates were beginning to rise, and the price of the 2 percent bonds was therefore beginning to fall. (Who would have paid 100 cents on the dollar for the privilege of receiving a stream of income at a below-market rate?) From 1946 to 1981, the government was a chronic issuer of depreciating bonds. Year by year, interest rates rose and (to say the same thing) bond prices fell. This state of affairs seemed to cause the governments of that period no moral distress. At least, no American President was heard to say, as Taft implied, that the government had an obligation to the holders of the bonds to maintain their market prices. Taft reasoned that because the government had forced the bonds on the national banks, the government was responsible for helping the banks to get out of them whole. This duty the postal savings system would conveniently discharge. It would buy the 2 percent bonds at par, or face value, and pay out a 2 percent rate of return to people who expected no more.

This feature, at least, of the postal savings scheme might have been expected to appeal to Wall Street. It did not. Why the government should offer depositors half the rate they were then earning at perfectly sound savings banks was beyond the imagining of bankers. *Bankers Magazine* put its finger on the nub of the proposition: ". . . essentially the postal savings measure is designed as a Federal guaranty of savings deposits." Not that depositors seemed to need much protection. With no federal impetus, savings-bank deposits had grown enormously, and losses were rare. In the twenty years up to 1909, the number of depositors had doubled, to 8 million, and the volume of deposits had more than doubled, to $3.7 billion. "The savings banks of New York," noted a Chicago banker, "hold nearly a billion and a half dollars of deposits—or more than the savings banks of any foreign country excepting Germany. If the savings banks of New York State were all to go out of business and turn their deposits over to the proposed postal savings bank, the depositors would lose over $25,000,000 a year in the shrinkage of the earnings of their deposits. And that is more than twenty-five times as much as the total losses to savings depositors in New York State in the last thirty years."

The Taft administration won the day if not the debate, and the postal savings system was enacted on June 25, 1910. Everything about its beginnings was small. A trial run was ordered in which only one post office in each of the forty-eight states and territories was selected to participate. Nobody could deposit more than $100 a month or more than $500 in all. The initial congressional appropriation for the system was only $100,000, which happened to equal the original capital of the Provident Loan Society of New York. Wallace B. Hunter of 181 Remsen Street, Cohoes, New York, was the first resident of New York State to make a deposit in a postal savings bank. He turned over five one-dollar bills. (Cohoes, like the other forty-seven trial sites, was selected, in part, for its large immigrant population. It was believed, correctly, that foreign-born Americans would be more responsive to the idea of a government-owned bank than the natives. Within six years, foreign-born depositors controlled three-quarters of the funds in the postal savings system, with Russians and Italians in the lead.)

Opponents of the system had feared it would create a new army of federal jobholders, but clerical expense was held to a minimum. Interest was credited only once a year, for instance, and the system dealt only in round sums, not fractional ones. There was, in any case, no money with which to build a new federal empire. Opponents had also raised the specter of an exodus of funds from private, uninsured banks to the nation's post offices, but neither did that happen. At the end of the first year, deposits totaled $20 million, most of which had been coaxed out of hiding. On one count, however, the critics had been vindicated absolutely. They had warned of paternalism, and the system laid it on with a trowel. Carter B. Keene, director of postal savings, issued an especially unctuous pronouncement in 1913. The system was not meant to yield a profit, Keene said. "Its aim is infinitely higher and more important. Its mission is to encourage thrift and economy among all classes of citizens. It stands for good citizenship and tends to diminish crime. It places savings facilities at the very doors of those living in remote sections, and it also affords opportunity for safeguarding the savings of thousands who have absolute confidence in the Government and will trust no other institution."

This confidence had been tested already. Seven months after the system opened, in July 1911, depositors were given the opportunity to exchange their 2 percent savings accounts for 2½ percent government bonds. The bonds would mature in twenty years, at which time the investor would be handed back his principal. This principal, of course, he already had. The proposition was that a 2½ percent interest rate would remain competitive for the life of the bond. It would not be, starting almost right away. By November 1911, the 2½ percent government bonds, due to mature in twenty years, had fallen to an indicated price of 92½ cents on the dollar from 100 cents, which is what the bank-fearing depositors had paid for them. Only a handful had actually availed themselves of this opportunity, and to them the paper loss was severe. The bond for which they had paid $200 was, within five months, worth $185, a 7½ percent shrinkage in principal. The loss represented three years' painstaking accumulation of interest paid at the 2½ percent annual rate. (As for the moral obligation of the government to make good the losses of its own depositors, the postal savings system promptly offered to purchase the bonds at 100 cents on the dollar on the application of any holder. For better or worse, this gesture did not constitute any lasting precedent in the American government bond market.)

Here was a brief but unforgettable lesson in the varieties of risk. The obvious way to lose money was in a bank failure, and fearful savers opened accounts in post offices to protect themselves against that contingency. However, it was also possible to lose money in a government bond if market interest rates went up, as they were then doing in Britain and France as well as in the United States. As if to anticipate World War I and the end of the international gold standard, long-term British bonds in 1911 had fallen to their lowest prices since the late 1870s. Interest rates were still low by the standards of the late twentieth century, but there could be no consolation in that to the holders of perpetual 2½ percent British government bonds. At their low ebb in 1911, the bonds, known universally as "consols," traded at 76⅜ percent of face value. As recently as 1906, they had changed hands at 91 percent of face value. As the Taft administration was inviting American postal investors to lock up their money for twenty years at 2½ percent, a British bank was reported to be in trouble for a novel reason. The Yorkshire Penny Bank, which, true to its name, catered to small savers, was forced to seek a merger. It had had deposits of the equivalent of $90 million and a blue-chip investment policy. It had purchased government bonds. There was nothing obviously wrong with the credit of the British government, but the market was busily marking down the prices of British obligations. These losses forced the Yorkshire bank to the brink of collapse. It was rescued, but other banks in similar circumstances were not so lucky.

In these circumstances, *The New York Times* scratched its head over the unflagging faith of the postal service savings customer. "This confidence is touching in high degree, and is amazing," the paper commented. "There is no business scandal which is not outdone by Government scandals. It is hardly too much to say that the Government is as conspicuous for inefficiency as many private corporations are for efficiency, and that on the average general trade is better conducted than Government business. Yet the poor prefer to trust the Government, taking 3 per cent from the Government rather than 4 from private savings banks, and more in private investments. This sentiment is an asset of Government, and can hardly be overvalued."

"I Believe in You"

Far from Wall Street, one man trusted the poor. Arthur J. Morris was born in Tarboro, North Carolina, in 1881 and was educated and trained in the law at the University of Virginia, Class of 1901. He began his practice in Norfolk and specialized in banking and corporate law.

Besides a reputation as an up-and-coming young lawyer, Morris was known for his ready signature on a loan application. Once a railroad clerk, solidly employed for fourteen years and earning an annual salary of $2,500, came to him at wits' end. He needed $500 to pay for his wife's operation, and no Norfolk bank would lend it to him. (In turn-of-the-century Virginia, the law itself made this difficult. The maximum legal interest rate, 6 percent, was one at which no profit-making lender could afford to lend.) Economic theory supposes that an entrepreneur, confronted with an unmet social need, will take profit-making action. Annoyed by the darkness, he or she will light a candle. In consumer finance at that time and place, Morris was this man of theory come to life. He endorsed the clerk's loan, and many others besides. Undertaking a survey, he convinced himself that 80 percent of the American public was being denied adequate banking services. He devised a technique of circumventing the usury laws without alienating the respectable people who needed to borrow from him. He set up in the lending business, lawfully, with the intention of making a profit. The credit-union movement was just then getting started, and the Provident Loan Society was almost twenty years old. The Russell Sage Foundation was spreading the gospel of so-called remedial lending. What distinguished Morris, first and foremost, was his interest in making a business of personal debt.

Morris was not yet thirty when he applied for a charter to open a new kind of bank. "Dear Arthur," wrote the chairman of the State Corporation Commission in reply, "I have carefully considered your application for a charter for your hybrid and mongrel institution. Frankly, I don't know what it is. It isn't a savings bank; it isn't a state or national bank; it isn't anything I ever heard of before. Its principles seem sound, however, and its purpose admirable. But the reason that I am going to give you a charter is because I believe in you."

The first Morris Plan bank, the Fidelity Savings & Trust Co., was opened in Norfolk in 1910. The idea was to lend at a high rate of interest on the twin collateral of "character and earning power." The borrower would repay the loan in installments over the course of a year, four times longer than the maturity of the conventional bank loan (when obtainable). Through an elaborate legal fiction, the effective interest rate on the loan would be a multiple of the legal rate.

A man in need of $100 would apply at Morris's bank. In lieu of a mortgage, common stocks, a piano, jewelry, or other collateral, he would present the names of two endorsers, or "co-makers." If the

A Thomas Jefferson of consumer debt, Arthur J. Morris, preparing to set sail on the SS Paris, *1925* (BETTMANN ARCHIVE)

loan was approved, the borrower would receive not the $100 he had applied for, but the $100 minus a commission of 2 percent and minus the legal interest rate of 6 percent. Proceeds to the borrower were therefore $92. There was another important step. The borrower would purchase from the bank, on the installment plan, a pair of "investment certificates" in the face amount of $100. He would pledge to pay $1.00 a week on each of them. When the payments were finished, he would present the certificates to the bank and thereby discharge his debt. Clearly, the borrower paid more than 6 percent for the privilege. He paid far more than 8 percent, if the 2 percent "commission" was rightly treated as interest expense. Because he was repaying the loan at the rate of $2.00 a week, he did not have full use of what he borrowed over the full year. The effective interest rate was, in fact, in excess of 19 percent. Penalties were assessed on delinquent balances at the stunning rate of 5 percent a week.

But credit unions, just then coming into existence in the United States, charged only a little less. Alphonse Desjardins, a Canadian journalist, helped to organize the first American specimen, La Caisse Populaire Ste. Marie, for the benefit of French-Canadian parishioners in Manchester, New Hampshire. Also in 1909, and also with Desjardin's assistance, Massachusetts passed a law to permit the creation of credit unions. By 1920, 142 such cooperative societies were gathering up their members' savings and lending them out again. Like the Morris Plan, the credit unions lent against the collateral of endorsed notes, not versus things or securities. Also like the Morris Plan, the credit unions required that loans be repaid in periodic installments and that delinquent borrowers pay fines. Unlike Morris, however, Desjardins and his followers eschewed the profit motive. Theirs was a work of cooperation.

The Morris Plan idea traveled well. It was successfully transplanted, with local management, in Atlanta, Washington, Richmond, New York, Chicago, and Baltimore, among other cities. It was taken to Wall Street by Morris himself around 1914. The entrepreneur told the bankers with whom he met, "The industrial supremacy of this country depends on mass production. Mass consumption must be in order that mass production may be. Mass credit must be in order that mass consumption may be. Where there is mass production and mass consumption properly coordinated, it follows as the night follows day that mass employment and the continuity of employment are assured." Some $5 million was forthcoming for Morris's proposed expansion.

Morris was credited with developing the first bank holding company to connect the far-flung Morris Plan organization and with the invention of credit life insurance to protect co-makers (and his own company) in case of the death of the borrower. His slogan was: "No man's debts shall survive him." He helped to pioneer the factory financing of automobiles in 1919, for the Studebaker Corporation. Morris lived long enough to accept congratulations from President Dwight D. Eisenhower on the fiftieth anniversary of the organization of the first Morris Plan bank, in 1960, and from President Lyndon B. Johnson on the fiftieth anniversary of the founding of the Morris Plan Insurance Society, in 1967. As an honored, rich, and still active old man, he became a proselytizer for credit. Consumer debt was no mere technique for rearranging the timing of outlays and incomes. It was a force for democracy against world communism that Morris compared not unfavorably with the hydrogen bomb. He cast himself almost as a missionary—which, in point of fact, he was. (In 1910, the year that Morris started, a leading banker was quoted about the automobile: "I decry the use of the machine for purposes of pleasure by classes who must go into debt or give up their savings to indulge that pleasure.") To Morris, his life's work was not installment debt but consumer credit, and he did not underestimate its financial, cultural, or geopolitical significance. It was a "remarkable lever in the realization of human hope," and if one united that with the Bill of Rights (Morris saw nothing lopsided in the comparison), "we weld together two of the great elements that have justified my coinage of the expression: 'Democratization of Credit.' "

When at last he died in 1973 at the ripe old age of ninety-two (leaving four daughters, six grandchildren, and fourteen great-grandchildren and a law library named in his honor at his alma mater), a headline in his obituary described a "Financier Who Opened Way for Workers' Loans." Consumer debt had taken its place by hearth and home.

The Irony of Farm Credit

The uplifting spirit of the Progressive age made its mark on credit, and farmers were singled out by reformers as the deserving recipients of more and cheaper loans. With the closing of the frontier in the 1880s, the era of free federal land had come to an end. Thus, the would-be owner of a farm was bound to show either the color of his money or the strength of his borrowing power.

As we have already seen, real-estate lending was not then in the banking mainstream. Even when allowed, it was sometimes regulated, as under the laws of New York, Ohio, Pennsylvania, South Carolina, and Texas. Real-estate loans were prohibited under the National Bank Act, and complaints about scarce or expensive farm credit echoed down through the late nineteenth century. Demonstrably, it was possible to incur farm debt, as many Americans did so after the Civil War. In the postwar inflation, wheat fetched $2.00 a bushel, and many debtors fell into the error of projecting that high price out into the future. "[A]ll a man seemed to want to do was buy a farm, no matter what the price was," a West Virginia farmer recalled of that optimistic time. But in the 1870s, wheat fetched little more than a dollar a bushel, and then, in the 1880s, less than a dollar. This witness—Alexander Clohan, the postmaster of Martinsburg—testified that the farms purchased at inflated postwar prices proved heavy burdens to those who had borrowed to buy. "[T]hey kept struggling and struggling and trying and were able to pay their interest up to, probably, 1893, when the panic came on, and a great many of them had to go into liquidation, you know, and there have been quite a lot that were sold out."

Clohan made his remarks before the U.S. Industrial Commission, a body of congressmen, senators, and private citizens that undertook a panoramic study of American working life around the turn of the century. It wasn't the last such enterprise. In 1908, under President Theodore Roosevelt, a Country Life Commission criticized the "lack of any adequate system of agricultural credit, whereby the farmer may readily secure loans on fair terms." In 1910, the National Monetary Commission reported a favorable view of the operations of the German *Landschaft* system of cooperative agricultural credit. In 1912, President William Howard Taft called on American ambassadors in Europe to report on the workings of the cooperative rural credit systems in the countries to which they were posted. Similar studies were undertaken by, among others, the American Bankers Association, the New York State Bankers Association, and the Southern Commercial Congress. Perhaps the truest bellwether of public sentiment was that each of the three major political parties in 1912 endorsed the idea of making farm credit more accessible.

Presently, this highly charged political atmosphere would yield the lightning bolt of federally sponsored credit. By 1916, however, when the Federal Farm Loan Act was passed, American agriculture was thriving—in fact, it was flourishing for years before World War I put up the prices of crops—and there was more than a little truth to the complaint of *The New York Times*'s editorial page that "any farmer who pays too much for his mortgage, or who cannot get a mortgage, in these days of $10,000,000,000 crops and improving farm values has himself to blame more than the system."

Such was not the case in 1899 and 1900, however, when the Industrial Commission was asking Americans questions about their workaday lives. The opinions of a handful of interested parties, even if delivered under oath, may not constitute clinching scientific evidence, but the transcripts are nonetheless revealing about individual experiences. They suggest that, in the South, agriculture was up against the almost insurmountable hurdle of 15 or 20 percent per annum interest rates—the punitive level of rates that prevailed in the junk-bond market some nine decades later. In the Dakotas, mortgage rates were frequently lower than that, and the burden of debt was correspondingly lighter—although still heavy enough to cause mortgage companies to foreclose on one-sixth of the land in South Dakota. Reading the testimony, one is reminded of how little is new under the sun. Frequently, people borrow at inopportune moments: against the collateral of petroleum reserves at the top of the oil market, for instance, or against the collateral of farmland at the peak of a great inflation. High and rising markets bring out the J. P. Morgan in even the humblest saver, whereas low and falling markets make cowards of moguls. In a more perfect world, people would be bold at the bottom (when, by definition, prices have fallen as low as they are going to get) and cautious at the top. Taking life as it is, however, one will not be surprised by the recollections of Charles A. Wieting, Commissioner of Agriculture of New York State, concerning the state of farm credit in the post-Civil War period: "Farm products bringing high prices made the value of lands high, and farms were sold at high prices. Many of them were bought on time and mortgaged. After the close of the war, the demand for farm products gradually grew less, prices became less and the price of land shrank accordingly, so that many farmers of the State of New York, who had bought lands and mortgaged them, lost them by shrinkage of value."

As the Industrial Commission heard the evidence, money was borrowed with a lighter heart in the West than in the East or South. In the South, indeed, tragedy was a silent partner in the dealings between farmers and creditors. Out West, "there seems to be something in the atmosphere out there favorable to [debt]," testified the secretary of South Dakota's Board of Regents, M. F. Greeley. "A man who, in the East, would not go into debt for 50 cents, after a year in Dakota would unhesitatingly run in debt that many thousand if he could get trusted for the amount." Seven percent was the legal interest rate, Greeley stated, but more was usually charged—"10 percent almost invariably, and from that up to 15 percent and 20 [percent], according to how tight a place a man is in or how poor pay he is." He added the opinion that there was some justice in this. The bankruptcy laws were lenient, for one thing. For another, the idea of repudiation enjoyed a certain measure of legitimacy. Perhaps Greeley had in mind the succession of collectivist political ideologies that had flourished in the Midwest, from Grangerism to Greenbackism to Populism, in the years since the Civil War. In any case, he went on, "owing to pernicious political teaching in nearly every Western community, a few can be found who are still looking to legislation, politics and Presidents to get them out of debt, but this misguided class are fast waking up to the fact that politics and mortgage lifting do not run on the same range."

In the crisply argued view of Brynjolf Prom, banker and farmer of Milton, North Dakota, there was nothing immoral about debt. Asked if his neighbors and he could have made a start without borrowing, he answered "no." "Most of our farms are bought on credit," he said. "We deem it wise to buy on credit." In a typical transaction, a farmer would dedicate half of his annual crop to debt service. And then? Prom was asked. What does a farmer do when he gets out of debt? "Buys more land," the witness replied. "They are restless people up here; they can not lie still."

It was a far cry from the Dakotas to the old Confederacy and from the optimism of Brynjolf Prom to the fatalism of Lawrence Winkler Youmans, cotton planter and merchant of Fairfax, South Carolina. Youmans was born in 1844 on his father's plantation outside of Gillisonville, South Carolina. After service in the Confederate Army, he was elected to the South Carolina General Assembly in 1868 and to the State Senate in 1894. Like the witnesses from New York and West Virginia, Youmans traced the problem of farm indebtedness back thirty-five years to the dislocations caused by the Civil War: "The old original landholders got in debt early. Cotton in 1866 down there dropped very heavily, and they all got involved, and their land has nearly all been parceled out, and the parties who have been more thrifty got them, and those lands in turn are being run out of the hands of the second parties now. I can scarcely hold my property now, and I made it since the war. It is a struggle with me, not to make money, but to hold my property. You do not have any idea of it. I have been trying to give you an idea of it. I have not overstated the case at all."

Up North, in the years immediately following the Civil War, the buyers of farmland overpaid and overborrowed. For years and sometimes decades, they struggled. In the South, farmers and planters struggled too, but not for the same reasons. For one thing, in the 1890s, cotton prices fell. For another, money and credit were in chronic short supply. In need of working capital, a Southern farmer would hand over a lien on his unharvested crop. He would often deal with a store, or "furnishing merchant," not a bank. Frequently, the coin of these banker-storekeepers was not cash but clothing and supplies. This merchandise was available at one price to buyers with cash and at another to buyers without. Paying the higher price reserved for credit customers was what William Faulkner's character Flem Snopes referred to as shopping with "six-bit," or seventy-five-cent dollars.

The implicit interest rates in a crop-lien transaction were devastating. According to one historian of the cotton economy, they ranged between 30 percent and 110 percent per annum. As hard as it was to obtain short-term credit, it was next to impossible to find long-term mortgage capital. Southern bankers, not unlike some Northern bankers, were reluctant to make land loans, even if they had the capital to spare, which, usually, they did not. All this the Fairfax cotton planter tried to convey to the members of the Industrial Commission.

"We pay 13 percent to the banks for money now," Youmans testified. "I pay it. . . . I started to raise cotton on the basis of 7 cents. When I sold my crop, it did not average me over 4½ cents a pound. You see very easily I could have made money if I had got 7 cents or even 6 cents, but when I got only 4½ cents, I met with a loss, and so did every man who advanced on the cotton crop. Cotton has been deflating steadily since 1873. There have been reactions, but the tendency is downward."

So saying, Youmans revealed himself to be a cycles man, like Sewell Avery: a believer in the tendency of prices to follow predictable patterns over weeks, months, or years. By the sound of his testimony, which was dispirited, he had not entertained the possibility that the prices of farmland and cotton were even then hitting bottom and beginning a recovery that would usher in two decades of national agricultural prosperity—which, in fact, they were.

He told the panel that he had 4,000 acres, but that only 1,300 to 1,400 were under cultivation. He said that he had made money until 1890 but not in the nine years since. He said he had farmed for thirty years. He contested—successfully, a modern reader will judge—the charge that wages paid to agricultural labor were extravagant. "Take my plowmen, for instance," Youmans testified. "I employ them by the month, and they make 5½ days' honest good work each week. . . . it is all that is counted and a little more than we got from the slaves before the war; and these hands on my plantation I allow to have 2 acres of land, and the plowmen, if I do not need the animals, have the use of them on Saturday evenings. But when I settle with them at 12 o'clock on Saturday or Friday night, I pay these hands for their 5½ days' work, in addition to their rations of 1 peck of meal and 3 pounds of bacon and salt, 90 cents in trade, to be traded out in the stores at 50 percent profit, and 20 cents in cash; this is all they get for 5½ days' labor."

Amplifying, Youmans said that he paid monthly wages of $5.20. He explained that he operated a store in conjunction with the plantation and that his retailing policy was to mark up prices by 50 percent. And he said, "I will say that my labor is about as well paid, as well clothed and I think the best satisfied labor in that vicinity."

Youmans was at a loss to explain what had gone wrong in the 1890s. "I cannot say it is from any vicissitudes of the season, from any lack of industry on the part of the people or from any failure in the soil to respond to cultivation. . . . There must be some cause for it and the cause must be artificial. We cannot charge it to natural circumstances. To claim that the triumphs of art or the bounty of nature would result in an overproduction of the good things of life and therefore bring about hardship and distress, it seems would be to argue an absurdity."

Pretty clearly, Youmans believed that the lack of credit was one such artificial depressant. "We have to pay a usurious rate of interest—the agricultural element of our country," he testified. "The discount is about 13 percent when they can borrow from the bank; and when a man has not got good collateral he has to borrow from the country merchant and has to give 50 to 75 percent profit."

Why 13 percent? Youmans was asked.

"I cannot go to New York and borrow money," he replied. "I cannot go to Augusta and get money. I went there to make the experiment, and I said to the president of the bank: 'I want to borrow money.'

" 'What security do you propose to give?'

" 'Real estate.'

" 'We do not loan money on real estate.'

"That throws me back to the country banks, where I can borrow money, but I have to pay 13 percent. When money congests at these trade centers there is no automatic power to redistribute it. It stays there."

Next, Youmans made an observation on the burden of high interest expense that would have applied with equal force to corporate finance in the 1980s. "[Y]ou gentlemen know as well as I that there is no business except for successful mining and gambling that can stand 13 percent; but that is what our people pay, and a great many pay more."

The witness was asked if the country banks in Barnwell, South Carolina, made much money. They were, after all, the presumed beneficiaries of ultra-high interest rates.

"One of those banks has gone out of business," Youmans answered. "I do not think they made money. The president told me that they have a certain paid up capital; it amounts to $40,000 or $50,000. They very soon loan that. They get a certain line of securities and they arrange with New York banks to borrow money, and they pay 6 percent. They bring that money back and have to make that 6 percent, and they have to put it on their profit. Everything is declining. Land is going down. Men took mortgages on land 5 or 6 years ago when it was worth more than now, and they can not realize what they advanced on the land. There is a general decline in prices."

This deflationary cycle was, in fact, ending. In his annual report for 1909, the Secretary of Agriculture, James Wilson, would be able to marvel: "The value of farm products is so incomprehensively large that it has become merely a row of figures." Yet the bumper crops did not stand in the way of a wonderful bull market in agricultural products. By 1910, crop prices, on average, were up by 89 percent from 1899. Farm land prices climbed even faster: by 189 percent in the first decade of the new century, according to the Commerce Department. Brynjolf Prom, the optimistic witness, had not been bullish enough. The price of an average farm in North Dakota jumped by 152 percent, of an average farm in South Dakota by 209 percent. Not only was mortgage debt free of sin. It was, in hindsight, the most prudent debt a Midwestern farmer could have incurred. "Whether he realized it or not," a pair of agricultural historians noted later, "the average middle western landowner had made his money not so much from good farming as from the unearned increment that came from the ownership of farm lands. To a considerable extent, he was only a successful speculator."

Like bull markets in stocks, the bull market in farmland engendered the belief that prices would rise forever. "Speculators who had no interest whatever in farming bought land for the 6 percent or 8 percent annual rise that seemed a certainty throughout the early years of the century," the same historians wrote. *Wallaces' Farmer*, in 1909, heaped scorn on the speculators who seemed to "regard the farm as something like the old-fashioned coupon bond, from which they can clip coupons twice a year on the particular day or date on which they are due, whether crops are good or bad." Although eminently sane, this piece of advice would prove highly unprofitable for many years. The rise in farmland prices had only begun.

There was irony in the boom. Vast new deposits of gold were being discovered in South Africa, Alaska, and Colorado even as William Jennings Bryan mounted the stump in the late 1890s. No sooner did the Populists go down to defeat on a platform of easy money than the production of gold began to accelerate. The result was a metallurgical, rather than a political, inflation. Between 1890 and 1914, the world's gold stock more than doubled. In consequence, American prices rose persistently (although not alarmingly by late-twentieth-century standards), as did British and European prices. The so-called gold inflation of the early twentieth century was therefore a rare event: a protracted, peacetime rise in prices. For American farmers, in comparison both with what preceded it and with what was to follow, it produced a golden age.

Yet it was this prosperity that sped reform. By 1912, most observers had swung around to the view that the existing American credit structure gave agriculture short shrift. State-chartered banks extended mortgage credit to farmers but often on hard terms: many loans were due and payable in a year. Life insurance companies also made mortgage loans on farmland, but frequently for no longer than five years. National banks, of course, made no mortgage loans on any terms. For another thing, the relationship between interest rates and land prices had become distorted. Thanks to the flyaway market in land, it was nearly impossible, in some sections of the country, to make a living on a mortgaged farm. One result of these circumstances was a rise in tenancy. Biding his time until he could sell at a high price, a farmer would retire to town and install a tenant to do his work. "Nothing is more important to this country," Theodore Roosevelt had proclaimed in 1914, "than the perpetuation of our system of medium sized farms worked by their owners. We do not want to see our farmers sink to the condition of the peasants in the old world." By 1914, however, it was estimated, almost 40 percent of the farms in the corn belt were being cultivated by tenants. The storied American yeoman was becoming a coupon clipper.

The political response to this phenomenon, inevitable but ill timed, was to facilitate lending on easier terms and thus to assure even higher farmland prices. In this questionable business, the states anticipated the federal government. Around the turn of the century, hundreds of little state-chartered country banks sprouted up. Even under the liberalized National Bank Act, the minimum capital for a new country bank was $25,000. It was only $5,000 under the state laws of Kansas, Nebraska, North Dakota, South Dakota, Oklahoma, and Wisconsin. In 1900, Iowa had 733 banks; in 1914, it had 1,558. Oklahoma had 106 banks in 1900 and 916 in 1914.

There were more banks and better buildings. Prior to the turn of the century, small-town banks rarely occupied their own premises. They frequently shared storefront quarters with such nonfinancial businesses as barbershops, meat markets, or residential apartments. The protracted rise in farm prices and land values inspired a renaissance of new bank construction, however. In 1905, the same year Frank Lloyd Wright built a bank in Dwight, Illinois, *Bankers Monthly* reported from Kansas that the farmers "are making money so rapidly in the wheat business that they find it necessary to get into some other line in order to keep their capital moving. Our people are harvesting the biggest wheat crop ever raised in the western counties and a number of new banks will start up this fall." In Grinnell, Iowa, in 1913, both of the leading banks decided to put up new buildings, one of them, the Merchants National Bank, commissioning what turned out to be a prairie masterpiece by Louis Sullivan.

Democracy in the Counting House

The architecture of the day was meant to be forward-looking and progressive, like the politics. Thus, in general, Roman columns were out and terra-cotta ornamentation was in. Sullivan built boxy brick buildings lit by huge semicircular windows. He built banks with community rooms, ladies' waiting rooms, and meeting rooms: space in which the bank could help to foster the life of the community. Sullivan's 1918 creation, the People's Savings and Loan Association in Sidney, Ohio, was built in the spirit of Arthur J. Morris. The *Sidney Daily News* caught the new, forward-looking philosophy: "The plan indeed, and in fact the entire arrangement and equipment may be described as 'democratic' in the sense that the mystery and secrecy of the older banking room arrangements wherein the banker was high priest, hidden from view behind many doors, has given way to so complete an openness of arrangement with the executive offices in full view, as to remove social barriers, and thereby to facilitate the transaction of business, through freedom of access, and to encourage confidence through the influence of personal contact. The careful consideration in the provision of rest rooms for the comfort and convenience of patrons, indicates a well defined tendency to make the institution, in a considerable degree, a social as well as a financial center."

Credit cooperatives sprouted in the same democratic soil. In 1913, Wisconsin provided for the incorporation of land-mortgage associations. They would lend to farmers from the proceeds of the sale of mortgage bonds. In 1914, the Land Bank of the State of New York, modeled on Prussian lines, was organized and empowered to issue bonds on the security of farm mortgages. In the same period, Idaho,

Indiana, Iowa, North Dakota, Oklahoma, Oregon, South Dakota, and Utah authorized the investment of school funds in farm mortgages. Missouri, Montana, New York, and Oklahoma passed laws to reduce the farmer's rate of interest on long-term mortgages below the then ruling market rates—in the cases of Montana and Oklahoma, for instance, to 6 percent or less.

When the Sixty-third Congress produced no fewer than seventy rural credit bills, it was therefore swimming with the tide. On July 17, 1916, President Woodrow Wilson signed the prevailing legislation, the Federal Farm Loan Bill, into law. The act created a dozen Federal Land Banks and empowered them to lend for up to forty years and at interest rates of 6 percent or less. Most private lenders resisted the measure, and it was to mollify them that the law made provision for the creation of Joint-Stock Land Banks. These banks would be privately owned but federally regulated. They too would issue tax-exempt bonds and invest the proceeds in farm mortgages.

Altogether, the nation was marshaling credit for farmers at what would prove to be a most inopportune moment. Farmland prices had been rising even before the federal government expanded the pool of lendable funds. When World War I furnished the final clinching argument for the American farmer to mortgage himself, he was almost accosted by willing lenders. Besides state-chartered banks, federally chartered banks, and state-chartered cooperatives, there was strong competition from the new Federal Land Banks and Joint-Stock Land Banks. "These Land Banks," wrote a historian of life insurance lending, "proved to be formidable competitors of the life companies. The competition for loans caused all lenders to relax their standards in order to secure business. This was especially unfortunate in view of the land boom conditions then obtaining."

The price of wheat was 62 cents a bushel in 1900. It was 99 cents in 1909, $1.43 in 1916, and $2.19 at the peak in 1919. To put $2.19 in perspective, it was a price not seen again until 1947. As for cotton, Lawrence Winkler Youmans would have been dumbfounded. Its price reached 35 cents a pound in 1919, a peak it would not regain until 1950. Not unlike the men they distrusted on Wall Street, farmers became bolder as markets went higher. In general, they did not believe (as *Wallaces' Farmer* predicted) that prices were bound to deflate with the peace. They did not seize the opportunity of record-high wheat, record-high cotton, and record-high land to reduce their indebtedness. Instead, they borrowed more. They did not trim sails in the wheat market in 1920 any more than Nelson Bunker Hunt stepped out of the silver market in 1979. They felt, with some justice, that a little prosperity was long overdue them. It was estimated that the average farmer earned no more than 75 cents an hour from his labor in bringing home the 1917 crop.

The collapse of prices in the early 1920s would have been devastating enough, but the damage was compounded by debt. By the summer of 1921, crop prices were down by no less than 85 percent from the postwar peak. Nebraskans, finding that corn had become cheaper than coal, burned it. As it does in every market, the fall in prices revealed the weaknesses in the structure of credit that had financed the rise. In 1915, according to the U.S. Department of Agriculture, banks "had outstanding to farmers, loans on personal and collateral security to the amount of $1,609,970,000." By 1918, this number had grown to $2,506,814,000. In 1920—a year in which every clairvoyant farmer was repaying debt and bracing for the worst—it reached $3,869,891,000.

In the heat of the moment, buyers in Iowa put down 10 percent or less in cash. It was understood that nothing could be safer, as the price of black earth only went up. Indeed, it had been going up for years. From $82.58 in 1910, the average Iowa acre rose to $199.52 in 1920. As usually occurs at the tops of speculative markets, experts were found on the bullish side of the issue. Because corn prices had risen, they explained, the value of land should rise too—never mind that corn prices had frequently slumped in the past and were, in fact, on the verge of a pratfall. "Iowans believe," according to the 1919 edition of the Iowa Yearbook of Agriculture, "that land is going higher, and that it can never be bought cheaper than at present. They buy therefore to avoid paying a higher price later on. They say there is but one corn belt to grow corn and hogs and the demand for these products is increasing and will continue to increase." That was the more or less clinical analysis. *Wallaces' Farmer* quoted an Iowa observer in the same year: "Half of the people are either land agents or speculators in land. Most of the men have never been farmers, and never will be farmers. The game is to buy and sell, and many are boasting of making thirty and forty thousand dollars in a few months. And then they say the boom is just started."

If the farm credit boom of the early twentieth century was anything like the corporate credit boom of the late twentieth century, the doubting Thomases were discredited long before the peak. It could be shown with paper and pencil that the prices paid for cropland were, in many cases, uneconomic. The economist George E. Putnam, writing in 1915 about the raft of state initiatives to make farm credit more accessible, forehandedly warned that "a lower rate [of interest] would only add to the present speculative element in farm land investments." War and excess credit sustained the boom and sowed the seeds for the inevitable bust. "Loans from the Federal Farm Loan System were available, with rates of interest perhaps 0.5 percent lower than had been customary before its advent and with the longer period of amortization of the loan," wrote the agricultural historians Theodore Saloutos and John D. Hicks. "Life insurance companies also had an abundance of money on hand for real estate loans. But the local small-town bankers, many with huge surplus deposits that they were eager to put to work, literally pressed money upon the not unwilling farmers and speculators. New banks were established by men who knew next to nothing about banking. From 1914 to 1920 more than 1,700 new banks began operations in eleven typical agricultural states. Often two or three banks appeared where one would have been enough."

The problem of surplus banks was presently addressed with a vengeance. The Armistice did not, after all, produce an immediate business recession. Early in 1919, a commercial boom was touched off by a businessmen's race to reenter peacetime production. Inventories were accumulated and commodity prices bid up. Banks lent to their corporate and agricultural customers, and the brand-new Federal Reserve System lent to the banks. Indeed, the rates at which banks were able to borrow from the Federal Reserve were profitably lower than the rates they were able to get in the market. Whereas the banks obtained between 5 percent and 7 percent, they paid between 4 percent and 4½ percent at the Federal. Inflation became the order of the day.

What followed was a uniquely vicious deflation. One by one, the props under high prices were kicked away. The Federal Reserve raised interest rates and gold left the country. (A word on gold: Its export was outlawed during the war. Following the peace, in 1919, the embargo was lifted. Thus, gold *could* be shipped out, if its owners could find more profitable uses for it abroad. In growing numbers, they did. The loss of gold was then identical to a loss of money, and the loss of money usually stops inflation.) Expecting higher prices, businessmen built inventories, and they laid in too much. On May 3, 1920, the John Wanamaker department store in New York shattered inflationary expectations by advertising a sale on goods that the market had assumed to be scarce. Merchants began to complain about a "buyers' strike," and not a few retailers went bankrupt. (One of the victims was a Kansas City haberdashery owned, in part, by Harry S Truman.)

Bond prices fell, thereby introducing unseasoned American investors to the hard, indeed perverse, ways of Wall Street. In 1918, the public had been urged to buy Liberty bonds with borrowed money. In May 1920, the Fourth Liberty Loan, which paid an interest rate of 4¼ percent a year, was quoted at 83 cents on the dollar.

The postwar inflation was global, and so was the succeeding deflation. The only countries to be spared this downdraft were the ones, like Germany, that fell into hyperinflation. As North Dakota wheat rose and fell, so did Cuban sugar. The changeableness of prices turned the sound loan of 1920 into the defaulted loan of 1921 and the solvent banker into a humbled petitioner. Between May 1920 and June 1921, wholesale prices in the United States fell by no less than 44 percent. Even more startling than the magnitude of the break was its compression in time: more than three-quarters of the damage was done in the six months from August 1920 to February 1921. Surveying the monetary history of the United States between 1867 and 1960, Milton Friedman and Anna Schwartz could find nothing quite like it.

As collateral values shrank, the number of bank failures rose. There were 63 in 1919, 155 in 1920, and 506 in 1921. One of the oddities of the 1920s was that banks continued to fail, the Coolidge bull market notwithstanding. From 1921 to 1928, no fewer than 5,214 institutions shut their doors. No other country suffered a comparable banking epidemic. One reason for this high mortality rate, certainly, was United States banking law. There were (and are to this day) federal- and state-chartered institutions, and competitions have periodically developed between the two levels of government to offer the more liberal regulatory environment. Public policy had consistently favored small institutions and even microscopic ones. It is an axiom nowadays that no bank fails for lack of capital; unprofitable lending is always the underlying cause. However that may be, $5,000 of capital furnished little enough insulation from the shock of one of the most violent setbacks in American business and financial history.

Given that the post-Civil War inflation was still a sore point with some farmers in 1900, it was reasonable to expect that the economic dislocations of World War I would survive the peace. Compounding the troubles of the twenties were the unintended consequences of the teens. If, as so many agreed, agriculture had been denied its fair share of credit, full amends were made in the Wilson years. With the advent of state and federal cooperative banks and with the liberalization of real-estate lending under the Federal Reserve Act, debt was pressed on farmers. As in urban bull markets, the boom in farmland elicited not more caution among lenders but less. Between 1910 and 1920, according to the U.S. Department of Agriculture, total farm mortgage debt in the United States jumped to $7.9 billion from $3.3 billion, a rise of 137 percent. It continued to rise in the early 1920s. Not all the money was lent in the late, or manic, phase of the cycle. Of the sum total of farm mortgages held by life insurance companies in 1928, only 20 percent were based on appraisals made in the boom years of 1920–21. Twenty percent was enough to cause trouble, however. In effect, in those years, the American heartland was being traded with margin debt.

Overwhelmingly, the bank casualties of the 1920s were small and rural, but one, at least, was large and urban. Not unlike little banks in Iowa, the National City Bank lent optimistically in Cuba. Its error, that sugar prices would hold at inflated wartime levels, was different in degree but not in kind from its country cousins' conviction that wheat could only appreciate. It might be noted that City Bank arrived at this 1980s-style belief in what was still the age of orthodoxy. The dollar was still convertible into gold, the government had not yet entered the deposit-insurance business, and no bank was thought to be too big to fail. City Bank's stock was closely held by private investors (mainly the family trusts of the former presidents James Stillman and Moses Taylor), so it cannot be said that the employees had lost sight of who was paying their salaries. Pure rationalists would like to believe that monetary systems are to blame for the bouts of zeal and black despair that periodically seize lenders. Different schools of reform advance different explanations for this fact. For the boom and bust of the 1920 era, one may logically blame the war and the credit reforms of the Progressive era. More fatalistically, but no less relevantly, one may observe that most of the bankers and farmers were bullish together, at the top. The reason why crowds think the same thing at the wrong time seems to vary. What is constant, however, is the tendency of crowds to be brave when they might be timid, and vice versa. In any case, at the Armistice in 1918, sugar fetched 4 cents a pound. In 1919, when Russia, distracted by revolution, failed to deliver its hoped-for sugar-beet crop, the price doubled to 8 cents. In 1920, speculative buying pushed it to 22 cents.

"In 1918–1919, National City plunged deeply into Cuba," according to the bank's official history. "It spread offices across the island, opening 22 new branches in 1919 and one more in 1920. . . . [It] made loans to finance the working capital of existing mills and to finance local merchants and suppliers to the sugar industry. By mid-1920 the bank's branches had become a major factor in the Cuban banking scene. By June 30, 1920, National City had nearly 20 percent of the total of loans outstanding in the Cuban banking system." In all but name, City Bank was the central bank of Cuba.

At the peak, the bank's Cuban loans totaled $79 million—the equivalent of 80 percent of the bank's capital. Capital was what the stockholders owned: the sum of what the investors had paid into the bank and what the bank had earned but had not paid out to the investors. The wiping out of capital is the definition of insolvency. Had the sugar predicament not been successfully resolved, therefore, as Charles E. Mitchell, City Bank's president in the 1920s, later reflected, "it would have meant pretty nearly the destruction of the bank."

"Management's bet on this single commodity had been imprudent to the point of folly," the official history acknowledges, even if Chase National and Guaranty Trust had also become deeply involved. A sign of things to come: City Bank was no more alone in Cuba in 1920 than it was a solitary lender to Brazil, Argentina, or Mexico in 1980.

What happened next was also a portent for a later day. The problem became intractable. To start with, Cuba declared a debt moratorium; City Bank's sugar loans were frozen. (With this, James A. Stillman, son of and successor to James Stillman, resigned from the presidency of the bank. He had never relished the job; now it overwhelmed him.) Next, the bank was confronted with the always knotty problem of whether to throw good money after what was possibly bad money. The specific issue was some unfinished sugar mills. Should the mills be completed, at additional cost, or should the loan, for $25 million, be written off? Consultants were retained. Their advice, on which the bank acted, was to finish the job. Presently, the price of sugar rebounded to 5 cents a pound from about 4 cents. The consultants were clapped on the back and elected to the board of directors; so far, so good.

But then the price of sugar weakened, and not even City Bank's state-of-the-art mills could make a profit. In 1927, the National City Co. issued some common stock and with part of the proceeds it purchased the mills. It thereby shifted them from one department of the bank to another; from the bank proper to the holding company. The net of that transaction, for the stockholders, was zero—they still owned the mills. It did constitute a benefit for the depositors, however. The mills had long become what is known in the trade as "slow loans." They had, in fact, become long-term investments, and it would have been hard to carve them up and present them to the depositors in case of a run on the bank. At the time, nobody in the Senate Banking Committee protested this circuitous transaction. At the bottom of the Depression, however, many things looked different, and Ferdinand Pecora, the Senate's chief investigator into goings-on at the New York Stock Exchange in the late 1920s, referred to "this $25,000,000 bailing out." It was an acute embarrassment for City Bank, if only one of many.

Even before the Depression, sugar prices had fallen, and they naturally continued to drop in the 1930s. City Bank had had the chance to get out of its Cuban loans and investments in 1927 at a break-even price, but decided to hang on. It could repent this choice at its leisure. Not until World War II did sugar prices recover, and not until 1945 were the mills sold.

5

Banking on Confidence

Charles A. Hanna, national bank examiner for New York, had no criticism to make of Baker's bank in January 1910 except to say that its vault was overcrowded. So it had been at other New York institutions. Prosperity was outstripping the space in which to house it.

Stillman's bank, National City, anticipating just such a problem, had bought the U.S. Custom House at the corner of Wall and William streets in 1899. (Going right to the top to negotiate the purchase of the building, the banker had dealt with his opposite number at the Treasury Department, Secretary Lyman Gage. It was the same Gage who, at about the same time, had directed Stillman to increase City Bank's capital if he wanted to keep the Treasury's deposits.) The building was designed by Isaiah Rogers and opened in 1841 as the Merchants' Exchange. Although only four stories high, it occupied a full city block and was said to be one of the costliest structures in the country. Concerning the investment value of fine art, Stillman had once quipped, "When tempted to buy, I find myself mentally calculating on the back of the canvas what the interest on the money would amount to at 6 percent." He did not hold back on the Custom House restoration, however, but chose to model the new plans for the interior after the Pantheon. Following architectural consultations and a field trip by a City Bank vice president to inspect the Roman temple in person, work was at last begun. The year, unpropitiously, was 1907.

Four new stories were built on top of the original four, and a new Corinthian colonnade was superimposed above an existing Ionic one. Inside, a new banking hall, lit by a vast skylight, soared fifty-nine feet in the air. "Rising like an altar in the center of the main banking floor was a square white marble box," wrote John K. Winkler, the caustic, Depression-era writer on Stillman and his bank. "Light from the huge glass dome fell full upon it, while the ecclesiastical effect was further emphasized by two giant illuminated fixtures, resembling thuribles, which depended from the niched ceiling at either side. A temple to Mammon, indeed, for the dominating white marble sarcophagus was none other than the resting place of GOLD—the National City's vault." Mindful that the new quarters might tend to weaken organizational discipline, Stillman urged his protégé, Frank A. Vanderlip, "Keep down expenses all you can and keep the new building from spoiling the clerical force and giving them false notions."

Customer Service for the Very Eccentric

In keeping with the tendency of new financial construction to mark the top of markets, City Bank opened its new office in December 1908, a year after the panic ended. Chemical Bank, also chafing under the lack of office space, actually opened a new building in May 1907, which turned out to be the first month of the 1907–8 recession. When Chemical put up its old building at 270 Broadway in 1887, its officers expected that move would be their last. But by 1905 they were hiring architects and laying plans for a monumental new headquarters suitable to the bank's reputation. By gamely paying out gold coin in the Panic of 1857 when almost every other bank in the country was either unwilling or unable to, Chemical had earned for itself the million-dollar sobriquet "Old Bullion." Hetty Green, the fabulously wealthy and bizarre "Witch of Wall Street," banked at Chemical and it wasn't for the interest she earned on her ample deposits. As a matter of prudent banking practice, Chemical refused to pay any interest (thereby distinguishing itself from the great Wall Street banks, which, like Baker's, paid 2 percent). It was for the safety of her principal, which substantially enlarged Chemical's deposits, and for the bank's indulgent, even heroic, service.

When George Gilbert Williams, Chemical's longtime president, was asked for the secret of his success, he replied, firmly but quietly, "The fear of God." He might have added "the patience of a saint," for he set a long-suffering example for his employees in catering to the eccentric needs of Mrs. Green. Choosing to forgo a regular address to exempt herself from New York State taxes, Mrs. Green for years made Chemical her headquarters. She hung her dresses in its vault and stored a wagon and a buggy (dismantled, as an accommodation to the bank) on its second floor. She refused the kindly intended offer of a permanent office, thinking that perhaps Williams was merely trying to get her out of the way. She moved instead from desk to desk, when a desk was available. At other times she sat on the floor, cross-legged, sorting checks or clipping coupons. When lunchtime rolled around, she would produce an unwrapped ham sandwich from the darkness of a pocket and eat as she worked.

Like Williams, who was born in 1826, Chemical had attained a venerable position by 1900, and people were apt to say that both he and his bank were behind the times. ("But, after all," one observer was heard to add, "there is only one Chemical Bank. We need it, just as an example.") Williams died in 1903, at the age of seventy-seven. He had only recently stopped walking two or three miles to his office every morning. The new Chemical Bank building that he didn't live to see was done up classically in gray granite and Chippolino marble. The vaulted ceiling in the main banking room rose eighty-five feet above the floor and, anticipating Stillman, admitted sunlight through a dome of heavy glass. On the pendentives below the dome were four allegorical figures, Ceres, Boreas, Helios, and Neptune, signifying the elements of earth, air, fire, and water. There was nothing like it at the National Shoe and Leather Bank, Chemical's towering Broadway neighbor.

The Panic of 1907 alone did not cause the formation of the Federal Reserve System, the postal savings system, or—at a later date—the Federal Deposit Insurance Corporation. Each had had a running start in the nineteenth century. Deposit insurance had been tried and found wanting before Franklin D. Roosevelt, with considerable reluctance, signed the bill creating the FDIC in 1933. American antecedents to the Federal Reserve System—the First and Second Banks of the United States—had come and gone by 1836, and the progenitor of all modern central banks, the Swedish Riksbank, was founded in 1668. The very architecture of the new prairie banks reflected the gathering Progressive impulse. (Not yet in downtown Manhattan, however: tastes there still ran to hardwood and marble.) The democratization of credit was an idea that, though rarely expressed in just those words, was entering a long and glorious bull market.

What the panic did produce was a critical mass of disillusionment with the financial system as it was. The Progressive backlash to the collapse took the now familiar shape of demands for federal intervention. Anticipating events in early 1907, James Stillman said that he looked forward to the next panic for the excesses it would remove, but he didn't anticipate its likely political consequences. "I have felt for some time," he wrote his deputy at City Bank in February, "that

*Hetty Green's home away from home: the new Chemical National Bank Building, corner of Broadway and Chambers Street, New York (*WURTS COLLECTION, MUSEUM OF THE CITY OF NEW YORK*)*

the next panic and low interest rates following would straighten out a good many things that have of late years crept into banking." Stillman did not elaborate, but he perhaps had in mind the boom in trust companies, the loosely regulated savings institutions that enticed depositors with high interest rates. For a time, in the fall of 1907, the most disillusioned people in America were the depositors of the Knick-erbocker Trust Co. In 1903, the New York Clearing House Association served notice on the trust companies to boost their reserves or lose their clearing privileges. In 1906, hoping to head off trouble, the New York State legislature fixed the minimum reserve at 15 percent—for every dollar of customer deposits, a trust company would have to keep 15 cents in cash. Whether or not 15 percent was intrinsically unsound, it was 10 percentage points lower than the minimum required of a nationally chartered commercial bank in New York.

In a latter-day touch, the president of the Knickerbocker, Charles T. Barney, was pulled down in the collapse of a speculation. Barney, a rich man's son, was one of the guiding lights of the New York City subway system, and he applied his confidential knowledge of the future subway map to turn a large personal profit by buying parcels of land, especially on the Upper West Side and Washington Heights, from those not so well informed. His downfall was the stock of United Copper Company, which Frederick Augustus Heinze, a collaborator of Barney's, unsuccessfully tried to corner. Heinze's bank, the Mercantile National Bank, was forced to go hat in hand to the Clearing House Association for an emergency loan, and the Knickerbocker's depositors, 18,000 strong, soon feared for their money. A delegation of Knickerbocker officers called at J. P. Morgan & Co. to forestall what seemed a certain run. They had forced out Barney, but feared the effect of the disclosure of that news on their nervous depositors. All that afternoon and evening, the Knickerbocker men sat huddled with the Morgan men—the second-class passengers come to petition the captain's table. No plan was produced, but the Knickerbocker agreed to open its books to an inspection. If the Morgan examiners found a solvent bank with serviceable assets, a loan would be arranged.

Hurriedly next morning, a handful of Morgan men sifted through documents in the rear office of the Knickerbocker Trust at Fifth Avenue and Thirty-fourth Street. They could hear the milling depositors outside—"Give us back our dough!" they began to chant—and could easily imagine the tapping of feet inside the Morgan bank (and at Baker's bank too) on Wall Street. They had been sent to decide if the Knickerbocker was solvent, but there wasn't enough time to get the facts. "I well remember," wrote Benjamin Strong, the head of the small auditing group and the future governor of the Federal Reserve Bank of New York, "the anxiety with which we discussed what should be said to Mr. Baker and Mr. Morgan who were awaiting our word.

Most reluctantly, and with some appreciation of the possible consequences, we . . . agreed that honesty and fairness to everybody required us to say it was absolutely impossible in the length of time
allowed to us to . . . make any reliable report."

The consequences were shattering. The Knickerbocker failed, precipitating a run on other trust companies. Less than a month later,
Barney, its former president, shot himself to death. Yet so improbable
was the bullet's angle of entry—through the banker's abdomen—that
the coroner declared he had never, in a dozen years, seen another
suicide just like it. Although still solvent himself, Barney had been
humiliated by his failure and by the abuse he had suffered in the
newspapers. But his dying did not still his critics. The day after his
death, the man who succeeded him as president of the Knickerbocker
told the afternoon press, "Mr. Barney was not a God-fearing man."
(He was not as bad a banker as he seemed, however, and certainly
better than many of his professional descendants in the savings and
loan industry. Even at the time of his death, it was expected that the
failed bank would, in time, yield full value to its depositors. In 1910,
it did.)

The troubles of 1907 were broadly distributed. Besides the run on
the trust companies, there was a banking panic, a bear market in stocks,
and a thirteen-month business recession. In the fall and early winter
of 1907–8, banks across the country refused to convert deposits into
gold coins or currency at the request of their depositors. Not even Old
Bullion broke ranks to pay out scarce cash.

With the death in 1903 of George Williams, the grand old man of
Chemical Bank, the presidency had passed to William H. Porter,
Williams's vice president and chosen successor. Even under Williams,
Chemical had not lived up to its mythical reputation each and every
day. From time to time, federal examiners would find that the bank's
reserve had fallen short or that it had lent to a particular borrower
beyond the legal limit imposed by the National Bank Act. Indeed,
under Porter, as with Williams (and, earlier, with James Stillman), this
latter infraction was routine. Under the law, a national bank could
lend no more than the equivalent of 10 percent of its capital to a single
customer. Under the same law, however, the stockholders of a national
bank were liable to an assessment for up to 100 percent of that capital
to satisfy the claims of depositors in the event of a bankruptcy. The
two laws pulled bank directors in opposite directions. It was in the
clear interest of the stockholders to admit to as little legal capital as
they could—there would be that much less to pay out under the

double-liability rule if worst should ever come to worst. By minimizing its capital, however, a bank also reduced its capacity to make large loans. Chemical's legal capital amounted to just $300,000. Thus, the maximum loan it was allowed to make under the law was just $30,000. However, year after year, examiners compiled long lists of "excessive loans," some of which (as to the American Car & Foundry Co., American Woolen Co., and Swift & Co. in 1903) pushed $500,000.

The Comptroller resolutely looked the other way. One mitigating circumstance was that legal capital was only a tiny proportion of real, financial capital. In 1904, for instance, the bank showed what today would be called stockholders equity—what the owners of the bank could claim as their own—of some $8 million. It was an exceptionally conservative and fat account even for that day and age (representing almost 19 percent of the bank's combined assets and some 38 percent of its individual deposits). In an economic sense, this capital was indistinguishable from the $300,000 that constituted the store of legal capital. "The small capital of this bank makes excessive loans very numerous," an examiner wrote in 1904, "but the capital and surplus being nearly eight millions eliminates any danger from this source."

Chemical entered the panic season of 1907 in its customary strong position but not without the accumulated bruises of any institution that lends money at risk. In 1904, an employee of twenty-two years, one E. C. Hoyt, had embezzled $22,000. (When George Baker was staggered by a $700,000 embezzlement in 1899, Williams had written him sympathetically: "Wait—patiently—wait—time will heal.") In 1905, a federal examiner, noting a rise in Chemical's questionable loans, had written to Washington: "The bank makes considerable losses; but has great earning power, as it pays no interest, and is enabled to write off its losses and show good profits." In 1906, the bank acceded to a tenfold rise in its legal capital. "There has always been a great deal of pride by the management in the large proportion of profits to Capital," the examiner noted, "but they state they are now willing to sacrifice that to eliminate any further violations of the law in regard to [excessive] loans."

High time. Not many months later, a provocative and threatening question was raised by an examiner with the Comptroller of the Currency. Might not, the examiner wondered, the directors of the bank be held personally liable for past losses on so-called excessive loans? By countenancing loans in excess of the legal limit, the directors had, in fact, broken the law. Never mind that for years the law had been routinely winked at by bankers and regulators alike. The answer seems not to have survived, but the mere raising of the question must have given the directors a turn. It is enough to know that, not many years ago, the owners and directors of a bank were held personally responsible for a great deal of what happened underneath their vaulted roofs.

In the past, Chemical had gained by panics, as depositors in less rock-ribbed institutions had fled to the safety and soundness of Old Bullion. It was no different in 1907. In December 1906, deposits by individuals at Chemical totaled $20 million. In late November 1907, in the midst of the storm, they stood at $29 million, including $2.8 million in the name of Mrs. Green. Chemical was still her kind of bank. (But not for many years afterward. Her falling out was caused by a case of food poisoning she suffered after lunch one day in the Chemical directors' room. "[A]nd the funniest thing," she told a reporter from the *New York Herald*, "was that there was no one else but me taken sick." She said—the interview was in 1912—that she subsequently moved her business out to the presumably safer precincts of the Park National Bank.)

On November 23, 1907, Chemical's reserve was discovered to have been $384,285 below the legal minimum, but the bank was quick to protest to the Comptroller's office that the shortage was unavoidable. "Notwithstanding that we imported $2,000,000 of gold from Europe," the president, William Porter, wrote, "we found that we could not consistently increase our supply of cash in the existing panic, proportionate to the rapid and extraordinary increase in our deposits." One further detail of Chemical's experience in the 1907 affair is instructive. It is that this most conservative bank was carrying a $200,000 loan to the soon to be notorious capitalist Frederick Augustus Heinze. Along with the stock manipulator Charles W. Morse, Heinze was one of the human catalysts for the collapse and one of the political villains of its aftermath. Chemical quickly moved to write off one-half of the loan and was perhaps moved to reflect on the difficulty of reconciling a reputation for absolute safety with the necessity of earning a profit.

Credit Shrinks

As might be imagined, it was hard to get a loan in the crisis, in or out of New York. Real-estate developers found themselves out in the cold in 1907 as they would more than eight decades later. In connection with Barney's death, it was reported that the builders who had acquired property through Barney had found it impossible to find permanent financing or to sell their buildings at a decent profit. "If these building loans are foreclosed, as seems likely to be done in many cases," the *Evening Post* commented, "there will be trouble for the builders." A few days later, Westinghouse Electric and Manufacturing Co. and other corporations identified with the inventor of the air brake, George Westinghouse, sought the protection of the bankruptcy courts; Westinghouse blamed the "acute financial stringency and consequent inability to renew our maturing paper." Employment, industrial production, and freight-car loadings were severely reduced. With clairvoyance, politicians of the day would have judged that, really, things could have been worse—and, indeed, that before the passage of twenty years, monetary and banking reform notwithstanding, they would be.

In time, historians would almost reflexively blame depressions and panics on the Federal Reserve Board, but in 1907 that all-purpose scapegoat was still unavailable. Six years before the passage of the Federal Reserve Act, the closest thing to central bankers in America was J. P. Morgan, ably assisted by Baker, Stillman, and, in the public sector, the Treasury Department. However, it was not the Treasury Secretary who made the front page of *The New York Times* two days after the Knickerbocker failure, but Morgan, then seventy. He had a head cold. The Treasury Department deposited a much-needed $25 million in the city's national banks in an attempt to relieve the money market, an act of intervention foreshadowing many more. But it was Morgan, with his deputies, who stopped the trust-company panic, who rescued the credit of New York City (in need of help even then), and who acted to bring down interest rates on overnight loans to brokerage firms from the panic-stricken heights of 150 percent or more. According to one's politics, Morgan's role in the autumn of 1907 was heroic or sinister. In *The Money-Changers*, a roman à clef by Upton Sinclair that appeared in 1908, a plutocrat very much resembling Morgan provoked a financial panic and turned the people's misery to his own sordid gain. In real life, Senator Robert M. La Follette, the Wisconsin Progressive, charged that a "group of financiers who withhold and dispense prosperity" had "deliberately brought on the late panic," for their own profit. To these wild charges, Morgan, Baker, and Stillman characteristically said nothing.

Not foreseeing the future, reformers set to work on improving it. Nearly everybody agreed that the existing structure was deficient. At banks across the country, depositors had been told that they could not withdraw their own money. The experience was both infuriating and repetitive—as recently as September 1902, banks had been so hard pressed that the Treasury had rushed to their aid with emergency deposits. In January 1908, after the banking panic had subsided, the leading financial commentator of the day, Alexander D. Noyes, appraised the situation in what was then a leading egghead New York newspaper, the *Evening Post*. "No doubt," Noyes led off, feinting,

> the most palatable comment would be congratulations to our financial institutions for having emerged from so formidable a crisis with relatively so little of outright insolvency. We shall not take this view. What, to our mind, stands out paramount in this panic episode is the refusal by the deposit institutions of this country, during nine successive weeks, to return to its owners, on their request, the money deposited by them in trust with such institutions; the public sale at a discount during all this period, and in amounts running to the tens of millions, of certified checks on powerful and solvent banks, and, finally, the forcing upon wage earners by employers in half a dozen cities of makeshift currency not exchangeable for real money in the city of its issue and not receivable for payments in any other locality.
>
> Everyone knows that this is a plain and accurate statement of what has happened; had such a state of things occurred in any other country than our own, our people would have described it as a shameful exhibition of weakness and bad faith. Why, of all nations, should the United States, which a very few years ago was claiming title to the financial center of the world, have been the scene of this extraordinary performance?

The Economist, watching from London, held that the moral dimension was uppermost. "From one point of view," the magazine allowed, "credit may be defined as the power to attract gold; but public credit really depends on public confidence, just as private credit depends on private confidence. The financial crisis in America is really a moral crisis, caused by the series of proofs which the American public has received that the leading financiers who control banks, trust companies and industrial corporations are often imprudent, and not seldom dishonest. They have mismanaged trust funds and used them freely for speculative purposes. Hence the alarm of depositors, and a general collapse of credit."

The bear-market view of a bull market is often reproachful. The truth of the indictment is sometimes less important than the need to express it. Similarly, to an older generation who may not appreciate how much richer the world has become since their own youth, new-fangled ways will often seem extravagant and the precursors to a justly deserved fall. So in the wake of the Panic of 1907. The assigners of causes took note (after the fact, generally) of a sharp, premonitory sell-off in Japan. There was excess speculation in America, especially in real estate, they said. There was an overextension of credit, then a contraction. Bankers had made too many loans, then called them in. A. Barton Hepburn, a man who spoke absolutely ex cathedra on all banking matters—he was president of Chase National Bank, a former Comptroller of the Currency, and former Superintendent of Banking in New York State—ascribed the panic to four years of spec-ulation, on and off Wall Street. "Every locality had its form of adven-ture," said Hepburn in December. "City, town and village lots, farms, wild farm lands, ore properties of every kind, timber and timberlands, especially the latter, have been purchased on the partial-payment plan at constantly advancing prices."

It is easy enough to understand the frustration of a bank depositor in the throes of the panic. From a distance of years, however, it is harder to grasp the nature of the problem. How could a solvent bank—and the vast majority were not bankrupt—fail to produce the money to pay its own customers? If the depositors wanted currency, why couldn't the banks get it? In this day and age, the least of a banker's problems is obtaining United States currency. At the turn of the century, however, the process was anything but automatic.

The National Bank Act established a link of expediency between national bank notes, or currency, and the public debt. It was to finance the Civil War that the national banking system was created. And it was to promote the purchase of bonds by the banks that the bonds were invested with the characteristic of collateral. To obtain national bank notes, a bank had to purchase an equal dollar amount of gov-ernment bonds. These bonds it tendered to the Treasury as collateral against the notes. In return, the Treasury handed the appropriate number of bank notes back to the bank, which furnished them to its customers. In wartime, of course, the size of the government debt was ever expanding; there was plenty of collateral to go around. With the peace, the rate of public borrowing declined, and the government's debt commanded a premium in the open market. In 1900–2, the United States 2 percent bonds, due in 1930, changed hands at the lofty price of 109⅝, meaning 109⅝ percent of face value. It was not that investors clamored for an investment that yielded only about 1.6

percent. They did not. It was that banks were prepared to pay a premium for bonds so that they might obtain the currency with which to satisfy their customers. Over and above any consideration of yield, Treasury bonds constituted the means with which to secure dollar bills from the Treasury.

Before the National Bank Act, as we have seen, the hallmark of American currency was its diversity. It was only as good as the bank that issued it (and promised to redeem it, on demand, in gold). Some was good and some was bad, but little was guaranteed by the national government. The Civil War banking legislation changed all that. The new national bank notes were first cousins to government money. They were to be received in payment by every other national bank and were redeemable at the Treasury at any time, whether or not the issuing bank was solvent. Thus, an important step down the long road of the socialization of credit risk: a currency that carried the government's guarantee; the issuing bank's guarantee had become redundant.

Certainly to foreigners, and possibly to native-born Americans as well, the country's monetary and banking system had become maddeningly complex. The dollar was indeed defined as a fixed weight of gold. But national bank notes were backed by government bonds, and sometimes, in moments of stringency after 1900, by municipal bonds too. So the dollar was secured by debts (that is, bonds) as well as gold. President Roosevelt excoriated the "trusts," but the trust companies had nothing to do with monopolies. They were, as mentioned, the thrifts of their time. They paid more for deposits than banks and were permitted to engage in a more speculative class of lending business than banks could. Besides national banks, there were state-chartered banks, each type with its separate regulatory apparatus.

To the monetary reformers of the day, the connection between currency and the government debt was an arbitrary, outmoded, and illogical one. How much better if the volume of currency were connected to the volume of trade, they said. Thus the cry went up for an "elastic" currency, one that, accordion fashion, would expand and contract with the business cycle.

In 1908, a stopgap measure was passed, the Aldrich-Vreeland Currency Act, which provided for the issuance of an emergency currency by groups of national banks in case of future panic. A National Monetary Commission was empaneled to give the matter of money and banking deliberate study. The commission was a godsend for the infrequently patronized art of financial history: some twenty-four volumes were commissioned and published, including some, like

O. M. W. Sprague's *History of Crises under the National Banking System*, that made a lasting scholarly mark. The studies identified four major defects in the American financial system: banks were decentralized, the currency was inelastic, clearing methods were inefficient, and the federal government's huge cash balances were badly distributed. Early in 1911, the commission produced a plan, the Reserve Association of America, that was meant to solve each shortcoming. Republican senator Nelson W. Aldrich of Rhode Island, the principal sponsor, had favored a central bank, like the Bank of England. As the very phrase stuck in the public's craw, however, he disowned it. The only "central" feature about the Reserve Association, he said, was the mechanism by which it would improve the coordination among 7,000 national banks. Otherwise, the association would be regional. Ownership would be scattered among the banks themselves. A board of directors would represent banking, the government, and business. Gradually, the association would release the currency from the arbitrary fetter of the public debt. Additional currency would be issued, secured not only by bonds but also by gold and commercial paper.

"The true basis of sound banking is commercial paper," *The Economist* stated, also ex cathedra, in the middle of the crisis. Then, as now, commercial paper was a short-term corporate IOU. A company would issue commercial paper to finance a rise in its inventories. It would stop issuing it, or redeem what it had outstanding, as it reduced its inventories. What *The Economist* and other banking authorities liked about this kind of instrument was its short life. Its length was limited by the nature of the business it facilitated. A mortgage financed the purchase of a building. Commercial paper financed the shipment of pig iron. The building might be salable; then again it might not be. The pig iron in transit was almost certainly salable, however. As the depositors of a bank sometimes wished to turn their claims into cash, it greatly aided a bank to hold assets—for example, commercial paper—that it could turn into cash as well. Thus, theory had it, the introduction of commercial paper into the monetary equation would lend the currency its hoped-for elasticity. There would be neither too much currency nor too little.

Assault on the "Money Trust"

In time, the Republican Aldrich plan would bear fruit as the Democratic Federal Reserve System. But the time was not yet right. It remained for Congress to investigate the possibility that a Money Trust was lording it over American credit. It was the heyday of trusts, and to many it seemed a foregone conclusion that U.S. Steel, Standard Oil, and American Tobacco had their counterpart on Wall Street. Whether or not Morgan, Baker, and Stillman had saved the day in 1907, they had made themselves, and their wealth and power, conspicuous. How much weight any one banker should be allowed to throw around in a republic became an impassioned public issue. When Charles A. Lindbergh, a Progressive congressman from Minnesota and father of the future aviator, took up the call for an investigation of "financial combinations in restraint of trade," in 1911, he received an outpouring of public support and encouragement.

The Wall Street Journal, always impatient with lay opinion, replied that if there was no Money Trust, one should be organized as quickly as possible, as no country was in greater need of a monetary authority than the United States. In the paper's editorial opinion, the trouble with American banking was that it was uncoordinated, and it drew an unfavorable comparison between domestic and foreign methods:

> They do these things differently in Europe. There the community of interest among banks is much closer than in America, but the machinery is up to date, well-oiled and works without friction. There is competition between the banks, but it is sane competition. The individual borrower who is not sound has a much harder time proving the excellence of his collateral than he does in America, where if he fails at one bank he has about 19,999 others to which he can make application.
>
> Under the European system it is difficult to over-extend credit to the same extent as here; there are no banking panics, because the combined financial resources of the community are adequate to meet emergencies; and there are few opportunities afforded for such culpable acts as taking over derelict enterprises at a sacrifice because their securities have been hypothecated to an unwarranted extent, and at unwarranted prices, with speculative banks.

It was one thing for Representative Lindbergh, "a Swede who dreams," as he was known in the House, to condemn the Wall Street interests. It was another for Samuel Untermyer, one of the foremost Wall Street lawyers of his day, to ask the question "Is there a Money Trust?" and to answer it, as he did before the Finance Forum of New

York City in December 1911, in the affirmative. Untermyer did not claim that the banks had consciously formed an illegal conspiracy. But he did say that the dominance of the big New York banks—namely, Morgan's, Baker's, Stillman's—constituted a monopoly in all but name and a dangerous concentration of power.

In the Money Trust issue, agitation began at the fringe of politics and worked its way into the center, so that Lindbergh presently found himself in unfamiliar, established company. The up-and-coming governor of New Jersey, Woodrow Wilson, declared, following Untermyer, that "the greatest monopoly in the country is the money monopoly. So long as it exists our old variety of freedom and individual energy of development are out of the question." One of the country's most accomplished financial writers, Garet Garrett, indicted the bankers' competence in *Collier's*, and wrote that, in view of the lamentable record of 1907, "it is not surprising that a plan [the Reserve Association of America] proposed and supported by the banking interests to enlarge the instrumentalities of credit should be regarded with symptoms of suspicion."

Even *The Wall Street Journal*, though not falling in with the bank-baiters, did concede that perhaps too much financial power was concentrated in lower Manhattan. "So long as Congress will not give us what every other civilized country possesses, a central bank, it forces Wall Street to improvise something of the kind itself," the *Journal* said. In fact, the bankers had rigged up even more than the *Journal* let on. Following an investigation into insurance-company practices in 1905 by a committee headed by New York State Senator William Armstrong, the Equitable Life Assurance Society and the Mutual Life Insurance Co. were ordered to divest themselves of their controlling interest in the No. 2 New York City bank, the National Bank of Commerce. This stock the triumvirate of Morgan, Baker, and Stillman promptly purchased. Fraternally, they agreed to share control of the Commerce, appointing a finance committee to manage it. With this consolidating stroke, Morgan et al. cemented their position as the nation's central bankers without portfolio. Stillman controlled National City and had much to say about the running of the Hanover National. Besides the First National Bank, Baker owned a majority of the stock in Chase National. And Morgan shared control of the National Bank of Commerce with Baker and Stillman. In 1910, those five commercial banks held most of the funds deposited in New York institutions by out-of-town bankers. If this was not a Money Trust, it was something close enough to set off Charles Lindbergh.

In any case, the *Journal* commented, "the result is that one large house, with its satellites, secures many of the profits and privileges of such an institution without its responsibilities or its power to protect the money market. . . . If there is to be any constructive legislation," it added of the Money Trust investigation,

> may it be suggested that it shall be also in the way of restricting what is called "financial banking"? The banker ought to be a merchant in credit, just that and no more—not a stock broker, or a bond salesman, or a public trustee, or an underwriter of new issues, or any of the other side-lines which present conditions have made profitable.
>
> There is no use in mincing words about it; there are more than enough great banks, well known to everybody, where the soda fountain is bigger than the drug store.

Baker's soda fountain—its securities underwriting and venture-capital business—was the envy of Wall Street.* Almost from the day it was chartered, the First National Bank had dealt in securities, especially government bonds, more than in ordinary loans. Baker, a connoisseur of stocks and bonds, invested for the bank as well as for himself. In his own mind, it must have been difficult to distinguish one from the other. Examiners might have objected even before the Panic of 1907 to the equities that Baker was buying. It seems they did not. A national bank was prohibited from owning common stocks, and when the Comptroller of the Currency, in February 1908, chose to enforce the law literally, the bank had no choice but to yield. (The Comptroller's letter criticized the bank on a number of counts. It had made a loan secured, in part, by real estate; had broken some technical rules concerning borrowed bonds; and had put itself in the position

---

* As was his bank's profitability. Paul J. Isaac, a managing director of Mabon Securities Corp., has appraised the First National Bank's financial statement from a late-twentieth-century perspective. "In not a *great* year, 1906," writes Isaac, "the bank showed a return on equity of almost 20 percent in an environment of 5 percent to 6 percent interest rates on corporate debt obligations. Small wonder that the stock sold for 200 percent of true book value!" As for the First National Bank balance sheet, Isaac continues, it resembles "nothing so much as the present-day balance sheet of Bear, Stearns & Co.—a lot of clearance deposits and obligations, sizable securities positions but not huge relative to net worth, small cash customers' obligations, and short maturities on most of the asset and liabilities structure." One of Baker's secrets was to have a balance sheet of unassailable strength. Showing this face to the world, the First was able to borrow cheaply and to garner the lucrative banking business of its country correspondents.

of becoming the guarantor of some loans it had made for some out-of-town banks. If the Comptroller's zeal owed something to the universal human impulse to lock the barn door after the horse has gotten out, so be it. It would be unusual if the contretemps over the alleged crackdown by the Comptroller's office during the real-estate downturn of the late 1980s and early 1990s was unprecedented. In financial markets, almost nothing is unprecedented.)

Confronted with the letter of the law, Baker responded with a technicality of his own. The entity to which the First National Bank sold its stocks—the portfolio included American Telephone & Telegraph, of which Baker was an enthusiastic director—was a newly formed affiliate. The stocks were thus put out of the bank, but not out of the Baker banking organization. The First Security Co. owned them, and the stockholders of the First National Bank owned the First Security Co. In yielding to the law, Baker made a multimillion-dollar gift to the new affiliate. As Hanna, the examiner, explained it to Washington, Baker had realized an unexpected windfall in connection with the recapitalization of the First National Bank in 1901. This sum of money was his by right, and he invested it. Just the same, he had decided "to hold the profits derived by him from the operation for the future benefit of the Bank, rather than to benefit by it himself. This he has done during the past seven years, investing the same chiefly in stocks of other banks and by that means increasing the business and influence of his own Bank." Sheridan Logan, his sympathetic biographer, called this decision of Baker's the greatest act of generosity in the history of banking.

Still, it made no mitigating impression on the subcommittee of the House Banking and Currency Committee that was established to get to the bottom of the Money Trust. The subcommittee was under the chairmanship of Arsène P. Pujo, Democrat of Louisiana, but Pujo played second fiddle to the subcommittee's counsel, Samuel Untermyer. It was Untermyer's speech in 1911 that legitimized the idea that a Money Trust might actually exist. Made rich by his work for Wall Street clients, Untermyer espoused Progressive views and was ambitious for political office. To Pujo's hearing, he brought his withering skills as a courtroom examiner and an encyclopedic knowledge of the workings of Wall Street.

In reply to a letter from the subcommittee, in May 1912, requesting financial information of the First National Bank, the directors respectfully said that they could not comply, on advice of counsel. The subcommittee persisted and the bank regretted, until late that year it

Baker laying down the law in his garden in Tuxedo Park, New York (GEORGE F. BAKER TRUST)

became apparent that George F. Baker himself would have to testify. Baker was seventy-two years old. Four years earlier, in January 1909, he had resigned as president of the First National Bank and assumed the title (then purely an honorific one) of chairman of the board. His distaste for public speaking amounted to almost a phobia. It was as clear to him as it was to Morgan that this would be no impartial seeking after the truth but a kind of public disrobing. All in all, it is hard to imagine any piece of correspondence less welcome than the inescapable request for his presence before the Money Trust investigation in Washington, D.C., on Thursday, January 9, 1913, at 11 a.m.

He was sworn in. Sitting in the witness chair, Baker was the very picture of the successful capitalist. His hair was black and abundant and his muttonchop whiskers were flecked with gray. His gray-blue eyes shone from under his heavy brows. For all his dread of public speech, "smiles played frequently across his broad features," a reporter noticed. Sitting close at hand were his son, George F. Baker, Jr., his lawyer and seventy-five-year-old uncle, Fisher A. Baker, and another counsel, former senator John C. Spooner of Wisconsin.

Getting down to business, Untermyer said that the First National Bank and its securities affiliate in fact constituted "absolutely one concern, a big speculative outfit using the bank's capital, hiding the assets in the security company's treasury on which 'No reports are ever made.' " And he asked Baker what was the purpose of it.

BAKER: Exactly as stated there in that circular.

UNTERMYER: How do you state the purpose?

BAKER: For doing business that was not specially authorized by the banking act. We held some securities that in the early days were considered perfectly proper, but under some later decisions of the courts the holding of bank stock or other stock was prohibited; at any rate, the Comptroller prohibited it.

UNTERMYER: Was this company formed for the purpose of enabling you and your associates to deal more freely in stock?

BAKER: In any of the securities. If you came there and wanted a loan on your property of $1,000 and put it up as collateral, under the national banking act we have no right to do it. Today in the security company we can make this loan.

Untermyer wanted to know if the real purpose of the securities affiliate was to let Baker do some trading. Baker denied it. He ventured that purchases of stock by the First Security Co. had probably averaged less than 100 shares a day since it was organized in 1908.

Untermyer next delved into the cross-ownership of the large New York banks. He asked Baker if, in 1908, the year of the organization of the security affiliate, he had personally owned any stock in the Chase National Bank. Baker warily admitted that he had owned a lot.

UNTERMYER: It was a clear control of the bank?

BAKER: It was a majority; yes, sir.

Baker said that, while he bought the stock with his own funds, it was held in the "interest" of the bank. Untermyer tried to understand that transaction.

UNTERMYER: Had it not been paid for out of the bank's property?

BAKER: No, sir.

UNTERMYER: . . . It was never carried among the First National Bank
    property as an asset?
BAKER: I think not.
UNTERMYER: Was there any paper or document of any kind showing
    it belonged to the First National Bank?
BAKER: No, sir.
UNTERMYER: It was just a matter of your word, was it?
BAKER: Yes, sir. I do not know that I ever expressed a word.

Try as he might, Untermyer could not quite crack the matter of
ownership. "I understood you to say that this bank stock of the Chase
Bank was held for the account of the First National Bank," he tried
again.

BAKER: No; I do not think so.
UNTERMYER: You never did?
BAKER: No, sir.
UNTERMYER: It never belonged to the bank?
BAKER: No, sir.
UNTERMYER: It was never considered a part of the bank's assets or
    property?
BAKER: No, sir.
UNTERMYER: Was it sold for the account of the bank? When you sold
    it did you sell it for the account of the bank?
BAKER: I do not understand. It was not sold.

Fog had now closed in on Untermyer's few remaining landmarks.
He groped helplessly for a few minutes, asking about accounting details and the chronology of Baker's purchases, before plunging back
into the dark. In what sense, he asked Baker, was the Chase stock—
the stock that he, Baker, bought with his own money—"in the interest" of the First National Bank?

BAKER: That I bought them [sic] myself.
UNTERMYER: You paid for them, and with the idea that the stock-
    holders of the First National Bank should get the benefit of them?
BAKER: Indirectly they got a benefit from them; and when they or-
    ganized the security company they were turned over to that
    company.

If Untermyer thought he knew anything about Wall Street, it was that Baker controlled the First National Bank. Baker did not, in fact, control a majority of the stock, but his personal holdings, combined with those of his son, George F. Baker, Jr., and of his ally, J. P. Morgan & Co., amounted to 40 percent of the total. For all intents and purposes, it *was* Baker's bank.

UNTERMYER: There is no question, is there, that you control the First National Bank, in its management and affairs?
BAKER: I would not be so conceited as to say that.
UNTERMYER: Would you be so honest as to say it?
BAKER: Yes; I would like to be honest.
UNTERMYER: There is no doubt about it, is there?
BAKER: Oh, I think so.
UNTERMYER: You think there is doubt about what?
BAKER: I could not control it if I wanted to do anything that the others did not want to have done.
UNTERMYER: As a matter of fact, Mr. Baker, do you not, and have you not, for many years past, controlled the management of that bank?
BAKER: There has never been any dispute about the control.
UNTERMYER: There has never been any dispute about your control?
BAKER: About mine any more than anybody's.
UNTERMYER: Nobody has disputed your control?
BAKER: No, sir; and I have not disputed anybody else's control.

When, presently, Baker testified that nobody controls the bank, Untermyer could hardly believe his ears. "I understand," he said. "It controls itself." Choosing not to pick up on this note of sarcasm, Baker responded earnestly, "Practically. We are a very harmonious family, Mr. Untermyer, I am happy to say, and we can not get up any quarrels."

One reform proposal of the day was that banks should disclose more information about their loans and investments—should, in their financial reporting, anticipate the all-glass design of the 1950s Manufacturers Trust branch on Fifth Avenue. Knowing what assets a particular bank held, a depositor or investor could make an informed decision about whether or not to entrust his funds. The sunshine of publicity would deter the kind of reckless lending that sometimes produced failures. Baker, not seeing the point of the idea, opposed it.

"Why should not the assets, and the detailed assets, be a matter of public knowledge?" Untermyer asked him.

BAKER: Business would come to rather a standstill.
UNTERMYER: I want you to explain to the committee why.
BAKER: I can not explain it.
UNTERMYER: You mean you can give us no reason?
BAKER: It would be exposing all the details of that business to the whole world.

Through the Socratic method, Untermyer tried to show Baker his error, but the banker only dug in deeper. He said at last, "If they [the depositors] are not satisfied, they had better take their account somewhere else." Untermyer seized this reactionary nugget.

UNTERMYER: Your answer to the suggestion that a bank should be required to disclose its assets is that if the depositors do not like it they should go elsewhere? Is that it?
BAKER: They can; yes.
UNTERMYER: And that is your position on it, anyway?
BAKER: Yes; that is my position.
UNTERMYER: That is your position?
BAKER: Yes.

So much for the depositors. As for the stockholders, Baker conceded their right to know something about the assets of the bank, but he added that few of them ever cared enough to ask. Nor did they have to ask. Their representatives, the directors, knew the details perfectly well. Untermyer doubled back to the depositors.

UNTERMYER: . . . [D]o you not recognize that it is important to the security of the depositors and to fair dealing in banking institutions that the assets of the bank should be open to inspection?
BAKER: No, sir; I do not.
UNTERMYER: . . . So that you do not think there ought to be any way in which anybody can find out whether the statement of assets that is contained in gross on the balance sheet represents more or less than the real value?
BAKER: There is a way. In the first place, there is a board of directors elected for that purpose. Then, taking the First National Bank, in New York City, there is [sic] the clearing house examiners that

we have had, especially of late years. Then we have the Comptroller, who makes an examination through his bank examiners twice a year, and then we send to him a report five times a year. There are eight reports a year of the assets of the First National Bank.

But to Baker, a man of the nineteenth century, the first and last lines of defense of the depositor were the honor and competence of men like himself. Again, Untermyer asked him, "Why should the public do business on confidence when it can get the facts?" and again Baker offered the politically unfashionable answer. "Mr. Untermyer," the witness stated, "the fundamental principle of banking, perhaps more than some others, is credit."

UNTERMYER: We have had a good deal of that, and we will take that up a little later.
BAKER: Then I do not need to say anything, if you know all about it.
UNTERMYER: By credit you mean confidence in the men who are running the concern?
BAKER: Yes, sir.
UNTERMYER: You think the public should just blindly follow on confidence and should not know anything about the facts?
BAKER: I do not think they do it very blindly.

Still, Untermyer could not believe his ears, and he put the question to Baker again. "You do not think they ought to rely on confidence? You think they ought to have the facts, do you not?"

BAKER: No; I do not think that.
UNTERMYER: Which do you think they should have, confidence or facts, or both?
BAKER: I think they ought to have confidence.
UNTERMYER: Without the facts?
BAKER: Without the facts, in detail.

By "confidence," Baker meant faith in the banking system as then established, not exclusively in bankers. He included federal regulators, the New York Clearing House Association, and boards of directors among the institutions deserving of public trust. He excluded the new regulatory apparatus that seemed to figure on Untermyer's agenda.

"Have you said all you wanted to say on that subject?" the counsel asked him at last. "Yes, sir," said Baker, dryly, "and more, too."

Untermyer had no trouble establishing the continental reach of Baker's banking and corporate affiliations. On the second day of testimony, in answer to a question about the number of his directorships, Baker said disarmingly, "I know I have too many." In fact, as Untermyer brought out, he and his fellow directors of the First National Bank were directors of eighty-eight corporations. As for Baker personally, Untermyer mentioned company after company, asking if Baker sat on its board. The answer was invariably "yes." Some of the companies he mentioned competed with each other, or could potentially compete, Untermyer noted. Did Baker see any impropriety in serving all of them? He did not, and cited an old, capitalist authority.

UNTERMYER: What I should like to find out, Mr. Baker, is whether you think, from a business point of view, that competition can be quite as freely exercised when there is an identity of directors as where there is a diversity of directors?

BAKER: I do not see why not. Mr. Jay Gould used to say, and he told me once, that the greatest success he had was in being on two boards, where he could adjust differences that might have created a great deal of disturbance.

UNTERMYER: You consider him a good authority, do you?

BAKER: On that business, yes.

J. P. Morgan, preceding Baker as a witness, had uttered his now famous remark about credit. "Is not commercial credit based primarily upon money or property?" Untermyer had asked him. "No, sir; the first thing is character," Morgan replied. "Before money or property?" Untermyer asked. "Before money or anything else. Money cannot buy it." Evidently, Untermyer was unconvinced, because he doubled back to the same question, which Morgan answered even more emphatically. "Because a man I do not trust," said the banker, "could not get money from me on all the bonds in Christendom."

In other words, the principal source of credit was moral, not legal or regulatory. Baker seemed to believe that—he testified that there were people on the Stock Exchange to whom he would not lend no matter how much collateral they gave him—but he also conceded, in an exchange that set the galleries buzzing, that Untermyer had a point too.

UNTERMYER: I suppose you would see no harm, would you, in having the control of credit, as represented by the control of banks and trust companies, still further concentrated? Do you think that would be dangerous?

BAKER: I think it has gone about far enough.

Now, at last (at the end of the second and final day of questioning), the issue was joined. Surprised by this gift of Baker's, Untermyer reached for another. "You think it would be dangerous to go further?" he asked, inviting the witness to prescribe the kind of legislation that the country would eventually get. Baker, however, balked. "It might not be dangerous, but still it has gone about far enough," he replied. "In good hands, I do not see that it would do any harm. If it got into bad hands, it would be very bad." Still, Untermyer pressed. "If it got into bad hands," he asked hopefully, "it would wreck the country?"

BAKER: Yes; but I do not believe it could get into bad hands.

UNTERMYER: You admit that if this concentration, to the point to which it has gone, were by any action to get into bad hands, it would wreck the country?

BAKER: I can not imagine such a condition.

UNTERMYER: I thought you said so.

BAKER: I said it would be bad, but I do not think it would wreck the country. I do not think bad hands could manage it. They could not retain the deposits nor the securities.

Untermyer, a farsighted man, did not imagine to ask whether, under a regime of federal deposit insurance, bad hands might not retain hundreds of billions of dollars in deposits and securities indefinitely; if the insured depositors had nothing personally to lose, why should they worry? Nor did Baker think to suggest such a possibility.

Reform Triumphant

The issue of deposit insurance was, in fact, an old source of contention in American banking. In 1894, Charles G. Dawes, an up-and-coming banker, a future Comptroller of the Currency, and a future Vice President of the United States, advocated a tax on the national banks for the purpose of creating an insurance fund to reimburse the depositors of failed institutions. If the hard times of the 1890s produced a debate on deposit insurance, the Panic of 1907 stirred action. In 1908, Oklahoma became the first state in the new century to pass a deposit-insurance act. Kansas, Nebraska, South Dakota, and Texas followed. In 1908, the Democratic Party wrote a federal-deposit-insurance plank into its presidential platform, and in 1911 the Supreme Court ruled unanimously that the Oklahoma Depositors' Guaranty Fund was, in fact, constitutional. In 1913, under the shadow of the Federal Reserve Bill and the Money Trust investigation, the federal-deposit-insurance idea came up for debate on the floor of the Senate.

It was Justice Oliver Wendell Holmes who delivered the high court's opinion in the deposit-insurance matter in 1911, and he made a curious argument. The Noble State Bank had sued the governor of Oklahoma over the new insurance fund. The assessment was compulsory, not voluntary, the bank noted. Furthermore, the fund was not to be used for any governmental purpose but distributed among private citizens who happened to be depositors of an insolvent bank—a bank that might very well have competed with Noble. Holmes admitted the plaintiffs had a point—the Fourteenth Amendment, which prohibits the taking of property without compensation, might have been infringed—but he said that, in effect, the end justified the means. The end in this case was the safety and soundness of banks, and the means was the insurance of deposits. The historical record, he seemed to claim, was all on the side of deposit insurance. "The power to compel, beforehand, cooperation, and thus, it is believed, to make a failure unlikely and a general panic almost impossible, must be recognized, if government is to do its proper work, unless we can say that the means have no reasonable relation to the end . . . ," Holmes wrote. "So far is that from being the case that the device is a familiar one. It was adopted by some States the better part of a century ago, and seems never to have been questioned until now."

As a matter of fact, the historical record of the state-deposit-insurance schemes was checkered at best. The first such undertaking, the New York Safety Fund, was launched in 1829 over the trenchant objection that its mere existence would tend to relax "public scrutiny and watchfulness which now serve to restrain or detect malconduct." In time, the edges of this argument would become beveled with repeated use, and the pro-deposit-insurance forces would roll their eyes when they heard it, just as Progressives would smile at the oft-heard bankers' claim that character was the basis of credit.

In New York, proponents of the Safety Fund scheme argued that the state's banks had a common interest in each other's solvency and that the state, which chartered them, had an overriding interest of its own. Joshua Forman, a civic-minded lawyer and promoter of the Erie Canal, made a number of modern-sounding arguments. It wasn't enough that banks should be insured, he said. They must also be well run. They should make short-term commercial loans only. When these loans fell due, the borrowers should be required to repay them: no amiable extensions allowed. He claimed, convincingly, that the losses caused by insolvent banks were nothing compared to the losses caused by solvent but badly managed banks. "He had in mind," a historian of the Safety Fund wrote, "the custom of banks of discounting and lending beyond the limit of safety and then suddenly calling their loans to meet obligations, to the ruin of many and the inconvenience of many more." But the Safety Fund was not to be the next Erie Canal. It was swamped by losses resulting from the Panic of 1837, which it did not prevent. By 1842, it was reduced to the insurance of bank notes only—that is, to the currency of the day, not to checks or deposits. But even that task proved beyond its meager means, and by 1860, when the fund was melting away, its assets were sufficient to cover only 2 percent of what the state's banks owed to their depositors.

New York was an example of a weak deposit-insurance plan; within a decade of its founding, a bank could elect to leave it (as a strong bank would naturally do). Similar voluntary plans in Vermont and Michigan also came a cropper. Indiana and Ohio fared better with involuntary plans but at a price: the protected banks cooperated beyond the brink of collusion.

Even before Holmes had delivered the Supreme Court's decision on the constitutionality of state-deposit-insurance plans in 1911, events had rendered a verdict of their own. In 1910, practically all of Oklahoma's brand-new deposit-guarantee fund was tied up in a single bank failure, and *The New York Times* chose to caption its editorial on the Holmes decision (and on state deposit insurance in general), "Constitutional, But Worthless." That did not quite settle the matter, however.

In 1913, an up-to-date version of the Dawes plan of 1894 came up for consideration in the Senate. Instead of taxing the national banks to set up a deposit-insurance fund, the government would tax the new Federal Reserve banks. Proceeds would finance a fund for the benefit of Federal Reserve depositors, in case one of the new banks should fail. The Fed was then on the drawing board, and anything seemed possible. Plainly, the proposal was no universal deposit-guarantee scheme, but it stirred passions as if it were.

The anti forces won the debate and their arguments will strike a sympathetic chord with the taxpayer of the 1990s. In the Senate, it was the East vs. the West. John W. Weeks of Massachusetts, a Naval Academy graduate, veteran of the Spanish-American War, and former banker, carried the water for the Atlantic coast. It was the right time and the right place to be making the Weeks argument, as the nation was prosperous and the historical record was clear. It was easy to show that, from New York to Oklahoma, state deposit-insurance schemes had failed to live up to expectations. As for the Oklahoma fund, Weeks quoted a rueful assessment by the Oklahoma State Banking Commissioner himself, giving six reasons for its coming to grief. Each has a familiar, contemporary ring: "(1) The banking department was for a long time in politics. (2) Unsound banks were admitted and guaranteed at the outset. (3) The record of bankers has not been properly traced. (4) There has been procrastination in closing insolvent banks and timidity in the face of losses. (5) Economic conditions have been somewhat adverse. (6) The guaranty of deposits has relieved depositors of all necessity for care in selecting banks."

Weeks attacked the proposal on both ethical and practical grounds. He did not forget to state that character is the basis of credit, and, quoting a University of Chicago economist, J. Lawrence Laughlin, he questioned the moral claim of a crooked or badly managed bank on the earnings of an honest and solvent one. "Mr. President," said the senator, addressing the chamber, "this whole system, in my judgment, is the confiscation of good character. It is putting a man without reputation or record on the same level as a man who has a record and reputation."

Exhibiting considerable foresight, Weeks invited his colleagues to imagine the subversive effect of deposit insurance on the marketplace. In his natural, uninsured state, the senator led off,

> the banker appeals for business, using various arguments, such as the amount of his capital, the accumulation of surplus which he has made, and, especially, through the personality of the bank's management; but if we are to adopt this system, all of those elements may be waived, and people, closing their eyes, may drop into the first bank they come to, make the best trade they can for the best rates of interest or unusual accommodation, and feel perfectly sure that they are going to receive their money when they need it. If it is well to make the individual a nonentity, this may be a desirable move, but, in my judgment, he should

be taught to be solicitous for his own personal welfare by keeping his eyes open and his mind exercised to protect his personal interests. It is a form of socialism which must be repulsive to anyone who deplores the socialistic tendencies of the day, and is added evidence that the socialist is looking to the State to provide for him what he has not been able to provide for himself.

If the debate proved nothing else, it was that great economic issues, like large cities, never seem to be finished. Rising to debate with Weeks was the freshman Democratic senator from Nevada, Key Pittman. Weeks illustrated his argument with a real-life story of an imprudent Boston bank that offered its depositors 4 percent interest instead of the 2 percent that prudent institutions—Weeks's, situated across the street, for instance—paid. The 4 percent bank inevitably failed. "Why did it fail?" Weeks rhetorically asked. "Because it was paying 4 percent interest on deposits, and in the city of Boston no commercial bank paying 4 percent interest can invest its money safely and make any profit." Pittman shot back:

Then, as I understand it, the Senator wants that condition to exist. He thinks it better for those people to lose their money so that he may continue a flourishing banking business at their expense and do without a law that will make that condition impossible in the future?

WEEKS: Mr. President, I want to ask the Senator from Nevada why I should lose my business because somebody was offering an extravagant inducement for taking it away, and then be assessed because that somebody lost his money when he did not use any judgment in depositing it in another bank?
PITTMAN: If the depositors had been guaranteed, even if that bank failed, the depositors could not have lost any money, could they?
WEEKS: Mr. President, the bank to which I refer as the other bank would have been assessed to pay the losses sustained by those depositors.
PITTMAN: But the depositors would not have lost their money.
WEEKS: They would not.
PITTMAN: We consider the interests of the depositors above the interests of any bank.
WEEKS: If the Senator from Nevada wants to guarantee people against

folly and lack of wisdom by national laws, this is the way to do it.

The signing into law of the Federal Reserve Act on December 23, 1913, moved the United Cigar Stores Co. to extend public congratulations to one and all. In full-page newspaper advertisements, the retail chain hailed the new legislation as a national Christmas present and the more or less certain agent of lasting prosperity. It predicted that the highly technical law would take its place alongside the Declaration of Independence in the hearts and minds of the American people. As for financial panics, the copy stiffly promised, they "should under this new system become effete."

Many people, in and out of the cigar business, thought the same thing. Paul M. Warburg, the distinguished partner of Kuhn, Loeb & Co., declared that the nation's banking system was well launched on a new era. A new era was, indeed, at hand. But as is so often the way with radical change, it was not exactly the era that people had imagined.

Clearly, things would never be the same again. Short-term interest rates would no longer soar to 10 percent or 20 percent under the annual strain of crop-moving season. Private citizens like J. P. Morgan would no longer be pressed into emergency service as central bankers. Now the nation had a dozen regional central banks joined in a national system. Through networks of correspondent relationships—a bank in Nebraska, for instance, clearing through Chemical—a de facto central banking system had evolved. Country bankers deposited their excess balances with Baker, Morgan, or Stillman. Those gentlemen re-lent the money on the floor of the New York Stock Exchange. It went down badly with Representative Lindbergh that the savings of ordinary Americans should wind up in Wall Street, and it annoyed the editors of *The New York Times* that call-money rates were sometimes 9 percent in America when they were 4 percent in France. Henceforth, country banks—indeed, all banks belonging to the new system—would keep a large portion of their idle funds on deposit at the Federal Reserve banks. It was expected that Wall Street's loss would be America's gain. For one thing, the seasonal migration of bankers' balances in and out of Wall Street would no longer precipitate financial crises. For another, the solid, but now illiquid, business loans of the nation's commercial lenders would be mobilized. A national bank in need of funds could call on its local Federal Reserve bank, present its collateral, and take away cash. (The number of Federal Reserve banks was fixed at a dozen so that no commercial banker would be more than one night's train ride away from accommodation. In case of trouble, the president of a threatened institution could pack his bag with 30-, 60-, or 90-day commercial paper, climb aboard a city-bound train, and be able to wire home the next morning that he had cashed, or discounted, enough of the loans to satisfy the demands of the frightened depositors.) The Federal Reserve banks would therefore turn short-term loans into ready cash. They would be in a position to stop bank runs before they started. They would cut the nation's currency to the cloth of the nation's business, making money more or less abundant as business conditions warranted. Why should panics *not* become effete?

Carter Glass, the Virginian who introduced the legislation into the House in the summer of 1913, was certain, in advance, about the character of the Federal Reserve. "It is an altruistic institution," he declared, "a part of the Government itself, representing the American people, with powers such as no man would dare misuse." It would be as benign as the Interstate Commerce Commission.

Sponsors of the legislation tried, without much success, to set their creation apart from the central bank envisioned in the Aldrich plan or from the existing central banks of Europe. To the suspicious Progressive mind, "central" was exactly the wrong idea. The correct adjective was "decentralized," or "federal," and it was hoped that the Federal Reserve would reverse the trend identified by the Pujo Committee only months earlier: "a great and rapidly growing concentration of money and credit."

But the reform, insofar as the concentration of financial power was concerned, boomeranged. The great New York banks lost much of their correspondent business, as the act intended they would. But they were handsomely compensated in ways that the lawmakers perhaps did not anticipate. As the big banks were no longer obliged to cultivate the little banks for deposit balances, they were free to compete with them, and this they proceeded to do. The National City Bank, for instance, sent officers to comb the country for new, midsize business borrowers, and the number of corporate accounts jumped by almost 100 percent between September 1912 and July 1916.

To appease the opposition, the pro-Federal Reserve System forces had promised to uphold the gold standard and to defend the new Federal Reserve notes against the well-observed tendency of government-backed currencies to depreciate. It would take decades before inflation became chronic in the United States, but the expansive influence of politics on the banking system was felt right away. For big-city banks, reserve requirements were sharply reduced. For every dollar on deposit in a checking account, for instance, a bank like Baker's or Stillman's was bound to set aside only 18 cents, down from 25 cents under the old National Bank Act. Also, a new type of savings deposit was created for which it was necessary to hold just 5 cents on the dollar. Inasmuch as the Federal Reserve would now perform the functions of a central bank, profit-making banks were allowed to become a little less like central banks. They were allowed to become less conservative.

The Federal Reserve Act relaxed the rules against real-estate lending for all but the largest banks, and it allowed national banks like City, for the first time, to establish foreign branches. The irony of this post-Pujo liberalization was not lost on Frank Vanderlip, Stillman's second-in-command. The Federal Reserve Act, Vanderlip wrote his mentor, "was designed to curb the great New York banks in their growth. Instead of that, it has given them the broadest opportunities for development. . . . It has made the City Bank far more a national bank than ever before." It did not, however, diminish the financial responsibility of the stockholders of a national bank for the debts of their bank in the event of its failure. The principle of "double liability," borrowed from the old National Bank Act, was written into the new law.

When Elihu Root, Republican senator from New York, rose to speak against the Federal Reserve bill on December 13, the die was already cast. Secretary of War under President McKinley, Secretary of State under President Roosevelt, and recipient of the Nobel Peace Prize, Root was one of the most formidable voices in the Senate. Details of the bill were still under negotiation, but its passage was as inevitable as Christmas Day. Still, Root spoke passionately for three hours, attacking theory, ethics, and practice and predicting troubles that would be duly visited on the lawmakers' grandchildren.

His main argument against the Federal Reserve was that it could be inflationary. He conceded that it didn't have to be, but insisted that it would be. To the proponents' claims that the nation was going to be the lucky recipient of an "elastic" currency, Root retorted that it would rather be an "expansive" one—all growth and no contraction. He assailed the specious popular notion that bank credit would not be inflationary if created in the service of trade. More than most of his colleagues, Root understood the dynamics of a credit inflation, and he offered a schematic example to the senators. "Little by little, business is enlarged with easy money," he said, continuing:

With the exhaustless reservoir of the Government of the United States furnishing easy money, the sales increase, the businesses enlarge, more new enterprises are started, the spirit of optimism pervades the community.

Bankers are not free from it. They are human. The members of the Federal Reserve board will not be free of it. They are human. Regional bankers will not be free of it. They are human. All the world moves along upon a growing tide of optimism. Everyone is making money. Everyone is growing rich. It goes up and up, the margin between cost and sales continually growing smaller as a result of the operation of inevitable laws, until finally someone whose judgment was bad, someone whose capacity for business was small, breaks; and as he falls he hits the next brick in the row, and then another, and then another, and down comes the whole structure.

That, sir, is no dream. That is the history of every movement of inflation since the world's business began, and it is the history of many a period in our own country. That is what happened to greater or less degree before the panic of 1837, of 1857, of 1873, of 1893, and of 1907. The precise formula which the students of economic movements have evolved to describe the reason for the crash following this universal process is that when credit exceeds the legitimate demands of the country the currency becomes suspected and gold leaves the country.

It must have disheartened the opposition to realize that Root was only warming up. He warned against the reduction in bank reserves and against the certainty that, following the inevitable inflation, foreigners would sell American securities. He did not grapple directly with the proponents' contention that the Federal Reserve would hold down interest rates just as the Interstate Commerce Commission had held down rail rates. He did note, however, that the ICC had brought about a squeeze on railroad earnings and dividends and that foreign investors, taking the measure of this policy, were bound to reappraise the creditworthiness of American railroads. Much more of the spirit of the ICC, he suggested, and they would begin to reappraise the dollar. Root was more farsighted than he could have known. The dollar crisis to which he alluded was fifty years away, and the first recognition of the loss of the government's creditworthiness was even further off in the future (though there would be many false alarms along the way). It would be overly narrow to lay the savings and loan debacle, for instance, at the doorstep of the Federal Reserve Act. Surely, it was the gradual socialization of financial risk, rather than any one act of reform, that led to the disaster-prone (and boom-prone too) credit structure of the present day. Root, however, saw the Federal Reserve legislation for what it signified as much as for what it stipulated. "[B]ehind the system under which we are working," he said, "and under which we have grown so great and strong, stands always the Government of the United States, with its credit unimpaired, with its solvency undoubted, always ready to come to the rescue by the sale of its securities to bring gold. This bill proposes, however, to put in pawn the credit of the United States; and when your time of need comes, it is the United States that is discredited by the inflation of its demand obligations which it can not pay." Eventually, but not yet.

6

Loans for Nearly Everyone

World War I marked a great divide in American credit. As we have noticed before (and will have reason to observe again), the wheels of debt rarely grind at one speed for very long. The chances are that, at any given moment, it is becoming easier to get a loan or it is becoming harder. In the 1920s, as in the 1980s, it was becoming easier. During the war, Americans lent patriotically to their own government. After the war, they lent to foreign governments, not all of which would subsequently have the means to pay them back. They lent to industrial corporations, public utilities, and real-estate companies. Americans for decades had purchased pianos, sewing machines, and the Encyclopedia Americana on time. Now, en masse, they borrowed to buy automobiles. In the 1920s, the personal lending business became institutionalized—City Bank, responding to the appeal of the New York State attorney general for help in putting down loan sharks, started to make personal loans in 1928—and "down payment" entered the American language. Lending and borrowing entered the social mainstream.

Prior to the Liberty bond campaigns of 1917 and 1918, the bond business had been the August afternoon of finance. Traveling salesmen produced engraved certificates from leather valises for perusal by members of the creditor class. "Chamberlain," one young salesman was addressed by the manager of the bank that had just hired him, "this business, like any other, has its disadvantages, but one thing you may be sure of, you will never have to make apologies for your profession."

Lawrence Chamberlain was the ideal of the Belle Epoque bond man. An alumnus of Phillips Andover Academy, he was graduated from Yale as a Porter fellow in English literature in 1903 and briefly taught rhetoric at Dartmouth. In 1906, he entered the bond world, taking his first job in Boston. In 1909, he moved to New York, where he helped to found the New York Stock Exchange member firm of

Hemphill, White & Chamberlain. In 1911, he produced what would become a definitive text, *The Principles of Bond Investment*. The next year—the last one of the old, pre-Federal Reserve era—a charming sequel, *The Work of the Bond House*, appeared. It, and the business that Chamberlain affectionately described, were almost immediately rendered obsolete by events. In 1913 came the Federal Reserve Act and the income-tax amendment to the U.S. Constitution. In 1914, there was war in Europe, and in 1917 American entry into the war. Belligerency brought economic as well as human mobilization: towering tax rates and the first mass government borrowing programs of the century. Up until World War I, the largest U.S. government loan on record was the $200 million bond issue that was raised to defeat the Spaniards in 1898. The first Liberty Loan of 1917 was ten times larger, yet it was priced at the exceptionally low yield of 3½ percent. Was the rate of interest too low to attract the public's savings? "Anybody who declines to subscribe for that reason," said Charles G. Dawes, chairman of the Liberty Loan Drive and future winner of the Nobel Peace Prize, "knock him down."

In prewar days, the widows of Salem and the capitalists of Hartford were susceptible to persuasion and the force of personality. They knew Chamberlain and his kind, and they knew that certain things about bonds were unquestionably true. They understood, for instance, that railroad issues were on the top of the fixed-income heap. On the other hand, corporation bonds bore the stigma of speculation and were for that reason unsuitable as investments. "Except under unusually favorable circumstances," Chamberlain adjured, "the highest grade of bond houses will not purchase bonds of industrial corporations, mining or irrigation companies, etc."

In *The Work of the Bond House*, Chamberlain did not get around to mentioning interest rates until page 39, which gives an accurate picture of the stability of the times. Rates had been gently rising since the turn of the century, but there was no panic in New England over that tendency, and the author ventured only that "good railroad refunding issues" might be permanently headed to 4½ percent from 4 percent. (At the bottom of the Depression, in 1931, Justice Oliver Wendell Holmes, still practicing the form of thrift favored in Boston, periodically visited his safe-deposit box at the Riggs Bank in Washington to "fish in the pool," hunting through his collection of railroad bonds for coupons to clip.) This did not seem to sit well with Chamberlain, any more than did the popularity of what today are called convertible bonds: straight corporate loans enhanced by an equity, or ownership, interest in the borrowing company. "Apart from the unholiness of stock in general," Chamberlain reflected, "once the investor gets the bonus habit he is hard to cure." Another modern irritation was the prevalence of accessible price quotations. When dealing with women, especially, Chamberlain would recommend unlisted bonds, the price of which an emotional investor could not check in the morning newspaper. Not that they always listened to him—not by a long shot! Once, Chamberlain related, a lady was ushered into his office. She said that she wanted to buy a certain preferred stock. He heard her out and made another, more conservative suggestion: a good, sensible public utility bond—unlisted, of course, for her own good. Then the office manager, sticking his head into the meeting, asked him (right in front of the customer, a breach of sales etiquette) if "a certain underlying divisional railroad issue" might not be more appropriate for her. "To be sure," Chamberlain reflected. "But I knew that there was no profit there to speak of, for a scant 4 percent has no attractions to people who look takingly at high-yield industrial preferred stocks."

Then, as later, people *would* look takingly at high-yield securities. The great division between the prewar and the postwar financial world was the weight of government debt. Beginning in 1917, the U.S. Treasury became a mighty force in the debt markets. In Chamberlain's time, it was an inconspicuous one, and *The Work of the Bond House* accorded the Treasury's bonds less space than it did railroad debt. Chamberlain couldn't imagine why anybody except a bank would buy Treasury bonds. He scoffed at the idea that they were absolutely secure. They seemed risky enough at the low ebb of the Civil War (and, he also might have mentioned, during the monetary crisis of the 1890s). All in all, he concluded, "nothing but unfamiliarity with investment principles is an excuse for private buying of United States bonds to net 2½ percent. The Federal Government encourages this merely to prevent the worse habit of hoarding. It does not seek or want for its 2½ percent funds the money of *investors*."

What Chamberlain didn't imagine (and who could have imagined it in 1912?) was that the government would be levying surtaxes on income at rates up to 77 percent, manipulating interest rates and the value of the dollar, and borrowing $21 billion, all within six years. The prewar population of bond-buying Americans was estimated at only 350,000, and experts warned the Treasury not to try to raise more than $500 million in the first Liberty Loan. Instead, the government pointed for $2 billion, and four million new members of the creditor class subscribed for more than $3 billion.

How Americans learned to invest: a Liberty Loan drive at the corner of Broad and Wall, World War I (CULVER PICTURES)

The outpouring was zealous but not wholly spontaneous. In place of prewar selling methods, there emerged Liberty Loan committees, patriotic posters, slogans ("every dollar a crack at the Kaiser"), speeches by Four-Minute men between the acts of plays, movies with Douglas Fairbanks, war-exhibit trains, aerial demonstrations by Allied aces, and public appearances by wounded veterans. In May 1917, a

National Women's Liberty Loan Committee was organized in the belief "that the women of the Nation would constitute a powerful moral force in war finance." More than 100,000 clergymen of all denominations delivered Liberty Loan sermons. Instead of the commissions for which Chamberlain had worked in peacetime, salesmen earned captured German helmets—85,000 were handed out. Champion worker-investors won medals cast from German cannon, and cities competed for honor flags.

American industry threw itself into the war-loan campaigns. In Providence, Rhode Island, the Browne & Sharpe Manufacturing Co. stood ready to deduct the cost of a bond from a workman's pay, and almost every workman stood ready to cooperate (though few had known what a bond was before they were prevailed upon to buy one). Competition was organized among departments, and foremen carried the patriotic message home to the shop floor. Luther D. Burlingame, the company's industrial superintendent, shared some of his most effective selling methods with the readers of the *American Machinist*. Beyond pitting the electrical department, for instance, against the milling-machine department, or the boxing or hardening departments, he wrote, "a spirit of competition was . . . encouraged between different alien races, testing to that extent their loyalty." He elaborated on the ethnic slant: "While the canvass was in progress it was found that certain nationalities were not responding as readily as others. Where this appeared to be an organized opposition such men were brought together and given a forceful talk by an official of the company, who pointed out to them that they should be ready to serve the country in which they had made their homes and were bringing up their families, and that if they were not ready to give it loyal support it was their duty to pack up and leave at the earliest opportunity." This line of persuasion produced good results, and not only among the foreign-born. Many a native American was made to feel that "he should not be outclassed by aliens, even if it meant a sacrifice on his part to subscribe."

Still Spry, Still Bullish

On January 26, 1918, George F. Baker, then in his seventy-eighth year, wrote to his son and namesake about the future. He recalled the advice that Morgan's father had given to *his* son: "As J.P.'s father told him when he went into business, while he might make many mistakes, never to be a bear on his country or he would surely go broke. That advice is as good today as it was then." Baker was bullish in all seasons, and he became more hopeful with age. With the declaration of war in 1917, he eagerly resumed the business of war finance, the work that had launched his bank in the first place.

In the first Liberty Loan campaign, the First National Bank of New York turned in more subscriptions than any other bank in the country. It was clear to the Treasury Department that the people's savings would fall short of the needs of the government. To augment the stock of real capital, the government directed the banking system to loan would-be investors the price of their bonds. The Federal Reserve, in turn, would lend to the banks. In effect, the worker-investors would buy on margin—an experience that some of them would repeat in the stock-market boom of the 1920s. Baker's bank became the very model of the patriotic financial institution. It purchased Liberty bonds for its own account, lent to facilitate their purchase by others, and took the extra, and at the time novel, step of borrowing from the Federal Reserve Bank of New York to extend its reach. Not many bankers had then developed the self-assurance to knock on the door of the new institution to ask for a loan. Baker had it, and he once carried away $50 million. (The hesitancy felt by the other New York banks was short-lived. A few borrowed so much that they subsequently had trouble paying it back.)

Baker was made chairman of the city's Liberty Loan Committee, and (so a colleague at the bank recalled) "he trotted the legs off those younger fellows." Once in 1917, an emergency meeting was called on short notice for 3 p.m. at the office of Benjamin Strong, governor of the Federal Reserve Bank of New York. "Shortly before the meeting," as Strong reminisced, "a very severe thunderstorm broke over the city, and I had not the slightest expectation that the members of the committee would appear. On the contrary, however, Mr. Baker came into my office promptly at 3:00 o'clock, dripping wet, and ready, as always, for whatever new development was at hand." In fair or foul weather, Baker would personally solicit Liberty bond subscriptions on his way to work in the morning, arriving at his desk with pledges stuffed in his pockets.*

As it had in Sherman's time, the Treasury expressed its gratitude

---

* Baker, resplendent in Dundreary whiskers and flat-top derby, arrived at the bank with a flourish. Weather permitting, the top of his Rolls-Royce convertible would be down. As the car reached the corner of Broadway and Wall Street, a policeman (one Cunningham) would stop the traffic to allow Baker's driver to make a U-turn. Baker, having attracted a small crowd, would alight from the automobile and swing through the doors of his bank.

to Baker's bank. One spring day in 1917, Baker was visiting Birmingham, Alabama, on some business for U.S. Steel (he was a member of its board of directors). William G. McAdoo, Secretary of the Treasury, was also in town to address a Liberty bond meeting, and he invited the banker to join him on the stage. Turning to Baker, McAdoo presented him with a bouquet. "I congratulate Birmingham on having present today one of the nation's great patriot bankers," said the Secretary. "This man told me in New York recently that if it were needed he was willing to contribute half his total income to help whip Germany." *Half* of his income? Baker's wealth was legendary. Did this pledge of support, no doubt earnestly offered, fall flat in the public retelling? Was there a tittering in the audience over what might have been interpreted as a little joke at Baker's expense? Evidently not, for the crowd cheered, and Baker acknowledged the tribute with tears in his eyes.

No more than every citizen-soldier in the U.S. Army knew what he was doing, not every newly minted investor knew what he or she was buying. "Many workmen," the magazine *Factory* reported in 1918, "thought their subscriptions were outright gifts to the government." Stories made the rounds of the novice Liberty bond buyer who showed up at a bank on the day that interest was payable. Incorrectly assuming that *he* owed the government, rather than the other way around, he passed the appropriate amount of money over to the teller. Other investors forgot to claim their principal. There had been similar misunderstandings in the past—the government was still holding payment for blocks of unclaimed securities that had been sold to the masses by Jay Cooke & Co. in the Civil War—but never before had the investing population grown so quickly in so short a period of time as it had in 1917–18. In 1914, England made no special appeal to the small investor, but Germany, taking a page out of Jay Cooke's book, did. Later in the war, Britain was obliged to follow suit.

Wars cause inflation, and inflation brings high interest rates. Rising interest rates are identical to falling bond prices. Thus, a strong investment case against Liberty bonds could have been made at the time they were issued, and should have been made, too, in the light of the disasters visited upon creditors worldwide after the war. In the United States, however, the advocate of that bearish argument would have had to defend himself as much as his logic. The safety of capital was an unpopular subject in the heat of the war and, besides, the government and the banking establishment were more than accommodating to the would-be saver who happened to be without money.

Banks lent the full purchase price of a bond, and the interest rate they charged was exactly the rate that the bond paid.

Patriotism and bank credit proved a marketing juggernaut, but the bonds, although well sold at the outset, did not always stay sold. With the peace, inflation heated up, and the high cost of living squeezed the people's savings. "Reckless wastefulness and extravagance of the people characterized the year," was the assessment of 1919 by the bond house of C. F. Childs & Co. It was just what a representative of the old creditor class would say of a time like that, but the public had plenty to worry about, extravagance notwithstanding. Consumer prices were climbing and interest rates were going up, which meant (among other things) that the prices of Liberty bonds were going down. An estimated 18 million Americans had bought the government's securities. Now, in the first year of the peace, 10,000 a day were selling out.

Lawrence Chamberlain didn't approve of bond prices being noised about in public, and it must have pained him to see quotations for Liberty bonds in the newspapers. Still, even by the end of 1919, the public losses were relatively light. The bear market began in 1920.

For the Wilson administration, the Federal Reserve System was not established one day too soon. Like conscription or the federal income tax, it was a wartime necessity. In the bond market that Chamberlain had known, interest rates were determined in private, broker to client. Government policies exerted influence but almost never control. Beginning in World War I, and continuing up until today, interest rates became the public's business.

No less was debt. In a 1927 edition of *The Principles of Bond Investment*, Chamberlain could show that the United States public debt was constantly shrinking. "Since 1865," he wrote, "in spite of large bond issues to facilitate the resumption of specie payment in 1879, and to increase the gold reserves in 1894, 1895 and 1896, and to finance the Spanish War in 1898, and to purchase the Philippines in 1904, and to build the Panama Canal in 1906, 1908 and 1911, our debt has shown a constant tendency to decrease, and is now approximately $1,000,000,000, with the smallest interest charge of any of the great powers except Germany." Baker, Morgan, or Stillman might have given the same reason for this blessing as the one advanced by Chamberlain: "credit is confidence," and "confidence is fostered by the prompt discharge of obligations." No country was more deserving of confidence or quicker to pay a debt than this one, Chamberlain went on. "The history of our own public debt is a record of obligations almost unavoidably created and speedily discharged."

If the war was unavoidable, so was the cost and therefore the debt. In 1911, the going rate of interest on a long-term Treasury obligation had been about 2 percent; or 2 percent with extenuating circumstances. The law required that national banks hold government securities, and that regulation created a strong noninvestment demand for bonds that Chamberlain and his clients saw no point in owning. After 1914, wartime inflation caused a general rise in interest rates. A blue-chip corporation that had borrowed at 3¾ percent in early 1910 was paying upwards of 5 percent by late 1917. Plainly, the days of 2 percent government bond yields were over. But what rate would the Treasury have to pay?

The answer developed: less than the market would demand, had it had its voice and its wits about it. At the outbreak of war, the Federal Reserve System got into the business of suppressing interest rates. Not even Elihu Root, the most pessimistic man in the Senate in the 1913 monetary debate, had predicted that the system would be suborned by the Treasury Department within four years of its founding. If the government in Washington had had to negotiate a rate of interest with the creditors of Hartford, for instance, the result would probably have been 5 percent or 6 percent. Certainly, it would not have been 3½ percent or 4¼ percent, the actual yields obtained.

The Federal Reserve became the Treasury's bond-selling affiliate. If investors could be led to believe that 3½ percent or 4¼ percent was a fair rate of interest in an inflationary time, they would buy Liberty bonds, perhaps with borrowed money. This patriotic deception the Federal Reserve authorities succeeded in bringing off. The Reserve banks created credit, and the commercial banks created more of it. The public availed itself of the opportunity to borrow. Thus, low interest rates stimulated the expansion of lending and, ultimately, the rise in prices. Not for the last time in our story, low interest rates led to high ones.

Unlike Britain, the United States clung to the technical letter of the gold standard during the war, but it too abandoned the substance as well as the spirit. In the great Edwardian peace, governments submitted to an almost constitutional check on their traditional sovereign prerogatives in money. When the people chose to exchange the national currency unit for the appropriate measure of gold coins, a government allowed it; when foreigners chose to take their gold home, a government did not try to stop them. The war changed all that. In the United States, the dollar was still defined as 25.8 grains of gold, nine-tenths fine, and the Federal Reserve banks were still directed to hold a gold reserve against the paper money they issued. But Americans were discouraged from using gold coins, even for Christmas presents, and foreigners, between October 1917 and June 1919, were refused the right to repatriate their gold. Also, in a preview of monetary policies of the future, the nation's gold reserves were collected by government order in the Federal Reserve banks. Before the advent of a government central bank, commercial banks held their own reserves in their own vaults, or in the vaults of a trusted big-city bank like Baker's. Friends of the Federal Reserve legislation anticipated that, come the day of reform, the banks would cede the reserve-holding function to the Federal Reserve System. The war furnished the reason or pretext for ordering this surrender on the ground that a centralized monetary reserve was more effective than a decentralized one, especially in a national crisis. Congress and the Treasury agreed with that contention. So did the advisory council of private bankers that the Federal Reserve law had created. Editorial voices to the contrary argued in vain—though not without force, considering the rise in postwar consumer prices—that the measure was inflationary.

Over the century, control of credit has moved to the public sector from the private sector. It has evolved from a system of rules to one of administrative discretion. In the 1890s, as we saw, the U.S. Treasury was a supplicant in the world capital market. A hundred years later, the Treasury is again a borrower, but it must no longer treat directly with the owners of gold. With the demonetization of gold, the character of money has changed radically, and from the point of view of the government, expediently. Paper money requires no mining and in theory is infinitely expandable. As for the Federal Reserve System, it is no longer constrained by the need for a gold reserve. It may create credit in the volume and at the price that the market will bear. Gathering as much information as its automated staff can absorb and interpret, it improvises.

World War I sped the evolution of the financial system toward the extreme of improvisation, but there were vestiges of the old ways still. One of these was that the Treasury Department should establish a sinking fund to retire the national war debt; not merely to push it forward, borrowing even to pay the interest, but to pay off the principal year by year. (The Treasury was morally bound to do so, the 1919 annual report of the Secretary of the Treasury stated: "Any thought in the future of suspending the operation of the cumulative sinking fund or of meeting its charges through the sale of securities would not only be unwise in the extreme from the standpoint of the Government's finances and the ultimate wiping out of the war debt, but would be a breach of faith with every subscriber to the Victory loan and with every holder of the Liberty bonds." Handsome, nineteenth-century words! The Treasury's sinking fund recorded its last transaction on August 15, 1960.) Another such vestige was the idea that a central bank *was* a bank, not just another regulatory body. Being a bank, it should conform to sound banking practice. Every one of the dozen reserve banks was therefore held to a minimum reserve ratio (measured as a percentage of gold to deposits and note circulation) of 40 percent. No matter that the reserve banks were quasi-governmental institutions; they were expected to conduct their affairs as if they were the National City Bank. From that code followed this possibility: a Federal Reserve Bank, no less than National City, could become overextended. It could lend beyond its legal means. In early 1920, the Federal Reserve Bank of New York, then as now the system's flagship, faced just this dilemma. So much had it lent in the war years and so great was the demand for loans in the peace that it had reached the end of its rope. Its reserves had fallen to their legal minimum. Indeed, as it subsequently came to light, the New York bank was compelled to borrow from other Federal Reserve banks "in order to maintain its legal reserve percentage." As Alexander D. Noyes, then the financial editor of *The New York Times*, wrote of the period: "This was pretty nearly a signal of distress."

The autumn of 1918 brought a welcome break from custom. A war crowded in on the traditional crop-moving season, yet the cost of overnight funds never rose above 6 percent. Was any further proof required that the Federal was a national blessing? But the central bankers' application to their wartime duties also loomed large in the postwar toboggan ride of inflation and deflation. Throughout the war, the reserve banks had kept the discount rate below the market rate of interest. In other words, they had kept the rate at which a bank might borrow below the rate at which a bank might lend. In part for that reason, credit expanded rapidly. People applied for loans at banks, and banks—hard pressed to accommodate the traffic—applied for loans at the Federal Reserve. What was the Federal to do? To continue to lend indefinitely at bargain rates would imperil the standing of the Federal Reserve Bank of New York. It was, in fact, within the system's power to suspend the gold-reserve rules but, to quote Milton Friedman and Anna Schwartz, "it could hardly have justified doing so when the declining reserves were so clearly the result of [domestic] inflation fed by Federal Reserve credit creation."

So it must raise its discount rate. But what would become of the holders of Liberty bonds? Their number was legion, and they came in all sizes. The U.S. Steel Corp., no doubt at Baker's urging, bought more than $125 million worth. So full were American corporations of Liberty bonds that the securities literally seeped from them; in 1918 and 1919, companies paid Liberty bond dividends. Banks bought bonds for their accounts as well as for their customers'. "Before the $6,000,000,000 loan of October 1918 was offered," Noyes wrote, "Congress by special act enlarged the authorized powers of national banks to lend on Liberty bond collateral, and practically all large banks, as a result of pressure by loans committees and of special facilities granted by the Federal Reserve, announced through public advertisements to subscribers that 'we will lend you money secured by the Fourth Liberty Loan at 4¼ percent [the interest rate on the loan itself] for 90 days, with renewals at the same rate covering the entire period of one year.' " The success of this offer can be measured by the lending it incited. In March 1918, the national banks held $341 million in war bonds as collateral for loans. In September 1919, they held $1.2 billion worth.

All the while, the riot of luxury and extravagance (the inflationary boom so much deplored by the partners of C. F. Childs & Co.) continued. National City Bank turned on the spigots in Cuba, and small-town banks financed the bull market in Iowa farmland. The Federal Reserve looked down on this groaning banquet table and proceeded to tip it over. On January 22, 1920, the Federal Reserve Bank of New York raised its discount rate to 6 percent from 4¾ percent, the sharpest single boost in that key lending rate in Federal Reserve history.

In the 1980s, it became a cynical rule of thumb on Wall Street that the type of collateral most favored by bankers—office buildings, for example—was bound to depreciate and must not, on pain of certain loss, be purchased for investment. In other words, whatever the bankers did enthusiastically would turn out to be wrong. In 1918 and 1919, bankers lent freely against bonds; and the bond market presently broke. Between January and May 1920, the average yield on a prime corporate issue rose by one-half of 1 percent, to 5.56 percent, the highest rate of interest on a high-grade corporate obligation in the United States until 1967. Treasury Secretary David F. Houston declared that the United States was under no obligation "to guarantee the holders of Liberty bonds against variations in money-market conditions or to guarantee a market at par for the bonds." Nor did it. In early 1920, short-term interest rates climbed. In fact, the shorter the maturity, the higher the yield. For the year, commercial paper rates averaged 7½ percent, the high-water mark of the commercial-paper market until 1969. By the spring, the 6 percent discount rate at the Federal Reserve Bank of New York no longer looked punitive. It was, in fact, a standing invitation to perpetuate the war-induced credit bubble. On May 29, the discount rate was pushed to 7 percent. Why would anyone pay 7 percent and up to buy a Liberty bond that yielded 4¼ percent? Obviously, nobody would; certainly no bank could borrow at a high rate to carry bonds yielding a lower one. The 4¼ percent Liberty issues now fetched 83 cents on the dollar, not just a low price but a disturbing one. "The market's rating of the government's credit was on an interest basis higher than 5 percent," Noyes observed; "something which could not have been said even in the panic of 1873. These prices of May were the lowest ever reached." They were, in fact, so low that they could only rise. And to their supreme credit, the savings banks of the day (not yet the "thrifts" of so much well-earned derision) shrewdly bought them. For the next twenty-six years, bond prices would tend to rise and interest rates to fall. "The holders of Liberty bonds who save and hold their bonds will not, in the opinion of the Treasury, regret it, nor will they suffer by reason of the present depreciation in market prices," the Treasury Secretary said. For once, the government's investment advice was right on the money.

Prince of Thrift

On August 11, 1915, the International Congress for Thrift—the first such event of its kind ever to be held in the United States—opened in San Francisco. The first speaker was Simon W. Straus, forty-eight, a salesman of real-estate bonds and the first president of the American Society for Thrift. In his inaugural remarks at the birth of the American Society one year earlier, Straus had urged the nation's schoolchildren to put their summer vacations to productive use by cultivating gardens. The sense of the meeting was that vegetable gardening would go a long way to solving the nation's economic problems.

The International Congress was set in the San Francisco Exposition Grounds and was convened on the first-ever "Thrift Day," officially recognized and proclaimed by California governor Hiram Johnson. The governor had asked that the people of the Golden State devote their thoughts that day, as fully as possible, to the subject of thrift. Somewhat out of keeping with that spirit, Straus spared no rhetorical expense. His was, of course, the kickoff address. "In addressing you at the opening of this, the first Congress for Thrift ever held in the world, I feel a deep sense of personal humility. The movement is so broad, and of so far-reaching importance to all humanity, that, as president of the Thrift Society, I feel a certain sense of littleness—like that which overwhelms us when we contemplate the starry heavens at night. Words are incapable of describing the magnitude, significance and possibilities of this movement, if we are faithful to our duties and our opportunities. For if we shall lead humanity into more thrifty ways, and especially our fellow American citizens, we shall, in reality, be turning many a human soul from penury to prosperity, from want to affluence, from failure in everything to success in everything."

Straus, obviously, was a man in search of a larger canvas, and he collected his thoughts on thrift in a book that was published in 1920. *History of the Thrift Movement in America* was as much a moral as an economic essay. To Straus, thrift was an ideal. It concerned planning, prudence, foresight, and patriotism as much as it did frugality. It was not to be confused with miserliness any more than it was with extravagance. It was a way of life, like vegetarianism.

Thrift promotes character—is indistinguishable from character— and Straus saluted the strength of the thrifty Belgians in the face of the German onslaught. He commended the French too, but withheld his highest praise, for even though the French kitchen was properly celebrated for its efficiency (nothing was wasted, not even chicken feet), the French blackberry went uneaten. It evidently took all the author's self-restraint to temper his indictment of American profligacy. There was waste in canning salmon and cutting lumber. Insects, rats, forest fires caused preventable havoc. "In our great cities," wrote Straus, "people break down in health or reach premature senility because of late hours, loss of sleep, fast pleasures, and headlong, nerve-racking methods of existence. Without regard to the laws of nature, we have been guilty of overeating, have brought about ill-health, and have incapacitated ourselves for effective work by the improper mastication of our food."

Looking the reader in the eye, Straus asked him a direct question: "Has it ever occurred to you that every wasted moment means that someone, somewhere, must make up for it? If there were no wasted days anywhere, how much more easily and quickly the world's work would be accomplished! If all mankind were thrifty, how much happier and better this world would be, and how greatly improved living conditions would be for everyone!"

Living conditions for Straus and his firm could hardly have been any better than they presently became. In 1921, the new $4 million headquarters of S. W. Straus & Co. opened in Manhattan at Fifth Avenue and Forty-sixth Street. The architects, Warren & Wetmore, seemed to think of everything except their client's devotion to frugality. In the basement was an infirmary, a library, a dormitory, dining rooms (one for women and one for men), and a kitchen. The main banking room, to which one ascended on a grand staircase, had a vaulted ceiling forty feet above a glistening marble floor. Marble was the principal material in the interior of the banking room, and the wood finish of the private offices was walnut. Metal railings and grilles were embellished with gold.

The American Architect remarked on the choice of a midtown location by a thriving downtown business, taking it as a hopeful sign for the evolution of finance. "Years ago," the magazine commented, "the 'financial district' was Wall street and its vicinage. To that district went men and groups of men—corporations—to find money to float for all the many schemes, sound and 'wildcat,' that man's ingenuity and rush for wealth could invent. There was no well drawn line between operations in money that, on the one hand, sought out safe and sure investment, or on the other took all the hazards of a gambler in mad orgies of speculative gambling. No matter how carefully or conservatively certain groups of men tried to segregate the mad elements of speculation from the saner seeking out of safe investment opportunity, there was the taint of the gambler over it all. Clients, feeling they were classified with the 'lambs,' were loath to trust those who lived so intimately with the 'bulls and bears' of finance." Hence the move uptown. S. W. Straus & Co. had joined the carriage trade.

Straus's business was real-estate-mortgage bonds, and he had been at it for years. His father, born to a long line of bankers, emigrated to the United States from his native Prussia in 1852. He settled in Auburn, Indiana, and later moved to Ligonier, where he founded the Citizens Bank. Moving next to Chicago, he started F. W. Straus & Co., dealer in mortgages. Simon entered the firm at the age of eighteen and took control at twenty, when his father retired. After that, it was S. W. Straus & Co.

Straus was credited with originating the first mortgage real-estate bond in 1909. A real-estate bond was a security with a senior claim

Structurally, if not financially, impregnable: the headquarters of S. W. Straus & Co., Fifth Avenue and Forty-sixth Street, 1921 (UNDERHILL COLLECTION, MUSEUM OF THE CITY OF NEW YORK)

on a building, and Straus became a leading financier of skyscrapers. The bonds were sold to the public at high rates of interest and in small denominations. Typically, a Straus bond yielded 6 percent, twice the rate paid on a commercial-bank savings deposit and more than two percentage points higher than the rate offered by savings banks. It competed for the high-yield-investment dollar with a host of foreign-government bonds that came to the American market in the 1920s (and which, like all too many mortgage bonds, wound up in default in the 1930s). Straus's advertisements were distinctive and appealing. They claimed that, since 1882, no customer had lost a cent in a Straus investment. "Thirty-five years without loss to any investor," said the 1917 edition.

In December 1917, in the wake of the Second Liberty Loan, S. W. Straus & Co. addressed the public with a wartime message: "In times of war, demand safety doubly safeguarded. Only the soundest investments should be purchased in times like these. Furthermore" —the advertisement sought to check any patriotic qualms against investing for profit—"you are fully justified in requiring the best interest return on your invested funds, sufficient to meet the increased cost of living and the burdens the war imposes on all of us."

Now the volume was turned up: "The first mortgage bonds, safeguarded under the *Straus Plan*, meet these requirements in every detail. They are thoroughly fortified against commercial strains and stresses and adverse economic conditions. They yield 6 percent net and they do not decline in value."

The war advanced the democratization of credit and therefore the fortunes of Straus. Liberalizing tendencies were visible throughout American business and finance. Up until 1910, for example, automobiles had been sold for cash, and even the visionary Arthur Morris was reluctantly led to share the prejudice of the day: as a car was a luxury, it must not be paid for with borrowed money. L. F. Weaver, of San Francisco, the man who is credited with first making the potent match of loans and automobiles, prospered, but only after listening to the discouraging advice of local bankers. "[I] was over-cautious in the beginning," Weaver recalled, "and always looking out for trouble." That was in 1913. By 1919, the year John J. Raskob founded the General Motors Acceptance Corp., a revolution was well under way.

The swelling of the creditor class was all to the good, as was the postwar slump in government-bond prices. In Germany, Britain, and the United States, the patriotic investor suffered losses ranging from large to catastrophic. Not so the holders of Straus bonds, which, as advertised, did not decline in value.

S. W. Straus & Co. was the promoter of Straus bonds, not their unconditional guarantor; the credit behind a given Straus issue was the earning power of a particular mortgaged building. In the public's estimation, however, the Straus name was generic. "Straus" was thought to constitute a separate investment class, like New York Central common or the Victory Loan. Although a leader in mortgage bonds, Straus did not own the field. There were Greenebaum bonds—"100 Percent Safe Since 1885"—and the bonds of G. L. Miller & Co. and of American Bond & Mortgage Co., among others. Each was represented to be bulletproof.

At the start of the 1920s, the Straus approach was, in fact, conservative. By the end of the decade, it was risky (and fraudulent too). The evolution was telling of the 1920s, and it anticipated the 1980s. In each decade, the terms and conditions of lending became progressively easier with the passage of years. Auto finance helps to illustrate the tendencies. To start with, cars were financed for a year and with a down payment of one-third to one-half of the purchase price. However, as Professor Edwin R. A. Seligman noted in 1927: "With the growing competition between dealers to increase the volume of their sales, the minimum cash payment was gradually reduced and the maximum period of installments was lengthened. It was not long before the minimum down payment was lowered to a third or even to a fourth of the selling price of new cars, while the series of monthly payments was increased to eighteen months, and even in some cases to longer periods." A conservative backlash followed. In 1924, the Annual Convention of the Finance Companies urged creditors to hold the line on one-third down and twelve months to pay. In 1926, the year in which Merriam-Webster admitted "down payment" into the language, a Chicago finance man warned the National Automobile Dealers' Association that an automotive credit crisis loomed. So closely watched was this particular pot, however, that no disaster boiled, either then or in the Depression.

No such reaction occurred in the mortgage-bond business. In the early 1920s, Simon W. Straus seemed a veritable Morgan. He recommended first mortgages—that is, senior claims—only. He insisted that every building have a solid foundation of equity: say, 40 percent of the market value. He demanded that a building throw off earnings sufficient to cover its mortgage debt and then some. "I do not believe in lending money on a property, no matter how big the land value or how proportionately small the loan," he advised the readers of *American Magazine* in 1922, "unless I am convinced that the earnings of that property will be two or three times the interest charges."

But in the gathering prosperity of the 1920s, lending standards generally softened. They were relaxed in the markets for foreign-government bonds, corporate bonds, and urban mortgages. After 1924, Straus dropped his opposition to junior liens. Besides first mortgage bonds, he began to offer seconds and thirds, which his marketing staff euphemistically called "general mortgages." He offered so-called collateral trust bonds—"a potpourri of indifferent subordinate mortgages owned by the borrower and pledged as security, besides debentures of corporations owning real estate," as a court subsequently discovered. Without saying anything to his customers, Straus entered the junk-bond business.

"Of late years," the *New York Evening Post* ventured in 1924, "real estate bonds have been sold perhaps more widely than any other type of bond; they have been placed with the small investor so well in cases that many have come to regard them as the personification of safe investing. Real estate mortgage bonds have probably done more to increase the investor class in this country than any other influences since the Government war bonds selling campaigns; they have demonstrated that new buyers of bonds, in large numbers, can be created by intensive merchandising methods (and not necessarily undignified methods). In doing this the real estate banker deserves no little appreciation from the bond business in general and from general business and the public at large."

High Yield, Low Risk

The intensive, yet not undignified, merchandising methods of the Straus company hammered away at safety and high yield. In Straus bonds, these two investment ideals, so long thought to be antithetical, were at last inseparably joined. One advertisement told the parable of Mrs. White, a seventy-two-year-old victim of "over-conservative" investment advice. She had invested in high-grade railroad bonds and governments that yielded next to nothing. They were highly marketable, of course, but so what? Mrs. White was an investor, not a trader. Luckily for Mrs. White, as the ad continued, her S. W. Straus representative was able to help. "When [the Straus] plan was explained and adopted," the copy said, "her capital, instead of returning 3.8%

returned 5.5%—raising her income from $112.00 a month to $162.00 a month. Thus Mrs. White was provided with all those little comforts she desired and feared she never would be able to obtain."

Always, it was the "Straus plan," or "Straus bonds," never this mortgage on that building. If an impression had been created that Straus guaranteed the bonds, that impression was allowed to stand. "And you did nothing to disabuse the minds of these people to the contrary?" a Straus salesman was asked in a proceeding in New York State Supreme Court. "Only when a customer would ask if they were guaranteed," he replied.

"Otherwise nothing was said about it?" was the next question.

"No."

Ambiguity was subsequently expunged from the securities-selling repertoire by the federal securities acts. In the modern age, Michael Milken's bonds were never represented, formally, to be Milken bonds; they were the debts of their corporate issuers, and Milken was under no obligation to make good the loss if they defaulted. If some of his devotees believed that he would prevent defaults (and many did), that was their right, but it was a hope without legal standing.

In the 1920s, the federal code had not yet impinged on an investment banker's freedom of speech. On the books of New York State was an antifraud statute, the Martin Act, and it was waved in the face of the real-estate bond industry, S. W. Straus & Co. included, later in the decade. But the elaborate federal apparatus governing every jot and tittle of a securities transaction was several years off in the future.

The failure of G. L. Miller & Co., one of Straus's smaller competitors, in 1926, set off a flurry of charges, investigations, reports, and speechmaking, but the weird circumstances of the failure itself were almost overlooked. It would come to light later on that the firm was perennially in trouble, but its reputation for solvency was intact and evidently unquestioned at the time of its bankruptcy. How intact is startling: less than three months earlier, G. L. Miller, the president and founder of the firm, had succeeded in selling it.

The buyers conspicuously included organized labor. The 1920s were the heyday of union-sponsored banks, and the unions involved in the purchase of G. L. Miller proposed to create a holding company. Ownership of the holding company would be shared by themselves, businessmen, and bankers. Luke J. Murphy, formerly executive vice president of the Brotherhood of Locomotive Engineers' Trust Company of New York, was chosen to succeed Miller in the presidency, and he expressed the hope that the workingman would thus be afforded a sound, new investment opportunity. "We will be able to extend to the small investor—the wage earner—the opportunity to purchase safe bonds, underwritten and distributed by an old established institution," Murphy said.

The sale was announced on July 1, 1926. Almost the first important undertaking of the new owners was to bail out. On September 3 the firm was placed in receivership. No trace of indignation at the brief elapsed time between sale and bankruptcy was hinted at in the news reports. (As for Miller, he kept his knack for timing. Only a few weeks before the New York failure and in the midst of a collapsing Florida real-estate market, he managed to unload his Florida interests on another set of buyers.) Albert Ottinger, New York State attorney general, while pointing to the need for new protective laws, advised the holders of Miller's bonds not to panic. Herbert Martin, a vice president of S. W. Straus & Co., remarked that the "first" real-estate mortgage bond business—the Straus organization still refused to acknowledge that it trucked in junior liens—would suffer no loss of public confidence. Certainly, the older "more responsible houses" remained beyond question. "The first mortgage real-estate bond business," declared Martin, "is too large, too important and too well established to be affected by one failure. During the last half century the first mortgage real-estate bond business has been one of the most important factors in the rebuilding of the United States, and we believe this business is destined to play a still greater part in the future of the country."

As a matter of fact, the failure of G. L. Miller & Co. revealed exactly how this large, important, and well-established industry had been operating and why it was certain to fail. Significantly, Miller held little cash but considerable sums of its own real-estate bonds. These it had hoped to sell to the public, but the public, by the late summer of 1926, had had enough of them. What had driven Miller over the edge was its failure to meet a deadline to pay one of its investment-banking clients. The proceeds of the bond sale had not, as the investors might have assumed, been immediately turned over to the borrower. They had been lumped in with the Miller general accounts. When the 571 Park Avenue Corporation, Miller's client, demanded payment, Miller was in no position to oblige. This was on August 6, a little more than a month after the front page of *The New York Times* heralded a new era in labor-union investments.

To even a cursory reader of the *Times* report, it must have dawned that the Miller enterprise was a kind of Ponzi scheme. The real-estate mortgage bonds it sold were often construction bonds. The collateral behind the issues was frequently a hole in the ground. Sometimes the project succeeded and sometimes it did not. When not, Miller would tell the bondholders nothing but continue to pay them their interest and principal from the corporate pot. Each new wave of investors in effect paid the preceding wave. In the real-estate bond business, there was no such thing as an independent trustee to serve as the legal guardian of the bondholders' rights; G. L. Miller & Co. stood guard at the henhouse door itself.

Keyes Winter, deputy state attorney general of New York, disclosed that he had been hot on Miller's trail, that an investigation of the entire real-estate bond industry would be pressed, and that the immediate causes of the failure were "overappraisals of property values and placing their funds in frozen assets." It would emerge years later that inspectors from the U.S. Post Office had conducted an investigation as early as 1925 and that Haskins & Sells, Miller's accountants, had questioned the firm's procedures years before that. Unlike S. W. Straus & Co., which slid gradually into questionable practices, Miller seemed to have pioneered them. For instance, in 1921, it floated a $350,000 bond issue to finance the Harvey Court Apartments in Indianapolis. Out of that $350,000, no less than $73,500 was paid to Miller itself in "commissions." The contractor received only $222,000. At length, mechanics' liens were placed against the building, and in 1924 the lenders foreclosed. Miller & Co., telling the bondholders nothing, bought the building itself and continued paying the interest as if nothing had gone wrong. The next year, anxious to get rid of the title, Miller ordered a "sale" to a new corporation. But at what price? Not the $150,000 it would actually command. It would go badly for Miller if its competitors found out that a building with a $350,000 bond issue had fetched only $150,000. So the transfer was made at $500,000. A memo to G. L. Miller from a Miller vice president explained the procedure of faking the higher price: "This, of course, cost us $350 more in revenue stamps but you doubtless feel about it as I do."

Straus, the financier of the Westinghouse Building and the New York Athletic Club and the future banker to the Chanin and Chrysler buildings, had a reputation to uphold. He was the voice of the "first" mortgage business, and he rose to its defense after the Miller embarrassment. He reiterated his conservative views on the valuation of income-producing real estate. The appropriate test was the capacity of a building to produce net income, he said. He said that he welcomed federal regulation of the market—it was, in any case, inevitable—and he acknowledged that, in a regrettable minority of cases, unsound practices had been followed. Sometimes appraisals were overblown (although perhaps the appraisers' opinions were no worse than the opinions of the people who criticized them). Occasionally, construction funds had been commingled with the general accounts of the bond houses, and that abuse must stop. He complained about a "malicious whispering campaign" by the enemies of mortgage bonds and of investment securities in general.

"We are today standing on the threshold of a new era in the entire investment field," said Straus, "and I believe the day is not far off when the methods of treating and selling every type of investment offered to the American public will be in some manner under strict state or federal government supervision and control. How soon that day will come, I do not know, but it is as certain as tomorrow's sun."

A prescient forecast indeed; and Straus now hit his sanctimonious stride: "I am not unmindful of the fact that business can be hampered by over-regulation and over-supervision. But the tremendous growth of the investment field, especially with the advent of millions of Americans as investors in our Liberty Loan flotations, make it necessary that the American public be offered every possible protection."

Scrutiny, if not protection, was closer at hand than Straus might have imagined. The state attorney general's office was at work as he spoke. The investigation was to reveal that, contrary to advertising claims, defaults on real-estate mortgage bonds were commonplace: S. W. Straus alone had at least forty issues, totaling $54 million, under water. The attorney general could only hazard an educated guess about the default statistics, because the underwriting houses controlled them. No independent bond trustee monitored the affairs of the building corporations—the actual issuers of the bonds—or notified the investors in case of a missed interest payment. As Miller had done, Straus ate his losses, paid the interest out of his own ample funds— fees and commissions ran to 10 percent of every issue—and thereby perpetuated the literal truth of the claim (circa 1925) "Forty-three years without loss to any investor." The literal truth of that claim obscured a more important fact. Straus bonds (or Greenebaum bonds or Miller bonds) were safe only as long as Straus (or Greenebaum or Miller) remained solvent. Their solvency depended, in good part, on the public's willingness to invest in new real-estate bonds. In 1926, at least, the public was not to be denied. The volume of new real-estate bond issuance totaled almost $1 billion, up threefold from 1925.

As 1927 unfolded, Simon W. Straus and his colleagues were the objects of unwanted attention. A committee of the American Construction Council, chaired by Franklin D. Roosevelt, mounted an investigation of the real-estate bond business in tandem with the state attorney general's. The Construction Council's findings and conclusions, at least, posed no threat to the status quo: for instance, the practice of an issuing house serving as its own bond trustee was endorsed as sound and acceptable even though it was patently neither. The editorial board of *The New York Times*, which had had high hopes for the committee and its up-and-coming chairman, expressed disappointment. For his part, Attorney General Albert Ottinger laid down a set of rules intended to guide the real-estate bond business back into safe and fair dealing. Among these was a prohibition against the lumping of investment funds into a common bond-house account and a requirement to notify bondholders in case of default in their issues. If the bond house had a financial interest in the building or enterprise securing an issue of bonds, it was barred from serving also as bondholders' trustee.

This last reform was potentially subversive to the established order, and it must have given the bankers a turn. The real-estate bond market was a closed system. Straus and Miller and Greenebaum controlled not only the issuance of bonds but also their pricing. They controlled the flow of information to the bondholders (something that, in the 1980s, Drexel Burnham Lambert could only dream of doing). They themselves cynically occupied the office of bond trustees. Up until the late 1920s, a Straus employee was usually the trustee of a Straus issue. After the organization of the Straus National Bank and Trust Co., in 1928, it was a Straus banker. As no pet trustee would tell the bondholders bad news, let alone defend their legal rights, the issuers' control was complete. It remained so until the Depression, new rules notwithstanding.

A little like Lawrence Chamberlain, Simon Straus disapproved of active public markets in the bonds he sold, but his reasons were more specific than Chamberlain's. Straus had a proprietary interest in the reputation of that fraudulent generic security, the "Straus bond." To convey the impression that every Straus issue was equally creditworthy, he stood ready to purchase every one at 99 cents on the dollar, plus interest. Greenebaum and Miller (and the other mortgage-bond men) had identical policies. "Real-estate mortgage bonds are not listed on stock exchanges; so they are not subject to the vagaries of a wide active market," Straus wrote in 1922. "*They remain at par*—neither lessening nor appreciating in value. This may not appeal to the speculator, but it is an advantage to the legitimate *investor*, who should always see to it that he obtains the bonds from a reliable dealer." And who was more reliable than Straus?

The mild regulatory heat of 1927 seemed to cause Straus and his colleagues not even a wilted collar. Attorney General Ottinger, evidently, understood the system thoroughly, and his analysis of it was on the mark. "[T]he unsuccessful buildings are promoted at the expense of the successful holdings," he reported. As for the ubiquitous claims of decades without losses to any investor, "this method of financing building construction was practically unknown before 1916." For that matter, Philip L. Carret had brilliantly exposed the real-estate bond market for the hoax that it was in an article in *Barron's* as early as 1924. There was, in the Martin Act of the General Business Law of the State of New York, ample legal means to stop fraudulent practices in the securities markets, had the attorney general chosen to take action. But he contented himself with warnings, some of which were rendered sotto voce. For instance, although Straus was prohibited in 1927 from renewing the claim, "Forty-three years without a Loss," no public mention was made of that censure, and the press seemed not to notice the sudden editing of the familiar Straus ads. If the press turned its head, the public stopped its ears. The will to believe was unshaken through the first year of the Depression.

Certainly, the real-estate bond purveyors suffered no loss of public esteem. Less than a year after his knuckles were rapped by the New York State attorney general, Straus was made a Chevalier of the Legion of Honor in recognition of his charitable work in France. At about the same time, William J. Moore, president of American Bond & Mortgage Co., a competitor of Straus's, was presented with a key to the city of Boston by Mayor James M. Curley. Skyscrapers rose, and the men who financed them were counted as public benefactors.

Miss Kuhlmann's Revenge

On July 31, 1929, Cyrus C. Miller, president of the proposed New York Real Estate Securities Exchange, addressed a luncheon meeting of editors and publishers at the Uptown Club. The exchange, Miller told the newsmen, would open on October 1, and finishing touches were even then being applied to the new 25-by-100-foot trading floor. "For the real estate field," said Miller (who is not to be confused with

G. L. Miller), "it will function as the New York Stock Exchange does in its field." The new floor, situated at 12 East Forty-first Street, was being fitted out as a miniature of the Big Board at Broad and Wall streets, complete with trading posts and quotation boards.

Listening to Miller, the journalists might have detected an undercurrent of criticism of the state of real-estate finance. With the advent of skyscrapers, "financing by individuals has become incompatible with progress," he said. The time had come to apply the principle of "collective ownership" to real estate. And in a quite unmistakable dig at the Straus system, Miller went on: "Stabilization of the real estate market values will be an outstanding achievement through its tendency to curtail blind speculation and its strong emphasis on the aspect of sound investment."*

The new exchange could hardly have opened at a worse time. It was the month of the Great Crash. What almost nobody foresaw was the significance of that break to real estate or to the cozy business of real-estate bonds. The bear market was long and (true to form for most bear markets) lightly attended by public investors. On February 1, 1930, for example, the number of bonds changing hands on the New York Real Estate Securities Exchange floor was exactly two. Even without active trading, quoted prices fell. Thus, in the spring of 1930, the Chrysler Building 6 percent bonds of 1948 fetched 95 cents on the dollar. Two years later, they had fallen to 38.

Straus's timing, on the other hand, was in some respects enviable. He lived to see *Fortune* magazine praise him as the epitome of the constructive real-estate financier—the article was published in August 1930, fully a year into the Depression, by which time *Fortune* might have known better—but not to witness the collapse of the national real-estate market and of his own reputation.

At his death in September 1930 at the age of sixty-four, Straus was still, in the public's eyes, the benevolent financier, philanthropist, and exponent of thrift he had seemed in happier days. "Although a stern disciplinarian," said the *New York Sun* in its send-off, "Mr. Straus was a man of even temperament, who commanded great respect and affection among his employees. Not even the most timid office boy

* Seconders of these views were rounded up for an amiable Sunday piece in *The New York Times*'s real-estate section. "Many of the leading members of the American Economic Association have notified Cyrus C. Miller that they regard the New York Real Estate Exchange as an additional unit in the country's economic system," the story led off. Among those eminent authorities were Alvah H. Benton of the North Dakota Agricultural College Experiment Station and Albert S. Keister of the North Carolina College for Women.

feared to approach him, it is said. Many hard luck stories were heard by him, and no good cause was turned away. He had only two hobbies—charity and thrift." It came to light, however, that Straus was more a proponent of thrift than a living exemplar of it. During his critical illness, a police officer had been stationed on the sidewalk underneath his Park Avenue windows to prevent unnecessary noise from disturbing his rest. (The first word of Straus's critical illness came from the arrest of a motorist by the special police sentry; the offender, a Manhattan architect, had been leaning on his horn.) He lived in the Hotel Ambassador, an S. W. Straus & Co.-controlled property. It would later be told that he occupied the entire twelfth floor, that he had not paid rent in a decade (depriving the hotel of $500,000 in revenues), and that, before his death, he had given the apartment's furnishings, for which he had paid nothing, to his wife. All this, it was strongly suggested by the New York State attorney general, had come out of the hides of the S. W. Straus & Co. creditors. Subsequently, the Securities and Exchange Commission would charge that a 1928 debenture issue of the Ambassador Hotel Corporation, distributed by S. W. Straus & Co., was in effect a device by which the public had been led to bail out the Straus firm.

The unlucky successor to Straus as president of S. W. Straus & Co. was Nicholas Roberts; the new chairman was Samuel J. Tilden Straus, the financier-philanthropist's brother. Each man would invest a substantial portion of his time in legal proceedings in the next several years: defending the firm in lawsuits, reorganizing Straus-sponsored bond issues, and managing the bankruptcy of S. W. Straus & Co. itself. In sponsoring and dominating the so-called bondholder protective committees, Straus would blaze new trails in conflict of interest and help to inspire the drafting and passage of the Trust Indenture Act of 1939. In its decline, the firm would rub elbows with rising legal and political talent—for instance, William O. Douglas, the future Supreme Court Justice, who directed the SEC's searching inquiry into the committees that purported to protect the interests of bondholders in reorganizations; and Robert Moses, chairman of the New York State Council of Parks, who resigned as a receiver of S. W. Straus & Co. after only two weeks, saying that the Straus firm was "a shell" and that there was nothing that he (or his associate, William M. Calder, a former United States senator, who also resigned) could do to protect the holders of the bonds it had issued.

On October 8, 1932, S. W. Straus & Co. was ordered into receivership by a justice of the New York Supreme Court, Brooklyn, who cited, among other findings, the fraudulent fobbing off of junior bonds on customers who were under the impression they were buying first mortgages.

In March 1933, around the time of the Roosevelt bank holiday, a remnant of the Straus organization moved out of the palatial Fifth Avenue office for more modest quarters downtown as Straus Securities Company. S. J. T. Straus, retaining the title of chairman, declared that "one of the main purposes of the new company was to help out in every possible way" the customers of the old one (he said, further, that the defunct S. W. Straus & Co. had spent some $15 million in defending the interests of its customers). Just the same, Nicholas Roberts, the former S. W. Straus & Co. president, was arrested as he left an office building a few months later, charged with grand larceny by one of those customers, Miss Anna Kuhlmann, fifty-five, of 655 Greenwich Street. She recognized him as he exited 70 Pine Street, pointed him out to a pair of detectives, and watched as he was borne off to the Old Slip police station. Roberts received the full bear-market treatment: beyond the humiliating fact of the arrest, a report of it on the front page of the next day's *Times*. Miss Kuhlmann said that she and her sister, Katherine, fifty-two, were both unemployed. Anna told the *Times* that they had opened a joint account with S. W. Straus & Co. in 1928, invested $10,000 in what they thought were first mortgage bonds, and proceeded to lose their money. Their lawyer said that their case was similar to "thousands" of others. Or tens of thousands: in 1936, the sum total of defaulted Straus bonds was $214 million, and the number of afflicted investors was put at 60,000.

Loans for Peru

In January 1925, the investment editor of the monthly magazine *World's Work* addressed some practical advice to a widow's daughter. The woman had written to ask how $25,000 might safely produce an income of 7 percent a year—this at a time when Liberty bonds yielded only 4 percent. It was the eternal question. "There are in general only two investment fields in which it seems possible to-day to get 7 percent return on one's money with a good degree of safety," the editor replied. "Those are the foreign government field . . . and the real-estate mortgage bond field. As a rule we would not advise the placing of all of an inheritance, such as you and your mother have in hand, in any one or two investment fields. Greater safety is to be secured by greater diversification, and there are risks in these two fields that are not found in some other fields—that is what accounts for the higher rate of return."

So far, so good. High yields imply above-average risk. However, the editor continued, "the writer is inclined to believe the foreign field offers some of the most attractive investment possibilities to-day in such bonds as the new German 7s, French Republic 7½s, State of Queensland 6s, Belgian Government 6½s. But these are not securities that are usually recommended for a widow's investment.

"Coming back to your problem," he wound up, now strapping on the protective armor of the first person plural, "we think it would be well to place $4,000 of this money in Liberty bonds . . . and if you must have 7 percent income on the total, divide the rest between such foreign government issues as we have mentioned and real-estate mortgage bonds purchased through houses of high standing and long experience in that field."

Just as World War I created a new public market in the bonds of the United States government, so it opened a new domestic market in the bonds of foreign governments. War broadened the country's investment horizons. And the postwar decline in interest rates created a hunger for income that could only be satisfied (or so it seemed) by high-yield investments. The first important foreign-government issues to be marketed in the United States were the French and British war loans. They were followed by the postwar German reparations loans and by the issues of scores of governments in South America, Europe, and Asia.

Surveying the foreign-government bond market from the vantage point of the Great Depression, Max Winkler, a financial authority who had repeatedly warned against the excesses of the boom, wrote matter-of-factly: "The history of government borrowing is really the history of government defaults." Winkler's dictum was accurate if cynical. At intervals throughout the nineteenth and twentieth centuries—in the 1820s, the 1880s, 1910–14, and the 1920s, for instance—governments, especially in Latin America, had borrowed and defaulted. It was not surprising that governments would borrow over and over again as opportunity presented itself. What was remarkable was that bankers and bond buyers would pliably lend.

The foreign-government bond episode of the 1920s and 1930s naturally suggests comparisons with the Third World debt predicament of the 1970s and 1980s. The similarities and differences are both instructive. In each cycle of lending, worldwide dislocation was the precipitating event: war in the earlier period, oil prices in the second. In each cycle, lenders committed funds eagerly and almost innocently. They lent not only for profit, they said, but also out of duty. "If America wants to help in the reconstruction of Europe," wrote Thomas W. Lamont, a partner of J. P. Morgan, in 1920, "if America wants to continue her profitable export trade, she will have to sell her goods on credit—not all, but a good part. . . . America may well follow in the footsteps of the older countries in the field of foreign investment. Along that path, America will discharge her duties and her capacity for universal service, not without profit to herself." Charles E. Mitchell, chairman of the National City Bank, called to testify before the Senate Finance Committee in the Depression, sounded a purer eleemosynary note. "Many of us have found a real inspiration in the fact that in the issuance of this large volume of foreign loans we were playing a part in the development of American trade and industry," he said. "That is our first motive always."

One important financial difference stands out in comparing that period with the later one. Then, the creditors of foreign governments were bondholders. In the 1980s, they were the major banks. In the 1920s, the first order of business of a bank was still the safe and liquid keeping of its depositors' funds; the depositors, being uninsured by the federal government, insisted on it. As there was no legal prohibition against banks conducting an investment underwriting business, the banks sold bonds to the public. The consequence of this arrangement, come the Depression and the ensuing massive default of foreign bonds, was twofold. First, the solvency of banks and of the banking system was not imperiled by the financial breakdown of foreign governments (as it was in the early 1980s by the breakdown of Third World government finances). The German debt crisis threatened the National City Bank, to cite an important exception to that rule, but banks in general were not as exposed to risk by overseas loans as they were in the 1980s. Second, a hue and cry went up over the allegedly sloppy and fraudulent underwriting practices of the major banks in the 1920s. In subsequent reforms, the banks were excluded from investment banking, which would cost them dearly in future decades. It was, in part, to replace the profits lost to Wall Street that the commercial banks in the 1980s undertook some of the high-risk, low-reward business they did—for instance, real-estate lending.

Foreign-government bonds inspired some of the richest invective of the Depression literature. "In no single field of finance is the betrayal of the American investor more brilliantly demonstrated than in that of numerous issues of foreign bonds," wrote Bernard J. Reis. "And while the almost fraudulent trade was carried on," charged Winkler, "no one raised his voice in protest, not even the wall paper concerns who must have felt the competition very keenly." Writing without heat, modern-day scholars have found that a representative portfolio of foreign-government bonds of that day actually produced a higher return (provided they were not sold during the rough patch of the early thirties) than safe and sane Liberty bonds did. In truth, the legendary collapse of Peruvian bonds diverted attention from the honorable fiscal record of numerous other governments. "History tends to emphasize newsworthy defaults," as Sidney Homer taught, "and leaves in obscurity a great volume of routine periodic debt repayments between nations." Thus, lucky was the holder of the French Government 7s of 1949. Even in the darkest moments of the 1931 debt crisis, they were quoted comfortably above par, a reflection of the important monetary reforms earlier achieved by the governor of the Bank of France, Emile Moreau.

The indignation of the Depression-era writers was not without grounding in fact, however. Booms produce complacency in almost equal measure as wealth. The longer the good times last, the deeper the conviction grows that they will go on. As bull markets render skepticism unprofitable, doubting Thomases learn to hold their tongues, and short sellers (whose method of criticism is to try to sell high and buy low, in that order) become discouraged. It is near the top of the cycle, when the bears have turned to doubting their own senses, that the most fantastic offenses against conservative investing occur.

In 1951, the economist Ilse Mintz produced a study to show that the quality of foreign-government bonds issued in the United States had deteriorated in the 1920s. The evidence she offered was that bonds issued in the latter half of the decade suffered a higher rate of default than those issued earlier. Her conclusions subsequently became a source of scholarly contention. Thus, in 1959, Lawrence Fisher sought to justify the seeming gullibility of late-1920s investors by citing the steady economic growth of that decade and the growing marketability of the bonds themselves. More recently, Barry Eichengreen and Richard Portes have qualified Mintz's conclusions. But they have not refuted them and they have discovered that, in the case of sterling-denominated foreign-government bond issues, creditworthiness deteriorated as Mintz had described.

This abstruse debate is more relevant than it might appear. At bottom is the issue of the behavior of people—well dressed and well educated, most of them—in crowds. If they are no less rational than the calculating individual, there is really no issue at all. By inference, the leading, or even the sole, cause of recessions, depressions, and bear markets is the miscalculation of governments. It is a room-temperature world, this theory implies, and people will never exhibit an excess of optimism or pessimism. If Mintz is right, on the other hand, the diagnosis of business and financial crises becomes more interesting. Reading between her lines, one sees the germ of a theory of the credit cycle. It is the idea that bankers and investors in crowds are suggestible. What they will do, or will not do, is conditioned by circumstance as much as by any fixed calculus of risk and reward. Under the press of competition, investment bankers will cut corners. Eager to participate, investors will pay no attention. The result is the progressive relaxation of credit standards during a long expansion. Such a turn of events may or may not precipitate a business downturn. Even if it does not, however, the frail structures it has tended to create—overindebted corporations and shaky banks, for example—may deepen and prolong a slump. The evidence of the 1920s, no less than that of the 1980s, strongly suggests that Mintz was on to something.

The World Trusts

Certainly, the fantastic career of the swindler-financier Ivar Kreuger, culminating (from our point of view) in a big 1929 bond issue, is in harmony with her views. Kreuger, "the Match King," was a Swedish industrialist who lent to governments in exchange for monopolies on the sale of matches in their countries. His affairs were complex, cosmopolitan, and superficially brilliant. His American investment banker was the Boston firm of Lee, Higginson & Co., and his American auditor was the eminent Ernst & Ernst. His foreign bankers included N. M. Rothschild, Swiss Bank Corp., and Crédit Suisse. A little like Baker's, Kreuger's policy was to keep his own counsel (the Swede, of course, had compelling legal and business reasons for silence), but his public willingly indulged him in that. "International Match paid an absolutely regular 11 percent cash dividend," as John Train has written of one of Kreuger's U.S. subsidiaries. "The world was inclined to take the rest on faith."

It was Kreuger & Toll, the Match King's main corporate vehicle, that issued $50 million worth of 5 percent Secured Sinking Fund Gold

Debentures in March 1929. The sale, the largest corporate bond offering of the year up until that date, was heavily oversubscribed; *The
Wall Street Journal*'s bond writer could not withhold a reference to
Kreuger's "remarkable talents." Besides Lee, Higginson, the domestic
underwriters included National City Co., Dillon, Read & Co., and
Brown Brothers & Co., among others—in short, names connoting
probity and solvency. The bonds constituted no mere unsecured
claims, according to the prospectus, but amply collateralized ones.
Constituting the collateral were the bonds of major and minor governments, including those of France, Belgium, Yugoslavia, Latvia,
Ecuador, Poland, Greece, Romania, and Hungary. Anticipating the
1980s, the bankers stated that the collateral afforded the investor an
excess measure of protection. It was specified that the face value of
the pledged securities must, at all times, constitute 120 percent of the
face value of the outstanding Kreuger & Toll securities. But nothing
was said about market value, and substitutions could be made in the
collateral as long as the minimum ratio was maintained. Drastic substitutions were made almost instantly. Out went creditworthy French
and Belgian issues; in came Hungarian and Yugoslavian ones, issues
either then in default or on the brink of it. In truth, the latitude for
substitution was enormous, but the bondholders seemed not to mind
that. Nor did they object to the conspicuous absence from the prospectus of the signature of Kreuger's accountant, Ernst & Ernst. It
later came to light that the firm had refused to lend its name to a
balance sheet and income statement it was unable to verify.

Although the bonds were highly questionable, investors were not
in a doubting mood. Perhaps, by March 1929, they had been conditioned to believe. After all, prospectuses of numerous foreign-
government bond issues were shot through with factual error. Winkler
had called attention to them, but the bonds had sold nevertheless,
and the world was palpably growing richer. Nine months later, after
the Crash, *Time* magazine put the Match King on its cover and borrowed a quote he had bestowed on the publicist Isaac Marcosson a
few months before. "No market is sufficiently significant to be of
importance to us," said Kreuger. "The reason is that the whole world
is our field."

The deluge was preceded by optimistic investment reports on the
securities of Kreuger & Toll, now represented to be "undervalued"
by Lee, Higginson, and by belated doubts about Kreuger's solvency
on the part of his lenders. When, in March 1932, the Match King shot
himself to death—he had at last run out of borrowed money—*The New*

York Times's obituary reported that he was thought to be overextended. In the days before his death, Kreuger & Toll securities were marked down heavily on the New York Stock Exchange in active trading, constituting as much as a quarter of the total exchange volume. However, Marcosson confidently told the paper, "I feel confident, knowing Mr. Kreuger as I knew him, that his act was due to one thing, and one thing only—overwork."

The truth of his fakery, when it came to light in hastily ordered bankruptcy proceedings, caused a worldwide sensation. Although Kreuger was Swedish, blame was directed at his credulous Boston bankers. Gustav Cassel, the distinguished Swedish economist, wrote in the *Svenska Dagbladet*: "When such firms as Lee, Higginson & Company placed their names under Kreuger emissions, it was natural that we, in Sweden . . . , imagined that they had carefully examined the firm's position and that they exercised reliable and thorough supervision over its leadership. In this, we have been deceived." Relating this distressing tale, Winkler threw up his hands. "*Mundus vult decipi—ergo decipiatur*," he quoted: the world wants to be deceived—let it therefore be deceived. Of the financial world, the Romans might have added this note: It wants to be deceived in good times; prosperity makes it gullible.

Drainage-Ditch Finance

Caldwell & Co., of Nashville, Tennessee, made a great success in the boom and a flaming, instructive failure in the bust. Its rise and fall constitute a credit cycle in miniature, a domestic case study in the proposition that lenders and borrowers periodically suspend their judgment. Its motto was: "We Bank on the South," and it was, for a short time, the largest investment-banking firm that the South had ever seen. Its career anticipated the conglomerates of the 1960s and the junk-bond age of the 1980s. It owned or controlled banks, insurance companies, newspapers, textile mills, clothing manufacturers, building-products companies, a dairy, a laundry, a department-store chain, an oil company, a minor-league baseball franchise, an investment trust, and a municipal-bond brokerage firm. The municipal-bond firm was the first brick to be laid in the Caldwell & Co. house. Rogers Clarke Caldwell, the founder, was the son of a rich Nashville businessman. He enrolled at Vanderbilt University but quit his studies to join his father's insurance company. Specializing in tax-exempt bonds, he decided that Southern municipal issues (still stigmatized by the defaults of the carpetbag era) might be profitably traded and underwritten. In 1917, at the age of twenty-seven, he organized Caldwell & Co., and made one of the corporate bylaws read: "No officer or employee shall be retained in the service of the corporation whose expenditures seem to be profligate or to exceed his known income, or who is not sober and of good moral character."

The firm presently outgrew that policy, however, as it did its original municipal-bond business. In 1919, it founded a bank. In 1923, it branched out into first mortgage real-estate bonds, à la S. W. Straus & Co. In the same speculative vein, it did a large and disastrous business in drainage-ditch bonds, bringing some $4 million worth to market in sizes ranging from $7,000 up to several hundred thousand dollars. A Tennessee law of 1909 had provided for the creation of drainage districts. The districts dug the ditches and borrowed to pay for them. When, however, property owners stopped paying the high taxes necessary to support the debt service, the districts fell into arrears. Out of forty such issues underwritten by Caldwell & Co., forty defaulted, a perfect score.

Undaunted by this debacle, the firm undertook a much larger business in first mortgage real-estate bonds, which, as we have seen, were hot. Caldwell's issues were collateralized by liens on hotels, apartments, churches, hospitals, colleges, office buildings, parking garages, theaters, and lodges. In keeping with the drainage-ditch structure, each bore a high coupon (usually 6½ or 7 percent), but not every single one defaulted right away. In fact, real-estate bond defaults did not become costly until 1929, when they suddenly became overwhelming. By the mid-1930s, only one known Caldwell & Co. real-estate bond issuer, the Baptist General Convention of Texas, had *not* defaulted. Out of $20 million in Caldwell & Co. issues for which data were available, $19 million had fallen into arrears. No doubt, the Depression did the Caldwell underwriting record no good, but then neither did the Caldwell methods. John Berry McFerrin, the author of a splendid history of the firm, described the business difficulties of one of the firm's real-estate bond issuers:

The National Memphis Garage was located near one of the largest free parking areas in any city in the South. It set its prices, originally, higher than the general level in the city and attempted to attract customers by its uniformed attendants, its unique floor arrangement and officious but none too efficient service. The free parking area constituted too much competition for it and, although it has operated continuously, at no time has it earned enough to make the bonds on the building attractive even from a speculative standpoint.

From a credit point of view, the story of Caldwell & Co. was one of rising risk. Many of the speculative-grade bonds that the firm underwrote found their way into its own inventory. To help dispose of them, it acquired banks and insurance companies. It borrowed from the banks and sold bonds (its own unmarketable inventory) to the insurance companies. An important feature of the rapid Caldwell expansion was that it was financed by short-term deposits. As a condition of underwriting an issue of tax-exempt bonds for a Southern municipality, the firm would insist that the proceeds of the sale be deposited in it or with one of its banks. Trust agreements were drawn up. High-grade collateral would be pledged with a trustee in an amount sufficient to cover the deposits. Frequently, however, it was Caldwell & Co., or a Caldwell affiliate, that was named trustee. Then again, there developed a firm-wide shortage of eligible collateral—high-grade municipals, for instance—and a surplus of speculative-grade collateral. Quietly, Caldwell & Co. would substitute the latter for the former.

This systematic breach of faith helped the firm to grow and diversify. In 1926, it set up a corporate-finance department. As in the drainage-ditch and first mortgage real-estate businesses, the caliber of Caldwell's industrial clientele was mainly of speculative grade. Most probably, there were few non-speculative-grade issuers to be found in the South at that time. In any case, Caldwell's method in corporate finance was the familiar one. It obtained a sizable markup on the sale of its industrial clients' bonds (buying them at 90 cents on the dollar, selling them at 100 cents). It would direct its corporate clients, as it did its municipal ones, to deposit a large part of their unused cash at a Caldwell & Co. depository. These funds would help to finance the investment banker's increasingly far-flung operations.

Anticipating the "merchant banking" fashion of the 1980s, Caldwell & Co. acquired an ownership interest in many of its industrial clients. These ran the gamut of corporate enterprise, from the Cumberland Portland Cement Co. to Southern Department Stores to the Nashville Baseball Association. When, in 1927, the baseball team needed a new grandstand, Caldwell & Co. issued the bonds with which to build it to one of its very own Caldwell & Co. insurance companies.

The greater the prosperity, of course, the more valuable these equity investments—"bonus stocks," the firm called them—came to appear. Thus, the higher the value of the speculative-grade bonds in the Caldwell & Co. inventory. And, thus, the less culpable (in the firm's own eyes) the substitution of them for high-grade bonds in the trust accounts of unknowing municipalities must have seemed.

To a certain kind of economic determinist, the Depression was caused by an error of economic policy. Surely, however, prosperity must share some measure of the financial blame. The long expansion fostered strange lending practices and weak structures. In the 1980s, the widening socialization of risk in the banking business served to promote the extension of credit in the United States. But the career of Caldwell & Co. antedated deposit insurance; the creditors of the Caldwell banks had no claim on the U.S. Treasury, none except on the assets, judgment, and honor of Rogers Caldwell and the Caldwell companies. Why those banks resisted a run for as long as they did seems a question not of national policy but of crowd psychology. In the boom, people believed, whereas in the slump, they came to doubt. Their naïveté did not cause the downturn, but it allowed the creation of structures that began to fail even before the Depression began. Their collapse in 1930 must have contributed to the Depression's severity.

If anybody had personal experience with the corrosive powers of prosperity, it was Rogers Caldwell himself, and he began to sell the stock market short in 1927. But the campaign was premature, and the firm bore sizable losses. The stocks he picked to sell—American Can, American Telephone, Coca-Cola, General Motors, etc.—were the bull-market leaders, and they continued to rally. (In GM, at least, Caldwell had distinguished company. Bernard M. Baruch was also, independently, losing money on the short side of the automaker's stock.) "The short account was closed in June, 1929," McFerrin wrote—that is, only months before the Crash—"and, sad to relate, was not reopened."

The firm was increasingly short of cash. In the summer of 1929, its inventory of unsold stocks and bonds was burdensome. It labored to peg the falling price of stock in Shares-in-the-South, the investment trust it had brought to market in a gale of optimism in 1928. One of its affiliated banks, the Bank of Tennessee, suffered a growing deficiency in its legal cash reserve. The assets of Caldwell & Co. more and more consisted of unsalable or defaulted securities, interests in affiliated companies, and real estate. By the close of 1929, some $19.5 million, amounting to 55 percent of its total assets, was plainly and dangerously illiquid. As short-term deposits overwhelmingly comprised its liabilities, the firm was wide open to a run.

The Crash galvanized Rogers Caldwell. If the public was still complacent, he was not, and he turned for help to James B. Brown, president of BancoKentucky Corp., a holding company controlling the National Bank of Kentucky, Louisville. With that curious magnetic force that draws financial mountebanks to one another, Caldwell asked Brown to consider a merger of their two institutions. Each was on the brink of disaster, but neither man could admit the truth about his own affairs, or imagine the truth about the other's. In a masterful negotiating stroke, Caldwell got away with refusing Brown even a glimpse at the Caldwell & Co. financial statements before the deal was struck. (If the merger did not go through, Caldwell claimed, Brown would know too much, and the standing of Caldwell & Co. would be jeopardized.) For his part, Brown neglected to tell Caldwell about the grave condition of the National Bank of Kentucky. It was thus a marriage made in heaven. What Brown wanted from the merger was the help of Caldwell & Co.'s sales force in placing shares of stock in his company with the public; what Caldwell hoped to get from BancoKentucky Corp. was a loan. If Caldwell got the better of it, his advantage was short-lived. The combined assets of Caldwell's and Brown's businesses approached $600 million.

Still in extremis, Rogers Caldwell tried to arrange a last-ditch sale of the controlling interest in a Caldwell insurance company. The plan was dependent on financing, part of which was to be provided by St. Louis banks, part by Brown's flagship, the National Bank of Kentucky. "This plan was rumored in financial circles," McFerrin wrote, "and in St. Louis was mentioned to a national bank examiner who rather casually and tactlessly, perhaps, replied that the National Bank of Kentucky was in no condition to carry through such a deal for it had been practically insolvent for about five years." Now the public, docile in the boom, belatedly staged a run, only to find that there was hardly anything in the Caldwell banks to run for. When the Bank of Tennessee was closed on November 7, 1930, its deposits totaled $10 million. The actual cash in its till, however, was $32.55.

Caldwell & Co. itself failed on November 14, and a chain reaction of bankruptcy struck Tennessee, Arkansas, Kentucky, and North Carolina. The National Bank of Kentucky failed on November 16. By the end of that month, every Caldwell-affiliated bank but two had entered receivership. Most of the Caldwell-affiliated insurance companies entered bankruptcy before the Depression was over. The losses to depositors, policyholders, senior lenders, bondholders, and stockholders in the Caldwell enterprise were usually large and sometimes incredible. Banks recovered an average of 49 percent of what they had lent to the firm. However, the Third National Bank of Scranton, Pennsylvania, which had lent $185,000, salvaged only $202. Owing to its illegal substitution of low-grade for high-grade collateral, Caldwell's "secured" depositors fared worse than its bank creditors, recovering, on average, 26 percent of their claims. A $40,200 deposit of Weakley County, Tennessee, was secured by municipal bonds; that money was returned. Numerous other government depositors received little or nothing, their collateral consisting of real-estate mortgage bonds, industrial bonds, and other bull-market emissions of Caldwell & Co.

In studying the foreign-government bond market of the 1920s, Mintz found that the decay of credit quality was progressive. Caldwell & Co. exhibited a similar tendency, moving from municipal bonds (which, to be sure, included the essay in drainage-ditch finance) to real-estate mortgage bonds to "high-yield" corporates—in short, becoming more speculative as the country became more bullish. "Caldwell allowed his company to be carried along with the general trend

*An older Rogers Caldwell, years following his exploits at Caldwell & Co. (*NASHVILLE TENNESSEAN*)*

in investment banking toward the wholesale and disastrous relaxation of standards of safety and the underwriting of securities of the most speculative nature," McFerrin concluded. The last junk-bond deal to be underwritten by Caldwell & Co. was $1 million of 6 percent three-year notes of the Southern Department Stores, in 1930. The public bought almost none of them, but Caldwell & Co. and the Bank of Tennessee turned them to use as collateral for their own desperate borrowing. The loss on the notes—borne, in the end, by the creditors of Caldwell and the Bank of Tennessee—was almost complete.

A Road-Show Gold Standard

The call-loan market on the New York Stock Exchange—the post at which short-term loans, secured by stocks and bonds, were negotiated—was one of the financial institutions dearest to George F. Baker's heart. In the tumultuous days preceding the outbreak of war in July 1914, and the subsequent four-month suspension of trading, the First National Bank, alone among New York banks, continued to lend to brokers. And when the New York Stock Exchange reopened in December 1914, Baker's bank was the first to resume call lending. It was surely with some measure of annoyance, then, that Baker viewed the development of the call-loan market in the 1920s.

Before the Federal Reserve, long-term interest rates were steady, whereas short-term rates were variable (in later years, it has often been the other way around). Frequently, short rates were higher than long rates. In the case of call loans, secured by stocks and bonds and payable on demand, panics produced sky-high rates. In the heat of 1907, hard-up stockbrokers briefly paid 125 percent. The other side of the coin was slack times. Once in the ebb of 1908, call money fetched less than 1 percent.

With the coming of the Federal Reserve, it was expected that interest rates would lose their manic-depressive tendencies and excess funds would be put to constructive use in commerce or agriculture (as distinct from speculative use on Wall Street). In 1928, Andrew W. Mellon, Treasury Secretary and ex officio member of the Federal Reserve Board, declared that, thanks to the new central bank, there was no longer "any fear on the part of the banks or the business community that some sudden and temporary business crisis may develop and precipitate a financial panic such as visited the country in former years. . . . We are no longer the victims of the vagaries of business cycles. The Federal Reserve System is the antidote for money contraction and credit shortage."

Certainly, monetary contraction was not the top concern of the middle and late 1920s. Formerly, a government could try to prolong prosperity by lowering tax rates or juggling the tariff. With the coming of age of the postwar central bank, new horizons of governance were opened. If it seemed advisable to suppress a rise in interest rates, the Federal Reserve would suppress it. If a favored ally needed help to hold down *its* interest rates, that cooperation (if deemed desirable by the American authorities) was forthcoming. Thus, between 1922 and 1928, the Federal Reserve presided over a doubling in domestic bank credit and the great bull stock market.

This monetary intervention was largely accomplished through open-market operations. Here was a new financial development. In two major episodes—1924 and 1927—the Federal Reserve bought sizable quantities of government securities in the open market. So doing, it created new lending capacity in the commercial-banking system. Then, as now, central bankers had two principal policy-making levers at hand. One was the discount rate: the interest rate at which a commercial bank might borrow from the Federal Reserve banks. The other was open-market operations: buying or selling securities to influence the level of interest rates or the supply of lendable funds in the money market.

The discount rate had all the gold-standard tradition. A central bank was expected to lend without subsidy and against short-term, "self-liquidating" collateral. It was expected to lend freely in a crisis but at a rate that made a bank think twice about borrowing. What a central bank was not expected to do was to buy and sell government securities in the open market with an eye to achieving a hoped-for economic or political result, such as 4 percent growth in the gross national product or the reelection of the incumbent government. If the prevailing market interest rate were 3 percent, the Bank of England would not stoop to lend at 2¾ percent. It would lend at 3¼ percent or higher and typically against the collateral of commercial bills, or promissory notes. (Bankers of every stripe put great store in liquidity in prewar days. They preferred short maturities to long ones. The ideal short-term loan was one that would turn itself into cash in the normal course of business. It was a trade bill and absolutely not a mortgage.)

In the years 1880–1914, the international gold standard reached full flower, and no reader of the current financial headlines can study its workings without a sense of wonder. Nowadays, the balance sheet of the typical central bank is a study in circularity. The asset that "secures" the currency is the government's debt; but there is no connection, except in the most recondite law, between that asset and the corresponding liability. A Federal Reserve "note" is a promise to pay nothing. Under the gold standard, the asset that secured the currency was gold, and the gold and currency were interchangeable at a fixed rate. If the people became suspicious of their nation's money, they were free to exchange it for gold coins. Foreigners enjoyed the same privilege.

The consequence of a vote of no confidence was an outflow of gold. There was nothing political in this challenge to the financial integrity of the loser, and the certain response was also apolitical: interest rates were raised and the money supply was reduced. The result was that business activity was likely to weaken, securities prices to fall, and unemployment to rise. As the formerly suspect country mended its ways, however, gold began to return. Interest rates fell and business conditions brightened. Voters returned to work.

To the late-twentieth-century eye, one of the most remarkable aspects of the system was that the voters accepted it. Their belief was amply rewarded by results: low interest rates and stable prices were the hallmarks of the gold-standard experience—in England's case, over a hundred years long. Yet if one tries to imagine the institutions of 1914 superimposed on the politics of 1992, the picture will not quite come into focus. Central banks operated according to unwritten rules that governments, usually, did not attempt to override. One of these was never to obstruct an outflow of gold or to "sterilize" an inflow. To do so would be tantamount to icing a thermometer. To an extent that is almost impossible now for an American to credit, central banks based their policies not on the state of their domestic economies but on the gold value of their currencies.

Thus, open-market operations on the vast scale now routinely conducted were out of the question. Were market interest rates too high to suit a senior government official? The official could adjust his expectations to the facts of the money market. Very high interest rates would depress business activity, reduce employment, restrict lending, and—after sometimes painful adjustment—fall in on themselves. The last thing a governor of the Bank of England would expect to hear was instructions to bring them down. The bank did, in fact, conduct purchases and sales of government securities before the war, but its motive was frequently to earn a profit for itself (until 1946, this most illustrious central bank was owned by its stockholders, not the government). When it did try to influence the money market, it was usually to tighten it, but these transactions, in any case, were tiny.

They grew in the war. As honest writers took up propaganda work, the Bank of England inflated the British currency. For instance, it staged purchases of government bonds in the open market in the days leading up to public sales. The Federal Reserve System also picked up this trick—when the loan was closed, the Federal would deal its bonds back into the market. Worse things were done on the home front, of course, and the cost of the deception was not unbearably large. The significance of these wheel-greasing measures was that they marked the end of the prewar monetary order. They set the moral and financial tone for the successor systems of the 1920s and the even more makeshift monetary systems that followed the next world war.

"More" is the best brief description of the evolution of credit in the United States in the twentieth century. It also describes the evolution of the international monetary system. The integral feature of the gold standard of 1880–1914 was that a unit of money could be in only one place (on only one central-bank balance sheet) at one time. If country A ran a chronic payments deficit with respect to country B, A would lose gold to B. If A lost the confidence of its own citizens, the central bank of A would lose gold coins: the people would exchange them for the central bank's discredited paper money.

After the war, the system was financially and morally shattered. On the Continent, there was inflation and scandal. The Bank of France cooked its books, for example, covering up the fact that it had printed the money with which to finance its government's deficit and pay for its own real-estate construction. Germany dissolved into hyperinflation.

In the 1920s, offenses against the gold standard (the set of unwritten rules by which the banking world had functioned before the war) became the rule. For instance, central banks came to discriminate against gold coins. Nearly everywhere, even in France, no weight of gold smaller than a heavy bar was deemed eligible to be exchanged for paper money. Thus, under the pretext of economizing on gold, the monetary authorities disenfranchised the common man. In 1922, convening in Genoa, leading financial nations took steps to economize on gold even further, and with greater economic effect. They agreed to adopt the machinery of the gold-exchange standard.

The principal difference between the gold standard and the gold-exchange standard was one of rigor. Under the prewar system, gold moved freely in search of the highest available rate of return. Under the gold-exchange standard, its movement was officially stifled. In the old days, if Britain overissued sterling and if that sterling piled up in Paris, the French could be counted on to send it back and ask for gold in return. The process would continue until the British stopped producing excess credit. Under the gold-exchange standard, however, a new understanding developed. Central banks would not insist on gold in settling up accounts but would be content to hold foreign currency instead: a paper claim on the gold in a particular central bank. France, in a case that proved to be not hypothetical at all, retained excess sterling balances. Not having any use for these funds in Paris, it kept them on deposit in London. No pain was suffered, but, then again, no adjustment was made. Although Britain had run a deficit, it had lost no gold. It was able to resist the deflationary measures that, under the traditional gold standard, had been unavoidable for deficit countries. Procrastination now became an integral part of the international monetary system.*

The economic objection to the gold-exchange standard—that it postponed painful adjustments and encouraged excessive lending and borrowing—was exactly the quality that commended it to politicians and investors. It made possible a systematic overissue of credit, with the initial, happy result of rising prices. In the great expansion, central banks could pyramid their monetary reserves. Britain could keep its gold, and France its sterling, believing that the sterling was convertible into gold on demand.

Moreau Improves His Balance Sheet

Emile Moreau, governor of the Bank of France from 1926 to 1930, had his doubts about that. Moreau, a successful former governor of the Bank of Algeria, was a loyal son of his native Poitou. He hunted, worked his family estate, and looked every inch the French country-

---

* In one easy example, the economist Melchior Palyi showed how fundamentally the new ways differed from the old. Assume, he began, that Britain incurred a £100 million deficit with France. Under the classical gold standard, Britain would have had to ship £100 million worth of gold to France. Britain lost gold, France gained it; the joint monetary base of the two countries remained the same. Now, by substituting a debt certificate for gold, a part of the reserve assets of the two countries was doubled: £100 million gold remained in London and £100 million in foreign exchange was added to the French reserves. A deflationary pressure on London was avoided; the inflationary pressure in France increased; and the world as a whole experienced a corresponding increase in liquidity. The overall effect was inflationary.

man. He spoke little English, was not widely traveled, and was suspicious of clever people (especially of clever foreigners). "His relatives and friends who surround him, and to whom he is very faithful are, for the most part, solicitors, notaries, magistrates," wrote his monetary disciple, Jacques Rueff. Moreau had powerful shoulders, a tenacious mind, and an incorruptible character. He believed in the international gold standard, and he held nineteenth-century financial prejudices. When he was installed at the Bank of France in the spring of 1926, both the bank and the currency were at low ebb. Under Moreau, each recovered brilliantly. The bank regained its respect and the franc its purchasing power.

What Moreau actually did will now seem quaint. He restored the balance sheet of the Bank of France to shipshape gold-standard condition. This meant a purging of government loans—a clean break with the inflationary practice of financing state deficits—and an end to the accommodation of real-estate lending by French commercial banks. "[A] currency can be truly healthy only if it is actually backed by gold," the banker wrote in his diary. He instructed the director of the Le Havre branch of the bank: ". . . give broad acceptance to statutory paper which is strictly commercial, take agricultural paper in moderation [and] reject without mercy any real estate borrowing." In other words, lend against banking assets that might easily be turned into cash. Like the architects of the Federal Reserve System, Moreau believed that a central bank's balance sheet was the means to the end of a sound currency. The more liquid, or salable, the assets it held, the better the money it issued.

If he were a gold-standard purist, however, Moreau would not have countenanced some of his own policies. For instance, he would have had no part in neutralizing, or "sterilizing," inflows of gold into France. He would have allowed the inflationary consequences of such a monetary expansion to unfold naturally. He would have awaited the inevitable reaction to that inflation. One such reaction was a rise in the interest rates of the deficit countries that had lost gold to France. In time, the monetary flows would have to reverse themselves. "The only difference is now such automatic results must be obtained through conscious effort," wrote Moreau in 1927, echoing the received opinion of the day.

Moreau also told his diary, in the same year: "All this shows that theoretical arrangements, however refined and sophisticated, cannot replace the free play of natural laws." Thus, losing gold in 1927, Germany refused to raise its interest rates. Gaining gold, the United

States refused to let its interest rates fall (and its credit expand). In effect, the Federal Reserve stopped a gold-induced inflation before it could fairly get under way—a laudable policy, but one that short-circuited the gold-standard wiring. It preempted the chain of events whereby gold would, in time, be induced to return to the countries that had lost it. "If Strong let things develop naturally," Moreau reflected on the policies of the governor of the Federal Reserve Bank of New York, "gold flowing into the United States would raise prices there. The rise in American prices would attract European products and gold would return to Europe until equilibrium was restored. Instead of that, Strong seeks to prevent American prices from rising by withdrawing the imported gold from circulation. The result is that equilibrium is not achieved, Europe loses its gold and erects a credit structure on artificial foundations."

From time to time, Moreau's Anglo-Saxon colleagues would seem to get under his skin. He bristled at what he correctly interpreted to be their imperial designs on the money markets of Europe. Montagu Norman, governor of the Bank of England, was the Frenchman's polar opposite in style and substance. If Moreau was provincial, Norman was cosmopolitan. Whereas Moreau was short and squat, Norman was elongated. (To Moreau, Norman looked "like a painting by Van Dyck—tall, pointed goatee, great hat, like a courtier of the Stuarts.") Nevertheless, Moreau had the better balance sheet and the more elegant currency. The monetary reform undertaken by the Bank of France and the government of Raymond Poincaré, beginning in 1926, drew gold to France. It similarly attracted foreign currencies, conspicuously Norman's, the pound sterling.

It irritated Moreau to read in the English-language press (or to read in translation, for his English was weak) that in the postwar world no country except Britain and the United States should actually keep gold bullion. It was said that secondary powers, like France, should be satisfied to hold the bank notes of those two mighty financial nations, trusting to their gold and judgment. Moreau rejected this proposition—a principal tenet of the gold-exchange system—and he worried about Britain's capacity to redeem its notes on demand, in gold. His concern was well founded, for the British were daily becoming more overextended. Rejoining the gold standard in 1925, they had mistakenly insisted on redefining the pound at its old, prewar value, $4.8665. That error was the father of a long line of troubles: overpriced exports (because the pound was too high), a sluggish economy, and a chronic loss of money to more gainful employment overseas. Thus enfeebled, British industry needed bank credit and low interest rates, and these the Bank of England provided. It could hardly stop providing them now, Norman contended.

What was to be done? Before the war, a flight of funds to Paris would have created a similar movement of gold. An influx of gold to one country was, of course, the opposite side of the coin of the loss of gold by other countries. France's gain would have been the other countries' loss, and the losing countries would have responded in turn. They would have tightened credit and raised interest rates, thereby enticing money home again. However, Britain, taking stock of itself in the spring of 1927, decided that it was in no position to tighten. "To tell the truth," as Moreau described a meeting he had had with Montagu Norman that May, "the governor of the Bank of England believes that at present he could not do so without provoking a riot." It was, indeed, Norman's expressed belief that the Bank of France should lower *its* interest rates. Certainly, he was in no position to risk the social repercussions of a rise in British rates and, thus, of unemployment.

In a particularly trenchant diary entry in May 1927, Moreau reflected on what had happened. London had lost its long-standing monopoly as a center for European capital, he noted. It had been eclipsed, in part, by Paris. "Mr. Norman had not entertained the possibility of such a displacement," Moreau went on. "And as he has allowed the British central bank to commit itself excessively to the support of industry and commerce, he is now embarrassed and frightened. He has committed an error of management and he now feels its weight and dangerous consequences should we wish to oblige him to adhere strictly to the rule of the gold standard by converting our pounds to gold. . . . We have thus touched not only on the fragility of the British financial structure but also on the breakdown of the entire European economic system, where one can no longer play, as one could before the war, according to the normal monetary rules."

A couple of monetary generations later, in 1985, the United States prevailed on Japan to lower its interest rates. Japan at the time was a rising creditor nation, the United States a debtor (or, more severely, a falling creditor nation). Agreeing, Japan poured fuel on the fire of its own stock market and on equity markets around the world. So in 1927: in need of assistance, Britain turned to America, the United States then occupying the position filled by Japan in the 1980s.

In July 1927 on Long Island, four central bank chiefs met, at Norman's behest, to consider the state of the world. Besides the governor of the Bank of England, they included Benjamin Strong, governor of the Federal Reserve Bank of New York and the dominant figure in the Federal Reserve System; Hjalmar Schacht, governor of the German Reichsbank; and Charles Rist, deputy governor of the Bank of France, in place of Moreau.

Britain, as Moreau knew full well, wished to hold down its interest rates yet not relinquish its gold. It specifically wanted a commitment to easier money by the other central banks. Schacht and Rist held back, Schacht reportedly saying, "Don't give me a low rate. Give me a true rate, and then I shall know how to keep my house in order."

Strong, however, sided with Norman, and American interest rates quickly began to fall. On July 29, the Federal Reserve Bank of Kansas City, lamely citing the need to "help the farmer," became the first regional bank to cut its discount rate, to 3½ percent from 4 percent. The Federal Reserve Bank of Chicago, which was expected to follow suit, refused to do so until Washington ordered it to in September. (The management of the bank did not agree with Strong, and the *Chicago Tribune*, which demanded Strong's removal, did not agree that help for England should be at the top of the American monetary agenda.) Throughout the Federal Reserve System, purchases of U.S. Treasury securities were stepped up, another expansive thrust. At the central-bank governors' meeting early in July, Strong had made the excuse that the Treasury needed lower interest rates to facilitate its bond sales. He was also overheard to say that his policies would soon provide the stock market with "a little *coup de whiskey*." Light in the head, the market rose.

"Every Time Is Different"

Attention now turned to the liquor. Call loans were demand loans to brokerage firms secured by stocks and bonds. Also known as brokers' loans, they were the liquid banking asset most commonly available in the days before the advent of Treasury bills and so-called federal funds. The first comprehensive report on loans against such stock-exchange collateral was published in February 1926, and it showed some $3.5 billion outstanding. The market had expected a number on the order of $2.5 billion. At $3.5 billion, call loans constituted a little more than one-tenth of all loans outstanding at American banks (measured at the previous reporting date in June 1925). It was a strikingly large number. Was it therefore dangerous? A compelling case could be made that it wasn't. Since the war, American corporations had come to rely less on bank loans and more on the issuance of common stock. Increasingly, they had financed themselves in the securities markets. The *Literary Digest* quoted Moody's Investors Service: "Brokers' loans of $3,513,174,154 serve mainly to disclose the importance of the Wall Street market to the American people, and the large and fundamental way in which it contributes to the general prosperity. The petty questions whether these loans are larger than the public thinks they ought to be, and whether somebody is making profit enough to make somebody else envious, ought to be entirely forgotten in the larger truth that there is nothing which contributes so much to national prosperity as a great, free and responsive capital market."

By early 1929, however, the volume of brokers' loans—almost $6 billion and climbing fast—had begun to appear outsized. The number itself was not so troubling as the identity of the lenders and the expectations of the borrowers. The borrowers were willing to pay 6 percent or 8 percent to buy stocks that yielded considerably less than that. The lenders, increasingly, were corporations, not banks. Interest rates obtainable on Wall Street were higher than those available in banks. As for the risk of loss, it seemed to be manageable (as indeed it proved to be).*

By 1928, the Federal Reserve had reversed policy: now it pushed interest rates higher to discourage speculation in common stocks. The bull market pretended to take no notice of this change until March 1929, when call-money rates shot alarmingly to 20 percent. Was this what the central bank intended or what the country deserved? George F. Baker, for one, doubted it, and the First National Bank borrowed massively from the Federal to re-lend in the money market. It was Baker's personal monetary policy to bring the country easy money, and in particular to present it with a 6 percent call-loan rate.

Baker, as the chairman of Old Fort Sherman, had gradually come to identify the nation's interest with his bank's, and vice versa. He and Morgan had personally stilled the money market on many occasions, and Baker saw no reason why he (after the elder Morgan's death) should not engage in this constructive work alone. He knew full well that the Federal Reserve Bank of New York had a contrary policy. He

---

* S. W. Straus & Co. was one such source of speculative funds. It furnished millions of dollars in the call market in the late 1920s, money it had earmarked for nonspeculative purposes—that is, paying bondholders and putting up buildings. After the Crash, the SEC made hay over what by then, in the cold morning light of the Depression, appeared a very questionable practice indeed.

was also aware that the New York banking community was mainly on the Federal's side. But it was sufficient for him to believe that he was right.*

It was not sufficient for the governor of the New York Federal Reserve Bank, however. George L. Harrison, a former clerk to Justice Oliver Wendell Holmes who had succeeded Benjamin Strong in the most important post in the Federal Reserve System, was upset by the goings-on at Baker's bank. The First was far and away the largest borrower from the New York Fed—in April 1929, its indebtedness reached $52 million, twice as large as the amount loaned to the next-largest borrower in the district—and the Street was under the deepening impression that Baker was defying Harrison. Baker, at the age of eighty-nine, was having trouble getting around, and Harrison was happy to visit the First National Bank to try to reach an understanding. Baker and he met on April 23.

Harrison began with the innocuous observation that these were busy days for everyone. Laughingly, Baker said that he was surprised to hear that the Federal Reserve was ever busy. Harrison replied, evidently without laughing, that "some of our member banks kept us pretty busy." With that, the two got down to cases. At some length, Baker narrated the First's long history of service to the Treasury and remarked on the losses that its current government-bond investments had cost its stockholders. Harrison agreed that the bank had distinguished itself over many years. Still, he asked the question he had come to ask: Why was it borrowing so much? Baker replied that he was proud of the size of his debt to the Federal, that he meant to re-lend the money he borrowed on the call-loan market to bring down interest rates. He said that he had been doing this, in times of crisis or stringency, for the past forty years. As for his right to borrow what he needed, he insisted on it, and he cited a conversation he had had with Senator Nelson W. Aldrich, author of a landmark piece of monetary legislation antedating the Federal Reserve Act of 1913. To Baker, evidently, Aldrich was the first and last word on the subject.

Harrison replied, firmly, that the central bank was within its rights

---

* Baker was used to working on a big scale. Before the war, he had considered financing, single-handedly, the construction of a Hudson River bridge to connect New York and the New Jersey Palisades. The cost, regrettably, was prohibitive—$15 million for a suspension bridge—and Baker decided instead to endow other good works. Wistfully, however, he reflected on the pleasure it would have given him to imagine his children and grandchildren driving across the George F. Baker Bridge (rather than, say, the George Washington Bridge, the first such cross-Hudson span, which was finished in 1931). "I should rather like to have driven over it myself," he said.

to deny accommodation to any bank that had borrowed too much or too long. Baker replied that he should regret it very much if the First National Bank were cut off, but that the Federal Reserve might regret it too. If push came to shove, Baker threatened, he would dump big blocks of government bonds on the market, and who would want that to happen? Harrison evenly replied that he failed to see how such a course of action would help to bring lower interest rates to America.

Now Baker reverted to the role of elder statesman. He said he did not know how much longer he had to live but he wanted to make one last constructive campaign for easy money—he wanted it for the good of the country. But, Harrison parried, how would more lending suppress the rising speculative demand for funds, the cause of high call-money rates in the first place? Perhaps sensing that he was in the presence of a superior force, Baker fell back on the gentleman's code. He told Harrison that he would relent if his actions were embarrassing him "personally." Harrison, however, amicably refused any personal favor, and he made ready to leave. It was at one o'clock, Harrison wrote in his diary,

> when some gentleman, who I think was Mr. Baker's secretary, entered the room to say that he had a one o'clock engagement. Mr. Baker said that he was not interested in that and asked me to stay on to continue the discussion. Just then he asked this same gentleman what call money then was. He received the reply that shortly before it had advanced from 7½ to 8 percent and that $18,000,000 was wanted. Mr. Baker immediately turned to me more or less laughingly and asked me whether we had taken some $50,000,000 out of the market, saying that no one else in the circumstances could have advanced the call money from 7½ to 8 percent. I laughed and told him that it only demonstrated how futile it was for one bank to attempt to lower call money to 6 percent under present conditions. . . .
> Mr. Baker was very quiet for a few moments and then said that perhaps he was wrong and others were right, but that he still was not convinced; that he thought that he could and should ease money if possible to 6 percent. For a period of almost a minute he sat looking at me and then said, "If you were not here I would tell this man to put out an additional 10 million but, in the circumstances, knowing how you feel, I do not think I shall."

It was not Baker but Charles E. Mitchell, president of the National City Bank (he had succeeded James Stillman's son in 1921), who came to be identified with defiant opposition to Federal Reserve policy. In the brief money-market crisis of March 1929, a number of New York City banks undertook emergency lending operations. They did so with the tacit approval of Federal Reserve authorities, in New York and Washington. Mitchell, lacking Baker's legendary discretion, accompanied his action with an impolitic statement. "So far as this institution is concerned," he announced, "we feel that we have an obligation which is paramount to any Federal Reserve warning, or anything else, to avert, so far as lies in our power, any dangerous crisis in the money market." Those words were a little like Straus's loans: ill advised before the Crash and disastrous afterward. They would be recalled in the Depression and Mitchell would be pilloried, although he was, in fact, at the moment he lent, no more defiant a banker than Baker.

A surging volume in call loans may not have worried Baker, but it did disturb the press, lay and professional alike. In 1928, *The Wall Street Journal* wondered about a world in which industrial corporations could invest their surplus cash at 9 percent in the call-loan market yet earn just 4 or 4½ percent in their own lines of business. "Bootleg loans" was the name given to this nonbank business on Wall Street, and that was the title of a cautionary essay in the June 1929 *Atlantic Monthly*. "The most conservative bank in my town has a million dollars lent in Wall Street raising the prices of stocks which it advises its clients not to buy because they are too high," wrote Howard Douglas Dozier, thereby neatly identifying the chief financial paradox of the day.

But in financial markets, anxiety is sometimes misplaced. Worry over call loans might have been better directed at Straus bonds, Ivar Kreuger, Caldwell & Co., and the overwrought market in foreign-government debt. Thanks to the deft and unsung work of Wall Street's margin clerks, the call-loan market weathered the Crash. Benjamin Anderson, longtime economist at Chase National Bank, reminisced about a visit he paid to Chase's margin department one evening after an especially hard day. "The head of the department said that all such [margin] calls had been met except two or three," wrote the economist, "and that he was sure that additional collateral in those cases would come during the evening. Then he broke into a spontaneous panegyric on the immense fabric of good faith that held in Wall Street."

Baker watched the gathering clouds with perfect equanimity. In the 1920s, he was as full of honors as he was of years and wealth. In 1924,

"Old Fort Sherman," head-quarters of the First National Bank of New York, as seen from Trinity Church in August 1929, just before the deluge (GEORGE F. BAKER TRUST)

he consented to give $5 million to build the Harvard Business School if he could be allowed to build it alone. Harvard agreed, readily, and in 1926 it made him an honorary Doctor of Laws. ("It may not be the right kind of pride," Baker had said in explaining his desire to endow the school himself, "but I should like to feel that my descendants could point to the Harvard Graduate School of Business, the first of them, and know that I had done it.") In June 1927, the new buildings were dedicated, the library named after Baker himself, the adminis-tration building after his friend Morgan, and the others after various Treasury secretaries that the banker had admired or had been pleased to help with the public finances.

If the palpable excesses of the credit markets registered on Baker, he did not show it or let it color his view of the future. At the age of eighty-nine, he had never been more bullish, and he lost patience easily with those who doubted. The stock market (although not, in general, the New York City banking fraternity) shared his optimism.

The First Security Co., the bank's investment arm, became an object of wonderment. Throughout the 1920s, it had increased its stock-market investments, borrowing from the bank to finance them. As no details of these transactions were disclosed, the market was allowed to use its imagination. At the peak, it valued the bank and its security affiliate at $8,600 a share, more than twice the $4,000 book value, or stated net worth.

In the early 1920s, Baker's physician, George David Stewart, consulted with Baker about his personal finances. The doctor's savings included $50,000 in bonds. Under Baker's direction, these were deposited in the bank as security against a loan; common stocks were purchased with the proceeds. As the bull market ran and the doctor's balance grew, additional stocks were purchased. By 1929, the equity in the account totaled $700,000. Now the physician wanted out, but Baker wouldn't hear of it.* All his long life, reversals had been temporary, not protracted. Bear markets had spelled opportunity, not final loss. Others importuned Baker, but to no avail. Emerging from one contentious meeting with his father about the stock market, George F. Baker, Jr., was in tears.

Harry Sturgis, another officer of the bank, decided that one of the public-utility holding-company stocks in the First Security Co.'s portfolio was fantastically overvalued. "He consulted the Bonbright & Company partners who had originally issued the stock," Baker's biographer relates. "They confirmed his judgment and told him that they had sold every share they owned. He accordingly felt justified in selling that stock out of the Security Company inventory. To his amazement, Mr. Baker questioned the sale, and after Sturgis had explained his reasons—in his mind, compelling—Mr. Baker directed him to buy the stock back."

There seems to have been no question that Baker was perfectly lucid; he happened to be very bullish. His son, however, seeing that the "entire Baker family was sitting on a huge margin account" (again to quote Logan), sent Frank Rysavy, the old man's personal secretary, companion, and valet, on one last appeal. Baker heard him out but said of the men who doubted, "They are afraid, but they don't understand. As long as Charlie Mitchell and Al Wiggin [head of the Chase National Bank] are on the job, nothing is going to happen. Don't worry."

After the collapse, Baker said two things, one of them touching and

---

* Baker made it up to him in the same year, endowing Dr. Stewart's surgery department at the New York University Medical School with $1 million.

one of them wise. Once, forgetting the magnitude of things, he addressed Rysavy: "Frank, if I were a younger man, I'd take $10,000,000, go in there and turn this thing around." On another occasion, Rysavy and Baker were going over the accounts of the bank and the security affiliate. "Mr. Baker," ventured the secretary, "wouldn't it have been wonderful if you had sold out in 1929? With cash, you could now buy back twice as much." If Baker felt a murderous impulse, he suppressed it. "Frank," he replied, "if I had started selling things, I would have lost my position years ago. You see, you never know when you've reached the top." "But, Mr. Baker," Rysavy countered, "you know more about these swings than anybody else." "No, Frank, you can't know," said Baker, "because *every time is different.*"

7

The Welfare State of Credit

After the Crash, predictably enough, the focus of concern shifted from too much lending to too little. In the pages of *Fortune* magazine, only three years—1930 to 1933—separated the lionization of Simon W. Straus (bold entrepreneur) and the demonization of the officers of the failed Bank of United States (financial villains). In the same three years, the institutions of American credit underwent a profound overhaul. The nineteenth-century gold standard was abandoned, and individuals—depositors and bank stockholders—were increasingly relieved of the costs of bank failures. The government, which for generations had been looking over bankers' shoulders, now undertook to insure their deposits. Inveighing with bankers to be braver, it barred them from certain traditional lines of business—such as securities underwriting—but invited them to enter certain nontraditional ones —such as real-estate lending. When these measures failed to produce results, the government itself entered the lending business.

If there had been a pump of credit it might have been primed through legislation, but the process of lending and borrowing (then as now) was human, not hydraulic. Banks and corporations that had thronged the call-loan market in 1929 were absent from it. People who had borrowed to buy stocks at high prices now refused to buy them at low prices. In a panic in late 1931 and early 1932, Liberty bonds, Straus bonds, railroad-mortgage bonds, foreign-government bonds, and drainage-ditch bonds were all indiscriminately thrown on the market for sale. The crisis passed, as every previous crisis had passed, but there was no immediate recovery of credit. Lenders had lost their courage and nothing that the government did or said could seem to restore it.

On the sixty-ninth day of the Hundred Days of Franklin D. Roosevelt, May 12, 1933, the editors of the *American Banker* made their readers a proposition. Plainly, the new administration was determined to inflate the currency, the editors observed. Just as plainly, the demand for loans was almost nonexistent. What, then, was a bank to do with its depositors' money? Diffidently, the editors suggested an investment in second-grade corporate bonds, issues falling somewhere between blue chip and speculative grade on the credit-quality spectrum (that is, those rated Baa by Moody's Investors Service). Shunned by wary investors in the Depression, they would almost certainly recover following the inevitable business upturn. They had, indeed, already begun a major rally that would carry well into the next decade. At the time, the average bank lending rate was only 4½ percent. Second-tier bonds yielded 7¾ percent. In June 1932, at the bond market's low ebb, they had yielded 11½ percent, an extraordinary premium to the 3¾ percent yield available on governments. "Frankly," the editors wrote, "we see no reason why, with the intentions of the Federal administration so plainly advertised as 'inflation or bust,' a banker should not take on some of the bond issues which are adequately secured, and where indications point [to] an improved credit position as inflation develops. Such bonds, for instance, would appear to include issues like U.S. Rubber 5s of 1947, Western Union 5s of 1951, and Armour 5½s of 1943. Are we wrong? We invite readers to send in letters which will express their opinions on this question of investments."

Summing up, they asked, "[W]ould it be wise to speculate a little now consciously in the investment account with which bankers were speculating so unconsciously and unwisely in 1929?"

It would not be wise, the readers responded. It would be daft. By two to one, they rejected the *American Banker*'s suggestion. Seventy-one percent replied that a bank should buy high-grade bond issues only and have nothing to do with lower-rated ones. "There were numerous expressions of horror that we should even suggest such a thought," the editors reported. "No mid-Victorian lady could have been more shocked at the antics of a post-war flapper than some of the bankers now seem at the thought of buying low-priced industrial bonds on the theory that the President of the United States has practically said that he is going to restore 1926 commodity price levels. . . . The questionnaire showed clearly that the last four years has strengthened the real basis of conservative banking thought." Such is the way of crowds. In the same month that the *American Banker* disclosed that most of its readers would have nothing to do with credit risk, President Roosevelt signed the Banking Act of 1933, creating the Federal Deposit Insurance Corporation. Thus, the credit welfare state grew. The banking crisis and the Depression were over; the nation was embarked on a new expansion and the stock market on a new upswing. At a moment when risk had been largely wrung out of both the banking system and the national economy, the banking profession chose to dwell on the potential for loss.

Bank of United States

The timidity of the 1930s is as relevant to our story as the boldness of the 1920s. Before the Depression, the stock market assigned lofty valuations to bank stocks. In the slump, the same stocks went begging. So low were interest rates that it became difficult to operate a bank branch network profitably in New York City. Thus, in the 1930s, the Chase National Bank literally gave away five of its branches because it could not generate enough business to pay their overhead. (Chase was in fact one of the bolder lenders in New York in the Depression, but it was nevertheless cautious by the free and easy standards of the 1980s.) Responding to government complaints that the banks were withholding credit, it announced, in 1933, that it had invited a certain class of depositor to apply for a loan—anybody with $25,000 or more in the bank. This was the very class of person who didn't happen to need one, of course. The recipient of Chase's surplus branches, Manufacturers Trust Company, played a supporting role in one of the great financial dramas in the run-up to the Depression. In 1930, it was almost merged with the Bank of United States.

The omission of the definite article where it would naturally seem to fall—just preceding "United States"—was a concession by the founder to the objections of the New York State banking regulators. As the name was proposed, the state decided, unsophisticated depositors might confuse its credit with that of the federal government. Thus, it was the Bank of United States that opened for business, at the corner of Delancey and Orchard streets, on July 1, 1913.

The founder, Joseph S. Marcus, was born in Russia, kept store in East Prussia, and immigrated to the United States. Landing in the port of New York, he became a garment worker and later a clothing manufacturer. In 1906, now in his mid-forties, Marcus founded the Public Bank on Delancey Street. His bank and he weathered the Panic of 1907 and the simultaneous collapse of the East Side real-estate market. His reputation grew.

To his Yiddish-speaking customers, Marcus was a prudent steward of deposits. To his associates, he was a stick-in-the-mud. As a lender, one of his close friends later testified, the founder was "not fit, too careful and too much afraid." Regrettably, these traits—perfectly suited to the coming slump—were not passed along to his bright son Bernard, who succeeded to the presidency of the bank, at the age of thirty-seven, upon his father's death in 1927.

It was not as if the bank had stagnated under the elder Marcus. In 1923, at the end of its first ten years, its assets totaled $46 million; they had surged tenfold over the preceding five years. The bank had a main office and three branches. It was profitable and unquestionably solvent.

In the bull market of 1927, however, these seemed modest achievements. At least, Bernard K. Marcus and his deputy, Saul Singer, immediately set out to improve upon them. In August 1927, one month after the founder's death, the new generation created a subsidiary to engage in the buying and selling of securities. To give some sense of the supercharged speculative atmosphere of the time, the new common stock of the City Financial Corporation, as the subsidiary was called, was oversubscribed by 14½ times. Next, Marcus and Singer announced the formation of a syndicate to speculate in the shares of City Financial under their personal direction. Another subsidiary corporation, Bankus Corporation, was formed to pursue lines of business that the bank itself, under the New York State banking laws, could not engage in. Acquisitions followed: the Central Mercantile Bank in 1928; the Colonial Bank, the Bank of the Rockaways, and the Municipal Bank & Trust Company in 1929. So well regarded were Marcus and Singer, and so apparently slack were financial practices at that particular time, that the directors of the Municipal Bank & Trust, one of the leading banks in Brooklyn, made no independent investigation of Bank of United States before agreeing to merge with it. (Shades of the merger of BancoKentucky and Caldwell & Co.!)

In May 1929, after completion of all the mergers, Bank of United States was the prototype of the modern financial services company. Under its corporate ownership were three safe-deposit companies, numerous real-estate subsidiaries, an insurance company, a securities subsidiary, and a bank with fifty-seven branches throughout Manhattan, Brooklyn, the Bronx, and Queens, serving 440,000 depositors. Deposits totaled $220 million; assets—loans and securities—footed up to $315 million.

So fast was the expansion and so complete the control of Marcus and Singer that the directors of Bank of United States were reduced to the role of spectators and well-wishers. The board, which numbered more than thirty, sat around a long table in a room overlooking Fifth Avenue. It was hard to hear when the windows were open and the minutes of the latest executive-committee meeting were being read aloud at the customary unintelligible rate of 350 or 400 words per minute. It would have been hard for some of the directors to understand, even at a more measured gait of speech, because they did not understand the words and numbers (even when Marcus and Singer shared all the relevant numbers, which they frequently did not). One such inexperienced member, John F. Gilchrist, a former chairman of the New York City Transit Commission and president of the New York State Tax Commission, contributed some blunt testimony during the subsequent inquest.

"Mr. Gilchrist," the investigating attorney addressed him, "I think you know that I do not want to be insulting or anything of that sort, but would it be fair to say that you knew practically nothing about the bank?"

"Personally?"

"Yes."

"Yes."

Under oath, the insiders acknowledged the violation of a number of banking canons. Directors borrowed as they chose, and for whatever reasons they pleased, subject only to the approval of Marcus and Singer, which was predictably forthcoming. According to the historian of the bank, M. R. Werner: "These loans passed through the board with no discussion, the director mentioning how much he wanted for the year, and the board approving, for most of the men had loans themselves and were therefore in no position to disapprove those of their fellow directors." For another thing, some of the techniques the officers employed to sell the bank's own securities to a credulous public were not improved upon even by Charles Keating, the notorious savings and loan figure of the 1980s. Furthermore, the bank lent sizable sums to its own affiliates, a clear conflict of interest; in 1929, such loans amounted to 24 percent of the bank's capital and reserves. No doubt, Bank of United States was not alone in these abuses. Where it did stand apart from the banking mainstream was in real-estate finance. This it embraced wholeheartedly.

As we have seen, real-estate lending, never mind real-estate investment, was forbidden in the national banking legislation. New York State banking rules (the rules that applied to Marcus and Singer) were similarly restrictive in the matter of investment. They held that, if a bank did happen to come into the ownership of a piece of property, it must dispose of it within a reasonable period of time: five years was the limit. These rules, in spirit if not in letter, the Bank of United States systematically violated. To finance new Manhattan properties (and, in some cases, to take equity interests in them), it created a score of real-estate subsidiaries. Among the real-estate talent collected by the bank to manage its affairs was the builder Irwin S. Chanin (of Chanin Building fame). "It seemed to be the ambition, among others, of Marcus and Singer," wrote Werner,

> to change the face of Central Park West in New York City. On a plot of ground of about 40,000 square feet between Eighty-first and Eighty-second Streets on Central Park West, they financed a twenty-story apartment house, the Beresford, with 172 elegant, spacious apartments, which were to be rented at prices which were possible during the boom period, but which it was found impossible to get after the stock market crash of October, 1929, when the building was completed, at a cost of about $5,000,000. The City Financial Corporation financed another large apartment-house project, the San Remo Towers, at Central Park West between Seventy-fourth and Seventy-fifth Streets.

To Werner, both of these projects were "costly failures," a judgment colored by the unprosperous year in which it was written: 1933. Unlike the traditional, transitory commercial-bank collateral (that is, 90-day bills of exchange), Marcus and Singer's collateral was majestic and permanent. Architects praise it today, but it was, at the time, illiquid, and when the depositors wanted their money back, it proved unsalable.

Bank examiners, fresh from an inspection of the Bank of United States, in 1930 advised the New York State Superintendent of Banks that Marcus and Singer had overextended themselves. "Your examiners are quite certain that the funds tied up in notes receivable and capital stock of real estate subsidiaries would not be satisfactory to use in payment of liabilities to others," they wrote. They went on:

> It is admitted that if the real estate subsidiaries had been owned by outside interests and presented similar financial structures, the bank would not have advanced them a penny. It is simply another instance of the age-old fact that if people who are directly involved in outside ventures, they always over-expand because

Built with a loan from the Bank of United States: the majestic San Remo apartments, Central Park West between Seventy-fourth and Seventy-fifth streets, New York (NEW YORK PUBLIC LIBRARY)

it is so easy for them to obtain funds from their bank and the stability of the bank becomes jeopardized unless checked in time by supervising authorities.

The bank's real-estate ventures were drawn up in the boom, the examiners noted. But the boom was over, and the assumptions on which the depositors' money had been lent and invested were now dangerously outdated. "It is quite evident that these companies depend on the future for their market," they concluded, "and that the ventures are based exclusively on optimism instead of good business policies and sound judgment"—a comment that might have been written with equal force about banking practices in Florida in the 1920s and in Texas in the 1980s.

Like Rogers Caldwell, Marcus and Singer understood something of the gravity of their own predicament, and in the summer of 1929 they looked for a merger partner. The bank was not yet an outcast. Chase and National City Bank had lent it money to pursue its acquisitions, and J. & W. Seligman & Co. was receptive when Marcus and Singer, that August, proposed that the two institutions join forces. Seligman was receptive only up until the point when it began to delve into the condition of the Bank of United States, however. In late September, it abruptly broke off negotiations.

Marcus and Singer continued to look for help. Regulators, both state and federal, encouraged them, as the Depression was fast depleting the bank's net worth. In June 1930, examiners descended; their report, released in September, documented the obliteration of the capital of the bank's subsidiaries and the impairment of the capital of the bank itself. Marcus, as was his custom, withheld the report from the directors and caused an overoptimistic balance sheet to be disseminated to the public.

In the fall of 1930, the answer to the collective prayers of the officers and regulators appeared in the form of a four-bank merger. The Bank of United States would be combined with Manufacturers Trust, the International Trust Co., and—in a fine generational irony—the Public National Bank & Trust Co., the very same Public Bank the elder Marcus had founded in 1906. Marcus and Singer would take no part in the management of the new $1 billion institution, which shaped up as the fourth-largest in the city and the fifth-largest in the nation. Indeed, every prospective merger partner had insisted on their ouster. In a sign that the combination had won the blessing of the New York banking establishment, J. Herbert Case, chairman of the board of the Federal Reserve Bank of New York, was designated to be its new chairman. The $1 billion bank would apply for membership in the New York Clearing House Association, the establishment's self-regulatory body; clearly, everything was taken care of. "$1,000,000,000 Union of Banks Completed," *The New York Times* reported, prematurely, on November 25.

But snags developed. The negotiating banks were unable to decide on the apportionment of interest in the new institution. On December 2, Jackson E. Reynolds, president of both the First National Bank of New York (Baker still occupied the office of chairman) and the New York Clearing House Association, visited the White House to discuss, among other things, the difficulties of the Bank of United States. President Hoover said he doubted that there was really much trouble.

"What makes you so yellow, Jack?" the President asked Reynolds.

"You have known me for years, you know I have always been yellow," Reynolds amiably replied. "What's that got to do with it? We're talking about facts."

"Your attitude, in your position up there, is a fact all right, and you are unduly apprehensive."

"I'm glad you feel that way," said Reynolds, "because you are going to have something bust right in your face in a few days, and it will just smear you with garbage. And that's the Bank of the [sic] United States."

The denouement, although not earthy, was unhappy. Merger talks did, in fact, break down. As word of the impasse leaked out, depositors began a run on the bank's branches. On the evening of December 10, a summit conference was convened at the Federal Reserve Bank of New York. Top bank presidents and bank regulators met to decide on a course of action. Reynolds was there, as were Albert Wiggin, chairman of Chase National, and Charles E. Mitchell, chairman of National City, and others of comparable station. It was put to the bankers that the institutions of the New York Clearing House Association should rescue the Bank of United States by assuming control of its assets and liabilities. The New York State Superintendent of Banks, Joseph A. Broderick, after being made to wait for a chance to make his case, said that he considered the bank solvent as a going concern. He said that, if the bank was closed, it would set off a city-wide panic. Reynolds, speaking for the private sector, objected that "a great many of the assets" were questionable and that there was no telling what value they might realize in a liquidation. He said that the effect of the failure would be merely local. The Clearing House institutions would lend the hapless depositors 50 percent of the value of their net balances at an interest rate of 5 percent, pending the winding up of affairs. They would do no more.

The announcement next day of the failure of the bank—the largest such suspension in American history up until that time—would have constituted the starting pistol for a run, but as the bank was closed by order of the state, there was nothing to run on. Long queues of depositors in Manhattan, the Bronx, and Brooklyn heard the police say over and over again, inaccurately, "Everything is all right. Don't worry." In a journalistic tableau of the unfolding Depression, the Bank of United States shared the front page of the *New York Evening Post* with the human-interest news that the unemployed apple vendors on city streets had begun to sell tangerines. "Their sale at two for a nickel has met with enthusiasm," it was reported.

It came to light too that the bank and its securities affiliate, Bankus Corporation, were under investigation by the stock-fraud bureau of the attorney general's office. A number of depositors had complained that the bank had induced them to invest in the bank's securities on the false promise that, if the price should fall, the bank would make them whole. When the price did fall, the bank denied that any such promise had been made, or should have been made. In time, Marcus and Singer were indicted on charges of fraudulent banking practices, tried, found guilty, and sent to prison. Singer, a high liver, was obliged to let go his apartment at the Biltmore and his twenty-five-room country house on Long Island and to discharge his two chauffeurs and three gardeners. They were both the object of anti-Semitic digs in Werner's book, Marcus being described as "the Napoleon of New York's Jewry, with Saul Singer as his Marshal Ney." Reynolds, years later recalling his role in the failure of the bank, characterized Marcus's associates as "men of perhaps pawnbroking capacity, but not banking capacity."

This much, at least, can be said for the insiders. Some of them earnestly lost their own money too. Until the bitter end, Marcus and Singer continued to buy stock, or "units," in the combined bank and Bankus Corporation. (In June 1930, Marcus made his wife a birthday present of 10,000 units, on which she subsequently was assessed to

*Depositors of the Delancey Street branch of the Bank of United States stage a run, December 1930 (*BETTMANN ARCHIVE*)*

the tune of $250,000; the "double liability" law, which held bank stockholders financially responsible for the failure of their own institutions, was still on the books.) "I never sold any of the stock that I have had," the director Irwin Chanin later testified, "and the fact of the matter is that I had so much faith and confidence in the institution that on Wednesday night, the night before the closing of the bank, I was present at that famous meeting, and when I went out to dinner I called up the office and I spoke to my brother and he told me about the run and he said, 'What shall we do with the cash?' We were depositing cash from our hotels' and theaters' receipts. I said, 'Go ahead and deposit it,' and we deposited $20,000 in cash on that very night, and I could never believe that a thing like this would ever happen."

No doubt this was small consolation to the public depositors, but the crisis feared by Broderick and others did not immediately materialize. Manufacturers Trust, one of the potential participants in the hoped-for four-bank merger with the Bank of United States, repelled a small run (it was hurriedly admitted to the protective company of the New York Clearing House Association), but the solvency of the great New York banks remained unquestioned.

As for the Bank of United States, the most notorious bank in New York City and the biggest failure to date, it ultimately returned 83.3 cents on every depositor's dollar, four-fifths of that within two years of the bank's closing. It managed to return that respectable sum on the sale of assets at Depression values (and also on the assessment of stockholders who, in the Depression, were not overloaded with spare funds with which to meet the call). Clearly, its officers lacked judgment as well as honesty. The bank's published financial statements, if the examiners were right, were probably untrustworthy. However, there were almost certainly worse banks in the United States in the 1930s; there were many more worse banks in the 1980s. As Marcus and Singer were Jewish, whereas the Clearing House Association's leadership was not, the establishment's motives have been questioned down to this day. One piece of evidence suggesting prejudicial motives is the testimony of the State Superintendent of Banks. Joseph Broderick, for one, was not convinced, as the big New York banks were, that real estate was an intrinsically unsuitable class of banking collateral. "I told them I thought it was because none of the other banks had ever been interested in this field," the superintendent testified, "and therefore knew nothing about it." (Broderick himself was tried twice for alleged neglect in not closing the Bank of United States before he did. He was acquitted at his second trial, in 1932; his first ended in a mistrial.) What role did anti-Semitism play in the decline and fall of the Bank of United States? Real estate happened to attract Jewish businessmen in New York; the New York Clearing House Association was mainly run by non-Jews. But the anti-real-estate tradition in commercial banking was of long standing. Objectively, the Bank of United States had overreached. Worse, it had overreached in real estate on the eve of a depression, and it had acquired a well-founded reputation for false dealing. Perhaps a real-estate-freighted bank run by dishonest Gentiles would have won the sympathy of the banking establishment. But there were sound business reasons for Jackson Reynolds to decide as he did, and the Bank of United States became one of the Depression's first major financial casualties.

Things Come Unstuck

Jackson Eli Reynolds, a Columbia University law professor turned successful corporation lawyer, had been recruited to the First National Bank in 1917 by George F. Baker himself. The proposal had come out of the blue, and Reynolds, hearing it from the mouth of the most successful banker on Wall Street, then a venerable seventy-seven, had responded to it with a spontaneous burst of laughter.

"Have I said something funny?" Baker asked him.

"It sounds so to me," said Reynolds, "as I am expecting a telephone call any moment from Paderewski asking me to play a piano duet with him."

"Banking isn't quite as hard as piano playing," Baker assured him.

It was certainly easier in the 1920s. Reynolds was elected president of the First National Bank in 1922, at the age of forty-nine, and served as president of First Security Co., Baker's stock-and-bond affiliate, as well. So formidable was his reputation that, in September 1929, just before the Crash, he sailed to Baden-Baden, Germany, to chair the organizing committee of the Bank for International Settlements. The BIS, a central bankers' bank, was formed to implement the plan devised by Owen D. Young to solve the German reparations problem. When the United States government declined to participate in the new organization, the First National Bank assumed voting control of the United States portion of the stock.

Reynolds was one of the few men who were not struck dumb by Baker's wealth and reputation. He loved to joke with his mentor and to poke fun at his eccentricities. ("He always wrote memoranda on slit-up used envelopes," Reynolds reminisced. "If a clerk would bring him a statement on a sheet of paper eight by six inches and the memorandum covered only four of the eight inches, he'd send for that man and give him thunder about wasting that paper.") Neither was he overawed by Baker's pet philanthropy, the Harvard Business School. When Robert G. Fuller, Class of 1925, came to the bank to be interviewed for a job in the spring of his graduating year, he underwent the trial of a meeting with Reynolds. Asked what kind of degree the Baker-endowed institution conferred on its graduates, Fuller replied (with some chagrin, as the phrase struck him as a little pretentious), "Master of business administration." Reynolds's voice dripped with sarcasm. "We certainly need one of those around here," he said.*

But not even Reynolds could jolly Baker out of his optimism. The Crash and its aftershocks at first seemed to do the bank no real damage. In only one case was a broker's loan called, and no losses resulted on that loan or any other loan of its kind. The First was no real-estate lender, and its depositors were mainly correspondent banks and blue-chip corporations. As the stock market continued to fall, however, losses at the First Security Co. mounted. The affiliate, as always, was a heavy borrower from the bank. The collateral behind the loans was common stocks, and the prices of stocks were falling.

In truth, the financial world was coming undone. In June 1930 (as Marcus prepared to make his wife a costly present of his own bank stock), President Hoover signed the Smoot-Hawley Tariff Bill, creating the highest import duties in American history and speeding the breakdown of international trade. In May 1931, six months after the closing of the Bank of United States, the largest private Austrian bank, Credit Anstalt, collapsed. Financial crisis spread—to Austria itself, then Germany. In gold-standard times, we should bear in mind, countries, no less than banks, were subject to runs by the holders of their paper money. "With the collapse in Austria and in Germany," Benjamin Anderson, the Chase National Bank's economist, wrote, "there came a disposition to question the credit of other countries. Men and institutions outside England, who had an excess of pound sterling on their hands, readily grew worried. Was sterling as good as gold? They undertook to find out."

---

* Fuller, who made a great success at the bank, suffered keenly at first from low pay and lack of stimulation. The First's idea of a training program was to make the young man a messenger. When he married, in 1927, his wife took a job at Lord & Taylor, the department-store company, to help make ends meet.

They found it was not. As we have noted, the 1920s gold standard was a pale copy of the pre-World War I original. When, in the summer of 1930, gold left England for safer and more profitable shores, the government did not try to recapture it by the traditional means of raising interest rates. Instead, it borrowed more gold from the United States and France and bought government securities in the London money market—the last measure an attempt to push down interest rates. In prewar times, no country left the gold standard without leaving what was then believed to be the civilized world. (To have done so in 1894, Grover Cleveland judged, would have been a "national calamity" and "disgrace.") In a shocking departure from accepted good form, the British government and the Bank of England capitulated peaceably. On the day of the announcement that England would refuse to exchange sterling for gold bullion, in 1931, the lending rate of the Bank of England was a phlegmatic 4½ percent. In a crisis of similar gravity in 1913, the rate would certainly have climbed into the double digits.

Old Fort Sherman Falls

On May 2, 1931, following a brief illness, George F. Baker died of pneumonia. He was ninety-one and had only recently attended a directors' meeting of U.S. Steel Corp. ("Baker luck to the end," some of his friends said, "he died at the bottom, and taxes will greatly be reduced.") Baker did not live to see England abandon the gold standard, but he had seen many discouraging things, and his confidence in the future remained unbroken; as well it might be, considering his achievements as well as his net worth, even before adjusting for the Depression. "Vast Baker Wealth as yet Uncounted," *The New York Times* reported (the final appraisal of the estate, made in May 1934, was some $74 million; it was estimated to have shrunk by $100 million from the top in 1929). Charles E. Mitchell, chairman of the National City Bank and no small optimist himself, eulogized Baker as "the man who was always a bull. . . . The holdings of his bank were composed of old-line stocks like U.S. Steel, American Telephone and Telegraph and Western Union. Baker was essentially an American with a faith in his country that precluded any possibility of serious and lasting trouble due to poor business conditions and depressions."

What neither Mitchell nor Baker had seen was the closing of an era. The country would, indeed, recover, as it always had recovered from depressions and panics in the past, but it would do so with new institutions. The *Times*, speculating on the future of the First National Bank, did not grasp the change either. In a piece after Baker's death, it took approving notice of the bank's old-fashioned ways: it would not join the merger movement or build branch offices. The newspaper speculated that the Baker policies would be "enduring."

Within a few months, a superstitious person would have reason to doubt that. On October 10, 1931—two weeks after England shook the international monetary world—the First National Bank building at Broadway and Wall Street was declared unsafe by the New York City Bureau of Buildings. Fort Sherman was seen to be listing in a northerly direction as early as 1920. Concern grew over the structural integrity of the building when the new Irving Trust skyscraper at No. 1 Wall Street rose in 1929. Alarms went off when Bankers Trust began to excavate the foundation for an annex at No. 10 Wall Street in 1931. It was then seen that the First National Bank building was tilting eastward. Wedges were driven into the eastern brick wall, and wooden beams shored up the Wall Street side. It was part of the picturesque style of Baker's bank that the elevators sometimes had to be jimmied open with a crowbar. However, the 1931 settling process had upset even the old granite vault, which was buried on a foundation of large rocks set on wooden piles some twenty feet below street level. Every banking day brought the unnerving possibility that the safe could be rendered inoperable through some overnight settling—the threat of a geological, rather than financial, closing.

George F. Baker, Jr., who had moved into his father's office and assumed his title, got the sad news at sea, aboard his yacht, and promptly set course for home. His shipboard guests, who had expected to awaken Saturday morning on Chesapeake Bay, instead blinked their eyes at the Statue of Liberty. Hurrying ashore to lead the search for emergency quarters, Baker found them in space recently vacated by the National City Co. (City Bank's stock-and-bond subsidiary). On Sunday morning, moving men filed down the wide, bluestone stairs of the condemned old building carrying boxes of records and period furniture. Monday—a stroke of luck—was a holiday; an extra twenty-four hours was given to move, hook up telephone service, and resettle tenants into other buildings. On Tuesday morning, the First National Bank reopened without incident at 52 Wall Street.

But the easy transition was a poor symbol of the upheaval in worldwide finance. The world of the senior Baker, like that of No. 2 Wall Street, was condemned, but the world was without clear prospects for immediate reconstruction. For more than a generation, access to credit had been expanding in the United States, and that trend would persist even through the Great Depression. This movement was now joined by another, and it too would carry into the last decade of the twentieth century. It was the socialization of lending and borrowing, and its principal architect was not Franklin Roosevelt but Herbert Hoover.

As the libertarian historian and economist Murray Rothbard has pointed out, the 1929–33 depression was the first in American history to be met by active federal government intervention. Hoover, although a Republican President in a more or less orthodox age, was no disciple of laissez-faire, and he chose to intervene in markets rather than to suffer them. Creditors were urged not to foreclose on overdue debts, short sellers not to hammer common stocks, and lenders, generally, not to say no. As prices were falling, the burden of debts denominated in dollars was rising. It was the administration's plan to spar for time: to forestall bankruptcies while attempting to restore prosperity. If prices could be made to rise, the debtors' burden would, by definition, be made lighter. Thus, a new institutional skyline began to take shape in the early to middle 1930s, and it is not too much to say (as Rothbard, for instance, has said) that the principal points of interest are as much of Hoover's design as of Roosevelt's.

The first of the new landmarks was the National Credit Corp., enacted in the fall of 1931. It was Hoover's idea but the private sector's burden. Some $400 million was subscribed by the big commercial banks to lend to lesser banks. The needy institutions were illiquid but solvent. That is, they had assets to put up as collateral for a loan but not the simon-pure collateral (mainly government securities and first-class commercial bills) required by the Federal Reserve banks. To meet depositors' withdrawals as the Depression deepened, weaker banks had sold their better assets. In contrast, the strong New York banks only became more prudent, laying in cash and government securities and prompting Owen D. Young, chairman of the board of General Electric and a director of the Federal Reserve Bank of New York, to register a complaint: "[I]f the rest of the country looks to New York [banks] for leadership in recovery . . . we shall not get anywhere, and banks will become no more than safe deposit boxes."

Young's voice presently became a chorus, but the bankers had more pressing concerns on their minds than the perception that they were a little too liquid for the country's good. One was the lending capacity of the Federal Reserve itself. It had been the hope of the system's founders that the Federal would be a liberating force in commercial lending. National City and the First National Bank, for instance, which had acted as de facto central banks, could lend a little more freely. They could lay in less capital and not fear quite as acutely for their own safety. If, on the other hand, the Federal Reserve itself would soon become impaired, the big banks could ill afford to let down their guard. Unnerved by Britain's departure from gold, foreign holders of dollars had begun a run on the gold reserves of the United States. Under law, the Federal Reserve could lend only so much, that limit being determined by its gold reserve. Let that reserve fall below the minimum, and the Federal itself would become impaired. It would be bound to turn away loan applicants to comply with the law. A minute taker at a meeting that fall reported Mitchell as saying: "[T]he banks, individually, were trying to maintain liquidity and . . . they would not lend nor invest freely, either at home or abroad, even though the Federal Reserve promised to bail them out if the necessity arose."

By late 1931, the inhibiting rules of the gold standard had been marked for early revision. Henceforth, the Federal Reserve would be less an independent bank and more an arm of government. At its founding only eighteen years earlier, the system was charged with public duties but was given a private form. It was expected to observe the conventions of traditional banking—to present a balance sheet both liquid and well capitalized—as well as to smooth out the business cycle and to serve (in a crisis) as the lender of last resort.

Under the Hoover administration, the outright annexation of the Federal Reserve System by the government was begun. Year by year in the Great Depression, the forms and conventions of the gold standard were abandoned. Monetary rules gave way to the discretion of policy makers, and the Federal came to look less like a bank and more like a federal regulatory body—the Interstate Commerce Commission, for instance. In fact, contended a Federal Reserve official, Karl R. Bopp, writing in the mid-1940s, the shift away from laissez-faire had begun decades earlier. However that may be, it was proposed in 1935 that the government itself should acquire the stock of each of the Reserve Banks, thereby achieving legally what it had already accomplished in fact. The measure failed, but it distilled the sentiment of the times.

Herbert Hoover's New Deal

Landmark legislation in the matter of monetary control was achieved with the passage of the Glass-Steagall Act of 1932 (not to be confused with another historic measure by the same two legislators in 1933). The authors of the original Federal Reserve Act in 1913 had intended the nation's currency to be elastic; it would expand and contract with the nation's business. To that end, the new Federal Reserve notes were collateralized with commercial paper as well as gold. They were, of course, convertible into gold. An upturn in business activity would stimulate commercial lending, and this lending, in turn, would support the issue of additional currency. As long as the incremental dollar was collateralized by the extra dollar's worth of business or agricultural credit, the currency would never become redundant. There would be no inflation, or, for that matter, deflation. It was a theory of deceptive neatness, implying that the Federal Reserve could dispense credit more or less automatically through the technique of "rediscounting" commercial loans. A bank would lend to a merchant, and a Federal Reserve Bank, in turn, would lend to the bank. If the merchant's loan was short-term and productive, it was, by definition, wholesome and noninflationary.

Fault had been found with this idea as long ago as 1802. Presently the Federal Reserve itself acknowledged that money was money and that "speculative" and "productive" credit all looked the same in the nation's payment stream. It followed, therefore, that strict eligibility rules for member-bank collateral served no useful purpose. Certainly it made no sense to insist that a bank in need of a loan present prime commercial loans as collateral; probably, in 1931, it wasn't making any. Hence the significance of Glass-Steagall. Passed in February 1932, it allowed a Federal Reserve Bank to extend credit to member banks even if they had no "eligible paper." More significantly, it added Treasury securities to gold and commercial paper as assets that might legally back the nation's currency. The public debt was hardly the ideal of the "elastic" monetary asset (if one accepted, as few economists believe today, that "elasticity" is a desirable monetary property). It did not expand or contract with trade, and it was not, like gold, the essence of money. The long-term fiscal record of governments was disreputable and who was to say that the United States itself might not choose to borrow or print its way out of some future jam? One of the purposes of the Federal Reserve Act was to sever the link between the government's debt (which, until the war, was insignificant, and even in the 1920s was shrinking rather than growing) and the nation's money. Now the debt would be monetized all over again. To the Hoover administration in late 1931, however, there were more urgent things to worry about than the appearance of the Federal Reserve's balance sheet. The gross national product was on its way to falling by 7.7 percent in that one year, the unemployment rate stood at 25 percent, and the universal direction of securities markets, bonds and stocks alike, was down. Banks were failing at a record rate. Furthermore, as there was a run on the nation's gold, the Federal Reserve Board was bound, under time-honored practice, to raise American interest rates. It did so.

The National Credit Corp. (to which the National City Bank, noblesse oblige, subscribed $20 million) was a stopgap. It failed to reverse the process by which bankers chose not to lend and would-be borrowers could not bring themselves to borrow. In January 1932, the government itself entered the lending business with enactment of the Reconstruction Finance Corp. "With [RFC]," wrote Benjamin Anderson, "we had put ourselves in position to give banks with assets which were good but slow, opportunity to mobilize their slow assets to meet quick liabilities. With the Glass-Steagall Act we had put it into the power of the Federal Reserve Banks to buy government securities so as to relieve money market pressure."

This was putting the best face on a very bad time. The trouble lay not only with banks but also (and more fundamentally) with the collateral against which banks could lend: its value was relentlessly falling. The Federal Reserve duly stepped up its purchases of government securities. Although instantly thrilling to the stock market, this new *"coup de whiskey"* gave no lasting relief. It is true enough, in general, that as central banks expand their assets, commercial banks expand theirs. But it is true only if loan committees and boards of directors of profit-making organizations choose to act. The hallmark of a depression is that they do not. In the 1920s, as we have seen, there was an excess of courage. In the 1930s, there was an epidemic of caution. Thus, in 1931 and early 1932, when government bonds yielded 4 percent, apparently no inducement of yield or capital gain could tempt investors into 8½ percent utility bonds or 12 percent railroad bonds. As the prosperity of the 1920s had appeared to investors as a permanent condition, so now did the long night of distress. "In fact," as Barrie Wigmore has written, "between September 1931 and December 1932, banks liquidated 4 percent of their long-term U.S. Treasury bonds and increased their holdings of shorter-maturity U.S. Treasury bills and notes by 90 percent, even though yields on these latter securities probably averaged under 1 percent." Late in 1932, Treasury bill yields actually became negative; investors paid the Treasury for the privilege of lending to it. Anxiety-racked Americans poured money into postal savings accounts and (as Hetty Green had done in 1907) into the still unquestioned vaults of the New York banks.

More important to posterity than the crisis was the government's response to it. Contrary to the conventional historical indictment, the Hoover administration refused to do nothing. It intervened at once, creating policies that anticipated the New Deal and leaving a legacy of institutions that, come the 1980s, would produce a distinctly un-Hoover-like record of profligacy. Under Herbert Hoover, politics took a statist turn. In the name of recovery, the national good became supreme, and woe betide the short seller or banker who seemed to hinder it. In November 1932, Atlee Pomerene, chairman of the RFC, harangued fearful lenders: "Now . . . and I measure my words, the bank that is 75 percent liquid or more and refuses to make loans when proper security is offered, under present circumstances, is a parasite on the community." In June, twenty leading New York banks, acting at the behest of the Federal Reserve Bank of New York, organized the American Securities Investing Corp. to try to prop up the bond market, then in a state of near-collapse. It was a case of perfect timing. The corporation raised $116 million with which to buy distressed bonds (which then included virtually every bond extant), bought less than $50 million worth, but helped to lift *The New York Times*'s bond average by some 40 percent within two months. Not until the inflation-beset markets of the 1970s would corporate bond yields ever be higher or prices lower than the ones at which the bankers' pool was fortunate enough to buy. (After taxes and incidental expenses, just the same, the pool earned nothing.)

Also in June, a blue-ribbon committee of bank presidents and corporate executives was organized, also under the sponsorship of the New York Federal Reserve, to encourage new lending. The *Philadelphia Inquirer*, grasping at straws, hailed it as "the most significant step since the beginning of the depression." In July 1932—the month the stock market finally stopped going down—the Emergency Relief and Construction Act was signed into law. It was, symbolically, among the most radical measures of the Hoover recovery program. It authorized the Federal Reserve Banks to lend directly to corporations, individuals, or partnerships, bypassing commercial banks entirely and suggesting strongly that if the private sector was unwilling or unable to lend, the public sector was not. Still, the funk of credit would not lift. By the end of 1932, only twenty-three such Federal Reserve advances had been made, amounting to less than $1 million.

The Hoover program yielded few tangible results in the Depression but contributed mightily to the expansion of credit in subsequent generations. The Federal Home Loan Bank Board was one of its chief legacies. In the fall of 1931, the administration proposed a grandiose scheme to relieve distress in the real-estate and mortgage markets. At one of his signature White House conferences, Hoover described a far-flung network of federal mortgage discount banks serving the insurance, thrift, and commercial-banking industries. Insurance executives blanched at the prospect of wide-open federal intervention, however, as did many savings bankers. In deference to their criticism, it was a watered-down version of its mortgage plan that the administration brought to Congress in the spring of 1932.

Even so, it was a massive undertaking. A dozen Federal Home Loan Banks, under the direction of a Federal Home Loan Bank Board, were created in a system closely modeled on the Federal Reserve. The Treasury subscribed $125 million in capital. The hope was to liquefy the nation's building and loan societies, later to be called savings and loans. Their membership in the system would be compulsory; insurance companies and savings banks would not, after all, be compelled to join. A building and loan in need of ready cash would be entitled to borrow from one of the banks against the collateral of its residential mortgages. The measure, enacted in July 1932, slowly produced results. At the beginning of 1933, loans outstanding had still not reached $1 million. But the total hit $94 million by the end of the year. In the 1980s—when the Home Loan Bank System helped to finance the fateful bull market in commercial real estate—system-wide loans outstanding reached $152.8 billion.

But nothing in the federal arsenal of economic policy was able to rejuvenate private lending and borrowing. From June 1929 to December 1932, loans outstanding on business and real-estate collateral dropped from $14.8 billion to $8.8 billion. It is an accounting truism that an expansion of bank lending is tantamount to an expansion in the money supply. In making a loan, a banker creates a deposit. It is no less true that by calling a loan, or by not renewing it, a banker destroys a deposit. Thus, a shrinkage in lending is the same as a decline in the money supply (or tends to be). As long as the Depression lasted, the reluctance of the bankers was understandable. It was all well and good for the RFC to make risky loans; it was the taxpayers' money that it was risking. It was an entirely different matter for a private banker to lend when the only certain feature of business and financial markets seemed the prevailing direction of everything: lower. The mystery (which deepened with every passing year) was the continued stagnation of credit despite the 1933 upturn in business activity.

The election of Franklin D. Roosevelt on a platform of gold-standard orthodoxy and economy in government held out the initial promise of less experimentation in credit, not more. Great hay was made by conservative Democrats in the 1932 campaign about the extravagance and wild-haired policies of Herbert Hoover. There were solid, non-partisan grounds too for believing that the economy was over the hump. A second run on the dollar by foreigners had spent itself in the spring; the dollar was, in fact, as good as gold. The stock market made its low on July 8, when the Dow Jones Industrial Average touched 41.22, representing a loss of no less than 88 percent from the 1929 peak. (John D. Rockefeller, who had issued more than one prematurely bullish comment on the way down, redeemed his predictive reputation with one on the precise low-water mark, July 8, his ninety-third birthday. "These are days when many are discouraged," he said. "In the 93 years of my life, depressions have come and gone. Prosperity has always returned, and will again.") In the next seven weeks, the Dow vaulted by 81 percent from this admittedly low base. A blight of bank runs in and around Chicago in the late spring and early summer had been stopped, thanks in part by loans from the RFC. Charles G. Dawes, the former Vice President, former head of the Liberty Loan Committee, and former boy-wonder Comptroller of the Currency, had resigned from his then current post as head of the RFC to return to Chicago to help to rescue the Central Republic Bank & Trust Co. In another career, Dawes had been head of that institution too. Now a private citizen again, he applied to the agency he had just quit, the RFC, for a loan. Properly, the request was granted; inevitably, however, the Democrats became suspicious of it and of the politics of federal assistance all around.

Except for World War I, the ersatz gold-exchange standard might not have displaced the genuine article; if so, the 1929 stock-market panic might have been as short-lived and as economically inconse-quential as the Panic of 1907. Except for the Smoot-Hawley Tariff of 1930, the recession of 1929 might not have become the Great Depres-sion of 1929–33. Except for Britain's sudden abrogation of gold, the international monetary crisis of 1931–32 might not have erupted. Finally, with a little bit of luck and even a modicum of cooperation between the incoming and outgoing American Presidents, the bank holiday of March 1933 might not have broken what little remained of the nation's financial spirit.

As it was, scenes of almost ritual panic interrupted the transition between Herbert Hoover and Franklin D. Roosevelt. In 1929 in the stock market and in 1931–32 in the bond and currency markets, public fear was spontaneous. People were sincerely frightened in 1933 as well, but by then fear had become reflexive. One would have expected the liquidation of bad debt to have long since run its course. S. W. Straus & Co., Caldwell & Co., Kreuger & Toll, and Bank of United States—summertime institutions all—had failed, arguably on merit. By 1933, the survivors were, by definition, hardy specimens. What Darwinian purpose would be served by one more plunge into the abyss? If depressions and liquidations served the useful if painful purpose of purging financial excess, what excess could have possibly remained after three and a half years of depression? The only one, surely, as Roosevelt would soon declare, was fear itself.

"Out of wrath come none but misbegotten offspring," instructed *Fortune* in December 1932, one month into the Hoover lame-duck term. "Our danger now is that we shall legislate in wrath, letting the desire to punish our present banks outstrip our efforts to obtain a better banking system." The country was feeling punitive; "banksters" were being called before Congress to explain themselves. Charles E. Mitchell, chairman of the National City Bank, whom Senator Carter Glass had never forgiven for daring to lend in the call-loan market during the Federal Reserve-induced stringency of 1929 (and for other boom-time offenses, for instance, the manipulation of City Bank stock by City Bank's own stock-and-bond subsidiary), was a frequent witness. He was called as an expert at first but later, as the country's mood turned black, as a defendant. Looking every inch the banker, strong-voiced and self-assured, Mitchell was a scapegoat out of central casting. By our own lights, what was most striking about the National City Bank of that time was its eminent solvency. (In March 1933, *Time* magazine called City's balance sheet "the envy of every bank in the United States.") To members of the Senate Banking Committee, however, that achievement was considerably less relevant than the alleged role of the bank in the insolvency of others. Thus, the sale, by the bank's underwriting subsidiary, of Peruvian bonds to public investors was condemned not as a mistake but as an act of cynicism. Similarly, the worst possible light was cast on the bank's misadventures in Cuban sugar and its ill-conceived investment in the stock of Anaconda Copper. These were financial matters, however, and the committee wanted flesh. It found it in Mitchell, who had earned over $1 million in salary and bonus in 1929 but had paid no income tax because of a capital loss he had incurred through the timely sale of some stock (National City Bank stock, as it happened) to his wife.

Never had a banker, any banker, seemed less worthy of a million tax-free dollars than Mitchell did in February 1932. Standing in cold lines outside closed banks, Americans had ample time to reflect on the difference between their lot and his. In the *American Mercury*, Clifford Reeves had written a few months earlier: "The title of banker, formerly regarded as a mark of esteem in the United States, is now almost a term of opprobrium. There seems some danger, in fact, that in forthcoming editions of the dictionary it may be necessary to define the word as a peculiar American colloquialism, synonymous with rascal . . . and we may even see the day when to be called the son-of-a-banker will be regarded as justifiable grounds for the commission of assault and mayhem."

The griddle on which Mitchell sat was warmed by politics. As we have noted, the Democrats were either suspicious or envious of the RFC and its loan to Charles Dawes's bank. With the start of the presidential-nomination season in the summer of 1932, the Speaker of the House of Representatives, John Nance Garner, demanded public disclosure of the banks that had availed themselves of RFC funds. Although a loan from the agency was no proof of insolvency—it was RFC policy, in fact, to lend to still solvent banks that were trying to work their way out of difficulty—the public was inclined to run first and ask questions later. Bankers expected that the publication of a list of weakened banks would cause an immediate run, but the public only slowly edged to the door. It listened anxiously after Hoover's defeat, hoping that the President-elect and the President would agree on a course of action over the next several months. Would the nation follow Britain off the gold standard? Would debts be payable at 100 cents on the dollar or at a discount? Was Roosevelt cast in the mold of Cleveland or of Bryan? In the absence of a confidence-building statement from Roosevelt himself, creditors were left to wonder. For three and a half years, optimism had been a money-losing state of mind. The successful investor had been the timid investor (the exact inversion of the long and lucrative experience of the elder Baker). In January 1933, rumors circulated that Roosevelt was, in fact, planning to leave the gold standard, in effect preparing a colossal redistribution of wealth in favor of debtors. The lack of the expected denial galvanized fear. Through all the loss and dismemberment of the Depression years, the American public had never doubted the capacity or will of its government to pay out an ounce of gold for each $20.67 presented for exchange. Now it entertained grave doubts. There had been runs on banks, of course, and runs by foreigners on the dollar itself. But there had been no run by American citizens on gold. Starting in January 1933, however, the people descended on solvent banks. They withdrew money—paper dollars—to exchange for gold coins, obtainable at the nearest Federal Reserve bank. These they hid under the mattress.

The "X" Account

It was in this nascent panic that Baker's bank, the First National, was paid one of the handsomest compliments it (or any other private bank) could hope to receive. In house, the employees discreetly referred to one account as the "X" account. It belonged to the Bank of England, and by January 1933 it had grown to $55 million. This was a staggering sum by any measure: in absolute terms, in terms of the overall deposits of the First National Bank (14 percent), or in the light of custom. As a rule, central banks deposited money only in other central banks. It is not clear why the Bank of England chose to venture outside the Federal Reserve Bank of New York—possibly, it wanted to earn some return on its cash balances, something that the Federal could not offer. So deciding, however, it picked what it must have believed to be the most impregnable depository in New York City.* It was the bank in which Bernard M. Baruch, another discerning customer, had deposited $3.4 million during an earlier (and no less harrowing) financial crisis,

---

* In mid-January 1933, George L. Harrison, governor of the Federal Reserve Bank of New York, twice called the deputy governor of the Bank of England, Sir Ernest Harvey, to suggest that the First National Bank deposit be reduced. There was certainly nothing to worry about, Harrison assured Sir Ernest. On the other hand, it was undesirable that any commercial bank take on so large a sum just then, particularly when it might be withdrawn at any moment. Besides, money-market rates in New York were so low—Baker's favorite interest rate, the call-loan rate, was quoted at 1 percent—that the First was unable to put the money to work at a profit. Harrison's record of the conversation, the only one extant, describes good feelings all around. Sir Ernest was grateful for the "hint," and Jackson Reynolds, the First National's president, was happy to be out from under the burden of so large a deposit. On January 18, it was reduced by $18.5 million.

that surrounding the sterling crisis of November 1931. It was Baruch's largest single deposit.

One by one, the states declared banking "holidays," unfestive suspensions of cash payments. The first of consequence was Michigan's, on February 14. In Detroit, real estate had grown up with the automobile business, and Michigan banks had lent liberally against inflated property values. Heroic efforts were made to contain the crisis. New York banks lent heavily to their Detroit correspondents, Herbert Hoover called Henry Ford on the telephone, and detectives fanned out across the state: 15 to guard an incoming shipment of gold and 350 (dispatched by the head of the U.S. Secret Service, William H. Moran) to watch out for "scandal-mongers and others who might spread unfounded rumors." To no avail. Before the month was out, Indiana, Maryland, Arkansas, and Ohio had followed Michigan.

Beginning on March 1, the states capitulated in blocs, with New York, the biggest banking state, throwing in the towel only at 3:30 a.m. on March 4, inauguration day; at that small hour, depositors were already lining up outside the banks to take their money out. (From February 1 to March 3, the National City Bank, in no way helped by Mitchell's public ordeal, lost 29 percent of its domestic deposits; except for advances from the Federal Reserve Bank of New York, it might have had to close.) It was full-scale panic, and there was an unmistakable tone of reproach in the Clearing House news release, which said in part:

> The unthinking attempt of the public to convert over $40,000,000,000 of deposits into currency at one time is on its face impossible.
>
> While the condition of the Clearing House banks in New York is such that they could, through the facilities of the Federal Reserve Bank, pay on demand every dollar of their deposits, the . . . tremendous withdrawals through the country as a whole, and upon a rapidly increasing scale, render imperative a halt to enable the proper authorities to consider and adopt remedies, not only for New York primarily but for the nation as a whole.

Remedies were forthcoming, but they would not appeal to the Clearing House Association. The expectations of Jackson Reynolds of First National were low to begin with. They were tempered by his knowledge of the President-elect in their days together at the Columbia University School of Law. "[He] was not much of a student and nothing of a lawyer afterward," said Reynolds, who taught Roosevelt in a pair of courses, gave him low grades, and watched him leave without a degree.

Roosevelt seized the activist torch from Hoover. However, in the judgment of the new administration, the shambles of the American economy was not the doing of Hoover's statism but of Coolidge's inattention. Hoover had not intervened too heavily but too little. It was not the RFC or the White House that had stalled the process of recovery (by pushing off into the future the inevitable adjustment of debts and incomes) but the ineptness of the institutions that were meant to assist. Hoover had little enough faith in the ability of markets to coordinate human action in ways great and invisible. Roosevelt had less. What the new President saw, in March 1933, was the failure of the old regime. As for the bankers, they were as discredited as the stocks and bonds they had foisted on an unsuspecting public. The system of Mitchell and Baker and Kreuger and Caldwell had failed (on that Roosevelt had no doubt). Certainly, no harm could come from changing it.

The pre-inaugural financial crisis inspired radical plans for credit. On March 2 (the National City Bank was then repulsing a run), Adolf Berle, one of the President's inner circle, met with Jackson Reynolds and the Treasury Secretary-to-be, William Woodin, at the Federal Reserve Bank of New York. Berle had a scheme to discuss. "His plan," as Reynolds remembered it, "was that the United States government should guarantee the deposits of all the banks of the country. The government had absolutely no authority to do any such thing, but that was a mere bag of shells, he could remedy that instantly. We had to discuss it on its merits, and I said that I thought it was the most foolish idea I had ever heard about to pledge the credit of the whole United States to buttress the banks that could be carried along by the Reconstruction Finance Corporation and our own Clearing House groups. I asserted it was a usurpation of power and there was no emergency to justify any such constitutional invasion. I thought it ought not to be done. It was never heard of again. I don't know why, because they brought up one scheme more foolish than that later on."

The more foolish scheme, in Reynolds's opinion, was a bond-buying plan conceived by the President-elect himself. Woodin explained it to him. "I was with [Roosevelt] last night," Woodin told Reynolds, "and he has an idea that all we need is a bold gesture of confidence and a demonstration that we don't fear anything. Therefore he is going to propose the United States instantly redeem all of its outstanding bonds in paper money, no matter what the maturity of the bond should be. If it has fifty years to run, just buy it with nice, new printed money immediately." But neither did this bombshell immediately burst.

Two days after the inauguration—March 6, a Monday—Roosevelt made the first bold gesture of many. He declared a four-day national banking holiday. Every bank in the country, including the safe-and-sound First National, which could have paid off its depositors in cash, would be shut for the next four days: neither deposits nor withdrawals would be permitted. As for the constitutional authority for this drastic measure, Roosevelt invoked the Trading with the Enemy Act of 1917. Already, Hoover seemed a piker. On March 9, Congress took only a few hours to pass the Emergency Banking Act, which validated what Roosevelt had already done and gave him free play for monetary experimentation in the future. Employing it, on April 5, he confiscated gold. By executive order, it was declared illegal to hold or own gold coins, bullion, or certificates. No American citizen could export gold except under license by the Treasury. Under law, the dollar was still convertible into gold at $20.67 an ounce, but the government, in practice, had stopped converting it.

Now what? The American creditor was at sea. In Lawrence Chamberlain's day, investors had confidently purchased railroad bonds of a half century's maturity in the belief that the value of the dollar was as fixed and unmovable as the city of Boston. The definition of the dollar was 25.8 grains of gold, nine-tenths fine. It would remain so. (At the turn of the century, extreme optimists could purchase the West Shore Railroad 4 percent bonds maturing in the year 2361: as financial time was measured, beyond kingdom come.) Investors continued to buy Treasury securities in which payment of interest and principal was specified in dollars of the customary gold weight.

However, only days after the gold order, a new and disturbing phrase entered the legal language of credit. Monroe County, which borders Lake Ontario in upstate New York, advertised a sale of $350,000 in Emergency Bonds. Concerning the manner of repayment, the copy said, "Both principal and interest payable in gold coin *or its equivalent in lawful money of the United States.*" Since time out of mind, such boilerplate had said, without qualification: "Principal and interest are payable in gold coin of the United States of America, of or equal to the present standards of weights and fineness." Now Monroe County, alert to the shifting monetary tides, reserved for itself the right to pay "lawful money" in discharge of its debts, whatever lawful money might be.

The *American Banker*, in reporting on this unsettling turn of events, jumped to no alarming conclusions:

> The presumption is that the emergency in which gold is contraband for private hoardings or for unlimited shipment abroad will soon pass, and that in a matter of a few months, normal freedom will be restored to the right to demand gold for gold certificates, gold bonds and other forms of gold futures contracts.
> And when that time comes, it is hardly likely that the psychology of considering gold more desirable than gold paper will continue. If gold is freely available, it will likely be little desired. Possessing other things will probably be more profitable.

"Doubts About the Currency"

It soon developed, however, that the banking emergency was anything but temporary. On May 12 came the Thomas Amendment to the Agricultural Adjustment Act, which invited the President to devalue the dollar in terms of gold and to direct the Secretary of the Treasury to issue up to $3 billion of greenbacks with which to retire outstanding federal debt—the President's pre-inaugural bond-purchase idea returned to life. On June 5, in the same leveling vein, Congress declared null and void the traditional gold-clause contract. In other words, if Congress chose to devalue the dollar (and it then seemed certain it would), no creditor could demand payment in the old, weightier dollar specified in the pre-devaluation loan agreements. Monroe County had been on the cutting edge of finance after all.

Insecure creditors had demanded protection from the threat of a devaluation of money since the late Middle Ages. In American monetary history, successive disasters in Revolutionary War continentals, state bank notes, and Civil War greenbacks preceded the silver agitation of the 1890s. Thus were creditors drawn to the gold clause. It was standard in long-term contracts—such as mortgage deeds, life insurance policies, and railroad bonds—to warrant that the quality of money repaid would be identical to the quality of money lent. In 1933, it was estimated, $100 billion of gold-denominated contracts were outstanding in the United States. The gold clause was a staple in Germany (a legacy both of pre-World War I agrarian politics and of the titanic postwar inflation), France, Denmark, and Sweden. There were gold stipulations in the reparations clauses of the World War I peace treaties. The only victorious power to forbear to require a gold clause was Britain. In London, it was understood that sterling and gold were permanently and honorably interchangeable.

Obviously, however, this was changing. In November 1931, two months after Britain abandoned the gold standard, Bernard Baruch, the speculator and political figure, counted more shares of Alaska Juneau Gold Mining Co. in his portfolio than shares of any other company. The price of the stock was $15 a share; in the roaring bull market of 1927, it had fetched only $1. In April 1932, Baruch went to the extreme length of buying gold bullion itself. He directed his mine to send him bars to his vault in New York (the Glass-Steagall Act had just authorized the Federal Reserve System to begin to collateralize the dollar with Treasury bonds). In the normal course of events, of course, there was every reason not to buy gold, which was difficult to transport, bore no interest, and cost money to assay and store. Years later, when a suspicious Treasury Secretary asked him to explain his motives, Baruch replied, laconically, ". . . because I was commencing to have doubts about the currency."

It was because the monetary issue is always open to doubt that the gold clause had become a mainstay of American contract law. To those who equated gold with money and the sanctity of contract with civil order, the June 5 congressional resolution was nothing less than revolutionary. Senator Elmer Thomas, the Oklahoma inflationist, called it "the most important proposition that has ever come before any parliamentary body of any nation of the world" (possibly excepting the last war, he added) and rubbed his hands at the prospective transfer of wealth from creditors to debtors.

The case for abrogation was variously couched in terms of expediency, collectivism, and constitutional theory, according to the taste of the disputant. There had been a financial emergency, and the government, exercising its powers to regulate money and to borrow on the credit of the United States, had properly intervened. No mere private contracts could impede the exercise of this authority. The "sanctity of contract" was no mean phrase itself. However, in dollar terms, the price of gold was rising and would probably continue to rise. To demand repayment of debts in gold coin or its equivalent at the old rate was to insist on the ruin of debtors. If a man had borrowed $20.67, pure and simple—just the twenty paper bills and some spare change—the price of gold would be immaterial to him. He would be bound to repay those twenty bills and that spare change. If, on the other hand, he had borrowed $20.67 under the terms of the standard gold-clause contract, he would be bound to repay the equivalent in gold coin. As it happened, $20.67 was the equivalent of one ounce of gold coin, exactly. In January 1934, $35 was made the equivalent of one ounce: the dollar was devalued. If the literal language of the gold-clause contracts was allowed to stand, a debtor who owed $100 "in gold coin of the present weight and fineness" would be set back. He would need $169 to satisfy his obligation in gold. On the other hand, he would need only $100 to satisfy it in paper. A report of the House Committee on Money and Banking noted the high incidence of gold hoarding and capital flight in the late banking crisis. Both of these acts, it explained, had rendered "the enforcement of the gold clause incompatible with the public interest." In other words, people owned gold on sufferance of the government. They were free to exchange dollars for gold but only until such time as an uncomfortably large number of them chose to do so. It then fell to the government to take their gold away from them.

Conservative reaction to this revolution in the relation of debtor to creditor and of man to state was swift and anguished. "It's dishonor, sir," Senator Carter Glass said to a friend on the day the Thomas Amendment was announced. "This great government, strong in gold, is breaking its promises to pay gold to widows and orphans to whom it has sold government bonds with a pledge to pay gold coin of the present standard of value." Senator Thomas P. Gore of Oklahoma, blind from the age of twelve but respected both for his political courage and for his study of economics, had been asked by Roosevelt for his opinion on the gold-clause resolution before it was put to a vote. "Why, that's just plain stealing, isn't it, Mr. President?" he directly replied.

So it seemed to other creditors—in London, the Treasury's refusal to pay gold was called "the American default"—and litigation flowered. Almost nobody had doubted that Congress would act as it did. The question was whether it had acted constitutionally. The Supreme Court heard arguments for the gold-clause cases (there were four) in January 1935 and handed down its decisions in February.

In keeping with the gravity of the issue, Attorney General Homer S. Cummings argued the government's case himself. He invited the court to recall the near miss of March 6, 1933, and reviewed the government's strenuous policies to restore confidence. He mentioned the bank holiday, the Emergency Banking Act, the Agricultural Adjustment Act, and the Joint Resolution dated June 5. He noted that, at the beginning of March 1933, only the dollar, the Swiss franc, and the Dutch guilder had not been devalued in terms of gold. He cited the Gold Reserve Act of January 30, 1934. It was the Gold Reserve Act that created a lighter, more inflationary dollar, one defined as 15⁵⁄₂₁ grains of gold, instead of the old weight of 25.8 grains. The devaluation meant that an ounce of gold was henceforth equivalent to $35, compared with the customary $20.67. "Thus," said Cummings,

> in a hectic period of eleven months, a sweeping change was effected in the financial and monetary structure of our country. Our system was completely reorganized. Gold and gold bullion were swept into the Treasury of the United States; gold certificates were placed where they were readily within the control of the Government of the United States; foreign exchange was regulated; banks were being reopened; gold hoarding was brought under control; parity was maintained; and a complete transition was effected from the old gold-coin standard to the gold-bullion standard, with the weight of the dollar fixed at an endurable amount.

What the court must understand, the Attorney General continued, was the coherence of the administration's monetary policies. Let one be struck down and they all would be the worse for it. Shifting from policy to morality, he observed that the bondholders had wrapped themselves in the flag of contract. "I hesitate to venture upon the high ground of ethics and morality so completely occupied by those who argue for the sanctity of the written word, and who assert that it should be maintained at all hazards," he said, waxing sarcastic. "That field has been pretty thoroughly occupied by counsel for the bondholders. Such arguments make me feel a stranger in this preempted territory."

And what if the old contracts were deemed valid and enforceable? What would be the consequence of marking up the outstanding value of the nation's gold-clause contracts to the then current value of gold? The arithmetic was appalling: $100 billion worth of gold-clause contracts were in existence. If the higher gold price were held enforceable, the face value of those contracts would instantly become $169 billion. "Should the claims of the owners of these gold obligations be approved," said Cummings, now seeming to borrow from Senator Thomas, "it would create a privileged class which, in character, in immunity, in power, has hitherto been unparalleled in the history of the human race. I feel the walls of this courtroom expand. I see, waiting upon this decision, the hopes, the fears and the welfare of millions of our fellow citizens."

The great fact about gold in the twentieth century is its loss of official monetary standing. In 1935, however, it was still regarded as the ultimate standard of value, and Cummings used that fact in the service of his constitutional argument. "Gold is not an ordinary commodity," he told the court. "It is a thing apart, and upon it rests, under our form of civilization, the whole structure of our finance and the welfare of our people. Gold is affected with a public interest. These gold contracts, therefore, deal with the very essence of sovereignty, for they require that the Government must surrender a portion of that sovereignty." Radical for their day, Cummings's views on gold presently came to appear reactionary. In the 1970s, successive Republican administrations would contend that gold was, in fact, a mere commodity. Its value would have as little bearing on American credit policy as the vicissitudes of the pork-belly market.

Surely, by the time the gold-clause cases reached the Supreme Court, the die was cast. Bankers Trust, arguing for the bondholders, made a strong and plausible-sounding constitutional case. The June 5, 1933, resolution had nothing to do with the power to "coin money" or to "regulate the value thereof," it stated. "On the contrary, its sole purpose and its effect are, not to regulate the value of money, but directly and immediately, not indirectly nor incidentally, to change these contracts by destroying their most valued obligation. Thus the Resolution not only undertakes to restrict the expressed and vastly important power of Congress to borrow money on the credit of the United States, but it directly violates the limitation of power imposed by the Fifth Amendment."

What the bondholders and their lawyers could not have then imagined was how little the government's borrowing power would be impaired or how resilient its credit would prove to be, gold clause or no. In June 1933, the month and year of the congressional nullification, the yield on government bonds was 3.21 percent. By February 1935, when the Supreme Court voted 5–4 to uphold Congress's action, the yield had fallen to 2.79 percent. It would keep right on dropping, the second, third, and fourth Roosevelt terms notwithstanding, until it reached 2.03 percent in April 1946.

The court, in its majority opinion, said it was not concerned by the government's contention that a 69 percent markup of the nation's gold-indexed debts would plunge the economy back into chaos. What did concern it, the majority stated, was the constitutional power of Congress over the national monetary system and its attempted frustration. Justice James C. McReynolds delivered the dissenting opinion in considerable heat with his Southern voice pitched high. "The record," he declared,

> reveals a clear purpose to bring about confiscation of private rights and repudiation of national obligations. To us these things are abhorrent. . . . The Constitution as many of us have understood it, the instrument that has meant so much to us, is gone. The guarantees heretofore supposed to protect against arbitrary action have been swept away. The powers of Congress have been so enlarged that now no man can tell their limitations. Guarantees heretofore supposed to prevent arbitrary action are in discord.

It exasperated McReynolds that the government itself had issued $500 million worth of gold-clause bonds in May, only to have Congress in June declare the gold contract null and void. He concluded his dissent on a note of near-despair:

> We are confronted by a dollar reduced to sixty cents, with the possibility of twenty tomorrow, ten the next day, and then one.
> This thing we utterly abhor. We have earnestly tried to prevent its incorporation in our system without success.
> It is said that the National Government has made by these transactions $2,800,000,000 and that all gold hypothecated to the Treasury now may be used to discharge public obligations! If the dollar be depreciated to five cents or possibly one, then, through fraud, all Government obligations could be discharged quite simply.
> Shame and humiliation are upon us now. Moral and financial chaos may confidently be expected.

But there was no financial chaos, not even in the upheaval of the Hundred Days. Instead, a long funk followed euphoria. So little chaos descended on the government bond market that an auction of Treasury securities on June 15, 1933, was six times oversubscribed. Congress had abrogated the gold clause only ten days before. "We are rich in money in the bank, it seems," the *American Banker* remarked, "but unhealthily poor in commercial enterprise and initiative in which such funds should be productively employed."

One would have expected more of it. The Depression was ending, the stock market was rallying, and the government had selectively reopened the banks. In the Banking Act of 1933, signed in June,

Roosevelt swallowed his own long-standing objections to deposit insurance and rejected the banking industry's. (Attacking federal deposit insurance on principle, the National City Bank proved more prescient than it could have imagined. "The element of character in the choice of a bank is eliminated," said the bank's July monthly letter, "and the competitive appeal is shifted to other and lower standards, such as liberality in making loans. The natural result is that the standards of management are lowered, bankers may take greater risks for the sake of larger profits and the economic loss which accompanies bad bank management increases." It was, in fact, a chillingly accurate prediction of the bank's own future predicament.) The RFC continued to lend to banks in need. In short, the bad news was out and recovery was palpably under way. In retrospect, there was no safer moment to begin insuring bank deposits. The government's market timing was merely impeccable.

The mystery of the 1930s (and for that matter of the 1940s) was why the mood of lenders and borrowers was so glum for so long. Viewed from the perspective of the 1980s, the 1930s are a financial riddle. Interest rates then were startlingly low, while corporate and individual tax rates (particularly after 1936) were prohibitively high. Then as now, interest expense was deductible for a corporation, whereas dividend payments were not—that is, it paid to borrow. Banks were brimful with lendable funds. The stock market had barely begun to recover its bear-market losses. Yet lending and borrowing remained at a virtual standstill.

The Government Commands

Not for lack of federal exhortation. In September 1933, Jesse H. Jones, chairman of the RFC, browbeat the plenum of the American Bankers Association in Chicago. "I came to talk about preferred stocks for banks," the President's man led off, "but before referring to that subject I should like to impress upon you how very important it is that bankers cooperate wholeheartedly with the President's recovery program, and by cooperation I do not mean merely by the purchase of more government bonds, as desirable as that may be, nor do I mean the cashing of a few highly liquid bills or drafts."

What Jones meant was risk-taking (surely the bankers remembered what that was): "Banks must provide credit to accommodate agriculture, commerce and industry based upon a going country, otherwise the government will have to do so." The private ownership of banks was a little like the private ownership of gold. The government's tolerance of it was contingent on the production of constructive results. Anticipating the frustrations of the early 1990s, Jones criticized overly zealous bank examiners. He sympathized with the bankers to the extent of acknowledging that the supply of "liquid loans" was short. But what was to be done about that? "Will we continue to force liquidation or will we take the pressure off and allow our borrowers a little freedom to work out their problems, and probably to employ somebody and buy something?"

Was the shortage of bank capital an impediment to lending? Congress had recently legislated a solution to the problem: it had authorized the RFC to buy preferred stock in commercial banks, both state and national, to permit them to lend more. "I am aware that many of you—most of you, perhaps—will say you cannot lend the money that you now have," Jones continued, "and I venture to suggest that you probably are not making very much actual effort for the simple reason that you are still waiting. You are afraid of a recurrence of conditions through which we have just passed. Some of you are afraid we will have inflation, and some of you are afraid we will not have inflation. After all, it is fear, and I ask, is it not time that we uncross our fingers and follow the President's lead?"

Sounding for all the world like Atlee Pomerene, Hoover's RFC chairman, Jones roughly adjured them:

> Be smart for once. Take the government in partnership with you, and then go partners with the President in the recovery program without stint. Every other business is required to perform under the NRA [National Recovery Administration]—why not banks—all banks? Not merely by raising the salaries of a few underpaid clerks, but in providing credit and in performing the normal functions of a bank. I do not mean loose credit—no one expects that—but credit that can be put on a safe basis if the banks will really try to find a way to make it so.
>
> It is easy to say "no," and if that is the program and if we want the government to do our banking, what is to become of our high-priced bank talent? The office boy can say "no," and the note teller can collect the notes if they are good. Why not use our bank talent to find ways and means to provide the necessary credit for home requirements in cooperation with the NRA?

Here was a business proposition such as the Internal Revenue Service annually made to the American taxpayer. By the sound of Jones's voice, it was lend—or else. But lend on what collateral, and for what purposes? The American banking system—indeed, the whole credit structure—had just passed through the ordeal of the Great Depression and the trial by fire of the 1933 panic. If the surviving lenders knew anything, it was that it was better to be safe than sorry. On the same day that Jones implored the bankers to lend, Francis H. Sisson, vice president of the Guaranty Trust Company of New York and president of the American Bankers Association, reminded them of their prudential duty to be liquid. Sisson warned particularly of the dangers of real-estate lending. "Many of the banks that have come to grief in this country," he told the convention, "have done so largely because they allowed themselves to become involved to a shocking extent in real estate financing. The bankers of the United States need to take renewed devotion to this time-honored fundamental principle of commercial banking." As for federal deposit insurance and the other key provisions of the 1933 Banking Act, Sisson added, he was against them.

The National City Bank had long since succeeded Bank of United States as the country's most notorious financial institution, and its immediate post-Depression goal was to restore its good name. Early in 1934, it "went partners" with the President, in Jones's phrase, selling $50 million in preferred stock to the RFC. James H. Perkins, who succeeded the disgraced Mitchell in 1933, elected to take what, in accounting jargon, is known as a "big bath." "Let's clean up this bank once and for all," he told the directors, and he did. Some $60 million of additional credits were written off, bringing the grand total of losses borne by the bank since 1929 to $167 million (net of recoveries). To put $167 million in perspective, it amounted to 68 percent of what the stockholders counted as their equity at the end of 1929. Even at this depleted level, however, stockholders' equity amounted to 8½ percent of the conservatively valued assets, a far higher ratio than most banks, and certainly Citibank, the direct descendant of National City, can show at this writing.

Having restored the National City Bank to strength, Perkins refused to risk new losses. Writing to the stockholders in December 1933, three months after Jones's harangue, he advised them that, "in these times the obligation of a commercial bank to its depositors, customers and shareholders is to pursue a conservative policy, maintain an adequate degree of liquidity, reduce expenses and increase reserves"— in other words, to attend to its own agenda, not to the President's.

For all Perkins knew, the depositors might again run for their money, as they had in March 1933, and he took precautionary measures. The bank did make some loans—United Parcel Service proved a valued customer, its loss-making record in 1930, 1931, and 1932 notwithstanding—but mostly it laid in Treasury securities. It favored Treasury bills, which entailed no risk at all, not even the risk of rising interest rates (expecting a rise, Perkins refused to invest in long-term bonds). The other side of the coin of negligible risk was infinitesimal reward. In 1936, when bills came to constitute more than half of City Bank's portfolio of government securities, they yielded less than three-tenths of 1 percent. It was literally less than the cost of handling them. If City Bank was fearful, so were many of its former corporate borrowers. Loan demand was chronically weak. In March 1934, Perkins threw up his hands. "It is almost impossible to lend money to anybody from whom you have a reasonable chance of getting it back."

In general, the National City Bank was a shadow of its former self. At the end of 1929, its balance sheet had footed to more than $2 billion. Its loans had totaled $1.2 billion, its deposits, $1.5 billion. Five dispiriting years later, loans had fallen to $490 million, deposits to $1.2 billion. It was not so much that the public had lost confidence in City Bank—deposits had fallen by only 20 percent as against a 59 percent drop in loans—as that the bank had lost confidence in the country or the future or the economy.

What posterity knows is that the nadir of credit occurred in 1933, that interest rates would fall for more than a decade, and that risk in the banking system would be increasingly borne by the government. There would, in fact, be no reenactment of the panic of February and March 1933, but bankers (frightened out of their wits by the Depression, in many cases themselves in financial difficulties and resentful of policies in Washington) would continue to fear one. But at this moment of greatest obsession with the past, the future veered off in an unexpected direction.

Things were different even when they appeared to be the same. "J. Pierpont Morgan called on George F. Baker at the First National Bank Building at 2 Wall Street yesterday afternoon," the *American Banker* reported on April 18, 1933. "To be sure, it was the second J. Pierpont Morgan and the second George F. Baker, and the occasion of the visit was the opening of the second First National Bank Building at the historic corner of Wall and Broadway." But the only propitious omen of the neo-Greek structure was its cost: only two million Depression dollars.

The truth was that the time of the First National Bank was passing. In January 1932, less than a year after the death of the elder Baker, the bank's investment subsidiary, First Security Co., became technically insolvent. It was propped up by loans from the directors, including the younger Baker, whose bearish market judgment had been roundly vindicated after all. In the same year, the dividend, although duly paid, was unearned (in effect, it was paid in borrowed money), and the bank's profit-sharing plan was rescinded. Clerks were hard hit by the new austerity: many were accustomed to bonuses equivalent to a full year's salary. Some, hoping to cash in on what had seemed a perennial sure thing, had borrowed from the First Security Co. to purchase their own First National Bank stock. They planned to repay the debt with proceeds of future bonuses or, perhaps, from the sale of the stock itself. Did it not always go up? If the clerks had expected the senior Baker to make provisions in his will for the forgiveness of their margin debt, however, they were disappointed. And the price of the stock, in most un-Baker-like fashion, kept falling. In the spring of 1934, when Baker's estate was appraised, it was quoted at $2,640 a share. In 1929, it had sold for $8,600 a share. Those who had borrowed to buy near the top of the market had inadvertently climbed on a treadmill. Their debts (some of which were still the topic of resentful office gossip after World War II) had availed them nothing except a loss.

Nor, for the bank, was that the worst of it. It had hardly opened the one-piece, cast-iron doors of its new building when the Banking Act of 1933 was signed into law. Glass-Steagall, as that seminal legislation was called, forced commercial banks to abandon their activities in corporate securities underwriting. First National's career as a vastly successful Wall Street investment bank was over. ("This is a huge money-making machine," a bank examiner had marveled of Baker's institution in 1896, "having little to do with commercial risks and making a large percentage of its profits from stock and bond dealings and investments.") There would be no more First Security Co. and no more lucrative underwritings of corporate bonds and stocks. From 1922 to 1933, investment-banking profits had averaged almost $1 million a year. There was nothing on the horizon to replace them.

Glass-Steagall dealt one blow to the First National's business prospects. The Federal Deposit Insurance Corporation, which the 1933 law had also created, signified the beginning of the end of the economic value of safety in American banking. Deposits, in the beginning, were insured only up to $2,500, but the drift of things was clear enough.

In time, the government's credit, in the estimation of the average public depositor, would supersede the credit of the bank that kept his money. By the 1980s, with the evolution of the doctrine that some banks were too big to fail, the government would become the silent partner of even uninsured depositors. The stock-in-trade of the First National Bank was, in good part, its impregnability. Solvent and liquid in all financial weather, it was the epitome of safety and soundness. (In 1931, the First made application to the Federal Reserve and Clearing House authorities to write down the value of its bond portfolio to the then depreciated market prices. As such an uncompromising act would reflect badly on the weaker banks, however, permission was denied.) As depositors were taught that banks would no longer fail, the First National Bank lost one of its reasons for being.

Subsidized Loans Go Begging

Jesse Jones's threat to the bankers in the fall of 1933 was no idle bluster. Seeing no revival in lending, the administration drafted legislation to create a dozen industrial-loan banks under the direction of the Federal Reserve. Congress accepted the administration's overture but drafted its own legislation, a bill to invest the Federal itself (in conjunction with the RFC) with new and significant banking powers. Revising Section 13b of the Federal Reserve Act, the act would empower the Reserve Banks to subsidize private lending to industrial companies. In extraordinary circumstances, they could bypass the private banking system altogether, lending to customers directly. Private banks were made what appeared an irresistible offer. If they would lend to creditworthy corporate borrowers at 6 percent, for a term of five years, a Federal Reserve Bank would guarantee 80 percent of the loan. "A long-term loan," as a Federal Reserve official reasonably pointed out, "that may be discounted at the Federal Reserve Bank at any time without recourse as to 80 percent of any loss, is, from the point of view of the commercial bank, as liquid as any earning asset it may hold." The bill became law—it was passed in the House with just four dissenting votes—in June 1934. But the bankers would not be cheered up. A year later, only 17 percent of the Federal Reserve's $280 million loan allotment was in use.

The *Commercial & Financial Chronicle*, as unswervingly opposed to statism under Roosevelt as it had been under Hoover, condemned the new measure as "the essence of inflation." But at least, the editors added resignedly, "we should at length have a test of the truth of the charge so often made that the banks of the country generally are at present so unduly niggardly in the extension of credit as to hamper the return of prosperity." (At best, the charge must be judged unproven.)

By the fall, the strife-weary bankers were ready for an honorable peace, and they traveled in record numbers (some 4,000 strong, including, for the first time, a delegation from J. P. Morgan & Co.) to Washington, D.C., for the American Bankers Association annual convention. The keynote speaker was none other than Franklin D. Roosevelt. Preceding him was his former law professor, now the president of the First National Bank, Jackson E. Reynolds.

"My remarks will be brief, simple and earnest," said Reynolds, leading off. He promised his fellow bankers that they would not surrender on the principles of finance, yet the tone of his remarks was almost contrite. What he didn't say was that the White House, insisting on getting an advance look at his speech, had excised some ironic or unflattering passages, including one concerning Roosevelt's embarrassing law-school record. Roosevelt responded with some magnanimous words of his own—departing from his text, he emphasized his own "acceptance" of the profit system—but he returned to the theme that Jones had pounded home the year before. "In March 1933, I asked the people of this country to renew their confidence in banks," the President said. "They took me at my word. Tonight I ask the bankers of this country to renew their confidence in the people of this country. I hope you will take me at my word."

Reynolds, for one, refused. At the next annual meeting of the First National Bank, in January 1935, he spoke freely and scathingly of policy in Washington. He said that he would rather keep the bank's money in the cellar than lend it out at 6 percent and jeopardize the principal. In response to a stockholder who asked if the bank was not, by that stance, opening itself up to attack, he replied, in reference to the First's own indelible experience in the 1933 panic, "Two years ago, deposits in this bank were $447,000,000. Two weeks later, deposits had declined to $172,000,000. We don't suggest that there is a possibility of another such wallop, but it would be simple to have one-half of this proportion. . . . A large proportion of the deposits represented by our excess reserves is placed here for safety . . . and we don't want to put it where we can't get at it when we want it."

By expanding its role in credit, the administration hoped to foster both recovery in business and safety in banking. Assisted by the Federal Deposit Insurance Corporation, the Federal Reserve, and the RFC, it believed, a banker might logically do less worrying and more lending. He could put aside the fetish of liquidity, the fixation on the readiness with which his loans and investments might be turned into cash to satisfy the demands of his depositors. But in 1935 the banking community was unconverted. "We have been opposed . . . to any principle under which A pays B's debts," said Reynolds, thereby rejecting the fundamental principle of the New Deal. To many of the nation's bankers, who believed that a balanced federal budget was a prerequisite to economic recovery, the probable future costs of the Federal Deposit Insurance Corporation, the Federal Farm Mortgage Corporation, the Home Owners' Loan Corporation, et al. were more worrisome than confidence-building. Reynolds criticized a then pending bill that would put federal deposit insurance on a permanent basis and double the maximum deposit-insurance coverage per deposit, to $5,000. Under the temporary 1933 version of the law, banks had been assessed on their insured deposits alone; now they would pay a levy on their overall deposits, a costly change for the First National, which hardly dealt with the public and which expected its depositors to keep a good deal more than $5,000 on the premises to remain in good standing with the management. "It looks as though these modifications will go into effect by mid-year," Reynolds said. "However, the proposal is so unfair that its sponsors may not have the face to approve it."

The cycle of decay and renewal is as much a part of capitalism as it is of the forest floor, and there were signs, even in the deep funk of 1935, that banks were developing new lines of business. Consumer lending—the lifeline of banking in the 1980s and early 1990s—was slowly gaining adherents, and long-term business lending was coming into its own. "With the Government doing so large a share of the large-scale lending," *Bankers Magazine* noted, "the banks must . . . seek elsewhere a fresh outlet for loans if they are to continue to operate at a profit. The banks, having large excess reserves, can not forever remain indifferent to the comparative lack of demand for loans."

But the truth was that something in the normal regenerative process was missing. There was no decisive recovery from the business-cycle bottom. People had lost their speculative courage, and the more the government legislated and taxed, the more that credit sulked. Perhaps the reformers had created a vacuum. They had investigated, overhauled, or eliminated the institutions of the prewar gold standard. What would support or replace them? The government would, it developed.

Federal participation in the process of lending and borrowing did not begin with Wilson, let alone with Hoover or Roosevelt. But it was in the Depression that the government first offered its guarantee wholesale in lieu of the credit of banks and individuals. The consequences of this epochal change were slow in coming, awaiting the time when the existing generation of lenders, whom the Depression had scarred for life, were ready to move on. In time, the socialization of risk—in which A paid B's debts, and perhaps Z's—would help to ignite the greatest credit expansion in American annals. More than by any other single piece of legislation, the Banking Act of 1935 crystallized and codified the new era.

It was more radical than even Reynolds seemed to know. It centralized power within the Federal Reserve Board (shifting it to Washington from New York) and enlarged the board's powers over interest rates, bank reserve requirements, and stock-market margin requirements. It institutionalized federal deposit insurance and eliminated the so-called double liability on bank stocks. Proceeding from the view that the liquidity of the assets of an individual bank was no longer of paramount public concern, it further liberalized the rules under which banks might borrow from the Federal Reserve. It reversed the long-standing discrimination against real-estate lending contained in the national banking law.

Altogether, the administration's bill marked a departure from the traditional idea that a banker's first obligation was to the safety of his depositors. Nowhere did reformers endorse reckless lending, bank wrecking, or the renunciation of individual responsibility in favor of social responsibility. They proposed a resumption of lending with neither the abuses of the boom nor the fears (unwarranted, they believed) of the Depression.

To the old guard, the 1935 Banking Act was just about the last straw. "I think that to accept any such measure, to allow it to go to the statute book, and to attempt to continue to do business under it, is practically suicide," said H. Parker Willis, one of the guiding lights of the Federal Reserve Act and a professor of banking at Columbia University. He condemned the centralization of power within the Federal Reserve Board and the abandonment of the theory (to which he still subscribed) that banks should devote themselves to short-term, "self-liquidating" loans. As for federal deposit insurance, his critique has come to sound less hysterical in recent years than it must have seemed to his opponents at the time. "[I]t is far better, both for the depositor and the banker," he said, "that the actual net irreducible losses growing out of bank failure should fall where they belong. The universal experience with this type of insurance—if it may be called —has pointed to the danger of increasing losses as the result of bad banking management induced by belief in deposit guarantee." (The Comptroller of the Currency, J. F. T. O'Connor, was no less prescient in his remarks. "Mr. Congressman," he said in testimony, "I do not think it is possible to frighten depositors today, with the Federal Deposit Insurance Corporation.")

Not even Willis shed many tears over the proposed repeal of the double-liability law on bank stocks—the assessment visited on sometimes unsuspecting holders of common stocks in failed banks to help defray unpaid debts. The disastrous record of bank failures in the 1920s and early 1930s was proof enough that this Sword of Damocles was not unerring. Certainly it did not prevent abuses at the Bank of United States or stave off unsound lending in Chicago or Detroit. Still, the fact of the double-liability law had served as a symbol of where, in gold-standard days, ultimate responsibility for the safety of banks lay. Its repeal was no less symbolic of the changes that lay ahead.

In the provisions to expand real-estate lending, symbol and substance were joined. Marriner Eccles, governor of the Federal Reserve Board and chief administration proponent for the 1935 act, brushed aside the objection that it was not the place of banks to make long-term loans, certainly not against the notoriously slow collateral of real estate. In the first place, he noted, the national banks had been making real-estate loans (albeit on a small scale) for twenty years, under the liberalizing terms of the Federal Reserve Act. In the second place, the construction industry needed help. "Member banks," Eccles testified, "are suffering from the competition of many Government and other agencies that are entering the field of real-estate loans, and it is a matter of self-preservation for the banks to be able to expand their activities in this field."

Eccles and the other witnesses were testifying with an eye to the conditions of the 1930s, of course, not to the 1990s, but it is impossible to read the record sixty years later without savoring its irony. As the chairman of the Federal Reserve Board favored the expansion of real-estate lending in 1935, the chairman of the Chase National Bank (forerunner to the real-estate benighted Chase Manhattan Bank) resisted it. "I am opposed to any change in the law which tends to weaken the banking structure and prevent it from doing its duty in times of emergency," testified Winthrop W. Aldrich. "Accordingly, in the light of the experience many banks, especially country banks, have had in recent years with real-estate loans, I seriously doubt the wisdom of relaxing the existing loan conditions. To the real-estate speculator, easier credit terms would no doubt be advantageous, but to the lending bank they might well prove the reverse."

But the double prize for prescience and irony goes posthumously to Morton Bodfish, an economist and executive vice president of the U.S. Building and Loan League (forerunner to the U.S. League of Savings Institutions). It was not surprising that Bodfish would oppose the liberalization of real-estate lending by commercial banks: thrift institutions could hardly have welcomed new competition from that quarter. But his arguments transcended self-interest and rose to the higher ironical plane. For starters, he noted that the government itself had become a major dispenser of home-mortgage credit. For another thing, he pointed out that commercial banks had traditionally lent for the short term and that when they did not they frequently landed in trouble. "The dramatic bank failures of the recent depression in Detroit and Chicago and many other localities," he said, "was convincing evidence that extensive mortgage lending was not sound banking."

Now Bodfish reached full flight, addressing not only the Congress but also posterity. "Building activity has not been deterred for lack of reasonable safe credit," he testified. "The price of present properties in relation to costs of construction, vacancies, unemployment and general unwillingness to incur debts on the part of prudent citizens and conservative businesses explain the lack of volume of construction at the present time. Of course, there are speculative builders and others who would build office building upon office building and hotel upon hotel and apartment upon apartment if the now regretted 100 percent mortgage credit of 1927–29 were available." The passage of two financial generations made Bodfish a prophet.

8

False Alarms

On the night of the grand opening of the Mount Washington Hotel in 1902, its builder, the New Hampshire coal baron Joseph Stickney, raised an ironic toast to himself, "the damn fool who built this white elephant." The hotel was just as he described it. Its 234 rooms made it the largest structure in New Hampshire. The perimeter of its front porch measured one-fifth of a mile, and its interior hallways rolled on like the sea. Its windows gave on the near-wilderness of the Presidential Range of the White Mountains.

Well conceived or not, it soon became a favorite resort of the kind of person to whom Lawrence Chamberlain sold sensible railroad bonds. In addition, then and later, came the rich and the famous: the Vanderbilts, Astors, and Rockefellers, Babe Ruth and Winston Churchill. The Depression reduced its clientele—the hotel shut down for the 1930 season—and World War II almost put it into bankruptcy. It was closed in the summer of 1943, owing to war-induced shortages, but 1944 brought a reprieve. Through a stroke of federal lightning, the hotel was chosen as the site of the United Nations Monetary and Financial Conference, better known to posterity as "Bretton Woods," after the hotel's mailing address. Here the postwar monetary order would be designed.

In June, as Allied troops stormed ashore at Normandy, frenzied preparations began at the hotel for the imminent arrival of sixteen ministers of finance and delegations from forty-five nations. (The second-largest contingent, behind the American one, which numbered almost two hundred people, was China's; it had more than forty.) Joining the hotel's staff in the double-time preparatory work were casual laborers, Army MPs, and government officials of all ranks. Arriving delegates found only small signs of disorder; mainly, in the chill of the mountains, they felt the need of heat and sweaters.

John Maynard Keynes, leader of the British delegation and the most influential economist of his day, had what he would call, in another context and at a later date, a "brain wave." The postwar monetary order he envisioned was a drastic departure from the international gold standard. Currencies would continue to be defined as a measure of gold. But governments would intervene, as they had become accustomed to doing in the war, to reduce interest rates and forestall unfavorable movements in exchange rates. Needy governments could apply to a new International Monetary Fund for short-term accommodation. An International Bank for Reconstruction and Development would lend to governments for capital projects, thereby avoiding (or so it was hoped) the excesses of enthusiasm that had characterized international lending by private bankers after World War I. A country that suffered a persistent deficit position in its international payments would no longer have to face the music of high interest rates and a shrinking money supply. It could implement exchange controls, devalue its currency, or have recourse to international credit. In other words, it could continue to run a deficit. If the pre-World War I gold standard had been more or less self-regulating, the Bretton Woods system would be consciously managed. If the gold standard was evolved, Bretton Woods was created. Whereas the gold standard had been transparently simple, Bretton Woods would be complex—bafflingly so, as its critics contended.

One of these critics was the fifth president of the First National Bank of New York. Leon Fraser succeeded Jackson Reynolds in 1937 (George F. Baker, Jr., then the chairman, died aboard his yacht a few months after Fraser's appointment). Fraser was a man of a thousand credentials. He was a former president and chairman of the Bank for International Settlements in Basle, Switzerland. He was an international lawyer, "a banker who never worked in a bank," as he sometimes self-deprecatingly joked. He had served with distinction as a judge advocate in the American Expeditionary Force in France (rising from private to major, in part on the strength of his fluent French, and taking home a pride of international medals and commendations, including one making him a commander of the Order of St. Sava of Yugoslavia). He had worked for a year as a reporter on the old *New York World*, had taught law at Columbia University (an experience he shared with Reynolds), and earned B.A., M.A., Litt. B., and Ph.D. degrees, also from Columbia, in the space of five years, from 1910 to 1915. He had never earned a law degree but passed the New York State bar examination in 1914. A pacifist in the years leading up to the American declaration of war in 1917, he had opposed the Platts-burgh military training camps. Anybody who attended, he was sup-posed to have told a campus rally, was a "benighted fool." For this, Columbia fired him from his teaching post, but it later embraced him (a rich and successful prodigal son) as a trustee.

His clubs included the Knickerbocker, but Fraser was a self-made man and a simple one. His mother had died at his birth and his father had given him for adoption to friends. He was raised on a farm in North Granville, New York, by his adoptive parents until he was sent to New York City and the Trinity School, at the age of thirteen, to prepare for Columbia. In Paris in 1922, he married a former showgirl and government clerk, Margaret M. Maury. They adopted their only child, James, who lived at boarding school at Deerfield, Massachusetts. Fraser did not golf, and he had no use for ceremonial evenings out. "He expressed a distaste for such affairs," a colleague recalled, "saying that he preferred to have a quiet dinner at home with his bottle of wine." In the office, as the spirit moved him, he would kick off his shoes and pad around his desk in his stocking feet. As Reynolds was at ease with Baker, so was Fraser unawed by Reynolds. Once, in the 1930s, Reynolds delivered a stern lecture to the employees about the urgent need to cut costs. At the officers' meeting the next morning, Fraser (who was brought into the bank expressly to succeed Reynolds) subversively and puckishly asked, "[W]hen do we start raising salaries?"

Between 1924 and 1936, there was hardly an international monetary conference that Fraser did not attend. He participated in the Dawes and Young plans for German reparations and in 1933 was a member of the commission of experts at the London Monetary and Economic Conference. By joining Baker's bank, he had, of course, put all that behind him. Mr. Baker had seen no reason to conduct a foreign banking business, and Fraser, after he became president, in 1937, made no change in that policy. Nevertheless, Fraser's reputation as an inter-nationalist was still intact (he was, for instance, a member of the Council on Foreign Relations), and in March 1945 he was called to testify before Congress on the Bretton Woods proposals.

Fraser didn't like them. He said there was nothing wrong with the World Bank (as the Bank for Reconstruction and Development has universally come to be known), but he criticized the International Monetary Fund as an engine of waste and inflation. Fraser spoke easily and colloquially, and the congressmen, to whom he apologized several times for droning on, heard no audible evidence of his long years at the lamp or the law. "Remember, of course," he testified, "that in these countries we have ministers of finance; that each of them wishes to make a good showing before his people, and when he sees a pot of money, believe me, he is going to try to get his nose in it."

Conservative critics of the Bretton Woods scheme directed their fire at its principal architect, Lord Keynes. To Benjamin Anderson, formerly of the Chase National, and to academics like Melchior Palyi and Edwin Kemmerer, Keynes was the plan incarnate, and they spoke to him even when he wasn't there. ("Lord Keynes has been quoted more than any forty men since we have been hearing testimony on this provision," a congressman observed on the day Fraser testified, "and I am wondering if there was anybody there except Lord Keynes.") It was Keynes who understood the future, however. In the United States in the latter half of the twentieth century, debt would lose much of its stigma (as would even bankruptcy). Credit would become more accessible and the terms of repayment less onerous. Under the proposed articles of the International Monetary Fund, borrowing would become, as Fraser put it, "impersonal." A country in need of a loan could borrow from the fund without the political embarrassment attached to borrowing directly from the United States, for example, or from France or Portugal or Britain. The fund, in theory, would not be a lending institution. It would be a mechanism for converting local currencies contributed by member countries into a "pool" of international reserves—that is to say, money. Each country could draw on this pool in proportion to its contribution. Fraser, with his customary bluntness, explained the essence of the plan to the congressmen. "The curiosity in the Monetary Fund," he said,

> is that there is a huge pool of money out of which persons may draw, not automatically, but who, under the wording as I recall it, are "entitled" to draw, under certain conditions which are extremely elastic and to which there are great exceptions, and they make no promise to pay back this sum. We are told that, by a happy fiction, they do not borrow anything; that they purchase some other kind of exchange with their own exchange.
>
> They put in lei, lits, lats and rubles, and they take out dollars. We are entitled to use the lei, the lits, the lats and the rubles. We are told that there is only a service charge, when, of course, the ordinary man would say that such modest charges as they are, are interest charges.

When Fraser, a Depression-era banker, rhetorically asked the congressmen, "Is there not enough debt in the world?" and "Do we want to create some more?" he already knew that the answers were "yes" and "no," respectively. "Fundamentally," he testified, "money trouble is a symptom of some underlying disease, and it cannot be cured without removing the symptom." It was as if a lawyer had borne witness against litigation or a surgeon had endorsed the water cure.

Fraser, however, endorsed the World Bank. American creditors had been badly burned by loans to South America, Poland, and the Balkans, and he guessed that they were not eager to return to those parts. Would the private sector make good loans? "The catch is in the word 'good' and how it is interpreted," said Fraser. "I think there are a lot of 'maybe good' loans which the banks would hesitate to take because of their experience." He might have added that their domestic experience was seared almost as deeply into their ultraconservative subconscious.

At Columbia, Fraser had been captain of the varsity debating team. He had been a graduate assistant to Charles A. Beard, the brilliant constitutional historian, and had earned his doctorate in politics. Driven from Columbia for his principles, Fraser had decided to turn over a new leaf. He had resolved to abandon reform and accept the world as it was. The world was at war in the spring of 1917, and Fraser harmoniously joined the Army. As a grown man at the head of a leading New York bank in the 1930s, he had quietly criticized the New Deal. Now, at the hearings in 1945, the congressmen asked him where he stood on the politics of Bretton Woods. Fraser asserted some libertarian views, but humbly hedged them. "It is my fear that the fund, as distinguished from the bank," he said of the proposed IMF and World Bank, "runs the risk of being an international bureaucracy, due to the provisions it has for exchange controls. That is merely a view and I do not assert that it is necessarily a correct view."

His disapproval of the IMF was complete and unqualified, however, and his views were echoed by some of the subsequent witnesses. Edwin Kemmerer, emeritus professor of international finance at Princeton University, noted that, under the Bretton Woods scheme, the gold par value of currencies was open to revision. "In fact," said the professor, "in sharp contrast to the gold standard, frequent changes of par value seem to be contemplated as an important instrument of monetary policy. We did not change our par value except slightly by metallic adjustment from the time of the establishment of the mint under Alexander Hamilton until 1934." Now the economists proposed that the world change its money as it did its mind, or its governments.

Melchior Palyi, another witness with whom Fraser might have had something to talk about, had been chief economist at the Deutsche Bank and later an economist at the German central bank (after Hitler came in, he packed up for America). Palyi did not agree that frequent changes in the gold content of currencies posed a practical threat to the monetary order proposed by Bretton Woods. The fund would have the right to review them, he noted. A far more immediate danger to the honest settling of international accounts, he said, were policies to stifle the free movement of foreign exchange across national borders. He disarmingly told the congressmen that he was "a specialized student of these monetary tricks," meaning the stifling of the free movement of foreign currencies by governments; Germany had excelled at them in the early 1930s. Under the international gold standard, foreign-exchange controls would have been an absurdity. The unchecked movement of gold among countries was the mainspring of the monetary mechanism. Unless a deficit country lost gold bullion (thereby causing it to stop inflating) the system would have dissolved into nonsense. Not only had the Bretton Woods attendees admitted the possibility of exchange controls, but also, alarmingly, they seemed to sanction them. "Members may exercise such controls as are necessary to regulate international capital movements," said Palyi, reading from Article VI, Section 3, of the Bretton Woods constitution. Warming to his theme, he testified that "for the first time in history" creditor nations had sanctioned the nonpayment of debts—after all, what was advance approval of currency manipulation except an invitation, however carefully phrased, to renege in the settling of accounts? He said that the resulting moral damage could not be easily calculated.

Fraser, having given up quixotic causes in his youth, spoke more guardedly, and Representative Wright Patman, Democrat of Texas, pressed him for his judgment. "If you were a member of Congress, Mr. Fraser . . . and you could not get the bill amended and it is a question of voting for or against it, how would you vote?"

"I would go to my farm that day," said the witness.

Later that day, which was March 22, Fraser reiterated his unhedged view of the IMF. "In my judgment," he said, "it would not bring the desired results and I will bet you a nickel that five or ten years from now, if we are alive, we will look back and say, 'I wish we had not done that.' "

"If we are alive"—the remark was unlikely to strike anyone as literally morbid. Nor would the casual listener have drawn any hidden significance from Fraser's escapist answer to the question of how he would vote if he had to. As for his farm in North Granville, which a few years before had undergone extensive remodeling, it was situated near his boyhood home. He visited it now as a widower.

Fraser returned to New York and to congratulations (we may be sure) all around on Wall Street. So pleased was the bank that it published his testimony and distributed it to its friends and clients. On Friday afternoon, April 6, Fraser left the office to spend the weekend alone upstate. Margaret, his wife, had died in 1943. The visit took his caretaker by surprise; Fraser had not been on the farm since February, when, with Under Secretary of State Joseph C. Grew, he had addressed the Warren County Bankers Association at Glens Falls. Returning Sunday to drive the banker to the train station, the caretaker came upon a pair of notes in the den of the farmhouse. (The door was unlocked, and Fraser had not responded to the doorbell.) One note was addressed to Fraser's son and another to his neighbors. Addressing his business associates, Fraser had also written: "No [cause] other than melancholia in mental depression that I have forgot for years leads to this. Keep losing ground. Put shortly, I have long been unhappy. . . . My deep love for my only son. My will is in my account book in my desk drawer lower left. It leaves everything to him and he can be comfortable for life." By Fraser's side—the caretaker first searched the house, then the grounds, where he came across the body of his employer in back of a small storage house—was a .32 caliber revolver. After a short investigation, the local authorities listed his death as a suicide. Fraser was fifty-five years old.

The news on the radio that weekend left at least one of his colleagues incredulous; to Robert Fuller, Fraser had always seemed the most poised and even-keeled of men. He had the capacity to take life as it was, Fuller reflected, unlike Jackson Reynolds, for instance, who had become increasingly bitter over the domination of American politics by his former inept student, Franklin Roosevelt. Later, going through the things on his desk, Fraser's fellow officers came across the page on the calendar for the Friday before he left the office for the last time. On it, Fraser had written: "Finis?"

So loyal and capable a steward had he been that his death caused no apprehension among the bank's depositors. Nor should it have. Although in certain decline, the First National Bank was as liquid and well capitalized as it had ever been. Its fundamental problem was that the world was passing it by. Presiding over his last annual meeting in January 1945, Fraser had warned the stockholders not to expect the restoration of the old $100-per-share dividend any time soon; starved for interest income, the bank, for the prior three years, had paid $80. It was no small effort to earn that. When, in 1944, the First had had to surrender its Coolidge-era 4 percent government bonds for early redemption, it replaced them with an issue of 2 percents. Fraser anxiously admitted that the bank had earned some money in the last year in securities transactions. "But I want to dispel any idea that we are trading in securities, in and out of the market for a turn," he told the stockholders, some of whom might otherwise have gone into shock. The profits resulted from the early call of such high-yielding issues (extravagant for the time) as the New York Central 3¾s.

Some weeks after the shock of Fraser's death had worn off, a newsman asked the new president, Alexander C. Nagle, if he had any idea of changing things. "No," Nagle replied. "We just hope to stay as we are." Nagle's election had come as no surprise, but the New York newspapers had no picture of him in their files to publish with the story of his promotion. Outside the bank, he was an unknown quantity. George F. Baker was titanic; Reynolds and Fraser each were men of very specific professional gravity. Nagle's chief credentials were long tenure (he had started as a "bench boy," or runner, at the age of sixteen), his unswerving competence, and his photographic memory. Except for a stint in the Army Tank Corps in World War I, Nagle had made his entire career at the First. He trained at the Baker school by day and at New York University at night. In 1925, eighteen years after he was hired, he was made an officer of the bank with the title of manager of the credit department. Baker delivered the good news himself in his own inimitable style. "Nagle," he said, "you have been elected manager of the credit department. It's all right, but of course you know there are only two jobs in the bank that are any good— cashier and president." Baker was speaking from deeply felt personal experience. They were the jobs that he had held.

Fortune, in 1945, described the First as a place that made a "fetish of tradition, convention and opposition to change." It reported that apparently no outsider had been considered for the presidency or the chairmanship (the latter post had gone, at the same time as Nagle's election, to Samuel Welldon, another First National career man). As change is the law of capitalism, however, tradition and convention frequently clog the evolutionary gears. The truth was that the First National Bank was moving backwards.

World War II had brought a cornucopia of public deposits to the bank, but the war was over and deposits, by 1949, were down by half from the peak year of 1945. Earnings were down in 1949 too, even if the average interest rate that the bank was able to garner on its loans was higher: 1.89 percent per annum in 1948 vs. an only slightly more derisory 1.72 percent in 1947. (Even those rates constituted an improvement. Starting in the mid-1930s and continuing until after the war, the First had made term loans at rates of as little as 1½ percent a year.) As for losses, the reserve for bad debts stood at $100,000, a minuscule sum reflecting the bank's almost unblemished credit record over the previous twenty years. Taking few risks, it had lost almost no money.

The somnolent financial mood in New York City in the late 1940s was strongly in keeping with the postwar temper of Baker's bank. There was not much that Fraser could do, in the years leading up to World War II, to lift the bank out of the slough of near-zero interest rates. Wartime brought renewed activity; government bonds again became the focal point of the bank's activity, as they had been in Lincoln's time. Lending, much of it subsidized or guaranteed by the government, was stepped up. It was not capitalism as the first Baker had practiced it—the Federal Reserve, by pegging interest rates, virtually guaranteed the banks a small profit—but the First was at least earning its reduced dividend.

The First Stands Pat

James Fuller, of Hartford, Connecticut, the owner of one share of common stock of the First National Bank of New York, was not satisfied with that small consolation. Nor did he seem to appreciate the traditions and amenities of the bank. (Nagle did, certainly; in his home in Scarsdale was the bench on which he had sat in 1907 as an errand boy to Mr. Baker.) The reason it had no branch offices, no foreign department, no retail deposit base, and no savings deposits was that it had never had them. Its employees always lunched on the premises, the officers between the hours of 12:30 and 2 p.m. in their own dining room. The officers worked at sixty-year-old rolltop desks in the hushed open space of the main banking room. If an officer was in, he would put his hat on the top of his desk to indicate that fact. Nobody would smoke before 3 p.m.*

Fuller did not seem to care about these things, however. At the 1949 annual meeting, he asked about the reduced deposits and the wisdom of ignoring smaller depositors. He asked that the management become more "modernly stockholder-minded." Observing that the First was known as a "blue-blood bank," he asked if it might not profitably reach out for other classes of business. When a reporter's voice from the back of the room commanded him to "shut up," there was laughter and applause from the fifty or so people in attendance. Another stockholder, seeking to clear the air of this uncharacteristic rancor, closed the meeting with a motion to congratulate the management and board on their outstanding achievements.

Sewell Avery was not alone in fearing a postwar collapse. Anxiety was widespread (in 1947, deposits in the fastness of the postal savings system reached a record-high $3 billion). The National City Bank had warned its stockholders that the likely outcome of another world war would be a new depression. But 1946 dawned bright and inflationary. The rate of growth in bank lending nationwide in 1946 and 1947— an astonishing 46 percent—was the highest of any two-year period of the twentieth century up until that time. Loans against the collateral of commercial real estate doubled.† Consumer loans, which had atrophied under wartime controls, climbed by 140 percent. (Partly offsetting those gains was a 70 percent drop in loans for the purpose of

---

* In 1946, a visiting reporter from *The New Yorker* had described the bank as "Dickensian," seeing *Fortune*'s "fetish of tradition" and raising it one. "The First National is regarded in financial circles as the most select in the country," the magazine reported in an item headed, in a nice atavism, "Baker's Bank."

"It has only twelve hundred depositors (most local banks couldn't hold their façades up if they didn't have at least fifteen thousand), but its accounts total in excess of $715,000,000, an average of $600,000, and its capital, surplus, and undivided profits add up to more than $135,000,000. . . . Unlike less formidable institutions of finance, the First National does not insist that its clients—many, but by no means all, of whom are railroads and other sixteen-cylinder corporations—maintain a minimum balance. The thin, cool, hoary air of the place has always discouraged pikers with only a hundred thousand or so in homeless cash."

† The Depression still cast its shadow, however, even over residential real-estate finance. Reacting to the postwar chill in the formerly red-hot California house market, many local banks reduced their loans to 35 to 50 percent of the purchase price. Bank of America made waves by continuing to lend to what was then the legal maximum of 60 percent. "Bankers wondered if that was wise," *Time* reported, and it quoted a competitor of A. P. Giannini, the bank's guiding light: "I guess Giannini knows what he is doing . . . but you can't get a damn cent out of real-estate loans when the bottom falls out." What conservative bankers failed to see was for how long the bottom would not fall out.

financing securities, the result of the cessation of the war-loan drives. Thus, the New York banks, which had taken the lead in war finance, failed to thrive as much as banks in other regions, particularly California.) Between 1945 and 1948, City's personal-loan volume tripled, to $167 million.

But people continued to resist the obvious, bullish conclusion. Of so little faith was City Bank that as late as June 1948 its portfolio of domestic earning assets—loans and investments—consisted mainly of government securities. Gordon S. Rentschler, City's chairman, conceded, in a message to shareholders, that "so far as industrial activity and employment are concerned, the immediate prospect could hardly be more satisfactory. It also seems to be true, however, that uneasiness over the outlook is increasing. The country is riding the boom not confidently and comfortably but rather with a sense that the position becomes precarious as time goes on." At rock bottom in 1933, City Bank had passed up the opportunity to open a branch in Geneva, Switzerland, perhaps for the reason that nothing was certain anymore. Still not ready to climb out on a limb, the bank did not get around to reopening its Paris branch, closed during the war, until 1948. (Even then it warily refused to put "National City Bank" on the door; the place went by the anonymous-sounding name of International Banking Corporation. The staff was years in recovering its bruised self-esteem.)

When, in 1948, the postwar recession did materialize, it seemed to confirm every doubt. City Bank, fearing the worst, sharply reduced its lending. The City Bank Farmers Trust Company, sharing its parent's excessive caution, refused to warm to investments in common stocks. Although the bond market had peaked in 1946—it would be downhill until 1981—the City Bank investment managers loyally clung to it. What they knew was the recent past, and the bond market had risen for almost twenty years.

Meanwhile, the First National Bank was losing ground more quickly than Fuller, its fault-finding stockholder, could have known. The First, with its copper-bottomed balance sheet, excelled in perilous times. There was uncertainty in the postwar world, and no end of worry, but the corporate depositors to whom the First chiefly catered could sense no peril. Credit risk, as measured by the bad-debt experience of the nation's banks, was receding (and had been since 1935). In the same vein, federal deposit insurance was beginning to pose a competitive threat to the banks that didn't need it. Coverage was being extended, by law and through administration. In 1933, the maximum insured sum was set at $2,500 per *depositor*, but in practice anyone could keep as many different insured deposits as he chose. In 1934, the limit was raised to $5,000. For the year 1938, the FDIC was able to report that it had come to the rescue of depositors in seventy-four sinking banks and that 99.5 percent of these were made whole. The insurance fund itself was not the sole agent of protection in each and every case. However, in twenty-four of them, the corporation had extended loans to facilitate the merger of stricken banks with stronger ones. "In effect," as the FDIC explained, "the depositors of the absorbed bank have been paid off in full."

By 1944, the FDIC was pushing hard for an increase in the insurance ceiling. It noted that the nation's bank balances had risen threefold since Congress had fixed the $5,000 limit in 1934. The size of the average deposit was up too, it said, and that fact argued for a higher limit. "The cost to the Corporation of additional coverage is not likely to be large," the agency contended. "It is believed that the indirect benefits of increased coverage resulting from the increased confidence in the safety of bank deposits, combined with broadened powers of the Corporation to assist banks in difficulties, would more than compensate for the relatively small increase in expenditure which might be experienced because of higher insurance coverage." What the FDIC had in mind in the way of "broadened powers" was the authority to buy preferred stock in banks that, by definition, nobody else in his right mind would willingly invest in. It also asked for the authority to lend to them, much as the Reconstruction Finance Corporation had lent to weakened banks (and invested in them too) in the 1930s. "With increased coverage and broadened powers of reorganization," the agency wrote hopefully, "the task of rehabilitation could be adjusted to the needs of the particular situation. There would be no necessity for a hastily conceived merger or the establishment of a new bank in order that the banking service in the community may be maintained without interruption."

The FDIC did not get its way with Congress, but it broadened its coverage nevertheless. It continued to do what it had already begun to do in the 1930s, lending to banks in jeopardy with the end of merging them with strong institutions. The effect was to protect each and every depositor. But it went beyond loans to the outright purchase of the assets of broken banks. By taking outright title to them, it was able to dispose of them without legal interference. Looking back from 1950, the corporation was able to point to a five-year period in which no depositor, insured or not, had lost a dime.

It was the golden age of deposit insurance. "This record of safety for depositors is without parallel in the history of American banking," the FDIC proudly stated. It claimed that confidence in the banking system was "universal" and that the technique of purchasing outright the loans and investments of failing banks constituted a "far-reaching improvement. Its importance is highlighted by the fact that it is basically a mutual self-help arrangement which is so vital to the preservation of the American free enterprise dual banking system. By encouraging and sponsoring the use of this method of protecting depositors, the Corporation believes that it is fulfilling in the highest degree the ultimate purposes of Federal deposit insurance."

All well and good: but when did Congress authorize a program of universal coverage? Senator J. William Fulbright, Democrat of Arkansas, pointedly asked that question of some FDIC officials during a routine hearing in 1951. In 1950, with considerable fanfare, the deposit-insurance limit had been doubled, to $10,000. But the failure, also in 1950, of the First National Bank of Cecil, Pennsylvania, underscored the fact that the limit was increasingly moot. The Cecil Township School District, which had $80,000 on deposit, or eight times the legal limit, had suffered no loss. Under the new regime, an acquisition was always arranged, and a neighboring bank absorbed the Cecil bank. The FDIC instantly advanced $500,000 to facilitate the transaction but could not have known the ultimate cost to the taxpayers when it agreed to make everyone whole. The Cecil vice president had killed himself; two-thirds of the bank's money was not even posted in the books. It was found stuffed in vaults, boxes, and desks. Yet the FDIC intervened to arrange a merger, as it had made a practice of doing since 1944. Small wonder that confidence ran high.

In Cecil, the bank had attracted deposits by offering high interest rates. "It would seem to me maybe your policy is encouraging this method; knowing that nobody is going to lose anything anyway," said Fulbright, "everybody is going to be happy." A man from the FDIC concurred.

"That is an interesting aspect of it," the senator continued. "I was wondering about that the other day when I noticed the second defalcation in New Kensington, Pennsylvania, within six months, I believe. I wondered if this policy might not have a tendency, by relieving the directors of certainly part of their responsibility as citizens to their fellow citizens in the community, they knowing that regardless of what happens everybody is going to be happy, I wonder if that does not tend to cause a letdown in the alertness and the concern of the directors in the bank."

That would be posterity's lookout. Bank failures, rare though they were in the immediate postwar years, left a favorable trail of publicity concerning the FDIC and its widening net of protection. Certainly, the *Valley News* of Tarentum, Pennsylvania, commenting in 1951 on the matter described by Senator Fulbright, did not choose to dwell on the long-range implications of the socialization of financial risk or the disenfranchisement of character as a competitive element in banking. "How times have changed!" the paper marveled. "Only a few years ago the news that a bank president had looted the bank of $500,000 or only $60,000 would have thrown any small community into a state of panic and frenzy. Yet there was hardly a ripple on the surface of New Kensington's business life last week when that very thing happened. Along with the announcement came assurance that no depositor would lose more than a single penny because the deposits were insured by the Federal Deposit Insurance Corporation."*

The competitive threat posed to the First National Bank of New York by the rescue of each and every depositor of the First National Bank of Cecil was not as yet clear. What was becoming obvious, however, was the decline in the value of the strong-and-silent-type balance sheet in the competitive world. To the extent that the American depositor had come to believe that his money was really in the government's hands, to just that extent was an ultraconservative bank at a competitive disadvantage. Money lying fallow in reserve might more profitably, in the new world, be put out on loan.

In anxious times, money had come to the First for safekeeping (March 1933 being a notable exception, as it was for almost every other bank). In slack times, it was left there for lack of better employment. The Ford Motor Company had kept as much as $50 million on deposit at the First, earning nothing. The National Biscuit Co.'s deposit ranged from $20 million to $30 million, and similar lucrative arrangements had existed with General Motors, the American Can Co., and U.S. Steel. As interest rates finally began to rise in the late 1940s and early 1950s, however, corporate treasurers came to reconsider the cost

---

* Bank directors were still liable under the law for negligence or malfeasance, John H. Russell, counsel to the FDIC, reminded Senator Fulbright, and that liability existed whether or not the FDIC elected to make every depositor whole. In one recent failure, said Russell, "the reason we were able to pay off the so-called innocent stockholders, those who were nondirectors, was because we wrung guilty directors, put them through the wringer for their directors' liability, and they had to put back their stock, and in the process of that had to buy back $45,000 of stock that the [Reconstruction Finance Corporation] put up." In that special sense, therefore, a form of double liability in bank common stock still existed (and exists today).

of these idle balances. Naturally, they decided to make do with fewer of them.

The First was well aware of these problems, and it did what it felt was within its means to address them. In the 1930s and early 1940s, Wall Street had attracted precious little new blood. It was not until the mid-1950s that the National City Bank tried, without much success, to recruit junior executives at the Harvard Business School. After the war, the First began to hire more officers (the complement was almost doubled, from sixteen to thirty-one, between 1945 and 1954) and rearranged its clublike main floor to make room for them. It hired more young men to call on corporate customers and even to beat the bushes for new business. (Reynolds, a lawyer, did not believe in soliciting for deposits any more than he did in chasing ambulances. By asking for someone's business, he said, a banker put himself in the position of committing himself to decisions that he might later come to regret.) It did not entirely refuse to take risks in lending. Thus, it helped to facilitate the purchase of Spencer Chemical Co. by J. H. Whitney & Co., an early leveraged buyout. During the war, the government had built a synthetic-nitrogen plant at Pittsburg, Kansas, for use in producing explosives. With the peace, it had leased the facility to the man who had run it, Kenneth A. Spencer. The proposition that Spencer took to Jock Whitney's new venture-capital firm was that he (with Whitney's help) buy it. The acquisition was the first big investment for Whitney & Co., and it proved to be a home run. Although readily agreeing to provide the bank financing, Alexander Nagle, chairman of the First, had vetoed any equity participation in the deal by the First's officers. It must be a purely arm's-length credit decision, he decided, without the distracting hope that, if the deal worked out, the bank or its officers would also participate in a huge capital gain. In the old days, the decision might have gone the other way.

The First, never big in staff or overhead, was now small in almost every respect. Its senior officers had unusual autonomy—they might casually dictate a three- or four-paragraph loan agreement in the presence of a corporate loan applicant and sign it on the spot, without consulting with the home office, bypassing the committee structure of big banks and insurance companies—but they could lend no more than $11 million, later $13 million, to any one customer. The rule was frequently bypassed as it had always been bypassed, but it nevertheless put the bank at a competitive disadvantage. More and more American companies looked abroad for new markets, and the First had no foreign outlets. In 1946, for the first time since the Depression, American industrial corporations became net issuers of bonds, securities that the First was no longer allowed to underwrite.

James Fuller continued to be a source of unsolicited hints to the management at annual meetings. He suggested that a branch be built at Rockefeller Center and that blood lines be discounted in the selection of directors. In 1950, he questioned the nomination to the board of Harold S. Vanderbilt: "All that I know about him is that his name is Vanderbilt, and so I'm 'agin' him."

Not only was financial safety in banking losing some of its competitive significance (the government was seeing to that), but also the democratization of credit was proceeding at a gallop. As Fuller had correctly sensed, ordinary people were becoming a force in lending and borrowing. The postwar years gave rise to the first modern credit cards—Diner's Club came along in 1950—and to no-down-payment, federally guaranteed home mortgages. Car loans were proliferating, and their terms were becoming easier. Second mortgages were reappearing after a long hiatus in the 1930s and 1940s. (It was a sign of the times that the Provident Loan Society, the most active Depression-era consumer-lending institution in New York, did its peak business in 1939. After the war, it faced rising competition from profit-making lenders.) The First National Bank of New York could not bring itself to open a midtown branch office, much less to embark on the uncharted seas of consumer credit. In any case, Alex Nagle was not inclined to refashion at that late date the institution to which he had devoted his life.

Arguably, it was too late. Bank deposits were moving out of New York City, and the First National Bank's share of what remained was on the decline. It no longer seemed to matter that Baker's bank showed the highest ratio of capital to deposits of any bank in the Clearing House Association. It too was a member of the FDIC (although most of its deposits were, of course, over the legal insurance limit, the First paid assessments to the FDIC of more than $8 million from 1933 to 1955; in some lean years, the bank had missed the money). What the world no longer feared, in the late 1940s and early 1950s, was a reenactment of the Panic of 1907. In 1952, the First cut its dividend. It simultaneously split its stock, three shares for one, hoping to attract a wider range of investors—a small, belated concession to Fuller's plea to become more "modernly stockholder-minded." But in the next three years, the number of its stockholders actually fell, to 7,631 from 8,194.

By the end of 1954, all agreed that the time had come to merge or die. Fittingly, the National City Bank was selected as the merger partner and First National City Bank as the name of the consolidated enterprise. It was City that had taken in the First that weekend in 1931 when the city's building inspectors had temporarily made it homeless, and it was Stillman, City's old chairman, with whom Baker and Morgan had consorted so profitably at the turn of the century. The acquisition price agreed to was the equivalent of $1,650 a share on the old First National stock, a small premium to book value, or net worth. In the glory days of 1929, the price had reached $8,600.

As it turned out, Baker's bank had been largely Baker himself. Uniquely suited to the era preceding the Federal Reserve, the FDIC, and the Securities and Exchange Commission, it had failed to adjust to the new ways. Ironically, its original and most valued client, the United States government, had overwhelmed it by regulation. The bank's unique strength—its balance sheet, but also its character, in the presence of Baker, Reynolds, Fraser, and many talented younger men—could no longer be capitalized so easily. Credit had been democratized and its risks had become socialized, and there was nothing to be done but bend to the times. *The New York Times*'s editorial page exactly understood the merger's significance:

> The passing of the First National as an entity in its own right through purchase by the National City Bank dramatizes more strikingly than the other recent bank mergers, perhaps, the changes that have occurred in this field in a comparatively short span of years. Ironically, the niche that George F. Baker had carved for the First became less important with the end of the Bank Holiday, the early Thirties and the establishment of deposit insurance. When people began to cease worrying about the safety of their deposits the premium declined on a bank that made a name for itself as the very epitome of conservatism. The next blow suffered by the First came from the cheap money policy of the past few years, since the chief earnings asset of the First had been Government bonds.
>
> This venerable institution had prospered and increased its prestige by raising specialization to a high degree—specialization in conservatism and in the size and quality of its clients. This was to be a handicap with changing times, when the successful bank was the one that was prepared to become a veritable department store of banking, with branches in the expanding met-

ropolitan areas and even abroad. If George Baker's First National had to choose between compromising with its own tradition and compromising with the times, it was inevitable that it would choose the latter by becoming a part of the splendid, modern banking organization with which it now proposes to join hands.

Too Much Debt? Not Yet

In separate reviews of the United States economy for 1955, American and Soviet authorities both harped on the growth of indebtedness. Not unlike Sewell Avery, with whom they shared not one other square inch of common intellectual ground, the Soviets had confidently expected a postwar capitalist depression. They blamed prosperity on the boom in American consumer credit, seeming to view it as an unfair breach of the rules of ideological engagement.* President Dwight D. Eisenhower, approaching the same data from the nontotalitarian perspective, also expressed concern. His annual "Economic Report" explored the rise in borrowing—stock-market, automotive, and mortgage—and warned that credit controls might have to be employed as a kind of financial sedative.

For the first time since 1937 (and arguably since Coolidge), a genuine speculative boom was in progress, and the nation alternately counted its money and worried about losing it. As so few young people had come down to Wall Street or entered commercial banking in the 1930s and 1940s, the collective memory of American finance was still preoccupied by the Crash, the Depression, and, in general, the risks associated with going overboard.

In 1955, the American financial system was fording a river between the Depression and the 1980s. As at any such juncture, there was confusion among the travelers and anxiety about the destination. A full generation had passed since the economy functioned more or less autonomously, without comprehensive federal controls on the credit markets. First in the New Deal and later during World War II, regulation had become ubiquitous. By the early 1950s, it had come to embrace interest rates, which were fixed to accommodate Treasury borrowing, and the very terms and conditions of an automobile loan.

But after the Korean peace, capitalist sap was rising again. The great

---

* From time to time, the Kremlin could sound more orthodox than the Morgan bank. In 1974, *Pravda* urged the West to return to the gold standard, advice that might have been colored by the Soviet Union's role as a major gold producer.

bull stock market, which got under way in the fall of 1953, roared into 1955, and the nation's commercial banks confidently reentered the lending business. At long last, the Comptroller of the Currency could report that outstanding loans of the national banks had surpassed the size of their investment accounts—that is, government bonds, in the main, with which they had been stuffed during the war.

Possibly for that reason, the boom of 1955 was an unusually introspective one. On two occasions, in January and April, the Federal Reserve Board raised margin requirements on loans to buy securities (in April to a punitive 70 percent), although the level of brokers' loans had not even begun to approach the extremes of 1929. The discount rate, the rate at which the Federal Reserve lent to its member commercial banks, was raised four times that year—finally, in November, to 2½ percent. In April, as the Senate Banking Committee was preparing to release its report on the suspiciously frothy stock market, *The Great Crash*, John Kenneth Galbraith's cautionary essay on 1929, was published to admiring reviews.

Lenders were making it easier to borrow, and that tendency too provoked concern. In the Coolidge boom, the term of an auto loan was twelve months (when, under the force of competition, it began to work its way beyond twelve months, creditors did their best to restore it to a year). Two-year maturities had come in after the war, and now, in 1955, there was movement toward loans of thirty months and even three years. If repossessions and delinquencies were still low, the warning signs of future trouble were unmistakable. In the summer, following repeated warnings by dealers' groups about "crazy credit" and phantom down payments, the national press speculated about the possible reimposition of federal credit controls. In August, General Motors Acceptance Corp. warned, specifically, that a three-year loan coupled with a 25 percent down payment was probably a little too easy for comfort.

The Wall Street Journal asked the trick question: What is wrong with debt? "Isn't it helping to make us all prosperous? Perhaps. But there comes a point where the accumulation of debt ceases to be normal and becomes a menace to the economy. Where that point is nobody ever knows in advance, but once the pyramid's peak is scaled, look out below. Even now, if one thinks about it, there is perhaps something disquieting in the spectacle of millions of people riding around in twelve and a half billions of bright-hued debt."

Dated as such views may seem to a debt-hardened posterity, the rate of growth in borrowing in 1955 seemed alarming. Consumer installment credit (excluding mortgages) was on its way to a 25 percent increase; auto loans would climb by 37.5 percent.* There was exuberance too in real estate, but a leading source of the credit for new home mortgages was now the government. In the 1920s, mortgages were usually unamortized, or "bullet," loans of six years' maturity, requiring down payments of 25 to 30 percent. The contract was between an insurance company or a building and loan society, on the one hand, and an individual, on the other. In the New Deal, fundamental changes were brought about. Down payments were lowered, maturities were stretched, and—most significantly—credit was nationalized. Loans extended by, or through, the Home Owners' Loan Corporation (1933) or the Federal Housing Administration (1934) were underwritten, or insured by, the federal government. Thus emboldened, lenders made loans they would not otherwise have dared to touch. In 1955, under FHA sponsorship, a $12,000 house could be had for 10 percent down and as long as thirty years in which to pay the balance. If the buyer was a veteran, the house could be had on his signature. The immediate results of the substitution of public for private credit were a rise in land prices, a surge in construction activity, and a shortage of building materials. *Barron's*, contrasting the government's investigation of the stock market with its unstinting subsidy of the real-estate market, observed that the terms then available on subsidized mortgages "would have appalled an old-time bucket-shop operator."

In Christmas Week 1955, Geoffrey H. Moore, the distinguished business-cycle economist, addressed a joint meeting of the American Finance Association and the American Statistical Association in New York on the year's burning financial topic. "Changes in the Quality of Credit: The Quality of Credit in Booms and Depressions" was the title of his scholarly paper on the dynamics of lending and borrowing. New research had brought to light a deterioration in the quality of credit in the years leading up to the Depression. Moore did not blame the Depression on bad lending, but he did venture that the weakened structure of credit had "helped to make the Depression much deeper and longer than it might otherwise have been." He went on to ask: "Is a similar deterioration accompanying the present boom, and

---

* In "Family Fortunes," a series of stories on Americans in debt, *The Wall Street Journal* examined the daily lives of overextended consumers. One installment concerned a young physician: "Young Dr. B.'s Income Soars 1,000%, But His Quick Assets Total $700; Years of Schooling Give Way to Buying Binge; Cadillac and Electrocardiograph; The Patients Pay Up Slowly." A reader was led to wonder where the doctor's next meal was going to come from.

thereby increasing the vulnerability of the economy if a recession should, for one reason or another, occur?"

The answer, he said, was unavailable with the information at hand. But those gaps notwithstanding, he did describe the economic conditions that, in the past, were associated with credit deterioration. "What are these conditions?" he asked his audience. "First and foremost is a rapid increase in the volume of credit or debt. Second, a rapid, speculative increase in the prices of the assets that are bought with the rapidly increasing credit, such as real estate, common stocks, or commodity inventories. Third, vigorous competition among lenders for new business. Fourth, relaxation of credit terms and lending standards. Fifth, a reduction in the risk premiums sought or obtained by lenders."

Possibly, at this point in the lecture, members of the audience exchanged nudges and knowing glances. What Moore had just described was 1955. He continued:

"Total private debt increased 21 percent between 1925 and 1930; it increased nearly three times as fast, 62 percent, between 1949 and 1954. In state and local government debt the differences are less extreme; nevertheless, the relative increase was twice as great in 1949–54 as in 1925–30 (85 percent compared with 41 percent). Changes in federal debt were modest in both periods: a decline of 19 percent in 1925–30, a rise of 5 percent, from a very much higher base, in 1949 to 1954."

As for the second condition, Moore cited the bull markets in stocks and real estate. There was no shortage of evidence pointing to heightened competition among lenders (condition number three): finance companies were advertising for customers on the promise that they would not pry into their credit or employment histories. The three-year car loan and no-down-payment mortgage he held up to show that the terms and conditions of borrowing were becoming easier (condition number four). As for a decline in the interest-rate premium demanded by lenders of risky borrowers (number five), he said it had been a fact for some time.

Moore, continuing, said that he did not mean to imply that the news was all bad or that the monetary authorities were complacent. Neither did he mean to cast doubts on the efficacy of the great financial reforms of the past generation—such as federal mortgage insurance, deposit insurance, and securities regulation. He noted, however, that the government was far from being a universal guarantor. Some 42 percent of the mortgage debt on nonfarm homes was government-underwritten, he noted, but risks in the multifamily and commercial sectors were still borne by the private sector, and these had produced some of the highest loss rates in the Depression.

Turning now to the past, Moore reviewed the findings of some scholarly studies of the evolution of credit in the 1920s. Five markets were carefully examined: foreign-government bonds issued in the United States, domestic corporate bonds, urban mortgage loans on dwellings, urban mortgage loans on business properties, and farm mortgage loans. "All but the last of these types of credit underwent a marked expansion in volume during the twenties," he said. "All but the last showed marked deterioration in quality; that is, the proportion of funds advanced that later went into default or foreclosure (mostly after 1929) was much greater for advances made in the second half than in the first half of the decade."*

One implication of Moore's work must have spoken directly to the investors in the audience. It was that in the great bull market people became suggestible. Under the influence of prosperity, they took risks that they would not have stood in a more anxious state of mind. There was every intuitive reason to believe that people's emotions influenced their investment decisions. Perhaps people in markets were especially susceptible to emotions, both on the upside and the downside. ("The more intense the craze," a rueful investment banker said of the 1920s, "the higher the type of intellect that succumbs to it.") How else to explain the urgency to buy Ivar Kreuger's bonds in 1929 or the refusal to lend with an 80 percent federal guarantee in 1935? If, as Moore suggested, lenders become brash and careless at the top of the market, it followed that they also became timid and risk-averse at the bottom. It only remained for the shrewd judge of markets to identify the extremes at which crowds held sway.

Nineteen fifty-five, however, was not one of them. If the growth in borrowing shocked conservative lenders, that was because they were so out of practice at lending. The truth was that the country had forgotten how to have a boom and its misgivings were the reflex of a generation that had come to associate good times with the worst time in American economic history. "Some people are scared to death of prosperity," said William McChesney Martin, chairman of the Federal Reserve Board, in evident exasperation. "They work like slaves to get it, and when they get it, they're scared to death of it because they say there may be hazards in the future. Well, there always are."

* The exception to the rule of decay in the 1920s, the farm mortgage market, suffered its own deflationary collapse (as we have seen) in 1921.

"There exists, and has always existed, a bias against debt itself," wrote Sidney E. Rolfe in 1956 in a persuasive debunking of the critics of the rise in debt, especially of consumer borrowing, which he published in the *Harvard Business Review*. "It is found in the ancient Judaic law, which forbade lending; in the Catholic-medieval concepts of usury; in the Elizabethan drama as a pound of flesh; in the windy strictures of Polonius, who argues 'neither a borrower nor a lender be'; and indeed in virtually every preindustrial society known." Thus dispatching old-fogeyism, Rolfe moved on to deflate the importance of the statistics that purported to describe the relationship between debt and personal income. In the first place, he wrote, a "silent but thorough revolution" in income redistribution had vastly enlarged the American middle class. This fact alone would invalidate comparisons of contemporary and historical data. Because the rise in average incomes had made many more families eligible to borrow, it seemed—falsely—that the nation had gone debt-happy. Then, too, patterns of consumption and spending had changed, again for the better: "The families which in 1929 or 1935 were spending so much per week on the iceman and so much for the laundryman were engaged in the consumption of these services through weekly cash payments without limit of time. But when the iceman was replaced by an electric refrigerator, and the laundryman by an electric washing machine, the *same* expenditures became installment payments and were duly reported in the credit totals by the Federal Reserve Board—only to contribute to the concern over expanding installment debt."

Furthermore, debt was not yet universal. As many as 57 percent of all American families had no consumer debt at all (defined as personal debt excluding business debt, mortgage debt, and charge accounts). For another, the families that did were likely to be those with young children. Finally, one-third of the indebted consumers held liquid assets—that is, cash and marketable bonds and stocks—in excess of their short-term debts.

If this weren't enough, Rolfe pointed out that credit-related losses, repossessions, and delinquencies had been "historically low in the postwar years and especially in 1955–56"—a circumstance it was hard to square with the view that lenders had gone off the deep end. Nor could the critics draw support even from Depression-era rates of default on consumer debts. "[I]t is impossible to level serious charges against the actual performance of consumer debt at any time in the past, in any sector of the economy," Rolfe pointed out. "Indeed, in the last major downswing (1930–32) consumers behaved so well in paying their outstanding debt that one of the then formidable opponents of consumer credit—the banking fraternity—made peace with it and now provides a good part of it for the economy." Far more striking than the excesses of the mid-1950s was their relative sedateness, especially in banking and corporate finance. There were many good reasons for corporations to plunge into debt in those days. Interest rates were low (the prime rate on commercial loans was less than 3½ percent in 1955) and tax rates were high. As it does now, the tax system favored debt financing over equity capital—that is, bonds over stocks. A dollar of corporate earnings, if paid out in the form of a dividend to the stockholders, was taxed twice: first at the corporate tax rate (which was as high as 52 percent); then at the individual tax rate (as high as 91 percent). If the same dollar of corporate earnings was paid in the form of interest expense, however, it was tax-deductible to the corporation. It would be taxed only once, as income to its recipient. But for all the compelling logic of debt, American corporations continued to rely on equity. For every dollar of bonds they issued in 1955, they sold $5.40 worth of stock.

Notwithstanding every good reason to rush the calendar and to hold the 1980s three decades early, however, American business would not be rushed. Using borrowed money to buy a company was not unknown but it was exotic, and the technique did not find acceptance in a straitlaced population that was shocked by a figurative glimpse of stocking in a three-year automobile loan. If proof were needed that Depression attitudes persisted, even in 1955, it could still be found in the bull stock market. The fact was that equities continued to yield more—that is, their dividends alone yielded more—than prime corporate bonds. At the low ebb of stock valuation in 1950, stocks had yielded 7 percent, while high-grade corporate bonds yielded less than 3 percent. Never mind that bond yields almost literally had nowhere to go but up or that the United States, geopolitically, had just inherited the earth. Investors demanded safety—bonds, it was universally believed, were safe—even to the point of relinquishing capital gains in some future bull market. But as bond prices fell and stock prices rose, the Depression-era gulf between stock and bond yields began to close. In early 1955, as the Senate was investigating the possibility that another great crash was around the corner, the gap had closed to less than one and a half percentage points, causing even H. C. Nelson, the usually bullish *Barron's* columnist, to become contemplative. "It is one thing," Nelson ventured, "when stocks yield over 6 percent and bonds 3⅝ percent, producing a favorable spread for the stock buyer of better than 2⅜ percent, as was the case in mid-September 1953 [when the bull market began]. It is another matter when, as now, stocks yield 4½ percent and the spread above the highest-grade bond return of 3.07 percent is approaching 1⅜ percent." To Nelson's readers, it went without saying that the narrowing gap implied caution, although no such course of action was in fact advisable. Before 1959 was out, bonds would outyield stocks, and would continue to outyield stocks through this writing, frequently by wide margins.

The trouble with received opinion in the 1950s was that it was conditioned by the abysmal experience of the 1930s and 1940s. In comparison with no speculation, for instance, even a little bit of speculation seemed to resemble a lit fuse. In comparison with not lending, the resumption of normal banking conjured up memories of Charles E. Mitchell on the witness stand in Washington. By the standards of the 1980s, the banks of the mid-1950s were impregnable. However, they did not look overly sound in comparison with the banks of the mid-1930s. "In most recent years," stated the 1955 annual report of the Federal Deposit Insurance Corporation, "capital accounts of banks have increased more rapidly than either bank assets or bank deposits, thus resulting in gradually rising ratios of capital accounts to assets and deposits." Well and good. However, the FDIC continued, "the ratios of the capital accounts of the banks to their assets and deposits are now substantially lower than they were two decades earlier." What was the standard to rally around? Prosperity or depression?

Concern focused specifically on the soaring ratio of loans to deposits. In the 1920s, banks had typically lent a high proportion of their deposits: in June 1929, it was 80 percent. As war followed depression, loans were replaced by government bonds; by the end of the war the ratio of loans to deposits had fallen to 20 percent. Naturally, peacetime brought a revival in the demand for credit. New lending rose, and the ratio of loans to deposits climbed, in 1955 to 50 percent. Was this, or was this not, the end of the line? Raymond Rodgers, writing in *Bankers Monthly*, presciently argued that it was really only the beginning. "The long-term trend of loans is bound to be upward," he wrote, understating matters, "because the long-term trend of business is upward, and there are no consequential changes or developments in our economy which will reduce loan demand. On the contrary, our new patterns of production and consumption, especially the increasing reliance on consumer credit as a basic pillar of prosperity, point to increasing utilization of credit."

As for the First National City Bank (the name of the new, combined entity, Baker's bank and City), it summed up the boom year in the diffident style of an ex-convict who wants to avoid giving offense to his parole officer. "We recognize that banking has at all times a responsibility to promote stable economic progress and the general welfare," said First National,

> and in years like 1955 this responsibility is a heavy one. In some manufacturing industries immediate demand is greater than present capacity can satisfy. To add excessively to demand through unwise credit expansion, when an equivalent increase in output cannot be achieved, could only have inflationary effects. It is appropriate in these circumstances to remind both lenders and borrowers that it is necessary to use credit with discrimination. This is the effect of the policy which the Federal Reserve authorities are now following. In our opinion this policy is being carried out with skill and moderation. It has put a brake on the expansion of the money supply, which is desirable in the present state of optimism and increased use of borrowed money, but it has not closed the door to credit extension for purposes consistent with stable economic growth.

Euphemism is the lingua franca of central banking, and the international monetary establishment was even more oblique about the stirrings of price inflation than First National City was, or could be. In the early postwar years, the only dollar problem was one of scarcity. It was the currency that everyone wanted and there was not enough of it to be had. Technically, under Bretton Woods, the dollar was the world's chief "reserve currency." It was convertible into gold (for those so foolish as to prefer a non-interest-bearing brick to a fecund dollar). Lesser currencies, in time, would be made convertible into dollars. The dollar was the sun of the postwar monetary system and pounds, marks, francs, and rubles were the planets, moons, meteors, and asteroids. Ultimately, the authors of Bretton Woods intended, every currency in the system would be defined as a measure of dollars, while the dollar would be defined as a measure of gold (35 of them to the ounce). In theory, the dollar, like the sun, might one day fall in on itself, bringing down chaos, but that would not happen for a very long time.

For all the foreboding of Keynes's critics, Bretton Woods did not immediately dissolve into chaos or hyperinflation. On the contrary, world trade expanded and war-ravaged economies recovered. "In continental Europe," wrote the author Angus Maddison, "the decade of the 1950s was brilliant, with growth of output, consumption, productivity, investment and employment surpassing any recorded historical experience, and the rhythm of development virtually uninterrupted by recession."

The Employment Act of 1946 was (as we can see now) a declaration of inflationary intent for the postwar American economy, but the rise in the cost of living in the 1950s was restrained. From 1953 to 1959, a broad measure of prices rose by 20 percent in Europe but by only 14 percent in the United States. Bank credit was growing and indebtedness was coming back into vogue, but interest rates were low and the overseas demand for dollars continued high.

At first, the trouble with the dollar was disguised as a blessing. Starting in 1950, the United States disbursed more dollars abroad than it received from abroad. It earned a surplus of dollars in trade but suffered an overall deficit (foreign aid, military expenditures, and foreign investment were some of the things that canceled the trade surplus). In the jargon of economists, the United States balance of payments was in deficit, but the economists too spoke euphemistically. In lieu of "deficit," they would say that the country had had "net transfers of gold and dollars to the rest of the world." Welcoming that fact, they did not stigmatize it. In 1946, the world was deficient in dollars. By the late 1950s, thanks to years of United States deficits, it was having its fill.

In its solar capacity in the Bretton Woods system, the dollar was uniquely privileged. Running a deficit with the rest of the world, the United States was obliged to settle its accounts by paying its creditors. But the currency in which it paid was dollars. And its creditors, having no use for dollars at home, at once returned them to the United States, the deficit country, for investment or deposit in a bank. The dollar, after all, was a "reserve currency." It was as good as gold.

Or was it? If there had been no doubt, it is unlikely that many creditors would have demanded payment in gold. More and more did, however, until, in 1959, the American gold stock dropped below $20 billion, a loss of $3.3 billion in a decade. Jarring new turns of phrase began to crop up in official monetary reviews. In its 1959 annual report, the Organization for European Economic Cooperation noted that its member countries were accumulating ever larger holdings of dollars and gold—the monetary spoor of the persistent American deficits. "The growth of the gold and dollar holdings of European countries over most of the last decade has represented a beneficial and necessary redistribution of world reserves," the report said. "But the continuation of large overall European surpluses on the scale experienced during the past two years would pose considerable problems for the rest of the world. . . . The United States could not for very long provide an outflow of reserves on the present scale, although its reserves are still large in regard to any probable fluctuations in its balance of payments and to claims on the dollar as a reserve currency."

The Dollar on Trial

Under the international gold standard, "outflows of reserves" meant the loss of gold. A loss of gold brought unhappy consequences to the losing country, notably higher interest rates and a shrunken money supply. Under Bretton Woods, the phrase had a more ambiguous meaning. "Reserves" included dollars, and an "outflow" of dollars, for the United States, was not an immediate loss at all, because most of the dollars were redeposited in the United States. It was as if a man bought a suit and paid his tailor, and the tailor turned around and lent the man the money again. Under such a system, observed Jacques Rueff, the leading critic of the monetary arrangements of the day, a man might accumulate an impressive wardrobe.

Rueff made a brilliant career, fluently combining the qualities of the *croyant* and the *pratiquant*. Imbued at the Ecole Polytechnique with Cartesian logic and a faith in the application of mathematical techniques to social problems, he entered the French civil service and the European intelligentsia. If others in public employment shrank from controversy, Rueff embraced it. In 1931, while serving in the French embassy in London, he contributed a pair of pieces to *The Times* that blamed British unemployment on British unemployment insurance. The sum and substance of his advice in the depths of the Great Depression was to abolish the dole and thus to begin to cure the economic problems of which joblessness was only a symptom. The British government diplomatically pretended not to take notice.

Charles de Gaulle did listen, however, in 1958. In that year Rueff helped to put over the financial reform that launched France on the great prosperity of the 1960s. The program was the essence of Rueff's thought: the franc was devalued and anchored as a weight of gold. Subsidies were reduced or eliminated and import quotas were abolished. Thus the French economy was subjected to the bracing competition of the Common Market. "It worked," *The Times* of London later succinctly noted.

As he was prepared to contend against unemployment insurance in Britain in 1931, so did he champion the cause of hard money in America in the 1960s. Rueff believed that there was one true gold standard: that of the years preceding World War I. Similarly, there was one impostor: the system in place since the early 1920s. According to Rueff, the gold-exchange standard was responsible for most of the world's financial ills. It had caused the bubble of the 1920s and the Depression of the 1930s. It had done this by institutionalizing delay in the settlement of international accounts. As we have seen, the hallmark of the gold-exchange standard was the unequal status of the participating countries. The exalted few were the "reserve currency" countries, notably Britain in the 1920s and America in the 1950s. It was the privilege of a reserve-currency country that lesser countries would accept its money in payment for goods and services. More than accept it: hold it. A drone country, acquiring sterling (in the 1920s) or dollars (in the 1950s) would not then do what was customarily done between 1870 and 1914. It would not exchange the money for gold. Instead, as we have seen, the creditor would redeposit the sterling in London or the dollars in New York. In the Rueff parable, it would play the role of the gullible tailor. "Thus," wrote the French economist, "the United States did not have to settle that part of their balance-of-payments deficit with other countries. Everything took place on the monetary plane as if the deficit had not existed. In this way, the gold-exchange standard brought about an immense revolution and produced the secret of a deficit without tears. It allowed the countries in possession of a currency benefiting from international prestige to give without taking, to lend without borrowing and to acquire without paying."

However, the dollar's prestige was waning. In 1959, the American trade surplus vanished. In 1960, a most untoward event occurred in London: on October 11, the price of gold touched $40.50 an ounce, $5.50 higher than the official dollar conversion rate. By deeds more damning than words, investors expressed the conviction that the Federal Reserve System, abetted by the American banking system, had overexpanded. In relation to America's gold, there were too many dollars abroad. No doubt, every international holder of dollars would not elect simultaneously to present his currency to the Treasury for exchange into gold at the statutory, $35-per-ounce rate. However, the arithmetic began to suggest that if one were of a mind to switch, it would be better to do so sooner rather than later. As recently as 1958, the dollar value of American gold reserves had exceeded the dollars held by foreigners. In 1959, the ratio of gold to foreign-held dollars was even. In 1960, alarmingly, it became uneven. Dollars in foreigners' hands—that is, dollars that might potentially be exchanged for gold—totaled $20.9 billion. United States gold reserves amounted to $17.8 billion.

In truth, a $40.50 gold price smacked of the run in Cleveland's day. There was open speculation about a devaluation of the dollar (meaning a higher official gold price), which Senator John F. Kennedy, in the last lap of his 1960 presidential campaign, tried to quash: "If elected President, I shall not devalue the dollar from the present rate. Rather, I shall defend its present value and soundness."

But the "value and soundness" of the dollar was exactly the issue. Under the classical gold standard, the gain or loss of gold was the cue for action, and central banks would take appropriate remedial steps in small increments. No dams burst, because no reservoir was filled to overflowing with unpaid international bills. Under the gold-exchange standard, however, the principal countries procrastinated as a matter of policy. Had there been, in the late 1940s, a worldwide "dollar shortage"? The world needed "reserves," and these the United States supplied by spending dollars. Was the world's gold unevenly distributed? By running a deficit, thereby losing gold (though by no means all it might have lost had not foreign creditors so eagerly clung to dollars), the United States helped to redistribute it. In other words, the existence of surplus dollars was not the prima facie evidence of a too liberal monetary policy. It was a kind of global public service. By the time the international monetary establishment had come around to agreeing that the chronic American payments deficits constituted a "problem," it was 1960, and the problem was ten years old. The solution was fewer dollars and a lower inflation rate, but the United States was not inclined to accept it. Rueff wisely quipped: ". . . the gold-exchange standard places the whole economy in the situation of a man falling from the tenth floor: everything goes well at the start, but he can be sure that he is going to crash to the ground."

Even if not yet in crisis, the dollar was becoming a source of international embarrassment. Late in 1960, a delegation of U.S. officials visited Europe to seek financial assistance from the onetime beneficiaries of the Marshall Plan.

From 1950 to 1957, the U.S. gold stock had fallen by $1.7 billion. Between 1958 and 1960, it dropped by $5.1 billion. On January 16,

1961, just before leaving office, President Eisenhower issued an order forbidding Americans from holding gold abroad. Thereby he joined hands historically with Franklin D. Roosevelt, who had outlawed the ownership of gold at home in 1933. (Henry C. Alexander, chairman of the Morgan Guaranty Trust Co. of New York and by virtue of that position one of the nation's leading bankers, must have been gratified to hear it. In November, Alexander had declared that the holding of gold by Americans abroad "can have very unfortunate side effects," since foreigners may interpret buying by "speculators or eccentrics" as a lack of confidence in the dollar on the part of "responsible people.")

Nineteen sixty-one was a banner year for palliatives. The Federal Reserve undertook a maneuver to raise short-term interest rates and simultaneously to lower long-term interest rates. Operation Twist, as the scheme was called, was intended to induce foreigners to hold more dollars (and, it was supposed, to carry away less of the Treasury's gold). So-called swap arrangements were negotiated by the Treasury with foreign central banks, also to thwart the unwanted exchange of dollars for gold. Banding together in the wake of the surge in the free-market gold price in October 1960, central banks formed the London Gold Pool to suppress any such future speculative outbreak. "Roosa bonds," which took the name of their inventor, Under Secretary of the Treasury Robert V. Roosa, were sold to foreign central banks; otherwise volatile short-term dollar deposits would be temporarily taken out of circulation. An expansion of the IMF's resources was planned against the day, formerly unimaginable, when the United States itself might apply for a loan.

At the supermarket checkout counter in the early 1960s, there was no dollar crisis. Inflationary stirrings were unmistakable abroad but nascent at home. The economy grew slowly in 1962 and 1963, and the rate of domestic price inflation, 0.7 percent in 1963, was the envy of the industrialized world. In 1961 and 1962, the overall balance-of-payments deficit was below the level of 1960. After the October 1960 dollar panic, the world's gold fever had apparently broken. Far from selling into a roiled and rising market, the London Gold Pool was able to purchase unwanted gold in a quiet market. It was possible to believe that the international monetary storm had passed. Rueff, however, did not believe it, and he struck a foreboding note in the July 1961 issue of *Fortune*: "A grave peril hangs over the economy of the West. Every day its situation more and more resembles the one that turned the 1929 recession into the great depression." This menace, as students of Rueff's writings did not need to be reminded, was the gold-exchange standard, and the economist pleaded for immediate reform.

As usual, the Americans declined. In 1964, capital controls were enacted, a stopgap of the kind that Leon Fraser had warned against in 1945. The regulations took the form of an "interest equalization tax" designed to keep dollars at home and out of the hands of foreigners. It taxed Americans who purchased foreign securities and foreigners who raised funds in the United States. (Also in that year, the Treasury announced it would no longer pay out silver dollars, a concession that the commodity value of the coins had come to exceed their purchasing power. The inflation of the dollar had reached the coinage; indeed, silver coins had been disappearing from circulation since the late 1950s.)

The fundamental problem of an excess of dollars went unaddressed, but the world was not cast into darkness on account of that fact. There was no 1929, and there was no 1931. The credit structure of the United States was undergirded by federal deposit insurance and the "universal confidence" in banks of which the regulators had boasted. The institutional memory of the Great Depression was still intact and perhaps for that reason the time was not yet right for the reincarnation of S. W. Straus & Co. or the Bank of United States. Booms are made of attitudes, and the state of mind of American lenders and borrowers (to judge by what they would and would not do in the early 1960s) was still, by latter-day standards, conservative.

To the undoubted secret annoyance of the American monetary establishment, Rueff in 1964 was accorded the honor of election to the Académie Française. He was the first economist to be so honored (the man he succeeded was a poet, Jean Cocteau), and his rising star augured badly for the dollar. His considerable influence on monetary thought in France was evident in the policies of the President, Charles de Gaulle, who frankly described his resentment of the dollar in a press conference on February 4, 1965. Echoing Rueff, de Gaulle recited the inequities of the gold-exchange standard, including, especially, the privileged position of America. "[W]hat the United States owes to foreign countries it pays—at least in part—with dollars that it can simply issue if it chooses to," said the general. Reform was needed, but on what terms? "Actually," de Gaulle declared,

it is difficult to envision in this regard any other criterion, any other standard than gold. Yes, gold, which does not change in nature, which can be made into either bars, ingots, or coins, which has no nationality, which is considered, in all places and all times, the immutable and fiduciary value par excellence. Furthermore, despite all that it was possible to imagine, say, write or do in the midst of major events, it is a fact that even today no currency has any value except by direct or indirect relation to gold, real or supposed. Doubtless, no one would think of dictating to any country how to manage its domestic affairs. But the supreme law, the golden rule . . . is the duty to balance, from one monetary area to another, by effective inflows and outflows of gold, the balance of payments resulting from their exchanges.

It was sentiment worthy of Grover Cleveland, but the American government was now headed by Lyndon Johnson. On the day of the press conference, the Treasury Department issued a statement rejecting a return to the international gold standard (that is, to the real McCoy, as opposed to the gold-exchange standard that de Gaulle and Rueff, and before them Emile Moreau, had criticized). It insisted, however, that the $35-per-ounce official exchange rate was inviolable. It was what governments in such compromised circumstances had always said. The United States was losing gold year by year. Yet also, year by year, it was issuing new dollars. The proliferation of dollars coupled with the loss of gold strongly pointed to devaluation—that is, to an increase in the number of dollars required to buy an ounce of gold. The facts were in the public domain. It was up to the government to convince the country's foreign creditors that there would be no devaluation, the facts notwithstanding.

The root of the problem was still inflation. The Vietnam War was widening, consumer prices were rising (though moderately), and the money supply was expanding. The reason to have a gold standard was to anchor the value of money. It was to limit the ability of governments to do exactly what the Johnson administration was doing. The orthodox response to inflation—higher interest rates, fiscal restraint, etc.—did not have appeal to the Johnson White House even in a nonelection year. (Nor was it a foregone conclusion on Wall Street that inflation was becoming a significant problem. The years 1961 to 1965, in the words of Sidney Homer, marked "the most unusual period of stability in the postwar period. Prime corporate bond yields remained close to 4.50 percent for five years." In October 1965, *U.S. News & World Report* published an article that explained to its readers: "Why Workers

Don't Mind a Little Inflation.") Instead, the administration elected to stretch the gold it still had on hand.

In March 1965, this sum amounted to $14.6 billion. Not all of it was available to meet the demands of the French and other disgruntled foreign holders of dollars, however. It was the law of the land that gold must stand behind the currency itself: greenbacks in circulation in the United States and money on deposit ("bank reserves") at the Federal Reserve. The amount of backing, or "cover," specified was 25 percent. As no American citizen enjoyed the right to exchange his dollars at the $35-per-ounce rate, the law could be viewed as a monetary throwback, and the administration chose to seek its revision. On March 4, legislation authorizing partial repeal of the gold-cover requirement was signed into law. The currency would still be backed by gold, but money on deposit at the Federal Reserve banks would not be. Some $1.8 billion in gold was thereby "released," as *The New York Times* put it, "for use in meeting foreign demands and for the expanding money supply needed by an expanding economy." Still, there were many more potential foreign claims on the nation's gold than there was gold to pay them. Thus, the administration saw to it that foreign central banks received a higher interest rate on their dollar balances than Americans did. If foreigners could be induced not to exchange their dollars for gold, there would be no gold problem.

There would be no functioning gold standard either, but Washington hardly minded that. The Johnson administration, simultaneously waging war and building the "Great Society," had no use for limits. In urgent need of latitude, it continued to short-circuit the warning device of the gold standard, or what remained of it. Its financial policies suggested a man slyly jamming a penny into a fuse box.

By the mid-1960s in the United States, monetary orthodoxy was heresy, and vice versa. Makeshift was the national policy, and orthodoxy (in the shape of a rigorous gold standard) was outside the bounds of informed discussion. Rueff, therefore, was a heretic, and his proposal that the United States should double the gold price—thereby effecting a 50 percent devaluation of the dollar—aroused exasperation. "When a prophet of doom comes to America—as does Jacques Rueff—mantled as the only economist worthy of membership in the French Academy and bearing the favor of General de Gaulle," *Business Week* commented in April 1965, "it is difficult to write him off as a nut." The magazine came close, however. As for the devaluation, ". . . [it] would reward all those who speculated against the dollar; and would punish those who upheld it; it would be a permanent windfall to the big gold producers, the Soviet Union and South Africa. But, far worse, rather than strengthening the world's monetary system, it would weaken it, as faith in national currencies declined in anticipation of further hikes in the price of gold." Concerning Rueff's prescription for the international monetary system—a return to the kind of gold standard in which the deficit countries relinquished gold and the surplus countries gained it—that too was out of the question. Surely, the editors suggested, the wit of man could contrive a better device than gold bricks. "The time is past," they wrote, "when any sane nation will limit the growth of its money supply to the growth of its gold reserves or accept a system that forces it into deflation, depression and mass unemployment as the price of protecting its gold reserve."

If this was the test of sanity, the United States was eminently sound of mind. When the Federal Reserve banks raised their discount rates in December 1965 by one-half point, to 4½ percent, President Johnson publicly rebuked them. The President was not indifferent to the gathering signs of inflation, but he preferred to address the problem on the person-to-person level. He appealed to businessmen to postpone unneeded capital investment, to mayors to defer bond issues, and to women to "get out their lead pencil and put on their glasses and look at some of those price lists and see where these shortages are occurring, and see where prices are advancing, and say, 'goodbye to those products that insist on going up and up.' " He identified the source of inflation as the rising prices of butter, pork, fresh vegetables, copper, lead, and zinc. He did not quote from Rueff or de Gaulle or mention the Federal Reserve Board. He predicted that interest rates would be falling.

Monetizing the Debt

It was a colossal error, of course. Rising prices were the symptom of the problem, not the cause. The primary cause was the growing tendency of the Federal Reserve to purchase the administration's notes and bonds with newly created dollars. The process is easily described. The Fed would buy some Treasury bills from a commercial bank. In payment, it would credit the bank's reserve account. Banks kept such deposits for one reason only: to serve as a legal reserve against lending. Therefore, an increase in reserve accounts was tantamount to an invitation to step up the pace of lending. More lending created more dollars and thus (in an economy overheated by war) the certainty of rising prices. Literally, the government's debt was "monetized," or turned into money.

In the 1950s, except during the Korean War, the Federal Reserve only rarely augmented its holdings of government securities from one year to the next. In the 1960s, however, under the chairmanship of William McChesney Martin, it did so routinely. In the mid-1960s, a 10 percent rate of expansion in its portfolio of Treasury bills and notes became the norm. Nothing could be more inflationary—surely, nobody in the Federal Reserve could expect the economy to grow by 10 percent a year before inflation—but that was not the fact on which the central bank dwelled in its public discussion of the inflation problem. Looking back on 1967, for example, the Federal Reserve Bank of New York fastened blame on taxes, deficits, wages, prices, the war, and the "stresses of 1966." (In that year, market interest rates had risen over the limit imposed by the Federal Reserve's Regulation Q. The result was a "money crunch" that briefly traumatized the mortgage market.) What it did not get around to discussing, except by indirection, was the blatant monetization of the public debt by itself and the other reserve banks. At the end of 1967, the Federal Reserve System owned 10.8 percent more of the government's securities than it did at the end of 1966.

Small wonder that prices and interest rates were climbing. For the full twelve months of 1967, the broadest measure of inflation registered the biggest rise in a decade: 3 percent. The bond market put in a harrowing year. In June, Illinois Bell Telephone borrowed at an interest cost of 6.04 percent, the highest such rate since 1921. Long-dated Treasury yields climbed to 5.64 percent from less than 4.50 percent at the start of the year, and prime tax-exempt yields rose to 4.30 percent from 3.35 percent. It had been thought that 6 percent constituted the upper limit of corporate new-issue bond yields; by the end of the year, investors were hoping that 7 percent was the top (it proved not to be). It began to appear that the bond market was becoming extinct.

In November 1967, the British pound, a chronically weak currency, reentered the hospital. Its exchange rate was devalued to $2.40 from $2.80, and the world's attention was directed to the dollar once more. In its day, sterling had been the world's premier currency.* Its dilap-

---

* One legacy of the pound's former glory is the way it is quoted in foreign-exchange markets. There are always so many dollars to the pound—e.g., $1.90. On the other hand, there are always so many yen (and francs and marks) to the dollar.

idation was a morbid reminder of the fate of paper money down through the ages. On the date of the devaluation, Saturday, November 18, President Johnson issued a statement "unequivocally" reaffirming the United States' commitment to buy and sell gold at the existing, $35-per-ounce dollar rate. Central banks, led by the Federal Reserve, intervened in the London gold market, selling heavily to all speculative takers. The Federal Reserve banks promptly raised their discount rates to 5 percent from 4½ percent. By raising the yield on dollar deposits, the American authorities hoped to discourage speculators—the proverbial "gnomes of Zurich" whom a Labour politician had conjured up in an earlier sterling crisis—from buying gold against an imagined future devaluation. The higher the interest rate, the more a gnome was out of pocket by holding gold, an asset that paid no interest.

Subsequent elements of the administration's dollar-defense program borrowed heavily from the brain-wave school of monetary control. Even before the latest sterling crisis, Robert Solomon, a ranking Federal Reserve official, had conceived the ultimate refinement on the gold-exchange standard. Central banks would continue to sell gold in London to dampen speculation against the existing $35-per-ounce rate. However—here was the refinement—they would not really lose the gold they sold. They would receive a new reserve asset, a "gold certificate," in return. (For the time being, the idea went nowhere; central banks were not yet willing to make that kind of a trade.)

The consensus of official opinion in 1967 and early 1968 was that the $35-per-ounce dollar exchange rate was the gravitational force in international trade and finance. If the rate was changed, the world would fly apart. In comparison with that terrible possibility, Treasury officials may not have expended undue worry over the manhandling of some official data. The statistics concerned the classification of dollars held by foreign central banks. All of those dollars were potential claims on the ever-dwindling American gold stock. However, only the dollars invested in short-term instruments contributed to the closely watched "liquidity deficit." The definition of short-term was less than a year. The Treasury, therefore, prevailed on central banks to place a portion of their dollars in American securities maturing in more than a year. By such makeshift did Washington get through the day.

However, none of these things—higher interest rates, heavy gold sales in London, and imaginatively edited data—was enough, and President Johnson announced new stopgaps on January 1, 1968. "To the average citizen," he said, "the balance of payments, and the strength of the dollar and of the international monetary system, are meaningless phrases. They seem to have little relevance to our daily lives." But Johnson proceeded to invest them with relevance. He ordered the curtailment of direct overseas investment by American corporations, restrictions on overseas lending by American banks, and limitations on overseas travel by American citizens. All of this, it was hoped, would keep dollars at home and out of the hands of the unreliable foreigners.

Soon another administration proposal reached Congress: repeal of the remaining domestic gold-cover legislation. Under law, currency in circulation was still assigned a 25 percent gold backing, but either there was too little gold or there were too many dollars. Altogether, Fort Knox held $12 billion worth of gold, of which $10.7 billion was required for domestic cover. That left $1.3 billion worth available to meet potential foreign claims. These totaled not less than $39 billion (counting all dollars held by all foreigners). Anyway, the administration contended, the domestic gold-cover rule was an anachronism. No American citizen could own gold, let alone demand it in exchange for currency. The Federal Reserve was already empowered to suspend the gold-cover requirement for a period up to thirty days (and to renew that suspension every fifteen days indefinitely), but permanent relief was needed to assure America's foreign creditors that the United States was prepared to defend the dollar down to the last gold brick.

"Removal of this requirement," the chairman of the Federal Reserve Board, William McChesney Martin, testified, "would in no way reduce our determination to preserve the soundness of the dollar."

Sylvia Porter, the personal-finance writer, had echoed the administration's views on this matter, and a column of hers was approvingly read into the record of the hearings of the House Banking Committee. She used questions and answers:

Q. Would this [measure] encourage the Treasury to print more money?

A. It is the Federal Reserve System which controls the money supply through its policies determining the availability of credit. Cash represents only about one-fourth of the total money supply; the balance is "checkbook money." This fear is unfounded.

Q. Is this a sign of weakness?

A. It is certainly another warning to get U.S. budgets under better control. What the country is doing is buying time to put accounts in shape and to build a stronger world monetary system. The dollar remains the only reserve currency in the world, the only truly international money. Gold is not its strength, the economy is.

There was reason to doubt that establishment view. The Treasury was in the position of any deposit-taking bank. It ran the risk that the depositors would all descend at once to reclaim their money. Most banks do not invite that debacle, but the Treasury's depositors (the foreign holders of $39 billion) had every good reason to be suspicious. Not every solvent bank is liquid, and the Treasury, although solvent, was clearly illiquid. It was without the gold to meet a run. The Federal Reserve Board chairman had pledged his customary determination in the job of fighting inflation, but only his customary determination. The gnomes of Zurich were up in the driver's seat.

"The conception that our dollar is as good as gold was rudely shattered by the gold buying abroad triggered by the devaluation of the British pound, which only too clearly demonstrated weakness and distrust of the American dollar as a store of value." So one deeply interested party, the chairman of Homestake Mining Co., Donald H. McLaughlin, wrote to the House Banking Committee in late January. He was against repeal of the gold-cover legislation. The American Bankers Association also opposed it, but the Federal Reserve System, the Treasury, and David Rockefeller, president of the Chase Manhattan Bank, supported it. (One Treasury Department witness observed that France was behind on its World War I debt to the extent of $6,850 million and that not a dime of interest or principal had been paid since 1931. He did not have to point out that Rueff and de Gaulle were French or that the Bank of France had shown an annoying preference for gold over dollars.)

Whatever the dollar's utility as a long-term store of value may or may not have been, the temptation to speculate against it in the short term was irresistible. To place a bet, a gnome bought gold in the London market. The price would not go down: $35 to the ounce was the law. In case of a devaluation, it could only go up.

In February 1968, the principal seller of gold was the London Gold Pool, a consortium of eight central banks led by the United States. What galvanized the pool members was a determination to hold the $35 line. ("We will use our gold down to the last bar," Joseph W. Barr, Under Secretary of the Treasury, had testified in January. "We are not going to raise the price.") United States officials repeatedly said that nothing less than the future of world trade hung in the balance.

Even for so worthy a cause, the cost of the battle became prohibitive. Early in March, gold changed hands in London at a price fractionally above the official rate, $35.22 an ounce. But that price was only an earnest of gains to come. As speculation rose, the volume of turnover increased, from 30 tons a day in the first week of March to 100 tons on March 8 to 225 tons on Thursday, March 14. Almost by definition, for every speculative buyer there was an official seller, and the buyers were in the far stronger position. They couldn't lose. On Thursday, the Gold Pool members capitulated. They closed the London gold market (effective Friday) and boarded aircraft for a conference in Washington. In their wake, in other world markets, the price of gold was bid up to $43 an ounce.

In Washington over the weekend, a communiqué was released on behalf of the governors of the seven participating central banks, the managing director of the International Monetary Fund, and the general manager of the Bank for International Settlements. The document was a masterpiece of dignity, conceding the inevitable in such a way as to convey the distinct impression that the monetary establishment had only done what it had wanted to do all along. "The Governors," said the statement,

> noted that it is the determined policy of the U.S. Government to defend the value of the dollar through appropriate fiscal and monetary measures and that substantial improvement of the U.S. balance of payments is a high-priority objective. . . .
>
> They noted that the U.S. Government will continue to buy and sell gold at the existing price of $35 an ounce in transactions with monetary authorities. The Governors support this policy and believe it contributes to the maintenance of exchange stability.

The news of the surrender, couched as an improvement in methods, was withheld until the seventh paragraph. It said:

> The Governors believe that henceforth officially held gold should be used only to effect transfers among monetary authorities and, therefore, they decided no longer to supply gold to the London gold market or to any other gold market. Moreover, as the existing stock of monetary gold is sufficient in view of the

prospective establishment of the facility for Special Drawing Rights, they no longer feel it is necessary to buy gold from the market.

In plain English, the Gold Pool was dissolved, and the gold market was set free to establish whatever price it would. Central banks would continue to conduct their business at $35 to the ounce. Special Drawing Rights—so-called paper gold—were on the drawing board to augment the supply of dollars and monetary gold. All in all, the world of international finance had never been more mystifying. What had been simple and reassuringly tangible—losers lost gold and winners gained it—now became abstract and overarchingly clever. The Federal Reserve Bank of New York tried to explain the new ways: "In effect the decision to terminate official intervention separated the circuit of monetary gold movements from private trading, and thereby insulated the stock of monetary gold from speculative and industrial demands." But what did this mean? In essence that the movement of monetary gold had lost its traditional role as the means to compel adjustments among nations. The persistent drain of gold from the United States was nothing more than the mirror to American inflation. Wishing to spend heavily at home and abroad, the administration was not prepared to do what had to be done. It was still less inclined to submit to the discipline of the gold standard. It refused to suffer the loss of more gold to foreign "speculators," yet it also refused to devalue the dollar. The policy on which Johnson settled, therefore, was to make gold inert. It would no longer travel abroad in settlement of accounts but instead would remain stacked in the vaults of Fort Knox. When, on August 15, 1971, President Richard M. Nixon finished the work so long in progress—declaring that the dollar would no longer be convertible into gold at any price—he did it by playing to the populist galleries. "This action will not win us any friends among the international money traders," he told the nation. But among the many winning features of the gold system was its genuine populism. Until 1933, anyone could exchange his unwanted dollars for gold. Until Nixon's time, any foreign central bank could do the same. With all its faults, the gold standard represented the rule of law in monetary affairs. People could take the government's money or they could leave it; the government was beholden to the people, some of whom were called speculators.

From Moscow's perspective, the significance of the events of March 1968 was simple, and the Communist Party chairman, Leonid Brezhnev, explained them clearly and with none of the defensiveness of the New York Fed: "After the devaluation of the pound, we are now witnessing the beginning of the devaluation of the United States dollar, and in such circumstances the possibility of a profound crisis of the capitalist system should not be excluded." Jacques Rueff himself could have said it no more emphatically.

9

It's a Wonderful World

In 1969, interest rates were higher than they had ever been before. When the New York Telephone Company issued forty-year bonds bearing a 7½ percent coupon, in March, the underwriters were besieged by eager individual buyers. "The customers came at us like Coxey's army," a bond dealer marveled. By the end of the year, however, the typical well-regarded utility was paying 9 percent. Since the time of Queen Anne, long-term, investment-grade bond yields had rarely risen above 6 percent. Something was plainly awry.

In May, *Institutional Investor* magazine, a dinosaur scene pictured on its cover, published an article that proposed that the bond market was becoming extinct. It was a plausible thesis that had occurred to more than one loss-ridden investor. Bond prices had been falling since 1946. They had not fallen every day, but they had fallen almost every year. In the 1950s and early 1960s, inflationary trends were latent; by the late 1960s, they had become overt. It was clear to anyone who visited a supermarket that the purchasing power of the dollar was shrinking.

"There was a moment only a few weeks ago," wrote John F. Lyons, the magazine's staff writer, "when everyone who held a bond had a loss in it." It was a fact that condemned an entire generation of investors as patsies. They had believed in 1946 that 2½ percent was a fair rate of interest at which to lend for the long run. They had entertained similar delusions about 3½ percent in 1956, about 4½ percent in 1959, and about 5½ percent in 1966. When successive Presidents, Treasury Secretaries, and Federal Reserve Board chairmen had promised balanced budgets, lower interest rates, and sound money, they had believed them. It was one of the longest losing streaks in the annals of investments.

"It takes a while for the impulses of pain to travel from the source to the nerve centers of some of the larger institutions, but it is safe to say, by now, that the pain impulses have reached all the nerve centers," Lyons went on. He noted that university endowments were turning away from bonds and that state pension funds were pressing for legislative permission to buy more stocks. He interviewed some of the financial descendants of the New England bond salesman Lawrence Chamberlain. One of these authorities was S. Coe Scruggs, an investor of private capital and former financial vice president of the American General Insurance Co. Scruggs was not optimistic. "The bond market as we know it is dead," he said, asserting that "we can only have a bull market in bonds if the nation returns to the days of McKinley and sets up Calvinism as its national philosophy. Now what are the chances of that happening?"

It was possible to trade bonds profitably, and Scruggs described that kind of speculation as "an aesthetic experience and lots of fun." But as for investing—doing what Chamberlain had faithfully done— Scruggs almost scoffed. "[T]he market is only good for nickels and dimes," he said. In the opinion of Lyons and his informants, the past was irretrievable. Inflation was now a permanent condition of American life. It was, indeed, a necessary condition of growth. "The fact of the matter is," wrote Lyons, "that markets which are good for bonds are bad for people in the social sense. Long-term bull markets in bonds have typically been associated with major economic slowdowns, stock-market panics, and depressions. The last great bull market in bonds, for instance, started in May 1920 but didn't gather momentum until the Great Depression of the 1930s."

Never mind that low interest rates were the rule in American history, not the exception, and that the country's growth had not been stunted by the lack of inflation in gold-standard times. An important school of thought on Wall Street had become defeatist. Because the dollar would be debased, it held, no sane person would continue to lend at fixed rates of interest over years or decades. Investors would demand and receive protection against inflation. They would lend for months, not years. In exchange for a loan to a corporation, they would receive the right to participate in the borrower's profits. Mortgage lenders would demand cost-of-living adjustments from their tenants. All of these adaptations would supplant the straight, fixed-rate, long-term bond of old. "As a bond portfolio manager today," said John H. Larkin, senior vice president of the First National City Bank and the senior officer in the bank's bond department, "I often feel like a funeral director presiding over the funeral."

"And finally," wrote Lyons, "though bond men do not talk about it very much, there is the nagging suspicion that bonds as they have existed in the past are something of an anachronism as a modern investment vehicle. The point is this. In an era when everything seems to be growing by multiple leaps—from compounding company growth rates to whole new industries like the one which has emerged from space exploration—simple percent returns from fixed income securities tend to pale. In effect, who wants a fixed percentage return through 1997, when they can get a double or a triple in a matter of years?"

Here was brave, inflationary talk. Why *not* a "double" or "triple" every few years? Why not buy growth stocks and simply watch them grow? Well, somebody would have to lend to the future growth companies of America just the same. If the bond market was becoming extinct, a new, hardier species of market must evolve to succeed it.

One potential successor was the commercial-paper market. Commercial paper is a corporate IOU maturing, typically, in ninety days. Unlike a mortgage, it is an unsecured debt. The claim of the lender is against the general credit of the issuing corporation, not specifically against its railcars, real estate, or inventories. In the 1960s, the commercial-paper market was thriving. Measured by volume of issuance, it quadrupled between 1966 and early 1970, from $10 billion worth to upwards of $40 billion worth.

There seemed nothing untoward in that remarkable expansion. W. Braddock Hickman, the great bond scholar, had written that meteoric growth in any debt market usually foretold trouble ahead; sound lending was measured, not manic. However, Hickman was writing about ancient times, the first four decades of the twentieth century. No shadow of fear hung over the 1960s. The economy was booming and bank failures were rare: not one marred the prosperity of 1968. When, inevitably, a bank did shut its doors, the usual precipitating cause was mismanagement or defalcation, not the stringent economic conditions that had characterized the 1920s, let alone the 1930s. In March 1968, the National Credit Office, then the sole arbiter of creditworthiness in the commercial-paper market, remarked on the market's "growing exclusiveness." It noted, hopefully, that "the ready availability of top-quality paper, coupled with financial problems of a few finance companies, has tended to weed out lesser rated paper and many smaller firms have dropped out of the market."

Penn Central Affair

Set in this clear blue sky, the Penn Central Transportation Co. was a cloud hardly bigger than a man's hand. The company was the product of the 1968 merger of the Pennsylvania Railroad Co. and the New York Central Railroad. It was a potluck supper of businesses, including real estate, railcar leasing, truck leasing, and oil pipelines. It was the nation's largest railroad and sixth-largest nonfinancial corporation. Among its real-estate assets, wholly or partially owned, were the Waldorf-Astoria Hotel, the Pan Am Building, the Graybar Building, and some fifteen other presumably valuable properties in midtown Manhattan. Its railroad lines, wholly or partially owned, included the Lehigh Valley, the Northern Central (including, for instance, the Shamokin Valley & Pottsville Railroad Co.), the Cleveland, Cincinnati, Chicago & St. Louis Railway, the Philadelphia, Baltimore & Washington Railroad Co., the United New Jersey Railroad & Canal Co., the Michigan Central Railroad, the Wabash Railroad Co., the Illinois Northern Railway Co., the Norfolk & Western Railway Co., the Toledo, Peoria & Western Railway Co., and the West Jersey & Seashore Railroad (among dozens of others). For a time, Penn Central was a 1960s wonder stock. In September 1968, it changed hands at a price equivalent to 19 times expected 1968 profits. What is clear to posterity was not unfathomable at the time: railroads faced crippling competition and regulation, and Penn Central was beset by a host of financial and operating difficulties. However, the company borrowed from the leading banks—such as the First National City Bank—and sold commercial paper through the top dealer—Goldman, Sachs & Co. It received the National Credit Office's highest rating.

What made the commercial-paper market ideal for an inflationary time was its short time horizon and low interest cost. Besides, it was exempt from the registration and disclosure requirements of the federal securities laws. Money was lent for days or months rather than for years. The risk of a German-style hyperinflation, all could agree, was remote. But it was considerably more remote in the short term than it was over the next twenty years. There was always the theoretical possibility that an issuing company would go bankrupt. In the late 1960s, however, that risk too was viewed as distant, or antique. Investors had come to believe that commercial paper entailed no more risk than Treasury bills. Shattering this complacency, Penn Central was to anticipate the 1980s, but it did so only with effort and application.

Investors of the go-go era were as implacably optimistic, and ill informed, about credit as their fathers (in the 1930s and 1940s) had been
hypersensitive.

One telling feature of the commercial-paper market of the day was
the aforementioned National Credit Office. A subsidiary of Dun &
Bradstreet, NCO had been in business since 1920, but it was ossified
beyond its years. It employed only three or four analysts to monitor
500 or 600 companies, and the depth of its research was commensurate
with the level of its staffing. In general, NCO personnel worked from
annual reports and other public documents; from time to time, seeking
another opinion, they would pick up the telephone and call a commercial-paper dealer. As the dealers were habitual owners of commercial paper (they sold it from their own inventories), they were also
habitually bullish. Certainly, Goldman, Sachs had only good words for
Penn Central, and NCO guilelessly believed them. (In testimony
before the Securities and Exchange Commission, a man from NCO
swore that he had no reason to doubt them. Of his friend at Goldman,
the analyst said, "He is a responsible man and well recognized in the
commercial-paper market.")

The Federal Reserve Bank of New York criticized the rating agency
for failing to see that the commercial-paper market had become less
creditworthy. "There are, of course, no statistics on commercial-paper
quality," the bank commented in a Penn Central postmortem late in
1970, "but the fact that a number of firms in the market by 1970 had
very high debt to equity ratios and/or income flows of dubious quality
(some conglomerate, franchising and leasing companies, for example)
suggests such a deterioration in the quality of outstanding paper."

It was easy enough to see that in hindsight. As it was happening,
few seemed to notice or take action. By late 1969, $200 million worth
of Penn Central commercial paper was outstanding. How would the
company redeem it? It would issue new paper, as issuers habitually
did. What would it do if it found no buyers? It would then mobilize
its "backup lines of credit"—promises by banks to tide it over pending
receipt of permanent financing. Backup credit was then, and is today,
an integral part of the commercial-paper market. Few issuing companies have it within their means to redeem their maturing paper for
cash on demand. That was (and remains) the role of the banks.

In 1969, Penn Central had a backup line of credit in the sum of
$100 million. It was not unusual that this insurance policy should be
smaller than the volume of paper outstanding ($100 million less than
the maximum level of issuance), and NCO approved the arrangement.

"From this office's point of view," the agency tried to explain in the fall of 1969, "the commercial-paper standing of this company is not affected because of the readily salable assets of the subject, if the need arose." In other words, Penn Central could sell a railroad or a coal company.

It could do nothing of the kind in a pinch, however. It could sell unpledged corporate possessions, but not on the spur of the moment or in the heat of a crisis. In November 1969, Penn Central suspended its dividend. In April 1970, it reported a $79 million operating loss for the January–March quarter; the company had expected a loss of $49 million, at worst. *Institutional Investor* had been wrong about the stock market serving up doubles and triples in perpetuity. For the hapless investor who had bought at the peak of November 1961, the net gain for the decade of the 1960s (before receipt of dividends) had been exactly 66 Dow points, or 9 percent. (In fact, according to the Dow Theory school of analysis, a bear market had been in progress since 1966; it would not end until 1974.) As for the bond market, it seemed to be vanishing according to script. Under the press of inflation and tight money, interest rates were rising. In 1970, Penn Central had hoped to borrow $100 million for the long run, supplementing the $200 million it had raised for the short run, via the paper market, but the bond market proved inhospitable.

The paper market belatedly came to its senses too—Penn Central's new annual report, released in March 1970, was a calamity—and by late April, a buyers' strike had begun. What was to be done? David C. Bevan, the railroad company's chief financial officer, spent sleepless nights mentally canvassing the private sector. Convinced that nobody would lend to the company voluntarily, he arranged a meeting with President Nixon's Secretary of the Treasury, David Kennedy, in effect to wring an involuntary loan from the taxpayers. A former Chicago banker, Kennedy listened to Bevan describe the company's plight and the possibility that it might reverberate. Hearing this, Bevan recalled, the Treasury Secretary "paled perceptibly." Kennedy responded that he was not certain of his powers but he "understood the problem and everything would be done" to help.

Penn Central wanted a government-guaranteed loan, and its bankers wanted it to have one. Walter Wriston, chairman of the First National City Bank, was a frequent and biting critic of government intervention, but it was his bank that submitted an application for a $200 million loan guarantee to the Federal Reserve Bank of New York on June 2.

City Bank (which spoke for seventy-three others) had overappraised the credit of Penn Central. Now the bankers asked that their risk, or part of it, be federalized. The legal authority for this request was given as the Defense Production Act of 1950; the guaranteeing agency was to be the Navy Department. The claim, of course, was specious. There was no imaginable connection between the landlocked Penn Central and American sea power. Besides, as the editor of *Barron's*, Robert M. Bleiberg, wrote at the time, "bankrupt or not, many railroads operated throughout World War II, and several are running that way today." The chairman of the House Banking and Currency Committee, Wright Patman of Texas, challenged the legality of the proposed guarantee, and he asked how much the government could theoretically lose in case Penn Central went bankrupt anyway. The answer (furnished by the New York Fed) was the entire $225 million that the company and its bankers had asked it to pledge. Patman refused, and the administration withdrew its request. On Sunday, June 21, 1970, Penn Central filed for protection under Section 77 of the federal bankruptcy act.

By then, Penn Central had been forced to reduce its paper issuance to $82 million, down from $200 million at the peak in 1969. One might have supposed that by then the bad news was out. Penn Central's common stock had collapsed and even the National Credit Office had gotten around to demoting it from "prime." (NCO acted on June 1, only three weeks before the bankruptcy. Among the things that the agency did not get wind of that spring was that Goldman, Sachs, on May 20, had ceased to offer Penn Central's commercial paper. As late as May 28, NCO was still credulously asking the brokerage house for its opinion of Penn Central's finances. The broker at Goldman was still saying that he thought they were fine.)

Like a man waking up with a start from a deep sleep, however, the commercial-paper market stumbled out of bed and crashed into the furniture. The logical and cold-blooded reaction to the news—Penn Central deserved to fail, and indeed had been failing for years—was not the one that the market chose. The Federal Reserve Bank of New York described the anxieties of the day: "Holders of paper issued by other large corporations became apprehensive about the low level of corporate liquidity as well as about the ability of borrowers to refinance existing debt, given the tight position of the banking system. The difficulties encountered by a number of brokerage firms, including some of the oldest and largest houses, and the fact that stock prices continued to fluctuate erratically added to the widespread uneasiness. Moreover, the Penn Central default came at a time when the amount of maturing commercial paper was seasonally high because of the midyear statement date."

In the week ended July 1, 1970, the volume of "nonbank" commercial paper outstanding—promissory notes issued by businesses—fell by $2.25 billion; in the next two weeks, it declined by another $714 million. Thus, in short order, one vital segment of the commercial-paper market had shrunk by almost 10 percent. Commercial-paper investors now conceived a rapt, belated interest in the creditworthiness of the companies in which they invested. Only the best companies would do; second-tier issuers were obliged to pay a premium, and all corporate issuers were forced to pay significantly more to borrow than the Treasury paid.

The Treasury was not a party to the quick resolution of this crisis, but the Federal Reserve System intervened decisively. It encouraged banks to lend to corporations as it lent liberally to banks. It suspended the interest-rate ceilings above which banks had not been able to bid for new deposits. Harking back to the makeshifts of the 1930s, it prepared what it subsequently described as "standby procedures to make credit available to worthy borrowers facing unusual liquidity requirements that could not be met by obtaining funds from other sources." If this meant that the inflation was a lesser evil than a domestic financial crisis, so be it: ". . . the System recognized that it might have to let the money supply and bank credit temporarily grow faster than desirable over the longer run in order to maintain financial-market stability."

One of the original purposes of the Federal Reserve System was to foster the growth of a commercial-paper market. As inflation is a monetary phenomenon, the system had inadvertently done its duty. By suffering a rise in inflation, it had undermined the bond market. To buy a forty-year bond required a faith in the purchasing power of the dollar that no newspaper-reading investor could possess in 1970. The mirror image of the loss of faith was the growth in the commercial-paper market. Anybody would lend for ninety days.

Only seventy-two investors had been stuck with Penn Central commercial paper (many more with its bonds and stock, of course), and one of them, the treasurer of a small Pennsylvania college, gave an affidavit describing his experience to the Securities and Exchange Commission. He had made his final purchase in March 1970, the month that the company issued its damning 1969 annual report:

At this point the availability of Penn Central was mentioned. I hesitated because the college already held $400,000 in Penn Central. On asking for pertinent information from the latest financial report, I was informed the company reported consolidated revenues of $2,251,716,000 compared with $2,102,770,000 the previous year and preliminary earnings of $4,388,000 versus $86,961,000. At this point the problems of consolidation as a result of the merger were pointed out. I next questioned the current asset to current liability ratio, which was indicated at approximately one to one. When I indicated my concern over this, the representative reassured there was no need for concern since total assets exceeded 6½ billion. With some hesitancy I agreed to the purchase of 300M [$300,000] of Penn Central paper.

On April 3, 1970, I received the letter of confirmation and a copy of the financial data on Penn Central. I was dismayed to learn the information conveyed over the phone was as of December 31, 1968, and not December 31, 1969. This, coupled with reports to the newspapers of the increased financial plight of the company, prompted me to call our representative to attempt to sell the paper held by the college. I was informed our representative accepted another job and the college had been assigned a new representative. I do not know what efforts were taken by Goldman, Sachs & Co. to resell the paper, but in any event they were unsuccessful.

For all the world, the college treasurer sounded like an unlucky customer of S. W. Straus & Co. pouring out his heart to the New York State attorney general in the Great Depression. What had financial reform wrought? As for the National Credit Office, it too seemed a throwback to the bad old days. "It would seem apparent," the SEC had related, ". . . that NCO's commercial-paper department was relatively disorganized and of scant importance in the D.&B. corporate complex as the person selected to manage same is a veteran functionary of limited skills and experience in this area and as he received no training or ongoing guidance in the performance of these duties."

It was discouraging to consider that a $40 billion market had allowed itself to be misled by one dim bulb at the NCO. The fault was not his alone: the press had been deaf and Wall Street dumb. As for the Nixon administration, its attempt to nationalize the cost of poor lending decisions had been frustrated by a Texas populist. All in all, it was a spectacle that called to mind the truth that progress in financial affairs is cyclical, not cumulative. Putting a man on the moon, scientists had stood on the shoulders of giants. Overlending to Penn Central, bankers had re-created the errors of their fathers.

In markets, however, no disaster is unmitigated, and the wreck of the Penn Central created a dazzling investment opportunity. The country was then embarked on a real-estate boom, and the shattered railroad company was a major landlord and property holder. It had been accumulating real estate for more than a century. So far-flung were its holdings (and so mixed up was its management) that no reliable inventory of its real estate existed. Receivers, however, counted 8,500 parcels, including the Commodore Hotel on East Forty-second Street in New York, which was eventually sold to a brash young developer named Donald Trump.

Real Estate Becomes Respectable

The original prohibition against real-estate lending in the National Bank Act of 1864 was strict and uncompromising. The history of American banking was strewn with failures, runs, and panics that could be traced to an excessive enthusiasm for real-estate collateral. Whatever the theoretical value of a tract of land might be, it was hard to realize that value at the drop of a hat. If, all at once, depositors chose to demand their money in gold, a land bank (or a real-estate-oriented commercial bank) might be unable to accommodate them. The Second Bank of the United States vividly illustrated the shortfalls of real estate as a banking asset. Opened in 1817, the bank one year later was foreclosing on sizable loans against Western property, including choice farmland in Ohio and Kentucky and a great deal of the city of Cincinnati. Alexander Hamilton in 1790 had warned against mixing a commercial-banking business, in which liquidity was paramount, with a land-lending business, in which liquidity was, in the nature of things, unattainable. (On the other hand, of course, land was the preeminent American asset, and in pre-industrial days there were not many alternative assets.) Hamilton and hard-won experience notwithstanding, state-chartered banks continued to lend actively against land and buildings. A history of Chicago real estate, written from the vantage point of the Great Depression by Homer Hoyt, connected the boom of 1836 with "note issues of the State Bank of Illinois and the issues of Michigan banks that were issued against wild land. The collapse of these banks with the forced liquidation of their holdings intensified the gloom of the depression in 1841 and 1843. The rise of the new state banks of issue in Illinois in 1852 accelerated the rise to the new peaks of 1857."

The Federal Reserve Act of 1913 softened the original real-estate prohibitions of the national banking law. They were further relaxed in 1927 and 1935, and again in the decades of the 1960s and 1970s. In 1961, a subcommittee of the House Banking and Currency Committee conducted hearings into the advisability of increasing the limits on real-estate lending to the equivalent of 70 percent of the amount of a bank's savings deposits, up from 60 percent. The Federal Deposit Insurance Corporation, seeing no risk in the proposal to the banks or their depositors, voiced no objection to it. Neither did the Treasury Department. The American Bankers Association supported it enthusiastically. The association's witness, Harry P. Bergmann, testified that as many as one-quarter of the nation's banks were bumping up against their legal real-estate lending capacity. The existing limit dated from the 1930s. "Since that time," Bergmann said, "many developments have occurred in connection with real-estate mortgage practices, particularly the development of the amortized loan. There can be no question that the present form of real estate mortgage lending provides a much safer type of investment which in itself would appear to warrant the modest increase in the aggregate amount of such mortgages."

The traditional view was that real-estate collateral was hard to "realize," or to sell. Bergmann doubted the relevance of that concern in the modern day. "We do not think this will impair the liquidity of banks," he said. "It has been demonstrated that in times of recession or economic weakness the time or savings deposits of banks tend to increase rather than decrease." Representative Henry Reuss, Democrat of Wisconsin, put his finger on another important change. The advent of deposit insurance had enabled the banks to make illiquid loans. "Before we had deposit insurance to protect depositors in banks," he said, "there was a great deal to be said, it seems to me, for the proposition that we should not let banks put too much of their total lending power in long-term, relatively frozen assets like long-term mortgages on homes for fifteen or twenty years. If you put your whole lending power in long-term mortgages like that and more people want their money you will not be able to meet their demands." That, at least, was the historical reason.

Then Reuss asked Bergmann: "Would you say the success of deposit insurance gives you greater freedom in the way of long-term mortgage investments than would be the case if depositors had no insurance whatever?"

"That is very correct, sir," the witness replied.

The Office of the Comptroller of the Currency was also inclined to see things in a new light. "Earlier regulatory concepts . . . ," its 1963 annual report stated, "were molded by past custom and past economic conditions, and in part by unnecessary conservatism, rather than by statutory mandate."

Unnecessary conservatism had had its day. The time had come for unnecessary risk-taking. Inflation is a goad to speculation (both reasoned and gratuitous), and so, in the real-estate field, was federal legislation. In 1960, Congress passed legislation to create the real-estate investment trust, or REIT. The law was a lubricant to the boom. It held that if a REIT derived three-quarters of its income from real estate and if it paid out 90 percent of its earnings in dividends, it was exempt from corporate income tax. Soon there were REITs by the score, many of them sponsored by banks (or, more exactly, by bank holding companies). They invested in property or lent to finance construction.

In 1968, the Federal Housing Act became law. President Johnson, as he signed it, declared it the "Magna Carta" of the cities. The law, which set a national goal of creating or refurbishing 2.6 million housing units a year for a decade, built on the foundation of the REITs and of years of inflationary monetary policy. "Millions of jobs as well as millions of homes . . . ," said *U.S. News & World Report.* "That is what the nation can expect from the new housing law in years ahead. It is the biggest infusion of money into the building industry in history."

Barron's acclaimed REITs as the "No. 1 glamor stocks of 1969." Money was tight, and banks, which usually met the borrowing needs of real-estate developers, could not keep up with the inflation-swollen demand. In stepped the "mortgage trusts," REITs that invested in mortgages rather than directly in properties. Borrowing at 6 percent or less, they lent to builders at 12 percent or more. First Mortgage Investors, for instance, grew brilliantly, and in 1969 investors bid up its shares to a price 33 times more than its earnings. One of the secrets to FMI's success was uninhibited borrowing. Most successful businesses generated capital by keeping the profits they earned, by selling new stock, or by borrowing. Bound by law to distribute 90 percent of what they earned, REITs chose to borrow.

On Wall Street, success quickly elicits the highest form of flattery, and imitators crowded the mortgage-lending field. Life insurance companies, banks, and construction companies sponsored REITs. In 1970, Chase Manhattan Bank, the nation's largest lender for commercial construction, created what would prove the largest (and among the most ill starred) of REITs, the Chase Manhattan Mortgage & Realty Trust. "Chase" and "Trust" proved to be a highly marketable choice of names, and the company, borrowing from the luster of its sponsor, attracted a wide public following. Borrowing freely, it financed the construction of office buildings, resorts, condominiums, and shopping centers. Within five years, its assets—that is, loans—reached $1 billion.

By long tradition, bankers had turned a dour face to the world. It was a dull depositor who would hand over his money to a hail-fellow-well-met. Besides, if the wildest dreams of a promoter should ever be realized, what would that gain his lender? All that a banker could hope to gain in any loan was the return of his money, with interest. In Atlanta in the late 1960s, however, Mills Lane, chairman of Citizens & Southern National Bank, lived and lent by the motto "It's a Wonderful World!" The legend was posted on a sign above the entrance to his office and printed on neckties that he handed out to callers. The approved institutional attitude at C&S was joie de vivre, and the burden of proof fell to those who would not lend rather than to those who would say "yes." The bank lent eagerly against the collateral of real estate, trucks, and food-service franchises. Any of Lane's loan officers, seasoned or green, could commit the bank for up to $5 million, its legal limit. Few of them were inhibited by firsthand experience in the Depression or even with postwar recessions. "We had a lot of people lending who weren't even *born* until 1946," a C&S banker reflected later. "The last couple of recessions hadn't even touched Atlanta. You couldn't tell them that things might go bad."

It was into this hopeful world that the Chase Manhattan Mortgage & Realty Trust was born. Inflation was rising, but what of it? Real-estate values were rising too, and developers were paying more to borrow. Deposit interest rates were still regulated by the Federal Reserve Board; as market interest rates rose above the lawful ceiling, banks lost deposits to more lucrative investment outlets. Because they lost deposits, they were obliged to turn away eager potential borrowers, including real-estate developers. The latter flew into the waiting arms of the REITs, which operated under no Federal Reserve constraints. The Chase REIT grew by $250 million a year.

"You had to beat them off with a stick, they wanted to give you money so badly," said Jerome C. Berlin, a Florida lawyer with real-estate interests. The REITs of the 1970s anticipated the savings and loans of the 1980s. In the heat of competition, they lent not only at the full value of a project but at more than full value. "A builder could put $200,000 or $300,000 in his pocket," said Berlin, "and it was only when the real trouble started that he had to reach in for money, which is the time that many simply walked away." In a special report, "The New American Land Rush," in 1973, *Time* related the story of a thirty-acre parcel of land near Orlando, Florida, fifteen miles from Disney World. Sold in the spring of 1973 for $285,000, it was resold two weeks later for $375,000. "One week later," according to the magazine, "a subdivision developer bought it for $525,000. Several months later, the developer turned down an offer of $750,000 for the property, upon which he is now constructing apartments."

The afternoon of real estate was followed in due course by cocktails and darkness. To grow, the REITs had borrowed: from banks, in the bond market, and in the commercial-paper market. When the developers to whom they lent encountered credit problems in the 1974–75 recession, the REITs too fell behind on their debts. At the Chase Manhattan Mortgage & Realty Trust in 1976, bad loans constituted fully 71 percent of the overall portfolio. Hoping to keep its banks at bay, the trust offered to exchange some of its buildings (acquired in foreclosure) for the forgiveness of some of its debts. In vain, however: in 1979, the Chase REIT filed for bankruptcy; by the early 1980s, thirteen REITs had joined it. (As for Citizens & Southern Bank, it survived the 1974–75 recession under new, less ebullient management.)

A man with a long memory reflected at the time on what had gone wrong. It was what usually went wrong, William T. Ward, a partner at Peat, Marwick, Mitchell & Co., the nation's largest accounting firm and the auditor for thirty-five of the REITs, told *Business Week*. "Money was just too easy," he said, recalling the California real-estate slump of the 1960s. "This time around, we had another ready-made vehicle that had a very sexy name—trust. I mean, who wouldn't believe in 'trust'?"

Mr. Wriston's New World

For the first time since the 1920s, Citicorp—the new name for the holding company of the First National City Bank—was a hot stock.

It was trading as if it were not in the banking business at all but in some fast-growing branch of the aerospace industry. "Fat City" the brokers affectionately called it, but the bank grew not in girth but in stature. The energy crisis, successive international monetary crises, and misguided federal regulation of prices and interest rates seemed to roll off the sides of its midtown headquarters (it had moved its main office to 399 Park Avenue in 1961, choosing glass and steel over the classical look favored by James Stillman). Citicorp not only prospered in that inflationary time but also lectured others on the futility of worry.

The chairman of Citicorp, Walter B. Wriston, was a new-age man to his bones. He was the brilliant son of Henry M. Wriston, an accomplished historian of diplomacy and a onetime president of Brown University. The younger Wriston studied diplomatic history at Wesleyan University and prepared for a career in the Foreign Service at Tufts University's Fletcher School of International Law and Diplomacy. His State Department career lasted eight months; he joined the National City Bank in June 1946. When, later on, a senior officer asked for the name of the ablest young man in the bank, Wriston's was the name provided. At the time, the future chairman was a drone in the controller's office, counting things in the branches and absorbing the misinformation that the most important asset in the bank was the corporate-bond portfolio. This was just about the time that the bond market was beginning its forty-year decline.

Wriston's mentor, George S. Moore, has recalled: "In the minds of some members of the board, even as late as the 1960s, Citibank was still living down the aggressiveness of the 1920s." All the more notable, then, that Wriston, the historian's son, was able to focus so singlemindedly on the future. He shared Moore's vision of a global, "universal bank." He had a problem-solving intelligence, and the problem he solved in 1961 was that of attracting and retaining deposits. The time had passed when a bank could expect to obtain its inventory— namely, its money—for free. The Federal Reserve Bank of New York invited the banks under its wing to devise a new investment vehicle for attracting funds, and Wriston was chiefly responsible for producing it. His innovation was the negotiable certificate of deposit. Under the law, a bank could not pay interest on checking-account balances. As interest rates rose in the inflation of the 1950s, the cost of maintaining large, non-interest-bearing deposits rose with them. (Failing to adjust, Baker's bank, the old First National, had had to seek its merger with City, and it was Wriston who oversaw the integration of the two operations.) The solution, Wriston saw, was to offer a corporate treasurer a certificate of deposit that might be sold with no more difficulty than a Treasury bill.

The negotiable CD fundamentally altered banking. Frank Vanderlip, Stillman's protégé in the early years of the century, had hoped that the Federal Reserve would revolutionize the business by lending against the collateral of illiquid (meaning unsalable) loans. It would thereby enable a bank to lay in fewer low-yield assets, such as government securities, and more high-yield ones, such as corporate loans. It could lend a greater percentage of its deposits than it might before, knowing that in a time of need it could borrow. The system did not evolve in just that way, but the negotiable CD held out hope that the Vanderlip vision might be realized in another way. In effect, deposits were no longer specific to a bank but universal to the market. Money was a gurgling brook, and any solvent bank might fill its ladle if it offered the right interest rate. In days gone by, as we have seen, the National City Bank had appealed to a class of depositor who did not entirely trust government bonds. However, the safety franchise in banking was fast vanishing—who, in 1961, expected another money panic?—and it was necessary to adapt to the new facts. To his credit, Wriston had done just that.*

In communications with shareholders, Wriston did not confine himself to the bank's achievements, as large as they were. Known and feared in the bank for his wit, he also liked to tax those who worried unduly about the safety and soundness of the banking system. "There was no shortage in the use of the word 'crisis' during 1973," the annual report of that year led off.

> Stern warnings of impending disaster were communicated almost instantly around the world every day but, as usual, predictions of doomsday were premature. The demise of what had been called a fixed exchange rate system did not halt the growth of world trade and investment as many had predicted. A floating rate system handled massive movements of funds efficiently and

---

* Warren Marcus, a New York investor who for many years was a bank-stock analyst, recalls the introduction of the negotiable CD as a great divide in American banking. Before this innovation, a bank had two principal sources of funds: corporate demand deposits (that is, checking accounts) and retail savings accounts. The advent of the new CD widened those vistas enormously. However, as the banks were prepared to pay premium rates to get the extra deposit dollar, so they were obliged to find higher-yielding loans to employ it at a profit. Thus, a new competitive urgency entered banking. "It [the negotiable CD] turned banks into competitive and aggressive institutions," Marcus commented, "and we've had asset problems ever since."

proved once again that free markets have a resiliency and capacity to absorb shock that no administered control system has ever attained. . . . It was a good year to remind ourselves that the recuperative powers of the world are enormous and the ability of its three and three-quarter billion people to develop in new ways to handle new situations has always exceeded the imagination of the doomsday prophet.

Certainly, Wall Street was in hearty accord with that view. In 1973, Citicorp's stock achieved an all-time high price of $51.50 a share, and Wriston, breaking a long National City tradition of taciturnity, agreed to appear before the New York Society of Security Analysts. "I understand it is usual on occasions such as this one for companies to distribute samples of their products," the speech began. "Unfortunately, federal regulations and a few other considerations prevent me from following that custom."

If Wriston did not at that moment have his audience in the palm of his hand, the next item of business must have delivered them. "We come here at a good moment in the history of our corporation," said the banker. "Our earnings were up 20 percent last year to $201 million. It was the eleventh year in a row in which our earnings rose on a year-to-year basis, and it was the second successive year in which we surpassed our internal target of 15 percent earnings growth per year. Over the past five years our compound growth rate is now 13 percent."

Citicorp and its forerunners had never addressed the New York Society of Security Analysts before. Until 1972, they had not pointed themselves publicly toward any specific annual rate of earnings growth, much less 15 percent. In the long history of the National City Bank, earnings had grown, but they had not grown every single year. There were lush times, slack times, and periods in between. In 1900, under James Stillman (who made it a point never to say anything in public, general or specific), the bank had earned $1.2 million. In 1970, under Wriston, it had earned $140.6 million. Over those seven decades, which encompassed near-disaster as well as success, earnings had grown at the average annual compound rate of 7 percent. They had grown by nearly 11 percent in the booming 1960s. They had, as Wriston had noted, grown by 13 percent in the five years through 1972, but they had not grown by 15 percent.

To grow at 15 percent a year is to double in size every five years and to triple every eight years. It was common enough in the days of growth stocks for companies to propose even faster expansion, but a bank was still a bank. If the National City Bank's earnings had grown at 15 percent a year since 1900, they would have reached $28.1 billion by 1972. As it was, they came in at $201 million.

The 15 percent declaration electrified Wall Street. Heretofore, according to the bank analyst George Salem, "growth was not a goal. Bank stocks were stodgy, frumpy, yield-oriented investments, like utilities." All that changed after Citicorp said its piece. "Compared to today," recalled another bank analyst, Mark Biderman, "the banks were overcapitalized, and they began to leverage"—in other words, to borrow. In 1963, the Comptroller of the Currency, James J. Saxon, ruled that a bank might borrow new capital rather than earn it. As a rule, banks earned profits and paid dividends. The difference between what they earned and what they paid was the measure of the growth in their capital. This was "equity" capital or "retained earnings." Now a bank might supplement this homegrown capital with debt, expanding both its vistas and its risk in the process. "Although so-called 'senior' securities are considered entirely acceptable capital instruments in other industries," the Office of the Comptroller of the Currency explained in its 1963 annual report, "the attitude of this Office had been that they were inappropriate for banks. Apparently, this attitude stemmed from the fact that the Reconstruction Finance Corporation had purchased preferred stock and capital notes from banks during the Depression, so that the issuance of such securities was viewed somehow as a reflection on the banks' soundness. We rejected this reasoning and issued an opinion that it was both legal and appropriate for national banks to raise capital by these means."

In any case, before Citicorp's announcement, banks in general had erred on the side of caution. Many would continue to do so, but a new idea had entered the marketplace. It was that banks were, or could be, exciting, that they could fly like Avon Products, rather than walk like Consolidated Edison.

How did Wriston propose to convert what was almost a regulated public utility into a dynamic business? Some of the more experienced bank analysts were doubtful. "Corporate lending was the major part of their business—not consumer lending or the credit-card business," said Warren Marcus, who was also around at the time on Wall Street. "There was a feeling, 'How could an entity that large grow that much?' What was the growth rate of the economy? Three or 4 percent?"

According to Wriston, there would be growth in the domestic consumer business and growth abroad. There *had* been growth; in 1972, domestic earnings had fallen slightly, but overseas earnings, vaulting by 55 percent, had more than compensated. "Citicorp made the case that when you looked beyond the total numbers, there were a lot of little businesses in many parts of the world," said Marcus. For another thing, costs would come under strict control, and the average Citibanker would become more productive. "Whenever there is a national emergency—or there's an emergency around here, which there is on a regular basis—the output that people can produce is just astonishing," Wriston said. "I realize you couldn't operate that way all of the time, but I remember when our earnings were growing at 5 percent to 6 percent a year, everybody said, 'that's great.' And when we set a target of 15 percent, many said it was not—well, 'sensible.' "

For another thing, as Wriston told the security analysts, the bank would continue to diversify its sources of earnings. The banner year of 1972 was the first in which more than half of net earnings had come from abroad. Citicorp had offices in ninety countries. In 1970, it had earned $1 million or more in only nine of them; in 1972, it earned $1 million or more in twenty-seven of them. "The pattern, I think, is pretty clear," said Wriston, who was personally instrumental in building the foreign-branch network. "As our overseas investments continue to ripen, our earnings from these countries become more significant. This broadened diversity of earnings streams also tends to reduce our dependency on earnings streams from any single set of countries." The world was Citicorp's oyster, the more so with every passing year.

As for the United States, Wriston reiterated his ambition to make the bank a national financial services organization, complete with leasing, mortgage banking, and other "nonbanking" activities (a corporation, in short, as unlike Baker's bank as could be imagined). In 1967, there had been just one American Citicorp branch office outside New York State. In 1973, there were 130 offices in twenty-four states outside New York.

One more lending activity was coming to the fore. Up until about 1960, Citibank had had little to do with commercial real estate. With inflation, however, had come the need for higher-yielding loans. And with the advent of the negotiable CD, bankers could worry a little less about the liquidity of their loans. If it were possible to raise new deposits continuously by paying the going interest rate, there was no longer any good reason not to lend against real estate (except, of course, if one were lending to finance the construction of redundant buildings, which was to be the characteristic error of the 1980s). In the unlikely event that the depositors conceived a sudden urge to demand their money in cash, the thinking went, a bank could borrow as needed in the open market. Thus, in the late 1960s, real-estate lending emerged as a major opportunity, and the bank staffed its new real-estate department with bright and ambitious lending officers. "The results have been quite dramatic," Wriston told the analysts. "Since 1968 the volume of our real-estate loans has risen from an almost negligible position to the point where we now rank among the top real-estate lenders in the U.S." He closed imperially: "Our overall corporate strategy is as ambitious as it is simple. We intend to sell every financial service everywhere in the world where we can do so legally and at a profit."

Consumers Come into Their Own

For years, American bankers had failed to see the great potential banking market that was under their very noses. The "workingman," nowadays known as the consumer, was the stepchild of credit, consigned by the financial establishment to apply for a loan at an eleemosynary institution like the Provident Loan Society or with loan sharks like Daniel Tolman. A. P. Giannini, visionary founder of Bank of America, had understood the business potential of consumer lending, as had Arthur Morris, founder of the Morris Plan. But in New York banking circles, the individual in search of a loan was viewed as a charitable case more than a business prospect.

All that was changed in 1928 when the New York State attorney general appealed to commercial banks to enter the personal-lending business to combat loan sharking. Only one bank answered the call, and that was National City. City had already met the public and liked what it saw. Starting in 1921, it had offered savings accounts (in observance of state law that reserved the word "savings" for savings banks, it called them "compound interest accounts") in denominations of as little as $1.00. The interest rate it paid was 3 percent, compounded semiannually on balances of $5.00 or more. Savings banks paid 4 percent, but there was no federal deposit insurance, and City Bank was thought to be a fortress. That it was able to compete is a reminder of how potent financial safety was in the days before the federal government undertook to socialize the risk of loss.

Roger Steffan, a journalist turned banker, was City's man in charge of personal banking, and he was able to convince Charles E. Mitchell of the profit in personal lending. "Our contact with this great number of small depositors has brought us to an understanding of their problems [and] their periodic necessitous financial requirements . . . ," said Mitchell in explaining the bank's entry into the seemingly incongruous business of small loans. "Our contact with people of this class has given to us a confidence in the integrity and character of the average individual. While it is not our purpose to encourage anyone to borrow except under the stress of circumstances, we have faith that loans so made can and will be paid."

"Except under the stress of circumstances." Applicants filled out a form and produced the signatures of two co-signers. A measure of the Calvinist freight that still burdened personal lending was the irresistible arithmetic of the business. In spite of it, banks were reluctant to enter. Steffan was able to fund the loans at 3 percent; the interest cost to the borrowers was 12 percent. Loss experience was favorable. It was, in short, a business so inviting that the refusal of the rest of the banks to compete could only be explained by a belief that there was something unwholesome about it.

It turned out, however, that nearly everyone had overestimated the stigma of borrowing and had correspondingly underestimated the willingness of ordinary people to go into debt. On opening day at City Bank's personal loan department, 500 applications poured in. The next three days brought another 2,500. "The men outnumber the women," a City Bank officer related in May 1928, "and the married men outnumber the single men. There are policemen and firemen and mail-carriers and clerks and stenographers—mostly office workers. And they have piled in in streams that have upset all our calculations."

The press heralded City Bank's decision not only as a blow against loan sharking but also as a milestone in the democratization of credit. A cartoon in the *New York Evening World* pictured a money bag, labeled "Personal Small Loan Department," being brought down smartly on the head of a bloated man, labeled "Loan Shark." Wielding the bag was a well-tailored arm labeled "National City Bank." "The National City's new adventure in democratic finance will justify itself because average men and women are honest and proud of it," commented the *Newark* (N.J.) *News*. "Pioneering in human confidence, it will have imitators."

Steffan, who would later serve the cause of the democratization of credit in the Roosevelt administration by promoting the government's program for home-improvement loans, had a saying: "The clerk is a better risk than the boss and the boss is a better risk than the company he works for." He meant that a clerk could continue to pay his bills if he should ever lose his job, because he could quickly find another job. His boss might not be as easily employable, however, if the same

Sandbagged!

*1928: National City Bank gets a hero's welcome as it enters
the consumer-lending business (*NEW YORK EVENING WORLD*)*

thing should happen to him, and the company for which both of them
worked might vanish into bankruptcy.

As few commercial bankers in New York at the time seemed to do,
Steffan understood the possibilities of consumer credit. "Our credit
losses are about three-tenths of 1 percent, and our costs of analyzing
borrowers run about 3 percent, and that means we must be wasting a
lot of time asking stupid questions," he would say. Over the years,
City Bank's personal-loan questionnaires got shorter, and the volume
of personal lending grew larger. ("If a fellow had borrowed from us
before and paid it back, and held the job he'd held before, we made
the loan 99 percent of the time, whatever the answers were to the
other questions," George Moore explained.)

By the 1960s, the consumer was well on his way to becoming
the most important patron in the First National City Bank. It was "the

only bank your family ever needs," in the words of its advertising. Between mid-1959 and mid-1967, the volume of its home-mortgage lending increased ninefold. In 1958, following the lead of the First National Bank of Boston, it began to offer "ready credit," a preapproved loan that the consumer could draw upon by simply writing a check.* In 1966, the bank bought a controlling interest in Carte Blanche, the No. 3 nonbank credit card measured by volume, but the government raised antitrust objections. Backpedaling, City Bank sold it. The next year, 1967, it began to offer its own credit card, the "Everything Card," which it converted in 1969 to MasterCharge. In 1972, a string of consumer finance offices, Nationwide Finance Corporation, was acquired. In 1973, Bess Myerson, the former Miss America and onetime Consumer Affairs Commissioner of the City of New York, was retained as a consultant: "She will help us in designing new products and new services as well as in reviewing existing operations from the consumer's viewpoint," the bank explained.

There was growth and activity to spare, but not yet a grand plan. This the bank proceeded to rectify, and in 1974 it produced a comprehensive "consumer strategy." Year after year in the annual report, the Citicorp hierarchy had denied that the financial system was unsound. There were problems, of course, but there was no rot, despite inflation, floating exchange rates, oil shocks, and monetary improvisation. ("A difficult situation was exacerbated by a constant stream of widespread and strident predictions of the imminent breakdown of the world's financial system," the 1974 edition stated, a little defensively. "The system did not break down.") True to its faith in the world economy, Citicorp set out to make its mark on the descendants of Roger Steffan's policemen, firemen, mail carriers, clerks, and stenographers.

The bank was its usual hopeful self, but its determination to do more business with "the ordinary person with a job" was driven in part by worry. In the late twentieth century, commercial banking has

---

* "First Check-Credit Account," created by Roger C. Damon, then senior vice president, later president, of the First National Bank of Boston, was a hit from the day of its introduction, on February 15, 1955. Participating customers could write themselves a loan at the cost of 1 percent per month of the outstanding loan balance. In the first few weeks, according to the Bank of Boston's in-house newsletter, "over 2,000 applications were sent through the mail. . . . The coupon coming the greatest distance was from Texas, and for telephone calls, Cincinnati."

John W. Calkins, retired head of corporate communications at the bank, recalled that the new service elicited little or no criticism in fiscally conservative Boston. "No one would have said anything against the First National Bank of Boston, which sat just on the left hand of God, you know?" he said, only half in jest.

seen the successive exhaustion of profitable fields of lending, from corporate to Third World to consumer. In 1974, only the weakness in corporate lending was obvious (the Third World boom had scarcely begun), but that was enough to worry Wriston and his protégé, John Reed. If the bank was to make good on its promise of expanding its profits by 15 percent a year, it must find new worlds to conquer.

"Potentially," as Citicorp's official history pointed out, "the credit card was a remarkable invention. It would allow a bank to do a nationwide consumer credit business without local branches." In days gone by, a bank's architecture was its public face. It was the expression of the sterling qualities that, the depositors might hope, could be found in its income statement and balance sheet. In the new era, there might be no architecture at all. The bank of the future could be an unmanned suburban kiosk or a computer terminal. Neither of these things was calculated to project an image of impregnability to depositors, but the depositors hardly seemed to need reassurance. Money itself was becoming an abstraction. Workmen in the gold vault of the Federal Reserve Bank of New York wore magnesium boots to protect their toes against the palpable weight of real money. The newfangled monetary material—so-called Special Drawing Rights and dollar bills convertible into nothing—was lighter than air. As for credit, the promise to pay money, it was an abstraction once removed. (It had become a plastic one in 1959, when American Express issued the first plastic credit cards.) Reed of Citicorp saw that Visa and MasterCharge cards constituted a kind of partial banking "system," and that this plastic system could operate at one-fifth the cost of a branch network.

For decades in America, it had been difficult or impossible for the working man or woman to borrow at a nonusurious interest rate. At long last, it was possible to get a loan, but interest rates had become punitive everywhere. In New York State, it was illegal for a bank to charge a customer more than 18 percent for the first $500 he borrowed and 12 percent for amounts above that. The law had been on the books since 1963 and for most of that time it had been moot. In the late 1970s, however, it began to cramp the style of the lenders, Citibank among them.

Interest rates were a vital part of the grand consumer strategy of 1974. If the cost of deposits did not crowd the maximum legal interest rate, consumer lending could become a lucrative business. The cost that mattered was the average cost of the extra deposit over the long run. What Reed had to anticipate was the "marginal cost of funds," in economist's jargon. The Citicorp bureaucracy produced an official interest-rate forecast that Wriston, eschewing economist's jargon, called "Swami's best guess." Late in 1974, looking out over the next decade, Swami guessed an average of 8¼ percent.

"At that level," wrote Carol Loomis in *Fortune* magazine some years later, "Reed anticipated that a restructured, better-managed consumer lending business could make a lot of money. In fact, he thought it could make money at marginal rates considerably higher. It is good he thought that, because the Swami has since changed his mind several times and now suspects that the long-term marginal rate will be 10 percent."

In 1977, opportunity came knocking. BankAmericard, one of the original bank credit cards, was changing its name to Visa. Reed wanted to sign up credit-card customers outside New York. The Citibank name, as he knew, was not well known outside its home market, but the bank's name hardly mattered to prospective cardholders. "Visa" mattered, and people would accept a Visa card if the terms were right no matter which bank was behind it. Mailing lists were bought by the job lot, and 26 million letters were sent to prospects across the country, representing more than a third of what Reed estimated to be the size of the national consumer banking market. Five million people agreed to accept a card, a response that the bank judged gratifying. Heretofore, a consumer would own one Visa card or one MasterCard or one of each kind, issued by his local bank. With the advent of national marketing, people could begin to collect the cards of different banks.

"Citicorp felt very good about this, but only briefly," as Loomis reported. "Not only did interest rates begin to march upward, but an unexpectedly large number of the new card holders were discovered to be bad credits (which is no doubt part of the reason so many were delighted to accept this generous offer of a card). Citicorp's loan losses on the cards ballooned, and the company is still working, after two years, to get them down."

Dawn of the Great Inflation

For years, lending and borrowing had elicited guilt and anxiety in Americans of all stations. The growing popularity of credit cards heightened those feelings and compounded them with a sense of public amazement. In 1959, *Life* magazine told the story of a nineteen-year-old youth who traveled cross-country on a credit card, charging car rentals, a puppy, and a silver mink coat, among other goods and services, at a cost of $10,000. In 1969, Congress heard testimony concerning the mailing of credit cards to people long dead, including the author Bernard De Voto, who was twice solicited a dozen years after his well-publicized death in 1955, as well as to bankrupts and minors. A now familiar genre of news, the credit-card howler, began to appear—for instance, the story of Tony Benitez of Tampa, Florida, who might have used his new MasterCharge card to travel to Europe except for the fact that he was five years old. In Washington, Robert N. C. Nix, chairman of the House Postal Operations subcommittee, sounded off:

> An advertisement pamphlet put out by the American Express Company describes credit cards as the "new money." A more accurate description would be "funny money." Credit cards now account for well over $13 billion in outstanding debt. Retailers pay from 3 percent to 5 percent for the service of having their bills collected by the big credit-card companies. Consumers pay an average of 18 percent a year for credit-card debt. This is highly expensive borrowing. How then is credit-card borrowing so wide-spread? One answer is the indiscriminate use of unsolicited mailed credit cards. You get a credit card whether you want it or not. If debts are run up against you, you are subject to losing your credit rating if you don't pay up.

Interest rates were rising unnervingly. Although credit cards were not the only cause of that trend, they constituted a ready source of blame. "Money which used to be available for loans to consumers and for home loans has left for the mass credit-card market," said Representative Nix, striking the truth only a glancing blow. "We are a million homes a year behind our national goals, yet there is no mortgage money because it pays only 8 percent a year. If this keeps up, all loans for homes and other necessities could be driven up to the 18 percent a year bracket." In time, the congressman's interest-rate forecast would be duly borne out, although not for the reason he gave. Credit cards were a symptom rather than a cause of rising inflation (and were hardly even a symptom insofar as consumers used them in lieu of cash or a check). The underlying cause was monetary, the pell-mell creation of surplus credit by the Federal Reserve System.

By the late 1970s, the national attitude toward consumer debt had shifted decisively from puritanism to tolerance and here and there to hedonism. One sign of liberality was the growth of debt among low-income Americans. In 1970, only 22.9 percent of households in the $4,000 to $6,000 annual income bracket had installment debt outstanding. In 1977, 30.7 percent did. Credit was not exactly money. It was the capacity to obtain money on the promise of repayment. But the promises demanded of debtors were becoming less stringent and the consequences of nonpayment more lenient. (The federal Bankruptcy Code, newly revised in 1978, was the most forgiving bankruptcy law in the nation's history. The spirit of the reform was conveyed in the substitution of the word "debtor" for the stigmatizing term "bankrupt.") One had to look no further to explain this trend than the fact that it actually paid to borrow. There were other reasons too, including the high number of young adults in need of a loan to set up housekeeping, and the evolutionary truism that since the turn of the century it had become progressively easier to borrow. But these factors were overshadowed in the late 1970s by the simple arithmetic of debt. Interest rates were rising, but the inflation rate was rising faster. The dollars that debtors owed were steadily depreciating in value. In a happy mirror image, the assets that they borrowed to buy were frequently appreciating.

In its review of 1978, the Federal Reserve Bank of New York noted that consumer installment debt had climbed by 21 percent and that the real-estate market was white hot. It observed that the maturities of new auto loans were lengthening, a mitigating circumstance so far as the burden of debt was concerned: more time to pay meant a more affordable loan. Demographics explained part of the boom in indebtedness, as did the fact that interest payments were deductible from income for those who itemized deductions in calculating their income tax. Still and all, said the bank, "repayments of consumer installment and mortgage debt ate up a record share of disposable income," and it called the speculative aspect of the buildup in consumer debt "disturbing."

The Fed was not the only concerned party, and the kind of distraught financial journalism that so annoyed the Citicorp hierarchy began to appear as it had in the 1955 expansion (and would again, with greater factual underpinning, in the late 1980s). Thus, *U.S. News & World Report* of November 20, 1978:

The mountain of debt has grown so high in this country that many economists fear the United States is unusually vulnerable if a recession occurs.

Most analysts expect any business downturn in 1979 to be

mild, but some fret that a load of personal debt will make a recession more severe than it would otherwise be.

In only 3½ years since the end of the last slump, Americans have added a trillion dollars to their financial obligations. Today, government, corporations and individuals owe more than 3.5 trillion dollars, equal to nearly $16,000 for every man, woman and child in the country.

A rush for loans played a major role in the strong recovery the U.S. has made from the 1973–75 recession. The question now being raised is whether a day of reckoning is at hand.

In 1979, a remarkable speculative fact was recorded in southwestern Wisconsin. A 200-acre parcel of farmland that a third-generation farmer, Ted Griswold, had purchased for $12,000 in 1963 was valued at $200,000, indicating a compounded rate of return on the order of 21 percent a year. "Right now I owe more money than I ever did," Griswold told *Newsweek* in January 1979. "But I own more property and have greater net worth than I ever did, too." It had come to Griswold, as it had to a number of other Americans, including Nelson Bunker Hunt, of silver-fiasco fame, that "a dollar saved has meant half a dollar lost in this business. It kills me to think how much I struggled to make life-insurance payments when I would have been so much better off if I'd put my money into anything real." To Griswold, the dollar was unreal, and he added (again anticipating the Hunts), "I'd like to think this inflation could go on forever."

Forces were then in motion to see that it did not. On October 6, 1979, Paul A. Volcker, chairman of the Federal Reserve Board, told a rare Saturday press conference that certain technical changes would be implemented to reduce the rate of growth in the nation's money supply. Over breakfast on Sunday morning, Americans read the details and scratched their heads. The discount rate would be raised to a record 12 percent from 11 percent, the Federal Reserve would henceforth focus its attention on the supply of money and credit rather than on interest rates, and an 8 percent reserve requirement would be applied to certain kinds of bank deposits, including jumbo certificates of deposit and Eurodollar borrowings. What in the world did it mean?

Central bankers by custom spoke in tongues (once, after Volcker had delivered an especially opaque remark, Representative Frank Annunzio, a Democrat from Chicago, told him that he would make an excellent prisoner of war). On deciphering, what Volcker said was significant in the extreme. It was a vow to attack inflation and to let interest rates do whatever they would do. Certainly, interest rates would go up, but nobody—neither Reed nor Griswold nor Volcker— could imagine by how much or with what consequences.

Volcker was called to the chairmanship amid crisis. The dollar was falling at home and abroad. It was weak in terms of consumer goods, commodities, foreign currencies, and gold. When Richard Nixon suspended the right of foreign central banks to exchange their dollars for gold on August 15, 1971 (thereby erasing the last vestige of the gold standard), the price of gold was $35 an ounce. In September 1979, it touched $450 an ounce. No harsher verdict on the financial policies of the United States could have been meted out.

The purpose of the October 6 program was to restore the dollar to gold-standard soundness without restoring the gold standard. The heart of the program was a commitment to controlling the nation's money supply. The logic of the monetary theory was simplicity itself: Too much money would cause prices to rise; too little would cause them to fall. Inflation threatened at one extreme and deflation at the other. The Federal Reserve would count the nation's money, classify it according to its economic significance (checking accounts had a higher octane rating than savings accounts, for instance), and control it. The means of control would be the great commercial banks. When more money was desired, the Fed would encourage the banks to make more loans. Making a loan, a bank simultaneously created a new deposit. When the objective was less money, the Fed would choke off new lending. Fewer loans meant the creation of fewer dollars.

All this was more easily said than done. There was, to start with, the mundane matter of counting the dollars that the Fed presumed to control. Less than a month after the October 6 press conference, the bond market was shocked by a massive downward revision in the basic money supply. The Fed had erroneously reported that M-1, the sum of currency and checking accounts, had risen by $2.8 billion in the week of October 10. The news caused apoplexy in the bond market, as a rising money supply was what Volcker had promised to throttle. In fact, a big New York bank, Manufacturers Hanover, had miscounted *its* money, and the nation's money supply had not risen by $2.8 billion in that one week after all. It had actually fallen by $200 million. The error prompted one embittered trader to complain that if the Fed were held to the standards of the federal securities laws, it would have to answer in court for the damage that its data had done to investors.

The Federal Reserve placed itself in the same untenable position as the central planning committee of any socialist country. The information it needed to know was unavailable through any existing channel. Not only did it have to define the money supply and count it accurately, taking account of seasonal patterns of trade, but it was also bound to consider the speed at which money moved from hand to hand (or from computer to computer) in the economy. It was obliged to control the tangible money supply—that is, dollar bills and checking accounts—and also to reckon with the intangible one. Ted Griswold, the Wisconsin farmer, believed that it was foolish not to borrow, and his expansive state of mind was itself a kind of monetary engine. Expecting that credit would be forthcoming indefinitely on advantageous terms, he and others like him acted accordingly. The knowledge that one had recourse to a line of credit (and the conviction that one should use it) did not appear in any of the Federal Reserve's monetary aggregates, but it was no less potent for that omission.

It was a fine mess—inflation out of control, the prime rate at 15¼ percent, Treasury bills at 12 percent, each rate unheard of—and there seemed no precedent for it except in the great inflations of the distant past. The Bank of New York, which Alexander Hamilton had founded at another anxious moment in American financial history, distributed as a public service handsomely bound copies of Andrew Dickson White's nineteenth-century essay, *Fiat Money Inflation in France*. White, the co-founder and president of Cornell University, had begun research for his monetary essay before the Civil War, and he recalled years later, "as if it were yesterday, my feeling of regret at being obliged to bestow so much care and labor upon a subject to all appearances so utterly devoid of practical value." But the greenback agitation and later the Bryanite silver movement (and still later the debate leading up to the enactment of the Federal Reserve) frightened monied people and thus created a recurrent demand for the fruits of White's research. The difference between Grover Cleveland's time and Jimmy Carter's was that monetary orthodoxy under Carter was identical to monetary heresy under Cleveland. The Volcker Federal Reserve had embarked on the efficient management of a paper-money regime. What White and Cleveland had condemned was "fiat," or paper, money itself.

Was it pure coincidence that the great inflation of the 1970s had followed the abrogation of the gold standard* culminating in 1971? It

---

* Or, more exactly, the gold-exchange standard.

hardly seemed so. For the century preceding World War I, prices and interest rates had been remarkably stable. There had been peaks and valleys, of course, but the financial discombobulation of the 1970s was unprecedented in modern American history. In the war scare surrounding the election of Abraham Lincoln, in 1860, the Union government had been forced to pay interest rates of as high as 12 percent to borrow for a year. However, the war itself was financed by the Treasury (with young George Baker's assistance) at rates of 7 percent or less, even when the Union was in mortal danger. The price of oil soared in Carter's term, but inflation is defined as a fall in the value of money, not as the rise in a price, even one so critical as oil. Only so much of the country's financial distress could be blamed on the Organization of Petroleum Exporting Countries or the strange goings-on in commodity prices. It was mainly for monetary reasons that Griswold and others like him decided to spend and borrow.

The Volcker anti-inflation program at first produced high hopes but perverse results. Interest rates and commodity prices continued to rise, and the gold price spiraled, to $850 an ounce from $440 an ounce between the October 6 announcement and the middle of January. Evidently, the dollar was quickly going the way of the French assignat. What was the Fed doing?

Late in January 1980, a remarkable essay by Lewis E. Lehrman attempted to explain. Lehrman, forty-one years old, had solved his own personal economic problem by building the Rite Aid drugstore chain. It could not be said of him, as it was of the French theorists of 1790, that he had no head for money. ("It began to be especially noted," White had written, "that men who had never shown any ability to make or increase fortunes for themselves abounded in brilliant plans for creating or increasing wealth for the country at large.") Lehrman had studied at Yale and Harvard and accumulated such an improbably lustrous résumé that an Army sergeant once flatly told Private Lehrman that he refused to believe it. Lehrman was a student of central banking and an apostle of Jacques Rueff. He was impartially hostile to the opposite wings of conventional economic thought, Keynesian and monetarist, and single-mindedly devoted to the ideas of the classical gold standard, which, in their very obsolescence, had acquired an avant-garde capacity to shock. Morgan Stanley & Co., a top-tier investment bank that was not usually moved to champion long-shot causes, agreed to publish the Lehrman essay, all forty-four pages of it, "Monetary Policy, the Federal Reserve System, and Gold." (In an introductory note, Barton M. Biggs, the head of investment research at Morgan Stanley, speculated that Lehrman had hit on "what could be the economic and political issue of the 1980s—why the world must return to the discipline of the gold standard.")

Lehrman's diagnosis was elegantly simple and persuasive. He observed that the world's monetary system had been going downhill ever since 1914, retrogressing from the international gold standard to the gold-bullion standard to the gold-exchange standard and finally to the full-paper standard of 1971, each new regime less rigorous and more inflation-prone than the one preceding it. His prescription was equally simple but, again, in its very orthodoxy, discordant to many Morgan Stanley clients, for whom monetary heresy had long since become gospel. It was drawn in part from Rueff and in part from the nineteenth-century British thinker Walter Bagehot. The world must return to gold, Lehrman insisted, and the Federal Reserve must stop its frenetic buying and selling of government securities. It must throw in the towel on trying to control the nation's money supply, which it could not even count. (Lehrman, who also speculated in government securities, had borne a loss in the monetary counting error of the preceding October. If his monetary prose had bite, it was not without reason.)

Lehrman's objective was the remonetization of gold, and to effect this reform he tried to show that gold had never, as a matter of fact, lost its monetary properties. "Caught up in the specious present," he wrote:

> U.S. policymakers ignored the fact that gold is the oldest money of civilized man. Today, gold-price calculations still dominate large segments of the global trading system. Until a mere generation ago, gold was at the core of the fractional reserve banking system of all of Occidental civilization. The definitive rupture of this gold-backed monetary system in 1971 can be closely related to the price inflation of the past 10 years. The thirty- to forty-fold rise in the price of gold since 1932 is sufficient commentary on the effectiveness of the experts who ushered in the era of central bank-managed currencies. It bespeaks the termination of the fashionable monetary doctrines of our age, preeminently the age of inflation.

Lehrman quoted an errant prediction by Henry Reuss, chairman of the House Banking and Currency Committee, that if gold were ever demonetized it would fall to $6.00 an ounce. It was at that moment roaring to $850 an ounce. (The Wisconsin Democrat was not the first politician to hold misplaced hopes for his own paper money. It was widely expected that the brilliant success of the French assignats would coax gold coins out from the places in which they were hoarded.) In sum, Lehrman contended, gold was far from the "side show" that the Federal Reserve pretended it was. It was at center stage, and the run-up in its price proved irrefutably that the Fed was not stringent enough. As Lehrman noted, a commercial bank could borrow from the Federal Reserve at 12 percent and re-lend to a business at 15¼ percent. The difference between those key interest rates was the measure of the taxpayer subsidy to the creation of bank credit. If this was an anti-inflationary policy, heaven help the American consumer.

The Federal Reserve's Offensive

Lehrman's essay explored the tangible monetary issue. In March, the Carter administration addressed the intangible one. Inflation had not abated in the wake of the October 6 program (although commodity prices, including gold, had; they peaked in January for what would prove to be the next dozen years, at least). For a time in March, both the prime rate and the latest rate of consumer price inflation were quoted in the neighborhood of 18 percent. American finance was now certifiably deranged, and the administration, risking an election-year recession, embarked on its fourth anti-inflation program in less than four years.

"Just as our governments have been borrowing to make ends meet," President Jimmy Carter told the nation,

> so have individual Americans. But when we try to beat inflation with borrowed money, we just make the problem worse.
>
> Inflation is fed by credit-financed spending. Consumers have gone into debt too heavily. The savings rate in our nation is now the lowest in more than 25 years. . . .
>
> The traditional tools used by the Federal Reserve to control money and credit expansion are a basic part of the fight on inflation. But in present circumstances, those tools need to be reinforced so that effective restraint can be achieved in ways that spread the burden reasonably and fairly.
>
> I am therefore using my power under the Credit Control Act of 1969 to authorize the Federal Reserve to impose new restraints on the growth of credit on a limited and carefully targeted basis.

The Federal Reserve, for its part, outlined a half dozen restrictive measures, including, notably, a request that banks reduce the growth rate of their lending to an annual rate of 9 percent a year or less. In the twelve months ended January 1980, they had lent at the rate of nearly 18 percent. Volcker asked them not to finance corporate takeovers or to make unsecured loans to consumers. On the other hand, it was all right with the Fed if banks lent to individuals to purchase a car or a house. It was all right to lend to farmers and proprietors of small businesses. What was not acceptable to the Fed was lending for speculative purposes—for example, the purchase of commodities in the hope that their prices would rise.

The Fed did not know (and could hardly have been expected to know) that commodity prices had peaked or that a recession was already under way. It had begun in January. It no more knew those things than Jimmy Carter knew that the "savings rate" in 1980 would subsequently be revised from 4 percent to an encouraging 6 percent. Every competent American is an authority on his or her own savings rate and his or her personal money supply. But it is frequently beyond the ability of policy makers to measure the collective savings rate or the national money supply. Similarly, in 1980, no regulator could be sure how to distinguish between a worthy loan and an inflationary bauble.

Although parts of the March 14 program were self-explanatory, others were not. It was clear enough, for instance, that the administration wanted banks to reduce the rate of their lending. What was unclear was the technique by which this result would be obtained. When banks were asked to lay in non-interest-bearing reserve deposits equal to 15 percent of the amount of consumer credit extended over the amount of covered consumer credit outstanding on March 14, what did that mean? Bankers called the Federal Reserve banks, and the Reserve banks called the Federal Reserve Board. In just eight weeks, the board issued nine clarifying press releases.

Happily, the nation was rusty on credit controls, the last peacetime application of them dating back to Truman's time, in 1948–49. Controls had been reimposed in the Korean War, but the President's authority to order them in the future was rescinded in 1953 (a congressional subcommittee having found that they had not served their purpose well in 1950–52). In the late 1960s, inflation and high interest rates galvanized a new credit-control movement. Proponents contended that tight money was a blunt tool; better to cut out the expansion of excess credit surgically. In 1969, the president of the Federal Reserve Bank of St. Louis, Darryl R. Francis, forcefully argued the anti-controls case, and he noted, by the by, that the use of "selective" credit controls had a long and generally ineffectual history. Among these selective controls, he listed interest-rate ceilings, stock-market margin requirements, and the favoritism shown in the original Federal Reserve Act to short-term business loans as a form of collateral. However, Francis lost his fight, and President Nixon signed the Credit Control Act on Christmas Eve 1969. He did so reluctantly—"It would establish a complete credit police state," his own party had warned—and it was with considerable reluctance that President Carter invoked the act in 1980.

The March 14 program at first aroused the signature exasperation of the Carter term. "[It] is toothless, depends on other people, has no immediate effects on inflation but only ones which come much later—and we don't even know in what form," said a bond trader. After all, the controls were voluntary. As for the other points—such as a tripling in the staff of the Council on Wage and Price Stability to 240 and a 10-cent-per-gallon increase in the price of gasoline—they promised no miracles either.

Miracles there would be (or miracles-in-reverse), but they did not seem wonderful in advance. "What we're talking about is not a huge part of the credit scene," said Fed chairman Volcker of the curbs on consumer borrowing, "but it's a showy and symbolic one. We'll get some attention." Auto and housing credit were left untouched, as mentioned, and as for the rest of it, installment lending was fast becoming unprofitable anyway. The standard state usury ceiling of 18 percent was perilously close to the cost of funds to the lenders themselves.

A few hundred patriotic shoppers took scissors to their credit cards and mailed the pieces to the White House. Millions of others just kept them in their wallets, as if, even before the government's appeal, they had felt some latent guilt about using them. Sales on credit stopped cold at Sears, Roebuck. Visa, the national bank-card company, not only failed to add new customers but also started to lose existing ones. So improbable a figure as Russell E. Hogg, president of Interbank Card Association, a credit-card franchising company, appeared in a television advertisement to urge Americans not to use MasterCard except for "necessities and emergencies." A San Francisco man wrote Carter with the economically devastating news that he and his friends had "once again discovered parlour games, sing songs, lengthy walks and other means of 'old fashioned' entertainment."

The October 6 attack on the money supply was, to many or most Americans, bewildering. The March 14 thrust against credit, on the other hand, was reducible to an essence. As credit was a cause of inflation, it was better not to borrow. Appealing to the consumer, the President, in one televised stroke, was able to reduce that part of the "money supply" that is lodged in the minds of credit-using individuals. In a modern financial system, the possession of money itself is only one monetary medium. Another, far subtler, medium is the expectation of obtaining a loan. Credit is the promise to pay money. It is an abstraction. The expectation of receiving credit is a double abstraction. In a day and age of paper money, it is hard to be dogmatic about what in one's wallet is, and is not, tangible. A dollar bill is, literally, the Federal Reserve's "note." A note is the promise to pay. What payment does the Fed promise? Why, none. It will redeem $10 only in ten singles, two fives, or an appropriate weight of base-metal coins. As for a Visa card, it is a plastic borrowing ticket: at the end of the month, the debtor will remit to the creditor bank a certain sum of dollars, which, as noted, have no intrinsic value.

In any case, the March 14 appeal had immediate and drastic results. Outstanding consumer credit rose by $2.3 billion in February, the last month before the imposition of controls. It grew by only $1.4 billion in March and actually fell, by nearly $2 billion, in April. The decline was the largest in the thirty-seven years in which the government had been keeping records. But that record was toppled in May when the decline in consumer credit registered $3.4 billion. What had seemed an ineffectual rider to a weak anti-inflation program turned out to be a regulatory A-bomb. "It may have been symbolic," a spokesperson for the National Consumer Finance Association said of the campaign, "but it was shocking." *The New York Times*, which, in the wake of the announcement of the government's program in March, had quoted bankers disparaging its alleged toothlessness, in May published the bleak front-page headline: "Buying Habits Found Unexpectedly Curbed by Controls on Credit." The story cited a poll in which 58 percent of Americans said that they were using their credit cards less frequently, while only 5 percent said they were using them more. Another man-bites-dog feature, "Suburb Copes with Credit Curb," followed in ten days.

The government had not, in fact, killed inflation, but it had hit on a surefire antidote to consumer spending. In the three months ended June 1980, the national economy contracted at the annual rate of 9.1 percent, a statistic evoking the Great Depression and one that must have gratified the Soviet theoreticians who had explained away American prosperity as an artificial by-product of excessive borrowing. Housing activity collapsed, and contractors, in protest, affixed stamps to bricks and pieces of lumber and mailed them to members of the Federal Reserve Board. Frederic H. Schultz, vice chairman of the Federal Reserve Board, told the author William Greider that, on reflection, there had been a misunderstanding. "We really didn't think we had hit the mule with a two-by-four," said Schultz. "We thought we were using a light switch. The idea was not to make the economy go into the tank—it was supposed to allow the economy to grow but without the credit excesses. Instead, the consumer got it into his head that the government was telling him not to use credit. The darned economy just fell off a cliff."

Then it clambered right back up the cliff. On May 14, Volcker announced that the Federal Reserve Board was anticipating the dismantling of controls. In June, housing starts rebounded. Credit cards were drawn from wallets again. Real, or inflation-adjusted, retail sales rose at the annual rates of 12 percent in June and 21 percent in July. In July, the Federal Reserve, in the heat of the presidential nominating season, announced that the last of the controls would be phased out. The recession was over in August.

The decade of the 1980s could not have begun with a less accurate financial omen. Presently, stocks would be bought, cars and houses sold, and office buildings constructed on the confident expectation of a loan. That confidence was not misplaced.

10

"Crooked Banker Found Hanged"

George Champion began his banking career in the mail teller's department of the National Bank of Commerce, New York, immediately after his graduation from Dartmouth College in 1926. He got to work at 7:45 a.m., opened the mail, sorted and packaged checks, and turned to an adding machine. There was thirty-five minutes for lunch ("We didn't have thirty-six minutes," he recalled definitely). The workday ended promptly at 6 p.m. on weekdays (promptly, because the wage rate became time and a half beginning at 6:01) and at 2:30 p.m. on Saturdays. In accordance with bank policy, his tenure in the mail teller's department lasted for six months. He put in stints in the foreign department, where he handled documents and clearings, and the credit department, where he learned the fine art of getting the bank's money back. At night he studied finance and accounting. His starting salary was $1,800 a year, which he remembered as lavish.

The National Bank of Commerce, one of the great discount banks of the time, merged with the Guaranty Trust Co. in 1929 (and the Guaranty Trust Co., many years later, merged with Morgan). Before the merger, on the invitation of a banker he had met by chance on Long Island, Champion joined the Equitable Trust Co. Before long, *it* had merged with the Chase National Bank. Champion, who had worked at four different institutions within the space of twelve months, now stayed put. In 1930, he was promoted to assistant cashier and sent to call on correspondent banks in Tennessee, Mississippi, and Louisiana. In 1931, he was dispatched to New Orleans as the junior member of a two-man team to rescue a bank in which Chase held a threatened interest, the Canal Bank & Trust Co. That experience, colored by prolonged exposure to Governor Huey Long, constituted a unique laboratory in politics and credit. Returning to work in New York in 1933 (the year in which Albert Wiggin, Chase's longtime chairman, was disgraced, in part for trading extensively on inside information, in part, and more particularly, for selling short the stock of Chase itself), Champion began his rise through the executive ranks. He was named vice president in 1939, head of the Southeast District in 1942, senior vice president in 1949, and head of the "United States department," the national banking division, in 1953. In 1955, he became executive vice president of what was by then Chase Manhattan Bank. He was president of Chase Manhattan from 1957 to 1961 and chairman from 1961 until his retirement in 1969, sharing the duties of chief executive with David Rockefeller. Rockefeller and he were oil and water.

Champion left a sound and prosperous organization, but what was most significant about his tenure (as seen from the vantage point of the Rockefeller, Butcher, and Lebreque tenures that followed) was the list of things that he would not do. In general, for example, he would not lend to foreign governments. He would not lend to corporations for the purpose of piling on debt or financing hostile takeovers. He would make no Wriston-like projections of future growth, and he preferred to show higher reserves than larger profits. He would have no truck with the movement to create umbrella organizations called bank holding companies. It would have been interesting to see Champion in action during the Third World lending mania of the late 1970s and the real-estate lending binge of the mid-1980s. It is tempting to believe that if anyone might have withstood the pressures of the crowd to conform and throw other people's money around, it was he. In any case, the disastrous Chase real-estate investment trust was organized the year after he retired.

In 1978, eight years into the stewardship of David Rockefeller, Champion sat down with an archivist (the Chase had its own) to discuss his career and unburden himself about banking. He was in a difficult diplomatic position. Rockefeller and he had disagreed on matters great and small. For instance, the year after Champion left, the annual report, formerly plain, blossomed with photographs and sans serif type. Three years after he retired, a monumental, forty-two-foot-high sculpture, called "Group of Four Trees," by Jean Dubuffet, was unveiled outdoors at One Chase Manhattan Plaza. "The sculpture is being provided for the enjoyment of the financial community by David Rockefeller, chairman of the Chase Manhattan Bank, to mark his 25th anniversary on Wall Street," the press release said.

Champion was a home-market man, Rockefeller a cosmopolitan. Champion golfed with Dwight D. Eisenhower and shot with Lucius

D. Clay; Rockefeller dined with Zhou Enlai and consulted with Henry Kissinger. (Once Rockefeller rattled off a list of people he had visited on one of his frequent sojourns abroad: "Marshal Tito, the President of Germany, the Prime Minister of Italy and so forth and so on.") In 1973, Chase became the first American bank since 1929 to open a representative Moscow office. "We established relations with the People's Republic of China," the 1973 annual report also disclosed, sounding a little like the State Department annual, "being named sole American correspondent for the Bank of China."

Chase was a Rockefeller institution—in the 1930s, John D. Rockefeller was its largest shareholder—and David Rockefeller had it all over the other trainees when he joined the bank in 1946. He was immediately named assistant manager of the foreign department; by 1950, he was supervising Latin American operations. Conspicuously missing from his experience was the trial by fire through which Champion had passed in New Orleans and any number of bankers only slightly older than Rockefeller had borne in New York during the Depression and its long aftermath. As *The New York Times* described him in a glowing profile it published in 1980, Rockefeller was a "banker-statesman" as distinct from a banker. In his single-minded cultivation of heads of state, Rockefeller expressed the contemporary union of government and banking. In their stripes-and-plaid incompatibility, Champion was an exemplar of laissez-faire and Rockefeller of interventionism.

On the other hand, the Chase was Champion's bank too, and the interview was being conducted on Chase Manhattan premises. Champion was therefore constrained. He talked about the Chase and of banking in general, starting with his arrival in New Orleans at the bottom of the Depression in 1931. What he found at the Canal Bank & Trust was a crisis of real-estate lending, which is what investors, many years later, would discover at Chase itself:

"The bank had never thought of getting any of them [the loans] paid down," said Champion. "They would make a ten-year loan on a house or a farm and never say, 'This should be amortized or cut down.' Consequently, when the values fell out of bed there was no way to liquidate the loans.

"This was a completely different atmosphere than today because the Federal Reserve did very little to cooperate with the banks in helping them with their problems. They were afraid of themselves and, while we had the RFC [Reconstruction Finance Corporation], we also had a political confrontation at the time."

Champion said that he made considerable progress after a year. Borrowers began to pay down their loans, even if only in small parts. The collateral behind the loans was top-flight, he recalled—the finest rice lands, cotton lands, and sugarcane in the world—but "there was nobody with any money to buy them. So, it was a frozen situation, and those frozen assets were not acceptable as collateral at the Federal Reserve. . . .

"On Friday evening, February 3 [1933], we were having a clearing house meeting on the problem of the debt of the City of New Orleans. They needed some more money. The only bank[er who] wasn't represented was Rudolph Hecht, president of the Hibernia. At ten o'clock at night, Huey Long called up and said, 'Rudolph Hecht is at my house; I want you to come out right now.' We all did and Rudolph announced that he would not open his bank the next day, Saturday.

"Now, that was a horrible thing to hear when your own bank wasn't the most liquid asset in the world. But you must remember, this is February 3, 1933. Huey Long called up the newspapers, the librarians, and asked them to look through the library, papers and records and find out what happened on February 4—battle fought, country founded, who was born, who died, and so forth, as we were going to have a holiday. One by one they called back and said, 'We can't find anything on February 4.' Huey, in language which I will not repeat, said, 'I know, nobody knows when that so-and-so [Jean] Lafitte was born, but I happen to know it was 150 years ago tomorrow.' He dictated, at eleven or eleven-thirty, a proclamation that made Washington look like a piker as far as [being] the savior of the country is concerned, and we had [a] banking holiday . . . on that Saturday morning."

As for the Canal Bank, according to Champion, it wound up paying off not only its depositors but also its junior creditors. "And the stock of the holding company which owned the assets became very valuable," he said. "Now, it's true, part of that was due to oil, but even without oil the assets of the bank represented real value."

Chase's experiences in the Depression made an indelible impression on Champion. The bank was overloaded with German bonds, Cuban credits, and the depreciating obligations of its newly acquired investment-banking subsidiary, Chase Harris Forbes. In fact, it was Chase Harris Forbes itself that had sold the public some stock in the Canal Bank a year earlier. And it was, in part, Wiggin's sense of responsibility for that transaction that led to the decision to dispatch Champion on his mission to New Orleans. Losses piled up. In 1931, every employee's salary was cut by 10 percent. In 1932, the dividend on Chase's stock was twice reduced; at the bottom of the market that year, a share of Chase stock fetched only 7 percent of its peak 1929 price.

If Champion would have nothing to do with holding companies or foreign loans, and if he would resist the return of commercial banks to the investment-banking business, there wasn't far to look for the reasons. However, the Chase's staying power and solvency were no less deeply impressed on him than its many embarrassments. "The great thing that really we can brag about is the fact that in that period of banking crisis, the Chase stood up better than any bank in America—and I guarantee you that's true—in terms of supporting management that was competent, both in banking and in industry," he said. "We loaned more than any other two or three banks together in New York City, loaned [to] banks [that is].

"Now, before we went down to New Orleans, Mr. [Oliver] Lucas, when he was taking a trip, would call me from Memphis—I remember it very well—and from Nashville, and Knoxville, etc., and say, 'I am putting a bundle of first mortgage notes in the mail for such and such a bank. Put a credit to their account tomorrow morning.' And we'd do it. This is when others were refusing to make this kind of commitment. For many years banks all over the country would say, 'You saved me. If it hadn't been for you, we would never have been able to see it through.' There was no other place to go."

Champion's interviewer asked him why the Chase was willing while other banks were not.

"The others were scared, apparently," he said. "It was Wiggin's policy of staying with the customers. We had any number of customers, some of them of national standing, that we saved. Make no mistake about it. It was his philosophy to stick with management that was good and it was a very sound thing to do. Nothing was lost. It was a great gain to the bank. . . . The Chase saved any number of the largest corporations in the country who became overextended in the Depression period such as Kelsey-Hayes Wheel [Co.]; Carson, Pirie, Scott [& Co.] of Chicago; Sears, Roebuck; any number of large companies that found, because of their cash flow, difficulty in meeting their financial needs. . . .

"In those days the Chase was a primary reserve bank for correspondents throughout the whole country. As I think I might have mentioned earlier, we at one time had loans to correspondent banks in the Depression period of the early 1930s that were more than double the total loan volume of any other New York banks. And, as a result, we cemented a relationship with these correspondents throughout the country who realized that they could depend upon Chase for help when it was needed. We were recognized for many years as the primary correspondent for banks throughout the country." Baker's bank had occupied a similar position around the turn of the century.

Champion added that these loans were not made against the collateral of government bonds. The needy banks had no such bonds that were not already pledged. He said that the Chase lent against miscellaneous notes.

He was asked about Wiggin.

"I'm not familiar with Mr. Wiggin's personal financial operations. I do know that many of the officers of the Chase were broke because of the stock market and because of holding Chase stock in particular. I was told that many had been discouraged from selling it when the market was going down. I don't know, but I do know this, that as far as sound banking is concerned and as far as contributions to supporting this country in banking, the vital importance of staying with companies that were in need of help, he stood out as the tops of all. It was his policy that made it possible for the lending officers of Chase to do this."

It came out that Champion was not quite the mossback that he must have seemed to the younger generation. He spoke enthusiastically of Chase's role in helping "the individual with character, energy and ability compete with the individual or corporation that had the money," and he contended that the United States had the only truly competitive banking system in the world. He described the Chase's lending to tobacco dealers, a business conducted without written contracts. He expressed admiration for some of the business that the Bank of Manhattan had done in the Depression, years before it merged with Chase. It had lent to D. K. Ludwig long before the future shipping titan was a billionaire. It was the first bank to lend to Henry Mercer, founder of States Marine, and it had lent to Reynolds Metals when that company owed more to the RFC than it showed in net worth. "These were the positions that the Bank of Manhattan took which were risk positions that worked out," said Champion. "You've got to give them credit for these things. Consolidated Groceries—Nate Cummings bought a little outfit down in Baltimore and the Bank of Manhattan financed him. The thing was busted, Nate was a great operator and it developed into Consolidated Groceries. They did the same thing with Norton Simon, and you can name others—Rockwell Kent was the name of the lending officer who did this. That was very profitable business because it was a high-rate business. It was that kind of thing that they did that was good for banking."

It was an article of faith among old-time bankers that a loan should run no longer than ninety days. In the mid-1930s, longer-dated loans—so-called term loans—came into being, a trend that Champion helped to pioneer. "I handled the second term loan we made," the banker said, "a five-year loan to a cotton mill. . . .

"What we did was to say, 'We will help you anticipate your expansion if your cash flow will show that you can meet these obligations as they mature.' And we worked up loan agreements which were very tight agreements in those days even for a five-year term loan. Those were the maximum years of term lending that we used at that time. It proved to be a great asset to the bank.

"Interestingly enough, when I was president [1957 to 1961], we were criticized by the Federal Reserve for the amount of term lending we had in the bank. And I went to the Federal Reserve and asked them the basis for their criticism. They said, 'There are just too many term loans.' I said, 'Are you talking about too many loans?' 'No, no. Term loans.' Well, I said, 'The average maturity of our term loans, all of them, is two and a half years. Every company has debt extinction as its objective and program. We have a lot of ninety-day paper in the bank that I'd be glad to call if you want us to. That will disrupt the economy like nobody's business because the ninety-day paper is not headed for debt extinction.'

" 'Oh, no, don't do that.'

"I said, 'You tell me why this term paper isn't the most liquid paper we have in the bank.' And they couldn't tell me why it wasn't, and they apologized for having said it.

"I said, 'When we run this bank wrong, we will know it far before you do.' They virtually apologized. It was new. I don't blame them. You had a group of examiners who were trying to protect themselves and didn't understand."

Innovative as he had been, Champion held prophetic reservations about the drift of affairs in the 1970s, and he spent the rest of the interview describing his sense of estrangement from the times. He said he disapproved of bank holding companies—Chase Manhattan Corporation was created following his retirement—on the ground that they distracted management from the business of banking. "Be the best bank," he adjured.

He complained about the pressure to compete with other banks by lowering one's own standards. Citicorp had dropped its 15 percent gauntlet, and Chase had not. "We've always had pressure, ever since I've been in it. They say, 'Oh, the Citibank is gaining on you.' So what? It doesn't make any difference to me.

"I never believed you should say, 'I'm going to have X increase in profits. I'm going to have X increase in expansion.' If you run the bank properly, all the rest will fall in line. That was the whole philosophy that we had. As a matter of fact, all the time that I was president or chairman, we only had one visit with the security analysts for just that reason. We said, 'We'll do the best we can in running the bank and all can be informed when we issue our reports and we'll answer all the questions publicly, not for any particular few. And we're not going to be pressured into showing profits.' We tried to put out the most conservative statement possible, to hide away anything we could, frankly, for the future. . . . We did everything we could to set up reserves wherever possible in terms of questionable loans. We didn't do anything that was illegal, but we knew that we would come into periods when we needed to call on reserves and the statutory limitation on reserves was so bad that there was no way to set up as much as we felt it was necessary to have, prudent to have. . . .

"Banking should be in such an unquestionably strong financial position that they should be able to tell the government what they're going to do and not have it vice versa. Banks should decide proper ratios that are right in terms of loans to capital, total risk assets to capital. They should say, 'These are the proper relationships, in terms of percentage of assets in countries, to countries, to industries and to individual companies, as it relates to the capital of each bank. . . .'

"I long have said what they ought to do is to increase the reserve for bad debts until they get to a point of having at least 5 percent of total loans. [This] would not be out of line in view of the enormous losses that had to be written off in the last few years. Take a quarter of 1 percent each year and add to the reserve for bad debts until you get 5 percent. Strengthen your capital position. Don't apply for privileges and be turned down in Washington, which banks have experienced. You lose your strength, you lose your independence. Don't get in a position where you are going to have to rely on government to bail you out. Remain strong, very strong, particularly in a period such as we are facing. This is basically the philosophy that I have always adhered to."

No reactionary as a lender, Champion had misgivings about the new twin pillars of American banking, loans to effect razzle-dazzle corporate consolidations and loans to Third World governments.

He addressed the first of these. "We have seen these conglomerates come along. I think Chase has been very good in this, they have never financed a conglomerate acquisition where the acquired company wasn't in favor of it. We were out of a great many, like Ling-Temco, where they pressured us to beat the band to come into that. Not at all, we wouldn't do it because we saw nothing constructive in this."

In Champion's day too, the tax advantages of corporate debt were enticing. Companies could deduct from taxable income the interest they paid on their debt but not the dividends they paid on their stock. Champion understood perfectly well why a rational, taxpaying company would want to borrow, but he nevertheless deplored the trend (which, really, had hardly begun). "Not constructive for the country," he said, and he described the prescient ideas for reform that he had vainly offered to Congress:

"As a matter of fact, I went to Wilbur Mills when he was still in the House and to Arthur Burns and I said, 'What you ought to do is cut corporation taxes in half. Have a maximum of 25 percent corporation tax and substitute a value-added tax for the difference so that the product that is to be sold will still carry the tax burden that it does now and the government will not be the sufferer as far as income is concerned.' I said, 'The reason I say that is because it is so attractive to substitute debt for equity that the conglomerate is the most prosperous vehicle that you have in terms of per-share earnings and it is unsound for the economy.'

"They both agreed that it was perfectly right, but, as Wilbur Mills said, 'This is a sales tax, that is a value-added.' I said, 'Wilbur, there is no tax that isn't a form of sales tax. When you pay a tax on profits, that has been added to the cost of the product that is sold, but this is a much sounder way of doing it. This will stop the conglomerate movement which you are disturbed about, which I am disturbed about.' I went down to David Kennedy when he was Secretary of the Treasury and he agreed, but nothing was done."

That left lending to Third World governments. Champion registered his disapproval of this fad too. "When I was in the bank," he said, "the Union Bank of California came and asked us if we would participate in a loan to develop a copper mine in Mexico. I asked the chairman who owned the mine. He said, 'The Mexican government.' I said, 'No way. We are not here to socialize the world.' Then I went over to Korea. David Kennedy had been there a few weeks ago and said he would go back to the United States and try to arrange a five-, seven-, ten-year, $50 million, $75 million, $100 million loan. The

One of the last of the great New York bankers: George Champion of the Chase Manhattan, 1963 (CHASE MANHATTAN ARCHIVE)

Finance Minister asked me if we would participate. I said, 'Not only will we not participate, but if you do this we'll cut down our branch lending here materially.'

"I said, 'There is no way for you to pay those loans. It's unsound.'

"We would not make any loans to any foreign government, none.* We made loans to foreign banks, to foreign central banks. All were relatively short-term, but history had shown that when countries became financially in trouble, the central banks in some way met their obligations. In the 1920s, we couldn't go over to Germany and collect loans. We couldn't go any place and collect the loans that had been made by the investment bankers but ended up in the portfolio of the commercial bankers. We didn't feel, at least I didn't feel, that lending to foreign governments was part of the commercial-banking responsibility, because there is no debt extinction planned and programmed."

* Asked for comment on this recollection, Walter Wriston, Champion's opposite number at Citicorp, smiled and said that he could recall at least one loan to a foreign government—that of France—in which Champion enthusiastically joined.

Lending to the Third World

In 1978, the same year Champion was anticipating the future ills of
the American banking system, a twenty-five-year-old lending officer
of the Cleveland Trust Co. (later Ameritrust) disembarked from an
airplane in Manila, proceeded to his hotel in a chauffeured red Jaguar
(finding in the back seat a twenty-year-old female companion whom
his client had thoughtfully provided for the duration of his visit), and
then to a first-class restaurant. Over dinner, this same attentive customer, the Construction and Development Corporation of the Philippines (CDCP), consented to borrow $10 million from the young
man's bank. The loan would be applied to the purchase of earth-
moving equipment from an American manufacturer, a company that
also happened to be a Cleveland Trust client.

The banker, S. C. Gwynne, had joined the bank in 1977. He first
underwent basic training in credit and was later assigned to international lending because of his fluency in French. His first assignment
was to the French-speaking Arab countries of North Africa, from which
point his career literally took off. In the six months preceding his stop
in Manila, he had visited twenty-eight countries.

"As a domestic credit analyst," Gwynne recalled, "I was taught to
develop reasonable asset security for all loans unless the borrower was
of impeccable means and integrity. As an international loan officer, I
was taught to forget about that, and instead to develop a set of ra-
tionales that would make the home office feel good about the loan,
even though, technically, it was 'unsecured.' " It is unlikely that
Champion would have approved. For one thing, CDCP was connected
to the family of President Ferdinand Marcos. For another, it was highly
leveraged. For every dollar of equity on its balance sheet, there were
seven dollars of debt. "One to one is considered healthy," stated
Gwynne, writing before the junk-bond revolution, "two to one
dangerous."

As fortification, Gwynne arranged a "standby letter of credit," an
undertaking by another bank to honor CDCP's debts in case of trouble.
"It takes only a month and a few dozen overseas phone calls to get
the guarantee from the Philippine bank, which is handing them out
these days like free samples. With the help of a cooperative credit
analyst, who is just three months out of . . . Ohio State, we package
a stunning little credit that sweeps through all of the loan committees
without even a flesh wound."

The loan went bad, but Gwynne was not around to see it; he had taken another job with another bank in the meantime. That was the way of the world in the late 1970s and early 1980s. So hot was the market for international lending officers that it behooved ambitious young bankers to keep moving. In consequence, as Gwynne noted, "many of the people who make the big international loans are not around to collect them when they go bad, and, conversely, the people who are collecting the bad loans are not the people who made them in the first place, and therefore feel only vaguely responsible."

Much as they had been in the 1820s, in the 1880s, in the early years of the twentieth century, and in the 1920s, rich creditors were embarked on a wholesale extension of credit to poor nations. As the lending was recurrent, so were defaults, and the same countries were prone to pull the wool over the eyes of successive generations of creditors. Thus, Peru defaulted in 1876, 1931, 1932, and 1985, and Brazil in 1898, 1914, 1931, 1987, and 1989. In one sense, therefore, this episode was no different than the others, the oil shock notwithstanding. Capitalists had lost their heads under the gold standard, and they were losing them now, without any recognizable monetary standard. They had overlent in the years before the socialization of credit risk, and they were overdoing it now under the regime of federal deposit insurance. Yet, in one key detail, the 1970s were unprecedented. What was unique was the position of the banks: they themselves had chosen to bear the risk of nonpayment. In times past, the banks had underwritten loans to foreign governments in the form of bonds. Then they had sold the bonds to investors. In the immediate postwar years, governments themselves, or international organizations like the World Bank, had lent overseas. In the 1970s, the commercial banks resumed lending but kept the loans themselves, bearing all associated risks, which were great, and rewards, which were small. The difference was vitally important. Defaults in the past had threatened the financial interests of specific bondholders. Defaults in the future would threaten individual banks and, for a time, as it seemed, the world banking system.

Champion had retired not a day too soon. In the 1970s, Chase and Citibank and the other leading New York institutions set out to violate each of his canons of sound practice. Not only did they lend to sovereign governments and delude themselves that governments never defaulted; they further lent at uneconomically low interest rates. The quadrupling of oil prices in 1973 effected a quadrupling of the dollar income of the oil producers and a meaningful increase in their bank accounts. A new monetary coinage, petrodollars, described the funds that piled up in their names in the major international banks. What would be done with the money? It would be lent, in part, to the countries that had bought the Organization of Petroleum Exporting Countries' oil.

Lawrence Dennis, formerly a banker with J. & W. Seligman & Co. and earlier an American diplomat, testified before the Senate Finance Committee in 1932 concerning the unproductive uses to which the proceeds of some foreign loans had been put. In the case of a 1928 bond issued by Dillon, Read & Co. for the government of Bolivia in the amount of $28 million, he said, "I was rather struck by the fact that the loan, or at least $5 million of it, went to pay for arms to Vickers in London. . . . I thought it was rather an unusual thing, because the arms were supposed to be paid for in five years, and the debt was funded in 34-year, 7 percent bonds." He continued, deadpan: "A phase of that loan which was interesting to me was that they took $3,904,000 to pay off deficits, which included quite a large item for delayed salaries of Government officials." Peru too had borrowed not wisely but too well—"Peruvian bond" subsequently entered the language as a term to connote worthlessness—and Dennis had seen first-hand to what use the proceeds of various foreign loans had been put. "You could see the real-estate suburban developments. They were building up real-estate suburbs, plotting land and paving streets out in the desert," he said. "It was an exhibition of all sorts of follies." So in the 1970s and 1980s. Another word was coined—"kleptocracy"—to describe a government of thieves, and many such regimes spirited off the proceeds of bank loans to the United States and Europe. "A significant portion of the loans was reinvested in the developed countries by LDC residents through 'flight capital,' " as the General Accounting Office put it.

According to scholars of the international debt predicament (the banking crisis presently created its own academic specialty), the rates obtained in the 1970s and 1980s were less remunerative to lenders than those that were paid to bondholders in the 1920s or before 1914. In times past, investment bankers had competed to underwrite the bonds of foreign governments. In the 1970s, commercial bankers competed to lend their own depositors' money. It was a twentieth-century first. The competition was international, pitting Chase not only against Citibank but also (among others) the Saudi International Bank, the Commercial Bank of Australia, Lloyds Bank, and Compagnie Financière de la Deutsche Bank. One and all regretted the thinness of lending margins and thus of profit margins. However, they also agreed that banks must lend, both for the high-minded reason of "recycling" OPEC's windfall and for the low-minded one of, in effect, keeping up with the Rockefellers.

In the spring of 1978, a pair of South Korean state banks and the National Bank of Hungary managed to borrow at less than one percentage point over LIBOR (the London interbank offered rate). LIBOR was, and is, the rate at which banks obtained funds in the international market for dollars. It was the inside, or wholesale, cost of money. In the world fashioned by Walter Wriston, no solvent bank had to wait for a depositor to walk through the door. A bank in need of funds could obtain them in the domestic certificate-of-deposit market or (as was more likely to be the case in the 1970s) in the Eurodollar market. As for the wafer-thin profit margins, an officer of the overseas subsidiary of Continental Illinois Bank & Trust Co., the lead lender in the Hungarian credit, explained: "There's so much liquidity chasing so few borrowers that we either do this deal now at the price we've negotiated, or do it next month at a lower spread."

By implication, there were excess dollars in the world, and Paul Volcker would in fact tackle that problem in 1979 and again in 1980. Also—and this afforded a preview of the next decade—there were too many banks that had not familiarized themselves with the precepts of George Champion or that felt that they could no longer afford them. (George Moore, Wriston's predecessor at Citicorp, came up, as Champion did, through the credit side of the bank in the Great Depression. Moore compiled a manual of lending disasters, including misfortunes abroad, for the use of the bank's trainees. According to Moore—and inference is plainly on the side of his recollection—the book was misplaced in the 1960s.) In an interview in 1977, David Rockefeller, "a symbol and spokesman" for international banking, as *Euromoney* put it, paid court to one of Champion's tenets when he observed that governments would not do what a private bank told them they must do. That was as far as he would go in that direction, however. As for Third World debt in general, the chairman of the Chase Manhattan Bank saw nothing threatening in it. "I think there has been an exaggerated concern because people have tended to aggregate loans to all LDCs—pick a global figure and then assume that most of the risk was in countries where there has been serious exposure. Everyone immediately mentions Zaire. The fact is that the . . . total exposure [of] private banks to Zaire is relatively very small compared to loans in general. In our own case, it's minuscule. Most of our loans to developing nations are to so-called wealthier ones—the Brazils and Mexicos and Taiwans—countries of that sort which, we think, may have temporarily gone a little far in extending themselves. But they are better off now and we have great confidence in them."

If, in fact, Rockefeller's confidence had been well founded, Chase would have done no better than to get its depositors' money back and to earn a rate of interest only slightly higher than its own cost of funds. It was not the way that Rockefeller's grandfather had gotten rich, nor had it been the way that George F. Baker had built a bank. If, on the other hand, Rockefeller's confidence had been misplaced, as it duly proved to be, Chase would have borne significant losses, which it did. It is striking how little attention was paid to loss and how much to an admittedly meager prospective gain. In 1977, Argentina, a disastrous Third World debtor in the making, was described (along with Chile, a better credit) in *Euromoney* as a "much needed sink-hole for excess banking liquidity." In 1978, an officer of the Saudi International Bank admitted that his institution and he were corks in the sea: "We're in the banking business, and if the world is doing ⅝ percent business [that is, lending at that margin over the cost of funds] we may be forced to participate." And a man from Dresdner Bank's Luxembourg subsidiary rejected the proposition that a bank could refuse to lend below a certain minimum threshold of profitability: "Once a bank is in the international market it wants to stay there, especially if it has a large volume of funds to lend. So the theory of limits rarely functions." For example, drawing the line at 1 percent would be counterproductive: "If any bank took a decision like that and stuck to it, its business would go to its competitors, while relations with its country clients would deteriorate," the Dresdner's man continued. "Whenever a good proposition comes along limits are given little priority." The interest rates at which Brazil, Argentina, Mexico, and the rest raised money were floating. However unremunerative the profit margins were to the banks, the absolute level of rates presently became punitive to the borrowers.

The term loans for which Chase was criticized by the Federal Reserve around 1960 had had an average life of two and a half years. By the late 1970s foreign governments were able to borrow for ten or twelve years. Beginning in 1982, as debtor after debtor obtained relief through "reschedulings," terms were successively lengthened until, by 1986–88, the average maturity of a Latin American loan was more than seventeen years. In fact, as the crisis deepened in 1987, loans to Brazil and Peru virtually became perpetual.

Although the son of a historian, Wriston clung to the misapprehension that sovereign governments did not default, and he reiterated, in the recession year of 1981 (which preceded the debt-deluge year of 1982), that there was nothing to worry about. "One by one," wrote Wriston, "we are seeing developing countries finally breaking through the vicious cycle of poverty. Far from despairing, I have great hopes for the future of the LDC in the remaining years of this century." Later in 1981, Citicorp's public affairs department produced a lovely, coffee-table-quality brochure on Brazil for which Wriston himself contributed the introduction ("Brazil's future can be summed up in a single word: *opportunity*") and set the upbeat analytical tone. "By borrowing a good deal more than it needed to cover its current-account deficits," the bank's authors wrote, "Brazil managed to add some $5.5 billion to its international reserves during the middle of the 1970s. This buildup strengthened the country's financial defenses against new unforeseen contingencies." It did not, however, strengthen them against the contingency of too much debt, which was all too predictable.

In the spring of 1982, contra Wriston, the Mexican Finance Minister, Jesús Silva Herzog, met regularly with Paul Volcker in Washington to discuss the looming prospect of Mexico's bankruptcy. The Mexican unemployment rate was 13 percent. Private capital was leaving the country and the largest Mexican corporation, Grupo Industrial Alfa, was on the verge of default. Foreign creditors of the Mexican government, which owed $80 billion, were chiefly American banks. "It was clear they were on a trajectory—they were going broke—but what could you do about it?" Volcker reflected with William Greider later on. "You just sat there and wondered: when is Mexico going to blow? Is it going to blow before the election or after?"

On July 4, the Mexican people would go to the polls and elect—there was no doubt about it—Miguel de la Madrid their next President. However, in the interest of a decent respect for political form, there could be no humiliating appeal to the International Monetary Fund, the usual source of a loan for a country in Mexico's circumstances, before election day. Making the best of a bad lot, the Federal Reserve on April 30 entered into a currency "swap" with Mexico. In exchange for what amounted to a short-term $600 million loan, the Fed received the equivalent of $600 million in Mexican pesos. Two more such swaps were conducted in June and July, each entailing the risk that Mexico would find itself unable to return the dollars. The offsetting (and far more urgent) risk, in the American government's eyes, was that Mexico would default on its debt and set off a run on America's largest banks, which were collectively overextended in loans to poor countries. In 1982, the nine top banks were owed the equivalent of more than 300 percent of their capital by Third World borrowers. In other words, if only one-third of the LDC debts had to be written off, the banks' stockholders would lose their investments.

On August 13, Herzog told the Fed that he needed a big loan, and quickly, to forestall a default. What financial posterity knows best about August 1982 was that it was the first month of the greatest bull market in modern times. By definition, of course, the news is always the worst at the bottom, and the news that summer was bleak. Setting the tone in banking was a front-page headline in the Sunday *New York Daily News* of June 20, 1982, concerning the death beneath a London bridge of an officer of a failed Italian bank. "Crooked Banker Found Hanged," it indelibly said. On Wall Street, alarming rumors circulated about Chase Manhattan, Continental Illinois, and a number of smaller institutions, including the First Security Bank of Horseshoe Bend, Arkansas. On August 12, Lombard-Wall, Inc., a government bond dealer, filed for bankruptcy protection, and International Harvester, in a full-page newspaper advertisement, promised that it wouldn't file: "We're not giving in. We're going on." The next day was a Friday, but a less unlucky Friday the 13th has rarely been seen in finance. No word of Herzog's mission reached Wall Street, but the stock market, reversing eight straight losing sessions and shrugging off reports of weak car sales and a still worrisome rate of price inflation, rose 11 points.

A Bull Market Begins

Interest rates were falling—Treasury bills the next Monday fetched 8.62 percent, their lowest yield since July 1980—and prospects for Third World debtors were brightening. Over the weekend of August 14–15, a huge federal bailout of Mexico was organized, the Departments of Energy and Agriculture pitching in with the Federal Reserve and the Treasury. Three and a half billion dollars was committed, thereby averting the sovereign equivalent of Chapter 11. As speculators chase markets with money, so theorists pursue them with explanations. It is a callow theorist who presumes to explain exactly why any market does anything at any particular moment. It is a fact that the recession officially ended in November 1982 and that interest rates had peaked in September 1981. But there was another potentially bullish development on the horizon. By intervening on behalf of Mexico and its creditors, the Federal Reserve had reinforced the presumption that no big American bank would be allowed to fail by reason of its own rash lending. No chain reaction of failure would be allowed to occur in the American banking system even if market forces seemed to demand it. Walter Bagehot, the Victorian master, had stipulated that a central bank in a time of a crisis should lend freely but at a high rate of interest. He meant that it should lend to solvent commercial banks. He foresaw no need to lend to a government to which a threatened bank had unwisely lent. Nevertheless, in the United States in 1982, it had come to that, and the Reagan administration was not prepared to stand on principle to explore the free-market consequences of a possible run. Insofar as the fear of a run had inhibited the over-expansion of credit in the past, that inhibition was being suppressed.

Tuesday, September 14, brought news of a plunge in auto sales, of a rise in the ratio of inventories to sales (not a propitious business indicator), and of a warning by the Democratic chairman of the House Ways and Means Committee, Dan Rostenkowski, that rising defense outlays could push up taxes. For the readers of *The New York Times*, however, the day had begun on a financially hopeful note. On the Op-Ed page was an optimistic appraisal of Third World lending by Walter Wriston himself.

It was indeed Wriston's moment. Stock prices were climbing, interest rates were falling, and the gloom of the recession was palpably lifting. (It was still thick at the annual meeting of the World Bank and International Monetary Fund, however, which Wriston had just attended in Toronto. "It was like the *Titanic*," he recalled of the mood of the meeting. "We were just rearranging the deck chairs.") The system had not cracked up, calamity howlers to the contrary notwithstanding. In 1982, not a very good year for business activity, Citicorp was on its way to showing a 35 percent jump in profits. It would earn 16.4 cents, after tax, for every dollar of stockholder investment.

Once more, Wriston's faith in the established market order had been vindicated, and he mentioned that fact in his essay at his earliest convenience. "Over the years," he reminded his public, "a lot of intellectual capital has been invested in the proposition that massive defaults by developing countries will eventually cause a severe world financial crisis. Those who took that view in 1973–74 have been proved wrong, and those of us who believed that the market would absorb the shock of skyrocketing oil prices proved correct. Despite this, the perception remains that some form of disaster is inevitable. It is not."

Perhaps Paul Volcker or Donald Regan, the Treasury Secretary, expectantly scanned Wriston's piece for any sign of thanks, however oblique, for pulling his chestnuts out of the fire with Mexico. If so, they were disappointed, for none was offered. In fact, considering the circumstances, Wriston's assessment of the federal credit might have been judged ungrateful:

> If we had a truth-in-Government act comparable to the truth-in-advertising law, every note issued by the Treasury would be obliged to include a sentence stating: "This note will be redeemed with the proceeds from an identical note which will be sold to the public when this one comes due."
>
> When this activity is carried out in the United States, as it is weekly, it is described as a Treasury bill auction. But when basically the same process is conducted abroad in a foreign language, our news media usually speak of a country's "rolling over its debts," with the implication that the world is about to go bankrupt and take the banking system down with it.

So far, George Champion could have found nothing to disagree with. Governments, as he had noted disapprovingly in 1978, got into debt without a single thought to getting out again. However, that was about as much common ground as he and the chairman of Citicorp shared. Conceding Champion's point, Wriston had nevertheless rejected his example (as Rockefeller did too) and lent billions abroad, with more than $3 billion to public-sector borrowers outstanding at year end 1982. It had been lending to foreign governments for seventy-five years, the bank reminded its stockholders in 1983, and it had no intention of stopping because of what *Time*, on the cover of its January 10, 1983, issue, chose to call "The Debt Bomb." It had found the public sector to be a more reliable borrower than the private sector, and its loan-loss experience abroad compared favorably with its loan-loss experience at home. Wriston, the inventor of the negotiable certificate of deposit, believed in progress. He believed in the American economy and in the world's banking system. He believed in technology (in 1982, Citicorp became the first financial institution to own its own satellite transponders) and in the possibility of enlightened regulation (the Federal Reserve was phasing out its restrictions on interest rates). If a creditworthy borrower needed a loan, Wriston believed that that borrower would be able to get one.

It followed that the principal criterion of a country's financial standing was not its ratio of debt to exports or the sum of its foreign reserves. It was its capacity to borrow. And even if worst should come to worst, Wriston believed, a country would not go broke: "Bankruptcy is a procedure developed in western law to forgive the obligations of a person or a company that owes more than it has," he wrote. "Any country, however badly off, will 'own' more than it 'owes.' The catch is cash flow and the cure is sound programs and time to let them work."

Investors not many years older than Wriston had had a very different experience with foreign-government obligations in the 1930s and 1940s, of course (Citicorp's forerunner, the National City Co., had underwritten some of those cats and dogs), but Wriston went so far as to imply that that unhappy episode had never occurred. He strongly implied that the "global financial market" was something new under the sun, like the automatic teller machine. "For the first time in history it is within the power of a less-developed country to obtain from external savings the capital needed for growth," he wrote, for the time being ignoring the capital market in which Brazil, Argentina, and Mexico, not to mention the United States, had borrowed for more than a century.

Thus, the banks should keep on doing what they had been doing (Wriston did not mention the Federal Reserve, the Treasury, the Department of Energy, the Department of Agriculture, or the rest of the federal apparatus that had served his institution so well in recent weeks): "We should remember that the proposition that commercial banks cannot or should not continue to finance the developing countries is really a disguised way of saying that those countries will not be successful in adjusting to the new challenges posed by a world economy growing much less rapidly, and thus will not continue to enjoy access to the market. That is not a statement of fact but a prophecy—one that has little basis in recent history."

Had it only been so! In one sense, of course, Wriston was magnificently right. There would be no credit collapse-cum-depression, for the next eight years, at least. In September 1982, that was the most lucrative opinion that any investor could have held. (One Saturday in the spring of 1982, a group of gloomy Guses, including the author, met for lunch at the University Club in New York, exchanged views about the likely collapse of banks such as Wriston's, and generally prepared themselves for every speculative contingency except for the one that brilliantly materialized in August.) Wriston, however, was a banker, not an investor. The best thing that could happen to Citi's portfolio of Third World loans was no default. It was a very different proposition than that of an investor buying common stock in a Brazilian corporation at an attractive discount to book value. If everything went exactly as Wriston predicted, Citicorp would not be materially richer. If it did not, however, the bank would be significantly poorer.

It did not. In December the governor of the Central Bank of Brazil, Carlos Geraldo Langoni, convened a meeting of Brazil's principal bank creditors at the Plaza Hotel in Manhattan to tell them that things were not going very well. Brazil, he admitted, had been shut out of the international credit markets. (He diplomatically did not mention that Wriston had all but ruled out that contingency only three months earlier.) "Our analysis shows that under present circumstances we cannot look to market forces to restore the levels of resource flows necessary to finance our external deficit in 1983," he said, preparing to lay the arm on his listeners. "Only a planned and coordinated effort can offset market uncertainties, with the commercial banks assuming a leading role side by side with official lenders." Put less obliquely, Brazil could not pay what it owed.

Langoni thanked the U.S. Treasury, the Federal Reserve, and the Bank for International Settlements for the $1 billion "bridge" loan they had recently advanced, and he alerted the commercial bankers that more would be asked of them. In particular, they should contribute, in the form of a new loan, the $4 billion that Brazil owed them in 1983. He did not mention the word "bankrupt." That fell to José Carlos Madeira Serrano, external director of the central bank, who

Walter Wriston, chairman of Citicorp, declaring in December 1982 that the odds of an international banking collapse were "close to zero"; an accurate enough prediction for the time (BETTMANN ARCHIVE)

told a news conference in Rio de Janeiro on December 30 that the deadline for action was March 1. "If the projects for new loans and debt rollover are not structured by then," he said, "Brazil would be insolvent."

Brazil, one of Citicorp's favorite countries, did not declare bankruptcy. However, it twice overtly defaulted on its external debts, in 1987 and 1989, and it sank deeper into its domestic rut of low growth and high inflation. According to a tabulation by Thomas Kamm of *The Wall Street Journal*, Brazil, in the decade of the 1980s, bore up under eight monetary stabilization plans, four different currencies, eleven different indices to measure inflation, five wage-and-price freezes, fourteen different wage policies, eighteen changes in foreign-exchange rules, fifty-four changes in price-control guidelines, twenty-one different foreign-debt negotiation proposals, and nineteen decrees on fiscal austerity. In 1990, the inflation rate hit 1,794 percent.

As Brazil's fortunes deteriorated, its borrowing costs paradoxically cheapened. Big banks continued to lend to forestall the even less desirable alternative of not lending—that is, of acknowledging the impairment of the loans they had previously made. Thus, the recurrent news of negotiation, delinquency, and outright default was interspersed with news of additional lending. The new dollars, frequently, were earmarked for the payment of interest on the banks' existing loans, and the newspapers came to treat this strange practice as merely standard. "Meanwhile," *The Wall Street Journal* reported on the occasion of a new agreement between Brazil and its lenders in November 1987, "the country's major bank creditors are pledging in the new agreement to gather bank loans of $3 billion to help Brazil settle $4.5 billion of interest payments to banks, most of which are now in arrears." Literally, Citibank, Chase, and the others lent Brazil the money with which Brazil paid them. They lent when existing Brazilian loans were quoted in the open market at a substantial discount from par, or face, value. Until John Reed, Wriston's successor, broke step with the other New York banks in 1987 by acknowledging that the Third World debt on Citi's books was not worth 100 cents on the dollar, the American banks were able to pretend that it was. The interest income that the banks did not, in fact, receive from Brazil in 1988 was nevertheless taken into the banks' income. It was taxed as income by the federal government and distributed as income to the stockholders in the form of dividends.

The farce was shortened by the evolution of a free market in Third World loans. Unless otherwise stipulated, a bank's loans are accounted for as if they were worth par. If a loan is doubtful, it is so classified, and reserves are established to absorb a possible future loss. Up until about 1987, there was no market in overseas bank loans and therefore no outside, running, public commentary on what a certain sovereign credit was actually worth. Such a market grew up in Third World debt because the accounting supposition of 100 cents on the dollar had become untenable. The big banks, having overlent to Third World countries, could hardly stop lending, let alone sell out their existing loan portfolios. To do so would have called down the wrath of the regulators on them. ("Don't get in a position where you are going to have to rely on government to bail you out," Champion had whistled into the wind in 1978. "Remain strong, very strong, particularly in a period such as we are facing.") On the other hand, the smaller regional banks were under no obligation to carry the water of public policy. Many of them, begging to disagree with the chairman of Citicorp about the possibility of a sovereign bankruptcy, chose to cut losses and be done with South America. They sold their loans to speculators or to corporations that, in turn, converted them into local currency at a favorable rate of exchange. They invested the currency.

By late 1987, Brazilian bank loans were offered at less than 50 cents on the dollar in the informal (and, for the money of the major banks, incriminating) loan market. Notably absent among the buyers of discounted loans were the big American banks that were so professedly bullish on Brazil. "They don't really believe what they say, of course," a former Brazilian minister turned banker told the writer Martin Mayer in 1988. "If they did, they'd buy our paper at 48 cents on the dollar and double their return. And none of them does—I keep track."

As in Brazil, American agriculture was caught in the scissors of rising interest rates and falling commodity prices. The inflationary prosperity of the 1970s had ended symbolically with the cresting of the gold market in the opening weeks of 1980. Thereafter, the going was rough for farmers, oil drillers, copper miners, and country bankers, among others, who had taken inflation into partnership with them. In the great inflation of the 1960s and 1970s, certain ideas had become gospel. For instance, it paid to borrow because prices invariably rose. Similarly, interest rates would never fall. Therefore, the nation's savers could depend on a permanent supply of high-yielding Treasury securities. Presently, both of these guides to living were rendered obsolete.

The drop in the inflation rate in 1983 had taken monetary theorists by surprise. Echoing Milton Friedman that inflation is "always and everywhere a monetary phenomenon," the monetarist school singlemindedly watched the growth of the money supply. Let there be too much of it, they believed, and prices must rise. The rate of growth in money had moderated in the months and years following the Volcker diktat of October 6, 1979, but it had by no means collapsed. Furthermore, beginning in early 1982, the Federal Reserve had resumed its expansionary ways. It bought, or "monetized," the public debt at boom-time rates. Here was a fact to reckon with. The money supply was the key to the inflation rate, and the Federal Reserve was the key to the money supply. In 1981, the Fed had been painfully tight; the rate of expansion of its assets, expressed in annual rates of growth, had fallen to less than 5 percent.* But by year end 1983, the Federal Reserve's balance sheet was expanding once more at double-digit rates, recalling the late 1970s and creating the strong suspicion that inflation was not dead but only resting.

Inflation in Reverse

Yet it remained dormant, Federal Reserve expansion notwithstanding. Between January 1981 and January 1983, the rate of rise in consumer prices tumbled to 3.7 percent from almost 12 percent. Various facts were advanced to explain this divergence of money and inflation. It is always easy to project the recent past into the distant future, and what the past had known was inflation. One new element in the price equation was the drop in oil prices. Another was the resurgence of the dollar in foreign-exchange markets: a strong dollar meant lower prices for imported merchandise and stiff competition for domestic businesses. There was a third fact to consider, although it was hardly a new one. It was the truism that no inflation lasts forever. "A long rise in prices and wages that has been caused by inflation must be supported by more inflation or it will collapse," said the New York investor William H. Tehan in 1981, and he went on to state a theory.

Tehan was fiftyish, balding, sleek, and custom-tailored. Early on, he had understood the process of inflation and the distortions it had caused in the American economy. He had made money in gold, and

---

* Most of these assets are Treasury securities. Others are the securities of foreign governments or the securities of federal agencies. Buying them, the Fed creates new credit. The dollars are called "reserves," because they are credited to the reserve accounts of commercial banks. The banking system's capacity to grow is constrained by the availability of reserve dollars. Let the Fed enlarge the pool, therefore, and the pace of lending may increase.

lost jobs on account of it, since his days with Hayden, Stone & Co., Dominick & Dominick, and White Weld in the 1960s. A friend of Tehan's had a mental image of the locker room of the University Club in the mid-1960s: of Tehan, by then notorious for his views on gold (prematurely bullish) and the stock market (prematurely and violently bearish), being addressed by a member of average brains and amiability. "You might be right about gold," the member, a stockbroker by trade, said, "but you've missed one whole year of a great stock market."

Tehan looked every inch the banker, and his speech had an unmistakable boardroom timbre. However, any misapprehension about his outlook was clarified moments after he began to speak. At cocktail parties, his voice carried clearly and often alarmingly across crowded rooms. Once he was heard to assert, with characteristic certainty, "IBM is a ten-dollar stock." The great blue chip was then selling for about $100. Heads turned to the source of this rank heresy, but Tehan was oblivious to them. He was prone to state matter-of-factly that certain leading New York banks were insolvent, and his favorite depository for his customers' funds was Fiduciary Trust Co., an institution that had the paramount advantage (by his reasoning) of not belonging to the Federal Reserve System.

For all his financial success, Tehan was an outsider, and what he said in 1981 was as jarring to those who had come to agree with him as to the many who had not. He stunned an inflation-minded audience at a conference in Acapulco by predicting a monetary and financial sea change. Tehan, whose vanity license plates were stamped "AU-1," after the chemical symbol for his favorite metal, seemed to be saying that the gold bull market was over. "Rather than a greater rate of inflation characterized by an expanding dollar surplus and higher prices for the goods and services which dollars buy, we are forecasting a shortage of dollars and a surplus of the things which dollars buy," he said, speaking for himself and for his firm, P. R. Herzig & Co., but chiefly for himself:

> In our view, inflation is dissipating and the purchasing power of the dollar is now rising, reversing the decline in dollar purchasing power which began in the late 1940s.
> The decline in foreign currencies and gold against the dollar, in our view, signals the first stage of a general forced liquidation of all the dollar hedges which have been accumulated in the post-World War II era. We feel that the developing *dollar shortage* has

the potential to degenerate beyond deflation of the price structure. One cannot ignore the possibility that this situation can go from mild deflation into financial crisis and economic depression.

In other words, the bell had tolled for every familiar inflation-era investment, from real-estate tax shelters to oil-drilling partnerships to natural-resource company common stocks. In the long inflation, people had lent and borrowed as if the value of money would always depreciate. It would not. Tehan was careful to draw a distinction between printing-press inflation and credit inflation—between the German-style proliferation of bank notes in the 1920s and the American-style proliferation of debt in the 1970s. He contended that no hyperinflation would result from this modern credit inflation. Rather, it would end in deflation, as bad debts engulfed the banking system. The date of his speech, June 27, 1981, preceded the peak of the then current business expansion by exactly three days. In 1983, a farsighted book by A. Gary Shilling and Kiril Sokoloff was published with the title *Is Inflation Ending? Are You Ready?* Tehan, as much as any man or woman in America, could answer both questions with a resounding "Yes!"

In 1920–21, the transition from wartime inflation to peacetime deflation had been short and violent. In the space of thirteen months, commodity prices had fallen by 43 percent. The money supply had actually fallen, by 9 percent; even in bad times, the stock of currency and checking accounts usually register a small increase. The only steeper fall in American monetary history occurred in the Great Depression.

In markets, history repeats itself but not so literally as to enrich historians. The 1920–21 episode did not repeat itself in 1946–47 (much to the chagrin of Sewell Avery, for instance) or, exactly, in 1981–82. In the Reagan slump, there was no general fall in prices and no across-the-board rise in the purchasing power of money; on the contrary, consumer price inflation persisted. There was no mass run on weak banks. (In February 1982, frightened depositors fell on Hartford Federal Savings & Loan in Hartford, Connecticut, to demand their money back, some of them willingly paying penalties of as much as $2,000 for the privilege of prematurely cashing federally insured certificates of deposit. That and similar episodes, however, even the failure of Continental Illinois, were merely the exceptions that proved the rule.) There was, however, a jarring dissonance between what people had come to expect from the economy and what they saw with their own eyes. What they expected was inflation. What they saw in agriculture,

for instance—most vividly in the market for Midwestern farmland—
was deflation. In Iowa in 1985, land prices registered their fourth
consecutive annual decline and had returned to the levels of the early
1970s. For the nation as a whole, between 1981 and 1987, agricultural
real-estate values fell by an estimated 35 percent. Corn prices and
farm incomes fell, and the burden of debt, which had seemed trifling
in the upswing, presently became oppressive. The chairman's message
in the 1985 annual report of the First Interstate Bank of Iowa was
direct and to the point. "Bankruptcies will continue to soar . . . ,"
wrote Kenneth M. Myers. "Farmland prices will continue to deteriorate. . . . As many as 20 percent of Iowa farm-related businesses may
fail in 1986 and 1987."

Many things had changed in credit since 1920–21, but nothing so
much as the government's role as lender and guarantor. By the early
1980s, the federal apparatus was not only the prime instigator of price
inflation but also a leading creator of credit. In 1980, the government
comprised far and away the largest "bank" in the country. Citicorp's
loans, on December 31, 1980, totaled $70 billion. By contrast, Wash-
ington's loans totaled $164 billion. The sum of its loan guarantees was
$299 billion. There were, besides, the direct loans of the so-called
government-sponsored enterprises, which totaled $151 billion. All of
this footed to $614 billion, not including Federal Reserve credit of
more than $120 billion. A bar chart describing the rise in "Federal
and Federally Assisted Credit Outstanding" in the 1980 federal budget
resembled the height of a healthy child measured at lengthy intervals.

There was an ominous circularity about the government's credit
activities. As the dollar was debased, interest rates rose. As interest
rates rose, the demand for subsidized, federally assisted credit increased. Such credit had grown more than fourfold in the decade of
the 1970s and by 1980 had come to constitute a significant share of
overall funds raised in the American capital markets. As recently as
1977, the share of total credit advanced under federal auspices had
been 11.9 percent. It was 23.2 percent in the recession year of 1980.

Government-Issue Mortgages

To the gratification of homeowners and home builders, the residential
mortgage market almost became a branch of government finance. It
had been moving in that direction since the Hoover administration.
In 1932, the Federal Home Loan Bank System was enacted to serve

thrift institutions as the Federal Reserve served banks. In 1933, the Home Owners' Loan Corporation was created to purchase delinquent mortgages and restructure them to the debtor's benefit, reducing interest rates and stretching out maturities. The purpose of both agencies was to roll back the tide of dispossession and foreclosure. By the end of 1935 the HOLC had accumulated more than one-sixth of the estimated urban home mortgage debt in the United States. The Federal Housing Administration was established in 1934 and the Federal National Mortgage Association in 1938. Liberalizing tendencies continued. In 1938, the FHA was authorized to insure a mortgage with a maturity of up to twenty-five years and a loan-to-value ratio of up to 90 percent; the original terms were 80 percent and twenty years, respectively.* Similarly, in 1939, the HOLC was permitted to make twenty-five-year mortgage loans, ten years longer than the maximum originally set in 1933. (To put twenty-five years, and even fifteen years, in perspective, the average length of contract for new mortgage loans made by twenty-four leading insurance companies in the 1920s was just six years.) In 1945, the Veterans Administration entered the mortgage insurance business, and in 1948, William J. Levitt, selling directly to veterans with easy access to public credit, built Levittown, 6,000 "bungalows," each of 4½ rooms, on 1,400 acres near Hicksville, Long Island. Thus, the government helped to invent suburbia. Still, it cannot be said that these federal initiatives created a riot of mortgage indebtedness. (*Fortune* reported in 1938 that the growing federal role in mortgage finance disturbed old-time bankers, "many of whom refuse to have anything to do with FHA activities despite the obvious

---

* By lending at up to 90 percent of the value of a property, or by insuring such a 90 percent loan, the government was putting itself in a potentially costly position. If house prices fell by more than 10 percent, the "equity" of hundreds of thousands of homeowners would be wiped out. "Under such circumstances," as *Fortune* noted in 1938, "the FHA might very well find itself the unwilling landlord of half a million or more houses."

   The fear that the real-estate market was indeed on the brink of collapse persisted long after the Depression ended. In 1948 a writer in *Harper's*, Eric Larrabee, speculated on what it might cost if the taxpayers became the unwitting receivers of Levitt & Sons' new Long Island project. "Nearly everyone is agreed that today's housing values are inflated and that collapse will have to come some day," Larrabee ventured; "the expectation is that the government, when that day comes, will back the veteran and take over the projects. Levitt might be able to sell all of the houses in the next two and a half years. After that, Levittown, which will represent an eventual investment of $52,000,000, could become the taxpayers' baby." With hindsight, it is easy to see how clear was the risk of inflation and how negligible was the risk of a new deflation. Not so at the time, however. Sewell Avery worried about a postwar depression, and the Treasury continued to borrow at an interest cost of less than 2½ percent.

attractions of a 5 percent investment guaranteed by the government.")
In 1950, fewer than half of American houses had outstanding mortgages. Of those houses with liens, the median loan-to-value ratio was
just 36 percent.

Until the early 1970s, "the government" in the mortgage world
connoted the Veterans Administration, the Government National
Mortgage Administration, the Federal Housing Authority, and the
Farmers Home Loan Administration. Each agency, by insuring or
guaranteeing the mortgage debts of individuals, stamped private transactions with the full faith and credit of the United States. With the
advent of mortgage-backed securities, the government's mortgage role
expanded once more. The new securities were frequently not the
explicit obligations of the federal government. They were the obligations of government-sponsored enterprises. Fannie Mae and Freddie
Mac—the companies formally known as the Federal National Mortgage Association and the Federal Home Loan Mortgage Corporation,
respectively—were the most important such enterprises in the mortgage market. They collected mortgages by the hundreds of billions of
dollars' worth. They packaged them for sale as mortgage-backed securities, and they guaranteed the securities against default. Investors
attached a certain value to those guarantees, but they attached an even
greater value to the understanding that the Treasury's guarantee stood
behind Fannie's and Freddie's. There was nothing explicit about this,
but it came to be treated as fact. Billions of dollars were invested on
the strength of the perception that if any financial institution in the
United States was too big to fail, Fannie Mae was it.

In 1970, the federal government bestowed its support, direct or
indirect, on $26 billion worth of residential mortgage debt. In 1980,
it supported $206.5 billion worth; in 1989, more than $1 trillion worth.
Mortgages with federal support of one kind or another, as a percentage
of residential mortgages outstanding, rose from 7.7 in 1970 to 18.8
percent in 1980 to 38.2 percent in 1989. In Republican and Democratic
years alike, capitalism coexisted with a very specific kind of American
socialism. As thrift institutions withdrew from mortgage lending, Fannie and Freddie expanded in it. Thus, the blowup of one federal
credit scheme, deposit insurance, helped to incite the growth of another, government-sponsored enterprises. Indeed, the relentless expansion of Fannie Mae helped to drive thrift institutions out of the
residential mortgage market and into more speculative lines of en-
deavor. The consequences of this change were almost certainly bullish
for housing activity. In July 1990, in the heat of a Washington debate

over the safety and soundness of the various government-sponsored enterprises, Kent Colton, executive of the National Association of Home Builders, vouched for Freddie and Fannie before a subcommittee of the House Banking Committee. If America is the world's best-housed nation it is largely thanks to them, said Colton, and he recited some eye-opening facts. "In 1989," he testified, "Fannie and Freddie supplied the funds for over half of all conventional mortgages originated. This represents a tenfold increase over the 5 percent they supplied in 1980. . . . They have done precisely what they were created to do, and they have done it well, accounting today for over 50 percent of the conventional mortgage market."

Colton proceeded to estimate that Fannie and Freddie had reduced the interest costs to home buyers by as much as one-half of one percentage point a year, and he conjured up a bleak picture for housing if they were forced to mimic the risk-averse behavior of private-sector banks (or of some private-sector banks: many were not in the least risk-averse). Colton was testifying in response to proposals that Freddie, Fannie, and other government-sponsored enterprises be held to the standards of a triple-A credit rating, the private sector's highest financial accolade. The argument in favor of doing so was that the best way to forestall a new financial calamity for the American taxpayer was to ensure that the government's wards did not go the way of the thrift industry. Fannie Mae did a lot of business without a lot of equity capital. In Wall Street argot, it was highly leveraged, yet that leverage, so Colton contended, was doing no one any harm. On the contrary, it was helping Americans to buy houses. If Fannie or Freddie were forced to raise capital, reduce lending, or both, he predicted, mortgage rates would rise, low-down-payment mortgage loans would become harder to obtain, and some of the nation's low- and moderate-income housing needs would go unmet.

The National Association of Home Builders was saying that the country had become accustomed to a dash of mortgage socialism and that it would miss it sorely if it were gone. It was not the kind of sentiment that a Republican Rip Van Winkle, nodding off during the Nixon administration, would have expected to hear upon awakening in 1990, but it was an accurate reflection of how Americans lent and borrowed. The dividing line between public and private sectors in residential mortgage credit was becoming a blur. Fortified by subsidized credit, home buyers bought what they otherwise might not have been able to afford. Builders put up the marginal house, and Maytag sold the extra washing machine. Purists might have objected that massive subsidies usually create a massive distortion which, although bullish in the short run, is often bearish, or jolting, in the longer run. Few people thought that, however, and even fewer said it. The federal mortgage juggernaut rolled on.

Enticing Farmers to Borrow

Another source of the manic growth in government-related debt was the Farm Credit System. The system was (and is) the oldest of the government-sponsored enterprises. It is not state-owned, but the government wishes it well and extends it special privileges, privileges that it shares with Freddie, Fannie, and the like. For instance, Farm Credit securities are exempt from registration under the federal securities law. They are lawful investments for federal trust funds, and national banks can buy them without limit. Such features constitute a kind of federal blessing, as does the system's government charter. Farm Credit is an implicit blood relation to the most fiscally important federal agencies, specifically the Treasury and the Federal Reserve. In the 1980s, they were the best kind of friends to have.

The Farm Credit System, a federation of credit cooperatives, expanded wing by wing, like an old house. The Federal Land Banks were created in Woodrow Wilson's administration, the Federal Intermediate Term Credit Banks in Warren G. Harding's, and the Banks for Cooperatives in Franklin D. Roosevelt's. The Farm Credit Act of 1933 relaxed the terms under which the Federal Land Banks could lend—to 75 percent of the income-producing value of a piece of land, up from 50 percent—and granted emergency powers to the Farm Credit System to refinance certain commercial bank loans. By 1936, the twentieth anniversary of its founding, the Farm Credit System had become the leading farm real-estate lender. However, the mere availability of easy credit proved no great stimulant to the market in agricultural real estate or to the proclivity of farmers to borrow. Between 1936 and 1945, the outstanding volume of farm real-estate debt was cut almost in half.

In 1987, the Farm Credit System, racked by loss, was streamlined, but up until that time its organization was far-flung and complex. The country was divided into twelve Farm Credit districts, and each had a Federal Land Bank, a Federal Intermediate Credit Bank, and a Bank for Cooperatives. There was also a Central Bank for Cooperatives, which made a grand total of thirty-seven Farm Credit Banks of one kind or another. The Land Banks made long-term loans secured by first mortgages on farm real estate. The Intermediate Credit Banks made short- and medium-term loans, mainly for production or operating purposes, to yet another class of Farm Credit enterprise, the Production Credit Associations. The Banks for Cooperatives lent to farm cooperatives. "Cooperative" was (and remains) the operative form of ownership in the system. In 1979, the Farm Credit System was owned by nearly a million farmers and by 4,000 of their marketing, supply, and business-service cooperatives.

As we have seen, the socialization of credit is a long-running trend in American finance, and it did not begin in the 1970s. What was new, in agriculture, was the scale of federal commitment and the liberality of the system's lending terms. The watershed event of the agricultural inflation was the Farm Credit Act of 1971. It permitted greater lending against the collateral of farmland: not against its income-producing value, as had been the custom, but against its market value. The change was revolutionary, and would soon prove devastating. By offering to lend against market values on the terms that it did, the system almost guaranteed that those values would rise and, ultimately, after the bubble burst, fall. Furthermore, the system was encouraged to lend more. Previously, it had advanced no more than 65 percent of the income-producing value of a property (75 percent was a temporary Depression expedient); now it was able to lend up to 85 percent of the *market* value. To put 85 percent in perspective, the federal home mortgage agencies could lend to a maximum of only 80 percent of the appraised value of a house. House prices could decline (and would, later on) but they were far less prone to bouts of weakness than farmland prices had historically been. The consequence of this change was literally earth-moving. It allowed, in some cases, a doubling in the maximum amount that a Federal Land Bank could lend on a given piece of property.

Inevitably, farmland prices soared and fell. In the decade-long bull market of 1971–80, its inflation-adjusted value almost doubled. It fell faster, however. By 1986, it was very nearly back to where it had started in 1971. The cycle was magnified by the Farm Credit System's unique interest-rate policy. Its members lent according to the average cost of their deposits. They did not lend, as profit-seeking banks tend to do, according to the marginal cost of deposits—that is, according to the cost of the extra deposit. An example will help to illustrate the disaster inherent in average pricing. Let us say that the cost of the average deposit dollar was 6 percent in year one but 8 percent in year two. To obtain the average deposit rate in year two, one would add 6 percent and 8 percent. The average of the two rates would be 7 percent, and that (to simplify) would be the deposit rate on which a Federal Land Bank would price a loan on a parcel of land. A commercial bank, also in the agricultural lending business, would offer a market rate, not an artificial average: it would probably lend at more than 8 percent. As might be imagined, the Farm Credit System became every farmer's best friend, and its share of the agricultural lending business expanded. Its lending rates rose in the inflation of the 1970s but their rise necessarily lagged behind the increase in market interest rates. For a time in 1979, when the prime rate was 19 percent, the Land Banks (and other units of the Farm Credit System) lent at 14 percent. Never before had interest rates risen as fast as they did in the Volcker years, and never before had the average deposit rate been a worse guide to pricing a new loan.

The Farm Credit System was a miniature of American credit in those years, emblematic not only in its ties to the federal government, but also in its openhandedness. The 1971 Farm Credit Act, besides relaxing the terms of lending, also permitted the Land Banks to advance credit to nonfarm rural homeowners and to exercise more discretion in making farm mortgages. In those expansive years, more discretion was tantamount to more lending. As the Land Banks themselves had been founded in an inflationary time (in 1916, war prosperity was lifting American prices), so was their lending authority redundantly expanded in the inflation of the 1970s (in August 1971, President Nixon had abandoned the gold standard; the Farm Credit Act was passed in December). "It could be said that the 1971 act made it possible for the land banks to lose money and they took full advantage of the opportunity," wrote Ben Sunbury, a chronicler and longtime employee of the Farm Credit System.

Years of rising land and commodity prices had instilled the idea that debt was a blessing. The thirty-seven primary banks of the Farm Credit System had hundreds of lending outlets. The outlets were run by local boards, and the boards were elected by farmers. The farmers saw quite clearly the riches that inflation had bestowed on them and their neighbors, and they lent in a headstrong, inflationary style. Corners were cut, rules bent, and exceptions admitted. "We just rolled along," Burgee Amdahl, the head of the system's biggest bank, in St. Paul, Minnesota, told *The Wall Street Journal* in 1985. "It was dreamland." Never had the system been audited by an outside auditor. Not for the first time in our story, the inevitable happened. The *Journal's* report continued:

Especially during the go-go 1970s, the system seemed to run wild. . . . Loans outstanding zoomed from less than $20 billion in 1972 to $66.2 billion by 1980 and continued to rise after inflation began to break.

Herbert Ashton, an Indiana fruit farmer, recalls being wined and dined at a local country club by bankers from his local system bank who extolled the virtues of inflation and offered to lend him $1 million on the spot. "I turned it down," he recalls. "But they sounded like a soap testimonial. They were giving money to whoever passed their way, and they didn't ask too many questions."

According to the *Journal*, one Farm Credit bank in Kentucky had financed a pornographic movie. Even in the nonpornographic lines of agricultural lending, credit procedures were often slipshod. "One former system banker in Iowa, for example, recalls inadequate documentation of collateral that resulted in 'blank stares when we went out to check a tractor a fella had put up on loan. We found out later that he'd never owned it,' " the paper said. From the Populist era to the Wilson administration, reformers had complained about the shortage of credit to farmers. If any such inequity existed—and it is doubtful, even in 1916, that the farmer was being starved—it was more than redressed by the early 1980s.

The full weight of the farm debt crisis was stamped on the Farm Credit System's 1985 financial results. The net loss was $2.7 billion; bad loans had overwhelmed the capital with which to absorb them. Anticipating the 1980s proper, the system in 1986 was permitted to employ accounting techniques to postpone the recognition of loss. Mirroring the Chrysler bailout of 1980, the system obtained federal relief, under the Agricultural Credit Act of 1987. A Financial Assistance Board was authorized to issue up to $4 billion of Treasury-guaranteed debt to tide the system through. At year end 1990, $1.3 billion worth of the credit line was in use.

Commentators on the Farm Credit affair, lacking the perspective afforded by the savings and loan calamity, the late-1980s crack-ups in junk bonds and commercial banking, and the decay of the finances of the federal government itself, were prone to exaggerate. "In scope and in terms of implications for government policy, this is far and away the biggest financial blowup since the Depression," an economist declared in 1985. It was destined not to be, of course. But it was at once costly—federal farm payments climbed in the wake of the farm-debt crisis—and symbolic. It symbolized the pain of withdrawal from inflation and the costs of socialized lending. It demonstrated the mischief inherent in the lightly controlled lending of other people's money. In the wild and woolly run-up in real-estate prices, from 1971 to 1980, the Farm Credit System and the Farmers Home Administration together accounted for 69 percent of the total increase in farm real-estate lending. It was a bubble blown in Washington.

Bert Ely, one of the earliest and most persistent critics of the savings and loan industry, also contributed (along with his associate, Vicki Vanderhoff) one of the most insightful critiques of the Farm Credit disaster. He blamed the boom and bust on the Farm Credit System and specifically on the 1971 relaxation of the rules of lending. "Removing these restraints enabled the borrower-dominated FCS to become a more venturesome and dangerous lender," he wrote. "Had this liberalization not been enacted, the farm crisis would have been much less severe, if it had occurred at all. Land prices might have continued to rise above the 1971 level, but not to the extent they did."

Amen to that. Still, the student of booms and busts will reflect on the episodes in which there was no federally subsidized lending and farmland prices rose, or in which there was federally subsidized lending and farmland prices did not rise. Thus, for example, the Farm Credit Act of 1933 failed to stimulate farmland prices in the 1930s and early 1940s. Also, paradoxically, the postwar upturn began despite a slight stiffening in the terms of system lending: in 1947, the maximum lending rate on farmland was reduced to 65 percent of agricultural value, from 75 percent.

There was no Farm Credit System to explain the origins of the bull market in farmland before World War I. Neither does the 1971 abrogation of the gold dollar fully explain the inflationary leap in real-estate values in the 1970s: In the pre-World War I episode, after all, the dollar was freely convertible into gold, and that fact did not forestall the agricultural boom and bust of the late teens and early 1920s. No doubt, as we have seen, the untimely advent of the Federal Land Banks in 1916 played an important role in the perpetuation of the boom. The overriding moral, probably, is that some monetary systems are more prone to inflation than others and that certain forms of ownership are more conducive to responsible lending than others. However, acting in crowds, people will do inexplicable things with money.

Lending à la "Monkeybrains"

The imposing headquarters of the Continental Illinois Bank & Trust Co. constituted a last line of defense against a potential loss of depositor confidence. Not many people, once inside the doors, could easily credit a rumor that the occupant of such a majestic building was anything but solvent. Its long colonnaded front borrowed liberally from the design of the Treasury Department in Washington and its Indiana limestone portico intentionally echoed the similarly grand portico of the Federal Reserve Bank of Chicago across La Salle Street. Those architectural details were prophetic as well as pleasing. In 1984, the year of the run and the government bailout, the bank would temporarily join the Treasury and the Fed in the public sector. (In 1934, Walter Cummings, the first chairman of the FDIC, left Washington to become the chairman and chief executive officer of the Continental Bank. That too was a foreshadowing touch.) Eight uplifting quotations on financial subjects decorated the main banking hall, one of them destined to be ironic. Credited to the English banker Sir Edward H. Holden, it said, "America has a system of banking which surpasses in strength and excellence any other banking system in the world."

For years Continental did not disprove Sir Edward. Between 1978 and 1982, its share of the corporate lending market doubled. "Behind that quiet façade," wrote a *New York Times* reporter in the fall of 1981, "Continental was paving the way to its current position as an acknowledged member of the nation's banking elite." In its inflation-era heyday, Continental's common stock commanded a premium valuation and up to the time of its collapse its reputation with dozens of correspondent banks was unquestioned.

As Wriston was optimistic about Brazil, Continental was bullish on oil, and it lent heavily in the Southwest. "In the High-Flying Field of Energy Finance, Continental Illinois Is Striking It Rich," *The Wall Street Journal* optimistically reported, also in the fall of 1981, a time when oil-drilling stocks were priced as if to discount the certain rise of a barrel of crude to $100 from the then prevailing $34.

In 1982, on the occasion of the 125th anniversary of the founding of its oldest predecessor bank, Continental issued a public-relations booklet extolling the vision and clearheadedness of its soon to be jettisoned senior management. Some lines by T. S. Eliot (a man who had once been an employee of a different bank) were quoted approvingly: "I have measured out my life with coffee spoons . . . indeed there will be time to wonder, 'Do I dare?' and 'Do I dare?' "

Continental did (though the man in Eliot's poem did not), particularly in the decision it made to stock up on energy loans originated by the Penn Square Bank of Oklahoma City. ". . . Continental reached for a larger share of progress and began making its daring moves toward a higher position of leadership among the major banks of the world," the booklet related. Neither it nor, apparently, the management dwelled long on the possibility of loss, yet the odds did not favor risk-taking. The upside, if all had gone according to plan, was modest— namely, the recovery of the depositors' money, with interest. The worst outcome, on the other hand, was embarrassment, loss of depositor confidence, and failure. It was the result that actually materialized.

What is meant by the words "banking system" is the interconnectedness of financial things. Penn Square, a shopping-center bank in Oklahoma City, originated loans and sold participations in them to the twenty-three-story Continental. Continental took deposits from scores of correspondent banks and from institutions abroad. Thus, Penn Square's failure threatened Continental, and Continental's weakness menaced correspondents and depositors worldwide. Every bank under the sun balances a book of loans on a sliver of capital. From this fact follow several vital banking concepts. The first is that the margin for error in lending is small. It is a strong bank that can show as much as $1 million in capital for every $6 million in loans. In such an exemplary institution the owners' interest would be threatened if only one loan in six blew up. As the failure of one big bank raises the possibility of a chain reaction of failure, the destruction of bank capital holds the risk of a serial contraction. Returning to the example of the bank with $1 million in capital and $6 million in loans: If its capital were reduced by $100,000 to $900,000, and if it wanted to maintain the same capital-to-loan ratio, it would have to reduce its loans by $600,000. If its capital were sawed in half, to $500,000, a not unusual occurrence in banking in the 1980s, and if its loans were reduced proportionately, the extinction of bank credit would amount to $3 million. As the expansion of banking capital is bullish, its contraction is bearish.

When, in June 1982, a federal regulator called the chairman of Continental Illinois, Roger Anderson, to apprise him of the troubles at Penn Square Bank, Anderson did not immediately catch the bank's name, even though Continental had purchased $1 billion of its loans. Like a smaller and more manic Citicorp, Penn Square had dedicated itself to growth. From 1977, around the start of the energy-lending boom, to mid-1982, around the time it ended, its assets had vaulted to $520 million from $77 million. However, Typhoid Mary fashion, it had sold, or "syndicated," another $2 billion in oil and gas participations to other banks, some of them noted for their conservatism (e.g., Northern Trust), others not (e.g., Chase Manhattan and Seattle First National Bank).

The odyssey of Continental Illinois since the Great Depression was turning into a round trip. The bank had virtually become a ward of the state in 1933, and with Penn Square it was moving toward an identical change of ownership in 1984. As many banks had done in the Depression, Continental had raised capital by selling preferred stock to the Reconstruction Finance Corporation. Although solvent, Continental had issued $50 million worth of preferred, which constituted two-thirds of owners' equity at year end 1933. What was unusual was not the fact of the transaction but its scale: the Continental, the biggest bank in the Midwest, had relinquished voting control to the RFC and thus to the national government. In 1934, the RFC chose to swing its weight and install its own man as chairman: the aforementioned Walter J. Cummings, fifty-four, a manufacturer of electrical railway equipment, a doctor of sick traction companies, the Roosevelt administration's designated "bank reopener" in the wake of the national banking holiday of 1933, and the first chairman of the Federal Deposit Insurance Corporation. "I believe that this protection afforded to these depositors marks one of the most forward steps ever taken in the history of banking in America," said Cummings, a Republican, of the new era.

It was talk that sat badly with libertarian elements of the Chicago business community. Sewell Avery resigned from the board of Continental Illinois rather than submit to RFC control. John M. (One Hundred Percent) Nichols, president of the First National Bank of Englewood, Illinois, refused outright to go along with the FDIC. His bank was safe, just as his nickname implied it would be, and he failed to see why he should subsidize the unsound competition. It was, in fact, 100 percent liquid: for every dollar on deposit there was one dollar available in cash or readily marketable securities.* In the panic of March 1933, Nichols actually invited nervous depositors to withdraw their money. In 1934, still protesting against the drift of the times, he ostentatiously wrote down from $24,000 to one dime the value of stock in the Federal Reserve Bank of Chicago that his bank was obliged to own. Under his command, the First became the only bank, among the nation's 6,000 Federal Reserve members, to refuse to pay its allotted share into the FDIC insurance fund. "I would just as soon give up this banking business, anyhow, it is nothing but grief, troubles and insults," he complained. "I could invest my money more profitably in some other business, and maybe I will if I can find out what the government is going to do." He called the federal deposit insurance scheme "a damnable piece of political trickery" and a pretext to engineer the nationalization of the banking industry. (In 1941, making good on a threat he had made on the eve of the 1940 election, Nichols closed the bank for "the duration of the Roosevelt concocted emergency." In 1943, he tore down the headquarters building, at a cost of $10,000, rather than sell it to willing buyers. He wanted to give the institution "an honorable burial," he said; he ordered the site covered with black soil.)

Albert W. Harris, chairman of the Harris Trust & Savings Bank and a longtime friend of Cummings's, also opposed the FDIC, at one time threatening to remove his bank from the Federal Reserve System in protest. Nevertheless, Harris was all for Cummings personally, and he summed up his friend's banking credentials this way: ". . . a good banker is supposed to know when to say no. In my opinion, this of itself does not make a good banker. He should also know how to say

---

* An unusual condition in and around Chicago. Real-estate lending was a hallmark of the boom, especially in the suburban banks. "They gathered the savings of their communities, which amounted in 1928 to more than the savings deposits of the Loop banks," wrote the historian Homer Hoyt, "and put them at the disposal of contractors, builders, storekeepers, etc., for the purpose of building stores, apartments, or theaters. Many of the bank presidents were also real estate operators, and in some cases real estate loans were the largest items on their balance sheet." By 1927 or 1928, according to Hoyt, first mortgages worth 100 percent of the cost of a property were commonly available, and another 20 percent might be borrowed in the form of a second mortgage.

The spirit of One Hundred Percent Nichols lived on in the 1980s in the person of V. O. Figge, chairman of the Davenport Bank & Trust Co., Davenport, Iowa. "We can pay our entire deposit liability on demand, and our depositors can sleep at night with complete confidence during both good and bad economic weather," Figge wrote to his stockholders in his 1989 annual report. He was then ninety and out of step with the new ways. "In closing, as I have repeatedly said," he wound up, "we are living in a world bordering on financial insolvency, be it personal, corporate or governmental, and surely if the truth is faced, we are flirting with moral bankruptcy as well."

John M. (One Hundred Per-
cent) Nichols, implacable foe of
federal deposit insurance, sets
his face against the New Deal,
1934 (CHICAGO TRIBUNE
CO.)

no, and this is one of the advantages that I think Mr. Cummings will have over the ordinary banker—he will know how to say it." In contrast to later years, the ability to say "yes" was not deemed an important banking skill in 1934, and Cummings, evidently, did not disappoint Harris by uttering the word too frequently. He retired from Continental in 1959, presiding over an era that, seen from the modern perspective, had a certain solvent charm.

The 125th anniversary brochure, published in 1982, enumerated the management's goals for the 1980s, and there is no clearer statement of the sea change in attitude. None of the goals was as simple as not losing the depositors' money, which had seemed uppermost for Cummings. ("It was in this climate as the new decade began that Continental's management laid down the guiding long-term objective of the corporation: To achieve sustained long-term growth in the value of the owners' interest and maintain the shares of the corporation as an attractive equity investment.") Then again, the safekeeping franchise had virtually been nationalized. Under the terms of a 1980 act, the Depository Institutions Deregulation and Monetary Control Act of

1980, federal deposit insurance applied to a maximum of $100,000, up from $40,000. The protective doctrine known as "too big to fail" had not yet been enunciated (that step awaited the failure of Continental Illinois itself), but in 1980 no big multinational bank was under suspicion.

The medium-size, regional Penn Square was under a regulatory cloud, however. Early in the year, federal examiners had found a pattern of lax and unsound practices, ranging from inadequate capital to excessively rapid growth to overlending to officers and directors. If Continental seemed not to notice these foibles, it might have been because it shared so many of them. It too was fast-growing, and the quality of its loan portfolio was subpar. It was short of capital and long of illiquid assets. It showed a high ratio of loans to deposits and a low ratio of loan-loss reserves to loans. In addition, it suffered the characteristic problem of a business bank without a branch network (Illinois banking law restricted the number of branches to three): it was without a stable base of consumer deposits. In short, Continental was in much the same situation as the First National Bank of New York in the early 1950s, except that it lacked the First's caution and it had fallen into the costly commercial company of Bill Patterson.

"Monkeybrains" was Patterson's unforgettable nickname at the University of Oklahoma (no "One Hundred Percent" for him), and it had followed him out of the Sigma Chi fraternity house and into the world of banking. As the chief of energy lending at Penn Square Bank, Patterson no longer put himself into potentially humiliating practical-joke situations, such as cooling his heels for an hour and a half in a garbage Dumpster, but neither did he give up cutting capers. "No one accused Patterson of being boring," as Mark Singer has written:

> He had a sense of humor that made it difficult at times to know whether he was joking. When he strolled through the Penn Square Bank lobby wearing Mickey Mouse ears and smoking a big cigar, that was a joke. When he perched on a conference table among a roomful of out-of-town bankers and howled like a hound—"because if you're gonna treat us like dogs we'll act like dogs"—that was only partly a joke.

Patterson also knew how to syndicate a loan. A bank no longer had to wait for a depositor to walk in the door. It could raise money in the Eurodollar market, in the market for negotiable certificates of deposit, or in the market for subordinated debt. As for Penn Square, it could, and did, raise money in the syndicated-loan market. Patterson excelled at this, as Singer elaborated:

> Patterson knew how to go to Chicago with a bunch of deals in a briefcase and return twenty-four hours later bearing commitments for ten million dollars' worth of loans. It might be ten million dollars all in one loan and the loan might be a 99 percent participation—meaning that Penn Square would lend only a hundred thousand dollars, and the rest of the deal would belong to, say, Continental Illinois. Penn Square's 1 percent loan origination fee would come to ninety-nine thousand dollars, and thus the bank would have earned, overnight, a 99 percent return on its portion of the credit. Most loan sale agreements depended upon a simpatico understanding, the equivalent of a handshake. The paperwork, the "documentation," would come later. If Continental Illinois was involved, that meant the greatest corporate lender in the country had agreed to buy the loan.

When the Penn Square Bank was declared insolvent by the Comptroller of the Currency on July 5, 1982, it became the fourth-largest commercial-bank failure in the United States and the largest payout in the history of the FDIC. So hopeless was its condition—80 percent of its loan portfolio was in oil and gas—that the FDIC declined to seek a buyer for it. There was nothing to buy. Overnight, the bank went from being the Penn Square Bank to the Deposit Insurance National Bank. When it opened for business on July 6, it was for the sole purpose of paying off the holders of $270 million of insured deposits. The holders of $190 million of uninsured deposits received no cash but merely a claim on the ultimate liquidation of the assets. The uninsured depositors were told that a liquidation is frequently a drawn-out process. Ten years was mentioned as a not atypical waiting period. "Four young men wearing cowboy hats parked their white Continental in a space directly in front of Penn Square," the *American Banker*'s man, Phillip L. Zweig, reported from Oklahoma City. "Asked if they were affiliated, one man in the front seat replied with a terse 'No comment.' He then buried his face in his hands and cried." An ambulance waited expectantly on the sidewalk.

To its acute embarrassment, Continental Illinois was publicly identified at the time of the seizure as the owner of $1 billion of Patterson's oil and gas participations. At the 1983 annual meeting, Roger Anderson, Continental's chairman (who by then had familiarized himself with the Oklahoma City bank), delivered a report to the stockholders concerning the Penn Square affair. His conclusion was: ". . . we had a people problem."

The great bank presently had a financial problem, of course, and so did the FDIC. The decay in Continental's loan portfolio was no longer the bank's secret, and the uninsured depositors began to make their way out the door, discreetly at first and then, in May 1984, all in a rush. On May 8, Reuters moved a story speculating on Continental's bankruptcy, and it quoted a bank spokesman calling the rumor "totally preposterous." Not every foreign depositor was encouraged by that denial, or by the fact that the bank had thought it necessary to make it, or by the fact that the question had been raised in the first place. In any event, a run was set in motion, not a queue in the grand banking room, but a rush of withdrawal messages in the wire room. It is an open question whether any crowd assembled in the main hall—French Hauteville marble underfoot, massive skylight fifty-three feet overhead, Ionic columns, and Jules Guerin murals at eye level—could have worked itself into a proper bank-run mood. There was no opportunity to find out. Continental, like Morgan Guaranty but unlike most other big American banks, had become dependent on foreign money: "hot money" was the term in Continental's case, "offshore funds," simply and neutrally, in Morgan's. The difference was that Morgan was solvent and liquid, whereas Continental was apparently neither. Thus, the electronic run continued.

What was the government to do? The Reagan administration favored capitalism in general, but not in every specific case. One such exception was going to be Continental Illinois. Panics, although helpful in restoring a sense of purpose and vigilance to banking, are not so clearly salutary that anyone has ever thought to espouse them in a political campaign. The payoff of Penn Square had strained the system (it had literally sent two top FDIC officials to the hospital with heart-attack symptoms, if not with actual cases), and it had assets of only a half billion dollars. Continental Illinois, the nation's eighth-largest bank, had assets of $41 billion. Insured deposits were estimated to total not much more than $4 billion, or barely 10 percent of its overall "funding base" (meaning the sum of its borrowed money). Irvine H. Sprague was a director of the FDIC during the Continental affair. "Various scenarios were laid out and they all signalled doomsday," he has written. "We were reduced to speculation. The only things that seemed clear were not only that the long-term cost of allowing Continental to fail could not be calculated, but also that it might be so much as to threaten the FDIC fund itself." In 1984, threats to the FDIC fund were still considered novel.

Thus, the only admissible question was one of technique. The issue was not whether the bank would be nationalized. It was how the nationalization would be produced, directed, and portrayed. The creditors of the Continental Illinois Bank would be saved, it was clear, as the creditors of the Greenwich Savings Bank in New York (1981) and the United Southern Bank in Nashville (1983) had been saved before. But would the same indulgence be extended to the bondholders and preferred-stock holders of the Continental Bank's corporate parent, Continental Illinois Corporation? The answer was "yes." It was not the answer that the Treasury Secretary, Donald T. Regan, was expecting, and he condemned it as "an unauthorized and unlegislated expansion of Federal guarantees." What Regan didn't have to say was that United States guarantees were growing at an alarming rate. However, the Secretary was overruled by the banking regulators. The Penn Square Bank, which was small and expendable, had been allowed to fail and the pieces to fall where they might. Continental Illinois, which was large and indispensable, had been allowed to fail but only in the particular sense that its ownership and management were changed. It had become an 80 percent-owned investment of the FDIC. (In 1933, the Continental was a two-thirds-owned investment of the RFC.) In the wake of federal intervention, there had been no ambulances parked on La Salle Street and no tearful depositors ruing the day they set foot in the place. Neither had there been a forced liquidation of the unwise loans that Continental had made or a chain reaction of failure among the banks that had unwisely lent to Continental.

In subsequent testimony, Comptroller of the Currency Todd Conover hinted that the eleven largest banks in the country were, in fact, too big to fail. Sprague had suggested that only Nos. 1 and 2 were absolutely safe, but no one could doubt that some number of large American banks had virtually become federal protectorates. As noted, 100 percent deposit insurance was long a de facto policy in America. However, its specific application to the nation's great banks seemed an anomaly. What was a great bank if not a safe one? George Champion had warned against favors from Washington and the regulatory intrusion that would inevitably follow. In this too he was vindicated. Taken together with the expansion of deposit-insurance coverage and the ever-widening federal presence in residential-mortgage finance, the "too big to fail" doctrine helped to get the 1980s up and running. Soon there were loans for nearly everyone.

11

Wild and Woolly

In 1971, the year in which Richard M. Nixon made history by imposing peacetime wage-price controls, consumer prices rose by an average of only 4.4 percent. In the decade of the 1980s, they were up at an annual average rate of 5.6 percent. In 1985, the Consumer Price Index was no longer the nation's top economic problem, but neither was it out of mind. The management of the Coffee, Sugar & Cocoa Exchange of New York had not forgotten, and it devised a new vehicle for speculating on a possible debasement of the currency: inflation futures contracts.

In the 1980s, there were "interest-rate swaps," "stock index futures," "Euroyen debt supported by a currency swap," "long-dated, exchange-traded currency warrants," "floating-rate, inflation-indexed notes," and "cumulative redeemable commodity-indexed preferred stock." Inflation futures seemed no more farfetched than those instruments—Milton Friedman and Paul Samuelson, both Nobel laureates, attested to their economic merit—and the exchange launched a promotional drive to interest Wall Street. It mailed 2,000 money clips to commodity brokers, attaching to each a Bolivian note for one million inflated pesos. It informed the brokers that the value of their note had fallen to the equivalent of 55 cents from the equivalent of $5,000 in little more than two and a half years. "It's our way of dramatizing the unpredictability of inflation and the protection CPI Futures Contracts offer you along with the opportunities for profit," the copy teased them, and it invited all comers to try their hand at estimating the American CPI for June 1986. First prize: a week's paid vacation to La Paz, Bolivia, the inflation Tahiti of the world. In 1985, Bolivian prices had climbed by 40,000 percent versus a mere 3.6 percent in America.

It was the right contest (won by a Chicago man, Michael Klotz, who disarmingly explained, "I guessed") at the wrong time. In 1986, the American CPI rose at the low, anti-Bolivian rate of 1.9 percent, and people briefly stopped worrying about it. Although the CPI increased every year for the rest of the decade, revisiting 5 percent territory in 1990, it was easy to dismiss inflation as yesterday's problem. Indeed, for farmers and oil drillers and real-estate developers, the greatest problem of the decade was the lack of inflation. The inflation futures contract expired, either ahead of its time or behind it, in 1991.

By the mid-1980s, price inflation was overshadowed by credit inflation. Money is the paper in one's wallet and credit is the plastic. Credit is the promise to pay money, and the inflation of credit was carried on through the proliferation of promises. Down payments were reduced, banks guaranteed, maturities extended, and risks of default increasingly borne by the federal government. The franchise of credit was extended in ways that George F. Baker might not have anticipated. One lurid example was a loan by the Lincoln Savings & Loan Association, headed by the soon to be notorious Charles H. Keating, Jr., to Covenant House, the soon to be scandal-plagued home for runaways, in 1984. The loan, for $12.75 million, was secured by a sixth mortgage.

Money, which is tangible, can be counted. Credit too can be counted, and it can also be imagined. Expecting to get a loan on easy terms, people may spend more than they would otherwise do. The anticipation of borrowed money, no less than that of ordinary income or capital gains, is a spur to business activity and speculation alike, and it played a vital if unsung role in the Reagan prosperity. In the expansion of the 1980s, credit (actual and anticipated) boosted car sales, house sales, real-estate construction, and corporate takeovers. It constituted the lever by which small sums of money could be made to do the service of large ones. D. Morier Evans, the nineteenth-century British financial historian, found he was unable to explain the boom of 1824–25 by the mere increase in money in circulation at the time. However, he observed, "such was the general confidence that real money was hardly needed; credit was the universal currency."

It was to temper the recurrent bouts of overconfidence in financial markets that the federal securities laws were enacted during the Depression. Henceforth, the reformers intended, no investor in a registered bond or stock would lose his money by reason of ignorance. It was a revolutionary change from the disclosure practices (or lack of them) in the 1920s, but it brought about no revolutionary change in the behavior of optimistic people in crowds.

Nobody except the principals knew at the time of the loan that Lincoln had taken a very junior lien on Covenant House. In the same month and year, however, everyone who cared to know could familiarize himself with the details of a $1.3 billion junk-bond sale by Metromedia Broadcasting Corporation. In compliance with the federal securities laws, Metromedia was bound to disclose every material fact. The stipulated medium for truth-telling is the prospectus, and the company and its investment bankers labored all night and into the early morning of November 29, 1984, to produce one. Two law firms, two investment banking firms, one accounting firm, and Metromedia itself detailed twenty-one persons to the Charles P. Young Co. on Varick Street in lower Manhattan.

A night at the financial printer's was a ritual of the bull market. Wall Street worked long hours in the boom, and young analysts were expected to show the stamina of medical interns. The printers, in turn, were expected to provide their customers with every possible amenity. If an analyst (or a lawyer or a banker) was hungry for lobster, lobster was provided, and it was served on china. Pool tables, pinball machines, and fully stocked refrigerators were furnished to help beguile the time between relays of page proofs.

Young's appointments were plush (one of its conference rooms, done in colonial motif, was called the Ben Franklin room) and the Metromedia team made itself at home. Presently, the fine carpets and reproduction Williamsburg tables accumulated the flotsam of a college all-nighter: crumpled papers, a discarded yellow highlighting marker, Styrofoam cups, and spent beverage cans. After-hours drinking was not unheard of at these sessions, but a senior lawyer, catching sight of a single empty beer bottle, said for the record, "Any lawyer who drinks on my deal will not be here on the next deal with me."

Free-lance proofreaders, most of whom were artists by day, pored over the text and the numbers. At 11:30 p.m., Leon Black, thirty-three, a managing director of the principal underwriter, Drexel Burnham Lambert, dropped in to check up on things. His previous engagement: a meeting at "21" with the corporate raider Carl Icahn. Icahn was raising some junk-bond money of his own. At 4 a.m., Gregg Siebert, twenty-nine, vice president of Bear, Stearns, the No. 2 underwriter, looked up from his proofreading to say, "The payoff comes in five or six hours when we're cleared by the SEC." At 8 a.m., Hector Alfalla, a printer's messenger, was on the air shuttle to Washington to deliver 12,000 pages of Metromedia documents to the SEC for regulatory review. No objection was raised.

Meanwhile, on Varick Street, the blue-collar shift began the work of printing, collating, stapling, and trimming the finished product. They stacked 32,000 booklets on wooden pallets and moved them around the floor on forklift trucks, like pig iron. The printer's bill came to $1.3 million, a lot of money except as a percentage of the face value of the bonds. It was one-tenth of 1 percent of $1.3 billion. Although required by law, the documents were not instrumental to the success of the Metromedia deal, because the bonds were spoken for, or "circled," even before the ink on the pages was wet. By law, each of the buyers was entitled to refuse to take delivery of his allotted share if, before the settlement date, in this case December 5, he read the prospectus and reconsidered. None so elected, however.

Metromedia Broadcasting was the direct descendant of the Du Mont Television Network, which had obtained one of the earliest experimental TV broadcasting licenses in the country, in 1939. Its pioneering founder, Allen Balcolm Du Mont, was a literal belt-and-suspenders conservative who, when asked why he didn't upgrade his office from its original battered entrepreneurial condition, replied, "You know, ever since we got successful, all the young fellas in the plant want big, fancy offices. I figure leaving mine this way saves me a lot of arguments." When, in 1959, John W. Kluge, a former food broker, purchased the Du Mont broadcasting stable, the company was producing earnings of just $1.5 million on sales of $16.5 million. A quarter century later, Metromedia, as Kluge had renamed the company, was producing earnings of $31 million on sales of $355 million. Metromedia owned nine radio stations and seven television stations. The TV stations, sometimes flatteringly described as a "fourth network," reached almost a quarter of the homes in the United States. They included WNEW in New York City and KTTV Los Angeles and WTTG in Washington, D.C. Kluge eschewed Du Mont's decorating tastes—a visitor to the Metromedia offices in 1965 spotted a Rembrandt and a Van Dyck—but demonstrated other eccentric frugal traits. When out to dine, for instance, the billionaire would leave his overcoat in the car rather than spend the dollar he would decently have to leave as a tip for the coatroom attendant inside the restaurant. "I just saved a buck," he would tell his companions.

Metromedia Inc., parent of Metromedia Broadcasting, had gone private in June 1984 in what was then, at $1.3 billion, the biggest leveraged buyout ever. The securities up for sale included both the plain and the exotic: "senior subordinated notes," "participating subordinated debentures," "senior exchangeable variable rate debentures," and "senior serial notes." The cause of this variety was necessity. Metromedia had taken out a $1.3 billion bank loan to finance the buyout of its public shareholders. The interest burden on this debt was onerous, because it was payable on the barrelhead. Not so the interest on every new junk bond; some of it was deferred. The average interest rate on the bank loan was 14.9 percent. The average interest rate on the pending sale of junk bonds was 15.4 percent. The vital difference was the liberal use of such procrastination securities as the serial notes* and "adjustable rate participating subordinated debentures."† The happy consequence of this deferral was an effective, cash interest rate on the junk bonds of approximately 10.3 percent, more than five percentage points less than the apparent rate. The resulting annual reduction in cash interest expense amounted to more than $50 million until 1989, at which time Metromedia would have to find some cash to begin redeeming its deferred-interest junk.

The prospectus was explicit on these points, and the artist-proofreaders might have wondered what the investors were getting themselves into. Jay Cooke & Co. had issued speculative bonds for the Northern Pacific Railroad after the Civil War, and S. W. Straus & Co. and innumerable foreign governments had issued prototypical junk bonds in the 1920s. What was new was not the risk or the reward but the thoroughness of the disclosure. The so-called paper entrepreneurship of the 1980s in fact produced high-quality paper. It yielded documents of fine accuracy and stupefying detail. At the bottom of the Depression, Wall Street and Washington alike had agreed that investors needed more information to forestall a repeat of the credit collapse of the 1930s. In October 1932, the Investment Bankers Association glumly considered the record of defaults in the debt of real-estate companies, industrial companies, public-utility holding companies, and Latin American governments. *The New York Times* reported on the consensus of the meeting: "It was freely predicted that in the future both the bankers and the investors would stress more

---

* A kind of zero-coupon bond. Zeros are issued at a discount to face value. They are redeemed at face value. The difference between the issue and redemption prices, measured over time, constitutes the measure of an investor's return.

† Adjustable rate participating subordinated debentures paid a 13⅛ percent interest rate through December 1, 1989, and a 17 percent rate thereafter (hence "adjustable rate"); also, the debenture holders would receive a dividend type of payment if the company's cash flow met certain targets (hence "participating"). As the debentures were junior in right of payment to the senior serial notes and the senior subordinated debentures, they were "subordinated."

strongly the question of the credit behind each issue, and that the investors would demand more detailed financial statements."

It was an accurate forecast, but it was not the investors themselves who demanded the detail. It was the government. So much information was required by the Securities Act of 1933, in fact, and so great and long-lasting was the liability for noncompliance, that new capital-markets issues briefly dried up. Fifty-one years later, when the Metromedia Broadcasting transaction was filed, all that had been forgotten. A few years earlier, in fact, the SEC had moved to simplify the disclosure requirements ("Rule 415") for investment-grade corporations. No such relaxation was permitted to speculative-grade debt issuers, however, and a veritable industry of disclosure had grown up to meet the demand. In the case of Metromedia Broadcasting, separate prospectuses were issued for each of the four kinds of junk bonds. The edition for the "senior exchangeable variable rate debentures," for instance, ran to 172 pages. It contained up-to-date financial information on both the broadcasting subsidiary and its parent, not skimping on the debt, deficits, and prospective burden of debt service. It described the debentures in detail and it spelled out the compensation of the senior management. (Kluge's salary, which he didn't really need, was $962,050.) It described the rising trend of programming costs. When Peat, Marwick, Mitchell & Co. signed off on the accountants' report concerning Metromedia Inc., on page A-34, it took pains to fix the date of its opinion as of February 9, 1984, except for the second paragraph of the first footnote, which it dated as of March 22, 1984. In short, every conceivable reason why a prudent investor would have nothing to do with the bonds was recorded. If a prospective buyer ignored or discounted the risk language—reasoning, perhaps, that lawyers were paid to write it—that was understandable. Kluge was one of the great twentieth-century American moneymakers, and it was, after all, a bull market. In those circumstances, it was possible (indeed, in retrospect, advisable) to close one's eyes and buy.

Even so, the Metromedia disclosure was unusually blunt:

> Based on current levels of operations (assuming no growth in revenues), the Company's cash flow would be insufficient to make interest payments on the Debt Securities (other than the Serial Senior Notes) and it would have to use other funds, to the extent available, to make such interest payments. However, the Company has historically experienced significant rates of growth

M O N E Y   O F   T H E   M I N D

in broadcast revenues and cash flow. Although the Company does
not expect its rate of revenue and cash flow growth to continue
at its historical level, it nevertheless expects continued growth
which, if attained, would generate sufficient cash flow to enable
it to make interest payments on the Debt Securities (other than
the Serial Senior Notes). Such payments would consume all or
substantially all of such cash flow. No assurance can be given,
however, that such anticipated levels of growth will occur.

In other words, if everything went very well, the company could
probably meet its interest payments. Could it service its principal
obligations on its exotic deferred-interest bonds? The answer sounded
very much like "maybe":

In addition, based on current levels of operations and anticipated growth, the Company does not expect to be able to generate sufficient cash flow to make all of the principal payments
due on the Senior Serial Notes, which commence on December
1, 1988, without taking action to refinance a portion of its indebtedness. No assurance can be given that such refinancing can
be successfully accomplished. If refinancing cannot be successfully accomplished, the Company may consider selling a portion
of its assets including equity securities to the public, although
no assurance can be given that any such sale could be successfully
accomplished.

Metromedia Broadcasting was a subsidiary of Metromedia Inc. It
was created by investment bankers for the express purpose of selling
bonds. To start out with, it showed no long-term debt and more than
a billion dollars in equity. Giving effect to the sale of the junk bonds,
however, the balance sheet was turned inside out, like a pocket.
Equity became a very small number and long-term debt a very large
one (precisely $1.3 billion). After the refinancing, in fact, long-term
debt constituted more than 100 percent of the capital. Metromedia
Broadcasting on paper looked not much different from a bankrupt.
     One customary test of the soundness of a bond issuer is the number
of times its earnings suffice to cover its interest expense. In general,
the stronger the company, the more redundant its coverage. The Metromedia Broadcasting prospectus showed that had the company been
capitalized as it would soon be capitalized, its earnings (technically,
"earnings before interest and taxes") would have fallen short of its

interest expense for the latest twelve months. In fact, for every dollar of cash interest expense the company could have produced only 60 cents in earnings (before interest and taxes).

What kind of heresy was this? The patron saints of conservative investing, Benjamin Graham and David Dodd, wrote in the 1930s that the acid test of a bond issuer was its capacity to withstand a severe recession. Metromedia could scarcely have withstood a lower level of prosperity. To meet its interest expense, it needed growth. To meet its obligations to the holders of its zero-coupon bonds, it needed to refinance its debts or to sell some assets. Graham and Dodd adjured that bond investing is a "negative art," one more properly concerned with loss than with gain. A bondholder was not so different from a banker. For neither was the upside so unimaginably wonderful.

Metromedia Broadcasting was the biggest junk-bond transaction up until that time, but it created no great controversy. *Fortune* magazine published a pleasant photo essay, "All Night at the Printer's," on the job of putting the prospectus to bed ("While most of New York City sleeps, some of the nation's ablest lawyers, accountants, and investment bankers are sequestered in sumptuously appointed and well-guarded rooms . . ."), but the magazine ventured no comment on the document's revolutionary content. The author's comment—surely, *Grant's* contended, so rank a speculation as Metromedia implied that the bond market itself was at risk—proved remarkably ill timed. In fact, bond prices would continue to rally until the spring of 1986, as they had rallied since the Continental Illinois failure in 1984. Far from heralding the end of a speculative boom, the Metromedia sale almost marked its beginning. And as for the stock-market significance of a growing junk-bond market, it would prove to be thoroughly bullish.

In times past, the benefit of the doubt in the valuation of a public company had gone to the stock market. With the shining examples of the early leveraged buyouts, however, people began to doubt and look elsewhere for guidance. It was becoming apparent that William Simon, architect of the fabulously successful Gibson Greetings buyout in 1982–83, for instance, was doing better for himself than the average mutual-fund investor.* First with bank credit and later with junk

---

* Simon's investor group purchased the Gibson greeting-card division of RCA in January 1982. Out of the $80 million purchase price, fully $79 million was borrowed. When, 18 months later, Gibson was taken public at a value of $290 million, Simon won the lottery. His personal cash investment of $330,000 was transformed into $66 million of cash and stock. "I keep on wondering why more people are not doing what we're doing," the former Treasury Secretary reflected. He reportedly made this statement, according to Michael M. Thomas, "with an air of genuine bafflement."

bonds, Kluge had demonstrated that the stock market had undervalued Metromedia's assets. He and his creditors had done a better job of appraising the company than public investors had done (or, perhaps, could do; after all, who knew more about Metromedia than Kluge?).

"Private market value" was not the only new idea that the bull market had put into circulation. It was becoming fashionable to believe that debt had a place on every modern balance sheet. To treat the absence of debt as the highest form of prudence was to ignore the arithmetic of the tax code (which favored debt over equity and had done so, in fact, since the inception of the income tax).* Moreover, it was increasingly heard, a company's debt should be put in the perspective of the value of assets it had gone to finance.

The accountants had their kind of balance sheet (done according to GAAP, meaning generally accepted accounting principles), and forward-thinking people had theirs. The progressive balance sheet was attuned to "market value" as opposed to "book value." For example, if a company borrowed $1 million, the debt was booked at $1 million. Frequently, however, the asset offsetting that debt had a market value that exceeded its book value. In consequence, the indebtedness of such a company was overstated, because the equity—the real, market-adjusted equity—was understated. In the case of Metromedia Broadcasting, junk-bond partisans made certain adjustments in the reported numbers. To start with, they marked up the TV stations to the full bull-market value and projected rising asset values into the future. For another, they disregarded the amortization of goodwill as a fiction that had nothing to do with a set of assets that were, in point of fact, appreciating in value. "In the final analysis," Drexel Burnham asserted, "if a company has significant and enduring values in the equity marketplace relative to debt, it will be a good fixed-income investment."

The Case for Junk

The source of that quotation was the 1984 edition of "The Case for High Yield Bonds," an annual apologia produced by Drexel and distributed to its clients at the annual Drexel Burnham High Yield Bond

---

* In 1943, a writer forcefully and convincingly condemned tax and regulating policy under Franklin D. Roosevelt for discouraging the formation of equity capital and promoting the use of debt. He was Henry M. Wriston, the banker's father. The law still favored debt in 1984, but there was nothing revolutionary about that fact.

Conference in Beverly Hills. On Wall Street, it is sometimes profitable to believe what others doubt, and vice versa. In such a formative state was the junk market in the spring of 1984 that "The Case" was still printed in black and white on plain, nontextured typing paper. That in itself was bullish.

"The Case" led off with a concise and compelling call to arms:

> Why buy "high yield" bonds? Because they offer the oppor-tunity for better performance without undue risk; a chance to earn an incremental rate of return compared either to risk-free Treasury bonds or investment-grade issues. This premise has been validated consistently over the years, and we believe that it will continue to hold true because of corporate bond ratings which exaggerate credit risk and institutions which cannot or will not participate in this area of the market because of such ratings. Moreover, we believe that bond ratings, even if accurate at a given point in time, do not reflect the corporate instinct for survival—the many internal and external avenues available to avoid the stigma, costs and uncertainties of reorganization under the bankruptcy laws.

The author of those ideas, if not the literal words, was Michael Milken, a corporate-finance power not yet forty years old, the creator and chief of the Drexel junk-bond department. In person, Milken was soft-spoken and unassuming. His suits and his hairpiece had an off-the-rack appearance, and his shoes were middle-class. If a phone rang, he would answer it, directly, "Mike." His eyes darted. Not seeming to meet yours, they would suddenly engage them. If, for the sake of small talk, you happened to suggest the two of you might one day have a beer, he would reply that he did not drink (or take caffeinated or carbonated beverages, either). In conversation there was no wit, no thrust and no parry. His style was literal, factual, and persistent. On the telephone, he was garrulous and given to broker's slogans, such as (in the heat of the 1987 boom) "What you have to understand is, the world's awash in liquidity," or "You've got to look at the United States as if it were a takeover candidate," or "Often, what's old is weak and what's new is strong." He used your first name like an index finger with which to poke you in the chest and keep your undivided attention. But in the middle of a monologue, he could also say some-thing unexpected. On the telephone in August 1987, for instance, he dropped this fact: that the fees and expenses associated with the leveraged buyout of Borg-Warner Holdings Corporation were greater than the equity of the company after the buyout. In other words, the bankers, lawyers, and accountants had taken more out of the business than the company could show in net worth. It seemed a stunning fact at the time (later there were many more such cases) and an uncharacteristic one. Borg-Warner was a Merrill Lynch deal, and Milken was scrupulous with me, at least, to say nothing derogatory about the competition (and, indeed, nothing derogatory about the junk-bond market, the world economy, or almost anything else). I was a notorious bear on his market, and he invested what must have been several hours in proselytizing telephone calls.

Milken, too, worried about banks, but about their spite more than their solvency. Recalling Saul Steinberg's failed attempt to take over Chemical Bank in the late 1960s, he advised never to get crosswise with it or with one like it. They were powerful and unforgiving institutions, he said, and he seemed to fear what they might try to do to him for taking so much of their corporate-finance business.

The 1984 edition of "The Case" continued:

> When investing in high-grades, the cost of credit deterioration is usually a more important consideration than the cost of bankruptcy (presuming one looks at the "market value" of one's holdings). When Chrysler was floundering and investors were wondering whether even Ford Motor was viable, the decline in the market value of Ford's debt securities, excluding the effect of changing interest rates, exceeded the total loss from all bankruptcies during the preceding 12 months. . . . If deteriorating fundamentals don't get you, you can lose quality overnight in this new era of "giant" mergers, such as Du Pont–Conoco and U.S. Steel–Marathon Oil.

As for defaults, Drexel could easily show that they had done no significant damage since the 1930s. The recent troubles of companies like Chrysler, Eastern Airlines, Mattel, and Allis-Chalmers had merely presented alert investors with the opportunity to make a killing. Furthermore, as "The Case" continued, "while bankruptcies grab most of the headlines, since 1977 there actually have been more 'instant upgrades' due to mergers. In the past few years, Prudential Insurance, presumably an 'AAA' credit, acquired Bache, 'A'-rated St. Regis Paper bought 'BB' Drum Financial, 'A' Corning Glass acquired 'B +' rated MetPath and 'AAA' Coca-Cola assumed Columbia Pictures' debt." As for "going private" transactions like Metromedia's, Drexel was not prepared to concede that even they would hurt creditors in the long run:

> Many times, while leverage initially increases, it is subsequently reduced through asset sales. More important, the new "owners" (whose equity is below the companies' debt obligations) have a greater incentive to perform. As a private company, decisions can be made which will have long-term benefit, without concern as to the impact on next quarter's earnings or other short-term yardsticks imposed on public companies by the investment community. Thus far, none of the companies which have gone private has missed an interest or principal payment on its public debt.

The message of "The Case for High Yield Bonds" was therefore one of radiant optimism. It could be inferred that there was no bad news. Opportunities were frequently disguised as bad news, but the downside, in fact, was insignificant.

Was any of this possible? If Milken was right, the late Lawrence Chamberlain was wrong. Every conservative New England creditor had missed a bet, and investors in government bonds had purchased an inferior security. Milken was fond of observing that the debt rating of a triple-A-rated corporation had nowhere to go but down, whereas the rating of a speculative-grade company (barring a bankruptcy) had almost nowhere to go but up. By tradition, the majority of bond investors had construed "speculative" to mean "dangerous." The majority, probably, were still unpersuaded by Drexel Burnham in 1984, but in growing numbers they were beginning to interpret "speculative" as "promising."

One thing, at least, was certain. If Metromedia Broadcasting was the wave of the future, the past was no longer a useful topic for study. From here on, companies could borrow billions while freely confessing that they might not be able to repay it. Down through the ages, debtors had dreamed of exactly those terms. The revolutionary feature of the Metromedia transaction was that creditors had come to accept them too.

Skeptics could hardly believe their eyes. The asymmetry of risk and reward was flagrant: to John W. Kluge, controlling owner of the TV and radio stations, would go the upside; to the bondholders, the downside. The thing could be demonstrated mathematically, as Michael

Marocco, an analyst with Morgan Stanley & Co., proceeded to do. The proof was elegantly simple. First, noted Marocco, the fair market value of the broadcasting properties in fact approximated their recorded book value. Under so-called purchase accounting guidelines, the value of the stations had been written up to market value at the time of the Metromedia leveraged buyout in June 1984. There was, in fact, no hidden value on the Metromedia Broadcasting balance sheet. Because the stations were carried at market value, and because the bonds constituted the entire capital, it followed that the value of the stations equaled the value of the debt. Assets, of course, equaled liabilities. Therefore, any future decline in the value of the stations would diminish the value of the debt. There was no cushion of equity. Finally, there was the matter of the zero-coupon bonds. By definition, zeros were issued at less than face value. In the case of Metromedia, the amount of the discount—that is, face value minus the issue price— was $600 million. This $600 million was exactly the measure by which the market value of the stations would have to appreciate, prior to the maturity of the zero-coupon bonds, to guarantee that the bondholders' investment would not become impaired. What it all boiled down to, Marocco continued, was the creation of what is known as a call. A call confers upon its holder the right to participate in the appreciation of a stock or an entire market above a specified price and during a specified time. If, in Kluge's case, the market value of the assets came to exceed the book value of the liabilities, the gain would be his. If the values fell, that would be the bondholders' problem. "Metromedia," wrote Marocco, "has effectively passed on the entire business risk of the broadcasting properties to the bondholders, while retaining a 100 percent interest in any future price appreciation above the book value of MBC's debt."

But events, as they so often did in those days, favored the bulls. In May 1985, only six months after the bond issue came to market, Rupert Murdoch, the Australian media titan, bought the Metromedia TV stations. The price he paid was $1.55 billion, which, expressed as a multiple of their estimated cash flow, was described as a record high. Expressed in dollars, it was substantially in excess of the value at which the assets were carried on Metromedia's books. In September 1986, all but one of the Metromedia radio stations were sold in a management-led buyout, once again at a fancy price.

Kluge's timing was exquisite. A frenzy had come over the media market, and price was no object in consideration of a television station or a cable franchise. If the price was exceptionally rich, one could pay in the newfangled scrip of zero-coupon, or deferred-interest, bonds. Going in, Metromedia Broadcasting had seemed a shot in the dark. Going out—that is, within months—it looked like a bull's-eye. Its success changed corporate finance. Drexel Burnham was a miracle firm, and worry was obsolete. "How to Invent Money," was the tag line on an advertisement that Drexel had run in December 1984. By the middle of 1985, it seemed a literal description of the firm's business.

Rewriting Braddock Hickman

Once Milken described himself as having the "soul of a professor," and the subject he chose to profess was credit. "The Case for High Yield Bonds" never failed to invoke the name and work of W. Braddock Hickman, the eminent student of the corporate bond market and author of the non-best-selling 1958 study *Corporate Bond Quality and Investor Experience*. It was Hickman, as Drexel's customers were annually reminded, who found that high-yield bonds—that is, junk—had produced a paradoxically higher investment return than high-grade bonds over the first four decades of the century. The perception of risk was greater, then and later, than the actual experience.

But Hickman said a good deal more that "The Case" did not address. Along with Geoffrey Moore and other scholars whose work was published by the National Bureau of Economic Research, Hickman delved into the apparent decline in credit quality of bonds issued late in the Coolidge boom. As Moore had shown in his 1955 paper, defaults occurred with greater frequency among bonds and mortgages issued late in the 1920s than with those issued early. The rise in the default rate stuck out, Hickman observed, because the tendency since the turn of the century was one of declining rates of default. Then, again, as we have seen (Hickman did not get into personalities), bull markets reward audacity, Rogers Caldwell and S. W. Straus being only some of the more conspicuous examples. Nor did Drexel get around to quoting George W. Edwards, a scholar who, from the perspective of the bottom of the Great Depression, wrote: "The history of business cycles shows that the stage of prosperity in general is marked by an ever-increasing inefficiency. In the field of security investment the buying public, swayed by overoptimism, seeks more and more after securities of higher yield, and investment bankers, under the stress of competition, issue securities of higher yield, greater risk and poorer quality."

Hickman, taking up the same general theme, made a study of default rates in the 1920s. His statistical work corroborated Edwards's hypothesis—namely, that prosperity seemed to tarnish the quality of corporate debt. Arthur F. Burns and Wesley C. Mitchell, other economists whose work was not cited in any edition of "The Case for High Yield Bonds," had proposed that vigilance among investors ebbed and flowed in cycles. "After a severe depression," they wrote in 1946, "industrial activity rebounds sharply, but speculation does not. The following contraction of business is mild, which leads people to be less cautious. Consequently, in the next two or three cycles, while the cyclical advances become progressively smaller in industrial activity, they become progressively larger in speculative activity. Finally, the speculative boom collapses and a drastic liquidation follows, which ends this cycle of cycles and brings us back to the starting point."

This was a sweeping proposition, and Hickman could not find the evidence to support it without qualification. "Nevertheless," he allowed, "the long swings in the data do provide some evidence of deteriorating credit conditions toward the end of 'major cycles,' and of a possible tightening up of credit standards near the beginning of new major cycles." Hickman wrote something else that, to any Wall Street practitioner, rang true. It was that credit quality tends to suffer as securities issuance rises. Hickman put it more carefully than that, of course: "It will be observed that the trends in default rates are roughly comparable with trends in net and gross new financing, default rates tending to be high on securities issued during years of high financial volume and vice versa. . . . This would seem to suggest that some issues, perhaps those of marginal quality, can find a ready market only when the market is buoyant, and that in periods of market pessimism only the top grade issues can be placed." Nor did the facts warrant anything like dogmatism on that point. Still, Hickman wound up, "the evidence, while hardly conclusive, seems sufficiently strong to suggest a need for possible review of present credit standards, particularly in view of the abrupt run-up in corporate bonded debt since World War II."

Hickman was writing in the second Eisenhower administration. If he was prepared to be concerned in 1958, it was a cinch that he would have been worried in 1985, when William Lilley III, senior vice president of CBS, said, "Prudence is putting debt on your balance sheet" (the TV broadcaster was worried about a hostile takeover), and when Robert Pirie, president of Rothschild Inc., told *The Wall Street Journal*, "You've got to be leveraged to the point where someone can't leverage off you." By the first anniversary of the Metromedia Broadcasting financing, debt had become the new Archimedes lever. Without much capital, small companies could acquire big companies and individuals could become very rich. Suzy, the *New York Post* gossip columnist, reported rhapsodically from the estate-warming party of John W. Kluge outside of Charlottesville, Virginia: "As your eyes register the pristine stately house in its glorious setting of gentle hills and valleys, you can only think that the Kluges have wrought a miracle. The exterior looks 18th Century—did they have billionaires then?"

Metromedia Broadcasting had set records by selling $1.3 billion worth of junk bonds. A year later, Storer Communications, which owned seven television stations and the fourth-largest American cable system, issued more than $1.9 billion worth of junk securities, bonds, and preferred stock, in financing *its* leveraged buyout. Kohlberg, Kravis, Roberts & Co. (KKR) directed the buyout of what was renamed SCI Holdings; Drexel Burnham Lambert performed the investment-banking duties. On form, and setting aside the arithmetic, there was every reason to believe that Storer would work.

In 1985, there was a bull market in junk bonds, Treasury bonds, television stations, cable properties, radio stations, and common stocks. More important, there was also a bull market in expectations. Like a bartender sampling the liquor, Charles P. Young, the financial printer that had produced the Metromedia Broadcasting prospectuses, issued $50 million worth of its own junk bonds; it defaulted after the 1987 crash. At a dinner party in Westport, Connecticut, one pretty summer night in 1985, the conversation turned to the problems of the rich, and a well-tanned middle-aged woman spoke up. If one's husband commutes to work by helicopter, she said, the helicopter must land on one's lawn. And if one's lawn had been freshly cut, the cuttings were bound to be scattered into one's swimming pool. Could nothing be done about this nuisance? In the past, bear markets had eventually dealt with the problems of excess income by removing it, but there was no bear market on the horizon. KKR had been earning 50 percent a year for its investors for almost a decade, and Drexel Burnham was the most brilliant comet in the Wall Street sky. In those circumstances, credit was freely forthcoming. Over lunch one day around the time of the Storer offering, a couple of broadcasting executives marveled at their newfound popularity among lenders. "The biggest problem we have is the bankers," one of them said. "They stop you and ask you how much you want. We're starting to feel like the South American countries did a few years ago when they had all that money pushed on them." Another man at the table produced a copy of a limited partnership memorandum that Kidder, Peabody & Co. had been circulating. The partnership had been organized to buy TV stations, and one of the stated reasons to be bullish was the availability of easy credit. The memo mentioned the "willingness of senior and mezzanine lenders to provide financing for as much as 85 percent of the purchase price of television stations because of low loan-loss experience and an increased recognition of underlying asset value."

In the case of Storer, however, a lender had to be more than willing. He had to be trusting. The junk-bond prospectus addressed the expected shortfall of income with all required bluntness. "Based upon current levels of operations and anticipated growth," it said, "it is not expected that sufficient cash flow will be generated to make all of the principal payments on the Debt Securities (which commence in 1991) and to make the scheduled redemptions of Preferred Stock (which commence in 1997)." Believing the prospectus, it was easy to become discouraged:

> It is anticipated that cash flow from operations, after debt service, will not be sufficient to fund all of the projected capital expenditure requirements necessary to enhance and maintain Storer's television broadcast and cable businesses during the next five years, absent sales of assets of Storer during such period. No decision has been made as to which assets will be sold or when sales will occur. . . . In the event sufficient funds are not available, [the company] will be required to curtail its capital expenditures, which could have an adverse effect on [the company's] business and operations.

But creditors were not discouraged. They bought the Storer securities and the next month they bought the 15⅞ percent junk bonds of Commonwealth Savings & Loan, Fort Lauderdale, Florida. What Commonwealth proposed to do with the proceeds (what it did, in fact, do) was to buy junk bonds and to make real-estate loans. It did enough of those things to ruin itself.

It was not sunk in 1985, however. To borrow from George Edwards, the buying public, swayed by overoptimism, was seeking more and more after securities of higher yield, but the search had hardly begun. By the standards of the late 1980s, the mid-1980s were an era of antique caution. In the fall of 1985, G. Chris Andersen, a Drexel Burnham managing director, testified before a subcommittee of the House Banking Committee on the suitability of junk debt as an investment for thrifts. He deemed it extremely suitable and recommended it as a vehicle for the restoration of the financial health of the savings and loan industry. By this time the use of junk bonds to finance hostile takeovers had become a source of controversy. The previous April, for instance, *The Washington Post* had urged a ban on the purchase of junk by all federally insured institutions. In June, the legendary investor Warren E. Buffett spoke out against junk bonds at a public forum at Columbia University. In Washington, Andersen favored the congressmen with a concise version of "The Case for High Yield Bonds." He testified that the incremental yield obtained by investors more than compensated them for the incremental risk. "Studies have demonstrated that actual returns average four to eight times the increase in risk," he said. "In fact, significantly more money has been lost in the bond markets through the downgrading of investment-grade debt than through defaults on non-investment-grade bonds."

In support of the essential "Case," Andersen cited the work of Marshall Blume and Donald Klein of the Wharton School of the University of Pennsylvania, and of Edward Altman of New York University. But he did not mention the work of Hickman, Edwards, Mintz, Moore, Mitchell, or Burns, the existence of a theory of the credit cycle, or the historical record of credit in the 1920s and 1930s. "Critics sometimes question the relevance of historic data on performance, citing the recent increases in volume of high-yield bonds," the witness said. "Our experience indicates that the credit quality for high-yield bond issuers has improved significantly over the past five years."

In fact, just as Hickman et al. could have predicted, the credit quality of junk-bond issuers was beginning what would prove a long slide. Leniency was the trend throughout the credit markets. The terms and conditions of automobile loans made credit more accessible, and the government was guaranteeing a growing percentage of residential mortgages (thereby extending the benefits of homeownership to a greater percentage of the population but putting the American taxpayer at risk of ultimate loss in case of a protracted bear market). Under the so-called Plaza Accord of September 1985, Japan was moving to lower its interest rates in the service of reducing the foreign-exchange value of the dollar. So doing, it touched off a speculative boom in Japanese stocks and real estate and, indirectly, in American markets as well. Big American banks had been slipping for years, and the rate of decline in their creditworthiness accelerated. The government's finances continued their bipartisan decay.

Conservatives wondered what the country was coming to. Bears, believing that they knew, sold stocks short in expectation of the inevitable break. (Some of them—James S. Chanos, William M. McGarr, Michael J. Harkins, and Edwin A. Levy—did so with consisent success, even in rising markets.) Around Wall Street, a graph tracing the rise in national indebtedness passed from hand to hand. It showed that at least for twenty years, in the decades leading up to the early 1980s, the ratio of total debt (personal, corporate, and governmental, excluding the debt of banks and other financial entities) to gross national product had been constant at around 135 percent. In the recession year of 1982, however, the ratio began to climb. By 1986, it was closing in on 180 percent.

The conservatives correctly deplored the ruination of the thrift industry, the impairment of the banking industry, and the widespread substitution of debt for equity in corporate finance. What they failed to grasp, however, was how perversely bullish those tendencies would be for the short term. The letting down of hair among creditors meant that the marginal debtor would get a loan and make the extra purchase. The GNP would expand and the stock market go up. None of this could go on indefinitely, but neither would it stop immediately.

America Swings Its Weight

So too in the monetary realm. Bad news was miraculously transformed into good news through roundabout governmental processes. The American payments deficit was vast and chronic, but that flaw became the agent of lower interest rates, not higher ones. One winning attribute of the international gold standard was its simplicity. The paper-currency system of the mid-1980s was, by contrast, complex.* In truth, it was not a unified system at all, but a series of political stopgaps. In 1985, the United States confronted deficits at home and abroad. Under gold-standard rules, it would have had to raise its interest rates to stanch the outflow of money, thereby deflating the structure of its domestic costs and restoring itself to competitive trim. Under the gold-

---

* Its rhetoric was correspondingly slick, sometimes to the point of unintelligibility. "Building consensus on the conceptual framework of policy coordination, to which the Plaza strategy continued, should continue to be encouraged through pragmatic approaches, such as Volcker's 'quiet mutual contingency planning,' " a prominent economic journalist wrote of the period from 1985 to 1987. What could the words have possibly meant?

exchange standard, as we have seen, those rules were relaxed; by 1985, without even a gold-exchange standard, they were forgotten.

The 1984 Republican Party platform did, in fact, endorse a return to gold convertibility, but it was an expression of hope rather than of intent. Following its reelection, the Reagan administration chose to prevail on foreign central banks to reduce *their* interest rates. It intervened to reduce the foreign-exchange value of the dollar. Thus, it shifted the burden of remedial action away from the United States (the debtor and deficit country) and on to Japan and Germany (the creditor and surplus countries). As we have seen, Britain, a former surplus country turned debtor, had pulled off a similar tactical victory in the 1920s. The immediate financial consequence, then and later, was expansive—as Benjamin Strong noted as he cut the American discount rate in 1927, the central bankers had made a gift to the stock market: a *coup de whiskey*.

Oddly for professed champions of the free market, the Republicans intervened often and with relish. The Treasury Department of James A. Baker III undertook to manage not only the United States economy but also the economies of the principal American trading partners. Urging tax cuts here, government spending programs there, and lower interest rates all around, it sought to prolong the boom. If the United States was going to reduce its imports (as its payments difficulties suggested it might) and its Treasury deficit (as Baker repeatedly promised), Japan and Germany would have to step up their growth.

To the public, the monetary drama of the mid-1980s was obscured by the soporific meetings from which it issued. Following hours or days of ministerial consultations, government officials would utter bland and (as it seemed) irrelevant statements. But in time the results were uplifting: bullish for financial markets and stimulative for business activity. After a greater span of time, however, the decisions would threaten the economic and financial stability of the alleged beneficiaries.

The first such meeting took place at the Plaza Hotel on September 22, 1985. Attending were the Finance Ministers and central bankers of the so-called Group of Five: Britain, France, West Germany, Japan, and the United States. The catalyst for the event was the familiar list of international "imbalances": Japanese surpluses, American deficits, lopsided growth. The item highest on the American agenda was the depreciation of the dollar in terms of foreign currencies. A low dollar was the opposite side of the coin of a high yen; a high yen implied high prices for Japanese exports and thus, it was hoped, fewer of them in the United States. The conference took place on a Sunday. Promptly the following Monday, the dollar lost 4.29 percent of its value against an index of foreign currencies, its biggest one-day drop on record.

What happened next was unorthodox and unexpected: late in October, the Bank of Japan raised its interest rates. What was this? America should have raised its rates, if that unpleasant duty had fallen to any country. It was the country with the debt and the deficits, after all. To know the times, the Treasury Secretary, and the GOP, however, was to know that it would not. The administration was concerned about the domestic economy and the upcoming congressional elections. The economy was weak, and subsequent revisions in the gross national product would reveal that output actually fell in the second quarter. The weakness was specific to manufacturing, however. Elsewhere, notably in housing, defense spending, and consumer spending, things were booming. Nevertheless, the administration, its eye fixed on the electoral calendar, was in no mood to take chances. Its interest in the forms and protocol of the international monetary system was, in comparison to that pressing concern, almost nonexistent.

Thus, the Japanese move was alarming. It threatened to turn the hoped-for decline of the dollar into a collapse and to strangle the growth of the Japanese economy; Volcker advised the Bank of Japan that the increase was, in his opinion, "unnecessary and unwise." (Washington saw no contradiction between wishing the Japanese well, on the one hand, and wishing for a smaller trade deficit, on the other. It took steps to bring about each result.)

If Chairman Volcker refused to raise rates, neither would he lower them. Standing pat, he alienated the new, Reagan-appointed members of the Federal Reserve Board, who believed that the economy required resuscitation. By February, the chairman found himself outnumbered. Over his opposition, the board voted 4–3 to cut the discount rate. Embarrassed and angry, Volcker almost resigned, thought better of it, and instead proposed a compromise. The Federal Reserve would delay its implementation of the discount-rate cut until it could enlist the support of the other leading central banks. On March 6 and 7, the deed was done. Germany, France, Japan, and the United States cut rates one after another.

They continued to hack away, the United States and Japan coordinating another rate reduction on April 21. Twice in the summer of 1986, the Federal Reserve Board lowered interest rates unilaterally. (Thanks to the fall in oil prices, inflation in producer prices was hardly visible; then, again, inflation in stock prices and real estate was proceeding briskly, and the overall inflation rate would soon return to the levels at which Richard Nixon had deemed it necessary to impose wage-price controls.) The second such action, on August 21, brought the discount rate to 5½ percent, its lowest level in almost nine years. Germany refused to follow, and Japan too hung back until after Baker met with Finance Minister Kiichi Miyazawa in September in San Francisco. To the Treasury Secretary's interest-rate reduction overtures, Miyazawa replied that the timing was difficult. He alluded to what would subsequently be known in Japan as the "bubble economy," that helium-like state in which houses, land, and common stocks were lifted to unheard-of valuations. In the end, however, Miyazawa saw things Baker's way: in return for tax reform and lower interest rates in Japan, the United States would stop reducing the value of the dollar. By any past lights, Baker's negotiating stance was nothing short of insolent. The world's great economic power, steward of the world's reserve currency, prying monetary and fiscal policies from its trading partners in exchange for a pledge from its Treasury Secretary not to mutilate the value of its own currency. It was as wild-eyed a monetary development as junk bonds were a corporate-finance development. It was, however, expedient: the Japanese authorities continued to ease. On February 20, 1987, the discount rate of the Bank of Japan was cut to 2.5 percent, the lowest in postwar Japanese history.

Nobody had to explain its significance to the world's stock markets. Money supply was booming, in the United States and Japan alike, and central banks, in deeds if not in words, had declared their intention to subordinate the fight against inflation to the battle for prosperity. The gold price climbed from $300 an ounce in January 1985 to more than $400 an ounce by the closing months of 1986. Speculative real-estate construction boomed in North America, Europe, and Japan, and the Japanese stock market took flight (by 1987 trading at more than 70 times earnings, a level unheard of in modern equity markets). To Gert von der Linde, one of Wall Street's most searching and farsighted economists, the synchronized interest-rate reductions of 1986 constituted the official monetary blessing of the boom. The policies of the administration and the Federal Reserve were rankly and cynically inflationary, he believed. In consequence, the upswing would carry farther than most people realized, and he reiterated that view (presciently, it developed) even after the stock-market crash of 1987.

In the summer of 1991, Wayne Angell, a Federal Reserve Board governor who had fallen in with the easy-money forces immediately upon his arrival in Washington in 1986, confessed to second thoughts. "Had a recession occurred then," *The Washington Post* paraphrased him as saying, "some of the serious excesses of the 1980s—including the massive amount of overbuilding of commercial real estate that has devastated that industry and has killed or is threatening the existence of hundreds of financial institutions—likely would never have taken place." It was a handsome concession and better late than never.*

To Wall Street, the most compelling reason to participate in the boom was not the tax code but the money. The cover of the January 20, 1986, issue of *Fortune* magazine featured "Mega-Dealmakers" Bruce Wasserstein and Joseph R. Perella along with the pulse-stirring headline "Those Mind-Bending Merger Fees." Wasserstein and Perella, however, worked for the First Boston Corporation, not Drexel Burnham (they would later start their own firm), and any superlatives about merger fees inside the magazine were deflated by the next Drexel mega-deal. In April 1986, Kohlberg, Kravis, Roberts & Co. paid $6.4 billion for Beatrice Companies, using bank debt and junk bonds and installing on the new board of directors an employee of theirs who happened to be twenty-eight years old.† Drexel, as usual, was the underwriter, and its fees exceeded $86 million. Furthermore, it was the recipient of warrants to purchase common stock in the new Beatrice, and these appreciated spectacularly. (Either the stock market, once again, had low-balled the value of an investor-owned company or the miracle of leverage had created additional value. Milken advanced the second explanation: "The company spent thirty to fifty million dollars on corporate-image advertising," he pointed out, adding that that would stop, much to the stockholders' benefit.) Drexel had

---

* Angell only conceded so much, however. In a subsequent letter to John D. Britton, amplifying on those remarks, he observed that a recession in 1986 would have damaged "many sectors of the U.S. economy that were already very depressed: agriculture, oil and gas, and the rust belt. It would have been a dramatic blow. In addition, a recession in 1986 would have caused a continued plunge of world commodity prices which likely would have collapsed third world debt repayments and money-center U.S. banks. So I *wonder*, but I do not know."

† Youth was served continuously. In October 1986, just before the Boesky indictment, executive search firms confronted a shortage of junk-bond analysts. The rarest of this scarce talent were people who had actually been through a bear market. "If you can find three years' worth of experience these days, you're lucky," said Linda Bialecki, a "head hunter" with a specialty in the high-yield bond market. "Three years ago you could get a seasoned individual for around $150,000 to $175,000, maybe. Today [in 1986], you're lucky to find a seasoned individual for twice that."

"*Of course I'm over 21. I'm a managing director of Morgan Stanley.*"

Usually, youth was no handicap
(GRANT'S INTEREST RATE
OBSERVER)

gone beyond mere investment banking. It had become its client's partner.

Talton C. Embry, an investor in junk bonds, remembered Beatrice as an important catalyst for the change in Wall Street opinion. "It started the real feeding frenzy," he said. "People looked at Beatrice and said, 'Jesus, Drexel just made $300 million on Beatrice, on the warrants.' That number was discredited a year later, but it made people crazy. Nobody knew what Mike Milken was making out there—they probably thought he was making $12 million a year and were jealous of that. When it turned out to be $125 million, they went crazy." About that time Milken visited Boston to make a rare public appearance. "There are at least five hundred people in this country worth one billion dollars," he told an audience of Lawrence Chamberlain's professional descendants. "That gives us all something to shoot for." Smiling, Milken did not discourage speculation that he was already one of the elect.

You could get rich by selling junk bonds or by creating the companies that used them: KKR and Drexel were the proof of that. But could you also get rich by buying them? The promised yield on junk bonds, approximately 13 percent, handsomely exceeded the long-term rate of return on common stocks, approximately 10 percent. In many cases, of course, the actual yield fell short of the promised yield, but the investors' return was not what preoccupied Wall Street in 1986. Fees did, along with warrants and Milken's compensation and the growing dominance of his employer. In July, Seven World Trade Center, the largest speculative office tower erected in New York and the designated

A *"map"—only slightly fanciful—of the sources of speculative credit in the 1980s*
(GRANT'S INTEREST RATE OBSERVER)

future home of Drexel Burnham, was topped off in a ceremony witnessed by, among other notables, Mayor Edward I. Koch and Governor Mario Cuomo. Drexel, being Drexel, had acquired a minority interest in the building besides committing to lease the entire premises—all forty-eight acres of it—for $100 million a year. The firm predicted that its New York employment would rise to 10,000 from the then current 4,300.

The firm, in fact, would never occupy Seven World Trade Center —Drexel's topping out occurred almost simultaneously with the building's—but there was no hint of that fact in the summer's financial press. In July, *Business Week* put Milken on its cover. "The only figure comparable to Milken who comes to mind is J. P. Morgan Sr.," Samuel L. Hayes III, professor of investment banking at the Harvard Business School, told the magazine. "Power on Wall Street" was the headline, and the copy said, "There's a new relationship between Wall Street and Corporate America—largely because of the work of one man: Drexel Burnham's Mike Milken. A classic outsider, Milken has created a huge financing network that can raise billions overnight for almost anyone. Drexel is now at the pinnacle of an emerging power structure that's changing the game—for investors, executives, and regulators." *Institutional Investor* outdid *Business Week* by one adjective in August. *II* called its story "Milken the Magnificent." Milken himself refused comment, as he almost always did, but his colleagues gave freely. James Balog, described by *Business Week* as "a widely respected Wall Street figure who's considered a force for moderation in the firm," said, "We built a brand-new market. We didn't ask anybody for it. We created it." Robert E. Linton, Drexel's chairman, said, "Michael wants to win the game. Michael wants to have it all. Michael wants to do every piece of business and every deal and make every dollar." Andersen, the Drexel investment banker and previous year's congressional witness, said, "This is Camelot. Do I give a damn who gets to play Merlin, who gets to play Lancelot, who wants to play Arthur? *I want to live in Camelot.*" The mood of the piece was set in the second paragraph by a comment from William Pike, manager of Fidelity's junk-bond fund in Boston. Said Pike of Milken, "You really don't want too much access to him. He's almost too important. It's like sitting down with President Reagan."

The indictment of Ivan Boesky in November 1986 on charges of insider trading jarred the junk-bond market only briefly (in the short ensuing decline, there seemed more bargain hunting than fear). Dennis Levine, the government's principal witness against Boesky, was a

Drexel Burnham banker, but the economic harm to Drexel was apparently small. Levine worked in the eastern branch of Camelot, not out west with Milken. Besides, Drexel was no longer a monopolist. If the other firms lacked its worshipful network of buyers, they compensated by taking extra risks and showing an extra increment of feelust.

Clinching evidence that the Ivan Boesky affair was of no immediate financial moment was the resumption of the bull market in early 1987. In March, the First Boston Corporation offered $800 million worth of junk bonds and 10 million shares of junk preferred for Allied Stores Corporation. One of the distinguishing features of the 1980s was that brokerage firms had come to believe their own investment research. Not only did they advise their clients to buy; they also risked their own capital. Unlike their clients, of course, the brokers elicited fees, which were frequently sizable, for their trouble. In this fashion, First Boston, late in 1986, lent $850 million to a subsidiary of Campeau Corporation so that that subsidiary could purchase Allied. The plan was that Allied would repay First Boston by selling junk bonds; creditors would be paid, in part, through the sale of assets. (Eight hundred and fifty million dollars was a meaningful percentage of First Boston's $959 million net worth. The close proximity of those figures infused First Boston's management and sales force with an understandable zeal to sell the bonds.)

Allied set new low standards for prudence, as the prospectus frankly disclosed. The document described a balance sheet consisting 12 percent of equity and 88 percent of debt. It revealed a deficiency in the ratio of earnings (liberally defined) to fixed charges. It stated that operating results must improve if the numbers were going to work. The graceful Caslon type of the cover page of the prospectus jarred with the financial content inside. From page 13:

> If non-cash charges to income for interest, depreciation and amortization were excluded, pro forma income before fixed charges and preferred stock dividends as adjusted for the offerings would have been inadequate to cover cash fixed charges and preferred stock cash dividends by $4 million for the year ended February 1, 1986, and by $99 million for the 39 weeks ended November 1, 1986, in each case before provision for capital expenditures.

To translate, the company, as it proposed to capitalize itself, was behind the eight ball. It would have to sell stores to reduce its otherwise unmanageable debt, and the stores it would try to sell were its least profitable (and therefore least marketable) ones. It would pay myriad fees to First Boston: a "commitment fee" for making the pre-junk-bond loan, called a "bridge" loan, a fee for serving as financial adviser, and a fee for writing a letter that rendered an opinion (favorable, of course) on Allied's solvency, among others. In short, it was Metromedia all over again but with the significant difference that the interest rates offered to the Allied bondholders were only in the neighborhood of 11 percent. To accommodate the overflow demand from professional investors, First Boston bumped up the size of the junk-bond offering to $900 million from $800 million. In the weeks that followed, the issues traded to a premium.

Skeptics despaired over this triumph of hope over fact, but Allied was merely a sign of the times. In Japan, the month before, shares of Nippon Telegraph & Telephone had come to market at the equivalent of $7,770 a share and instantly vaulted (despite a promised drop in 1987 earnings) to the equivalent of $17,582 a share. At the higher price, the stock changed hands at 234 times prospective earnings, or more than four times the average price-earnings multiple on the richly valued Tokyo Stock Exchange. "We're not talking about a stock market phenomenon," a British analyst in Tokyo commented. "We're talking about a social phenomenon. Everyone is buying because everyone else is buying."

Americans too were susceptible to the power of suggestion, and bull-market tendencies in lending and borrowing only intensified. The Dime Savings Bank of New York had caused a stir in 1986 by disclosing that it would lend up to $350,000 against a house without checking on the income statement of the borrower. One stipulation was that the borrower contribute a 20 percent down payment; another was that a "qualified appraisal" substantiate the value of the property. By early 1987, the no-questions-asked style of real-estate lending was catching on nationally. One reason was tax-related. Suppose, a banker mused at the time, a waiter earned $75,000 a year in cash but reported only $18,000 to the government. Would he not leap at a mortgage that required no disclosure of his tax returns? To ask the question was to answer it. Another reason was confidence-related. The Dime, in a 1986 prospectus, had chosen the word "rising" to describe the trend of real-estate prices in the New York metropolitan area. It did not state that they "had risen" until that moment and might be expected to continue to appreciate. Rather, they would just go on rising, and in holding to this faith Dime had plenty of company. Guardian Savings

& Loan Association of Long Beach, California, calculatedly lent to borrowers of checkered credit standing, provided that they held title to a house. It was the thrift's conviction that the value of the house would not decline. Thus the owner and president, Russell Jedinak (who was removed by federal regulators in 1991), said, "if the owner has a pulse, we'll give them a loan."*

Bad Deals Beget Worse

The tenth annual Drexel Burnham High Yield Bond Conference took place in Beverly Hills in April 1987, and it too was a mirror to the confident times. A reporter who did not attend interviewed a man who did, and the following report was filed:

Lots of foreigners in attendance—maybe 20 percent of the 3,000 or so people expected to pass through the turnstiles by Saturday. [Ted] Turner to speak Saturday on "macro-type subject," maybe arms control or world ecology. Aussie contingent conspicuous. Insurance companies well represented. Lots of equity-related types, too—maybe another 20 percent of gathering. Big push on for convertible bonds. Also—this an ominous note—a couple of dozen college professors on hand. (Has any important market ever topped out before academics blessed it?)

Much ado about recent improvement in the market-adjusted balance sheets of the junk issuers. Total equity (at market prices) of companies on hand to pitch conference was $6 billion in 1980. Now $60 billion. Market-adjusted debt-to-equity ratio of junk companies said to be at record low—say 30 percent vs. a post-recession high of 70 percent.

The first such Drexel confab, held in New York in 1978, drew 80 people, a remnant. The 10th—this one—may top 3,000, up from 2,500 or so in 1986.

Manic though credit might have been, it was prepared to become more so. King County Jail in Washington State began to accept bank

---

* In June 1991, Guardian was seized by the Resolution Trust Corp., and the immediate reason was also typical of the times. In 1978, the bank had paid $57 million to build its fourteen-story, heliport-bedecked headquarters. Thirteen years later, federal regulators pronounced that the building was worth only $29 million. So great was the necessary financial adjustment that it forced the bank into federal conservatorship.

credit cards in payment for bail, and a seventeen-year-old investment adviser predicted that the market would not look back. "I do not foresee, contrary to popular Wall Street opinion, any major correction in 1987," said Daniel Stein, of Greenwich High School in Connecticut. "The market should stay strong throughout the year." It had been strong, in fact, since he was twelve. Even when Citicorp chairman John Reed, in May, made the unexpected admission that the Third World debt on Citi's balance sheet was impaired and that he would set aside an allowance for possible future losses equivalent to 25 percent of the face amount of the loans, the ensuing disappointment was cushioned by the indulgent rules of regulatory accounting. The "allowance for possible credit losses" would be, as a layman might expect, treated as a charge against profits, and therefore as a reduction in the stockholders' investment. If that is where the matter had ended, Citi would have had to take hasty action to raise new capital (or to reduce its assets). But in 1987 that was not the last word on the subject. Under regulatory accounting, the "allowance" was treated as an addition to capital, not a reduction. In no other business but American banking, observed the author Martin Mayer, would such a miracle have been possible. The accounting rules presently became more stringent.

In July, Michael Milken, ordinarily as unapproachable as Garbo, gave *Forbes* an interview for the magazine's seventieth-birthday issue. "Milken is passionately committed to preaching the need for change—which happens to be the theme of this issue," said *Forbes*, explaining its readers' good fortune. The Milken of this unique interview was a financial statesman, futurologist, investor extraordinaire, and philosopher of the family. The interview touched on biographical details ("Young Mike had a head for numbers . . .") as well as on prescriptive ones ("In an industrial society, capital is a scarce resource but in today's information society, there's plenty of capital"). The measure of Milken's celebrity, however, was not the space accorded to his view on finance but the long exposition of his theory of the family. ("You can call me old-fashioned, but I think a child should be raised by both parents, and that children should grow up with discipline, a love of knowledge, security and respect for their elders.") The publicity of the federal investigation into his possible violation of the securities laws did not diminish his standing as a celebrity; rather the opposite.

Still, Drexel's bonds defaulted less frequently than those of many

*Indicted but not yet scorned: Michael Milken in the flesh (magnified by his own photographic image) addresses the Mexican and American Foundation's California Forum, 1989 (*BETTMANN ARCHIVE*)*

other Wall Street firms.* It was not Drexel Burnham but First Boston that underwrote the junk bonds for Harcourt Brace Jovanovich, the Orlando-based textbook publisher, amusement-park operator, and insurance underwriter, in September 1987. HBJ was a prime new-era specimen. To repel an attempted acquisition by Robert Maxwell, the

---

* Drexel issued $113 billion of junk bonds, of which (through September 1991) $20 billion defaulted. PaineWebber, for instance, issued $2.6 billion, of which $1.35 billion defaulted.

ill-fated British publisher, it had mounted its own "leveraged recapitalization," a maneuver entailing massive borrowings, a one-time dividend to the public stockholders, large repurchases of stock in the open market, and a memorable payday for the investment bankers, lawyers, and accountants who designed the transaction and who waited up all night at the printer's. (Fees totaled $67,256,000, a sum of money greater than Harcourt's net profits in the twelve months ended June 30, 1986.) The object was to make the company financially repellent—to reach the point, described in 1985 by Robert Pirie of Rothschild, "where someone can't leverage off you." HBJ took out a huge, preemptive mortgage.

The "discipline of debt" was a phrase on the tips of the tongues of the proponents of heavy borrowing, and the Harcourt management, as if it had just thought of the idea, pledged unstinting attention to cost control and the bottom line. Twenty-five percent of the company's new common stock would be sold to the management and employees, and the prospectus outlined the dividends that this change of ownership might pay:

> The company intends to reduce corporate overhead and generate cash by disposing of certain non-revenue-producing assets, including the sale of the company's airplanes, sale of apartments, and condominiums used by transient or newly hired employees, elimination of company-owned or -leased cars (except those needed in sales) and the sale of certain undeveloped land.

Seth Klarman, a Cambridge, Massachusetts, investor who attended a sales meeting in Boston for the Harcourt bonds, raised his hand when the subject of the corporate planes came up. "If you need them, why are you selling them," he asked, "and if you don't need them, why did you buy them?" Management answered with a rhetorical wink, and smiles crossed the faces of the underwriters. It was the kind of question that an experienced investor did not ask of a sophisticated investment banker in 1987.

As for the financial statements, they were no more appalling than usual, but no less appalling either. Long-term debt would be $2.8 billion and equity would be minus $1.6 billion. That, at least, was the stated value of the stockholders' investment on the balance sheet. The stock market, taking a far less jaundiced view of such transactions than accounting principles directed, valued the common at $500 million. The prospectus contained the customary warnings about the difficulties of servicing the debt, let alone redeeming it. Junk-bond buyers, however, as was their wont, read those warnings metaphorically rather than literally. The bonds found a ready market.

Before the television age, stock-market panics were fresh-air events. Crowds milled around the Stock Exchange and lined the steps of the Subtreasury Building. They fomented rumors and, in the days before deposit insurance, started bank runs. The collapse of October 19, 1987, despite a day of unsurpassed sunshine, was an indoor phenomenon. The principal loiterers outside the Stock Exchange doors were television crews. Nearly everybody else was in an office watching a screen.

Hardly had the dust settled when financial authorities were on the air explaining why the market had reduced its appraisal of American corporations by 22.6 percent in a single day. Drexel's chairman, Robert Linton, looked into a camera and condemned the federal budget deficit. Almost certainly, the deficit was not the cause—it had been considerably higher in years in which there had been no crash—but it was a handy and friendless target. At the peak of the market in August 1987, stocks were as richly valued as they had ever been. (On August 14, less than two weeks before the top, *The New York Times* foreshadowed events with an uncharacteristic stab at humor in the prose of its news summary: "The Dow gained, ho hum, another 22.17 points as Wall Street marked the fifth anniversary of the bull market.") The fad of "insuring" the value of one's stocks by attempting to sell futures contracts in a falling market introduced a new element of instability, and the popularity and prevalence of highly leveraged capital structures instilled the belief (until the crash, very much a minority opinion) that something terrible was likely to happen at any minute.

And then, after the crash, no abyss opened.* There was no recession, no bank run, and no collapse of junk-bond prices. Corporate earnings, which the stock market is allegedly in the business of anticipating, would in fact rise sharply in 1988. The break in Japanese stock prices was perfunctory and Japanese real-estate prices held their own. Because the price of a residence was hopelessly out of reach for the average Japanese buyer, banks began to offer the "two-generation" mortgage, in which the burden of debt was handed to son from father like an heirloom. The *New York Post* was presciently bullish (hold on,

---

* Even Drexel Burnham seemed prepared for one. Two days after the crash, on October 21, a Drexel-underwritten junk-bond issue, SCI Television, was offered with one of the most vivid regulatory disclaimers ever printed. "The Securities involve a high degree of risk," said the very front page of the prospectus, "and, accordingly, investors may lose their entire investment in the Securities." In fact, many investors came close.

the paper advised its mutual-fund-holding readers under the post-crash headline "Rally-ho"), while Irving Kristol, on the editorial page of *The Wall Street Journal*, was a little less forehanded, contending, ". . . there is practically no possibility of a collapse of the banking system." The system itself would not collapse but a sizable number of the banks comprising it would. The prices of bank loans to Third World countries (which by then were traded in the open market like bonds) actually rallied. On the Friday after the break, an all-news radio station in New York, WINS, broadcast a brief personal-finance commentary. Addressing any business executive engaged in a leveraged buyout, an authoritative-sounding voice advised that it was all right to take out a second mortgage on one's home to buy stock in one's heavily indebted company. In December, Southland Corporation, the company behind the 7-Eleven stores, raised some $4 billion in junk-grade debt and preferred stock to finance its own leveraged buyout. It offered yields so high—15¾ percent and up—as to be self-destructive. Literally, the company would not be able to pay the interest. However, the bonds were sold, proving that speculation was off the critical list and taking solid food again. (It was an old problem, and L. W. Youmans, the Fairfax, South Carolina, cotton planter, had crystallized it in testimony before the U.S. Industrial Commission around the turn of the century: "[Y]ou gentlemen know as well as I that there is no business except for successful mining and gambling that can stand 13 percent.")

Even granting the truism that history never exactly repeats itself, the wake of the crash was puzzling. The absence of any tangible economic damage was unexpected. So too was the almost immediate resumption of the speculative boom. However, facts were facts. October 19 was a panic, like 1907, as it developed, not a crash, like 1929. If the United States was carrying too much debt, that was itself (for the short term, at least) a sign of financial resiliency. It meant that creditors believed in debtors, or in the future, or in the government. Owing, in part, to the heavy element of federal subsidy in banking and mortgage credit, the country was able to carry more debt than it ever had before. Credit lay in the soft lap of the state. Not many market observers had noticed the advent of federalized credit, and not one in a thousand, probably, opposed it.* According to a school of economics identified with the Nobel laureate Friedrich von Hayek,

* Testifying before the Senate Banking Committee in June 1987, Walter B. Wriston, retired Citicorp chairman but active free-market proponent, fielded a question on federal deposit insurance. "How important is it to commercial banking or to those entities that now have insured deposits that they continue to have them?" Senator Donald Riegle (D., Mich.) asked him.

excessive credit creation elicits wasteful investments and diverts capital and labor from their most productive uses. Whatever its economic merits, it is a theory not calculated to change congressional votes. The political choices in 1988 were essentially these: (a) to suffer a contraction of credit and the attendant loss of jobs in the name of weaning the nation from subsidized credit in all its multibillion-dollar manifestations, thus avoiding bigger financial trouble down the road, or (b) to try to perpetuate the boom in the interest of getting reelected. It was (b) by a landslide.

Field Trip to Dallas

On February 25, 1988, Thomas Gale Moore, a member of the President's Council of Economic Advisers, said in a public talk that the United States could simply print the dollars it owes to foreign investors if it ever felt that it had to. He hastened to add that that was not his idea of sound policy. But, he said, the presses could roll if they must. The story moved on the Dow Jones news wire (although not in next day's financial press), and its lead was incendiary:

WASHINGTON—The U.S. transition to a net debtor nation is not a significant problem, in part because the country could pay off its creditors simply by running the currency printing press, Thomas Gale Moore, a member of the President's Council of Economic Advisers, said. . . .

"Well, I think it's very important," Wriston replied. ". . . My suggestion was that it should be limited to some reasonable amount which was designed to protect small people. One hundred thousand dollars in an inflationary world is O.K. That's very important."

When Wriston asserted that it was also important not to extend blanket guarantees, as the government had done to Continental Illinois, Riegle interjected another question. Is the banking system too fragile to absorb such a failure if one were allowed to occur?

Wriston said what he always had said to that question. He replied that the banking system was stronger and free markets more resilient than most people realized. However, in this one instance, he seemed to forget himself. "Goldman, Sachs remembers that the Penn Central had $300 million [$200 million, in fact, at the maximum] of commercial paper coming due one day, and the Fed was very excited about that and the market took it and the system worked."

What Wriston neglected to add was that Citibank, then under his leadership, had applied to the Federal Reserve Bank of New York for federal guarantees on $200 million of Penn Central bank debt. As already mentioned, the putative legal authority for this attempted raid on the Treasury was the Defense Production Act of 1950. No such accommodation was obtained. To that extent, "the system worked."

"We can pay off anybody by running a printing press, frankly," Moore said, "so it's not clear to me how bad that [the transition to net debtor status] is."

Those remarks elicited no direct reaction in the bond market. In a jittery time, they might have shattered the peace and undermined confidence, but the post-crash mood was unflappable. Credit expanded and the terms and conditions of lending continued to be relaxed. It presently became possible to borrow 95 percent of the cost of a Yugo automobile on five-year terms and (if one were Robert Campeau, the Canadian real-estate developer) to borrow $1.1 billion to purchase a department-store chain while serving a blunt and accurate warning to one's potential bondholders that they might never see their money again.

The stock market crash was not the only financial event of that time to occur in a seeming economic vacuum. The Texas real-estate market was also crashing, and Texas banks were failing, but the diversified Dallas economy was conspicuously not falling in on itself. In the 1980s, every important Texas bank went bankrupt or was merged or required assistance from the federal government. It was a wholesale rout—349 banks failed outright—and it made vivid the abstract proposition that credit risk is increasingly borne by the taxpayers. The big Dallas banks had weathered the Depression of the 1930s and the recession of the mid-1970s. It was the received wisdom of the 1970s and early 1980s that another depression was impossible, that modern banks do not fail (thanks to federal deposit insurance) and that inflation is a permanent American condition (as a result of the Employment Act of 1946). However, the impossible proceeded to happen.

Early in 1988, Frederick E. "Shad" Rowe, a Texas investor, declared that no one could understand American finance who did not understand Texas. At the time, the bear market in Texas assets had lost its power to shock. For instance, the price of Dallas office space had already fallen to $50 or $60 per square foot from the 1984 peak of perhaps $150 per square foot; the current level was substantially less than the cost of new construction. In growing numbers, Dallas homeowners were choosing to lease their houses rather than sell them, because the market price had fallen below the amount of the mortgage, wiping out their equity. The equivalent of the entire downtown Boston office market existed in Dallas as empty space. The average office vacancy rate in Austin, Dallas, Houston, and San Antonio was 30 percent, up from 16 percent in 1985, when the *Dallas Morning News*

disclosed that the local real-estate market was becoming a little overbuilt. The existence of the glut was no secret in real-estate circles,
but its public disclosure galvanized fear and the bulls began a long
and sullen rearguard action. ("It's overbuilt now, sure. A lot of people
get worried," a North Dallas land broker complained to the paper.
"But sometimes I think it's just more satisfying to write about
doomsayers.")

If the Texas fiasco had been a purely regional matter—a case of
weak oil prices and a few rogue thrift institutions, for example—there
would have been nothing to visit. However, as Rowe insisted, the
import was broader. The cause of the collapse in banking and real
estate was excessive lending and borrowing on generous and socialized
terms. "Basically," said Rowe, "a guy who drills oil wells will keep
drilling until he can't get any more money. And a guy who builds
office buildings will keep building until he runs out of money. And a
takeover artist will keep on buying companies until *he* runs out of
money. There's nothing different about Texas. If you wanted to know
how World War II was going to be fought, you had to see the Spanish
Revolution. Well, Dallas is the Spanish Revolution of finance. It's the
preview—we developed the Stuka dive bombers of leverage down
here—and you've got to come see it."

Rowe was irresistible, and I packed my bags. Dallas, Rowe promised, was a laboratory for a modern debt deflation. In previous deflations, the value of money rose, banks failed, the availability of credit
shrank, and interest rates charged to speculative borrowers went up.
No such event had occurred in North America since the 1930s, however, and contemporary Dallas presented a hybrid.* The cab ride in

---

* The collapse of the Chicago real-estate market in the Great Depression was described
in one efficient paragraph by Homer Hoyt. The experience in Texas in the mid-1980s
and in New England and New York a few years later exhibited similar tendencies,
certainly in the morale of creditors. One key difference, of course, was federal deposit
insurance. None was to be had in 1932:

"The contraction of credit began with the failure of owners to meet second-mortgage
charges which began in 1928. As rents declined, owners began to fail to meet even
the charges on the first mortgages . . . and, as the first mortgages were foreclosed, the
second mortgages were wiped out. After 1929 the outlying [i.e., suburban] banks with
their assets, including savings deposits largely in real estate, were unable to liquidate
on the dull and declining market, and the failure of 155 banks from October, 1929,
to July, 1932, reduced their number to 45. These failures absorbed community savings,
paralyzed business initiative in the vicinity, and rendered money for even conservative
real estate financing unavailable. The banks and insurance companies still solvent
passed from one extreme to another. Whereas in 1928 first-mortgage bonds were made
for as high as four or five times the inflated annual income, in 1932 a first-mortgage
loan could scarcely be made for over double the depressed income of a building in a
good location."

from the airport—$28, with tip—was not unlike the inflationary cab rides available in New York. The daily room rate at the Mansion Hotel—$225—also seemed high, for a deflationary region, and the average Dallasite on the street seemed oblivious that he or she was supposed to be living out scenes from the Hoover administration. The city's skyline shone, and one could not see through the vacant office buildings, even though they were called "see-throughs"; the window glass was tinted. Later, on a driving tour of the surplus real-estate district in North Dallas, Rowe noted the presence of cars in some of the parking lots serving the new office buildings. He expressed surprise, as a New Yorker might start at the sight of a deer in Central Park.

All in all, the incidence of money still seemed high. In fact, as the matter was later explained, Dallas had managed to post slight net increases in employment since the oil and real-estate depressions began. Also, in 1987, consumer prices in Dallas–Fort Worth rose by a nondeflationary 4.3 percent. Banks had fallen, the bankruptcy courts were full, and BMW sales had collapsed, but the nonspeculative economy had gone about its business. If, five years earlier, one had predicted that Texas banking would come a cropper but the Dallas economy would continue to function, one would probably have been branded a double lunatic. "It's been a depression of the rich," a developer said.

In a subsequent postmortem, the FDIC observed that the leading Texas banks were painfully slow to react to overbuilding. In fact, the percentage of assets devoted by Texas banks to construction and commercial real estate increased in lockstep with the rise in office vacancy rates. Describing boom-time lending practices, Preston Carter, a friend of Rowe's, related, "I used to pick up the phone. 'I just bought so and so,' I'd tell the bank. Deposit so much in my account. Will be by this afternoon. . . . The notes used to be so square," he said, holding a pair of index fingers six inches apart. " 'I promise to pay.' " Now, said Carter, indicating a telephone directory, the documents are "so thick." He said that the shorter ones were harder to get out of. "There is no defense for 'I promise to pay,' " he said.

"Bank holding company shareholders appear to have supported the shift toward commercial real-estate lending," the FDIC concluded. "Indeed, shareholders did not appear to have anticipated the consequences of increased lending to commercial real estate, as vacancy rates grew. Bank stock prices did, however, react quickly to reductions in profits. In addition," the agency continued, commendably questioning its own mandate, "uninsured depositors appear to have reacted more slowly than shareholders to the deteriorating condition of these banks. The slow reaction of uninsured depositors may have been due, in part, to their expectation that any failure resolution transaction [i.e., federal bailout] would have resulted in their full protection, as had been the case in the handling of Continental Illinois, the largest bank rescued to that point." And in fact, not a dime in uninsured deposits was lost. (On New Year's Eve 1988, a small, uninsured Texas bank closed its doors, not because it was insolvent but because its time was past. The D. & A. Oppenheimer Bank in San Antonio, founded before the Civil War, chose to liquidate. It gave among other reasons the burden of new regulations that the state had chosen to heap on it. "No one holds the banker accountable," a customer of the bank said sadly of the old regime. "I could hold Dan Oppenheimer responsible. That's what I miss.")

In Dallas, the question was asked: What went wrong? One banker replied by drawing a pair of curves on a sheet of paper. He labeled one curve "real estate" and the other "oil," and he observed that both had turned down at about the same time. He also mentioned the federal tax laws, recently made hostile to speculative real-estate transactions, and the administration's successful assault on inflation. He asked how the hell one could have foreseen all of that.

His theory—a confluence-of-fate idea—competed for adherents in Dallas with a conspiracy idea. (Few seemed to espouse the self-blame idea.) "They took our liquidity away," stated one theorist, blaming the Federal Reserve. Under questioning, the man, a real-estate developer who had been up in the boom and down in the bust, admitted that the Fed could hardly create credit in one state without creating it in all the others at the same time. That wasn't the point, he said. He identified the point as regulatory persecution. He said that the Fed could just as easily have sent its bank examiners into New York as into Texas.

Homer B. Vanderblue, a contemporary historian of the Florida land bubble of the 1920s, wrote futilely of Miami's skyscrapers: "These buildings should stand for a long time as monuments to folly, and by so standing they will warn against a recurrence of a boom psychology." Little did he suspect that reform ultimately, after the passage of generations, would make the banking system more boom-prone, not less so.

Junk Auto Loans

"They're like cows," said Carter of the Texas lenders he knew. "You open the gate, one goes out, and they all go out." A Gresham's law of credit was in operation in the 1980s, in and out of Texas. Lenient lending terms drove out conservative ones. The tendency was visible in all walks of financial life and in a variety of different markets. Automobile credit makes a particularly telling case study. No tax-related reasons explain the proliferation of easy lending. Neither did corporate control or the ideal of the Noble Entrepreneur (debt is good because it is such a hard taskmaster, the argument went) have anything to do with it. Competing to sell more cars, banks and finance companies offered longer maturities, smaller down payments, and lower interest rates. In the early 1970s, the average length of a new-car loan was three years; by the late 1980s, it was pushing five years. In the early 1970s, lenders financed 86 percent to 88 percent of the price of a new car; by the late 1980s, they were financing 94 percent. "These elements caused the monthly auto payment as a percent of disposable income per household to fall to 10 percent from the prevailing 12 percent to 13 percent level of the 1970s," noted the economist Susan Sterne.

For a time, the consequences of this liberalization were only happy ones. Auto sales climbed whereas delinquencies and repossessions did not. Thanks to longer loans and lower interest rates, a 30 percent rise in the selling price of the average new car between 1983 and 1988 became a 20 percent rise in the average monthly payment. By the summer of 1988, however, the "dealer insolvency issue" was coming to the fore, and the trade press was warning of the consequences of easy credit on retail trade-ins. It was well and good that more people had bought more cars in the early and middle years of the decade. What was increasingly uncertain was whether the same people would have the means to buy another new car in the late part of the decade. Trends were not propitious. A new phrase—"upside down"—entered the auto-finance vocabulary. It described the condition of a car owner who owed more on his outstanding loan than he could get in a trade-in. Such a person was in the same predicament as the Dallas home-owner whose mortgage was greater than the resale value of his house. In both cases, the temptation was strong to walk away, dropping the keys in the mailbox or sticking them above the sun visor.* By the end of the decade, repossessions were rising briskly (General Motors' were up by 23 percent in 1988 compared to 1987), and banks and automobile finance companies, in belated reaction to credit losses, had begun to tighten terms. In early 1991 it was estimated that as many as 30 percent of potential new-car buyers were unable to find a loan.

The ultimate auto-finance story of the 1980s was that of the Yugo, *Motor Trend Magazine*'s "Import Car of the Year" for 1985 and for a time the fastest-selling import in the under-$6,000 price range in America. The Yugo was the automotive epitome of excessive optimism. It was conceived by the entrepreneur Malcolm Bricklin and manufactured by Zavodi Crvena Zastava of Yugoslavia. As junk bonds were sold on yield, the Yugo GV ("great value") was sold on price: $3,990.

Right from the start, Yugo had its public detractors. In December 1985, only months after the first cars had rolled off the boat, a review in *The Washington Post* by Warren Brown ("If Yugo For It, You Could Be Sorry") served fair warning. "It is pitilessly uncomfortable," wrote Brown. "The Yugo does not handle well, certainly nowhere near as well as many rival subcompacts." *Consumer Reports* repeated the gist of that analysis in a preliminary review in 1986. Not until 1988, however, did the Yugo receive the magazine's full and undivided attention. For six pages, the dandy little import was ripped to shreds, but a prospective buyer could have saved himself time by skipping to the conclusion. "[I]f you can overlook the way it's put together, you're sure to tire of its weak performance, barely operable transmission, and Spartan accommodations. The money saved in buying a Yugo may well be spent in maintaining it. Damage to the car in our bumper-basher tests totaled $1,372. In addition, the model has a much-worse-than-average repair record with many trouble spots."

Trying to regroup, Yugo unveiled a new warranty (one year/12,000 miles) and a $500 rebate. Two months later, in March 1988, it bumped up the rebate to $750, the equivalent of 17 percent of the purchase

---

* Or in the cabin of a boat. Ultraliberal terms in marine finance had created a generation of upside-down boat owners. *Soundings Trade Only*, a marine paper published in Essex, Connecticut, reported in December 1989 that the problem had begun to crop up in 1988. Boat dealers complained to manufacturers, and manufacturers complained to lenders. "Influenced by the excellent performance of marine loans—they have lower late-payment and default rates than auto and credit-card loans—scores of lenders have entered the marine industry to generate new business," the paper said. "These lenders have offered lower down payments and longer terms to attract boat buyers." First Financial Group, Wall Township, New Jersey, offered a no-money-down loan on a purchase of $50,000 or less and a 10 percent-down loan on a purchase of more than $50,000. The interest rate was 12½ percent over fifteen years.

price. Still, consumers were wary, and in August, Yugo announced its pièce de résistance, a revolutionary, quintessentially 1980s finance plan: 5 percent down and five years to pay. Imperial Savings Association, later to be sunk by junk bonds, signed up to lend to the Yugo Credit Corporation.

Within four months, Imperial was setting aside reserves for possible credit losses against every Yugo advance it had made, $16 million worth. A few weeks later, in January 1989, Yugo America filed for protection under Chapter 11 of the federal bankruptcy code. As might be imagined, the news did not enhance the value of existing Yugos or improve the service at Yugo dealerships. It was the experience of more than one owner that the cars essentially blew up after the warranty period elapsed. It began with little things, like the window handles. Then it seemed that many parts of the plastic-quality interior were prone to dislocation. Presently, nonoptional equipment—the starter, for example—stopped working.

The Barnett Bank of West Florida in Pensacola did some of the lending against this short-lived collateral. It lent for forty-eight months and sometimes, when it couldn't be helped, for as many as sixty months. "Borrowers had broken-down cars, couldn't get 'em fixed, and were turning them back to the bank," Rick Masser, senior loan officer at Barnett (but not at the time of the debacle), recalled. He said that the car-loan maturities were lengthening under the press of competition. The choice for Barnett was to lend for the long pull or to relinquish the business to Chrysler Credit of Mobile, Alabama. Barnett lent, and it lent long-term. It financed the purchase of 1,500 Yugos, of which it repossessed 150. "Normally," Masser explained, "if we take back more than one in a hundred, we're not breaking even." Yugo was one of those less-than-break-even propositions.

Gordon Cain, the Great

There were many spectacularly successful propositions, of course, and they played an important inspirational role in prolonging the up cycle. Of these triumphs of debt, none was more brilliant than the purchase and sale of the Cain Chemical Company of Houston. Gordon A. Cain, a septuagenarian visionary, had accumulated a string of seven modern (but temporarily unwanted) petrochemical plants along the Gulf Coast of Texas for a cost of $1.1 billion. Only $25 million of this price was paid in equity; the balance was borrowed from banks and raised in the junk-bond market. Less than a year later, in April 1988, Occidental took the property off the owners' hands for $2.2 billion, a price that represented a 44-fold return on the equity investment ("an impressive rate of return," *The New York Times* laconically noted). The Chase Manhattan Bank and Morgan, Stanley & Co., Cain's financial advisers, lenders, and investment partners, each earned $120 million. Gordon Cain himself justly pocketed $100 million on an investment of $2.3 million. "He saw the industry turn before anyone else did," said a Wall Street analyst who was able to find some words, any words, to describe this dumbfounding feat. "He bought these plants at the absolute bottom of the market."

Gordon Cain was a genuine hero. Most of the 1,300 Cain employees received at least $100,000 apiece as their share of the investment windfall. Workers who joined the company too late to get into the employee stock-ownership program received an extra year's pay. Workers who had forgone the chance to contribute to the plan received $10,000 in consolation. Under Cain's brief ownership tenure, the plants had been revitalized by employees' active and enthusiastic participation in day-to-day management. It was a display of capitalism the likes of which, had it been publicized behind the Iron Curtain, might have started a workers' revolt against communist rule years ahead of historical schedule.

Charles Keating, the Miserable

But there was no gainsaying the collectivist side of the Republican financial boom. One of the leading beneficiaries of this public-private collaboration was Charles Keating, Jr., thrift executive, trafficker in political influence, founding father of Citizens for Decent Literature, Catholic layman, and college All-American swimmer. Keating purchased his thrift, Lincoln Savings and Loan Association, with the help of junk bonds issued by Drexel Burnham Lambert, in 1984. He wasted no time converting what had been a conventional mortgage-making institution into a buyer of junk bonds and a collector of commercial real estate. It was only to be expected that Lincoln would have a holding company. American Continental Corporation (ACC) was this inevitable entity, and it issued junk bonds to finance itself. It sold them through the twenty-nine branches of Lincoln Savings. One glance at the prospectus invited the suspicion that the American Continental bonds were among the worst investments available in America.

The savings and loan crisis in person: Charles H. Keating, Jr., brought to book, 1990 (WIDE WORLD PHOTOS)

As against putative net worth of $137 million, the company (that is, parent and subsidiary combined) held $622 million of junk bonds and $821 million in real estate—not real-estate loans but real-estate "investments." In fact, Lincoln, the principal subsidiary, was not a "thrift" at all but an enterprise to gather federally insured deposits for the purpose of gambling in securities and real estate. Its profits, such as they were, stemmed not from the difference between the cost of its funds and the yield on its loans. Rather, they were the product of gains on the sale of land, bonds, or buildings. American Continental, like any Wall Street hedge fund, was in the business of buying low and selling high, except that the Federal Savings and Loan Insurance Corporation generously insured its liabilities.

The Bank of United States, which existed before the dawn of federal securities regulation, kept its investors in the dark. American Continental, on the other hand, spelled out most of the incriminating details in its obligatory bond prospectuses. The cover page clearly specified that the bonds were not insured by the FSLIC (Lincoln's deposits were, but not the parent's bonds). However, that vital information was not conveyed to every buyer. Indeed, according to a memo addressed to the company's bond salesmen and later read, devastatingly, into the court record, the "meek, weak and ignorant" were the best sales prospects. (Keating said that he would recommend the bonds to Mother Teresa, although that was apparently not what the memo was driving at.)

In testimony reminiscent of the Congressional Committee to Investigate Real Estate Bond Reorganizations in 1935, Mark Johnson, a former clothing salesman who went to work for Lincoln Savings in 1986, said in a sworn statement: "As a teller, I was limited to what I could tell prospective clients about the bond program. As time went on, however, the sales policies became more lax. Eventually, the only thing I could not do as a teller was to sign the purchase agreement." Johnson said that he would call Lincoln depositors as their federally insured certificates of deposit were falling due. He would offer them a higher-yielding investment to replace what they had—that is, the uninsured junk bonds of American Continental Corporation. Skirting the lack of deposit insurance, Johnson said, he would let it drop that the bonds were "backed" by over $5 billion in assets. The assets furnished no such backing, of course, but a $5 billion number was calculated to sound impressive over the telephone. When, in April 1989, American Continental filed for bankruptcy protection and Lincoln Savings was seized by federal regulators, $200 million worth of American Continental's bonds were outstanding. They were, by then, virtually worthless. On September 19, 1990, the day after Keating was indicted for fraud and jailed, the *Los Angeles Times* reported that Martin Fowler, seventy-nine, had bought $14,000 in bonds without being given a prospectus and without being told that his investment was uninsured. "A resident of Bellflower," according to the paper, "Fowler said he needed the money to care for his forty-year-old daughter, who has Down's syndrome."

Campeau Rolls the Dice

A market that financed the speculative adventures of Charles Keating with almost no questions asked was a market that was prepared to finance almost anybody. "There are lots of people out there writing checks," said Bruce Wasserstein in the summer of 1988. "This is a very liquid world." Wasserstein, the Babe Ruth of the First Boston investment banking department, along with Joseph R. Perella, the Gehrig, had left First Boston to form their own "merchant bank," Wasserstein, Perella & Co., on February 2. On July 27, a 20 percent interest in the new firm was acquired by Nomura Securities for $100 million. The sale implied a market value for Wasserella (as the venture was instantly and irreverently known) of $500 million and a theoretical daily accretion of value of $2.8 million since the principals quit their jobs. Wasserstein had a point about the availability of funds. It was in the same summer that Sewell Avery's pride and joy, U.S. Gypsum, entered the junk-bond market to protect itself from a threatened take-over, following the lead of Harcourt, Brace.

There was gullibility as well as misjudgment. Jeff (Mad Dog) Beck, self-described war hero, former CIA agent, and tycoon (Beck's beer was a family brand, he said), got ahead on Wall Street. By the time he was exposed as a compulsive, big-screen liar, he had risen to the upper echelons of the investment banking department of Drexel Burnham. William J. Stoecker, a bearded, thirtyish former welder with a line of blarney about the rust-belt renaissance, was able to borrow some $400 million from a half dozen major banks on the putative value of the business he owned, Grabill Corporation (founded in 1981), as well as on his own alleged net worth and demonstrated business acumen. It presently came out that Stoecker was a faker and that the banks, especially the doomed Bank of New England, had, as Walter J. Connolly, Jr., the Bank of New England's chairman, put it, "misjudged the character of the borrower." An exchange between Stoecker and Ed Bradley of the television show *60 Minutes* in the summer of 1990 vividly illustrated Connolly's point. Bradley asked Stoecker about some financial statements that he, Stoecker, knew to be fraudulent:

BRADLEY: Then why, when you saw that figure, why didn't you call the banks and say, "Hey, guys, wait a minute, there's a problem here, these companies that my accounting firm, Laventhol and Horwath,* have certified as being worth $232 million are not worth

---

* Stoecker's auditors themselves filed for bankruptcy protection in 1990, an indirect casualty of the Stoecker affair and a bellwether of trouble for the office-building market. If professional firms too could fail, the outlook for white-collar employment was dimmed.

quite that much. And if there's a problem I think you ought to be aware of it"?
STOECKER: Why would I?

If, by emphasizing "character" as the basis of credit during his famous testimony at the Money Trust hearings of 1912, J. P. Morgan had sounded an antidemocratic or exclusionist note, Wall Street, by the late 1980s, was bending over backwards to make amends. Robert Campeau had hardly digested the acquisition of Allied Stores when he set his cap for the Federated Department Stores chain, owner of (among other properties) Bloomingdale's, Abraham & Straus, Burdines, Lazarus, Rich's, and Goldsmith's. This was in January 1988, and the price he proposed to pay, $4.2 billion, caused skeptics once more to press their temples hard with their fingertips. When, however, on April 1, he agreed to pay $6.6 billion, there was nothing left to do. Edward Finkelstein, chairman of R. H. Macy, who finished second to Campeau in the competition for Federated, heaved a sigh of relief. "We're both lucky to get out of this alive," he said, evidently from the heart. "I'm very pleased that I don't have to deal with it and he does."

Thus was clinched one of the least inhibited transactions of the era. Campeau was able to borrow nearly the entire purchase price: $3.25 billion from a dozen banks, $2.1 billion from a trio of brokerage houses (First Boston, PaineWebber, and Dillon Read), in the shape of a "bridge loan," and most of the $1.4 billion of "equity." Of the so-called equity, only $195 million was not borrowed. This hard core of equity, secured by the sale of an Allied Stores unit, Brooks Brothers, represented less than 3 percent of the purchase price. It was less than the $224 million in front-end fees that Campeau had agreed to pay to his banks.

The 1987 Campeau Corporation annual report appeared later that spring. It was opulent to the touch and its prose style was *faux* Churchillian. "In retailing and real estate," it said on page 4, "industries that have become predictably conservative over the years, Campeau is a company that is prepared to take calculated risks. Campeau Corporation has the visionary qualities to see what others do not, to act while others hesitate, and to create value in innovative ways."

Without the shortsightedness of his creditors, however, Campeau's vision might have been realized, even for the brief period preceding the bankruptcy of his department-store acquisitions on January 15, 1990. The Federated merger posed the usual startling asymmetry between the potential gains of the lenders and principals. If Campeau succeeded, his vistas were unlimited. In that happy event, the creditors would get their money back, which, however, they had before Campeau borrowed it. If (as duly happened) the speculation collapsed, the lenders would bear the brunt of the losses. The lead banks earned substantial fees for agreeing to lend, and those would cushion their losses. So too with the junk-bond underwriters. There were $27 million in underwriting fees, $133 million in merger and acquisition fees, $70 million in bridge-loan fees, $100 million in interest on the bridge loan, and $19 million (for First Boston alone) in advisory fees. Rank-and-file creditors had no similar protection, however. Their only line of defense was the creditworthiness of the borrower.

Still, worry was not the prevalent creditor attitude of the day. One hopeful headline in the *Christian Science Monitor* that June—"Bond funds with higher yields aren't necessarily riskier"—distilled the new outlook. In July, it came to light that Campeau, in the 1960s, had simultaneously kept two wives and two sets of children in Montreal, neither knowing about the existence of the other. The source of this information was *The New York Times Magazine*. It was not the kind of news that would have sped a loan application through a bank in Morgan's day, but it seemed to do Campeau no harm in Wasserstein and Perella's. Nor did the fact, as the *Times* piece also disclosed, that Campeau was subject to bouts of severe depression. (Campeau was not the only debtor celebrity in the public eye. At the Tyson-Spinks heavyweight title fight a few weeks earlier, one of the first notables to be introduced to the crowd from ringside was "Fi-nan-seer Carl Icahn!")

The evolution of the Federated chain raised provocative questions about the mountain of junk bonds that Campeau proposed to sell to the public. The great department-store merchants had helped to bring debt to Main Street in the first place. Fred Lazarus, Jr., born into a family of Columbus, Ohio, merchants, was credited with overhauling turn-of-the-century credit practices. "In his youth," according to the author Leon Harris, "the store had required a chattel mortgage on whatever it sold for only a down payment. But reclaimed merchandise usually sold for less than the cost of repossessing it, so Fred dropped the mortgages, steadily reduced the percentage of down payment until it reached 20 percent, and then declared, 'If we're willing to trust people for 80 percent, we might just as well trust them for all of it.' " Reading that, an introspective bear was bound to admit that he would probably have resisted the liberalizing tendencies in consumer credit had he been around to deplore them decades earlier. Lazarus and A. P. Giannini, Bank of America's progressive founder, had profited in a market that conservative businessmen shunned, and the expansion of personal borrowing had continued until that very day without noticeable ill effect.

F. & R. Lazarus & Co. did not become the biggest department store in the world, but it joined what would become the largest department-store chain. Federated Department Stores was incorporated in November 1929, a month after Crash No. 1. In its first year of operation, a Depression year, its net income covered its fixed charges by a factor of more than three. The new Federated, by contrast, had thus far failed to cover fixed charges by even a factor of one. It reported no net income, as a matter of fact; massive interest expense created net losses. In the late 1920s, corporate leverage was not yet orthodox, and when Bloomingdale's went public in 1926, *The New York Times* approvingly noted that it "has no funded debt and no bank loans and has not been a borrower for many years." Federated survived the Depression, and Bloomingdale's was able to produce record sales in 1932. On the other hand, the new, fashion-forward Federated saw its debt rating slashed to B2, or junk grade, from Aa2, or blue-chip grade, after the Campeau purchase in April 1988. The rating was cut another notch, to B3, by the time the bonds came to market in November. One source of investment competition for the new Federated bonds was the Allied Stores securities, issued by Campeau in 1986. These bore telltale yields. The $25 Allied preferred, for example, was offered at $15.50, for a promised return of no less than 54 percent by the hoped-for maturity of March 1990. "As a result of the increased level of debt and the related principal and interest obligations," the prospectus noted, "the company may be less able than it has been to meet its obligations in the event of a downturn in its business or the economy or any increase in competitive pressure (especially price pressure by less highly leveraged competitors)."

The facts and figures were frightening, as usual. For one thing, net sales in the latest six-month period had actually fallen, by 0.6 percent, versus the year-earlier period. In the future, they would have to increase merely to make the capital structure viable; standing still would not be good enough. For another thing, as the prospectus noted, the bondholders occupied the bottommost rung on the ladder of credit, below the bank lenders as well as "substantially all other publicly and privately held debt of the company." Equity investors in Campeau Corporation at least shared a harmony of interest with Campeau himself. Not so the Federated bondholders, whose interests, in fact, were antithetical to the owners'. If push came to shove, they could expect no help from the executive suite.

In 1930, the "Broad Street Gossip" column of *The Wall Street Journal* ventured, apropos of the debate on installment credit that was then raging: "The wage earner has as much right to do business on credit as the millionaire." In the 1980s, the ideology of corporate leverage was even more progressive. Like Milken, Campeau played the role of the outsider. Through debt, entrepreneurs could breach the walls of the establishment. Debt made you free (from the Wall Street vantage point, of course, the ideology was considerably more practical: the fees produced by underwriting debt made you rich). So strong was the appeal of that message that the Federated Department Stores junk, despite every good reason not to buy it, found a market.

Real Estate Resurgent

So numerous and widely scattered were the cases of reckless lending in the 1980s that it is tempting to lump them all together and lay the blame on some cosmic, nonfinancial, even extraterrestrial cause. Certainly, no one macroeconomic factor (the Tax Act of 1986, for instance) can begin to explain the rich variety of markets, and, indeed, countries, in which lenders lost their heads. In the United States, creditors ran amok in commercial real estate, among other things. As Texas went, so went the nation. As office vacancy rates climbed, so did the percentage of bank loans secured by office buildings. The serial failure of the big Texas banks seemed not to register on bankers in other parts of the country.* In New York, for instance, the rate of growth in real-estate lending exceeded 20 percent a year as recently as the first quarter of 1990, or just before the public embarrassment of the

---

* There was one brilliant exception at least, that of Edward J. Powers, director of research and consulting economist at William Witter, Inc. "Boston, the New Houston," was the incendiary title of Powers's two-page report of December 1989. "After 27 years as a regional bank stock analyst, I believe that the New England economy has entered into a six- to eight-year decline which will rival the Texas economic decline," he wrote, for reasons that proved to be all too prophetic. Real estate, financial services, technology, and defense spending, the four pillars of the New England economy, all were crumbling, he contended, at a time when "Boston is no Dallas" was the conventional wisdom. "So we have it," he concluded, "the same scenario as in Texas. Real-estate fortunes built on financial-service fortunes built on technology fortunes. In Texas, it was real-estate fortunes, built on oil fortunes, built on cotton and cattle fortunes. Each pillar or pyramid fed the other until the cash flow stopped."

Inventor of Real Estate, Donald J. Trump. Between 1984 and 1989, real-estate lending accounted for 60 percent of the net loan growth of the U.S. banking system.

As junk-bond buyers could have read the prospectuses, so bankers could have read the newspapers. It was in 1984, toward the beginning of the real-estate stampede, that *The Wall Street Journal* reported: "Office Construction Boom Persists Despite Record Rate for Vacancies." In the story, a Houston real-estate developer, defending the decision to build a fifty-three-story, one-million-square-foot tower in a city where 21 percent of the office space was already vacant, said, "Major oil companies are almost like the government; they don't contract that much." A New York developer said, "We're beating inflation with office buildings and hotels." And a California banker said, "Even with some hiccups and glitches in the market, real estate has always performed well." In fact, oil companies were shrinking, inflation was tapering down, and real-estate investments were lagging. "Banks are making such loans because their business-loan activity is suffering from competition with commercial paper," wrote the *Journal*'s reporter on his own authority. It was an accurate description of a principal motive for lending, but it begged the question of how, and in what condition, the money would ever be returned. Bankers had to lend: as the rate of return on liquid assets, like Treasury bills, was below the cost of paying depositors, there seemed to be no alternative. "Lenders, Needing to Lend, 'Go For Broke' in Soft Market," reported *Real Estate Times*, in 1988. It was a headline worth a thousand words.

More than one-third of the office space ever built in the United States was constructed in the 1980s, and a ten-year inventory overbore the national market in 1990. Coincidentally, in 1991, office employment turned down for the first time in a decade or more. Japanese investors, who for years had bid eagerly for American property, stepped back from the market. American pension funds, which, in the 1980s, had boosted their real-estate investment to $125 billion from $25 billion, reconsidered that commitment in the light of poor returns. Since late in 1986, real estate had posted a lower rate of return than the lowly three-month Treasury bill. By the late 1980s, real estate was eclipsing Third World debt as the nation's top banking problem.

It was also becoming one of the world's. Real-estate lending as a percentage of total loans outstanding had climbed in Japan and the United Kingdom as well as in the United States. For instance, according to the Bank for International Settlements, between the end of 1985 and 1989 construction loans by Japanese banks grew at the annual rate of 20 percent. In 1980, the BIS estimated, real-estate lending by Japanese banks constituted 11 percent of their overall loan portfolios. In 1989, it was 17 percent. "In the United States, but also in the United Kingdom and Japan," the BIS noted, "banks have lost some of their best corporate customers to the capital markets."

In the United States, many disturbing features of the real-estate lending crisis were unprecedented. The scale of involvement by big, nationally chartered banks was new, as was the concentration of lending in one particular troubled class of asset.* "When LDCs [less developed countries] were a problem," said Carole S. Berger, a banking analyst and senior vice president for C. J. Lawrence, Inc., in testimony before the Senate Banking Committee in early 1991, "they were a huge problem for the dozen largest banks, where exposures averaged under 12 percent of total loans. For the banking system as a whole, however, LDC debt never exceeded 5 percent of total loans." Neither did agricultural or energy loans.

Berger estimated that commercial real-estate mortgage loans accounted for 18 percent of the total loans of American banks. She said that real-estate construction loans amounted to another 7 percent of bank lending. In a worst case, she ventured (now receiving the full attention of the senators and staff), property values nationally might fall by 50 percent. Such a thing would be possible if cash flows fell by as much as they had already fallen in Boston and New York. In that case, she said, banks might ultimately have to charge off one-third of their real-estate loans. That would be the equivalent of 6 or 7 percent of their total assets and roughly equivalent to their entire equity and reserves. "Therefore," the witness wound up, "if these charge-offs were required quickly, it could cause the insolvency of the banking system." Clearly, no such hasty action would be required.

---

* Certainly, there was nothing new about excessive real-estate lending by small, state-chartered banks. In the March 1933 issue of the *American Economic Review*, Herbert D. Simpson, of the Institute for Economic Research of Northwestern University, wrote provocatively, if generally, about the scale of bank-financed real-estate speculation in the 1920s. "A particularly ominous development," according to Simpson, "was the expansion of the banking system itself for the specific purpose of financing real estate promotion and development. Real estate interests dominated the policies of many banks, and thousands of new banks were organized and chartered for the specific purpose of providing the credit for proposed real estate promotions. The greater proportion of these were state banks and trust companies, many of them located in the outlying sections of the larger cities or in suburban regions not fully occupied by older and more established banking institutions." What distinguished the real-estate boom of the 1980s was the leading role played by these very same "older and more established banking institutions," Citibank not least.

Nevertheless, that matters had come to that pass was a rough indictment of the allied endeavors of banking and bank regulation.

The later the date in the 1980s, the more imaginative a junk-bond issue, personal loan, mortgage contrivance, or automobile accommodation tended to be. Thus, 1988 yielded the Sotheby's Art Equity Loan—not its invention but its aggressive marketing. On January 30, 1989, *People* magazine devoted a page to the curious hobby of Walter Cavanagh, forty-five-year-old Santa Clara financial planner, owner of the "world's largest credit card collection." Also in 1989, the forty-year home mortgage came to Washington, D.C., the seven-year car loan came to Florida, and Church's Fried Chicken changed hands in a remarkable sale to a heavily indebted buyer. Some $57 million in fees and expenses in connection with the sale were paid to Wasserstein Perella, Merrill Lynch, and many others, a sum nearly equal to the chicken company's pretax earnings for the fiscal years 1985, 1986, 1987, and 1988. In a similar vein, again in 1989, it came to light that the interest expense of a certain leveraged television station was actually higher than its revenues for the prior fiscal year. That is, it owed its creditors more than its gross receipts. Apparently, this was a junk-bond first. WTVT Holdings, Tampa, formerly a subsidiary of SCI Television, was able to survive this debilitating financial condition because most of its debt took the form of zero-coupon notes. They would fall due but not right away. It was hoped that, by the time they did mature, in 1992, something would turn up.

Leveraging the Airlines

One of the most characteristic delusions was that it was a good thing to pile debt on an airline. UAL (parent of United Air Lines) was deemed a viable candidate for a leveraged buyout, as was NWA (the parent of Northwest Airlines). In the spring of 1989, Pan American World Airways, which had a $300 million hole in its net worth account and enough long-term debt to facilitate its bankruptcy less than two years later, had disclosed that it was contemplating a bid for NWA. It was as if Rhode Island had announced the annexation of California.

Nothing was ruled out. When, on August 7, Marvin Davis made a bid for UAL, the Dow Jones Transportation Average climbed by 94 points, to a record-high 1,344. As recently as 1957, the Dow Jones Railroad Average (forerunner to the Transports) had been quoted at 94.91. That was the level of the index. In 1989, it had become the

Man of the 1980s: Walter Cavanagh, a Santa Clara, California, financial planner, shows off his credit-card collection, the world's largest

Dog of the 1980s: Zabau, a two-year-old Chinese Shar-Pei, began to get credit cards in the mail in December 1989 at the home of her Earlysville, Virginia, master. Here Dudley, Zabau's eight-month-old puppy, looks on (MATTHEW GENTRY OF THE DAILY PROGRESS, CHARLOTTESVILLE, VIRGINIA)

increment of one spectacular, debt-propelled, daily move. When, in July, the Transportation Average snapped back to make a new post-1987-crash high, that too was a page out of the record books. Almost an investment lifetime passed before the Rails could recover the record they had set just before the 1929 crash. It was not until February 25, 1964, as a matter of fact, that the Railroad Average made its way back to 189.13, thereby fractionally exceeding its September 3, 1929, peak. More than thirty-four years had marched on.

In 1989, there was no such holding back. A consensus had formed on Wall Street that the airline industry was no longer a prisoner of the business cycle. It was, in that respect, like the allegedly noncyclical gypsum-wallboard industry. Indeed, as some economists contended, the business cycle itself was a thing of the past. The advent of lease finance would permit the rapid, economical acquisition of modern aircraft. Carriers could borrow to the hilt, as, for instance, Trans World Airlines, Carl Icahn's leveraged carrier, had already borrowed. They would no longer be constrained by the limits of their own balance sheets. ("TWA's cash flow is not expected to be sufficient to enable it to repay the principal amount of the senior notes due in 1992 and 1993 or the notes at maturity, in the absence of refinancings," said one frank and prophetic passage in a 1988 TWA junk-bond prospectus.) Ruinous competition was a thing of the past. Eight big domestic carriers would compete and, yet, not compete. Everybody would mind his own business.

So said the investment mainstream. Nevertheless, it was impossible to overlook the fact that Forstmann Little & Co. and Kohlberg, Kravis, Roberts & Co., pioneering the LBO in the late 1970s, did not begin with an airline. It was a decade before they, or anyone else in a senior position in American capitalism, even got around to considering it. The ideal candidate for a leveraged buyout was a steady and reliable producer of cash flow. It was unregulated, not unionized, and not susceptible to a sudden jump in fuel prices. Capital-intensive, unionized, cyclical, and regulated, the typical airline was, in fact, the antithesis of this ideal. UAL, for instance, had earned a record $377 million from continuing operations in 1988. But it had lost $4.2 million in 1987. There was no good reason to believe that these ups and downs would be ironed out in the future.

"We believe the airlines are a natural resource which should not be pillaged to satiate the larval greed of the Attilas of the stock market." Thus Morten S. Beyer, chairman of Avmark, an airline consulting firm, made himself heard over the din of the debt frenzy. Beyer's was a minority view, however. Certainly it was not shared at Bankers Trust, which financed the heavily leveraged acquisition of NWA by an ex-Marriott Corporation executive, Alfred Checchi, with its depositors' money. Asked about his debt-laden balance sheet, Checchi optimistically replied, "If the company never did any better than it's doing right now, I could service my debt." Never did better? Operating income in 1988 totaled $205 million, the best year on record. But it had been as low as $77 million as recently as 1985. And no less a company than AMR (parent to American Airlines) had shown net losses as recently as 1980 and 1982. In the fall of 1989, the airline euphoria would be shattered by the surprise withdrawal of bank financing for the proposed UAL buyout. The astonishing fact, however, was that the money had ever been pledged in the first place.

The Law of Decay

On June 8, 1989, the *American Banker* reported on the sea change in lenders' attitudes toward leveraged buyouts, especially toward loans at the bottom of the credit pile. No more would medium-size banks stand with their noses pressed against the glass of high finance, the story—"Regionals Seeking Share of LBO Jackpot"—suggested. It led off:

> After years of watching their big-city cousins amass huge equity and mezzanine-debt* portfolios in leveraged buyouts and other corporate restructurings, regional banks are chasing the risky but potentially lucrative investments. . . .
> A recent poll of corporate finance officers at regional banks found that 17 of 21 had a newfound willingness to buy subordinated debt or equity. Eighteen months earlier, only two said their banks would dip below the secure senior debt level, despite the low returns. . . .
> The thirst for new investments is hardly surprising. Yields of 35 percent to 50 percent on equity and 25 percent to 40 percent on subordinated debt have been commonplace in recent years, leaving returns on senior bank loans in the dust.
> "You can make a lot more money if you're willing to take some

* An intermediate level of debt: junior in standing to certain bank claims but senior to junk bonds.

risk," said J. G. Richards Roddey, managing director of NCNB Corp.'s investment banking subsidiary.

"Markets make opinions" is the Wall Street axiom, and the bull market in financial leverage made bankers accommodating. In the 1970s, two or three months had to pass before an up-and-coming LBO firm could wring a $10 million loan commitment from a major New York bank. In 1987, the same firm had to wait only twenty-four hours for a $1.3 billion loan commitment. In the 1970s, term loans rarely extended for longer than six years; in the late 1980s, there were ten-year maturities. Banks compromised their credit standards because they were paid to do so. "Leveraged corporate transactions generally provide fees (typically 1 percent to 2 percent of the principal amount committed for) and higher interest rates . . . than most other corporate loans," Chemical Banking Corporation disclosed in 1988, and it was easy to translate that dry prose into human and financial results. Credit concerns were abstract and distant, whereas fees and bonuses were tangible and immediate. In the typical big bank, lenders to leveraged companies earned more than lenders to investment-grade companies (indeed, the ordinary corporate lending officer was a vanishing breed; companies with investment-grade credit credentials could borrow more cheaply in the securities markets). Each might receive a base salary of $125,000 a year, but the "merchant" banker's bonus might represent 50 percent to 200 percent of that sum, the garden-variety lender's bonus 50 percent, tops. As for the bankers who collected bad loans, they earned no more than $75,000 a year, about the minimum bonus for the average rainmaker.

In the late 1970s, the investment logic of many LBOs was compelling. In the late 1980s, the investment logic was no longer irresistible, but the fees and expenses were. It was the process of closing a transaction that was beginning to drive the market, not the hoped-for investment results. In this evolutionary process, Dr Pepper, the century-old soft-drink maker, constituted a one-company controlled experiment. It underwent a leveraged buyout in 1984 with smashing results. It was sold in 1986, also in leveraged circumstances, and again in 1988, in still more leveraged circumstances but with ever less smashing results.

The initial buyout by Forstmann Little in 1984 had the superficial earmarks of rank speculation. The price paid was $521 million, or 52 times the latest year's net earnings, which conjured up the Tokyo Stock Exchange. Interest rates were high too, soft-drink competition was brisk, and management's hand was cold. Excursions into bottling and the acquisition, in 1982, of Canada Dry had failed. In 1983, the Dr Pepper board had reached the dispirited decision to sell out.

Under new ownership, the company got back to basics. It concentrated on its syrup business and sold redundant assets, including real estate and the Canada Dry subsidiary. When, in August 1986, Forstmann Little sold out, its $30 million equity investment had ballooned to $270 million. Although highly leveraged, the company was actually producing enough income to cover its interest expense. So far, so good.

The next purchaser, a team including Hicks & Haas, Shearson Lehman, and Cadbury Schweppes, was at a disadvantage right from the start. Unlike Forstmann Little, Hicks & Haas et al. purchased no surplus assets and had no obvious management reforms to effect. Under the new regime, change occurred at the margin: sales grew, interest expense increased, operating income rose, and ratios of income to interest expense declined. The first generation of revolutionary capitalists had sold out to the second.

There was one major change. Only a few months after buying Dr Pepper, Hicks & Haas also acquired 7-Up. It was a combined Dr Pepper and 7-Up that still a third set of buyers, led by Prudential-Bache Securities, acquired in 1988. This time even more debt was laid on. Long-term borrowings constituted 180 percent of the capitalization (as opposed to the 90 percent or so under the prior two sets of owners), and operating profit failed to cover interest expense. What did not change much were profit margins. Junk bonds were sold to finance this third, and highly derivative, Dr Pepper incarnation, and the prospectus was frankly pessimistic about anyone getting out of the transaction with his life. "[M]anagement," it said, "does not anticipate that the company and its subsidiaries will generate cash flow from operations to repay the entire principal amount of the discount notes at maturity. Accordingly, it will be necessary to obtain funds sufficient to repay a portion of the principal of the discount notes through additional borrowings, sales of assets or a combination of the foregoing."

Thus, a real-life study in the dynamics of financial decay. Innovators did what seemed to be the impossible. Imitators followed, taking greater risks than the innovators but doing what the majority had come to accept as commonplace. From Forstmann Little to Prudential-Bache Securities—alpha to omega in four short years.

It was not until the fall of 1989 that the law of decay in the junk-bond market was clarified: too late for anyone who had invested in

Allied Stores or SCI Television, for example, but not too late to illuminate the process by which so much had been lent against so little. Barrie A. Wigmore, a limited partner of Goldman, Sachs & Co., working in his spare time (as he had worked to produce an exhaustive study of the Great Depression, *The Crash and Its Aftermath*), discovered what Braddock Hickman might have predicted. It was that the quality of junk bonds declined as the volume of their issuance increased. The great divide was 1986. In 1986 to 1988, Wigmore noted, over 75 percent of junk-grade debt was incurred in the source of a merger or leveraged buyout. No longer was "earnings before interest and taxes" (EBIT), the conventional income parameter in bond-market analysis, expected to cover interest expense. The standard test became "earnings before interest, taxes, and depreciation" (EBITD). Depreciation, after all, entailed no outlay of cash. It was a "noncash" charge and therefore one that might be overlooked. And if depreciation was treated as an imaginary expense, a marginal debtor could be made to look very nearly solvent. Furthermore, according to bull-market convention, the formal interest-coverage arithmetic was obsolete anyway. Companies reconstituted in an LBO could always sell assets (as Metromedia and Cain had done). It was not intended that the LBO capitalization would be the permanent capitalization. Something would turn up to make everyone whole before the principal fell due. There were plenty of chairs for everyone, and, besides, the music would never stop.

Wigmore examined every underwritten junk-bond issue from 1980 to 1988 except those issued by financial institutions and public utilities. To these issues, 694 in all, he applied five standard tests of creditworthiness, and he computed the numbers himself. The fruit of this painstaking after-hours labor was a picture of decline in the quality of junk-bond issues, a decline that the full-time junk-bond analysts on Wall Street had managed to overlook or explain away. Thus, for instance, common equity (the owners' interest) amounted to just 3 percent and 4 percent of the capitalization of junk-bond-issuing companies in 1987 and 1988. In the first few years of the decade, it had averaged 35 percent. EBIT had sufficed to cover interest expense by two to one in the early going but by less than one to one in 1986–88.

In effect, Wigmore had psychoanalyzed the boom. It was a bull market in credit, and credit is the money of the mind. He had not delved into real-estate lending, boat lending, art lending, or automobile lending, but any thoughtful investor could see a unifying pattern across markets. Just after the first Dr Pepper transaction in 1984, Drexel Burnham had favored Carl Icahn with a revolutionary letter.

Icahn, at the time mounting a bid for Phillips Petroleum Company, was in need of a source of funds. Drexel, in a phrase that anticipated a great deal of what was still to come, stated that it was "highly confident that it can arrange . . . financing commitments necessary to consummate such tender offers." Highly confident indeed. It was the story of a decade.

Afterword

End of the Line

Booms have consequences. The Mount Washington Hotel in Bretton Woods, New Hampshire, site of the famous World War II monetary conference, was sold at a foreclosure auction on June 26, 1991. Heavily mortgaged in the fat years, the resort was unable to pay its debts in the lean ones. Its principal creditor, and stockholder too, was the Eliot Savings Bank, a formerly staid Boston thrift that underwent a drastic personality change during the New England real-estate frenzy of the late 1980s. More than $6 million of the depositors' money was secured by the Mount Washington's 97 acres and 250 rooms, including grand No. 219, in which John Maynard Keynes had slept in the electric summer of 1944. When, in June 1990, the bank became insolvent, ownership of the hotel legally passed to the Federal Deposit Insurance Corporation. Now, in June 1991, the property went on the auction block.

The sale was a symbol of the end of an era, and so was the price obtained. Rumor had it that the FDIC would settle for nothing less than $5.5 million, but no buyer responded when the auctioneer called out $5 million and then $4 million. At $3 million, someone piped up, "I bid $1.6 million." Up the bidding went from there. It stopped at $3.15 million, however, a price that represented little more than half of the hotel's mortgage debt. It was as if a $10,000 car carried a $20,000 loan.

The other principal monetary shrine on American soil, the Plaza Hotel, site of the 1985 "G-5" meeting at which the fate of the dollar was temporarily decided, was itself overmortgaged in the spring of 1991. Its nominal owner was Donald Trump, but the author of *The Art of the Deal* owed desperate debts. In April he proposed to convert the hotel into condominiums, thereby raising cash and holding his creditors at bay. Six months later, however, no condominiums had been sold, and the Plaza—in Trump's boom-time judgment, a "trophy" property without peer—continued to await a return of the 1980s.

One of Trump's principal lenders was Citibank, the largest American banking institution, heir to rich traditions of James Stillman and (through a collateral branch of the family) George F. Baker and to all the modern heresies. By 1990, its chairman, John Reed, had come to admit doubts about the company's balance sheet. In an extraordinary interview with the *Harvard Business Review* that autumn, Reed sounded an uncharacteristic note of humility. What did he have to say to the proposition that the bank had been financially weakened? his questioners wanted to know. "We're being criticized mainly on our real estate assets and on the capital front," said Reed.

> Both criticisms are valid, and I take them to heart. . . . I've gone deeply into the credit portfolio and the credit process, and it's fair to say I've been hurt by it. I haven't told the world that, because who cares? But I'm a little embarrassed professionally —maybe more than a little embarrassed—that I didn't jump on it sooner. We were warned about real estate two years ago, and we pooh-poohed it. Now I'm damn embarrassed because the critics were right and we were wrong. Sure, the market's changed; we didn't know two years ago what we know today. Values have gone down. But the fact is, they're more right and we're more wrong.
>
> The capital thing is also valid. Visibly, statistically we look a little naked. Now the statistics may not be worth that much— except everybody looks at them, so you have to pay attention.

Citibank had been brought low by the real-estate-freighted prosperity even more than by the recession of the early 1990s. So far had its reputation sunk that Representative John Dingell, Michigan Democrat, in July 1991 charged it with being "technically insolvent." "Irresponsible and untrue," Citi shot back, but on Wall Street the congressman's remark was viewed as curious rather than scandalous —hyperbolic, perhaps—and no spontaneous rebuke was heard from the people who owned the bank's securities. A few months later, Citicorp took the unprecedented, and previously heretical, step of omitting its dividend. It disclosed an $885 million quarterly loss and acknowledged that its tried-and-true consumer-lending business was slowing down and would continue to weaken in 1992. A share of Citicorp common slumped to less than $10, a new low price and one far below the $25 for which Reed himself had purchased 100,000 shares in the fall of 1988 (on October 19, 1988, in fact, the first anniversary of the 1987 crash).

Citi did not suffer alone. The credit cycle had turned, and the financial strength of businesses, consumers, and governments had taken a turn for the worse. As for corporations, they became less creditworthy, not more so, during the course of the Reagan expansion. In the 1970s Moody's Investors Service marked down the quality of long-term corporate bonds only slightly more frequently than it upgraded them; the ratio of downgrades to upgrades was 1.17:1. In the 1980s, the incidence of downgrades almost doubled, to 2.17:1. In the single year of 1990, the ratio closed in on 5:1. The great bull market of the first half of 1991 afforded debt-laden companies the chance to sell new stock. Many seized it, but the improvement in corporate-credit quality was modest, and the preponderance of downgrades to upgrades declined to no better than 3.5:1.

USG, Sewell Avery's gypsum company, tried to issue new stock but found no buyers, even in the great bull market. It was in the position of the Mount Washington Hotel, with more unpayable debts than net worth. It defaulted on December 31, 1990, thereby risking a formal bankruptcy proceeding and almost certainly causing Avery to roll over in his grave once again. Up until its default, Gypsum had met its crushing financial obligations on time. Selling assets, it had cut its original bank debt almost in half, but the optimistic hopes of its promoters went unfulfilled. New residential construction was weak for five years in a row, beginning in 1987, and the market for USG's mainstay product, gypsum wallboard, languished. (Standard, half-inch wallboard was quoted at approximately $83 a thousand square feet in 1988, the year that USG turned itself inside out. It fetched $69 in mid-1991. In the halcyon days of 1984–86, it routinely changed hands at over $100.) As we have seen, the architects of the 1988 recapitalization admitted no unfavorable contingencies into their projections, even while serving fair notice that the bondholders might go unpaid. In this respect, at least, the original prospectus was prescient: By late 1990, USG's junior debt, issued to the USG stockholders at 100 cents on the dollar, was trading at 6½ cents on the dollar.

USG mounted an appeal to its bondholders in April 1991 to exchange their high-interest-paying debt, which the company could not afford to service, for new and lower-yielding debt, which, the bankers hoped, it could. Salomon Brothers (along with Goldman Sachs) had helped to underwrite the initial, disastrous offering. Now it was retained (along with Lazard Frères) to manage the new one. The sequel transaction, euphemistically known as a "restructuring," amounted to an out-of-court bankruptcy proceeding. "The corporation's cash flows in 1990 were, and its projected cash flows are, substantially below the levels projected at the time of the 1988 recapitalization," the new bond prospectus confessed. If the investment bankers had reason to be embarrassed by their 1988 handiwork, they still did not agree to work for free in 1991. Fees and expenses associated with the "restructuring" would amount to $40 million, or twice as much as the company's earnings from continuing operations for 1989, the new prospectus disclosed. (This hefty document, entitled "Offers to Exchange and Solicitations of Consents for Certain Debt Securities," ran to 203 printed, Bible-weight pages; the original, 1988 edition had contained only 80.)*

American consumers too played their part in the process of withdrawal from easy credit. As a class, they had borrowed extensively in the 1980s. It is a truism that every debt is ultimately paid, if not by the debtor then eventually by the creditor. In the late 1980s and early 1990s more and more consumer debt was repaid, involuntarily, by the lenders through the process of the borrower's bankruptcy.

In May 1991, Risa Kugal, a fortyish Brooklyn woman who said that she was unemployed, was supported by her mother, and was separated from her husband, appeared at federal bankruptcy court on Clinton Street in Brooklyn Heights to seek protection from her creditors under Chapter 7 of the federal Bankruptcy Code. There was nothing about Kugal's appearance that said "bankrupt" or "do not lend to me," and in fact she had managed to run up more than $75,000 in credit-card debt. She owed a total of $18,000 to Citibank on five separate accounts. She owed $5,838 on her American Express card, $5,837 on her Optima card, and $6,300 on her American Express Gold card (she had no Platinum card, however). She owed money to MBNA America, Household Finance Corp., Republic National Bank of New York, and Macy's. She said that the sum total of her assets was $750 in household goods, clothing, and miscellaneous possessions: no cash, real estate, bank deposits, boats, livestock, farming implements, office equip-

* The April proposal was itself superseded in November. "The continued weakness in construction-based markets, coupled with the need to establish a long-term solution to USG's financial structure, has made it apparent to us that a more significant restructuring of USG's balance sheet is necessary," Eugene B. Connolly, the chairman and chief executive officer, said. "The restructuring proposal we filed last April would have left USG with too much debt." The recession—which, in the palmy days of 1988, the promoters and investment bankers had failed even to admit as a contingency—had made the numbers obsolete.

ment, machinery, inventory, patents, bonds, insurance policies, annuities, partnership interests, corporate interests or equitable or future interests, rights, or powers in personalty, she swore under oath.

On paper, the Chapter 7 procedure seems to be arduous. A bankrupt must surrender his assets, cooperate with the U.S. trustee, and meet with creditors to discuss the accuracy of his financial statements, if any should question them. Only then does he reach the promised land of "discharge"—relief from pre-bankruptcy obligations (except, for instance, from unpaid taxes and child support). In fact, however, the practice of bankruptcy is remarkably brisk and unintrusive. On May 29, the day of Kugal's appearance, twenty-seven cases were settled in less than three hours in the courtroom of Judge Conrad B. Duberstein. One took just two minutes and fifteen seconds. None of the debtors admitted to any assets, and none of the major creditors chose to contest that claim. As for Kugal, the Chapter 7 trustee, Richard O'Connell, asked her the usual questions—for instance, "Do you have an IRA?" He departed from script to ask how she had managed to run up so much credit-card debt. Smiling weakly, Kugal answered, "I used one to pay off another." Her case was dismissed, and her debts were wiped out. She was, from that moment (or, officially, ninety days after that moment), debt-free, courtesy of the U.S. bankruptcy system.

Since the days of the loan sharks, consumers had never collectively borrowed themselves into trouble. Generations of worry over chattel credit, department-store credit, and automobile credit had mainly been for naught; Americans more than vindicated the faith of the pioneers of the consumer-lending movement. By the early 1990s, however, there was reason to wonder if the popularization of credit had at last been carried too far. In 1990, for instance, the value of equity in American homes fell by more than $300 billion, or by nearly 16 percent, the result of higher "home equity" borrowing as well as lower house prices. The only other declines of the prior thirty years, in 1963 and 1981, were of 5 percent or less. According to the economist Susan Sterne, debt service amounted to 14.1 percent of disposable personal income in 1989 and 1990; they were the highest readings since at least 1960. U.S. household indebtedness had risen at an annual rate of 10 percent in the 1980s, or by one-third again as much as growth in after-tax income.

If the financial foundation of personal credit ended the decade the worse for wear, so did its moral underpinnings. As corporate-bond defaults and bank failures mounted, more and more individuals chose to avail themselves of the protection of the bankruptcy law. Personal bankruptcy filings shot up from 1.2 per thousand persons in the mid-1980s to more than 3 per thousand in 1991. People increasingly came to treat the decision to pay their debts as a morally neutral one, like the choice of a mutual fund. Indeed, new-fledged bankrupts occupied a paradoxically privileged position for the very reason that they could not, under the law, file another Chapter 7 proceeding for another six years. General Motors Acceptance Corporation was a frequent caller to the Brooklyn Bankruptcy Court. It wanted to know whether a particular individual had been given his or her discharge, and the hoped-for answer, interestingly enough, was "yes." The six years in which a debtor could not obtain another court-sanctioned discharge was longer, even, than the term of the average car loan.

Late in June 1991, Judge Marvin A. Holland delivered an inspirational talk to a new class of bankrupts in Brooklyn court. His listeners were bound to conclude that the social stigma against bankruptcy had been reduced (as, indeed, had the financial stigma; more and more debtors were able to carry some form of credit with them into bankruptcy). "I don't want anybody to leave this court feeling uncomfortable, guilty or ashamed because you just went through bankruptcy," the judge said. "I think you have a right to feel good about it. You should walk out of here with your head held high. You should feel proud because you've done it—you've put your problems behind you. You now have some options about what to do with the rest of your life, because those debts that were burying you are all behind you now." *Newsday* reported that some of the people in Holland's courtroom dabbed at their eyes and sniffed back tears.

It is well to record that most Americans did not file for bankruptcy and most corporations did not succumb to the financial fashions of the 1980s. Most banks survived without FDIC assistance, and the United States government in mid-1991 was able to borrow in the short term at an interest cost of 6 percent or less, the prospect of $300 billion deficits notwithstanding. Between 1983 and 1989, the gross national product grew at an average, inflation-adjusted annual rate of 3.9 percent, and the recession that officially began in July 1990 was not immediately classified as a depression. Junk bonds, put out with the trash in 1989–90, enjoyed a wonderful bull market in 1991, as did bank loans to Third World countries and the common stocks of companies that could count few business assets except a heavy short interest.* The dollar, basking in the luster of the Persian Gulf war, appreciated against gold and most foreign currencies. After a sharp but perfunctory drop in 1990, the stock market bounded to record highs despite lower corporate profits and weakened consumer income. The Soviet Union disowned communism—indeed, it disowned itself. For Wall Street's money, it was a cloudless, 72-degree world, perfect yet somehow getting better.

Banks and thrifts continued to fail, but there was no coast-to-coast run. Besides, of what significance were bank failures? The banking system, arguably, was obsolete. It had been regulated into irrelevance, and new structures were evolving to replace it (as new structures always evolved in capitalism). Corporations borrowed each other's surplus cash in the commercial-paper market at interest rates well below prime. Money-market mutual funds, which the government did not insure, took the public's deposits and invested them safely and profitably. Wall Street refashioned loans into securities, Merrill Lynch in the summer of 1991, for instance, creating bonds out of motorcycle loans, "wave-runner" loans, and all-terrain-vehicle loans. To be sure, banks were losing deposits, but so, in another time, had the postal savings system. The credit system, or so the argument went, was not dying but merely evolving.

The columnist Warren T. Brookes asked rhetorically, "Have we seen the end of banks?" and he answered enthusiastically "yes." Money, he contended, is nothing more than an "information system." Thinking about the classical form of money, gold bullion, "information system" was not the first descriptive phrase that came to mind. Brookes, however, anticipated that objection. He insisted that money is chiefly a medium for the purchase of goods and services. "Knowing this," he wrote, "it should not be surprising that as we have moved into the information age, and the telecommunications world of integrated global financial markets, banks whose only function is to trade in money (information) should have become an endangered institutional species. . . . If every bank is just an information system, then every information system has the capacity to be a bank, and every owner of an information system, from a desktop computer to a main

---

* "Short interest" is the number of shares of a stock that have been sold short—that is, in anticipation of a fall. A short seller borrows stock that he doesn't own and sells it. Closing out the trade, he buys stock in the open market and returns *it* to the lender. In the bull market of 1991, great sport was had by "running" the stocks with large short positions, stampeding the bears into buying.

frame terminal, can be a banker. In a totally wired world market place, anyone with a laptop computer is potentially carrying his or her bank around with him."

Believing Brookes, one would also believe that cycles of lending and borrowing were relics of the pre-information age. Information people, knowing things, would resist the manic-depressive tendencies that had colored the booms and busts of yesteryear. Brookes implied that "information" was pure and disembodied. It was a substance unfiltered by the variable perceptions of bankers, promoters, bond-holders, and loan applicants. To any student of the vicissitudes of market psychology, the idea seemed farfetched.

Lenders and borrowers, it was clear enough, had overdone it in the 1980s. Would they therefore underdo it in the 1990s? The fundamental question was whether the recession would conform to postwar script or to some earlier pattern of boom and bust. If the answer was the former, certain comforting beliefs could be clung to. First and fore-most, the Federal Reserve would inevitably foster recovery. Interest rates would be made to fall until prosperity was securely restored.

Among professional investors, this was the ruling faith of 1991. In days gone by, Wall Street had believed that Morgan or Stillman or Baker would protect it from harm. It later lodged that semi-mystical hope in the Federal Reserve System, the FDIC, and the other agencies of the credit welfare state. One of the leading Wall Street economists coined a mantra for the bull market of the early 1990s. "There are 775 basis points between the federal funds rate and zero," he declared in October 1990 when the key money-market interest rate was quoted at 7¾ percent. (The federal funds rate is the key short-term interest rate in the money market; 100 basis points make a percentage point.) The economist adjusted his slogan as interest rates continued to fall, until by December 1991 there were only 400 basis points between the funds rate and zero. At 3 percent, or 2 percent, presumably, something expansive and bullish was going to happen to the economy as it had already happened to the stock market. The Fed would no more drop the ball than Baker and Morgan had. It would create more credit but not so much as to worry the bond market or cause a run on the dollar.

What made the recession of the early 1990s unique in postwar ex-perience was that the Federal Reserve did not precipitate it. In the past, inflation had provided the cue for monetary stringency. As in-terest rates rose, the housing market fell. When rates had been under direct federal control—1966, for instance—the process was almost hydraulic. Pulling lever A, the Fed achieved recessionary result B.

Nothing of the kind had happened in 1990, however. Iraq had invaded Kuwait, but neither that event nor Federal Reserve policy could account for the reluctance of the average bank to lend to the vital, problematical customer.

In economics, change occurs at the margin. It is the extra increment of lending and borrowing that tends to foster growth. The key financial fact of the 1980s was that the marginal borrower received the benefit of the doubt. The result was highly accessible terms for the purchase of nearly everything. Witnessing this headlong expansion, anyone of a skeptical, let alone puritanical, cast of mind was moved to condemn it, for there was no question where it was leading. What the bears forgot, however, was that the process of bank- and thrift-wrecking is ironically bullish for as long as it lasts. Being able to borrow, people will borrow, and they will spend the proceeds. By 1990–91, the rate of growth in borrowing at every level—consumer, corporate, governmental—was collapsing. It fell from more than 14 percent a year in the mid-1980s to less than 5 percent in August 1991. It was the lowest rate in thirty years. Now the skeptics came to doubt their own senses. Cars went unsold, employees unhired, and inventories unstocked, because of either the recession or the lack of available financing, or both. Business activity sputtered. Yet the stock market, the legendary leading indicator, pretended not to notice. It did not ignore the bad news so much as feed on it. Granted, the expansion was bullish, the skeptics belatedly came to acknowledge. Still, they wondered, how could the contraction be anything but bearish?

In the early 1990s a number of long-running trends were apparently cresting. The "democratization of credit," as Arthur J. Morris had styled his crusade for the workingman, had reached a kind of epiphany. (Tommy Mullaney, eleven, of Crownsville, Maryland, returned home from camp in the summer of 1990 to find his name inscribed on a new gold MasterCard complete with a $5,000 credit line. "I jumped up and down and said 'Wow'—the hologram on it was cool," Tommy told *The Washington Post*. "But it sure made me wonder about who was running that bank.") Credit risk was in the process of being desocialized. The federal government, running out of money, was no longer able to subsidize the lending decisions of private lenders.

The government was not without experience in banking when the New Deal began, but the scale of federal participation in the 1930s was unprecedented. Loans were extended or guaranteed, and bank and thrift deposits were insured. It was a stimulative policy, and a cheap one, too, until the government's chits began to be redeemed for payment in the 1980s. The bankruptcy of the Federal Savings and Loan Insurance Corporation was followed by the threatened insolvency of the Bank Insurance Fund. The Farmers Home Administration, the Farm Credit System, and the Federal Housing Administration all ran up credit losses. The most visible evidence of the government's fiscal plight was the annual budget deficit, but there were great potential costs hidden beneath the surface. These were the present value of promises to pay future benefits, ranging from health insurance to deposit insurance subsidies. Roy H. Webb, economist at the Federal Reserve Bank of Richmond, put the overall, potential cost at more than $4 trillion. His estimate included $130 billion for savings and loan deposit insurance (but none for bank deposit insurance; for argument's sake, Webb assumed that the banking industry itself would be able to foot the bill for the losses of the Bank Insurance Fund, a very ambitious argument). It also included $1.1 trillion for retirement and disability benefits, $1.4 trillion for health benefits, $643 billion for civil service retirement and disability benefits, $77 billion for loans and loan guarantees by government agencies, and so on down the line. These commitments Webb called the "stealth budget," and he warned that $4 trillion was very likely an understatement. The cold war had ended not a day too soon.

The timing of the creation of federal deposit insurance was a brilliant historical accident. The Great Depression purged the banking system of speculative tendencies. Our story has traced the recovery of bankers' spirits in the decades that followed. Whether the 1980s would have roared in the absence of the $100,000 deposit-insurance ceiling (raised from $40,000 in 1980) is an open question. Certainly, other aspects of federal policy also made the decade unforgettable. The legacy of the great inflation of the 1970s and the regulatory changes of 1974 and 1982 propelled lenders into real-estate lending. The doctrine that some banks were too big to fail subverted the most basic banking franchise of all, safety; promising to protect its depositors' money at all hazards, a small, safe bank could make no competitive headway against a large, risky bank. The Treasury Department was the ultimate big-bank stockholder.

In the fall of 1991, with the next presidential election looming, the "credit crunch" became front-page news. Federal Reserve policy was easy, the stock market was boiling, and interest rates were falling. Nevertheless, banks were not lending as the Bush administration would have them lend, and steps were taken to encourage a reversion to expansive ways. It was true, as a number of Wall Street economists liked to observe, that the banks' share of lending to businesses was not what it used to be (less than 60 percent in the summer of 1991, down from some 73 percent in the early 1980s). The commercial-paper market was a boon to blue-chip-caliber companies, but it was closed to the myriad of companies of lower rank that really needed to borrow (the Securities and Exchange Commission, moving to protect the safety of money-market mutual fund depositors, insisted on it). For the majority of American businesses that could not issue bonds, sell commercial paper, or raise equity capital in the public market, the place to turn for a loan was a bank.

The reasons banks chose not to lend were numerous, logical, and (some of them) new. There was, to start with, a shortage of solvent, upstanding loan applicants, but that is the story of every recession. What made 1991 different was the straitened state of the banking system and the accommodative posture of the Federal Reserve. In previous bouts of stringency, interest rates were rising, because the Federal Reserve was tightening. Not so in 1991. Bank credit was stagnant despite the Fed, not because of it. Monetary economists were reluctant to admit that anything like a contraction in bank credit—a circumstance associated with the prehistoric times of the early 1930s—existed. So doubting, they closed their eyes to an impressive pile of evidence. For example, according to a study by the Federal Reserve Bank of New York, banks with bad balance sheets had reduced their business lending more than banks with good balance sheets. At the margin, in other words, the banking system was impaired by its own weakness. In view of the wild-haired practices of the 1980s, it was not exactly a surprise conclusion, but it flew in the face of the conventional wisdom.

"Assume," reflected Charles Peabody, a leading Wall Street analyst, "that 70 percent of a bank's assets are in loans and that real-estate loans make up 25 percent of the total. In that case, real-estate loans would amount to 17 percent or 18 percent of total assets. Equity capital amounts to 5 percent or 6 percent of total assets. Now, a Federal Reserve survey last year suggested that two-thirds of all real-estate loans were not being repaid on the original terms, that the borrowers were behind on interest or principal. So the implication is that about 12 percent of the asset base—two-thirds of that 17 percent or 18 percent—is illiquid. And that's just real estate. It says nothing about HLTs [that is, loans to heavily indebted companies], for instance." Peabody observed that 12 percent is a number that dwarfs net worth and constitutes a significant drag on lending capacity.

Then, too, there were the nonarithmetic factors. As credit is money of the mind, the decision to lend or borrow is based in part on morale. In July 1991, the FDIC sent a message to the American boardroom by bringing suit against 67 former directors of the failed First RepublicBank Corp., Texas. The complaint alleged that they had run the bank into the ground at an estimated cost to the Bank Insurance Fund of $3.4 billion; the specific charges literally ran the gamut from "a" to "z" and from "aa" to "bb." (Thoroughly limbered up by the time it had reached the letter "y," the government complained that the directors "chose to 'bet the bank' and to engage in aggressive and suicidal activity of plunging headlong into a cyclical market knowing full well the dangers of concentration of loan volume to a bank in utter disregard of the welfare of the bank and its depositors.") The suit stunned Dallas. The directors were prominent figures. Not all were as rich as they had formerly been, some were unwell, and some had resigned from the board a year or more before the bank was declared to be insolvent in 1988. The suit brought home to every incumbent bank director the personal risk of negligence (or of ignorance, misjudgment, or bad luck). The point could hardly be lost that there were worse things to be than unreasonably cautious. Before 1935, as we have seen, the stockholders of a failed national bank were liable to be assessed for up to the par value of their stock to help settle accounts with the depositors. The First RepublicBank suit (and hundreds that preceded it) constituted steps toward the restoration of the ideal of individual responsibility in banking. The credit welfare state was being toppled.

If not lending made more sense, so did not borrowing. Consumers earned 5 percent on their savings accounts, but paid 18 percent or 19 percent (at that, an expense no longer deductible from their federal taxable income) to borrow. The arithmetic of credit-card debt was, to the solvent consumer, nonsensical. In a deflation, the most compelling reason not to borrow is the depreciating value of the thing one wants to buy. There was no across-the-board deflation of prices in 1991. The prices of buildings and computers were falling, but there was little or no relief for the consumer at the drugstore or the university bursar's office. Nevertheless, symptoms of deflation were visible, particularly in banking. The nation's money supply scarcely grew. Indeed, the monetary aggregate most closely watched by the Federal Reserve Board ("M-2," roughly defined as the sum of cash, checking accounts, savings accounts, and money-market mutual funds) actually began to shrink in the third quarter of 1991, the first such occurrence since

1949. The Federal Reserve was expanding its balance sheet, but commercial banks were not expanding theirs. For once the shopworn, deflationary metaphor—"pushing on a string"—began to seem an apt description of the efficacy of monetary policy. Interest rates had fallen but the housing industry was strangely moribund. "To have the lowest mortgage rates in 14 years and still have very few people looking at houses is very disturbing," an economist at the National Association of Home Builders told the *Barron's* columnist John Liscio.

To interpret the 1980s as the culmination of purely American trends—the popularization of credit and the socialization of risk— would be to overlook the rest of the world. Bankers were turning away the marginal borrower in Australia, Europe, and Asia as well as in the United States. In the fall of 1991, there were banking crises in Norway, Finland, and Sweden. The chairman of the Industrial Bank of Japan resigned to atone for the vast and embarrassing loans his bank had extended to an Osaka restaurateur, stock-market plunger, mystic, and mah-jongg parlor operator, Nui Onoue. The Bank of England and the Bank for International Settlements disclosed a precipitous drop in so-called interbank lending in the first half of the year. Lacking confidence, stronger banks reduced their lending to weaker ones. From March to September 1991, outstanding loans at Japan's largest banks increased by only 1.5 percent, the lowest rate in thirty-seven years.

No specifically American explanation could account for the worldwide shrinkage, and an international theory of the rise and fall of credit is outside the scope of this work. Suffice it to say that for decades in the United States—in round years, from the mid-1930s to the late 1980s—credit grew, and it expanded at last at a gallop. Then it stopped growing, and at the margin it started to shrink. At countless banks and thrifts, the arithmetic of expansion, 1980s-style, stopped working. At the government's Bank Insurance Fund, it became ruinous. How far the contraction might carry shapes up as one of the great political questions of 1992. Knowing the Republican White House, and recalling the zeal with which the Hoover administration moved to scotch the deflation of 1930, a historically minded observer was bound to bet against laissez-faire. It was inconceivable that any living American politician, once impressed by the intractability of the recession, would do anything except try to print money. Trying to coax more lending and borrowing from an overextended banking system, the government would intervene early and often.

Understanding the past, one could not presume to cure the troubles of the present. The story of financial reform in America has been a story of problems displaced rather than solved. Gold-standard orthodoxy, although elegant, was severe, and not in keeping with democratic impulses. But central banking, federal subsidies, paper money, deposit insurance, and full disclosure have each fallen short of the claims of their respective promoters. Perhaps the recession of the early 1990s is no ordinary postwar slump but a deeper contraction that will force a return to an enlightened, risk-taking conservatism in banking and credit: a step or two in the direction of George F. Baker. I would welcome such a move but would not confuse it with a return to the Garden of Eden. Knowing the past, one reads the morning newspapers with a sense of fatalism. One believes in the powers of markets and reason but not in the perfectability of lenders and borrowers.

Notes

1. Gloomy Sewell

9 Details of the Herrlinger bid for Dayton-Hudson: *The Wall Street Journal*, June 23, 1987; *Business Week*, "Hey Wall Street, Wanna Buy the Brooklyn Bridge?" July 6, 1987; *Cincinnati Enquirer*, June 23, 24, 1987.

12 USG repulses the Belzbergs: *Chicago Sun-Times*, March 10, 1988.

12 Desert Partners withdraws its first takeover bid: Ibid., January 15, 1988.

12 " 'They're back' ": Ibid., February 25, 1988.

12 " 'The offer is a two-tiered . . .' ": Ibid., March 10, 1988.

14 Description of the risks, changes, and details of debt issuance concerning USG: USG prospectus, July 7, 1988, pp. 7–12.

15 "In 1986, the management of R. H. Macy & Co. . . .": R. H. Macy prospectus, p. 34.

15 135 bank lenders: *Crain's New York Business*, November 20, 1990.

16 Wallboard prices and housing construction statistics: National Association of Home Builders and trade sources.

16 " 'USG Corp. announced today . . .' ": *PR Newswire*, December 31, 1990.

16 "For one thing, National Gypsum . . .": *Grant's Interest Rate Observer*, July 22, 1988.

17 Settsu Corp. purchases USG stake: Ibid., July 4, 1988.

17 USG turns a profit in the bottom of the Depression: *Fortune*, "Gyp," February 1936, p. 88.

18 " 'The officers of the company . . .' ": *The Wall Street Journal*, January 20, 1902.

18 " 'At first the consolidations . . .' ": Arthur Stone Dewing, *The Financial Policy of Corporation*, Vol. 4 (New York, 1920), p. 36.

18 USG's original capital of $200,000: *Fortune*, February 1936.

19 Early life of Sewell Avery and changing name of the Alabaster Co.: *Fortune*, "Gyp," February 1936.

19 Early history of U.S. Gypsum: Ibid., pp. 89–91.

20 Gypsum's profitability during the 1920s: *Moody's Industrial Manual,* 1924 and 1927.

20 Gypsum's price war with Certain-teed: *Fortune,* February 1936, p. 91.

20 " 'Gloomy Sewell' ": *Business Week,* "Sewell Avery's Mail Order Job Is Concerned with Manpower," January 13, 1935.

20 " 'When building failed to show . . .' ": *Fortune,* February 1936, p. 92.

20 Gypsum's Fort Knox balance sheet: *Moody's Industrial Manual,* 1934.

20 Morgan discovers Sewell Avery: *Fortune,* February 1936; *Dictionary of American Biography,* Supplement 6, 1980, p. 27.

21 Montgomery Ward's performance during the 1920s: *Moody's Industrial Manual,* 1920–31.

21 Sewell Avery takes over at Montgomery Ward: Frank B. Latham, *1872–1972 A Century of Serving Consumers: The Story of Montgomery Ward,* March 1972, pp. 75–77.

21 " 'I banana-peeled into this place . . .' ": *Time,* "KO for Mr. Avery," May 31, 1948.

22 " 'I never saw such a mass movement . . .' ": *Fortune,* "The Stewardship of Sewell Avery," May 1946, p. 112.

22 Financial statistics on Ward during the early 1930s: *Moody's Industrial Manual,* 1930–37.

22 " 'pretty generally held to be . . .' ": *Fortune,* February 1936, p. 96.

22 " 'Some of our best business . . .' ": *Fortune,* January 1935, p. 74.

23 Ward and the NRA: Latham, *Story of Montgomery Ward,* p. 78.

23 " 'talks a lot . . .' ": Untitled pamphlet on Sewell Avery and Montgomery Ward, by Montgomery Ward Workers of Chicago, 1944, pp. 4–6.

23 " 'And what will happen? . . .' ": *Fortune,* January 1935, p. 74.

24 Prevailing interest rates during the late 1930s: Sidney Homer, *A History of Interest Rates* (New Brunswick, N.J., 1963), pp. 350–52.

24 Folsom asks Avery to stop haranguing employees: *Fortune,* May 1946, p. 180.

25 " 'With an average monthly payroll . . .' ": Latham, *Story of Montgomery Ward,* p. 79.

25 Montgomery Ward, the War Labor Board, and the unions: *Fortune,* "U.S. Gypsum: No Nonsense," September 1955; *Time,* May 8, 1944; *The New York Times,* May 11, 1944; and Latham, *Story of Montgomery Ward,* p. 79.

26 " 'most startling newspicture . . .' ": *Time,* May 8, 1944, p. 12.

26 " 'Did they actually . . .' ": *Chicago Daily News,* April 27, 1944.

28 " 'One of these days you will find . . .' ": FBI files on Sewell Avery.

28 Legality of occupation: Latham, *Story of Montgomery Ward,* p. 80.

28 " 'Who am I to argue . . .' ": *The New York Times,* April 23, 1955.

28 " 'As a result of a consistent . . .' ": *Fortune,* May 1946, p. 184.

29 " 'It meant squirreling . . .' ": Latham, *Story of Montgomery Ward,* p. 81.

29 " 'Sewell Avery's ideas . . .' ": Montgomery Ward workers' pamphlet, p. 6.

29 " 'Unlike the Sears management . . .' ": Latham, *Story of Montgomery Ward,* p. 82.

29 Shell Union Oil makes bond market history: *The Wall Street Journal*, April 17, 1946.

30 " 'bank with a storefront' ": *Fortune*, "Montgomery Ward, Prosperity Is Still Around the Corner," November 1960.

30 Gypsum invests during the 1950s: *Fortune*, September 1955, pp. 96–99.

30 Comparison of Ward's and Sears's stores: Godfrey M. Lebhar, *Chain Stores in America: 1859–1959* (New York, 1959), p. 379.

31 The Sears balance sheet: *Moody's Industrial Manual*, 1955.

31 Avery meddles at Ward: *Fortune*, September 1955, p. 100; "What Did Happen at Ward's," by Herrymon Maurer, *Fortune*, May 1956.

31 " 'Don't you know . . .' ": *Fortune*, May 1946, p. 182.

31 " 'resigned' ": *The Wall Street Journal*, August 27, 1954.

31 " 'Ward Runs Out . . .' ": *Newsweek*, April 25, 1949, p. 66.

31 " 'The trouble with Wall Street' ": *Fortune*, January 1935, p. 80.

31 Avery predicts bad things for the economy: *The New Yorker*, "Our Plunging Correspondents," by John Brooks, May 21, 1955, p. 100; *The New York Times*, April 25, 1953.

32 Louis Wolfson's press conference, and Avery's response: *The New Yorker*, May 21, 1955, p. 100; *The New York Times*, August 27, 1954; *The Wall Street Journal*, August 27, 1954.

33 " 'The trouble is that you had the Sewell Avery type . . .' ": *Corporate Finance*, "My Life as a Dealmaker," by Donald P. Kelly, July 1989, p. 29.

33 Individual shareownership: NYSE, *1956 Census of Shareholders*, p. 26.

33 " 'I invite all Montgomery Ward . . .' ": *The Wall Street Journal*, August 27, 1954.

33 Other contests at the time: *The New York Times*, April 17, 1954, and April 23, 1955.

34 " 'The Kefauver Crime Committee' " and the Wolfson response: *The New Yorker*, May 21, 1955, pp. 101–2.

34 Wolfson goes to jail: *The New York Times*, May 5, 1969.

34 " 'Gentlemen . . .' ": *The New Yorker*, May 21, 1955.

35 Description of Avery at the proxy fight, and Krider's parting shot: *The New York Times*, April 23, 1955; *The New Yorker*, May 21, 1955, p. 112.

35 " 'As the significance of this victory . . .' ": *The New York Times*, April 23, 1955.

36 Incentive financing: *Harvard Business Review*, "Incentive Financing—A New Opportunity," by Charles M. Williams and Howard A. Williams, March–April 1960.

36 " 'I'm on the right side . . .' ": *Chicago Tribune*, April 23, 1955.

36 " 'At the outset of the proxy contest . . .' ": *The New York Times*, May 10, 1955.

36 " 'because I sincerely believe . . .' ": *Chicago Tribune*, May 10, 1955.

36 " 'Immediately before word of the resignation . . .' ": *The New York Times*, May 10, 1955.

2. Mr. Baker's Bank

38 " 'Has it ever occurred to any architect . . .' ": Robert A. M. Stern, Gregory Gilmartin, and Thomas Mellins, *New York 1930: Architecture and Urbanism Between the Two World Wars* (Rizzoli International Publications, New York, 1987), p. 182.

38 Description of the Manufacturers Trust building: *The New York Times*, September 20, 1954; *Architectural Record*, November 1954.

39 " 'The thing about many another bank . . .' ": *The Wall Street Journal*, September 23, 1954.

40 " 'broke the masonry-fortress psychology . . .' ": *Progressive Architecture*, June 1973, p. 108.

40 " 'The bank appeared to be beckoning suggestively . . .' ": Museum of Fine Arts (Houston) and the Parnassus Foundation, *Money Matters: A Critical Look at Bank Architecture* (New York, 1990), p. 5.

40 " 'To Harold Miner . . .' ": *The New York Times*, October 5, 1954.

41 Blue-chip depositors of the First: Sheridan Logan, *George F. Baker and His Bank* (private printing, 1981), p. 278.

41 " 'Old Fort Sherman' " and description of the First: Ibid., pp. 120–23.

41 George F. Baker, biographical sketch, and description of youth: Ibid., pp. 10–51.

45 Details of John Thompson: Ibid., pp. 285–98.

49 " 'for many years somewhat notorious . . .' ": Bank examiner's report of the First National Bank of New York, National Archives, February 23, 1872.

49 Letter from George F. Baker's father: Logan, *George F. Baker and His Bank*, p. 55.

50 Description of the founding and early history of the First National Bank: Ibid., pp. 55–62.

50 " 'Is a young man . . .' ": Examiner's report, October 8, 1866.

50 Meigs's comments on the First in 1872, and mention of the First Mortgage Sinking Fund bonds: Examiner's report, February 23, 1872.

51 " 'In looking over their affairs . . .' ": Examiner's report, March 13, 1873.

52 "After Appomattox, Cooke became . . .": Robert Sobel, *The Big Board: A History of the New York Stock Market* (New York, 1965), pp. 96–97.

52 "Baker was on record . . .": Logan, *George F. Baker and His Bank*, p. 50.

52 History of failure of Jay Cooke & Co.: Ibid., pp. 75–80, 330–36. See also Henrietta M. Larson, *Jay Cooke: Private Banker* (Cambridge, Mass., 1936). For a sample of the Northern Pacific Railroad promotion, see Northern Pacific Railroad, "The Great Northern Pacific Crosses the Best Zone Between the Great Lakes and the Pacific" (New York, 1882).

52 "The land grant, the parodist explained . . .": Larson, *Jay Cooke*, p. 364.

54 First National Bank's loan to Jay Cooke & Co.: Examiner's report, April 6, 1874, and Logan, *George F. Baker and His Bank*, p. 120.

54 " 'loaded with bad debts . . .' ": Logan, *George F. Baker and His Bank*, p. 105.

55   Baker takes over at the First: Ibid., pp. 96–98.

56   " 'I have just come from . . .' ": Ibid., pp. 102–3.

56   " '[T]he late Panic has left its *mark* . . .' ": Examiner's report, April 6, 1874.

56   " 'So the panic didn't bother you . . .' ": U.S. Congress, House Committee on Banking and Currency, "Money Trust Investigation," 64th Congress, 1st Session, part 11, 1913, p. 1420.

57   Meigs works late at the bank: Examiner's reports, February 1, 1875, and December 11, 1875.

57   " 'Their great success in placing . . .' " and the Rochester Savings Bank case: Examiner's report, January 2, 1878.

59   Description of the new bank building: Building Record 1880–81, City of New York, 31 Chambers Street Building Archive.

59   Baker buys a carriage and gets rich: Logan, *George F. Baker and His Bank*, p. 114.

59   " 'Of a naturally speculative nature . . .' ": Examiner's report, February 18, 1884.

60   Baker and Central Railroad: Logan, *George F. Baker and His Bank*, pp. 114–15.

60   " 'The small number of Shareholders . . .' ": Examiner's report, February 18, 1884.

60   Grant & Ward comes to grief: Logan, *George F. Baker and His Bank*, pp. 115–17; Thomas P. Kane, *The Romance and Tragedy of Banking: Problems and Incidents of Government Supervision of the National Banks*, 2nd ed. (New York, 1923), pp. 125–26.

61   " 'The great experience of the managers . . .' ": Examiner's report of the First National Bank, April 7, 1885.

3. The Timid Bank

62   " 'ready money' ": Harold van B. Cleveland and Thomas F. Huertas, *Citibank: 1812–1920* (Cambridge, Mass., 1985), p. 25.

62   " 'makes 'em take an interest . . .' ": John K. Winkler, *The First Billion: The Stillmans and the National City Bank* (New York, 1934), p. 35.

62   " 'When a bank's safety became . . .' ": Cleveland and Huertas, *Citibank*, p. 29.

63   " 'Supposed to be fire proof' ": Examiner's report for the National City Bank, National Archives, March 29, 1897.

63   " 'There is no doubt that the elimination . . .' ": Kane, *Romance and Tragedy*, p. 86.

63   Hepburn's review of National City: Examiner's report, February 24, 1891.

65   "Stillman himself, for instance . . .": Cleveland and Huertas, *Citibank*, p. 35.

65   Double liability at Marine National Bank: Kane, *Romance and Tragedy*, p. 124.

65 National City Bank's capital in 1893: Examiner's report, March 7, 1893.

65 " 'The right to advertise . . .' ": Kane, *Romance and Tragedy*, p. 545.

66 " 'Businessmen of America . . .' ": *The New York Times*, May 3, 1931.

66 " 'The U.S.A. is a great and growing country' ": Winkler, *The First Billion*, p. 149.

66 Stillman " 'always looks on the dark side . . .' ": Logan, *George F. Baker and His Bank*, p. 181.

67 " 'A caller would enter Stillman's office . . .' ": Winkler, *The First Billion*, pp. 4–5.

67 " 'In the various reorganization syndicates . . .' ": Cleveland and Huertas, *Citibank*, p. 40.

67 National City's Fortune 500 directors: Ibid., p. 34.

67 " 'Punctuality was rigidly enforced . . .' ": Winkler, *The First Billion*, pp. 69–70.

68 Hepburn becomes director: Cleveland and Huertas, *Citibank*, p. 44.

68 " 'Its assets are clean . . .' ": Examiner's report, March 22, 1898.

69 Returns on National City's loans: Examiner's report, August 8, 1904.

69 " 'This bank is in its usual strong . . .' ": Examiner's report, February 11, 1896.

69 " 'The bank is free . . .' ": Examiner's report, February 18, 1895.

69 "Stillman lent to employees, dummies, and straw men . . .": Examiner's report, August 8, 1904.

69 " 'With the growth of the consolidation . . .' ": Forrest Raynor to the Comptroller of the Currency, December 12, 1901.

70 Description of "Stillman's time": Grover Cleveland, *Presidential Problems* (New York, 1904), p. 169.

71 Debate over the gold standard, and the Sherman Silver Purchase Act of 1890: Ibid., pp. 121–30.

73 " 'You do not want an honest dollar . . .' ": Richard H. Timberlake, *The Origins of Central Banking in the United States* (Cambridge, Mass., and London, 1978), pp. 161–62.

73 " 'If the threat to the gold standard . . .' ": Milton Friedman and Anna Schwartz, *A Monetary History of the United States, 1867–1960* (Princeton, 1963), p. 105n.

73 The gold crisis and Grover Cleveland: Cleveland, *Presidential Problems*, pp. 138–48.

74 " 'This bank has methods . . .' ": Examiner's report, December 6, 1892.

74 " 'Just prior to the panic . . .' ": Winkler, *The First Billion*, p. 74.

74 " 'goldbuggery and Shylockism' ": Vincent P. Carosso, *The Morgans, Private International Bankers 1854–1913* (Cambridge, Mass., 1987), p. 327.

74 " 'not with the enlightened nations . . .' ": Timberlake, *Origins*, p. 161.

75 " 'To have one's motives misinterpreted . . .' ": Carosso, *The Morgans*, p. 343.

75 National City bolsters capital at Gage's request: Cleveland and Huertas, *Citibank*, p. 49.

4. Democratizing Credit

76 "In the bond market in 1900 . . .": Sidney Homer, *A History of Interest Rates* (Rutgers, New Jersey, 1963), pp. 340–44.

77 "The Provident Loan Society of New York opened . . .": Provident Loan Society of New York, *Twenty Fifth Anniversary, 1894–1919* (New York, 1919).

77 Robert Morris: William Graham Sumner, *The Financier and Finances of the American Revolution* (New York, 1968, reprint of 1891 edition), pp. 281–92.

77 " 'Money to Loan . . .' ": Louis Robinson and Rolf Nugent, *Regulation of the Small Loan Business* (New York, 1935), p. 39.

78 For information on the origin of small-loan operations, see Robinson and Nugent, *Regulation*.

78 " 'he originated and perfected the well-known plan . . .' ": *The New York Times*, February 14, 1918.

79 *The Bawlerout*, by Forrest Halsey (New York, 1911).

82 " 'The net result . . .' ": Robinson and Nugent, *Regulation*, p. 76.

83 " 'Took Even Baby's Cradle' ": *The New York Times*, February 4, 1904.

83 Speyer obituary: Ibid., November 1, 1941.

83 Tolman obituary: Ibid., February 14, 1918.

83 News accounts concerning Tolman and loan sharking from the following *New York Times* stories: February 5, 1904; December 24, 1913; February 14, 1918; March 26, 1914; October 11, 1913.

84 " 'At the start . . .' ": Provident Loan Society, *Twenty Fifth Anniversary*, p. 11.

85 Profile of the Provident: Peter Schwed, *God Bless the Pawnbrokers* (New York, 1975); Rolf Nugent, *The Provident Loan Society of New York: An Account of the Largest Remedial Loan Society* (New York, 1932); and Provident Loan Society, *Twenty Fifth Anniversary*.

87 Postal savings: Wayne E. Fuller, *The American Mail: Enlarger of the Common Life* (Chicago and London, 1972), and Carl H. Scheele, *A Short History of the Mail Service* (Washington, D.C., 1970).

88 " 'safe deposit of the earnings . . .' ": People's Party Platform, *National Party Platforms*, Vol. 1: *1840–1956* (Urbana, Chicago, and London, 1978).

88 For a concise narrative of the postal savings bank controversy, see *Bankers Magazine*, March, May, and June 1910.

89 "It was believed . . .": *The New York Times*, January 4, 1911, and Edwin Kemmerer, "Six Years of Postal Savings in the United States," *American Economic Review*, March 1917.

90 Opponents of the system: See Henry Clews, *Financial, Economic, and Miscellaneous Speeches* (1910), p. 299.

90 " 'Its aim is infinitely higher . . .' ": *The New York Times*, October 12, 1913.

91 Government bond prices slump: Kemmerer, "Six Years of Postal Savings," *American Economic Review*, March 1917, and *The New York Times*, November 7, 1911.

91 World interest rates and the Yorkshire Penny Bank: Homer, *History of Interest Rates*, pp. 416, 436; *Times* (London), June 9, 1911.

91 " 'This confidence is touching . . .' ": *The New York Times*, August 3, 1911.

92 " 'Dear Arthur . . .' ": Norfolk Chamber of Commerce, *New Norfolk*, May 1966, p. 15.

92 For a discussion of the mechanics of the Morris Plan, as well as the origins of credit unions, see "The Morris Plan," by Louis N. Robinson, *American Economic Review*, June 1931, and Robinson and Nugent, *Regulation*.

94 " 'The industrial supremacy . . .' ": Major General George Olmstead, "Making America Strong at Home and Abroad: A Private Enterprise at Work" (New York, 1962).

94 " 'No man's debts . . .' ": *Lynchburg* (Va.) *News*, December 5, 1971.

94 "Morris lived long enough . . .": *The New York Times*, November 20, 1973.

95 " 'Democratization of Credit' ": "Fifty Years of Consumer Credit and Its Potentialities," address by Arthur J. Morris before the Consumer Bankers Association, October 21, 1960.

95 " 'Financier Who Opened Way . . .' ": *The New York Times*, November 20, 1973.

95 "Even when allowed . . .": Kemmerer, "Agricultural Credit in the United States," *American Economic Review*, December 1912, p. 853.

96 " '[T]hey kept struggling . . .' ": House of Representatives, "The Report of the Industrial Commission on Agriculture and Agricultural Labor," Vol. 10, 56th Congress, 2nd Session, 1901.

96 " 'lack of any adequate system . . .' ": Quoted in George E. Putnam, "The Federal Farm Loan Act," *American Economic Review*, December 1916, p. 770.

96 " 'any farmer who pays . . .' ": *The New York Times*, July 21, 1916.

97 " 'Farm products bringing high prices . . .' ": "Report of the Industrial Commission," testimony of Charles A. Wieting, p. 993.

97 " 'there seems to be something in the atmosphere . . .' ": Ibid., testimony of M. F. Greeley, p. 935.

98 " 'Most of our farms . . .' ": Ibid., testimony of Brynjolf Prom, p. 790.

98 " 'The old original landholders . . .' ": "Report of the Industrial Commission," testimony of Lawrence Winkler Youmans, pp. 117–20.

99 "According to one historian . . .": Harold D. Woodman, *King Cotton and His Retainers: Financing and Marketing the Cotton Crop of the South, 1800–1925* (Columbia, S.C., 1990), pp. 303, 350.

99 " 'We pay 13 percent . . .' ": "Report of the Industrial Commission," testimony of Lawrence Winkler Youmans, pp. 117–19.

101 " 'Whether he realized it or not . . .' ": Theodore Saloutos and John D. Hicks, *Twentieth Century Populism: Agricultural Discontent in the Middle West 1900–1939* (Lincoln, Nebr., 1951), p. 23.

102 " 'Nothing is more important . . .' ": Ibid., p. 14.

103 "farmers 'are making money . . .' ": Quoted in *Louis Sullivan: The Function of Ornament*, edited by Wim de Wit (Chicago, 1986), p. 164.

103 " 'The plan indeed . . .' ": Ibid., p. 171.

103 Credit cooperatives: George E. Putnam, "Agricultural Credit Legislation and the Tenancy Problem," *American Economic Review*, December 1915, pp. 805–6.

104 " 'These Land Banks . . .' ": Archibald Woodruff, *Farm Mortgage Loans of Life Insurance Companies* (New Haven, 1937), p. 24.

105 " 'had outstanding to farmers . . .' ": Saloutos and Hicks, *Twentieth Century Populism*, p. 103.

106 " 'a lower rate . . .' ": Putnam, "Agricultural Credit Legislation and the Tenancy Problem," *American Economic Review*, December 1915, p. 812.

106 " 'Loans from the Federal . . .' ": Saloutos and Hicks, *Twentieth Century Populism*, pp. 102–3.

107 "Surveying the monetary . . .": Friedman and Schwartz, *Monetary History*, p. 235.

107 "From 1921 to 1928 . . .": Edwin W. Kemmerer, *The ABC of the Federal Reserve System* (New York, 1950), p. 110.

108 "Of the sum . . .": Woodruff, *Farm Mortgage Loans*, p. 33.

108 City Bank in Cuba: Cleveland and Huertas, *Citibank*, pp. 104 and ff.

5. Banking on Confidence

111 " 'When tempted to buy . . .' ": Winkler, *The First Billion*, p. 160.

111 " 'Rising like an altar . . .' " and " 'Keep down . . .' ": Ibid., pp. 183–84.

112 The eccentric needs of Mrs. Green: Boyden Sparks and Samuel Taylor Moore, *The Witch of Wall Street, Hetty Green* (Garden City, N.Y., 1948).

113 " 'But, after all . . .' ": Edwin Lefevre, "Mr. Williams and the Chemical National Bank," *World's Work*, April 1902.

113 " 'I have felt . . .' ": Cleveland and Huertas, *Citibank*, p. 52.

115 " 'Give us back . . .' ": *The Economist*, 1811. See various articles in October and November 1907 *Economist* concerning the Panic of 1907.

115 " 'I well remember . . .' ": Carosso, *The Morgans*, p. 538.

116 " 'Mr. Barney was not . . .' ": *The New York Times*, November 16, 1907.

117 " 'The small capital . . .' ": Examiner's report of Chemical Bank, National Archives, April 7, 1904.

117 " 'Wait . . .' ": Logan, *George F. Baker and His Bank*, p. 126.

117 " 'The bank makes . . .' ": Examiner's report, March 27, 1905.

117 " 'There has always . . .' ": Ibid., December 10, 1906.

117 The directors' liability: Letter of Walter F. Albertson to William B. Ridgely, January 3, 1907. Part of the examiner's reports for the Chemical National Bank, National Archives.

118 " '[A]nd the funniest . . .' ": Sparks and Moore, *The Witch of Wall Street*, pp. 314–15.

118 " 'Notwithstanding that we . . .' ": Letter of William H. Porter to T. P. Kane, December 18, 1907. Part of the examiner's reports for the Chemical National Bank, National Archives.

119 " 'If these building loans . . .' ": *New York Evening Post*, November 14, 1907.

119 " 'acute financial stringency . . .' ": *The New York Times*, October 24, 1907.

119 " 'group of financiers . . .' ": Quoted in Carosso, *The Morgans*, p. 547.

120 " 'No doubt . . .' ": *Collier's*, January 13, 1912.

120 " 'From one point of view . . .' ": *The Economist*, November 2, 1907, p. 1856.

123 " 'The true basis . . .' ": Ibid., November 9, 1907, p. 1904.

124 "When Charles A. Lindbergh . . .": Ida Tarbell, "The Hunt for the Money Trust," *The American Magazine*, May 1913.

124 " 'They do these things differently . . .' ": *The Wall Street Journal*, August 1, 1911.

125 "The up-and-coming . . .": Ida Tarbell, "The Hunt for the Money Trust," *The American Magazine*, May 1913.

125 " 'it is not surprising . . .' ": "Finance, the Division of Wealth," by Garet Garrett, *Collier's*, January 13, 1912.

126 " 'the result is . . .' ": *The Wall Street Journal*, January 30, 1912.

126 The Comptroller's letter: Examiner's report of the First National Bank of New York, National Archives, T. P. Kane to Baker, February 1, 1908.

127 " 'to hold the profits . . .' ": Letter from Charles A. Hanna to T. P. Kane, July 7, 1908. Examiner's reports of the First National Bank of New York, National Archives.

127 "Sheridan Logan . . .": Logan, *George F. Baker and His Bank*, p. 152.

127 The Money Trust hearings: See U.S. Congress, House Subcommittee of the Committee on Banking and Currency, "Money Trust Investigation," 64th Congress, 1st Session, part 11, 1913.

135 Charles G. Dawes: Dawes, *The Banking System of the United States and Its Relation to the Money and Business of the Country* (New York, 1980, reprint of 1894 edition), pp. 69–70.

136 " 'The power to compel . . .' ": *Noble State Bank* v. *Haskell*, "Error to the Supreme Court of the State of Oklahoma," Opinion, p. 112.

136 " 'public scrutiny and watchfulness . . .' ": Eugene White, "Free Banking, Denominational Restrictions and Liability Insurance," *Durell Journal of Money and Banking*, November 1990, p. 28.

137 " 'He had in mind . . .' ": National Monetary Commission, *Safety Fund Banking System in New York*, pp. 260, 382–84.

137 " 'Constitutional, But Worthless . . .' ": *The New York Times*, February 22, 1911.

138 Weeks's testimony: *Congressional Record*, Senate, December 16, 1913, pp. 990–96.

140 " 'should under this new system . . .' ": *The New York Times*, December 24, 1913.

141 " 'It is an altruistic . . .' ": Timberlake, *Origins*, p. 193.

141 "To the suspicious . . .": Tarbell, "The Hunt for the Money Trust," *The American Magazine*, May 1913.

142 " 'was designed to curb . . .' ": Cleveland and Huertas, *Citibank*, p. 76.

142 Elihu Root's testimony on the Federal Reserve Act: *Congressional Record*, Senate, December 13, 1913, pp. 831–35.

6. Loans for Nearly Everyone

145 " 'this business . . .' ": Lawrence Chamberlain, *The Work of the Bond House* (New York, 1912), p. 149.
146 " 'Anybody who declines . . .' ": Homer, *History of Interest Rates*, p. 346.
146 " 'Except under . . .' ": Chamberlain, *The Work of the Bond House*, p. 16.
146 " 'good railroad refunding . . .' ": Ibid., p. 39.
146 "At the bottom . . .": Sheldon M. Novick, *Honorable Justice: The Life of Oliver Wendell Holmes* (Boston, 1989), p. 373.
147 " 'Apart from the . . .' ": Chamberlain, *The Work of the Bond House*, p. 40.
147 Selling bonds to women: Ibid., p. 92.
147 " 'nothing but unfamiliarity . . .' ": Ibid., p. 143.
148 " 'every dollar a crack at the Kaiser' ": *Iron Trade Review*, September 26, 1918, p. 719.
148 "In May 1917 . . .": 1919 Report of the Secretary of the Treasury, p. 66.
149 Competition among workers to sell Liberty bonds: *American Machinist*, April 4, 1918, pp. 565ff.
149 " 'As J.P.'s father . . .' ": Logan, *George F. Baker and His Bank*, p. 184.
150 "The hesitancy felt . . .": Benjamin Anderson, *Economics and the Public Welfare: A Financial and Economic History of the United States, 1914–1946* (Indianapolis, 1949, reprinted in 1979), p. 154.
150 " 'he trotted the legs off . . .' ": Interview with Jackson Reynolds, Columbia University Oral History Project, p. 100.
150 " 'Shortly before the meeting . . .' ": Quoted in Logan, *George F. Baker and His Bank*, pp. 195–96.
151 " 'I congratulate Birmingham . . .' ": Ibid., p. 197.
151 " 'Many workmen . . .' ": *Factory*, April 1918, Vol. 20, No. 4, p. 642.
151 "Stories made the rounds . . .": *Literary Digest*, March 31, 1923.
151 "Later in the war . . .": Alexander D. Noyes, *The War Period of American Finance: 1908–1925* (New York, 1926), p. 181.
152 " 'Reckless wastefulness . . .' ": C. F. Childs, *Concerning U.S. Government Securities* (Chicago, 1947), p. 132.
152 " 'Since 1865 . . .' ": Lawrence Chamberlain, *The Principles of Bond Investment* (New York, 1911 and 1927), pp. 116–17.
152 " 'credit is confidence . . .' ": Ibid., p. 117.
153 "If the government . . .": Noyes, *The War Period of American Finance*, p. 203.
154 " 'Any thought in the future . . .' ": 1919 Report of the Secretary of the Treasury, p. 85.
155 " 'in order to . . .' ": Noyes, *The War Period of American Finance*, p. 339.
156 " 'it could hardly have . . .' ": Friedman and Schwartz, *A Monetary History*, p. 229.

156 " 'Before the $6,000,000,000 . . .' ": Noyes, *The War Period of American Finance*, pp. 190–91.

157 " 'The holders of Liberty bonds . . .' ": Childs, *Concerning U.S. Government Securities*, p. 136.

158 " 'In addressing you . . .' ": S. W. Straus, *The History of the Thrift Movement in America* (New York, 1920), p. 106.

158 " 'In our great . . .' ": Ibid., pp. 54, 61.

159 " 'Years ago . . .' ": *The American Architect*, June 22, 1921, p. 637.

161 " 'In times of war . . .' ": *The Independent*, December 1, 1917, p. 455.

161 " '[I] was over-cautious in the beginning . . .' ": Edwin R. A. Seligman, *The Economics of Instalment Selling* (New York and London, 1927), p. 43.

162 "S. W. Straus & Co. was the promoter . . .": U.S. Securities and Exchange Commission, *Report on the Study and Investigation of the Work, Activities, Personnel, and Functions of Protective and Reorganization Committees*, Part III, "Committees for the Holders of Real Estate Bonds," Washington, D.C., June 3, 1936, pp. 71ff.

162 " 'With the growing competition . . .' ": Seligman, *The Economics of Instalment Selling*, p. 58.

162 " 'I do not . . .' ": *The American Magazine*, January 1922.

163 " 'a potpourri of indifferent . . .' ": New York State Supreme Court, *The People of the State of New York v. S. W. Straus & Co.*, September 3, 1935.

163 " 'Of late years . . .' ": *New York Evening Post*, December 23, 1924.

163 "Mrs. White": Bernard J. Reis, *False Security: The Betrayal of the American Investor* (New York, 1937).

165 " 'We will be able . . .' ": *The New York Times*, July 2, 1926.

165 G. L. Miller failure: Ibid., September 4, 1926.

166 " 'overappraisals of property . . .' ": Ibid., September 4, 1926.

166 Details leading up to the G. L. Miller failure: Reis, *False Security*, p. 144.

167 " 'malicious whispering campaign . . .' ": *The New York Times*, November 10, 1926.

167 " 'We are today . . .' ": *The Wall Street Journal*, November 10, 1926.

168 The American Construction Council committee investigates real-estate bond houses: *The New York Times*, February 7, 8, and 9, 1927.

168 Straus as trustee of the bonds: SEC, *Report on Protective and Reorganization Committees*, p. 12.

168 " 'Real-estate mortgage . . .' ": "What You Should Know About Lending and Borrowing Money on Mortgages," by S. W. Straus, *The American Magazine*, January 1922.

169 " '[T]he unsuccessful buildings . . .' ": *The New York Times*, February 8, 1927.

169 Opening of the real-estate exchange: *Commercial & Financial Chronicle*, August 3, 1929.

170 " 'Many of the leading . . .' ": *The New York Times*, August 25, 1929.

170 "Not until then . . .": Ibid., p. 70.

170 " 'Although a stern disciplinarian . . .' ": *New York Sun*, September 8, 1930.

171 Police officer below Straus's window, and details of Straus's living arrange-

ments: *The New York Times*, September 8, 1930, and September 21, 1932.

171 Robert Moses resigns from Straus protective committee: *The New York Times*, March 20, 1933.

172 " 'one of the main . . .' ": Ibid., March 20, 1933.

172 "Their lawyer said . . .": Ibid., August 30, 1933.

173 " 'The history of . . .' ": Max Winkler, *Foreign Bonds: An Autopsy* (Philadelphia, 1933), p. 10.

174 " 'If America wants to help . . .' ": Thomas Lamont, "Foreign Government Bonds," *Annals of the American Academy of Political and Social Science*, March 1920, p. 129.

174 " 'Many of us . . .' ": U.S. Congress, 72nd Congress, 1st Session, Senate Committee on Finance, "Hearings on the Sale of Foreign Bonds or Securities in the U.S.," December 1931–February 1932, p. 64.

174 " 'In no single field . . .' ": Reis, *False Security*, p. 85.

175 " 'And while the almost fraudulent . . .' ": Winkler, *Foreign Bonds: An Autopsy*, p. 67.

175 "Writing without heat . . .": Barry Eichengreen and Peter H. Lindert, *International Debt Crisis in Historical Perspective* (Cambridge, Mass., 1989), p. 35.

175 " 'History tends to . . .' ": Homer, *History of Interest Rates*, p. 202.

175 Mintz study: Ilse Mintz, *Deterioration in the Quality of Foreign Bonds Issued in the United States, 1920–1930* (Princeton, 1951).

175 "Thus, in 1959, Lawrence Fisher . . .": Cited in Cleveland and Huertas, *Citibank*, p. 404.

175 "More recently . . .": Eichengreen and Lindert, *International Debt Crisis*, p. 35.

176 " 'International Match paid . . .' ": John Train, *Famous Financial Fiascos* (New York, 1985), p. 64.

177 "Kreuger's 'remarkable talents' ": *The Wall Street Journal*, March 9, 1929.

177 "Out went creditworthy . . .": Winkler, *Foreign Bonds: An Autopsy*, p. 99.

177 "It later came to light . . .": Barrie Wigmore, *The Crash and Its Aftermath* (Westport, Conn., 1985), p. 412.

177 " 'No market is . . .' ": *Time*, November 18, 1929.

177 "The deluge was preceded . . .": Winkler, *Foreign Bonds: An Autopsy*, p. 100.

178 Kreuger's suicide and Kreuger & Toll securities at the time: *The New York Times*, March 13, 1932.

178 " 'When such firms as Lee, Higginson & Company . . .' ": Winkler, *Foreign Bonds: An Autopsy*, p. 99.

178 " '*Mundus vult* . . .' ": Ibid., p. 103.

178 "Its motto was . . .": John McFerrin, *Caldwell & Co.: A Southern Financial Empire* (Ithaca, 1969, reprint of 1939 edition), p. 2. McFerrin's superb book constitutes our sole source on Caldwell & Co.

184 " 'any fear on the part . . .' ": Cleveland and Huertas, *Citibank*, p. 162.

185 "Thus, between 1922 and 1928 . . .": Anderson, *Economics and the Public Welfare*, p. 146.

185 For descriptions of the mechanism of the international gold standard, see Melchior Palyi, *The Twilight of Gold 1914–1936: Myths and Realities* (Chicago, 1972), and Arthur I. Bloomfield, *Monetary Policy under the International Gold Standard, 1880–1914*, Federal Reserve Bank of New York, 1959.

187 "When it did try to influence the money market . . .": Anderson, *Economics and the Public Welfare*, p. 154.

188 "In one easy example . . .": Palyi, *The Twilight of Gold*, p. 157.

189 " 'His relatives . . .' ": Lester V. Chandler, *Benjamin Strong, Central Banker* (Washington, D.C., 1958), p. 364.

189 " '[A] currency can . . .' ": Emile Moreau, *The Golden Franc, Memoirs of a Governor of the Bank of France (1926–1928)* (Boulder, 1991), p. 326.

189 " 'give broad acceptance . . .' ": Ibid., p. 87.

189 " 'The only difference . . .' ": Ibid., p. 289.

190 " 'If Strong let things . . .' ": Ibid., p. xiii.

190 " 'like a painting . . .' ": Chandler, *Benjamin Strong*, p. 260.

191 " 'To tell the truth . . .' ": Moreau, *The Golden Franc*, p. 295.

192 " 'a little *coup de whiskey* . . .' ": Murray Rothbard, *America's Great Depression* (Kansas City, 1963), p. 142.

193 " 'Brokers' loans . . .' ": *Literary Digest*, February 27, 1926.

193 S. W. Straus call-loan lending: SEC, *Report on Protective and Reorganization Committees*.

194 George Washington Bridge: Logan, *George F. Baker and His Bank*, p. 237.

194 Baker and Harrison: From the Harrison papers at the New York Federal Reserve.

196 " 'So far as this . . .' ": Anderson, *Economics and the Public Welfare*, p. 212.

196 " 'The head of the . . .' ": Ibid., pp. 222–23.

197 " 'It may not be . . .' ": Logan, *George F. Baker and His Bank*, p. 237.

198 Baker's bullishness: Ibid., pp. 248–49.

7. *The Welfare State of Credit*

201 " 'Frankly . . .' ": *American Banker*, May 5, 1933.

201 " '[W]ould it be wise . . .' ": *American Banker*, June 3, 1933.

202 "literally gave away . . .": Champion Oral History, p. 26.

202 "Thus, it was the Bank of United States . . .": M. R. Werner, *Little Napoleons and Dummy Directors* (New York and London, 1933), p. 7. The following account draws chiefly on Werner.

207 Dialogue between Hoover and Jackson Reynolds: Interview with Jackson Reynolds, Oral History Project, Columbia University, pp. 145–46.

208 " 'a great many . . .' ": Ibid., p. 148.

208 " 'Everything is all right . . .' ": *New York Evening Post*, December 11, 1930.

209 " 'men of perhaps pawnbroking capacity . . .' ": Interview with Jackson Reynolds, Oral History Project, p. 147.

210 Bank of United States returns 83.3 cents on the dollar: 94th Annual Report of the New York State Superintendent of Banks, 1944, p. 80.

210 " 'I told them I thought it was because . . .' ": Friedman and Schwartz, *A Monetary History*, p. 310.

211 " 'Have I said something . . .' ": Interview with Jackson Reynolds, Oral History Project, p. 73.

212 " 'He always wrote . . .' ": Ibid., p. 79.

212 Fuller anecdote: Interview with Robert G. Fuller, June 12, 1991.

212 "In only one case was a broker's loan called . . .": Samuel A. Welldon, *The First National Bank of the City of New York* (manuscript), p. 51.

212 "In May 1931, six months after . . .": Anderson, *Economics and the Public Welfare*, p. 238.

213 " 'National calamity' ": Grover Cleveland, *Presidential Problems*, p. 138.

213 " 'Baker luck' ": Logan, *George F. Baker and His Bank*, p. 255.

213 " 'Vast Baker Wealth as yet Uncounted . . .' ": *The New York Times*, May 5, 1931.

213 " 'the man who was always a bull . . .' ": *The Wall Street Journal*, May 6, 1931.

214 " 'enduring . . .' ": *The New York Times*, May 5, 1931.

214 Description of the First National Bank building: Welldon, *The First National Bank*, p. 56.

215 " '[I]f the rest of the country looks . . .' ": Cleveland and Huertas, *Citibank*, p. 170.

216 " '[T]he banks, individually . . .' ": Ibid., p. 170.

216 "shift away from laissez-faire": Karl R. Bopp, "Central Banking at the Crossroads," *American Economic Review*, Supplement 34, 1944.

217 "Fault had been found with this idea . . .": Ibid., p. 267n.

218 " 'With [RFC] . . .' ": Anderson, *Economics and the Public Welfare*, p. 271.

218 Description of Treasurys in the Depression: Wigmore, *The Crash and Its Aftermath*, p. 552.

219 " 'Now . . . and I measure my words . . .' ": *The New York Times*, November 18, 1932.

219 American Securities Investing Corp.: Interview with Jackson Reynolds, Oral History Project, pp. 158–61.

219 " 'the most significant step since . . .' ": Quoted in *Literary Digest*, June 11, 1932.

219 Emergency Relief and Construction Act: Edwin Kemmerer, *ABC of the Federal Reserve System* (Princeton, 1950), p. 115.

220 Loans made by the Home Loan Banks: Rothbard, *America's Great Depression*, p. 244; *The New York Times*, October 8, 1931.

221 " 'These are days . . .' ": *The New York Times*, July 9, 1932.

222 " 'Out of wrath come none but misbegotten offspring . . .' ": *Fortune*, December 1932.

222 "and for other boom-time offenses . . .": Anderson, *Economics and the Public Welfare*, p. 282.

222 "In March 1933, *Time* . . .": Cleveland and Huertas, *Citibank*, p. 171.

223 " 'The title of banker . . .' ": Ibid., pp. 183–84.

224 "X" account: Interview with Robert G. Fuller; Harrison papers, January 12, 18, 1933; James Grant, *Bernard Baruch: The Adventures of a Wall Street Legend* (New York, 1983), p. 247.

225 " 'scandal-mongers and others . . .' ": *Commercial & Financial Chronicle*, February 18, 1933.

225 "From February 1 to March 3 . . .": Cleveland and Huertas, *Citibank*, p. 189.

225 " 'The unthinking attempt . . .' ": Ibid., pp. 189–90.

225 " '[He] was not . . .' ": Interview with Jackson Reynolds, Oral History Project, p. 41.

226 " 'His plan,' as Reynolds remembered it . . .": Ibid., pp. 165–66.

226 " 'I was with . . .' ": Ibid., p. 168.

228 " 'The presumption is that the emergency . . .' ": *American Banker*, April 14, 1933.

228 "In 1933, it was estimated . . .": Henry Mark Holzer, *The Gold Clause: What It Is and How to Use It Profitably* (New York, 1980), p. 265.

229 " 'because I was . . .' ": James Grant, *Bernard Baruch: Adventures of a Wall Street Legend* (New York, 1983), p. 250.

229 "Senator Elmer Thomas . . .": Holzer, *The Gold Clause*, p. 40.

230 " 'the enforcement . . .' ": Ibid., pp. 40–41.

230 " 'It's dishonor, sir . . .' ": Anderson, *Economics and the Public Welfare*, p. 315.

230 " 'Why, that's just plain stealing . . .' ": Ibid., p. 317.

230 " 'the American default . . .' ": *American Banker*, May 31, 1933.

231 " 'Thus in a hectic period . . .' ": Holzer, *The Gold Clause*, p. 255.

231 " 'Should the claims . . .' ": Ibid., pp. 266–68.

232 " 'Gold is not an ordinary commodity . . .' ": Ibid., p. 257.

232 " 'On the contrary . . .' ": Ibid., p. 283.

233 " 'The record reveals . . .' ": Ibid., pp. 92ff.

233 " 'We are rich in money in the bank . . .' ": *American Banker*, June 15, 1933.

235 Jesse Jones implores bankers to support recovery program: *The New York Times*, September 6, 1933.

236 " 'Many of the banks . . .' ": Ibid., September 6, 1933.

236 " 'in these times the obligation . . .' ": Cleveland and Huertas, *Citibank*, p. 199.

237 " 'It is almost impossible . . .' ": Ibid., p. 204.

237 "But the only propitious omen . . .": *Architectural Forum*, August 1933, p. 117.

238 " 'This is a huge money-making machine . . .' ": Examiner's report of the First National Bank of New York, National Archives, September 28, 1896.

238 "From 1922 to 1933 . . .": Welldon, *The First National Bank*, p. 60.

239 "In 1931, the First made . . .": Logan, *George F. Baker and His Bank*, p. 258.

239 Federal Reserve Section 13b passed: *Commercial & Financial Chronicle*, June 23, 1934.

239 "A year later . . .": *Bankers Magazine*, July 1935.

240 " 'we should at length have a test . . .' ": *Commercial & Financial Chronicle*, June 30, 1934.

240 Reynolds and Roosevelt speak before the American Bankers Association: *The New York Times*, October 25, 1934; John Brooks, *Once in Golconda: The True Drama of Wall Street 1920–1938* (New York, Evanston, and London, 1969), pp. 213–15.

240 " 'Two years ago, deposits at this bank . . .' ": *Literary Digest*, January 19, 1935.

241 " 'We have been opposed . . .' ": *Commercial & Financial Chronicle*, January 12, 1935.

241 " 'It looks as though these modifications . . .' ": *Literary Digest*, January 19, 1935.

241 " 'With the Government doing so large a share . . .' ": *Bankers Magazine*, June 1935.

242 Quoted testimony of H. Parker Willis on the 1935 Banking Act: *Commercial & Financial Chronicle*, June 15, 1935.

243 " 'Mr. Congressman, I do not think . . .' ": Hearings before the House Committee on Banking and Currency, "Banking Act of 1935," March 1, 1935, p. 155.

243 " 'Member banks are suffering . . .' ": Ibid., p. 184.

243 " 'I am opposed to any change in the law . . .' ": "Banking Act of 1935," Senate Hearings, p. 419.

244 Testimony of Morton Bodfish: Ibid., pp. 907ff.

8. False Alarms

245 " 'the damn fool . . .' ": *The New York Times*, June 27, 1991.

246 "John Maynard Keynes . . .": Bernard Baruch, *Public Years* (New York, 1960), p. 349.

246 " 'a banker who never worked in a bank' ": *The New York Times*, April 9, 1945.

247 " 'benighted fool . . .' ": Logan, *George F. Baker and His Bank*, p. 383.

247 " 'He expressed a distaste . . .' ": Robert G. Fuller to Benjamin Haggott Beckhart, May 26, 1969.

247 " '[W]hen do we start . . .' ": Ibid.

248 Fraser's monetary views and testimony: Hearings before the House Committee on Banking and Currency, "Bretton Woods Agreement Act," 79th Congress, 1st Session, March 1945, Washington, D.C.

249 "resolved to abandon reform . . .": Logan, *George F. Baker and His Bank*, p. 384.

249 Kemmerer's testimony: "Bretton Woods Agreement Act" hearings, p. 832.

250 Palyi's testimony: Ibid., pp. 892ff.

251 Fraser's suicide: *The New York Times*, April 9, 1945.

251 " 'Finis?' ": Fuller to Beckhart, May 26, 1969.

252 " 'But I want to dispel any idea . . .' ": *The New York Times* and *American Banker*, January 10, 1945.

252 " 'No, we just hope to stay as we are . . .' ": *Fortune*, July 1945.

252 " 'Nagle, you have been elected manager . . .' ": Logan, *George F. Baker and His Bank*, p. 388.

253 "World War II had brought . . .": Welldon, *The First National Bank*, pp. 67ff.

253 "Nagle did, certainly . . .": *Fortune*, July 1945.

254 *The New Yorker*'s description of the First National Bank of New York in 1946: December 21, 1946.

254 "The Depression still cast its shadow . . .": *Time*, June 17, 1946.

254 1949 annual meeting: *American Banker*, January 12, 1949.

254 "The National City Bank had warned . . .": Cleveland and Huertas, *Citibank*, p. 213.

254 Loan growth: 1947 FDIC Annual Report, p. 67.

255 "Between 1945 and 1948, City's personal-loan volume tripled . . .": Cleveland and Huertas, *Citibank*, p. 217.

255 City Bank's conservatism: Cleveland and Huertas, *Citibank*, pp. 205ff.

255 "Although the bond market had peaked in 1946 . . .": Ibid., p. 227.

255 "Credit risk, as measured by the bad-debt experience . . .": FDIC 1947 Annual Report, p. 73.

255 "In 1933, the maximum insured sum . . .": Melanie S. Tammen, "The Savings and Loan Crisis: Which Train Derailed—Deregulation or Deposit Insurance?" *Journal of Law and Politics*, Winter 1990, p. 316.

256 " 'In effect, the depositors of the absorbed bank . . .' ": FDIC 1938 Annual Report, p. 12.

256 " 'With increased coverage and broadened powers of reorganization . . .' ": FDIC 1944 Annual Report, p. 10.

256 " 'This record of safety for depositors . . .' ": FDIC 1950 Annual Report.

257 "But the failure, also in 1950 . . .": Hearings before a subcommittee of the Senate Committee on Banking and Currency, 82nd Congress, 1st Session, "On the Nominations of H. Earl Cook, etc.," 1951, p. 65.

257 "It was found stuffed in vaults, boxes, and desks . . .": Ibid., pp. 64, 72.

257 " 'It would seem to me maybe your policy . . .' ": Ibid., p. 81.

258 " 'How times have changed! . . .' ": Ibid., p. 51.

258 " 'the reason we were able to pay off . . .' ": Ibid., p. 82.

258 Blue-chip companies deposit at the First National Bank of New York: Logan, *George F. Baker and His Bank*, p. 278.

259 "It was not until the mid-1950s . . .": Cleveland and Huertas, *Citibank*, p. 285.

259 Reynolds's opposition to soliciting: Fuller interview.

259 Spencer Chemical transaction: Interview with Clarence F. Michalis, March 29, 1990; E. J. Kahn, Jr., *Jock: The Life and Times of John Hay Whitney* (New York, 1981), p. 188.

259 "but they could lend no more than $11 million . . .": Welldon, *The First National Bank*, p. 77.

260 "In 1946, for the first time since the Depression . . .": W. Braddock Hickman, *Corporate Bond Quality and Investor Experience* (Princeton, 1958), p. 251.

260 "Fuller continued to be . . .": *The Wall Street Journal*, January 11, 1950. Fuller is not identified by name, but his signature style is unmistakable.

260 "Second mortgages were reappearing": Geoffrey Moore, "Changes in the Quality of Credit," *Journal of Finance*, May 1956, p. 290.

260 "It was a sign of the times that the Provident Loan Society . . .": Schwed, *God Bless the Pawnbrokers*, p. 27.

260 "Arguably, it was too late . . .": Welldon, *The First National Bank*, pp. 64ff.

261 " 'The passing of the First National . . .' ": *The New York Times*, March 3, 1955.

262 "They blamed prosperity on the boom in American consumer credit . . .": *The New York Times*, February 12, 1956.

262 Eisenhower's concern: "Economic Report of the President," transmitted, January 24, 1956, p. 31.

262 "In 1974, *Pravda* urged the West . . .": Robert Solomon, *The International Monetary System, 1945–1981* (New York, 1982), p. 376.

263 "If repossessions and delinquencies were still low . . .": *Automotive News*, May 30, 1955.

263 " 'crazy credit' ": Ibid., August 15, 1955.

263 "In August, General Motors Acceptance Corp. . . .": *The Wall Street Journal*, August 10, 1955.

263 "What is wrong with debt?": Ibid., August 5, 1955.

264 1920s mortgage terms: The President's Conference on Home Ownership, "Home Finance and Taxation," 1932, p. 21.

264 "subsidized mortgages 'would have appalled . . .' ": *Barron's*, March 14, 1955.

264 " 'Young Dr. B.'s Income Soars 1,000% . . .' ": *The Wall Street Journal*, August 12, 1955.

264 Geoffrey Moore, "Changes in the Quality of Credit": *The Journal of Finance*, May 1956, pp. 288–300.

266 " 'The more intense the craze . . .' ": Anderson, *Economics and the Public Welfare*, p. 203.

266 " 'Some people are scared to death . . .' ": *Barron's*, April 11, 1955.

267 " 'There exists, and has always existed . . .' ": Sidney E. Rolfe, "Installment Credit: The $28 Billion Question," *Harvard Business Review*, July–August 1956, pp. 48–60.

267 Relative appeal of debt: *Bankers Monthly*, April 1956.

268 " 'It is one thing when stocks yield over 6 percent . . .' ": *Barron's*, February 28, 1955.

269 " 'In most recent years . . .' ": 1958 FDIC Annual Report.

269 "In the 1920s, banks had typically lent . . .": David Rogers, *Consumer Banking in New York* (New York, 1974), p. 17.

269 " 'The long-term trend of loans is bound to be upward . . .' ": *Bankers Monthly*, February 15, 1955.

270 " 'We recognize . . .' ": 1955 First National City Bank Annual Report, p. 19.

270 The relation of the dollar to gold: Hearings before the House Committee on Banking and Currency, "Removal of the Gold Cover," 90th Congress, 2nd Session, January–February 1968, p. 51.

270 " 'In continental Europe . . .' ": Solomon, *International Monetary System*, p. 21.

271 " 'The growth of the gold and dollar . . .' ": Ibid., p. 28.

272 Rueff's life: *The Times* (London), April 25, 1978.

273 " 'Thus, the United States . . .' ": Jacques Rueff, *The Monetary Sin of the West* (New York, 1972), p. 23.

274 " 'If elected President . . .' ": Solomon, *International Monetary System*, p. 35.

274 " 'the gold-exchange standard places the whole economy . . .' ": Rueff, *Monetary Sin*, p. 46.

274 " 'The gold-exchange standard is a misleading disguise . . .' ": Ibid., p. 47.

274 "Late in 1960, a delegation . . .": Ibid., p. 36.

275 "Henry C. Alexander, chairman of the Morgan Guaranty . . .": *The Wall Street Journal*, January 16, 1961.

275 "An expansion . . .": Solomon, *International Monetary System*, p. 43.

276 "The inflation of the dollar had reached . . .": William Rickenbacker, *Wooden Nickels, Or, The Decline and Fall of Silver Coins* (New Rochelle, N.Y., 1966), p. 21.

276 " '[W]hat the United States owes to foreign countries . . .' ": Rueff, *Monetary Sin*, pp. 72–74.

277 "The years 1961 to 1965, in the words of Sidney Homer . . .": Homer, *History of Interest Rates*, p. 366.

277 " 'Why Workers Don't Mind . . .' ": *U.S. News & World Report*, October 4, 1965, pp. 99–100.

278 "Some $1.8 billion in gold . . .": *The New York Times*, March 5, 1965.

278 *Business Week* rebuke: April 24, 1965, p. 176.

278 " 'get out their lead pencil and put on their glasses . . .' ": *The New York Times*, April 1, 1966.

281 "On the date of the devaluation . . .": Solomon, *International Monetary System*, p. 96.

281 "For the time being, the idea went nowhere . . .": Ibid., p. 116.

281 "The Treasury, therefore, prevailed on central banks . . .": Ibid., p. 104.

281 " 'To the average . . .' ": "Removal of the Gold Cover," Hearings, p. 19.

282 " 'Removal of this requirement . . .' ": Ibid., p. 23.

282 " 'Would this [measure] encourage . . .' ": Ibid., p. 88.

283 " 'The conception . . .' ": Ibid., p. 291.

283 "One Treasury Department witness . . .": Ibid., p. 55.

283 " 'We will use our gold down to the last bar . . .' ": Ibid., p. 71.

284 The statement announcing dissolution of the Gold Pool: Solomon, *International Monetary System*, pp. 121–22.

285 " 'In effect the decision to terminate . . .' ": Federal Reserve Bank of New York, 1968 Annual Report, p. 34.

285 " 'This action will not win us any friends . . .' ": Solomon, *International Monetary System*, p. 186.

286 " 'After the devaluation of the pound . . .' ": Jacques Rueff, *Monetary Sin*, p. 155.

9. It's a Wonderful World

287 " 'The customers came at us like Coxey's army . . .' ": *The Wall Street Journal*, March 12, 1969.

287 "Since the time of Queen Anne . . .": *Institutional Investor*, "Can the Bond Market Survive?" by John F. Lyons, May 1969.

287 Interest rates in 1956, 1959, and 1966: Homer, *History of Interest Rates*, p. 361.

288 Coe Scruggs and John H. Larkin on the bond market: *Institutional Investor*, May 1969.

289 "When, inevitably, a bank did shut its doors . . .": Federal Reserve Board, *Banking and Monetary Statistics*, p. 421.

289 " 'the ready availability . . .' ": Securities and Exchange Commission, Staff Report to the Special Subcommittee on Investigations, "The Financial Collapse of the Penn Central Company," Washington, D.C., 1972.

290 Description of Penn Central: "Recent Developments in the Commercial Paper Market," by Frederick Shadrock and Frederick Breimyer, New York Federal Reserve, *Monthly Review*, December 1970, p. 289; House of Representatives, "The Penn Central Failure and the Role of Financial Institutions," 92nd Congress, 1st Session, Staff Report of the Committee on Banking and Currency, January 3, 1972.

290 Commercial paper: SEC, "Financial Collapse . . . ," p. 272; New York Federal Reserve, *Monthly Review*, December 1970, p. 279.

291 Description of the National Credit Office: SEC, "Financial Collapse . . . ," pp. 272–300.

292 Kennedy, " 'paled perceptibly' ": Stephan Salsbury, *No Way to Run a Railroad: The Untold Story of the Penn Central Crisis* (New York, 1982), p. 181.

293 " 'bankrupt or not, many railroads . . .' ": *Barron's*, June 15, 1970.

293 " 'Holders of paper issued by other large corporations . . .' ": New York Federal Reserve, *Monthly Review*, December 1970, p. 289.

294 " 'the System recognized that it might . . .' ": Ibid., p. 290.

295 " 'At this point the availability . . .' ": SEC, "Financial Collapse . . . ," p. 289.

295 " 'It would seem apparent that NCO's . . .' ": Ibid., p. 295.

296 Property of Penn Central in receivership: *Dun's Review*, "Penn Central: Up from the Ashes," November 1978.

296 Alexander Hamilton and real-estate lending: Earl Sylvester Sparks and

Thomas N. Carver, *History and Theory of Agricultural Credit in the United States* (New York, 1932), p. 57.

296 " 'note issues of the State Bank of Illinois . . .' ": Homer Hoyt, *One Hundred Years of Land Values in Chicago* (Chicago, 1933), p. 445.

297 Reuss and Bergmann testimony: Subcommittee No. 1 of the House Committee on Banking and Currency, "National Bank Legislation," 87th Congress, 2nd Session, 1962.

298 Real-estate investment trusts: *Fortune*, "Sorting Out Real-Estate Investment Trusts," August 1970; Senate Committee on Banking, Housing, and Urban Affairs, "Real Estate Investment Trusts," 94th Congress, 2nd Session, May 27, 1976.

298 " 'Millions of jobs as well as millions of homes . . .' ": Ibid., p. 109; *U.S. News & World Report*, August 12, 1968.

298 First Mortgage Investors trades at 33 times earnings: *Fortune*, August 1970.

299 Chase Manhattan Mortgage & Realty Trust: *Business Week*, "Chase's REIT Keeps Afloat—Barely," April 5, 1976.

299 Citizens & Southern: *Forbes*, "The Morning After at Citizens & Southern," July 1, 1975.

300 "The New American Land Rush": *Time*, October 1, 1973.

301 " 'universal bank' ": George S. Moore, *The Banker's Life* (New York and London, 1987), p. 20.

302 Warren Marcus on the negotiable CD: Interview with Warren Marcus, March 20, 1991.

303 Walter Wriston speaks to the New York Society of Security Analysts: "Citicorp in the Seventies," remarks of Walter Wriston before the New York Society of Security Analysts, February 22, 1973.

304 Warren Marcus on Citibank and 15 percent growth: Interview with Warren Marcus, March 20, 1991.

305 " 'Whenever there is a national emergency . . .' ": *Institutional Investor*, September 1973, p. 103.

305 Wriston the foreign-branch builder: Cleveland and Huertas, *Citibank*, p. 262.

306 National City Bank enters the personal loan business: Ibid., p. 212.

307 " 'The men outnumber the women . . .' ": *Literary Digest*, "Our Biggest Bank to Serve Small Borrowers," May 19, 1928.

307 " 'The National City's new adventure . . .' ": Quoted in *Literary Digest*, May 19, 1928.

307 Roger Steffan on the common man as borrower: Moore, *The Banker's Life*, p. 158.

309 " 'She will help us . . .' ": National City Bank, 1973 Annual Report.

309 First Check-Credit Account: From a February edition of "About the First," an in-house newsletter of the First National Bank of Boston. Also interview with John W. Calkins, March 14, 1991.

310 " 'Potentially . . .' ": Cleveland and Huertas, *Citibank*, p. 273.

311 Citicorp and the credit card: *Fortune*, "Citicorp's Rocky Affair with the Consumer," by Carol Loomis, March 24, 1980, p. 78.

311 Citicorp's credit-card mailing campaign: *The New York Times*, July 23, 1978.

311 People collect cards of different banks: *Newsweek*, "Living in Debt," January 8, 1979.

312 1969 hearings on credit-card abuse: U.S. House Subcommittee on Postal Operations of the Committee on Post Office and Civil Service, "The Plastic Jungle," 91st Congress, 1st Session, October 29, 1969–January 28, 1970.

313 "In 1970, only 22.9 percent . . .": Charles A. Luckett, "Household Borrowing Behavior: Some Survey Evidence," 9th meeting of the Financial Management Association, Boston, October 11–13, 1979.

313 " 'repayments of consumer installment . . .' ": New York Federal Reserve Bank, Annual Report, 1978, pp. 10–11.

314 Ted Griswold: *Newsweek*, January 8, 1979, and interview, May 9, 1991.

314 Annunzio on Volcker: William Greider, *Secrets of the Temple: How the Federal Reserve Runs the Country* (New York, 1987), p. 181.

315 The Fed miscounts the money supply: *Barron's*, October 29, 1979.

317 "However, the war itself was financed . . .": Homer, *History of Interest Rates*, pp. 307ff.

317 " 'It began to be especially noted . . .' ": Andrew Dickson White, *Fiat Money Inflation in France* (New York, 1980, reprint of 1912 edition), p. 32.

318 " 'Caught up in the specious present . . .' ": Lewis E. Lehrman, "Monetary Policy, the Federal Reserve System, and Gold," Morgan Stanley, 1980, pp. 27–28.

319 "It was widely expected that the brilliant success . . .": White, *Fiat Money*, p. 31.

319 Fourth anti-inflation program: *Newsweek*, March 24, 1980.

319 " 'Just as our governments . . .' ": Stacey L. Schreft, "Credit Controls: 1980," Federal Reserve Bank of Richmond, *Economic Review*, p. 35.

321 Darryl Francis argues against credit controls: *Barron's*, "Choose Your Weapons: Selective Credit Controls Would Do More Harm Than Good," by Darryl R. Francis, December 8, 1969.

321 " 'It would establish . . .' ": Schreft, "Credit Controls," p. 28.

321 " '[It] is toothless . . .' ": *Newsweek*, March 24, 1980.

321 Consumers mail cut credit cards to White House: Greider, *Secrets*, p. 185.

321 " 'necessities and emergencies' ": *The New York Times*, May 9, 1980.

322 " 'once again discovered parlour games . . .' ": Schreft, "Credit Controls," p. 42.

322 " 'It may have been symbolic . . .' ": *The New York Times*, May 9, 1980.

323 Contractors mail bricks and lumber to the Fed: Greider, *Secrets*, p. 189.

323 " 'We really didn't think we had hit the mule . . .' ": Ibid., p. 187.

10. "Crooked Banker Found Hanged"

324 Description of Champion's early life: Interview with George Champion, July 7 and 12, 1978 (Chase Manhattan Bank Archives).

326 " 'Marshal Tito, the President of Germany . . .' ": *Fortune*, January 14, 1980.

326 "by 1950, he was supervising . . .": *The New York Times*, January 30, 1979.

327 Champion relates the crisis at Canal Bank & Trust and talks of Huey Long: Champion interview, 1978, pp. 6–19.

327 Chase "overloaded with German bonds . . .": *The New York Times*, October 26, 1933.

328 Chase stock in 1932: Wigmore, *The Crash and Its Aftermath*, p. 357.

330 " 'I handled the second term loan . . .' ": *Nation's Business*, March 1967.

330 Champion discusses his career, views on banking, and history of the Chase: Champion interview, 1978.

334 Description of S. C. Gwynne as Third World lender: S. C. Gwynne, *Selling Money* (New York, 1986); and *Harper's*, "Adventures in the Loan Trade," by S. C. Gwynne, September 1983.

336 Lawrence Dennis testimony: Senate Committee on Finance, "Hearings on the Sale of Foreign Bonds or Securities in the U.S.," 72nd Congress, 1st Session, 1932, p. 1585.

336 " 'For all the epidemic . . .' ": Eichengreen and Lindert, *International Debt Crisis*, p. 236.

336 "By 1982, the nine largest American banks . . .": GAO, "International Banking: Supervision of Overseas Lending Is Inadequate," May 1988, p. 14.

336 " 'A significant portion of the loans . . .' ": Ibid., p. 14.

337 " 'There's so much liquidity chasing so few borrowers . . .' ": *Euromoney*, "Buddy Can You Borrow a Dollar?" May 1978, p. 10.

337 George Moore's lending manual is lost: George S. Moore, speech before a *Grant's Interest Rate Observer* Credit Conference, 1986.

337 " 'I think there has been an exaggerated concern . . .' ": *Euromoney*, "The Problems That Concern David Rockefeller," September 1977, p. 13.

338 " 'much needed sink-hole for excess banking liquidity . . .' ": Ibid., "How Chile Reappeared on the Tombstones," June 1977, p. 101.

338 " 'We're in the banking business . . .' ": Ibid., May 1978, p. 13.

338 " 'Once a bank is in the international market . . .' ": Ibid., May 1978, p. 15.

338 Evolution of Third World lending terms: Eichengreen and Lindert, *International Debt Crisis*, p. 236.

339 " 'One by one . . .' ": Greider, *Secrets*, p. 436.

340 Mexico defaults: Ibid., pp. 483–87.

340 "Three and a half billion dollars . . .": Ibid., p. 518.

341 " 'It was like the *Titanic* . . .' ": *Euromoney*, "Champion of the Citi," by Peter Field and Nigel Adam, October 1983, p. 296.

341 Citicorp earnings in 1982: Citicorp 1982 Annual Report.

341 " 'Over the years . . .' ": *The New York Times*, September 14, 1982.

342 "Conceding Champion's point, Wriston had nevertheless . . .": Citicorp, 1982 Annual Report, p. 25.

344 " 'Our analysis shows that under present circumstances . . .' ": Carlos Geraldo Langoni, "Brazilian Strategy in the Recent Financial Crisis," address in New York City, December 20, 1982, p. 4.

345 " 'If the projects for new loans . . .' ": *The New York Times*, December 31, 1982.

345 " 'Meanwhile,' *The Wall Street Journal* reported . . .": *The Wall Street Journal*, November 6, 1987.

346 " 'Don't get in a position . . .' ": Champion interview, 1978, p. 67.

346 " 'They don't really believe what they say . . .' ": *American Banker*, September 9, 1988.

347 Tehan profile: *Grant's*, June 2, 1985.

348 " 'Rather than a greater rate of inflation . . .' ": William Tehan, "Shifting Gears from Inflation to Deflation," speech given in Acapulco, Mexico, June 27, 1981.

349 "In the space of thirteen months, commodity prices . . .": Anderson, *Economics and the Public Welfare*, p. 80.

349 "The only steeper fall . . .": Friedman and Schwartz, *A Monetary History*, p. 232.

349 "In February 1982, frightened depositors . . .": *Hartford Courant*, February 9, 1982.

350 "In Iowa in 1985, land prices . . .": *Grant's*, March 24, 1986.

350 "For the nation as a whole . . .": Ben Sunbury, *The Fall of the Farm Credit Empire* (Ames, Iowa, 1990), p. 233.

350 " 'Bankruptcies will continue to soar . . .' ": *Grant's*, April 21, 1986.

350 Growth of federal guarantees: Office of Management and Budget, *Special Analysis F*, 1982, pp. 182 and 181.

351 "By the end of 1935 the HOLC . . .": Donald Horton, *Long Term Debts in the United States* (Washington, D.C., 1937), p. 143.

351 "In 1938, the FHA was authorized . . .": *Fortune*, "The House Not-So-Beautiful," May 1938.

351 Levittown: *Harper's Weekly*, "The 6,000 Homes That Levitt Built," by Eric Larrabee, September 1948.

351 " 'many of whom refuse . . .' ": *Fortune*, "The House," May 1938, p. 94.

352 "In 1950, fewer than half of American houses . . .": William Clyde Phelps, *Financing the Instalment Purchases of the American Family*, Studies in Consumer Credit No. 3 (Baltimore, 1954), p. 25.

352 "In 1970, the federal government bestowed . . .": *Grant's*, April 12, 1991.

353 Kent Colton testimony: U.S. House Subcommittee on Housing and Community Development of the Committee on Banking, Housing and Urban Affairs, "The Role of Fannie Mae and Freddie Mac on the Mortgage Market," statement of the National Association of Home Builders, 101st Congress, 1st Session, July 26, 1990.

354 "The system was (and is) . . .": Thomas Stanton, *A State of Risk* (New York, 1991), pp. 20, 43.

354 "By 1936, the twentieth anniversary . . .": Bert Ely and Vicki Vanderhoff,

"The Farm Credit System: Reckless Lender to Rural America" (Washington, D.C., 1990), p. 7. Much of the material on Farm Credit comes from this excellent analysis.

355 "The Intermediate Term Credit Banks . . .": Farm Credit System, 1980 Annual Report, p. 7.

355 "The Banks for Cooperatives . . .": Sunbury, *The Fall of the Farm Credit Empire*, p. 7.

355 "In 1979, the Farm Credit System . . .": The Farm Credit System Fact Sheet.

356 "For a time in 1979 . . .": Sunbury, *The Fall of the Farm Credit Empire*, p. xiii.

356 " 'It could be said . . .' ": Ibid., p. 70.

356 The *Wall Street Journal* article on the Farm Credit System is dated September 4, 1985.

358 " 'Removing these restraints . . .' ": Ely and Vanderhoff, "The Farm Credit System," p. 22.

359 "In 1934, Walter Cummings . . .": *The New York Times*, August 21, 1967.

359 " 'America has a system . . .' ": Museum of Fine Arts (Houston), "Money Matters."

359 " 'Behind that quiet façade . . .' ": Continental Illinois, "Behind That Quiet Façade," 1982.

359 "In its inflation-era heyday . . .": Irvine H. Sprague, *Bailout: An Insider's Account of Bank Failures and Rescues* (New York, 1986), pp. 150, 155.

360 Continental quotes Eliot and " 'reached for a larger share of progress . . .' ": Continental Illinois, "Behind," p. 17.

361 Roger Anderson and Penn Square: Sprague, *Bailout*, pp. 111–13.

361 "Although solvent . . .": *The New York Times*, January 9, 1934.

361 " 'I believe that this protection . . .' ": *Newsweek*, January 20, 1934. Concerning Cummings's politics, see *The New York Times*, August 21, 1967.

361 Nichols refuses to capitulate to FDIC: *Newsweek*, January 6, 1934.

362 Nichols marks down his Federal Reserve stock: *Chicago Tribune*, June 14, 1972.

362 " 'I would just as soon give up . . .' ": *The New York Times*, January 7, 1934.

362 " 'a damnable piece of political trickery' ": Ibid., September 21, 1934.

362 Nichols closes bank, then destroys building and covers site with black soil: Ibid., August 21, 1941, and December 29, 1943.

362 " 'They gathered the savings . . .' ": Hoyt, *One Hundred Years of Land Values*, p. 445.

362 " 'a good banker is supposed to know . . .' ": *Chicago Tribune*, January 10, 1934.

364 "Early in the year, federal examiners had found . . .": Robert Sobel, *The Big Board: A History of the New York Stock Exchange* (New York, 1965), p. 73.

364 "it was without a stable base of consumer deposits . . .": *The Wall Street Journal*, July 12, 1984.

364 Profile of "Monkeybrains": Mark Singer, *Funny Money* (New York, 1985), pp. 59, 118–21.
365 " 'Four young men wearing cowboy hats . . .' ": *American Banker*, July 7, 1982.
366 " 'we had a people problem . . .' ": March 31, 1983, Continental Illinois report.
366 "On May 8 . . .": Singer, *Funny Money*, p. 153.
366 Description of the Continental Illinois architecture: "Money Matters," p. 214.
366 " 'Various scenarios were laid out . . .' ": Sprague, *Bailout*, p. 155.
367 " 'an unauthorized and unlegislated . . .' ": *The New York Times*, July 26, 1984.
367 "It had become an 80 percent-owned . . .": Sprague, *Bailout*, p. 188.
367 "In 1933, the Continental . . .": *The New York Times*, January 10, 1934.
367 "In subsequent testimony . . .": Sprague, *Bailout*, p. 259.

11. Wild and Woolly

368 " 'interest rate swaps,' " etc.: *Grant's*, April 20, 1987.
368 " 'It's our way . . .' ": Alex McCallum to James Grant, February 26, 1986.
369 Lincoln S & L loans to Covenant House: *Grant's*, March 30, 1990.
369 " 'such was the general confidence . . .' ": Ibid., April 28, 1989.
370 Description of putting the Metromedia prospectus to bed: *Fortune*, "All Night at the Printer's," January 21, 1985.
371 " 'You know, ever since we got successful . . .' ": *The New Yorker*, January 27, 1951.
371 "When, in 1959, John W. Kluge . . .": *Dun's Review*, "Metromedia's Creative Financier," December 1965.
371 " 'I just saved a buck . . .' ": *The Wall Street Journal*, May 8, 1985.
372 " 'It was freely predicted . . .' ": *Grant's*, January 14, 1985. For a review of the Investment Bankers Association proceedings, see *The New York Times*, October 23–28, 1932.
373 New issues market dried up in 1933: Wigmore, *The Crash and Its Aftermath*, p. 425.
373 " 'Based on current levels . . .' ": Metromedia Senior Exchangeable Variable Rate Debentures, prospectus, November 29, 1984, p. 9.
375 Gibson Greetings . . .: *New York*, "Windfall," August 8, 1983.
375 "In 1943, a writer . . .": Henry Wriston, *Challenge to Freedom* (New York and London, 1943). See also statement of Alan J. Auerbach before the House Committee on Ways and Means, "Leveraged Buyouts, Corporate Debt and the Role of Tax Policy," 101st Congress, 1st Session, February 1, 1989.
376 " 'In the final analysis . . .' ": Drexel Burnham Lambert, "The Case for High Yield Bonds," 1984, p. 6.
377 " 'Often, what's old is weak . . .' ": Connie Bruck, *The Predator's Ball: The*

Junk Bond Raiders and the Man Who Staked Them (New York, 1988), p. 272.

378 Milken talks of the fees associated with Borg-Warner Holdings: *Grant's*, August 10, 1987.

380 Michael Marocco article: "No Win Proposition at Metromedia," *High Performance*, Morgan Stanley, January 1985.

380 Rupert Murdoch buys Metromedia: *Broadcasting*, "Working Through the Financial Maze of Murdoch-Metromedia," August 19, 1985.

381 " 'The history of business cycles . . .' ": "Control of the Security Investment System," by George W. Edwards, *American Economic Review*, October 1933.

382 " 'After a severe depression . . .' ": Quoted in W. Braddock Hickman, *Corporate Bond Quality and Investor Experience* (Princeton, 1958), p. 108.

382 " 'Nevertheless,' he allowed . . .' ": Ibid., pp. 109–10.

383 " 'As your eyes register . . .' ": *Grant's*, November 18, 1985.

383 A dinner party in Westport: Ibid., February 8, 1988.

383 " 'The biggest problem we have . . .' ": Ibid., November 18, 1985.

384 " 'Based upon current levels of operations . . .' ": SCI Holdings prospectus, November 1, 1985.

385 *Washington Post* editorializes against junk: April 11, 1985.

385 Buffett speaks against junk: *Grant's*, June 17, 1985.

385 " 'Studies have demonstrated . . .' ": Statement of G. Chris Andersen before the House Subcommittee on General Oversight and Investigation of the Committee on Banking, Finance and Urban Affairs, 99th Congress, 1st Session, September 19, 1985, pp. 5–6.

387 Plaza meeting: Our main source is Yoichi Funabashi, *Managing the Dollar: From the Plaza to the Louvre* (Washington, D.C., 1988). The discussion of the Plaza Accord draws chiefly from this text.

390 " 'Had a recession occurred then . . .' ": *Washington Post National Weekly Edition*, July 8–14, 1991; letter from Wayne Angell to John Britton, July 25, 1991.

390 Beatrice buyout: BCI Holdings Corp. prospectus, April 10, 1986.

390 " 'The company spent . . .' ": Bruck, *Predator's Ball*, p. 273.

390 "Youth was served continuously . . .": *Grant's*, October 20, 1986.

391 " 'It started the real feeding frenzy . . .' ": Interview with Talton Embry, April 17, 1991.

391 " 'There are at least five hundred people . . .' ": Bruck, *Predator's Ball*, p. 274.

393 Drexel's new headquarters: *Grant's*, July 7, 1986.

393 " 'The only figure comparable to Milken . . .' ": *Business Week*, "Power on Wall Street," July 7, 1986.

395 "In the weeks that followed . . .": *Grant's*, March 23, 1987.

395 " 'We're not talking about a stock market phenomenon . . .' ": Ibid., March 9, 1987.

395 Dime Savings Bank waives credit checks: Ibid., April 6, 1987.

395 "Guardian Savings & Loan . . .": *National Mortgage News*, July 8, 1991.

396 " 'Lots of foreigners in attendance . . .' ": *Grant's*, April 6, 1987.

396   "In June 1991, Guardian . . .": *National Mortgage News*, July 8, 1991.
396   King County Jail accepts credit cards: *Grant's*, May 18, 1987.
397   " 'I do not foresee . . .' ": Ibid., July 5, 1987.
397   "In no other business . . .": Ibid., June 1, 1987.
397   " 'Milken is passionately committed . . .' ": *Forbes*, "A Chat with Michael Milken," July 13, 1987.
398   Drexel defaults . . . : Salomon Brothers, "High Yield Default Study," November 13, 1991.
399   " 'The company intends to reduce . . .' " and review of the Harcourt buyout: *Grant's*, October 5, 1987.
400   Robert Linton blames the budget deficit for the crash: Ibid., November 2, 1987.
400   " 'two-generation' mortgage": *International Herald Tribune*, December 9, 1987.
401   " 'Rally-ho' ": *New York Post*, November 2, 1987.
401   " 'there is practically no possibility . . .' ": *The Wall Street Journal*, November 2, 1987.
401   Southland bonds: *Grant's*, December 14, 1987.
401   " '[Y]ou gentlemen know as well as I . . .' ": U.S. House of Representatives, *Report of the Industrial Commission*, p. 135.
402   Wriston testimony: Hearings before the Senate Committee on Banking, Housing and Urban Affairs, "Status of the U.S. Financial System," 100th Congress, 1st Session, June 18, 1987, pp. 77–78.
402   " 'The U.S. transition . . .' ": *Grant's*, March 7, 1988.
403   Texas banking disaster: John O'Keefe, "The Texas Banking Crisis, Causes and Consequences: 1980–1989," FDIC (Washington, D.C., July 1990).
403   *Dallas Morning News* and "Shad" Rowe: *Grant's*, March 7, 1988.
404   " 'The contraction of credit . . .' ": Hoyt, *One Hundred Years of Land Values*, p. 446.
405   " 'It's been a depression of the rich' ": Interview with Preston M. Carter, November 13, 1989.
405   " 'I used to pick up the phone . . .' ": Interview with Carter, November 13, 1989.
405   " 'Bank holding company shareholders . . .' ": O'Keefe, "The Texas Banking Crisis."
406   " 'No one holds the banker accountable . . .' ": *The New York Times*, December 31, 1988.
406   " 'These buildings should stand . . .' ": *Grant's*, March 7, 1988.
407   Evolution of car loan terms: Ibid., January 20, 1989.
407   " 'dealer insolvency issue' ": Ibid., September 16, 1989.
408   Boat loans: *Grant's*, November 24, 1989.
408   "General Motors' were up . . .": *The New York Times*, February 17, 1989.
408   " 'If Yugo For It . . .' ": *The Washington Post*, December 20, 1985.
408   " '[I]f you can overlook . . .' ": *Consumer Reports*, February 1988.
408   Yugo's warranty and Imperial Savings: *The Wall Street Journal*, June 30, 1988; *San Diego Business Journal*, August 8, 1988.

409   Yugo files Chapter 11: *The Wall Street Journal*, January 30, 1989.
409   " 'Borrowers had broken-down cars . . .' ": Interview with Rick Masser, December 20, 1990.
409   Cain Chemical buyout: *The New York Times*, April 18, 1988.
410   Lincoln Savings and Loan: *Grant's*, May 13, 1988.
412   " 'meek, weak and ignorant' ": *Los Angeles Times*, September 19, 1990.
412   " 'As a teller . . .' ": Ibid., September 19, 1990.
413   Advent of Wasserstein and Perella: *Grant's*, August 5, 1988.
413   " 'misjudged the character of the borrower' ": *Boston Globe*, March 21, 1989.
413   Bradley-Stoecker exchange: *60 Minutes*, July 8, 1990.
413   "Stoecker's auditors themselves filed . . .": David Shulman et al., "Real Estate Market Review," Salomon Brothers, December 1990, p. 9.
414   " 'We're both lucky . . .' ": *The Wall Street Journal*, April 4, 1988.
414   "It was less than the $224 million . . .": *Corporate Finance*, June 1988.
414   " 'industries that have become . . .' ": *Grant's*, June 24, 1988.
415   " 'Bond funds with higher yields . . .' ": *Christian Science Monitor*, June 8, 1988.
415   Campeau's other family: *The New York Times Magazine*, July 17, 1988.
415   "At the Tyson-Spinks . . .": *Grant's*, July 8, 1988.
415   " 'In his youth . . .' ": Leon Harris, *Merchant Princes: An Intimate History of Jewish Families Who Built Great Department Stores* (New York, 1979), p. 340.
415   Main Federated source: *Grant's*, September 30, 1988.
417   " 'The wage earner has as much right . . .' ": Ibid., September 30, 1988.
418   "Between 1984 and 1989 . . .": Shulman, "Real Estate Market Review," p. 4.
418   " 'Office Construction Boom . . .' ": *The Wall Street Journal*, November 15, 1984.
418   "In fact, oil companies were shrinking . . .": Shulman, "Real Estate Market Review," p. 4.
418   " 'Lenders, Needing to Lend . . .' ": *Real Estate Times*, June 16, 1988.
418   Real-estate statistics: David L. Birch et al., *America's Future Office Space Needs: Preparing for the Year 2000* (1990), pp. 4–5.
419   " 'In the United States, but also in the United Kingdom . . .' ": *Grant's*, June 22, 1990.
419   " 'A particularly ominous development . . .' ": Herbert D. Simpson, "Real Estate Speculation and the Depression," *American Economic Review*, March 1933, p. 164.
419   " 'When LDCs were a problem . . .' ": Testimony of Carole S. Berger before the Senate Committee on Banking, Housing and Urban Affairs, 102nd Congress, 1st Session, February 21, 1991, p. 101.
420   Forty-year mortgage: *The Washington Post*, January 21, 1989.
420   Seven-year car loan: *Grant's*, November 24, 1989.
420   Church's Fried Chicken: Ibid., October 27, 1989.
420   Airline section: Main source is *Grant's*, August 18, 1989.

424   Dr Pepper buyout: *Grant's*, August 4, 1989.

426   "In 1986 to 1988, Wigmore noted . . .": Barrie Wigmore, "The Decline in Credit Quality of Junk Bond Issues: 1980–1988," p. 8.

427   " 'highly confident . . .' ": *PR Newswire*, February 8, 1985.

Afterword

429   Mount Washington Hotel and the Eliot Savings Bank: Unpublished memorandum by John Britton, June 27, 1991; *The New York Times*, June 27, 1991; *Boston Business*, October 1, 1990.

430   Reed interview: "Citicorp Faces the World: An Interview with John Reed," *Harvard Business Review*, November–December 1990.

430   Dingell charge: *American Banker*, August 1, 1991.

430   Citibank loss: *Bloomberg Business News*, October 16, 1991.

431   Corporate credit quality: "Changes in Corporate Credit Quality, 1970–1990," Moody's Investors Service, February 1991.

432   USG's travails: *The Wall Street Journal*, January 2, 1991, and April 25, 1991; "USG Corporation: Offers to Exchange and Solicitations of Consents for Certain Debt Securities," prospectus, April 24, 1991.

432   Risa Kugal story: *Grant's*, June 7, 1991.

433   Drop in home equity: "Surge in Borrowing Erodes Home Equity in U.S.," *International Herald Tribune*, May 29, 1991.

433   Rise in household indebtedness: "Payment of Household Debts," by Glenn B. Canner and Charles A. Luckett, *Federal Reserve Bulletin*, April 1991.

434   Incidence of personal bankruptcy: *The Business Picture*, Summer 1991.

434   Judge Holland's pep talk: *Grant's*, July 5, 1991.

435   Merrill Lynch's innovative securities: *Bond World*, July 1, 1991.

435   Brookes article: *Durell Journal of Money and Banking*, May 1991.

436   " 'There are 775 basis points . . .' ": Edward Yardeni, chief economist, C. J. Lawrence & Co., New York, October 1990.

437   Collapse in borrowing: "Weekly Money Report," October 14, 1991, International Strategy and Investment, New York.

437   Tommy Mullaney's credit card: *The Washington Post*, August 4, 1990.

438   "stealth budget": Roy H. Webb, Federal Reserve Bank of Richmond *Economic Review*, May–June 1991.

439   Banks' share of business lending: C. J. Lawrence "Weekly Economic Analysis," October 3, 1991.

439   New York Fed study: "The Bank Credit 'Crumble,' " by Ronald Johnson, Federal Reserve Bank of New York *Quarterly Review*, Summer 1991.

439   Peabody analysis: *Grant's*, September 27, 1991.

440   Directors' suit: *Federal Deposit Insurance Corporation* v. *H. R. Bright et al.*, July 25, 1991.

440 Shrinkage in M-2: "Weekly Money Report," October 14, 1991, International Strategy and Investment, New York.

441 " 'To have the lowest . . .' ": *Barron's*, October 28, 1991.

441 Interbank lending drought: "A Squeeze in the Interbank Loans Market," *Financial Times* (London), October 16, 1991.

441 Japanese lending slowdown: *Nikkei Weekly*, October 19, 1991.

Select Bibliography

Secondary sources

Anderson, Benjamin M. *Economics and the Public Welfare: A Financial and Economic History of the United States, 1914–1946*, Liberty Press, Indianapolis, 1979 (reprint of the 1949 edition).

Baird, Frieda, and Claude Benner. *Ten Years of Federal Intermediate Credits*, Brookings Institution, Washington, D.C., 1933.

Baruch, Bernard M. *Public Years*, Holt, Rinehart and Winston, New York, 1960.

Bemis, Albert Farwell. *The Evolving House*, Vol. 2: *The Economics of Shelter*, Technology Press, Massachusetts Institute of Technology, Cambridge, 1934.

Birch, David L., Susan M. Jain, William Parsons, and Zhu Xiao Di. *America's Future Office Space Needs: Preparing for the Year 2000*, NAIOP, 1990.

Bloomfield, Arthur Irving. *Monetary Policy Under the International Gold Standard, 1880–1914*, Federal Reserve Bank of New York, 1959.

Blume, Marshall E., and Donald B. Keim. "Risk and Return Characteristics of Lower-Grade Bonds," Wharton, University of Pennsylvania, December 1984.

Brooks, John. *Once in Golconda: The True Drama of Wall Street 1920–1938*, Harper & Row, New York, 1969.

Bruck, Connie. *The Predator's Ball: The Junk Bond Raiders and the Man Who Staked Them*, American Lawyer and Simon & Schuster, New York, 1988.

Carosso, Vincent P. *The Morgans, Private International Bankers, 1854–1913*, Harvard University Press, Cambridge, 1987.

Cassell, Francis. *Gold or Credit? The Economics and Politics of International Money*. Frederick Praeger, New York, 1965.

Catterall, Ralph C. H. *The Second Bank of the United States*, University of Chicago Press, Chicago, 1903.

Chaddock, Robert E. *The Safety Fund Banking System in New York*, National Monetary Commission, 1910.

Chamberlain, Lawrence. *The Principles of Bond Investment*, Henry Holt, New York, 1911 and 1927.

Chamberlain, Lawrence. *The Work of the Bond House*, Moody's Magazine Book Department, New York, 1912.

Chandler, Lester V. *Benjamin Strong, Central Banker*, Brookings Institution, Washington, D.C., 1958.

Chapman, John M., and Robert P. Shay. *Licensed Lending in New York*, Graduate School of Business, Columbia University, New York, 1970.

Chemical Bank. *The History of Chemical Bank*, private printing, New York, 1913.

Childs, C. F. *Concerning U.S. Government Securities*, C. F. Childs & Company, Chicago, 1947.

Citicorp. *Brazil: A Strategy for the 1980s*, New York, December 1981.

Cleveland, Grover. *Presidential Problems*, The Century Co., New York, 1904.

Cleveland, Harold van B., and Thomas F. Huertas. *Citibank: 1812–1920*, Harvard University Press, Cambridge, 1985.

Clews, Henry. *Financial, Economic, and Miscellaneous Speeches and Essays*, Irving Publishing Company, 1910.

Colean, Miles L. *The Impact of Government on Real Estate Finance in the United States*, National Bureau of Economic Research, New York, 1950.

Coleman, Peter J. *Debtors and Creditors in America: Insolvency, Imprisonment for Debt, and Bankruptcy, 1607–1900*, State Historical Society of Wisconsin, Madison, 1974.

Continental Illinois Bank. "Behind That Quiet Façade . . . ," 1982.

Dawes, Charles. *The Banking System of the United States and Its Relation to the Money and Business of the Country*, Arno Press, New York, 1980.

de Wit, Wim. *Louis Sullivan: The Function of Ornament*, Chicago Historical Society and St. Louis Art Museum, with W. W. Norton, 1986.

Drexel Burnham Lambert. "The Case for High Yield Bonds," 1984–87.

Economic Report of the President, January 24, 1956, Government Printing Office, Washington, D.C., 1956.

Eichengreen, Barry, and Peter H. Lindert. *The International Debt Crisis in Historical Perspective*, MIT Press, Cambridge, 1989.

Ely, Bert, and Vicki Vanderhoff. *The Farm Credit System: Reckless Lender to Rural America*, Ely & Co., November 1990.

Freidel, Frank. *Franklin D. Roosevelt*, Vol. 2: *The Ordeal*, Little, Brown, Boston, 1954.

Friedman, Milton, and Anna Schwartz. *A Monetary History of the United States, 1867–1960*, National Bureau of Economic Research, Princeton University Press, Princeton, 1963.

Fuller, Wayne E. *The American Mail: Enlarger of the Common Life*, University of Chicago Press, Chicago, 1972.

Funabashi, Yoichi. *Managing the Dollar: From the Plaza to the Louvre*, Institute for International Economics, 2nd ed., Washington, D.C., 1988.

Gallert, David, Walter Hilborn, and Geoffrey May. *Small Loan Legislation: A History of the Regulation of the Business of Lending Small Sums*, Russell Sage Foundation, New York, 1932.

Gould, John M. *The National Bank Act*, Little, Brown, Boston, 1904.

Grant, James. *Bernard Baruch: The Adventures of a Wall Street Legend*, Simon & Schuster, New York, 1983.

Greider, William. *Secrets of the Temple: How the Federal Reserve Runs the Country*, Simon & Schuster, New York, 1987.

Groves, Harold M. *Postwar Taxation and Economic Progress*, Committee for Economic Research Study, McGraw-Hill, New York, 1946.

Gwynne, S. C. *Selling Money*, Weidenfield & Nicolson, New York, 1986.

Halsey, Forrest. *The Bawlerout*, Desmond Fitzgerald, New York, 1911.

Harl, Neil E. *The Farm Debt Crisis of the 1980s*, Iowa State University, Ames, 1990.

Harris, Leon. *Merchant Princes: An Intimate History of Jewish Families Who Built Great Department Stores*, Harper & Row, New York, 1979.

Hickman, W. Braddock. *Corporate Bond Quality and Investor Experience*, National Bureau of Economic Research, Princeton University Press, Princeton, 1958.

Holzer, Henry Mark. *The Gold Clause: What It Is and How to Use It Profitably*, Books in Focus, Inc., New York, 1980.

Homer, Sidney. *A History of Interest Rates*, 2nd ed., Rutgers University Press, New Brunswick, N.J., 1963.

Hoyt, Homer. *One Hundred Years of Land Values in Chicago*, Chicago, 1933.

Horton, Donald. *Long Term Debts in the United States*, U.S. Department of Commerce, U.S. Government Printing Office, Washington, D.C., 1937.

Ibbottson, Roger, and Rex Sinquefield. *Stocks, Bonds, Bills & Inflation: Historical Returns (1926–1978)*, Financial Analysts Research Foundation, Charlottesville, 1979.

James, Marquis, and Bessie James. *Biography of a Bank: The Story of Bank of America, N.T. & S.A.*, Harper & Brothers, New York, 1954.

Kahn, E. J. *Jock: The Life and Times of John Hay Whitney*, Doubleday, New York, 1981.

Kane, Thomas P. *The Romance and Tragedy of Banking: Problems and Incidents of Government Supervision of National Banks*, 2nd ed., Bankers Publishing Co., New York, 1923.

Keller, Morton. *The Life Insurance Enterprise, 1885–1910: A Study in the Limits of Corporate Power*, Belknap Press (Harvard University Press), Cambridge, 1963.

Kemmerer, Edwin. *The ABC of the Federal Reserve System*, Princeton University Press, Princeton, 1950.

Larson, Henrietta M. *Jay Cooke: Private Banker*, Harvard University Press, Cambridge, 1936.

Latham, Frank B. *1872–1972 A Century of Serving Consumers: The Story of Montgomery Ward*, March 1972.

Lawton, Alexania Easterling, and Minnie Reeves Wilson. *Allendale on the Savannah*, Bamberg Herald Printers, Bamberg, S.C., 1970.

Lebhar, Godfrey M. *Chain Stores in America: 1859–1959*, Chain Store Publishing Corp., New York, 1959.

Lehrman, Lewis E. "Monetary Policy, the Federal Reserve System, and Gold," Morgan Stanley, 1980.

Logan, Sheridan A. *George F. Baker and His Bank, 1840–1955*, privately printed 1981.

McCulloch, Hugh. *Men and Measures of Half a Century*, Charles Scribner's Sons, New York, 1888.

McFerrin, John Berry. *Caldwell & Company, a Southern Financial Empire*, Vanderbilt University Press, Nashville, 1969 (reissue of 1939 edition).

Mills, Charles H. *Fraudulent Practices in Respect to Securities and Commodities*, W. C. Little & Co., Albany, N.Y., 1925.

Mintz, Ilse. *Deterioration in the Quality of Foreign Bonds Issued in the United States, 1920–1930*, National Bureau of Economic Research, Princeton University Press, Princeton, 1951.

Mitchell, Wesley Clair. *A History of Greenbacks: With Special Reference to the Economic Consequences of Their Issue: 1862–65*, University of Chicago Press, Chicago, 1903.

Moody's Investors Service, "Changes in Corporate Credit Quality, 1970–1990," February 1991.

Moore, George S. *The Banker's Life*, W. W. Norton, New York, 1987.

Moreau, Emile. *The Golden Franc: Memoirs of a Governor of the Bank of France: The Stabilization of the Franc (1926–1928)*, translated by Stephen D. Stoller and Trevor C. Roberts, Westview Press, Boulder, Colo., 1991.

Museum of Fine Arts (Houston) and the Parnassus Foundation. *Money Matters: A Critical Look at Bank Architecture*, McGraw-Hill, New York, 1990.

Myers, Margaret G. *The New York Money Market*, Vol. 1: *Origin and Development*, Columbia University Press, New York, 1931.

National Consumer Finance Association. *The Consumer Finance Industry*, Commission on Money and Credit, Prentice-Hall, Englewood Cliffs, N.J., 1962.

Neifeld, M. R. *Personal Finance Comes of Age*, Harper & Brothers, New York, 1939.

New York Stock Exchange. *Who Owns American Business? 1956 Census of Shareowners*.

Northern Pacific Railroad, "The Great Northern Pacific Crosses the Best Zone Between the Great Lakes and the Pacific," E. Wells Sackett & Rankin, New York, 1882.

Novick, Sheldon M. *Honorable Justice: The Life of Oliver Wendell Holmes*, Little, Brown, Boston, 1989.

Noyes, Alexander D. *The War Period of American Finance: 1908–1925*, G. P. Putnam's Sons, New York, and Knickerbocker Press, London, 1926.

Nugent, Rolf. *The Provident Loan Society of New York: An Account of the Largest Remedial Loan Society*, Russell Sage Foundation, New York, 1932.

Office of Management and Budget. *Special Analyses, Budget of the United States Government*, fiscal years 1974–90.

O'Keefe, John. "The Texas Banking Crisis, Causes and Consequences: 1980–1989," FDIC, Washington, D.C., July 1990.

Olmstead, Major General George. *Making America Strong at Home and Abroad: A Private Enterprise at Work*, Newcomen Society in North America, New York, 1962.

Palyi, Melchior. *The Twilight of Gold 1914–1936, Myths & Realities*, Henry Regnery Company, Chicago, 1972.

Pound, Arthur, and Samuel Taylor Moore. *They Told Barron: The Notes of Clarence W. Barron*, Harper & Brothers, New York, 1930.

Provident Loan Society of New York, The. *Twenty Fifth Anniversary, 1894–1919*, New York, 1919.

Rickenbacker, William F. *Wooden Nickels, Or, the Decline and Fall of Silver Coins*, Arlington House, New Rochelle, N.Y., 1966.

Robinson, Louis, and Rolf Nugent. *Regulation of the Small Loan Business*, Russell Sage Foundation, New York, 1935.

Robinson, Ross M. *The Comptroller and Bank Supervision: A Historical Appraisal*, Office of the Comptroller of the Currency, McCall Printing Co., Washington, D.C., 1968.

Rogers, David. *Consumer Banking in New York*, Trustees of Columbia University, 1974.

Rothbard, Murray N. *America's Great Depression*, Sheed & Ward, Subsidiary of Universal Press Syndicate, Kansas City, 1963.

Rubin, Robert M. *Defending the Dollar: The Gold Pool and the London Gold Market, 1960–1968*, Master's Thesis, Columbia University History Department, April 26, 1989.

Rueff, Jacques. *The Monetary Sin of the West*, Macmillan, New York, 1972.

Saloutos, Theodore, and John D. Hicks. *Twentieth-Century Populism: Agricultural Discontent in the Middle West 1900–1939*, University of Nebraska Press, Lincoln, 1951.

Salsbury, Stephan. *No Way to Run a Railroad: The Untold Story of the Penn Central Crisis*, McGraw-Hill, New York, 1982.

Saulnier, Raymond J. *Industrial Banking Companies and Their Credit Practices*, NBER Financial Research Program, Studies in Consumer Installment Financing, Vol. 4, New York, 1940.

Schachner, Nathan. *Alexander Hamilton*, D. Appleton-Century, New York, 1946.

Scheele, Carl H. *A Short History of the Mail Service*, Smithsonian Institution Press, Washington, D.C., 1970.

Schuyler, Montgomery. *American Architecture Studies*, Harper & Brothers, New York, 1892.

Schwed, Peter. *God Bless the Pawnbrokers*. Dodd, Mead, New York, 1975.

Seligman, Edwin R. A. *The Economics of Instalment Selling*, Harper & Brothers, New York, 1927.

Shulman, David, et al. "Real Estate Market Review," Salomon Brothers, December 1990.

Sinclair, Upton. *The Moneychangers*, B. W. Dodge & Co., New York, 1908.

Singer, Mark. *Funny Money*, Alfred A. Knopf, New York, 1985.

Sobel, Robert. *The Big Board: A History of the New York Stock Market*, The Free Press, New York, 1965.

Solomon, Robert. *The International Monetary System, 1945–1981*, Harper & Row, New York, 1982.

Sparks, Boyden, and Samuel Taylor Moore. *The Witch of Wall Street, Hetty Green*, Doubleday, Garden City, N.Y., 1948.

Sparks, Earl Sylvester, and Thomas N. Carver. *History and Theory of Agricultural Credit in the United States*, Thomas Y. Crowell, New York, 1932.

Sprague, Irvine H. *Bailout: An Insider's Account of Bank Failures and Rescues*, Basic Books, New York, 1986.

Sprague, O. M. W. *History of Crises under the National Banking System*, National Monetary Commission, Reprints of Economic Classics, Augustus M. Kelley, Publishers, New York, 1968 (original copyright 1910).

Stanton, Thomas H. *A State of Risk*, Harper Business, HarperCollins, 1991.

Stern, Robert A. M., Gregory Gilmartin, and John Montague Massengale. *New York 1900: Metropolitan Architecture and Urbanism, 1890–1915*, Rizzoli International Publications, New York, 1983.

Stern, Robert A. M., Gregory Gilmartin, and Thomas Mellins. *New York 1930: Architecture and Urbanism Between the Two World Wars*, Rizzoli International Publications, New York, 1987.

Stockman, David A. *The Triumph of Politics: How the Reagan Revolution Failed*, Harper & Row, New York, 1986.

Straus, S. W. *History of the Thrift Movement in America*, J. B. Lippincott, Philadelphia, 1920.

Sumner, William Graham. *The Financier and Finances of the American Revolution*, Vol. 2, 1891, Reprints of Economic Classics, Augustus M. Kelley, Publishers, New York, 1968.

Sunbury, Ben. *The Fall of the Farm Credit Empire*, Iowa State University Press, Ames, 1990.

Tehan, William H. "The U.S. Dollar and the World Monetary System: Calm Before the Storm," P. R. Herzig and Co., May 1970.

Tilden, Freeman. *A World in Debt*. Foreword and commentary by Albert D. Friedberg. Friedberg Commodity Management, Toronto, 1983.

Timberlake, Richard H. *The Origins of Central Banking in the United States*, Harvard University Press, Cambridge, 1978.

Train, John. *Famous Financial Fiascos*, Clarkson N. Potter, New York, 1985.

Udell, Gilman G. *Federal Reserve Act of 1913, With Amendments and Laws Relating to Banking*, U.S. Government Printing Office, Washington, D.C., 1976.

U.S. Congress, House:

The Report of the Industrial Commission on Agriculture and Agricultural Labor, Vol. 10, 56th Congress, 2nd Session, Washington, D.C., 1901.

Subcommittee of the Committee on Banking and Currency, "The Money Trust Investigation," 64th Congress, 1st Session, Part 11, 1913.

Committee on Banking and Currency, Report to accompany S. 3487, Report #1719, 73rd Congress, 2nd Session, 1934 (pertaining to Federal Reserve Act, Section 13b).

Committee on Banking and Currency, "Banking Act of 1935," 74th Congress, 1st Session, 1935.

Committee on Banking and Currency, "Bretton Woods Agreement Act," H.R. 2211, 79th Congress, 1st Session, March–May 1945.

Subcommittee #1 of the Committee on Banking and Currency, "National Bank Legislation," 87th Congress, 2nd Session, September 1961–July 1962.

Committee on Banking and Currency, Hearings on HR 14743, "Removal of Gold Cover," 90th Congress, 2nd Session, January–February 1968.

Subcommittee on Postal Operations, of the Committee on Post Office and Civil Service, "The Plastic Jungle," 91st Congress, 1st Session, October 29, 1969–January 28, 1970.

Committee on Banking and Currency, staff report: *The Penn Central Failure and the Role of Financial Institutions*, 92nd Congress, 1st Session, January 3, 1972.

Subcommittee on General Oversight and Investigations, Committee on Banking, Finance and Urban Affairs, testimony of G. Chris Andersen, 99th Congress, 1st Session, September 19, 1985.

Subcommittee on Conservation, Credit and Rural Development of the Committee on Agriculture, "Review of Implementation of the Farm Credit Amendments Act of 1985; GAO Report Assessing the Financial Condition of the Farm Credit System . . ." 99th Congress, 2nd Session, September 18, 1986.

Committee on Banking, Finance and Urban Affairs, testimony of Manuel H. Johnson, 101st Congress, 1st Session, January 5, 1989.

Committee on Ways and Means, testimony of Alan J. Auerbach, "Leveraged Buyouts, Corporate Debt, and the Role of Tax Policy," 101st Congress, 1st Session, February 1, 1989.

Subcommittee on Housing and Community Development of the Committee on Banking, Housing and Urban Affairs, "The Role of Fannie Mae and Freddie Mac on the Mortgage Market," statement of the National Association of Home Builders, 101st Congress, 2nd Session, July 26, 1990.

Committee on Banking, Finance and Urban Affairs, testimony of L. William Seidman, on "The Condition of the Bank Insurance Fund and Recapitalization," 102nd Congress, 1st Session, April 11, 1991.

U.S. Congress, Senate:

Committee on Finance, "Hearings on the Sale of Foreign Bonds or Securities in the U.S.," 72nd Congress, 1st Session, December 1931–February 1932.

Banking and Currency Committee, "Banking Act of 1935," 74th Congress, 1st Session, 1935.

Hearings before a subcommittee of the Banking and Currency Committee, "On the Nominations of H. Earl Cook, etc.," 82nd Congress, 1st Session, 1951.

Committee on Banking, Housing and Urban Affairs, "Real Estate Investment Trusts," 94th Congress, 2nd Session, May 27, 1976.

Subcommittee on International Finance and Monetary Policy of the Banking, Housing and Urban Affairs Committee, "International Debt," 98th Congress, 1st Session, February 1983.

Committee on Banking, Housing and Urban Affairs, "Status of the U.S. Financial System," 100th Congress, 1st Session, June 18, 1987.

Committee on Banking, Housing and Urban Affairs, "Federal Reserve's First

Monetary Policy Report for 1991," 102nd Congress, 1st Session, testimony of Carole S. Berger, February 20–21, 1991.

U.S. Congress, Joint:
  Joint Economic Committee, "The Federal Debt: On-Budget, Off-Budget and Contingent Liabilities," 98th Congress, 1st Session, June 8, 1983.

U.S. Congressional Record. Senate, December 13, 1913; December 16, 1913.

U.S. Department of the Treasury. *Review of Use of Cumulative Sinking Fund for Retirement of Public Debt Obligations, April 1961,* by the Comptroller General of the United States, September 1961.

U.S. Government Accounting Office. "International Banking: Supervision of Overseas Lending Is Inadequate," May 1988.

U.S. Securities and Exchange Commission. *Report on the Study and Investigation of the Work, Activities, Personnel, and Functions of Protective and Reorganization Committees,* Part III, "Committees for the Holders of Real Estate Bonds," Washington, D.C., June 3, 1936.

U.S. Securities and Exchange Commission, staff report to the Special Subcommittee on Investigations, *The Financial Collapse of the Penn Central Company,* 92nd Congress, 1st Session, Government Printing Office, Washington, D.C., 1972.

Warren, Charles. *Bankruptcy in U.S. History,* Harvard University Press, Cambridge, 1935.

Werner, M. R. *Little Napoleons and Dummy Directors,* Harper & Brothers, New York, 1933.

White, Andrew Dickson. *Fiat Money Inflation in France,* The Bank of New York, 1980 (reprint of 1912 edition).

White, Eugene N. "Free Banking, Denominational Restrictions and Liability Insurance," *Durell Journal of Money and Banking,* November 1990.

Wickens, David L. *Farm-Mortgage Credit,* USDA Technical Bulletin No. 288, Washington, D.C., February 1932.

Wigmore, Barrie A. *The Crash and Its Aftermath: A History of Securities Markets in the United States, 1929–1933,* Greenwood Press, Westport, Conn., 1985.

Wigmore, Barrie. "The Decline in Credit Quality of Junk Bond Issues: 1980–1988," 1988.

Wilson, Richard S. *Corporate Senior Securities,* Probus Publishing, Chicago, 1987.

Winkler, John K. *The First Billion: The Stillmans and the National City Bank,* Vanguard Press, New York, 1934.

Winkler, Max. *Foreign Bonds: An Autopsy,* Roland Swain Company, Philadelphia, 1933.

Woodman, Harold D. *King Cotton and His Retainers: Financing and Marketing the Cotton Crop of the South, 1800–1925,* University of South Carolina Press, Columbia, 1990.

Woodruff, Archibald M., Jr. *Farm Mortgage Loans of Life Insurance Companies,* Yale University Press, New Haven, 1937.

Wriston, Henry M. *Challenge to Freedom,* Literary Classics, New York, 1943.

Wynne, William H. *State Insolvency and Foreign Bondholders,* Vol. 2, Yale University Press, New Haven, 1951.

Zabel, Craig, and Susan Scott Munshower. *American Public Architecture: European Roots and Native Expressions*, Pennsylvania State University Press, University Park, 1989.

Reference

Banking and Monetary Statistics, 1941–70, The Federal Reserve Board, Washington, D.C., 1976.
Current Biography, 1961 (George Champion).
Dictionary of American Biography (Avery).
Moody's Banking and Finance Manual, 1939–40.
Moody's Industrial Manual, 1920–55.
Nation's Business, 1967 (George Champion).
National Cyclopedia of American Biography (Sewell Avery), Supplement 6, 1980.
National Party Platforms, Vol. 1: *1840–1956*, edited by Donald Bruce Johnson, University of Illinois Press, Urbana, 1978.

Primary sources

Bank examiner reports (National Archives):
  First National Bank of New York:
      5/8/1866; 2/23/1872; 3/13/1873; 4/6/1874; 2/1/1875; 12/11/1875; 1/2/1878; 1/27/1883; 2/18/1884; 4/7/1885; 4/27/1885; 9/6/1887; 1/2/1890; 12/16/1890; 1/5/1892; 12/6/1892; 10/5/1893; 11/1/1894; 9/24/1895; 9/28/1896; 9/13/1897; 9/20/1898; 4/4/1899; 11/14/1899; 10/26/1900; 10/15/1900; 10/15/1901; 4/1/1903; 7/18/1905; 1/8/1907; 1/14/1907.
  National City Bank:
      1/4/1888; 2/20/1889; 1/9/1890; 2/24/1891; 2/25/1892; 3/7/1893; 2/14/1894; 2/18/1895; 2/11/1896; 3/29/1897; 3/22/1898; 11/22/1900; 12/12/1901 (Forrest Raynor letter); 10/27/1902; 8/8/1904; 5/12/1905; 6/20/1906; 6/14/1907.
  Chemical National Bank:
      10/16/1902; 4/13/1903; 4/7/1904; 3/27/1905; 3/27/1906; 12/10/1906; 1/3/1907 (Walter Albertson to William B. Ridgely); 11/25/1907; 12/18/1907; 5/27/1908; 4/13/1909; 4/13/1910; 5/15/1911; 7/23/1912; 10/1/1913.
Building Record 1880–81, City of New York, 31 Chambers Street Building Archive.
Chase Manhattan Bank, annual reports: 1969, 1970, 1973, 1974, 1975, 1987.
Citibank, annual reports: 1980, 1981, 1982, 1990.
Desert Partners, proxy statement, April 19, 1988.
Diaries of George Harrison, second president of the Federal Reserve Bank of New York.
Fannie Mae, annual report: 1990.
Farm Credit Act of 1971, Public Law 92-181, December 10, 1971.

Farm Credit System, annual reports: 1980, 1989, 1990; 1991 Information Guide, Annual Information Statement, 1989.

Federal Deposit Insurance Corporation, annual reports: 1938, 1946, 1949, 1951–53, 1955, 1959, 1962, 1964–68.

Federal Home Loan Bank Board, reports: inception through December 1934.

Federal Reserve Bank of New York, annual reports: 1967–69, 1972–79.

First National Bank of New York, annual report: 1955.

Robert G. Fuller to Benjamin Haggot Beckhart, May 26, 1969.

GMAC, annual reports: 1930–36.

Harrison Papers, Federal Reserve Bank of New York Archives.

Interview with George Champion, conducted July 7 and 12, 1978: Chase Manhattan Bank Archives.

Interviews:
Mark Biderman, 3/4/91
John W. Calkins, 3/14/91
Preston M. Carter, 11/13/89
Silas Cathcart, 11/3/90
George Champion, 12/11/90
Talton Embry, 4/17/91
Robert G. Fuller, 6/12/91
Ted Griswold, 5/9/91
Warren Marcus, 3/20/91
Rick Masser, 12/20/90
Clarence F. Michalis, 3/29/90
George S. Moore, 3/18/91
George Salem, 3/4/91
Spencer Witty, 5/31/91
Walter Wriston, 5/8/91

Kaufman, George. "Are Some Banks Too Big to Fail?: Myth and Reality," Competitive Enterprise Institute address, April 1989.

Langoni, Carlos Geraldo. "Brazilian Strategy in the Recent Financial Crisis," address in New York, December 20, 1982.

Luckett, Charles A. "Household Borrowing Behavior: Some Survey Evidence," 9th Meeting of the Financial Management Association, Boston, October 11–13, 1979.

Montgomery Ward, semiannual reports: 1944–45.

Morris, Arthur J. "Fifty Years of Consumer Credit and Its Potentialities," address before the Consumer Bankers Association, White Sulphur Springs, W.Va., October 21, 1960.

Morris, Arthur J. Remarks at the University of Virginia, December 4, 1971.

New York Clearing House, records concerning Bank of United States.

New York State Superintendent of Banks, annual reports: 1931–35 part 1, schedule E (payoff of Bank of United States depositors).

Noble State Bank v. *Haskell*, "Error to the Supreme Court of the State of Oklahoma."

Office of the Comptroller of the Currency, annual reports: 1931, 1934, 1936, 1955–59, 1963, 1964, 1972–80.

Oral History Project at Columbia University. Interview with Jackson E. Reynolds.
Pamphlet on Sewell Avery and Montgomery Ward, by Montgomery Ward Workers of Chicago, 1944.
People of the State of New York v. *S. W. Straus and Co., Inc.,* Supreme Court of the State of New York, September 3, 1935.
Prospectuses:
  Allied Stores, March 10, 1987
  BCI Holdings, April 10, 1986
  Dr Pepper, August 19, 1987; June 15, 1989.
  Federated Stores, November 4, 1988
  Harcourt Brace Jovanovich, September 18, 1987
  R. H. Macy, 1986
  Metromedia Broadcasting, November 29, 1984
  Metropolitan Broadcasting, September 24, 1986
  SCI Holdings, November 1, 1985
  USG, July 7, 1988.
Tehan, William H. "Shifting Gears from Inflation to Deflation," speech at NCMR 7th annual summer conference, Acapulco, Mexico, June 27, 1981.
U.S. Department of Treasury, *Annual Report on the State of the Finances,* 1917–23.
Welldon, Samuel A. *The First National Bank of the City of New York, 1863–1935* (manuscript).
Wriston, Walter B. "Citicorp in the Seventies," remarks before the New York Society of Security Analysts, February 22, 1973.

Periodicals

Advertising Age, Avery obituary, November 7, 1960.
Agricultural Finance Review, May 1938; May 1940; May 1941; November 1947; November 1979.
American Architect, The, "Creating a New Investment Center in New York," June 22, 1921.
American Banker, March–June 1933, 1984–91.
American Economic Review, "The Aldrich Banking Plan," by William A. Scott, June 1911; "Agricultural Credit in the United States," by Edwin W. Kemmerer, December 1912; "Agricultural Credit Legislation and the Tenancy Problem," by George E. Putnam, December 1915; "The Federal Farm Loan Act," by George E. Putnam, December 1916; "Six Years of Postal Savings in the United States," by Edwin W. Kemmerer, March 1917; "The Federal Farm Loan Act," by C. W. Thompson, March 1917; "The Federal Farm Loan System," by George E. Putnam, March 1919; "The Morris Plan," by Louis N. Robinson, June 1931; "The Economics of Brokers' Loans," by Wilford J. Eiteman, March 1932; "Real Estate Speculation and the Depression," by Herbert D. Simpson, March 1933; "Central Banking at the Crossroads," by Karl R. Bopp, Supplement 34, 1944.

American Machinist, "A Liberty Loan Campaign in a Prominent Machine-Tool Factory," by Luther D. Burlingame, April 4, 1918.

American Magazine, The, "The Hunt for the Money Trust," by Ida M. Tarbell, May 1913; "What You Should Know about Lending and Borrowing Money on Mortgages," by S. W. Straus, January 1922.

Annals of the American Academy of Political and Social Science, "The Need for American Investment in Foreign Securities," by James Sheldon, Vol. 88, March 1920; "Foreign Government Bonds" by Thomas W. Lamont, Vol. 88, March 1920; "Preparation for War and the Liberty Loans," by Herbert J. Case, Vol. 99, January 1922; "Reaching the Individual Investor," by Albert W. Atwood, Vol. 75, January 1918.

Architectural Forum, "Wall Street's Neo-Greek Revival," by John Cushman Fistere, August 1933.

Architectural Record, "America's Largest Banking Institution in Its New Quarters," February 1909; "The New Chemical National Bank," July 1907; "Manufacturers Trust Company Builds Conversation Piece on Fifth Avenue," November 1954.

Atlantic Monthly, "The Significance of Political Parties," by Andrew C. McLaughlin, February 1908; "Bootleg Loans," by Howard Douglas Dozier, June 1929.

Automotive News, 1954–55.

Bankers Magazine, "The Unprecedented Situation in the United States," December 1907; March–June 1910 (postal savings system); August–November 1933 (banking bill).

Bankers Magazine of London, "Gaucho Banking," by W. R. Lawson, May 1891.

Bankers Monthly, "Financial Stringency at an End" and "Recovery of the New York Banks," February 1908; "Direct Credit Controls Inequities in the Savings Picture . . . ," by Aubrey G. Lanston, April 1956; "Debt Can Unstabilize," June 15, 1956; "Should FHA Title I Be Extended?" June 15, 1956; "How Significant Are Loan-Deposit Ratios?" by Raymond Rodgers, June 15, 1956; "Loan-Deposit Ratios," September 15, 1956; "Credit Restraint: Appraisal and Outlook," by Raymond Rodgers, February 15, 1957; "Instalment Credit Marks Its Fiftieth Anniversary," April 15, 1960.

Banking: Journal of the ABA, "Easy Terms: Heavy Debt," August 1954; "Too Much Instalment Credit?" September 1955.

Bankruptcy Developments Journal (Emory Law), "Origins of Voluntary Bankruptcy," by John C. McCoid II, Vol. 5, 1988.

Barron's, "Alive and Kicking: Penn Central Has Gone From Bankruptcy to Prosperity," by Bernard Shakin, March 19, 1979; "Banking on the Future: Will the Pay-off Finally Come for Walter Wriston and Citicorp?" by Fran Schumer, April 12, 1982; "Current Yield" column, 1980–81, complete; "Current Yield," August 23, 1982.

Broadcasting, "Working Through the Financial Maze of Murdoch-Metromedia," August 19, 1985; "Metromedia, Katz Radio Groups Sold in LBOs," March 31, 1986; "Joint AM Ownership Allowed by the FCC," April 10, 1989.

Business Week, "Sewell Avery's Mail Order Job Is Concerned with Manpower," January 13, 1935; "Missionary for Gold Wins Few U.S. Fans," April 24, 1965; "Bad Advice and Worse Logic," April 24, 1965; "Chase's REIT Keeps Afloat—Barely," April 5, 1976; "Wriston: The Leadership Comes from Citicorp," September 15, 1973; September 5, 1977 (Citibank/credit-card drive); May 15, 1978 (credit-card anecdotes); "Drexel Wins Big by Backing Dark Horses," February 20, 1984; "Can Malcolm Bricklin Really Sell Cars for $3990?" by Dunkin and Hampton, February 11, 1985; "Power on Wall Street," July 7, 1986; "Hey Wall Street, Wanna Buy the Brooklyn Bridge?" July 6, 1987.

Chicago Daily News, April–May 1945.

Chicago Sun-Times, February and March 1988 (Desert Partners).

Chicago Tribune, December 1933–January 1934 (Walter Cummings).

Cincinnati Enquirer (David Herrlinger), June 1987.

Commercial & Financial Chronicle, 1913–35.

Commercial Law Journal, "A History of American Bankruptcy Law," by Vern Countryman, June 1976, p. 226.

Corporate Finance, "My Life as a Dealmaker," by Donald P. Kelly, July 1989; "CP Worries Put Ratings on Agenda," December 1990.

Current Opinion, "Liberty Bonds Constitute 66% of the Public Debt," Vol. 74, January 1923.

Dartmouth Alumni Magazine, "Dartmouth's No. 1 Banker," May 1964.

Dun's Review, "Metromedia's Creative Financier," December 1965; "Penn Central: Up from the Ashes," November 1978.

Economist, The, "The Panic in New York," October 26, 1907; "The Progress of the American Crisis," November 2, 1907; "American Crisis and a Comparison," November 2, 1907; "American Currency and Banking," November 9, 1907; "The United States—The Crisis and the Outlook—Mr. Hepburn's Views," January 4, 1908; "Latin America's Debt: Muddling Can Be Just Fine," June 27, 1987.

Euromoney, "How Chile Reappeared on the Tombstones," June 1977; "The Problems That Concern David Rockefeller," September 1977; "Buddy Can You Borrow a Dollar?" May 1978; "Champion of the Citi," by Peter Field and Nigel Adam, October 1983.

Factory, "How to Get Workers to Invest in War Loans," April 1918.

Federal Register, Vol. 46, No. 176, August 9, 1983 (describes the real-estate lending rules for national banks).

Federal Reserve Bank of New York, *Monthly Review*, "Recent Developments in the Commercial Paper Market," by Frederick Shadrock and Frederick Breimyer, December 1970.

Federal Reserve Bank of Richmond, *Economic Review*, "Credit Controls: 1980," by Stacey L. Schreft, November–December 1990.

Federal Reserve Bank of St. Louis, *Review*, "Inflation: Assessing Its Recent Behavior and Future Prospects," by R. W. Hafer, August–September 1983.

Federal Reserve Bulletin, "Farm Sector Financial Experience," December 1985;

federal presence in the mortgage market taken from table 1.55, 1970–89.

Financial World, "Walter Wriston Talks about the Banks, the Country and World Currencies," interview with Alfred Kingon, April 15, 1976.

Forbes, "The Morning After at Citizens & Southern," July 1, 1975; October 15, 1979 (credit-card anecdotes); "Mike Milken's Marvelous Money Machine," November 19, 1984; "A Chat with Michael Milken," July 13, 1987.

Fortune, "Skyscrapers: Pyramids in Stock and Steel," August 1930; "Mr. Baker's Bank," July 1931; "Branch Banking: The First Step," December 1932; "The Biggest Bank Failure" by M. R. Werner, March 1933; "The Stores and the Catalogue," January 1935; "Gyp," February 1936; "The House Not-So-Beautiful," May 1938; " 'Sort of Like a Country Bank . . . ,' " July 1945; "The Stewardship of Sewell Avery," May 1946; "U.S. Gypsum: No Nonsense," September 1955; "What Did Happen at Ward's," by Herrymon Maurer, May 1956; "Barr of Montgomery Ward," May 1956; "De Gaulle's Audacious Economics," by Michael Heilperin and Charles Murphy, May 1959; "Montgomery Ward, Prosperity Is Still Around the Corner," November 1960; "The West Is Risking a Credit Collapse," by Jacques Rueff, July 1961; "The Strategy That Saved Montgomery Ward," May 1970; "Sorting Out Real-Estate Investment Trusts," August 1970; "It's a Stronger Bank That David Rockefeller Is Passing to His Successor," by Carol J. Loomis, January 14, 1980; "Citicorp's Rocky Affair with the Consumer," by Carol J. Loomis, March 24, 1980; "The Firm That Fed on Scraps," by Joel Dreyfuss, September 3, 1984; "All Night at the Printer's," January 21, 1985; "Can a Beetle Brain Stir a Yearning for Yugos?" by Jaclyn Fierman, May 13, 1985; "Merger Fees That Bend the Mind," by Peter Petre, January 20, 1986.

Forum, The, "Our National Banking System: An Ominous Situation," by William De Hertburn, Washington, June 1913.

Grant's Interest Rate Observer, 1983–91.

Harper's Weekly, "The 6,000 Homes That Levitt Built," by Eric Larrabee, September 1948. (*Harper's*) "Life on the Card," by Jack Richardson, July 1979; "Adventures in the Loan Trade," by S. C. Gwynne, September 1983.

Harvard Business Review, "Control of the Security Investment System," by George W. Edwards, October 1933; "The Current Merger Movement Analyzed," by A. D. H. Kaplan, May–June 1955; "Installment Credit: The $28 Billion Question," by Sidney E. Rolfe, July–August 1956; "Incentive Financing —A New Opportunity," by Charles M. Williams and Howard A. Williams, March–April 1960; "Let's Not Panic about Third World Debts," by A. W. Clausen, November–December 1983; "The World According to Walter," January–February 1986; "Citicorp Faces the World: An Interview with John Reed," November–December 1990.

High Performance, "No Win Proposition at Metromedia Broadcasting," by Michael Marocco, Morgan Stanley, January 1985.

Independent, The, "New York's Great Financial Institutions and Their Presidents," by Serano S. Pratt, December 22, 1904; "An Elastic Currency and a Bankers' Bank," December 25, 1913; March 16, 1914 (Federal Reserve System); "Foreign Government Bonds in the United States," by Luigi Criscuolo, October 2, 1916; "Liberty Loan Bonds 3½s or 4s," December 1, 1917.

Institutional Investor, "Can the Bond Market Survive?" by John F. Lyons, May 1969; "Walter Wriston on Walter Wriston," July 1983; "Milken the Magnificent," by Cary Reich, August 1986.

Investment Banking, "The Future of Real Estate Financing," by Louis K. Boysen, June 1931; "Report of the Real Estate Security Commission," November 28, 1934, and June 8, 1936.

Journal of Finance, "Changes in the Quality of Credit: Quality of Credit in Booms and Depressions," by Geoffrey H. Moore, May 1956.

Journal of Land and Public Utility Economics, The, Fred L. Garlock, "Bank Failures in Iowa," January 1926.

Journal of Law and Politics, "The Savings and Loan Crisis: Which Train Derailed—Deregulation or Deposit Insurance?" by Melanie S. Tammen, Winter 1990.

Journal of Political Economy, The, "The Banking and Currency Act of 1913," by J. Laurence Laughlin, April 1914; "The Financial Policy of Federal Reserve Banks," by Thomas Conway, Jr., April 1914; "Who Paid for the War?" by J. Viner, January 1920; "Brokers' Loans and Bank Deposits," by Calvin B. Hoover, December 1929.

Law and Contemporary Problems, "Combating the Loan Shark," Duke University Law School, Winter 1941.

Life, "Strong Man's Victory," May 2, 1949; "My $10,000 Credit Card Binge," J. R. Miraglia, October 26, 1959.

Literary Digest, The, "Recent Declines in Foreign Government Bonds," December 30, 1916; "Maxims for Our New Investors," August 4, 1917; "Wage-Earners as Government Bond Buyers," August 4, 1917; "Government Profits from Careless Investors," March 31, 1923; "Lending Three Billions to Wall Street," February 27, 1926; "Who Buys Foreign Bonds and Why?" January 29, 1927; "Government Bonds Collecting in Bank Vaults," May 21, 1927; "Our Biggest Bank to Serve Small Borrowers," May 19, 1928; " 'Bootleg' Money in Wall Street," August 18, 1928; "Bankers' Worries over Wall Street Loans," October 20, 1928; "Borrowers Wanted," June 11, 1932.

Living Age, The, "America under the Money Trust," March 1, 1913.

Mortgage Banking, "The American Model," April 1991.

Nation, The, "The Pujo Report," March 6, 1913; "Senator Root on the Banking Bill," December 18, 1913; "Finance: Public Opinion and the New Banking System," May 21, 1914; "Our Broadening Market for Foreign Bonds," September 7, 1918.

Nation's Business, "Preaching What You Practice" (George Champion), March 1967.

New Norfolk, Norfolk Chamber of Commerce (Arthur Morris), May 1966.

New York Evening Post.

New Yorker, The, "Our Plunging Correspondents," by John Brooks, May 21, 1955; "The Prudent Pioneer," January 27, 1951.

Newsweek, September 2, 1933, and January 6, 1934 (Walter Cummings); "Avery on the Carpet," April 25, 1949; "The Individualist: He Could Say 'No' " (Sewell Avery), November 14, 1960; "Living in Debt," January 8, 1979.

Outlook, The, "Liberties," by William Leavitt Stoddard, May 11, 1927; "Surplus Cash in the Market," by Thomas H. Gammack, August 15, 1928.

People Weekly, March 14, 1988 (credit-card anecdotes); January 30, 1989 (Walter Cavanagh).

Quarterly Journal of Economics, "The Federal Reserve Act of 1913," February 1914.

Real Estate News, "New Home for Huge Bank Merger," December 1922 Supplement.

Real Estate Times, "Lenders, Needing to Lend, 'Go For Broke,' in Soft Market," June 16, 1988.

Saturday Evening Post, The, "The Foreign Bond Epidemic," by Edwin Lefevre, April 11, 1925; "Wholesale and Retail Bond Selling," by Edwin Lefevre, May 30, 1925.

Time, "Monopolist," October 1929 (Ivar Kreuger); May 8, 1944 (Sewell Avery's bodily ejection); June 17, 1946 (Spencer Chemical); "KO for Mr. Avery," May 31, 1948; "Spring Cleaning," April 25, 1949 (Sewell Avery); "Hatchet Man Axed," August 16, 1954; "Man at the Top," November 14, 1960; "The New American Land Rush," October 1, 1973.

Times, The (London), Bankhaus Herrstatt Failure, June 27, 1974; Jacques Rueff obituary, April 25, 1978.

U.S. News & World Report, "Why Workers Don't Mind a Little Inflation," October 4, 1965; "Is the Strongest Economy in the World Going Bankrupt?" October 17, 1966; August 12, 1968 (Housing Act of 1968); "People Going Deeper in Debt: 'It's Really Worrisome,' " November 20, 1978.

World's Work, "Mr. Williams and the Chemical National Bank," by Edwin Lefevre, April 1902; "America Owns Itself at Last," by Albert W. Atwood, April 1917; "Call Money and Stock Gambling," June 1929; "Foreign Government Bonds," January 1925.

Index

DATE DUE

THE
CAVALCADE
OF
AMERICAN CREDIT

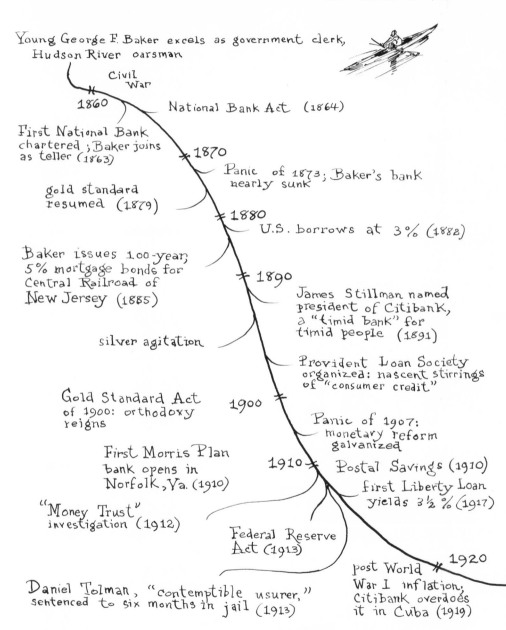

Young George F. Baker excels as government clerk, Hudson River oarsman

Civil War

1860

National Bank Act (1864)

First National Bank chartered; Baker joins as teller (1863)

1870

Panic of 1873; Baker's bank nearly sunk

gold standard resumed (1879)

1880

U.S. borrows at 3% (1882)

Baker issues 100-year, 5% mortgage bonds for Central Railroad of New Jersey (1885)

1890

James Stillman named president of Citibank, a "timid bank" for timid people (1891)

silver agitation

Provident Loan Society organized: nascent stirrings of "consumer credit"

Gold Standard Act of 1900: orthodoxy reigns

1900

Panic of 1907: monetary reform galvanized

First Morris Plan bank opens in Norfolk, Va. (1910)

1910

Postal Savings (1910)

first Liberty Loan yields 3½% (1917)

"Money Trust" investigation (1912)

Federal Reserve Act (1913)

1920

post World War I inflation; Citibank overdoes it in Cuba (1919)

Daniel Tolman, "contemptible usurer," sentenced to six months in jail (1913)